SECOND EDITION

Ethics and the Conduct of Business

JOHN R. BOATRIGHT

Loyola University Chicago

PRENTICE HALL, Upper Saddle River, New Jersey 07458

Library of Congress Cataloging-in-Publication Data

BOATRIGHT, JOHN RAYMOND
    Ethics and the conduct of buisness / John R. Boatright. — 2nd ed.
      p.   cm.
    Includes bibliographical references and index.
    ISBN 0–13–551798–2 (pbk.)
    1. Business ethics.   2. Social responsibility of business.
  I. Title.
HF5387.B6   1997
174′.4—dc20   96–20368
                                             CIP

Editorial director: *Charlyce Jones Owen*
Acquisitions editor: *Angie Stone*
Editorial/production supervision: *Merrill Peterson*
Interior design: *Joan Stone*
Copy editor: *Rebecca J. McDearmon*
Buyer: *Nick Sklitsis*

This book was set in 10/12 Baskerville by
Americomp and was printed and bound by RR
Donnelley & Sons Company. The cover was printed by
Phoenix Color Corp.

Acknowledgments appear on p. xi, which constitutes
a continuation of the copyright page.

Printed in the United States of America

10 9 8 7 6 5 4

ISBN   0-13-551798-2

PRENTICE-HALL INTERNATIONAL (UK) LIMITED, *London*
PRENTICE-HALL OF AUSTRALIA PTY. LIMITED, *Sydney*
PRENTICE-HALL CANADA INC., *Toronto*
PRENTICE-HALL HISPANOAMERICANA, S.A., *Mexico*
PRENTICE-HALL OF INDIA PRIVATE LIMITED, *New Delhi*
PRENTICE-HALL OF JAPAN, INC., *Tokyo*
SIMON & SCHUSTER ASIA PTE. LTD., *Singapore*
EDITORA PRENTICE-HALL DO BRASIL, LTDA., *Rio de Janeiro*

Contents

3 Kantian Ethics, Rights, and Virtue,   *51*

4 Justice and the Market System,   *76*

PART II   THE EMPLOYEE AND THE FIRM

5 Whistle-Blowing,   *109*

6 Trade Secrets and Conflict of Interest,   *132*

7 Privacy in the Workplace,   *161*

PART III   ETHICAL ISSUES IN EMPLOYEE RELATIONS

8 Discrimination and Affirmative Action,   *181*

9 Women and Family Issues,   *210*

PART V THE CORPORATION AND SOCIETY

14 Corporate Social Responsibility, *343*

15 Ethics in International Business, *370*

Preface

In little more than a decade, the field of business ethics has grown from the interest of a few philosophers into an interdisciplinary area of study that has found a secure niche in both the liberal arts and the standard business curriculum. Credit for this development belongs to many individuals—both philosophers and business scholars—who have succeeded in relating ethical theory to the various problems of ethics that arise in business. They have shown not only that business is a fruitful area for philosophical exploration but also that practicing managers in the world of business can benefit from the results.

Ethics and the Conduct of Business is a relatively comprehensive and up-to-date discussion of the most prominent issues in the field of business ethics and the major positions and arguments on these issues. There has been no attempt to develop a distinctive ethical system or to offer a supposed "right answer" in every instance. The field of business ethics is marked by diversity and reasonable disagreement, and a good text should reflect this.

The focus of the book is primarily on ethical issues that corporate decision makers face in developing policies about employees, customers, and the general public. The positions on these issues and the arguments for them are taken from a wide variety of sources, including economics and the law. The study of ethical issues in business is neither confined to a single academic discipline nor limited to the academic world. The issues selected for discussion are widely debated by legislators, judges, government regulators, business leaders, journalists, and, indeed, virtually everyone with an interest in business. Hence, readers wholly unacquainted with ethical theory will find most of the material in this book familiar and accessible.

An underlying assumption of this book, however, is that ethical theory is essential for a full understanding of the arguments commonly offered for positions on virtually every issue in business ethics. Fortunately, the amount of theory is relatively small, and its purpose is to clarify and further develop positions and arguments presented primarily by nonphilosophers. The book also contains a substantial amount of legal material, and an attempt has been made, whenever possible, to incorporate material from the functional areas of business and the actual practice of corporations. If the discussion of ethical issues in business is to have any relevance for management decision making, it must take into account both the legal framework in which problems occur and the role that managers fill in corporations. Although it has a strong philosophical orientation, this book is designed to be used as a text both in a strictly philosophical business ethics course and in one taught in a school of business.

The second edition is an opportunity not only to update the book to reflect recent developments and new concerns but also to change the format to some extent. The most substantial change is the addition of numerous short cases, forty-eight in all, that are intended to facilitate discussion of the issues raised in each chapter. A few of these cases were presented in the first edition and are now set off from the main text. Most of the cases, however, have been specially written for the second edition. All of the cases at the beginning of each chapter, except for Chapter 1, are real, whereas most of the other cases are fictional. Instructors who prefer longer case studies may wish to use one of many available casebooks. The casebook *Cases in Ethics and the Conduct of Business,* published by Prentice Hall, is designed to be a companion volume to this textbook.

A second substantial change occurs in Chapter 9. Two chapters in the first edition, one devoted to discrimination and a second to affirmative action, have been combined into a single chapter, and a new chapter on women and family issues has been created. This new chapter has sections on sexual harassment, comparable worth, and balancing family and work life. Other additions include coverage of virtue ethics in Chapter 3 and expanded discussions of competitor intelligence gathering and insider trading in Chapter 6.

Revision of this book has been aided by published reviews and by the advice of many instructors who have used it. To these contributors, whose names are too numerous to mention, I express my thanks. I also wish to thank the reviewers of this edition: Michael Harford, Morehead State University; Dennis Pelletier, University of Baltimore; and Richard Edwards, West Liberty State College. I am grateful for the support of Loyola University Chicago, especially the encouragement of Michael Keeley as chair of the Department of Management and the secretarial help of Kathleen King. I owe a special debt of gratitude for the expert research assistance of Carol Snell. Finally, my deepest expression of appreciation goes to my wife, Claudia, whose affection, patience, and support have been as essential for the revision of this book as they were for the completion of the first edition.

John R. Boatright

Acknowledgments

I would like to express my gratitude for permission to use material from the following published sources:

A. Carl Kotchian, "The Payoff: Lockheed's 70-Day Mission to Tokyo," *Saturday Review Magazine,* July 9, 1977, © 1977, reprinted by permission of *Saturday Review Magazine.*

Laura Bird, "Critics Cry Foul at Nike Spots with Actor," *Wall Street Journal,* December 16, 1993, p. B12. Reprinted by permission of the *Wall Street Journal.* © 1993 Dow Jones & Company, Inc. All rights reserved worldwide.

Sonia L. Nazario and Asra Q. Nomani, "Use of Staff Guinea Pigs Causes Squeals about Safety of Firms' Product Testing," *Wall Street Journal,* December 31, 1991, pp. B1, B4. Reprinted by permission of the *Wall Street Journal.* © 1991 Dow Jones & Company, Inc. All rights reserved worldwide.

R. Edward Freeman, "Joyce Roberts." Reprinted by permission of the author.

"Diller's Dilemma." Adapted by Karen Marquiss and Joanne B. Ciulla from, "H. B. Fuller in Honduras: Street Children and Substance Abuse," Norman Bowie and Stefanie Ann Lenway. Copyright 1991 by the Columbia Graduate School of Business. Reprinted by permission.

John R. Boatright, "Ethics and the Role of the Manager," *Journal of Business Ethics,* 7 (1988), © 1988, reprinted by permission of Kluwer Academic Publishers.

Thomas Donaldson and Lee E. Preston, "The Stakeholder Theory of the Corporation: Concepts, Evidence, and Implications," *Academy of Management Review,* 20 (1995), reprinted by permission.

Johnson & Johnson, the statement *Our Credo,* reprinted by permission.

1

Introduction:
Ethics in the World of Business

CASE 1.1   Four Business Decisions

The Sales Rep

A sales representative for a struggling computer supply firm has a chance to close a multimillion-dollar deal for an office system to be installed over a two-year period. The machines for the first delivery are in the company's warehouse, but the remainder would have to be ordered from the manufacturer. Because the manufacturer is having difficulty meeting the heavy demand for the popular model, the sales representative is not sure that subsequent deliveries can be made on time. Any delay in converting to the new system would be costly to the customer; however, the blame could be placed on the manufacturer. Should the sales representative close the deal without advising the customer of the problem?

The Research Director

The director of research in a large aerospace firm recently promoted a woman to head an engineering team charged with designing a critical component for a new plane. She was tapped for the job because of her superior knowledge of the engineering aspects of the project, but the men under her direction have been expressing resentment at working for a woman by subtly sabotaging the work of the team. The director believes that it is unfair to deprive the woman of advancement merely because of the prejudice of her male colleagues, but quick completion of the designs and the building of a prototype are vital to the success of the company. Should he remove the woman as head of the engineering team?

The Marketing VP

The vice president of marketing for a major brewing company is aware that college students account for a large proportion of beer sales and that people in this age group form lifelong loyalties to particular brands of beer. The executive is personally uncomfortable with the tasteless gimmicks used by her competitors in the industry to encourage drinking on campuses, including beach parties and beer-drinking contests. She worries about the company's contribution to underage drinking and alcohol abuse among college students. Should she go along with the competition?

The CEO

The CEO of a mid-size producer of a popular line of kitchen appliances is approached about merging with a larger company. The terms offered by the suitor are very advantageous to the CEO, who would receive a large severance package. The shareholders of the firm would also benefit, since the offer for their stock is substantially above the current market price. The CEO learns, however, that plans call for closing a plant that is the major employer in a small town. The firm has always taken its social responsibility seriously, but the CEO is now unsure of how to balance the welfare of the employees who would be thrown out of work and the community where the plant is located against the interests of the shareholders. He is also not sure how much to take his own interests into account. Should he bail out in order to enrich himself?

INTRODUCTION

These four hypothetical examples give some idea of the ethical issues that arise at all levels of business. The individuals in these cases are faced with questions about ethics in their relations with customers, employees, and members of the larger society. Frequently the ethically correct course of action is clear, and people in business act accordingly. Exceptions occur, however, when there is uncertainty about ethical obligations in particular situations or when considerations of ethics come into conflict with the practical demands of business. The sales representative might not be sure, for example, about the extent to which he is obligated to provide information about possible delays in delivery. And the director of research, although convinced that discrimination is wrong, might still feel that he has no choice but to remove the woman as head of the team in order to get the job done.

In deciding on an ethical course of action, we can rely to some extent on the rules of right conduct that we employ in everyday life. Deception is wrong, for example, whether we deceive a friend or a customer. And corporations no less than persons have an obligation not to discriminate or cause harm. Unfortunately, business activity also has some features that limit the applicability of our ordinary ethical views. What we ought to do depends to some extent on our situation and on the particular roles we occupy, and slightly different rules or codes of ethics are needed to guide us in the different departments of our lives. The CEO, by virtue of his position, has responsibilities to several different constituencies, and his problem is, in part, to find the proper balance.

One of the features that distinguishes business activity is its *economic* character. In the world of business, we interact with each other not as family members, friends, or neighbors but as buyers and sellers, employers and employees, and the like. Trading, for example, is often accompanied by hard bargaining, in which both sides conceal their full hand and perhaps engage in some bluffing. And a skilled salesperson is well versed in the art of arousing a customer's attention (sometimes by a bit of puffery) to clinch the sale. Still, there is an "ethics of trading" that prohibits the use of false or deceptive claims and tricks such as "bait-and-switch" advertising.

Employment is also recognized as a special relation with its own standards of right and wrong. Employers are generally entitled to hire and promote whomever they wish and to lay off or terminate workers without regard for the consequences. (This right is being increasingly challenged, however, by those who hold that employers ought to fire only for cause and to give employees an opportunity to defend themselves.) Employees also have some protections, such as a right not to be discriminated against or to be exposed to workplace hazards. There are many controversies in the workplace, such as the rights of employers and employees with regard to drug testing.

The ethics of business, then, is at least in part the ethics of economic relations—such as those involving buyers and sellers and employers and employees. So we need to ask, what are the rules that ought to govern these kinds of relations? And how do these rules differ from those that apply in other spheres of life?

A second distinguishing feature of business activity is that it typically takes place in large, impersonal *organizations*. An organization, according to organizational theory, is a hierarchical system of functionally defined positions designed to achieve some goal or set of goals. Consequently, the members of a business organization, in assuming a particular position—such as sales representative or vice president for marketing or CEO—take on new obligations to pursue the goals of the firm. Thus, the marketing executive is not free to act solely on her own standards of good taste and social responsibility at the expense of sales for the brewing company. Nor can the CEO rightfully ignore the interests of shareholders and consider only the impact of the merger on one group of employees and their community any more than he can consider only his self-interest.

This book is about the ethical issues that arise for managers—and, indeed, for all people, including employees, consumers, and members of the public. Corporate activities affect us all, and so the conduct of business is a matter of concern for everyone with a stake in ethical management. The ethical issues we will be examining are those considered by managers in the ordinary course of their work, but they are also issues that are discussed in the pages of the business press, debated in the halls of Congress, and scrutinized by the courts. This is because ethical issues in business are closely tied to important matters of public policy and to the legislative and judicial processes of government. They are often only part of a complex set of issues.

LEVELS OF ETHICAL DECISION MAKING

Decision making occurs on several distinct levels: the level of the individual, the level of the organization, and finally the level of the business system. Situations that confront individuals in the workplace and require that an individual make a decision concerning his or her own response are on the level of individual decision making. An employee with an unreasonably demanding boss, for example, or a boss who is discovered padding his expense account faces the question, What do *I* do? Whether to live with the difficult boss or to blow the whistle on the padding are questions to be answered by the individual and acted on accordingly.

Many ethical problems occur at the level of the organization in the sense that the individual decision maker is acting on behalf of the organization in bringing about some organizational change. Sexual harassment, for example, is an individual matter for the person suffering the abuse (and for the harasser), but a manager in an office where sexual harassment is taking place must take steps not only to rectify the situation but also to ensure that it does not occur again. The decision in this case may be a disciplinary action, which involves a manager acting within his or her organizational role. The manager may also institute training to prevent sexual harassment and possibly develop a sexual harassment policy, which not only prohibits certain behavior but also creates procedures for handling complaints. Developing a policy with regard to sexual harassment, as opposed to dealing with harassment of one's self, involves decisions on the organizational level rather than the level of the individual.

Problems that result from accepted business practices or from features of the economic system cannot be effectively addressed by any single organization, much less a lone individual. Sales practices within an industry, for example, are difficult for one company to change singlehandedly, because the company is constrained by competition with possibly less ethical competitors. The most effective solution is likely to be an industrywide code of ethics, agreed to by all. Similarly, the lower pay of women's work, which is discussed in Chapter 9, results from structural features of the labor market, which no one company or even industry can alter. A single employer can adopt a policy of comparable worth, which is one possible solution; but the problem is systemic, and any substantial change must be on the level of the system. Systemic problems are best solved by some form of regulation or economic reform.

Identifying the appropriate level for a decision is important, because an ethical problem may have no solution on the level at which it is approached. The beer marketer described in Case 1.1 may have little choice but to follow the competition in using tasteless gimmicks, because the problem has no real solution on the individual or organizational level. An effective response requires that she place the problem on the systemic level and seek a solution appropriate to that level. Richard T. DeGeorge has described such a move as "ethical displacement," which consists of addressing a problem on a level other than the one on which the problem appears.[1] The fact that some problems can be solved only by displacing them to a higher level is a source of great distress for individuals in difficult situations, because they must still find some less-than-perfect response on a lower level.

THE MORAL POINT OF VIEW

Decision making in business involves many factors, of which ethics is only one. In order to gain an understanding of the relevance of ethics for the conduct of business, it will be useful to begin with a description of three points of view from which decisions in business can be made: the moral, the economic, and the legal. Then we can see how these points of view can be integrated to form an approach to business decision making that can aid people facing the kinds of issues described at the beginning of this chapter.

A decision can be made from many different points of view. Closing the deal for the sale of an office computer system is good from a strictly economic or business point of view, as long as there are no repercussions. The quick completion of the design for the airplane component and increasing beer sales among college students are good for the same reason. The individuals involved might also evaluate different courses of action from the point of view of their own careers and ask, what is best for me? What should I do from the point of view of self-interest? Or the individuals involved might consider the law and take a legal point of view. Would removing the woman from her job as head of the engineering team be considered illegal sexual discrimination? Would it be legal to oppose the merger merely to avoid closing the plant? Finally, the individuals involved might consider the moral point of view when making their decisions. Morally speaking, what is the best thing to do?

In order to understand what it means to decide something from the moral point of view, let us consider the case of the sales representative. In deciding whether to disclose the possible delays in delivery, he might ask: What is accepted business practice? What would my boss expect me to do? What would other sales representatives in my company or the industry do? What kind of conduct is generally regarded as legally permissible? To proceed in these ways is to seek guidance from what is conventionally thought by one's peers or society at large to be right or wrong. Unable to find an answer, or perhaps wanting to make sure that he had found the correct one, the sales representative might push further and ask for the reasons that he ought to act in one way rather than another. Three reasons readily suggest themselves.

First, informing the customer about the possibility of a delay might result in losing the sale and a handsome commission. Judged purely by considerations of benefit to himself, he ought to close the deal, unless, of course, he would suffer greater harm if the company is unable to fulfill the contract. If benefit and harm to himself are reasons for acting in some way, why should he not consider the benefit and harm for the customer as well? The fact that the customer might suffer substantial losses would seem to be a morally relevant reason for revealing the possible delivery problems. But the sales representative might think, "I have no obligation to look out for this customer's welfare. If he suffers a loss, that's his problem, not mine; I am not going to pass up a sale to protect him."

On further reflection, however, he might realize that trust is essential in his line of work. If he and the company acquire a reputation for dishonesty, doing business will be more difficult in the future. In addition, if trust is lost in business as a whole—if buyers and sellers can no longer rely on each other's word in their dealings, then everyone suffers. Full disclosure in trade is of value because, on the whole, it helps everyone. In terms of benefit and harm for all concerned, therefore, it is a good policy to inform a customer of matters such as the possibility of delays.

Second, insofar as not revealing the information is misrepresentation, it is a form of lying; and we have been taught since childhood that lying is wrong. Misrepresentation does not require that something false actually be said. If the sales representative assures the customer that there will be no problem with the deliveries, then he is lying. But a person can lie by remaining silent or even saying something true. Consider a person selling a used car who says that the transmission was checked by a mechanic only last week but fails to add that the mechanic found serious problems. Since the seller's words would lead a hearer to conclude that the transmission is in sound condition, misrepresentation has occurred.

If we wish to push the matter further, we can ask, what is morally wrong with lying or misrepresentation? If we appeal to the harm done, so that the rule Do not lie is itself based on benefit and harm, then this second reason is no different from the first. However, a different line of reasoning can be sketched as follows. To intentionally bring about a false belief so that another person cannot make a rational decision about some matter of importance is to manipulate that person. Manipulating, or using, another person is morally objectionable because it involves treating people as "things" for satisfying our desires and preventing them from acting to satisfy their own desires. In short, manipulation shows a lack of respect for the essential humanity of others. And the idea of respect for persons is an important moral consideration—different from benefit and harm—that supports the commonly accepted view that lying is wrong.

Third, the sales representative might ask, how would my action appear to the customer were he to know the full facts? Or how would I view it if I were in the customer's place? Would I want to be treated in the same way? These questions suggest a line of reasoning that is commonly expressed by the Golden Rule: Do unto others as you would have them do unto you. Part of the force of this rule is its insistence on equality, which is an important element of fairness or justice. To treat others in ways that we would not like to be treated is to make exceptions for ourselves and hence to depart from strict equality. The point is also expressed in the familiar slogan "What's fair for one is fair for all." Assuming that the sales representative would not want to have important information withheld from him, then it would be wrong for him to withhold the information from the customer.

Features of the Moral Point of View

The moral point of view has two important features.[2] First is a willingness to seek out and act on *reasons*. The best action, according to one writer, is "the course of action which is supported by the best reasons."[3] This does not get us very far without some account of what are the best reasons, but it indicates a commitment to use reason in deliberating about what to do and to construct moral arguments that are persuasive to ourselves and others. Moral rules should not be accepted merely because they are a part of the prevailing morality. Rather, we should attempt to justify the rules we act on by means of the most general and comprehensive kind of reasons available.

Second, the moral point of view requires us to be *impartial*. We must regard the interests of everyone, including ourselves, as equally worthy of consideration and give all interests equal weight in deciding what to do. The moral point of view is the opposite of being purely self-interested. The idea of a personal morality—that is, a morality to be followed only by ourselves—is absurd. Morality by its very nature is public, in the sense that it involves a shared set of rules that can be observed by everyone.[4] A good test of the moral point of view is whether we would feel comfortable if our colleagues, friends, and family were to know about a decision we had made. Would we be willing to have an article on it appear on the front page of the local newspaper, for example? A decision made from the moral point of view can withstand and even invites this kind of openness and scrutiny.

Taking the moral point of view is easier said than done. Many people in business are apt to say, "I am able to take the moral point of view to determine what ought to be done in my personal life. But in business, decisions simply are not made that way. There is no place in business for the moral point of view." According to this response, the only relevant rules in business regard economic competition and the law. The sole purpose of business is to turn out some product or service at a profit. Every decision, therefore, must be made with an economic point of view. What is most profitable, not what is morally right, must be the overriding consideration—although what is legal must also be taken into account.

The people who say this do not mean that business is an immoral activity; rather, that business is an *a*moral activity, meaning that it is an activity conducted by rules of its own, so that moral considerations are not relevant.[5] According to those who take the *a*moral view of business, the law provides all the rules necessary for engaging in economic competition. Is it profitable and is it legal are the only two questions appropriate for making a business decision. Outside critics can, of course, take the moral point of view, and even people within an organization might pause to consider the morality of what they are doing. But the moral evaluation of business activity is not—and many would say, cannot be—a part of the business decision-making process.

Albert Z. Carr expressed this point in another way by arguing that ethical conduct, insofar as it occurs in business, is merely strategic behavior. In a well-known *Harvard Business Review* article, "Is Business Bluffing Ethical," Carr compared business to poker, which operates by different standards of right and wrong. He wrote:

Business is our main area of competition, and it has been ritualized into a game of strategy. The basic rules of the game have been set by government. . . . But as long as a company does not transgress the rules of the game set by law, it has the legal right to shape its strategy without reference to anything but its profits. If it takes a long-term view of its profits, it will preserve amicable relations, so far as possible, with those with whom it deals. A wise businessman will not seek advantage to the point where he generates dangerous hostility among employees, competitors, customers, government, or the public at large. But decisions in this area are, in the final test, decisions of strategy, not of ethics.[6]

Since a premise of this book is that the moral point of view is essential for business decision making along with the economic and legal points of view, the thesis that business is an amoral activity or that ethics is merely a matter of strategy needs to be met head on. One problem with the thesis is that it does not recognize the extent to which moral evaluation is already an integral part of business activity. Like Molière's famous bourgeois gentleman who discovers that he has been speaking prose all his life, managers and others frequently "speak ethics." The treatment of employees, customers, suppliers, the community, and other constituencies is often evaluated by businesspeople in explicitly moral terms. Second, Carr's distinction between ethics and strategy is not easily made in practice. The strategic benefits of ethical action (a commitment to customer satisfaction, for example) can be fully achieved only if the commitment is convincing; but people are unlikely to find a commitment convincing unless a company occasionally acts against its own self-interest, which is to say that the company sometimes acts nonstrategically, at least in the short run. As a result, a company that really believes in customer satisfaction will be more likely to act strategically in the long run than a company that seeks the strategic advantage of merely feigning such a commitment. Wholly strategic behavior without ethics may thus be impossible to achieve.

This is not to say that ethics does not need to be made more prominent and incorporated more explicitly into the corporate decision-making process. Still, the commonly held position that business decisions are and ought to be made solely from the economic and legal points of view is not an adequate description of business as it is currently practiced. Managers employ all three points of view—the economic and legal points of view, as well as the moral—and all three are absolutely essential for successfully managing a business firm.

In order to understand the relevance of the moral point of view in business, then, let us examine the other two points of view more fully.

CASE 1.2 Home Depot: Good Ethics or Shrewd Business?

When weather forecasters predicted that Hurricane Andrew would strike the Miami area with full force, customers rushed to stock up on plywood and other building materials.[7] That weekend the nineteen Home Depot stores in southern Florida sold more four-foot-by-eight-foot sheets of exterior plywood than they usually sell in two weeks. On August 24, 1992, the hurricane struck, destroying or damaging more than 75,000 homes, and in the wake of the devastation, individual price-gougers were able to sell basics like water and food as well as building materials at wildly inflated prices. But not Home Depot. The chain's stores initially kept prices on plywood at prehurricane levels, and when wholesale prices rose on average 28 percent, the company announced that they would sell plywood, roofing materials, and plastic sheeting at cost and take no profit on the sales. They did limit quantities, however, to prevent price gougers from reselling the goods at higher prices. In addition, Home Depot successfully negotiated with their suppliers of plywood, including Georgia-Pacific, the nation's largest plywood producer, to roll back prices to prehurricane levels. Georgia-Pacific, like Home Depot, has a large presence in Florida; the company runs sixteen mills and distribution centers in the state and owns 500,000 acres of timberland. Although prices increased early in anticipation of Hurricane Andrew, Home Depot was still able, with the cooperation of suppliers, to sell half-inch plywood sheets for $10.15 after the hurricane, compared with a price of $8.65 before, thereby limiting the increase to less than 18 percent. Home Depot executives explained their decision as an act of good ethics by not profiting from human misery. Others contend, however, that the company made a shrewd business decision.

THE ECONOMIC POINT OF VIEW

We are constantly reminded that businesses are profit-making organizations. They also provide us with valuable goods and services. In order to achieve this result, however, it is essential that business firms be operated primarily with profit in mind.

According to economic theory, firms in a free market utilize scarce resources or factors of production (labor, raw materials, and capital) in order to produce an output (goods and services). The demand for this output is determined by the preferences of individual consumers who select from among the available goods and services so as to maximize their own satisfaction. Firms seek to increase their output up to the point where the amount received from the sale of goods and services equals the amount spent for labor, raw materials, and capital—that is, where marginal revenues equal marginal costs. Under fully competitive conditions, the result is economic efficiency, which means the production of the maximum output for the least amount of input. Elaborate techniques have been developed by economists to determine the equilibrium point between marginal revenues and marginal costs that represents the most efficient utilization of resources for producing goods and services.

In order for business activity to result in benefit to the members of society, economic theory requires that certain conditions be satisfied. These include the observance of minimal moral restraints to prevent theft, fraud, and the like. Also, all costs of production must be reflected in the prices that firms and consumers pay. But as long as these conditions are satisfied, business managers need to be concerned only with maximizing profit. Profit maximization, according to some, is the only "morality" needed for managing a business enterprise.

In practice, this concern for profit maximization translates into taking the economic point of view in making decisions about virtually every aspect of a company's operations—from marketing and personnel matters to corporate strategy and long-range planning. And the decision-making process in most companies incorporates this point of view through the use of sophisticated techniques such as management by objectives (MBO), incentive plans tied to performance, and mathematical models for production and operations management and the evaluation of corporate financial performance. Given the extent to which decision making in the modern corporation has been refined and formalized, using elaborate management information systems and the latest theories of management consultants, it is not surprising that many people in business look upon the moral point of view as a potentially disruptive element in a rationally organized, smoothly functioning system.

Difficulties with the Economic Point of View

The difficulty with taking only the economic point of view, however, is that it is not and cannot be a complete guide to business decision making. This is so for three reasons. First, the economic theory underlying the economic point of view itself contains some ethical requirements for people's behavior, and the theory also makes many assumptions about perfect competition, the internalization of costs, and so on, which are not satisfied in the actual world. As a result, business activity cannot exclude moral considerations entirely; individuals in business need to observe certain moral standards, and firms must consider harmful consequences of their actions. Second, companies are not merely the abstract firms of economic theory but large-scale organizations that coordinate the activities of flesh-and-blood human beings. The task of organizing work so that people interact with each other productively requires some attention to ethics. The ethical climate of a workplace has a significant bearing on economic performance. Third, business firms operate in a complex environment with many constituencies to which they must constantly justify their activities. In recent years, oil companies, for example, have faced the wrath of consumers and the public over charges of price gouging at the gasoline pump, oil spills from ruptured supertankers, plans for offshore drilling, illegal political campaign contributions, and support for oppressive governments. A tarnished reputation from unethical conduct is a liability in doing business, not least because of the greater government regulation that it brings. Each of these reasons calls for some comment.

1. Ethics is required by the market system.   The need for ethics in business goes far beyond the obvious rules against theft and fraud. Bribery and kickbacks, conflict of interest, insider trading, and misappropriation of trade secrets are all practices that interfere with the efficient operation of a free market and hence cannot be permitted. Such matters are typically covered by corporate ethics codes—and, to a great extent, the law—but there are many gray areas where employee conduct cannot be adequately policed by rules, and judgment must be exercised.

Consider ethics in pricing. Under conditions of perfect competition, decisions concerning the price of products can be left to market forces. To the extent that markets are imperfect, however, other factors, including ethics, come into play. This point is illustrated by the controversy over the price of AZT, an experimental drug for the treatment of AIDS, which is manufactured by only one company, Burroughs Wellcome. As a result of the lack of competition, advanced victims of AIDS were being forced to pay around $8,000 a year for AZT. After months of mounting protests and charges of price gouging, Burroughs Wellcome finally agreed to lower the wholesale price by 20 percent. In explaining the company's decision, a spokesperson said, "We are certainly mindful of the needs of the patients and the desire for a price change in the medical community."[8]

Economists explain the behavior of companies like Home Depot (see Case 1.2) by the fact that considerations of fairness limit profit-seeking behavior. Consumers remember price gouging and other practices that they consider unfair and will punish the wrongdoers by ceasing to do business with them or even engaging in boycotts. One study found that people do not believe that scarcity is an acceptable reason for raising prices (despite what economists teach about supply and demand),[9] and so Home Depot and Georgia-Pacific, which are there for the long haul, have more to lose than gain by taking advantage of a natural disaster. Evidence also indicates that people in a natural disaster feel that everyone has to make some sacrifice, so that profit seeking by a few is perceived as shirking a fair share of the burden.[10]

Other examples are provided by such unintended consequences of business activity as job-related accidents, injuries to customers by defective products, and harm to the general public through pollution and the destruction of the environment. In economic theory, these are costs of production, and if they are factored into the prices that companies pay—that is, if they are internalized—then, economists argue, the market itself takes care of the problem. Forced to pay the true cost of pollution, for example, instead of being able to use air and water as free resources, companies have an incentive to stop polluting. However, the costs of pollution control are often not internalized but passed on to workers, consumers, and the public as spillover effects or *externalities*. When externalities are present, the economic point of view is inadequate to provide the needed protection, and the problem of environmental damage must be addressed directly in business decision making. Many of the problems of business ethics, as well as government regulation, concern situations involving externalities.

Finally, many social problems, including unemployment, urban decay, racial strife, malnutrition, and inadequate education and health care, stem from the distribution of income and wealth in this country—which is largely determined by the workings of the economy. Economists generally regard these matters as the responsibility of government. The only responsibility of business is to operate efficiently. If the result is inequality, then it is up to government to manage the equity/efficiency trade-off through tax-supported programs. To a great extent, this division of responsibility is appropriate for a free market system operating in a democracy, but questions remain about whether business can operate with no concern for the problems generated by our economic system.

2. Ethics is required for organizations. Economists tend to view business firms as a web of contractual relations, but working in an organization involves more than providing a service in return for a paycheck. Firms are groupings of human beings who must be motivated to cooperate with others in a mutual endeavor. Large modern corporations, in particular, are incredibly complex organizations with a largely hierarchical structure and a myriad of rules, procedures, and customs. Organizational theorists stress the need for a moral code to guide the behavior of individuals in an organization. In one of the classics of organizational theory literature, *The Functions of the Executive*, Chester I. Barnard describes the manager as the creator and maintainer of values in an organization. According to Barnard, "The distinguishing mark of executive responsibility is that it requires not merely conformance to a complex code of morals but also the creation of moral codes for others."[11] The main function of the executive is to communicate a common purpose which is not that of any individual alone.[12]

On a more practical level, Thomas J. Peters and Robert H. Waterman, Jr., the writers of the popular book *In Search of Excellence*, contend that making a profit requires that a corporation have a strong sense of values.[13] The best-run companies in their study do not concentrate solely on financial goals but have an obsession with quality that leads them to take a strong interest in the needs and interests of consumers and to show a respect for the dignity and worth of their own employees. They have written:

> Some colleagues who have heard us expound on the importance of values and distinctive cultures have said in effect, "That's swell, but isn't it a luxury? Doesn't the business have to make money first?" The answer is that, of course, a business has to be fiscally sound. And the excellent companies are among the most fiscally sound of all. But their value set *integrates* the notions of economic health, serving customers, and making meanings down the line. As one executive said to us, "Profit is like health. You need it, and the more the better. But it's not why you exist."[14]

3. Ethics is required by corporate constituencies. As a major institution in our society, the corporation is subject to demands from many diverse groups, and the ability to make a profit often depends on how well the managers handle the conflicting pressures. In *A Behavioral Theory of the Firm*, James G. March and Richard M. Cyert argue that corporations are coalitions of many constituencies which must be accommodated so as to avoid disruptive conflicts. Instead of pursuing some overriding goal, such as making a profit, managers give "sequential attention" to a variety of problems, solving them one at a time, in the manner of a politician who first satisfies one group then another.[15] Success consists in maintaining the organization against threats to its survival.

Not all the demands on corporations involve moral issues, of course, but many do. Some of the strongest pressure in recent years has come from organized campaigns to stop American investments in South Africa. Beginning in the 1970s, religious groups, such as the Interfaith Center on Corporate Responsibility, and other organized shareholders urged major U.S. corporations to withdraw entirely or at least to adopt a set of principles drawn up in 1977 by an African American minister, Leon Sullivan, from Philadelphia. The so-called Sullivan Code requires, among other things, that companies doing business in South Africa desegregate working facilities, pay equal wages for black and white workers performing similar work, advance blacks into higher-level positions, and improve living conditions for black workers.

The fact that ethical issues are raised by the constituencies of corporations does not require that managers consider them *as ethical issues.* They may respond to shareholder resolutions and consumer boycotts as problems to "get around" by any means available. However, some companies address ethical issues directly and incorporate ethics into the decision-making process. A few have established an ethics committee of the board of directors to monitor the corporation's ethical performance. Although the task of institutionalizing ethics in corporations is in its infancy, the movement is definitely growing.[16]

CASE 1.3 Hardball in the Toy World

Hardball tactics are often applauded in business, but when Child World was the victim, the toy retailer cried foul.[17] Their complaint was directed against a major competitor, Toys "R" Us, whose employees allegedly bought Child World inventory off the shelves during a promotion in which customers received $25 gift certificates for buying merchandise worth $100. The employees of Toys "R" Us were accused of selecting products that Child World sells close to cost, such as diapers, baby food, and infant formula. These items could be resold by Toys "R" Us at a profit, since the purchase price at Child World was barely above what a wholesaler would charge, and then Toys "R" Us could redeem the certificates for additional free merchandise, which could be resold at an even higher profit. Child World claims that their competitor bought up to $1.5 million worth of merchandise in this undercover manner and received as much as $375,000 worth of gift certificates. The practice is apparently legal, although Child World stated that the promotion excluded dealers, wholesalers, and retailers. Executives at Toys "R" Us do not deny the accusation and contend that the practice is common in the industry. Child World may have left themselves open to such a hardball tactic by slashing prices and offering the certificates in an effort to increase market share against their larger rival.

THE LEGAL POINT OF VIEW

Business activity takes place within an extensive framework of law, so that all business decisions need to be made from the legal as well as the economic point of view. Some people hold, however, that the law is *all* that is morally required in business. Their motto is, If it's legal, then it's morally okay.[18] This cannot be accepted as an adequate guide. It is necessary to take the moral point of view along with the economic and legal in making business decisions. In short, the law is not enough.

Why the Legal Point of View Is Inadequate

First, the law is inappropriate for regulating certain aspects of business activity. Not everything that is immoral is illegal. Murder, theft, and fraud are both immoral and illegal, and for good reason. But cheating at cards, although immoral, is not usually a legal offense. Some ethical issues in business are like cheating at cards in that they concern interpersonal relations at work or relations between competitors, which would be difficult to regulate by law. Taking credit for someone else's work, making unreasonable demands on subordinates, and unjustly reprimanding an employee are all ethically objectionable practices, but, as with cheating at cards, they are best left outside the law. Some hardball tactics against competitors may also be legal but ethically objectionable. Whether the effort of Toys "R" Us to sabotage a promotion by their competitor is acceptable behavior (see Case 1.3) is open to dispute, but not every legal competitive maneuver is ethical.

Generally, legislatures and the courts are reluctant to intervene in ordinary business decisions unless significant rights and interests are at stake. They rightly feel that outsiders should not second-guess the business judgment of people closer to a problem and impose broad rules for problems that require a more flexible approach. Companies also prefer to handle many problems without outside interference. Still, just because it is not illegal to take credit for someone else's work or to lie on a job application form or to sabotage a competitor does not mean that it is morally okay.

Second, the law is often slow to develop in new areas of concern. Christopher D. Stone points out that the law is primarily reactive, responding to problems that people in the business world can anticipate and deal with long before they come to public attention.[19] The legislative and judicial processes themselves take a long time, and meanwhile much damage can be done. He concluded:

> Thus, there is something grotesque—and socially dangerous—in encouraging corporate managers to believe that, until the law tells them otherwise, they have no responsibilities beyond the law. . . . We do not encourage human beings to suppose so. And the dangers to society seem all the more acute where corporations are concerned.[20]

This is true not only for unknown problems, such as those created by new technologies, but also for long-recognized problems where the law has lagged behind public awareness. For example, racial and sexual discrimination was legal—and widely practiced in business—before the passage of the Civil Rights Act of 1964. It should not take a major piece of legislation to make corporate managers aware that discrimination is wrong. They should have recognized this and changed their discriminatory practices long before Congress finally got around to passing a law. The motto If discrimination is legal, then it's morally okay cannot serve to defend employers who discriminated before 1964. At the present time, legal protection for employees who blow the whistle and those who are unjustly dismissed is just beginning to develop. Employers should not wait until they are forced by law to act on such matters of growing concern.

Third, the law itself often employs moral concepts that are not precisely defined, so it is impossible in some instances to take the legal point of view without also considering matters of morality. Norman E. Bowie argues that the motto If it's legal, then it's morally okay does not express a minimal conception of morality at all but, in fact, commits the holder to a very extensive set of moral standards.[21] The requirement of *good faith*, for example, is ubiquitous in law. The National Labor Relations Act requires employers and the representatives of employees to bargain "in good faith." One defense against a charge of price discrimination is that a lower price was offered in a good-faith attempt to meet the price of a competitor. Yet the notion of good faith is not precisely defined in either instance. Abiding by the law, therefore, requires decision makers to have an understanding of this key moral concept.

The *fiduciary duty* of a person, such as a trustee, to act in the best interests of a third party is another example. The classic statement of this duty was given by Justice Benjamin Cardozo in the case *Meinhard* v. *Salmon*:

> Many forms of conduct permissible in a workaday world for those acting at arm's length, are forbidden to those bound by fiduciary ties. A trustee is held to something stricter than the morals of the market place. Not honesty alone, but the punctilio of an honor the most sensitive, is then the standard of behavior.[22]

A person in a fiduciary relation, then, must act with reference to a very high standard that is properly a part of morality. As a final example, the law holds that a trade secret cannot be acquired by *improper* means, but this crucial notion is not itself defined. A court ruled, however, that flying over a plant under construction and taking aerial photographs to discover the method developed by Du Pont for producing methanol was an improper means. According to the opinion in the case:

> "Improper" will always be a word of many nuances, determined by time, place, and circumstance. We therefore need not proclaim a catalogue of commercial improprieties. Clearly, however, one of its commandments does say, "Thou shalt not appropriate a trade secret deviously under circumstances in which countervailing defenses are not reasonably available."[23]

A fourth argument, closely related to the one preceding, is that the law itself is often unsettled, so that whether some course of action is legal must be decided by the courts. And in making a decision, the courts are often guided by moral considerations. Many people have thought that their actions, although perhaps immoral, were still legal, only to discover otherwise. To illustrate this point, Ronald Dworkin cites an 1889 New York case in which a young man who killed his grandfather was named in the will as the legal heir of the estate. The court acknowledged that a literal reading of the will entitled the grandson to the inheritance. Still, the court reasoned:

> . . . all laws as well as contracts may be controlled in their operation and effect by general, fundamental maxims of the common law. No one shall be permitted to profit by his own fraud, or to take advantage of his own wrong, or to found any claim upon his own iniquity, or to acquire property by his own crime.[24]

The courts often refuse to interpret the law literally when doing so gives legal sanction to blatant immorality. Judges have some leeway or discretion in making decisions. In exercising this discretion, judges are not necessarily substituting morality for law but rather expressing a morality that is embodied in the law. Instead of the motto If it's legal, it's morally okay, another motto is perhaps more accurate: If it's morally wrong, it's probably also illegal. Where there is doubt about what the law is, morality is a good predictor of how the courts will decide.

Fifth, a pragmatic argument is that the law is a rather inefficient instrument, and an exclusive reliance on the legal point of view invites legislation and litigation where it is not necessary. Many landmark enactments, such as the Civil Rights Act of 1964, the National Environment Policy Act of 1969, the Occupational Safety and Health Act of 1970, and the Consumer Protection Act of 1972, were passed by Congress in response to public outrage over the well-documented failure of American businesses to act responsibly. Although business leaders lament the explosion of product liability suits by consumers injured by defective products, for example, consumers are left with little choice but to use the legal system when manufacturers themselves hide behind If it's legal, it's morally okay. Adopting this motto, then, is often shortsighted, and businesses may often advance their self-interest more effectively by considering the moral point of view in the making of decisions.

Reasons for Doing Only What the Law Requires

Despite these objections to the motto If it's legal, then it's morally okay, there are still good reasons for using the law as a guide for moral action and adhering closely to its requirements. The law provides a moral minimum, which sometimes is not very minimal! (Consider, for example, the extensive obligations imposed by antidiscrimination legislation or the Occupational Safety and Health Act.) And corporations sometimes go beyond the moral minimum of legality at their peril.

First, the law embodies many of our common moral beliefs and is often an adequate guide to right action. There is scarcely an ethical issue in business that has not been addressed at one time or another by a legislature, a regulatory agency, or the courts. These bodies have duly considered the moral arguments and come, in a great many instances, to well-thought-out conclusions. The law reflects the results of a sustained public discussion of most of the ethical issues that arise in business. The law has also benefited from a wealth of practical experience. Almost every conceivable problem that could arise with a contract, for example, has already occurred and been adjudicated. As a result, contract law has a richness of detail that could never be achieved by armchair theorizing.

Second, the law provides a clearly defined set of rules. Morality alone could never adequately regulate business activity because it lacks the means to formulate rules precisely and settle disputes over their interpretation. Laws for the sale of property, securities transactions, and the like are exceedingly detailed and complex, as they must be. Since so much is often at stake in business dealings, it is also essential that there be some authoritative means for resolving disagreements. In a dispute over a contractual matter, therefore, the law is more likely to yield a satisfactory resolution.

Third, the law consists of enforceable rules that apply to everyone. In a highly competitive activity such as business, it is important that everyone play by the same rules and that no one be disadvantaged by obeying the rules while others do not. If standards for deceptive advertising, for example, were left to individual judgment, without the Federal Trade Commission (FTC) or some other authoritative body, then ethical advertisers would be at a disadvantage. With the FTC, however, advertisers can refrain from using deceptive ads, knowing that their competitors cannot take unfair advantage. Legally enforceable rules prohibiting deceptive advertising, moreover, give advertisers some justification for adhering only to the letter of the law, because they would be at a disadvantage if they voluntarily adopted a higher standard. If a higher standard is warranted, then Congress or the FTC should act, so that everyone is held to the same rules. The same kind of argument can be used to justify using the law as a guide in matters concerning workplace hazards, product safety, pollution, and the like.

A fourth argument is that the law represents a consensus arrived at through long experience and extensive deliberation. On some issues, people hold sharply differing moral views, and a manager wanting to act morally has to question whose view to accept. Differences exist, for example, about the morality of advertising tobacco products. Enough of a consensus exists to support a legal ban on cigarette advertising on television and a law requiring warning labels. Opinion is divided, however, on whether all tobacco advertising should be prohibited. Until there is sufficient support for a complete advertising ban, tobacco manufacturers and the advertising industry may continue current practices.

Finally, the law is not wholly impartial. The political process by which laws are created and enforced is an arena of powerful competing forces, and business executives occasionally feel, perhaps not without some justification, that the law is an enemy to be fought whenever possible and obeyed with reluctance. On issues such as consumer protection, worker health and safety, and the environment, many groups lobby for legislation and more stringent regulations to achieve their own ends. Politicians and bureaucrats have interests that they attempt to advance as well. While an "us versus them" mentality is unfortunate, it is not wholly unwarranted in the response business takes to the law.

CASE 1.4   Johnson & Johnson: The Tylenol Crisis

On September 30, 1982, James Burke, the CEO of Johnson & Johnson received word that several deaths in the Chicago area might be linked to one of the company's products.[25] Reports were sketchy at first, but authorities eventually determined that seven people died from taking cyanide-laced capsules of Extra-Strength Tylenol. The news riveted the nation's attention, and Burke now faced the challenge of his career.

Tylenol is one of Johnson & Johnson's most successful products. The non-aspirin pain reliever was developed in the mid-1950s by McNeil Laboratories and sold initially as a prescription drug, primarily for hospital use. After Johnson & Johnson acquired McNeil Laboratories in 1959, the company recognized the drug's potential and gained approval to sell it as an over-the-counter medication. Sales increased slowly but steadily, and by 1982 Tylenol had captured over 35 percent of the one-billion-dollar analgesic market—over three times the market share of its nearest competitor. The product provided 7 percent of Johnson & Johnson sales and a whopping 17 percent of the company's profits.

Tylenol's success was achieved by heavy advertising and price reductions. Since the only active ingredient, acetaminophen, can be easily manufactured, the drug was open prey to competitors, and when Bristol Meyers introduced Datril in 1975, Johnson & Johnson had to move quickly. The company protected its market share by slashing prices by 30 percent and boosting advertising to $4 million in 1976 (from $142,000 the year before). The figure rose to $40 million in 1982, and during the seven-year period from 1976 to 1982, Johnson & Johnson spent over $155 million to promote the Tylenol brand. Developing a best-selling brand had been expensive, but by 1982 the company was reaping the rewards of its investment.

The cyanide that caused the deaths was placed in capsules of Extra-Strength Tylenol. Advertised as "the most potent pain reliever you can buy without a prescription," the extra-strength product—which contains 500 milligrams of acetaminophen as compared with 350 milligrams in regular Tylenol—was sold at the time in both capsule and tablet form. Extra-Strength Tylenol was instantly popular, and by 1979 it accounted for 70 percent of all Tylenol sales. The capsule form appealed to consumers because it was easier to swallow, and also because of an association of capsules with strength. Capsules are susceptible to tampering, however, because they can be pulled apart and refilled, and the fact that all of the deaths occurred in one area—and that only a few capsules in each of the bottles contained cyanide—suggested that someone (who has never been apprehended) took advantage of the ease with which capsules can be used to kill.

James Burke and his staff quickly concluded that the tampering had not occurred at a McNeil production facility, and so the company was not responsible for the cyanide contamination itself. Still, the poisonings were associated with the Tylenol name, and sales of the brand were dropping rapidly. The public reaction was fueled by confusion, which was furthered by false reports of Tylenol-related deaths in several other states, and the company feared a rash of copycat incidents, especially as Halloween approached.

Johnson & Johnson faced two problems. One was how to respond to public concerns—and to the possibility that more cyanide-laced capsules might still be found. What information should the company release to the media and to worried customers? What changes, if any, should be made in the advertising for Tylenol, or should all advertising be suspended? Should Johnson & Johnson recall capsules of Extra-Strength Tylenol only in the Chicago area, or should the company pull all capsules from store shelves nationwide? A nationwide recall would involve an estimated thirty-one million bottles with a retail value of $100 million. Removal of the product would also cede valuable shelf space to Tylenol's competitors and risk a permanent loss of market share.

The problem, moreover, was tampering, which could occur with any medication in capsule form, and indeed with any over-the-counter drug. The pharmaceutical industry, and not merely Johnson & Johnson, was threatened by the Tylenol poisonings. The cost of a recall outside of the Chicago area was out of proportion to the risk, and consumers faced far greater risk from adverse reactions to many pharmaceutical products that were regarded as safe. On the other hand, capsules of Extra-Strength Tylenol on store shelves (which no longer belonged to Johnson & Johnson) was so much "dead stock" that might never be sold, and the loss would be borne by distributors and retailers.

The second problem was whether—and if so, how—to save the Tylenol brand name. Many marketing experts were convinced that the brand was doomed —that the public would forever associate Tylenol with death—and that a new identity should be sought for an acetaminophen product before the company's competitors could capture the market. James Burke was convinced that the brand name could be saved if Johnson & Johnson restored public confidence quickly, but doing so would require not only reassuring words but steps to make tampering less likely. An aggressive campaign could backfire, however, if another poisoning occurred, since the company could be accused being more concerned with profits than consumer safety.

In addressing these problems, James Burke and others at Johnson & Johnson had the benefit of goodwill from a public that recognized that the company was also a victim of a senseless crime. The company also had an invaluable resource in the relation of trust that had been built through decades of adherence to the Johnson & Johnson credo. This declaration of the company's responsibility to customers, employees, and the community—as well as stockholders—had enabled Johnson & Johnson to prosper so far. Could it also be a guide in the current crisis?

AN INTEGRATED APPROACH

The approach advocated in this book is that decision making in business should involve an integration of all three points of view: the economic, the legal, and the moral. Business ethics is simply the attempt to think clearly and deeply about ethical issues in business and to arrive at conclusions that are supported by the strongest possible arguments. An integrated approach requires that we give proper weight to the economic and legal aspects of a problem, but to think that sound business decisions could be made solely from a perspective that excludes ethics is just as wrongheaded as it is to think that they could be made on the basis of ethical reasoning alone.

Integrating different points of view is nothing new; we do it all the time. Managers must juggle financial, production, marketing, personnel, and a host of other factors in taking just the economic point of view. Inevitably, there is tension between the three points of view, but the ideal resolution is not a trade-off between ethics and other considerations. The outcome, instead, should be a decision that is ethically defensible while at the same time satisfying the legitimate demands of economic performance and a company's legal obligations.

An illustration of an integrated approach is provided by Johnson & Johnson's response to the Tylenol crisis (see Case 1.4). Under the leadership of CEO James Burke, the company quickly cleared all bottles of Extra-Strength Tylenol capsules off store shelves in the Chicago area and recalled all bottles from the two batches that had been identified in the poisonings. A decision was made to be completely candid with the medical community, the media, and the public. Accordingly, the company issued warnings to physicians and hospitals around the world, briefed the press fully, and provided a toll-free telephone number for answering consumer inquiries. In addition, all advertising for Tylenol was temporarily suspended. On October 6, one week after the first Tylenol-related deaths, Johnson & Johnson instituted a nationwide recall of the thirty-one million bottles of Regular- and Extra-Strength Tylenol capsules that remained unsold.

James Burke was convinced that the Tylenol brand name could be saved with a well-designed strategy. The key was to protect consumers by developing a tamper-resistant package that would both discourage tampering and make tampering more evident. The Tylenol crisis had alerted the pharmaceutical industry to the need for tamper-resistant packaging, and on November 4 the Food and Drug Administration (FDA) made such protection mandatory. By acting quickly to develop the technology, Johnson & Johnson could establish an industry-leadership position. The company decided on a three-point protection system consisting of a tape seal on the box, a wrapper on the cap, and a seal over the mouth of the bottle. By late November, Extra-Strength Tylenol in capsule form was once again on store shelves. Advertising was resumed in December, and more than eighty million coupons were distributed for the product in its new tamper-resistant packaging. The direct cost for this recovery effort has been estimated at $150 million.

The response of Johnson & Johnson to the Tylenol crisis can be explained as sound business decision making. The effort to restore a valuable brand name was costly, but the high-stakes gamble paid off. The decision for a nationwide recall of all capsule products may appear obvious in retrospect because of the crucial role it played in assuring consumers of the company's commitment to safety. Strong arguments were made at the time against a recall, however, including the tremendous expense and the success of other companies in dismissing product tampering as isolated incidents.

An important factor in deciding on a recall was the Johnson & Johnson Credo (see Exhibit 1). Developed in the 1940s as an expression of the company's way of doing business, the Credo guided several generations of Johnson & Johnson employees. One of James Burke's first acts upon becoming CEO was to hold a series of Credo "challenges," to determine whether the document was still relevant to management decision making, and the outcome was a gratifying reaffirmation of the Credo's continuing force. Although economic and legal considerations played a role in Johnson & Johnson's response to the Tylenol crisis, the Credo served too,

Our Credo

We believe our first responsibility is to the doctors, nurses and patients, to mothers and fathers and all others who use our products and services. In meeting their needs everything we do must be of high quality. We must constantly strive to reduce our costs in order to maintain reasonable prices. Customers' orders must be serviced promptly and accurately. Our suppliers and distributors must have an opportunity to make a fair profit.

We are responsible to our employees, the men and women who work with us throughout the world. Everyone must be considered as an individual. We must respect their dignity and recognize their merit. They must have a sense of security in their jobs. Compensation must be fair and adequate, and working conditions clean, orderly and safe. We must be mindful of ways to help our employees fulfill their family responsibilities. Employees must feel free to make suggestions and complaints. There must be equal opportunity for employment, development, and advancement for those qualified. We must provide competent management, and their actions must be just and ethical.

We are responsible to the communities in which we live and work and to the world community as well. We must be good citizens—support good works and charities and bear our fair share of taxes. We must encourage civic improvements and better health and education. We must maintain in good order the property we are privileged to use, protecting the environment and natural resources.

Our final responsibility is to our stockholders. Business must make a sound profit. We must experiment with new ideas. Research must be carried on, innovative programs developed and mistakes paid for. New equipment must be purchased, new facilities provided and new products launched. Reserves must be created to provide for adverse times. When we operate according to these principles, the stockholders should realize a fair return.

Exhibit 1   Johnson & Johnson, the statement "Our Credo," reprinted by permission.

and the clear statements of responsibility that it contained enabled the company to make some really tough, but ultimately right, decisions.

In retrospect, however, the company might be faulted for one decision: to continue marketing Extra-Strength Tylenol in capsule form. Consumer surveys found that a segment of the market strongly preferred medication in a capsule. But a tampering incident three years later, in February 1986, took the life of a 23-year-old New York State woman and finally convinced Burke that the safety of capsules could not be assured, even with tamper-resistant packaging. Production of Tylenol in capsule form was terminated, and a new product, Tylenol caplets—tablets shaped like capsules—was introduced. At the time, approximately one-third of all Tylenol sold was in capsule form, and the change was estimated to reduce Tylenol sales by about 6 percent annually. Perhaps Johnson & Johnson should have taken this step three years earlier.

Integrating the three points of view requires an understanding of the ethical point of view in making decisions about problems that typically arise in business. Managers receive training in making decisions on the basis of purely economic considerations from their formal education and long years of experience. If they are unfamiliar with the law, company lawyers are there to give advice on the legal aspects of any problem. Many people assume, however, that taking the moral point of view requires nothing more than what we learned at home or the morality that we practice in our everyday life. Like the major functional areas in business education, philosophical ethics provides a set of concepts and theories for understanding and resolving complex issues. The first part of this book, therefore, covers important concepts and theories that form an essential foundation for the discussion of the specific ethical issues in business that follows.

MORALITY, ETHICS, AND ETHICAL THEORY

Before proceeding further, we need to clarify the meaning of the key terms *morality* and *ethics* and the cognates *moral* and *ethical* and *morally* and *ethically*. Generally, *morality* and *ethics*, *moral* and *ethical*, and so on are interchangeable. The presence of two words in the English language with the same meaning is due to the fact that they derive from different roots: *morality*, from the Latin word *moralitas*, and *ethics*, from the Greek *ethikos*. There is no difference, therefore, between describing discrimination as a moral issue or as an ethical issue, or between saying that discrimination is morally wrong or that it is ethically wrong. There are some subtle differences, however, between *morality* and *ethics*.

Morality is generally used to describe a sociological phenomenon; namely, the existence in a society of rules and standards of conduct. Every society has a morality, since this constitutes the basis for mutually beneficial interaction. Without such fundamental rules as Do not kill and Do not steal, for example, stable communities would be impossible. Not all rules and standards are part of morality, of course. Eating peas with a knife, for example, is a breach of etiquette but not a moral wrong, and the rule Look both ways before crossing the street is a rule of prudence, not morality. Etiquette and prudence, therefore, constitute sets of nonmoral rules and standards. Morality also has many complex ties to the law, as we have already observed.

Moralities are also specific to societies and exist at certain times and places. Thus, we can speak of the morality of the Trobriand Islanders or the colonial settlers. The morality of Americans in the 1990s is different from that in the 1950s or the 1850s. We can even speak, as Karl Marx did, of the morality of different classes in society. In a highly developed society such as our own, morality also includes a complex vocabulary and patterns of reasoning that permit the members of the society to engage in moral discourse for the purpose of evaluating the actions of individuals and the practices and institutions of the society. *Ethics* is roughly a synonym for *morality*, but it is often restricted to the rules and norms of specific kinds of conduct or the codes of conduct for specialized groups. Thus, we talk about the ethics of stockbrokers or the code of ethics for the accounting profession but usually not about the morality of these groups.

The term *ethics* also has another, quite different, use, which is to denote the field of *moral philosophy*. Ethics, along with logic, epistemology, and metaphysics, is a traditional area of philosophical inquiry that dates back to the time of the ancient Greeks. Ethics as a philosophical endeavor is the study of morality. Such a study is either *descriptive* or *normative*. Descriptive ethics may involve an empirical inquiry into the actual rules or standards of a particular group, or it could also consist of understanding the ethical reasoning process. A sociological study of the values of American business managers would be an example of the former; and the work of psychologists on moral development would illustrate the latter. Normative ethics is concerned largely with the possibility of justification. It takes morality as its subject matter and asks such questions as: Are there any means for showing that the rules and standards of our morality are the right ones? Are there any ultimate moral principles that can be used to resolve inconsistencies or conflicts? Normative ethics is concerned not with what people *believe* we ought to do but with what we *really* ought to do, which is determined by reasoning or moral argument. Philosophical ethics is not a substitute for morality; rather, it seeks to organize our ordinary moral beliefs in a precise and consistent manner and to discover whatever justification they have.

In the next few chapters, three major theories of ethics are presented as the basis for our beliefs about moral obligations, rights, and justice, and they are applied in discussions of a number of issues concerning the rights and obligations of employees in a firm, employee relations, the protection of employees and consumers, and the responsibility of corporations to the public at large. We will discover a large measure of disagreement between these ethical theories in their content and in the results of applying them to specific cases. The differences between theories should not lead us to despair of resolving ethical issues or to conclude that one resolution is as good as another. Nor should we be discouraged by the fact that agreement on complex ethical issues is seldom achieved. The best we can do is to analyze the issues as fully as possible, which means getting straight on the facts and achieving definitional clarity, and then develop the strongest and most complete arguments we can for what we consider to be the correct conclusions.

CASE 1.5   Joyce Roberts

Joyce Roberts, 29 years old, was a middle-level manager at Amalgamated Products, Inc. (API).[26] For the last nine months, she had been on special assignment to a key marketing-staff function at corporate headquarters, working directly with the marketing vice president, Bernard Peach, even though there were two levels of management between them. Peach had come to Roberts's boss and told him not to give her any other assignments—that Roberts was to work directly for Peach. In order to communicate more closely, Peach had Roberts install a high-tech phone system in her office and gave Roberts access to an executive secretary, perks that Roberts's boss did not enjoy.

API was a staid company, facing a number of changes in its external environment. It was highly centralized, and a number of key managers complained that the company was overly bureaucratic. Many older managers, like Roberts's boss (and her boss's boss) were looked upon as "dead wood," incapable of operating in the new environment. Nevertheless, change was normally a slow process at API, and on a number of matters Roberts found herself in direct conflict with her boss, even though she was acting on Peach's direct orders. She was unsure how much resentment was building up beneath the surface, but she found working directly with Peach, occasionally mentioned as a future CEO, exhilarating—even if she was frustrated by being caught in the middle of larger bureaucratic struggles.

Peach and Roberts worked together closely on a high-profile revamping of API's products, and by all measures the project promised to be quite successful. Two days before the presentation to API's Executive Committee, Peach dispatched Roberts to the resort where the meeting was to be held in order to double- and triple-check all of the arrangements. When Peach arrived, he called Roberts's room at 3 A.M. and together they checked the slide projector to be sure that the tops of the slides were straight when projected.

After the presentation, the committee adopted most of the recommendations, and two days later Bernard Peach was promoted to Group Vice President—Asia. Joyce Roberts went into her office to find two memos on her desk. The first was the announcement that Bernard Peach had been promoted and had already left for his new job. The second was a handwritten note from her boss requesting to talk about her performance problems over the last six months. Roberts wondered what she should do.

CASE 1.6   A Sticky Situation

Kent Graham is still on the telephone, receiving the good news that he has just secured his largest order as an account manager for Dura-Stick Label Products.[27] His joy is tinged with uncertainty, however.

Dura-Stick is a leader in label converting for the durable-products marketplace. Label converting consists of converting log rolls of various substrates (paper, polyester, vinyl) into die-cut, printed labels. The company specializes in high-performance labels for the automotive, lawn and garden, and appliance industries. Dura-Stick has a well-deserved reputation for quality, technical knowledge, and service that enables the company to command a premium price for their products in a very competitive market.

Kent Graham has been with Dura-Stick for two years. Because he came to the company with ten years in the label industry, he was able to negotiate a very good salary and compensation plan, but his accomplishments since joining Dura-Stick have been mediocre at best. Kent fears that his time with Dura-Stick might be limited unless he starts closing some big accounts. Furthermore, with a wife and two children to support, losing his job would be disastrous. Kent was on a mission to land a big account.

Kent called on Jack Olson at Spray-On Inc., a manufacturer of industrial spraying systems for the automotive painting industry. Dura-Stick has been providing Spray-On with various warning and instructional labels for about twenty years. Jack has been very pleased with Dura-Stick's performance, especially the quality of their manufacturing department under the direction of Tim Davis. After giving Kent another excellent vendor evaluation report, Jack began to describe a new project at Spray-On, a paint sprayer for household consumer use that needs a seven-color label with very precise graphics. This label is different from the industrial two-color labels that Dura-Stick currently supplies to Spray-On.

Jack explained that this was the biggest project that Spray-On has undertaken in recent years and that it would generate a very large order for some label company. Jack then asked Kent, "Does Dura-Stick produce these multicolor, consumer-type labels?" Kent thought for a moment. He knew that a "yes" would give him a better shot at the business, and Dura-Stick might be able to handle the job, even though the company's experience to date was only with two-color labels. Almost without thinking, he replied, "Sure we can handle it, Jack, that's right up our alley!" "That's great news," Jack shot back. "Now take this sample and give me your proposal by Monday. Oh, and by the way, I hope your proposal looks good, because I would really feel confident if this important project were in the hands of your production people!"

Kent gave the sample to Marty Klein, who is responsible for coordinating the costs and price quotes for new opportunities. Marty took one look at the sample and said emphatically, "We'll have to farm this one out." Kent's heart sank down to his shoes. He knew that Jack would want to work with Dura-Stick only if the labels were produced at Dura-Stick's facility. Yet, he still allowed Marty to put the numbers together for the proposal. Kent presented the proposal to Jack at Spray-On. "Gee, Kent, these prices are pretty high, about twenty percent higher than your competition. That's pretty hard to swallow."

Kent knew that the price would be high since it included the cost of another company producing the labels plus Dura-Stick's usual profit margin, but he countered cheerily, "You know the quality that we provide and how important this project is to your company. Isn't it worth the extra twenty percent for the peace of mind that you will have?"

"Let me think about," Jack replied.

The next day, Kent got a phone call from Jack. "Congratulations, Kent, Dura-Stick has been awarded the business. It was a tough sell to my people, but I convinced them that the extra money would be well spent because of the excellent production department that you have. If it wasn't for the fact that Tim Davis will personally oversee production, you guys probably would not have gotten this business."

Kent had to bite his tongue. He knew that Tim would not be involved because the labels would be produced in Kansas City by Labeltec, which would then send the finished labels to Dura-Stick for shipment to Spray-On's facility. Kent also knew that Jack would be completely satisfied with the quality of the labels. Besides, this order was crucial to his job security, not to mention the well-being of his company.

While Jack continued to explain Spray-On's decision, Kent pondered how he should close this conversation.

NOTES

1. RICHARD T. DEGEORGE, *Competing with Integrity in International Business* (New York: Oxford University Press, 1993), 97–99.

2. The concept of the moral point of view is developed in KURT BAIER, *The Moral Point of View: A Rational Basis of Ethics* (Ithaca: Cornell University Press, 1958). A similar account is offered in JAMES RACHELS, *The Elements of Moral Philosophy* (New York: Random House, 2nd ed., 1993), chap. 1.

3. BAIER, *The Moral Point of View*, 88.

4. BAIER, *The Moral Point of View*, 195–96.

5. For a fuller discussion of this point, see RICHARD T. DEGEORGE, *Business Ethics*, 4th ed. (Englewood Cliffs, NJ: Prentice Hall, 1995).

6. ALBERT Z. CARR, "Is Business Bluffing Ethical?" *Harvard Business Review*, 46 (January–February, 1968), 148.

7. This case is adapted from STEVE LOHR, "Lessons from a Hurricane: It Pays Not to Gouge," *New York Times*, 22 September 1992, D1, D2.

8. Quoted in PHILIP J. HILTS, "AIDS Drug's Maker Cuts Price by 20%," *New York Times*, 19 September 1989, A1.

9. DANIEL KAHNEMAN, JACK L. KNETCH, and RICHARD THALER, "Fairness as a Constraint of Profit-Seeking: Entitlements in the Market," *American Economic Review*, 76 (1986), 728–41.

10. DOUGLAS C. DACY and HOWARD KUNREUTHER, *The Economics of Natural Disasters* (New York: Free Press, 1969), 115–16.

11. CHESTER I. BARNARD, *The Functions of the Executive* (Cambridge: Harvard University Press, 1968), 279.

12. BARNARD, *The Functions of the Executive*, 217–27.

13. THOMAS J. PETERS and ROBERT H. WATERMAN, JR., *In Search of Excellence* (New York: Harper & Row, 1982).

14. PETERS and WATERMAN, *In Search of Excellence*, 103.

15. RICHARD M. CYERT and JAMES G. MARCH, *A Behavioral Theory of the Firm* (Englewood Cliffs, NJ: Prentice Hall, 1963), 118. Similar accounts are given in HERBERT A. SIMON and JAMES G. MARCH, *Organizations* (New York: Wiley, 1958); JEFFREY PFEFFER and GERALD SALANCIK, *The External Control of Organizations* (New York: Harper & Row, 1978); and from a public policy perspective, CHARLES E. LINDBLOM, *The Public Policy Process* (Englewood Cliffs, NJ: Prentice Hall, 1968).

16. See Center for Business Ethics, "Are Corporations Institutionalizing Ethics?" *Journal of Business Ethics*, 5 (1986), 85–91. An overview is provided by The Business Roundtable, *Corporate Ethics: A Prime Business Asset*, February 1988.

17. This case is adapted from SUZANNE ALEXANDER, "Child World Says Rival Cheats; Toys 'R' Us Answers: 'Grow Up'," *Wall Street Journal*, 19 September 1991, B1, B10.

18. This phrase is taken from NORMAN E. BOWIE, "Fair Markets," *Journal of Business Ethics*, 7 (1988), 89–98.

19. CHRISTOPHER D. STONE, *Where the Law Ends: The Social Control of Corporate Behavior* (New York: Harper & Row, 1975), 94.

20. STONE, *Where the Law Ends*, 94.

21. BOWIE, "Fair Markets." Much of the argument on this point is derived from Bowie's article.

22. *Meinhard* v. *Salmon*, 164 N.E. 545 (1928).

23. *E. I. du Pont de Nemours & Co.* v. *Christopher*, 431 F. 2d 1012 (5th Cir. 1970).

24. *Riggs* v. *Palmer*, 115 N.Y. 506 (1889). Discussed in RONALD DWORKIN, *Taking Rights Seriously* (Cambridge: Harvard University Press, 1978), 23.

25. Material on this case is taken from "James Burke: A Career in American Business (A) & (B)," Harvard Business School, 1989; "The 1982 Tylenol Poisoning Episode," in RONALD M. GREEN, *The Ethical Manager: A New Method for Business Ethics* (New York: Macmillan, 1994), 208–19; and ROBERT F. HARTLEY, *Business Ethics: Violations of Public Trust* (New York: Wiley, 1993), 295–309.

26. This case was prepared by R. Edward Freeman. Reprinted by permission.

27. This case was prepared by Kerry Winans under the supervision of Professor John R. Boatright. Copyright 1995 by John R. Boatright.

2

Utilitarianism

CASE 2.1   Lockheed in Japan

When Carl Kotchian, president of Lockheed Aircraft Corporation, made a trip to Japan in August 1972, the company he headed was in a very precarious financial situation. Lockheed had failed to get contracts with several major European carriers. Cost overruns on the C5A Galaxie transport plane and performance problems with the Cheyenne helicopter had caused the Defense Department to cancel its orders for these aircraft. And Lockheed had avoided bankruptcy in 1971 only with a $250 million loan guarantee from the federal government. The survival of Lockheed as a company was riding on the effort to sell the new L-1011 TriStar passenger jet to All Nippon Airways.

Shortly after landing in Tokyo, Kotchian asked a representative of the Marubeni Corporation, a trading company that Lockheed had engaged to aid in negotiations with All Nippon Airways (ANA), to arrange a meeting with Kakuei Tanaka, the prime minister of Japan.[1] Kotchian knew that Tanaka would be meeting with President Richard Nixon in Hawaii in a few days and that Nixon would ask him to improve the U.S. balance of payments by buying more American products. He felt that it was important for the prime minister to be informed beforehand about the merits of the TriStar.

The representative of Marubeni, Toshiharu Okubo, informed Kotchian that a "pledge" of five hundred million yen (about $1.6 million) would be required to set up such a meeting. Without specifically being told the destination of the money, Kotchian assumed that it was intended for the prime minister's office.

Kotchian was hesitant about making an irregular payment of this size to the highest official in the Japanese government, but he knew that refusing to do so would hamper Lockheed's efforts and that the blame for any failure would rest squarely on his shoulders. So he agreed to pledge the amount requested, and a meeting was held at seven thirty the next morning. At the meeting, which Kotchian did not attend, the president of Marubeni allegedly secured Tanaka's help on behalf of Lockheed with an offer of five hundred million yen.

After more than two months of complex negotiations, executives of ANA were on the verge of placing an order for six planes with an option to buy eight more. Late in the evening of Sunday, October 29, Carl Kotchian received a telephone call from Okubo informing him that the sale was assured if he would do three things. Two of them were minor, but the third was a bombshell. Kotchian was asked to have $400,000 in Japanese yen ready the next morning. Of this amount, $300,000, or ninety million yen, was to be paid to Tokuji Wakasa, the president of All Nippon Airways. This figure was based on $50,000 for each of the six planes ordered. The remaining $100,000, or thirty million yen, was to be divided among six Japanese politicians. When Kotchian protested that it would be impossible to raise that much cash so quickly, he was told the thirty million yen for the politicians was essential; the rest could wait.

By ten o'clock the next morning, thirty million yen in cash was delivered to Okubo, and the ninety-million-yen payment to the president of ANA was made a week later. Kotchian returned to the company's headquarters in Burbank, California, amid general celebration and apparently forgot about the pledge of five hundred million yen for Prime Minister Tanaka. Eight months later, though, Okubo called Kotchian to say that now was the time to follow through. Kotchian asked whether the payment was necessary since the deal had been concluded such a long time ago. Okubo assured him that if he did not honor the pledge, Lockheed would never be able to do business in Japan again, and he hinted darkly that the president of Marubeni, who had made the offer to Tanaka, would have to leave the country.

INTRODUCTION

The case of Lockheed in Japan presented Carl Kotchian with a complex ethical dilemma. He had to act quickly in a situation where he would be called upon to justify whatever decision he made. He could not decide what to do merely from an economic or legal point of view because his actions would be judged by his fellow executives and employees at Lockheed, by Lockheed customers and competitors, and by the public at large. Kotchian needed to think through the ethical implications of the alternatives and select a course of action that could be defended ethically.

Fortunately, Carl Kotchian has provided us with an account of the reasoning behind his decisions, which we can use not only to understand what it means to reason ethically but also to judge for ourselves the defense he offered. In an account of his experiences, Kotchian wrote:

After hanging up the telephone, I went home and thought about the matter overnight. I decided on the basis of what Okubo had told me that we could not possibly risk any retaliation against Lockheed or against Marubeni. If we did not make the payment on this matter, Hiyama [the president of Marubeni] would be forced into exile, Lockheed might not be able to sell anything in Japan again, and our relations with Marubeni might be completely disrupted. Consequently, the more I thought about it, the more I was convinced that there was no alternative but to make the payment. In the end, after talking it over with other Lockheed executives, I called Okubo and told him we would honor the pledge.[2]

Later, when All Nippon exercised the option to buy eight more TriStar planes, Okubo requested $400,000, based on $50,000 per plane. Kotchian again felt that he had no choice but to comply and ordered that the payment be made. In all, Lockheed paid about $12.5 million in bribes and commissions to sell twenty-one TriStars in Japan.

Kotchian explained his decision to approve the first payments to the president of ANA and the six politicians in the following way:

If some third party had heard this conversation, he could ask why I responded to this request for secret payments. However, I must admit that it was extremely persuasive and attractive at that time to have someone come up to me and confidently tell me, "If you do this, you will surely get ANA's order in twenty-four hours." What businessman who is dealing with commercial and trade matters could decline a request for certain amounts of money when that money would enable him to get the contract? For someone like myself, who had been struggling against plots and severe competition for over two months, it was almost impossible to dismiss this opportunity.[3]

And he justified all the payments for the sale of the TriStar by making three points:

The *first* is that the Lockheed payments in Japan, totaling about $12 million, were worthwhile from Lockheed's standpoint, since they amounted to less than 3 percent of the expected sum of about $430 million that we would receive from ANA for 21 TriStars. Further, as I've noted, such disbursements *did not violate American laws*. I should also like to stress that my decision to make such payments stemmed from my judgment that the TriStar payments to ANA would provide Lockheed workers with jobs and thus redound to the benefit of their dependents, their communities, and stockholders of the corporation.

Secondly, I should like to emphasize that the payments to the so-called "high Japanese government officials" were all requested by Okubo and were *not brought up from my side*. When he told me "five hundred million yen is necessary for such sales," from a purely ethical and moral standpoint I should have declined such a request. However, in that case, I would *most certainly* have sacrificed commercial success.

Finally, I want to make it clear that I never discussed money matters with Japanese politicians, government officials, or airline officials. . . . From my experience in international sales, I knew that if we wanted our product to have a chance to win on its own merits, we had to follow the functioning system. . . . [W]e understood that we would have to pay, or pledge to pay, substantial sums of money in addition to the contractual sales commissions. We never *sought* to make these extra payments. We would have preferred not to have the additional expenses for the sale. But, always, they were recommended by those whose experience and judgment we trusted and whose recommendations we followed.[4]

Evaluating Arguments for Bribery

Do these arguments serve to justify the actions of Lockheed in Japan? Although bribery is morally wrong in most situations, Lockheed officials contended that it is an accepted practice in many parts of the world and a necessity in a competitive climate where other companies do the same. If Lockheed had refused to make the requested payments, the company would quite possibly have lost the Japanese market to less scrupulous competitors. Carl Kotchian argued further that his actions did not constitute bribery but rather that Lockheed was an innocent victim of extortion demands made by the Japanese. Lockheed's motive in making the payments, moreover, was not to make a sale by corrupting Japanese officials; the company was simply trying to do business in an atmosphere tainted by the corruption of others. Finally, the payments were actually offered by the middlemen of the Marubeni Corporation, who were apparently well versed in the ways of decision making, Japanese style.[5]

The arguments used by Carl Kotchian appeal primarily to *consequences*. Tens of thousands of jobs were saved, thereby benefiting Lockheed workers, their families, and the communities in which they lived. The cost to the company was negligible given the size of the deal. Stockholders were saved from the loss that would have resulted from the collapse of the company. And the sale benefited the country as a whole by reducing the U.S. balance of payments problem. Kotchian insists that Lockheed violated no American law.[6] Besides, some people argue, no one really got hurt. The cost of the bribes would eventually be passed on to consumers and taxpayers, but these losses, they feel, are not significant when compared with the gains for Lockheed.

The appeal to consequences is not conclusive, however. Lockheed was competing for sales with two other American companies: Boeing with its 747 and McDonnell Douglas and the DC 10. So the jobs that were saved in Burbank, California, were lost in Seattle, St. Louis, and elsewhere, and the workers for these two companies, their families, subcontractors, and the stockholders of Boeing and McDonnell Douglas were all harmed as a result. Lockheed's success in taking business away from other American companies does nothing, moreover, to improve the balance of payments for the United States. In the aftermath of the Lockheed affair, many careers were destroyed. Carl Kotchian resigned from Lockheed. Prime Minister Tanaka was forced from office and prosecuted along with other Japanese officials. Many Japanese feel that the country itself was hurt because of the distrust of political institutions that the revelations created in Japan. Although the scandal prompted a movement toward reform, some observers believe that it also increased the strength of right-wing elements who think that Japan has been corrupted by modern life and ought to abandon parliamentary democracy and return to the old imperial system.

Consequences aside, some people hold that bribery is wrong because of the violation of *duty* it involves. Officials both in the Japanese government and at All Nippon Airways hold positions of trust, in which they are pledged to serve the interests of the people of Japan. They betrayed this trust by accepting the bribes, and

Lockheed, by paying the bribes, is guilty of complicity in their betrayal. Even if bribery has no adverse consequences, it is still wrong according to ethical theories based on the notion of duty because of the betrayal of trust that it involves.

Who is correct in this case? What is the best way to reason about these kinds of ethical issues? Are there any theories of ethics that can aid us in handling cases such as those faced by Carl Kotchian? This chapter examines one major ethical theory, known as utilitarianism, which looks for justification to the consequences of actions. In subsequent chapters we will look at other important theories, including some that base right action on the notion of duty. It will also be useful in this chapter to clarify the distinction already made between two types of ethical theories; namely, those based on consequences and those based on duty—or teleological and deontological theories, to use their technical names.

TWO TYPES OF ETHICAL THEORIES

It is customary to divide ethical theories into two groups, usually called teleological and deontological. The most prominent historical examples of a teleological and a deontological theory are utilitarianism and the ethical theory of Immanuel Kant, respectively. A third kind of ethical theory is one based on the concept of virtue, which is discussed in the next chapter. Aristotle's ethics is the best example of a theory of this kind.

Teleological theories hold that the rightness of actions is determined solely by the amount of good consequences they produce. The word *teleological* is derived from the Greek word *telos,* which refers to an end. Actions are justified on teleological theories by virtue of the end they achieve, rather than some feature of the actions themselves. Thus, the concept of goodness is fundamental in teleological theories, and the concepts of rightness and obligation, or duty, are defined in terms of goodness. According to utilitarianism, our obligation, or duty, in any situation is to perform the action that will result in the greatest possible balance of good over evil.

Obviously, a great deal depends on what is regarded as good and as evil. In classical utilitarianism, pleasure is taken to be ultimately the only good, and evil is the opposite of pleasure, or pain. But utilitarianism can be understood more broadly, so that goodness is human well-being. Whatever makes human beings generally better off or provides some benefit is good, and whatever makes them worse off or harms them is evil. Differences of opinion exist, of course, on what constitutes benefits and harms, or being better or worse off. Generally, utilitarianism does not attempt to resolve these differences but accepts each person's own conception of what being better off means for him or her.

The Strengths and Weaknesses of Teleological Theories

Teleological theories have many strengths. One is that they are in accord with much of our ordinary moral reasoning. The fact that an action would provide some benefit or inflict some harm is generally a morally relevant reason for or against performing it. So utilitarianism is able to explain why such actions as lying, breaking a promise, stealing, and assault are wrong and their opposites—truth telling, promise keeping, respect for property, and the like—are right. Lying, for example, creates false beliefs that often lead people to make disadvantageous choices, and if lying were to become common, then trust would be eroded, with a resulting decline in welfare for everyone. Having true beliefs, by contrast, is generally beneficial, and a society that values truth telling will have a higher level of welfare. Utilitarianism can also explain why lying in some circumstances is the right thing to do. It would be wrong to tell a murderer the location of an intended victim, for example, because the harm that would be done in this instance outweighs any benefit from telling the truth.

Second, teleological theories provide a relatively precise and objective method for moral decision making. Assuming that the goodness of consequences can be easily measured and compared, a teleological decision maker need only determine the possible courses of action and calculate the consequences of each one. For this reason, utilitarianism is attractive not only for matters of individual choice but also for decisions on issues of public policy. Utilitarian reasoning has also found favor among economists, who use the assumption that individuals seek to maximize their own utility or welfare to explain and predict a wide range of economic phenomena, such as prices and the allocation of resources. The ethical theory underlying classical economic theory is broadly utilitarian.

The weaknesses of teleological theories derive from the same features that constitute their strengths. Although much of our ordinary moral reasoning is teleological, some of it is decidedly nonteleological in character. Generally, we have an obligation to keep our promises, even when more good might be achieved by breaking them. If we promise another person to store some food that belongs to them, for example, it would be wrong to give the food away to hungry beggars merely because doing so would have better consequences. Indeed, in deciding whether to keep a promise, the consequences seem to be morally irrelevant, although there might be stronger obligations that override the keeping of a promise. If the food is needed to save the life of a person, for example, then we might have an obligation to provide it—not because of the good consequences, however, but because of a stronger obligation to save a life.

Role obligations, which occupy a prominent place in business, often seem to be nonteleological. Parents have obligations to their children, for example, that are created by the special relation of parenthood. There is nothing wrong with parents providing for their children—even when the money could be better spent on orphan relief. Indeed, parents who contribute to the good of more children by their donations to orphan relief while neglecting their own children would be properly regarded as failing to fulfill their duty as parents.

The concepts of rights and justice pose an especially difficult challenge for teleological theories. The right of free speech, for example, generally entitles us to speak freely—even when restricting this right might produce better consequences. The right of free speech protects not only the discussion of ideas that are essential to democracy and scientific progress but also the expression of views that are socially disruptive or deeply offensive to some people. Similarly, we believe that justice ought to be done regardless of consequences. Even if it could be shown that discrimination against women or racial minorities, on balance, produces better consequences, discrimination is morally wrong and ought not to be practiced, simply because it involves the violation of a basic principle of justice; namely, that equals ought to be treated alike. This principle of equal treatment, as with the right of free speech, seems to be nonteleological in character.

Deontological Theories

Those who argue that the actions of Lockheed in Japan were wrong not because of their *consequences* but because we have a *duty* not to bribe are taking a deontological rather than a teleological approach to ethical reasoning. Deontological theories, in contrast to teleological theories such as utilitarianism, deny that consequences are relevant to determining what we ought to do. Deontologists typically hold that certain actions are right not because of some benefit to ourselves or others but because of the nature of these actions or the rules from which they follow. Thus, bribery is wrong, some say, by its very nature, regardless of the consequences. Other examples of nonconsequentialist reasoning in ethics include arguments based on principles such as the Golden Rule (Do unto others as you would have them do unto you) and those that appeal to basic notions of human dignity and respect for other persons. Obligation, or duty, is the fundamental moral category in deontological theories, and goodness and other concepts are to be defined in terms of obligation, or duty. (The word *deontological* derives, in fact, from *deon,* the Greek word for duty.)

An example of a deontological theory consisting of a set of absolute moral rules is that presented by the twentieth-century British philosopher W. D. Ross. The seven rules in Ross's system are the following:

1. **Duties of fidelity**—to keep promises, both explicit and implicit, and to tell the truth.
2. **Duties of reparation**—to compensate people for injury that we have wrongfully inflicted on them.
3. **Duties of gratitude**—to return favors that others do for us.
4. **Duties of justice**—to ensure that goods are distributed according to people's merit or deserts.
5. **Duties of beneficence**—to do whatever we can to improve the condition of others.
6. **Duties of self-improvement**—to improve our own condition with respect to virtue and intelligence.
7. **Duties of nonmaleficence**—to avoid injury to others.[7]

One virtue of deontological theories such as Ross's is that they make sense of cases in which consequences seem to be irrelevant. Especially in justifying the obligations that arise from *relations,* such as contracts and roles, it is more plausible to appeal to the relations themselves than to the consequences. Thus, a manufacturer has an obligation to honor a warranty on a defective product even if the cost of doing so exceeds the benefit of satisfying a consumer. And an employee has an obligation to an employer to be loyal and to do his or her job. Another strength of deontological theories is the way they account for the role of *motives* in evaluating actions. Two people who give large amounts to charity—one out of genuine concern to alleviate suffering and the other to impress friends and associates—produce the same amount of good, yet we evaluate the two actions differently. The role of motives in evaluating actions is easily explained if we accept the belief of most deontologists that the rightness of actions depends wholly or in part on the motives from which they are performed and not on consequences.

The Weaknesses of Deontological Theories

The main weakness of deontological theories lies in the failure to provide a plausible account of how we can know our moral obligations and resolve problems of moral conflict. Although the rules in Ross's theory are plausible, no reason is offered for accepting these rules and not others. Ross's rules are also open to the charge of ethnocentrism; that is, of erroneously accepting the rules of our own society as though they were universal. People at different times and in different places might reject Ross's rules and regard others as being equally worthy. Worse, he suggests no order of priority among the rules, so that we have no guidance in cases where they conflict. For example, should we keep a promise or tell the truth, when doing so will harm someone? Or should gratitude for a past favor alter in some way a distribution of goods according to merit or desert?

Ross attempted to solve the problem of conflict among rules by making a distinction between *actual* and *prima facie* obligations. All rules have exceptions. Thus, the rule Tell the truth does not necessarily rule out harmless falsehoods or so-called white lies. In most cases of rule conflict, however, we do not make exceptions to rules, Ross claims. Rather, a rule that is overridden by another still applies and would be our actual duty if the other rule did not intervene. If we lie to save a person's life, for example, this case is not an exception to the rule Tell the truth. But the obligation that a rule creates is only a prima facie obligation. That is, it is an obligation that we ought to perform unless another prima facie obligation overrides it. In any given situation, we may have several prima facie obligations. Our actual obligation, though, is what we ought to do "on balance," or "all things considered."[8]

Although Ross's distinction provides a useful way to understand cases of conflict, it does nothing to solve the main problem with his theory. Instead of determining which rule applies, we now have to ask, which of our prima facie duties is our actual duty? Ross correctly refused to recognize any priority among the rules. Sometimes justice takes precedence over beneficence, for example; sometimes it does not. As a result, though, we are left with no guidance on how to apply the rules when they conflict. In order to better understand teleological theories, let us now examine in detail the most developed and influential theory of this kind: utilitarianism.

CLASSICAL UTILITARIANISM

Different parts of the utilitarian doctrine were advanced by philosophers as far back as the ancient Greeks, but it remained for two English reformers in the nineteenth century to fashion them into a single coherent whole.[9] The creators of classical utilitarianism were Jeremy Bentham (1748–1832) and John Stuart Mill (1806–1873). In their hands, utilitarianism was not an ivory tower philosophy but a powerful instrument for social, political, economic, and legal change. Bentham and Mill used the principle of utility as a practical guide in the English reform movement.

Jeremy Bentham

Bentham's version of utilitarianism is set forth in the following passage:

> By the principle of utility is meant that principle which approves or disapproves of every action whatsoever, according to the tendency which it appears to have to augment or diminish the happiness of the party whose interest is in question: or, what is the same thing in other words, to promote or to oppose that happiness.

So stated, the principle requires that consequences be measured in some way so that the pleasure and pain of different individuals can be added together and the results of different courses of action compared. Bentham assumed that a precise quantitative measurement of pleasure and pain was possible, and he outlined a procedure that he called the *hedonistic calculus* ("hedonistic" is derived from the Greek word for pleasure). The amount of pleasure and pain, according to Bentham, is determined by six factors. These include not only the intensity of a pleasure or a pain and its duration but also such matters as the likelihood of its occurring and its nearness in time. Thus, an immediate specific pleasure has more value than a less certain pleasure in the distant future. Bentham's procedure is to begin with any one individual whose interest is affected:

> Sum up all the values of all the *pleasures* on the one side, and those of all the pains on the other. The balance, if it be on the side of pleasure, will give the *good* tendency of the act upon the whole, with respect to the interests of that *individual* person; if on the side of pain, the *bad* tendency of it upon the whole.

If this process is repeated for all other individuals whose interests are affected, the resulting sums will show the good or bad tendency of an action for the whole community. Bentham's theory is open to some rather obvious objections. Among them is the longstanding opposition of many philosophers to the thesis of *hedonism*: that pleasure and pleasure alone is good. Critics at the time complained that pleasure is too low to constitute the good for human beings and pointed out that even pigs are capable of pleasure, which led to the charge that utilitarianism is a "pig philosophy" fit only for swine. One absurd consequence of Bentham's view, according to critics, is that it would be better to live the life of a satisfied pig than that of a dissatisfied human being such as Socrates.

John Stuart Mill

John Stuart Mill was aware of the objections to Bentham's theory, and in his major work on ethics, *Utilitarianism* (1863), he attempted to develop a more defensible version of the utilitarian position. His initial statement of the principle of utility is:

The creed which accepts as the foundation of morals, Utility, or the Greatest Happiness Principle, holds that actions are right in proportion as they tend to promote happiness, wrong as they tend to produce the reverse of happiness. By happiness is intended pleasure, and the absence of pain; by unhappiness, pain, and the privation of pleasure.

Mill departed from Bentham's strict quantitative treatment of pleasure by introducing the idea that pleasures also differ in their *quality*. The charge that utilitarianism is a "pig philosophy" can be met, Mill claimed, by holding that human beings are capable of enjoying higher pleasures than those experienced by swine. Because human beings, but not pigs, can enjoy the arts and intellectual pursuits, Mill concluded:

It is better to be a human being dissatisfied than a pig satisfied; better to be Socrates dissatisfied than a fool satisfied. And if the fool, or the pig, are of a different opinion, it is because they know only their side of the question.

Even if some pleasures are better than others, this insight does not succeed in saving the thesis of hedonism or the utilitarian principle that we ought to produce the greatest possible amount of pleasure. This is so because the higher pleasures enjoyed by a few people with elevated tastes are unlikely, in any actual society, to outweigh the total sum of the low pleasures enjoyed by the bulk of the population. As long as the number of people who prefer trashy television shows, for example, greatly exceeds the number who appreciate fine drama on television, a utilitarian decision maker would be forced, most likely, to give preference to soap operas and situation comedies over the plays of Shakespeare. In any event, Mill's writings give us no guidance for comparing the quality with the quantity of pleasure.

Utilitarianism does not require the thesis of hedonism, however, and many things besides pleasure have been regarded as good by utilitarian theorists, including friendship and aesthetic enjoyment. In his famous essay *On Liberty*, Mill himself moves close to the position that the development of our critical faculties and the capacity for autonomous action are worthwhile ends in themselves. More than two hundred years have elapsed since Bentham's formulation of the principle of utility, and in that time many refinements have been made. Contemporary utilitarianism takes many different forms that are more adequate than the classical theory. The next section deals with some of these forms of contemporary utilitarianism.

THE FORMS OF UTILITARIANISM

Classical utilitarianism can be stated formally as follows:

AN ACTION IS RIGHT IF AND ONLY IF IT PRODUCES THE GREATEST BALANCE OF PLEASURE OVER PAIN FOR EVERYONE.

So stated, the utilitarian principle involves four distinct theses:

1. **Consequentialism**. The principle holds that the rightness of actions is determined solely by their consequences. It is by virtue of this thesis that utilitarianism is a teleological theory.

2. **Hedonism**. Utility in this statement of the theory is identified with pleasure and the absence of pain. Hedonism is the thesis that pleasure and only pleasure is ultimately good.

3. **Maximalism**. A right action is one that has not merely some good consequences but the greatest amount of good consequences possible when the bad consequences are also taken into consideration.

4. **Universalism**. The consequences to be considered are those of everyone.

The first two theses have already been explained, but the last two call for some comment.

Virtually every action produces both pleasure and pain, and the principle of utility does not require that only pleasure and no pain result from a right action. An action may produce a great amount of pain and still be right on the utilitarian view as long as the amount of pleasure produced is, on balance, greater than the amount produced by any other action. Both Bentham and Mill assumed that the amount of pain produced by an action can be subtracted from the amount of pleasure to yield the net amount of pleasure—in the same way that an accountant subtracts debts from assets to determine net worth. Theories in which we are obligated merely to produce more pleasure than pain or a certain positive balance of pleasure over pain are possible forms of utilitarianism, but usually the principle is stated in the "maximalist" form, which obligates us to produce the *greatest* net amount of pleasure.

The thesis of universalism requires us to consider the pleasure and pain *of everyone alike*. Thus, we are not following the principle of utility by considering the consequences only for ourselves, for our family and friends, or for an organization of which we are a part. Utilitarianism does not require us to ignore our own interest, but we are permitted to place it no higher and no lower than the interest of anyone else. As Mill expressed the point:

> . . . [T]he happiness which forms the utilitarian standard of what is right in conduct, is not the agent's own happiness, but that of all concerned. As between his own happiness and that of others, utilitarianism requires him to be as strictly impartial as a disinterested and benevolent spectator.

The utilitarian principle does not insist that the interest of everyone be *promoted*, though. In deciding whether to close a polluting plant, for example, we need to consider the citizens of the community who suffer from the pollution, the workers who will lose their jobs if the plant is shut down, the owners of the company that operates the plant, and, possibly, consumers as well. No matter what decision is made, the interests of some people will be harmed. Utilitarian reasoning obligates us only to include the interests of everyone in our calculations, not to act in a way that advances every individual interest.

Act- and Rule-Utilitarianism

There is another formulation of the utilitarian principle that is significantly different and, in the view of some philosophers, more defensible. Based on the principle, as stated, an action is judged to be right by virtue of the consequences of performing *that action.* As a result, telling a lie or breaking a promise is right if it has better consequences than any alternative course of action. Utilitarian morality thus seems to place no value on observing rules, such as Tell the truth or Keep your promises, except perhaps as "rules of thumb"; that is, as distillations of past experience about the tendencies of actions that eliminate the need to calculate consequences in every case. This result can be avoided if we consider the consequences of performing not just particular actions but *actions of a certain kind.* Although some instances of lying have consequences that are better than telling the truth, lying in general does not. As a kind of action, then, truth telling is right by virtue of the consequences of performing actions of that kind, and any instance of truth telling is right because actions of that kind are right.

This suggestion leads to a version of utilitarianism in which rules are primary. Whether an action is right is determined by appealing to the relevant rule of morality, which is justified in turn by the consequences of observing that rule. Individuals, for the most part, do not need to calculate the consequences of specific actions in order to decide what they ought to do. A familiarity with common morality is generally sufficient. Some interpreters attribute this view to Mill, although it is unlikely that Mill was fully aware of the distinction.[10] This revised version of the theory is known as rule-utilitarianism (RU), and the principle of utility, as stated at the beginning of this section, is called act-utilitarianism (AU). Both may now be expressed formally in the following way:

(AU) AN ACTION IS RIGHT IF AND ONLY IF IT PRODUCES THE GREATEST BALANCE OF PLEASURE OVER PAIN FOR EVERYONE.

(RU) AN ACTION IS RIGHT IF AND ONLY IF IT CONFORMS TO A SET OF RULES THE GENERAL ACCEPTANCE OF WHICH WOULD PRODUCE THE GREATEST BALANCE OF PLEASURE OVER PAIN FOR EVERYONE.[11]

Act- and rule-utilitarianism each has its merits, and there is no consensus among philosophers about which is correct.[12] Act-utilitarianism is a simpler theory and provides an easily understood decision procedure. Rule-utilitarianism seems to give firmer ground, however, to the rules of morality and to role obligations, which are problems for all teleological theories. Society works better, rule-utilitarians argue, if individuals, for the most part, fulfill their assigned role and do not violate a role obligation—even if more good could be achieved in particular instances by doing so. A further advantage of rule-utilitarianism, according to its proponents, is that it eliminates the difficult task of calculating the consequences of each individual act.

Problems with Calculating Utility

Differences among utilitarians also occur as a result of problems with calculating utility. Classical utilitarianism requires that we be able to determine: (1) the amount of utility (that is, the balance of pleasure over pain) for each individual affected by an action, and (2) the amount of utility for a whole society. Whether we can measure utility in the way that utilitarianism requires has been a concern not only of philosophers but also of economists, since utility has been generally accepted as a basis for eco-

nomic theory. Because of the need in economics for precise calculations of utility—
and misgivings about Bentham's simplistic hedonistic calculus—economists have introduced a number of important refinements into the theory of utilitarianism.

There is little difficulty in calculating that some actions produce more pleasure for us than others. A decision to spend an evening at a concert is usually the result of a judgment that listening to music will give us more pleasure at that time than
any available alternative. Confronted with a range of alternatives, we can usually
rank them in order from the most pleasant to the least pleasant. A problem arises,
however, when we attempt to determine exactly how *much* pleasure each course of
action will produce, because pleasure cannot be precisely measured in terms of
quantity, much less quality. Utilitarianism also requires that we calculate the pleasure of alternative courses of action not only for ourselves but for everyone.

Some critics contend that this requirement imposes an information burden
on utilitarian decision makers that is difficult to meet. In order to buy a gift for a
friend that will produce the greatest amount of pleasure, for example, we need to
know something about that person's desires and tastes. Consider, for example, the
task faced by a utilitarian legislator who must decide whether to permit logging in a
public park. This person must identify all the people affected, determine the amount
of pleasure and pain for each one, and then compare the pleasure that hiking brings
to nature lovers versus the pain that would be caused to loggers if they lost their jobs.
The abilities of ordinary human beings are inadequate, critics complain, to acquire
and process the vast amount of relevant information in such a case. The response of
utilitarians to these problems is that we manage in practice to make educated guesses
by relying on past experience and limiting our attention to a few aspects of a situation.

Comparing the pleasure and pain of different people raises a further problem about the *interpersonal comparison of utility*. Imagine two people who each insist after attending a concert that he or she enjoyed it more. There seems to be no way in
principle to settle this dispute. Some philosophers and economists consider this
problem to be insoluble and a reason for rejecting utilitarianism both as an ethical
theory and as a basis for economics.[13] Others argue for the possibility of interpersonal comparisons on the basis that regardless of whether we can make such comparisons precisely, we do make them in everyday life with reasonable confidence.[14]
We may give away an extra ticket to a concert, for example, to the friend we believe
will enjoy it the most. Also, we assume that members of the Sierra Club who spend
their leisure time hiking value parks highly, and we weigh their feelings about logging
accordingly. The problem of the interpersonal comparison of utility is not insupera-
ble, therefore, as long as rough comparisons are sufficient for utilitarian calculations.

Applying the Two Principles

When applied to bribery in international business, act- and rule-utilitarianism seem
to yield different results. Carl Kotchian was reasoning as an act-utilitarian when he
defended Lockheed's expenditure of more than $12 million in Japan to secure the
sale of twenty-one TriStar aircraft to All Nippon Airways. Let us suppose for the sake
of argument that the benefit to Lockheed workers, their families and communities,
Lockheed shareholders, and the American public was sufficient to outweigh the

harm done to Japanese society, the consumers of ANA, Lockheed competitors, and others. If Kotchian saved Lockheed Aircraft Corporation from financial ruin, his otherwise unethical behavior might be justified on act-utilitarian grounds. Bribery as a general practice, though, is commonly recognized as having harmful consequences. It usually results in higher prices and reduced quality, since people are led by personal advantage to make decisions on considerations other than the value of the goods and services being offered. A widespread system of bribery would lead to less competitive conditions and a resulting decline in efficiency. On rule-utilitarian grounds, therefore, bribery is properly regarded as morally wrong.

One of Lockheed's defenses was, "We don't make the rules. And if we don't go along with the game as it's played, we only hurt ourselves and accomplish nothing." In a world in which others bribe, what should a utilitarian do? This question points up the fact that the consequences of our actions often depend on the actions of others. Lockheed alone cannot eliminate bribery in the sale of planes abroad, of course, but by engaging in the practice so readily, they perpetuate it and encourage others to do the same. (Officials of the Northrop Corporation who set up a special subsidiary in Switzerland to handle payments told a Senate investigative committee that "they learned how to do that from Lockheed.")[15] Moreover, Lockheed could take small steps to work with others who will cooperate to remove corruption wherever possible. In short, rule-utilitarianism draws attention to the need to create a mutually beneficial set of moral rules, and the obligation of each individual and business firm is to follow these rules. Furthermore, Lockheed's defense that the bribes were given by their Japanese agent is not entirely successful. The Marubeni Corporation was chosen by Lockheed officials to help conduct negotiations, so they were acting on Lockheed's behalf. In addition to Marubeni, Lockheed had also hired as an agent Yoshio Kodama, a notorious *kuromaku*, or "fixer," with known connections to organized crime. Kodama also served Lockheed in 1958 when the company beat out the Grumman Corporation for the sale of jet fighters to the Japanese Air Force, reportedly through the use of bribery. According to Japanese sources, Kodama was hired after Lockheed fired its previous agent, Dai Ichi Bussan, for resisting suggestions that payments be made. Japan was not the only country in which Lockheed had made payments. A scandal erupted in Italy when a president, Giovanni Leone, and two prime ministers, Aldo Moro and Mariano Rumor, were accused of accepting bribes from Lockheed for aiding in the sale of aircraft in that country. And Prince Bernhard, the husband of Queen Juliana of the Netherlands, was greatly embarrassed by the disclosure of a "gift" of more than $1 million for assisting in the sale of 138 F-104 Starfighter jets to the Dutch Air Force. Lockheed admitted to making questionable payments in a number of countries, totaling more than $30 million. Lockheed, it appears, was no stranger to the bribery game.

COST-BENEFIT ANALYSIS

Bentham's ideal of a precise quantitative method for decision making is most fully realized in *cost-benefit analysis*. This method differs from Bentham's hedonistic calculus primarily in the use of monetary units to express the benefits and drawbacks of various alternatives. Any project in which the dollar amount of the benefits exceeds the dollar amount of the damages is worth pursuing, according to cost-benefit analysis, and from among different projects, the one that promises the greatest net benefit, as measured in dollars, ought to be chosen.[16]

From an economic point of view, cost-benefit analysis is simply a means for achieving an efficient allocation of resources. Business decisions that evaluate investment opportunities in terms of their return are thus instances of cost-benefit analysis. However, there is an important difference between business decision making and what is usually described as cost-benefit analysis. Companies usually calculate the anticipated costs and benefits only for *themselves*, whereas legislators, social planners, regulators, and other users of cost-benefit analysis generally ask what the costs and benefits are for *everyone* who is affected.

The chief advantage of cost-benefit analysis is that the price of many goods is set by the market, so that the need to have knowledge of people's pleasures or preference rankings is largely eliminated. And the value of different goods is easily totaled to produce a figure that reflects the costs and benefits of different courses of action for all those concerned. Money also provides a common denominator for allocating resources among projects that cannot easily be compared otherwise. Would scarce resources be better spent on a Head Start program, for example, or on the development of new sources of energy? In cost-benefit analysis, decision makers have an analytic framework that enables them to decide among such disparate projects in a rational, objective manner.

Because of the narrow focus on economic efficiency in the allocation of resources, cost-benefit analysis is not commonly used as a basis for personal morality but as a means for making major investment decisions and decisions on broad matters of public policy. It is not a complete ethical theory, therefore, but a utilitarian form of reasoning with a limited but important range of application. Cost-benefit analysis is also not necessarily intended to be the *only* means for making decisions. It enables us to compare alternatives with respect to the two factors of cost and benefit, but other factors may also enter into a complete evaluation.

Utilitarians generally favor efficiency on the ground that it increases the welfare of society as a whole. But the rights of consumers in matters of product safety and the goal of protecting the environment, for example, sometimes override considerations of efficiency and lead to the adoption of regulations in which the costs exceed the immediate benefits. Still, determining the appropriate level of product safety or environmental protection requires an awareness of the costs and benefits of different regulatory schemes and of the trade-offs being made. Cost-benefit analysis, therefore, is an important tool that may be used even by nonutilitarian decision makers to provide one kind of morally relevant information.

A distinction is commonly made, moreover, between cost-benefit analysis and cost-effectiveness analysis. *Cost-effectiveness analysis* assumes that we already have some agreed-upon end, such as reducing injuries from defective products or protecting the environment, so that the only remaining question is, what is the most efficient means for achieving this end? *Cost-benefit analysis*, by contrast, is used to select both the means to ends and the ends themselves.[17] Nonutilitarians who reject the use of cost-benefit analysis to settle questions about ends, such as the rights of consumers and the value of environmental protection, should have no quarrel with a requirement that we pursue morally justified ends in the most efficient manner possible.

The Problems of Assigning Monetary Values

Cost-benefit analysis is criticized on many different grounds. First, not all costs and benefits have an easily determined monetary value. The value of the jobs that are provided by logging on public land can be expressed precisely in dollars, as can the value of the lumber produced. But because the opportunity for hikers to enjoy unspoiled vistas and fresh-smelling air is not something that is commonly bought and sold, it has no fixed market price. There is also no market to determine the price of peace and quiet, the enjoyment of the company of family and friends, and freedom from the risk of physical injury and death. And the same is true of many public goods, such as police protection, roads and bridges, and public health programs.

In addition, the market for some goods is distorted by various factors so that the price of these goods does not reflect their "true" value. In economic terms, the market price of goods does not always correspond to their opportunity cost, as determined by consumers' marginal rates of substitution, which economists regard as the proper measure of value. The fact that a yacht costs more than a college education, for example, does not entail that consumers value yachts more highly than education. It would be a mistake, therefore, to use cost-benefit analysis to support policies that foster the ownership of yachts by the rich while making it more difficult for the poor to attend college. Critics complain, however, that noneconomic goods and mispriced goods tend to be left out of cost-benefit analyses entirely or else are assigned arbitrary values.

Some applications of cost-benefit analysis require that a value be placed on human life. Although this may seem cold and heartless, it is necessary if cost-benefit analysis is to be used to determine how much to spend on prenatal care to improve the rate of infant mortality, for example, or on reducing the amount of cancer-causing emissions from factories. Reducing infant mortality or the death rate from cancer justifies the expenditure of some funds, but how much? Would further investment be justified if it reduced the amount available for education or medical care for the elderly? No matter where the line is drawn, some trade-off must be made between saving lives and securing other goods.

Experts in cost-benefit analysis attempt to overcome the problem of assigning a dollar figure to noneconomic goods with a technique known as *shadow pricing*. This consists of determining the value reflected by people's market and nonmarket behavior. For example, by comparing the prices of houses near airports, busy highways, and the like with the prices of similar houses in less noisy areas, it is possible to infer the value that people place on peace and quiet. The value of life and limb can be similarly estimated by considering the amount of extra pay that is needed to get workers to accept risky jobs. Several methods exist, in fact, for calculating the value of human life for purposes of cost-benefit analysis.[18] Among these are the discounted value of a person's future earnings over a normal lifetime, the value that existing social and political arrangements place on the life of individuals, and the value that is revealed by the amount that individuals are willing to pay to avoid the risk of injury and death. When people choose through their elected representatives or by their own consumer behavior not to spend additional amounts to improve automobile safety, for example, they implicitly indicate the value of the lives that would otherwise be saved. Using such indicators, economists calculate that middle-income Americans value their lives between $3 million to $5 million.[19]

The purpose of assigning a monetary value to life in a cost-benefit analysis is not to indicate how much a life is actually worth but to enable us to compare alternatives where life is at stake. If we know that spending $5 million on automobile safety will save one life whereas the same amount spent on childhood vaccinations will save two, then it is rational to spend the money on the latter, if a choice must be made. When we are comparing alternatives that can save lives, the dollar amount that we place on a life is irrelevant; all that counts is the number of lives saved. But we must also compare $5 million spent on childhood vaccinations to save two lives with the same amount spent on schooling that will create the opportunity for prosperous, rewarding lives for two hundred children. Now we are forced to compare the value of saving lives with other things that we value, and it would not be rational to spend all of our money on medical care and none on education. Beyond a certain dollar amount, the cost of saving a life is not worthwhile because of the other goods we could buy with those resources. Experts in risk assessment calculate that the "break even" point where the amount expended to save a life is worth the cost is about $10 million.[20] Thus, banning asbestos in brake linings, which will save lives at a cost of $230,000, is a good expenditure of resources. But should we ban asbestos in automatic transmission parts when the cost per life saved is estimated at $1.2 billion?

There are some pitfalls in using the technique of shadow pricing, especially when human life is involved. Many people buy houses in noisy areas or accept risky jobs because they are unable to afford decent housing anywhere else or to secure safer employment. Some home buyers and job seekers may not fully consider or appreciate the risks they face, especially when the hazards are unseen or speculative. Also, the people who buy homes near airports or accept work as steeplejacks are possibly less concerned with noise or danger than is the general population. We certainly do not want to assume, however, that workplace safety is of little value simply because a few people are so heedless of danger that they accept jobs that more cautious people avoid.[21]

Finally, people's individual and collective decisions are not always rational. People who drive without seat belts are probably aware of their benefit *for other people* but are convinced that nothing will happen *to them* because they are such good drivers.[22] As a result, they (irrationally) expose themselves to risks that do not accurately reflect the value they place on their own life. Mark Sagoff observes that the choices we make as consumers do not always correspond to those we make as citizens. He cites as examples the fact that he buys beverages in disposable containers but urges his state legislators to require returnable bottles and that he has a car with an Ecology Now sticker that leaks oil everywhere it is parked.[23]

Should All Things Be Assigned a Monetary Value?

A second criticism of cost-benefit analysis is that even if all the technical problems of shadow pricing could be solved, there are still good reasons for not assigning a monetary value to some things. Steven Kelman argues that placing a dollar value on some goods reduces their perceived value, since they are valued precisely because they cannot be bought and sold in a market. Friendship and love are obvious examples. "Imagine the reaction," Kelman observes, "if a practitioner of cost-benefit analysis computed the benefits of sex based on the price of prostitute service."[24] In *The Gift Relationship: From Human Blood to Social Policy*, Richard M. Titmuss very perceptively compares the American system of blood collection with that of the British. In the United States, about half of all blood is purchased from donors and sold to people who need transfusions.[25] The British system, by contrast, is purely voluntary. No one is paid for donating blood, and it is provided without charge to anyone in need. As a result, the giving of blood and blood itself have an entirely different significance. Peter Singer has observed that if blood has a price, then giving blood merely saves someone else an expense; but blood that cannot be bought and sold becomes a special gift that we make to others.[26]

Although some things are cheapened in people's eyes if they are made into commodities and traded in a market, this does not happen if goods are assigned a value merely for purposes of comparison. It is the actual buying and selling of blood that has the consequences Singer describes, not performing a cost-benefit analysis. Moreover, Titmuss himself argues in favor of the British system on the grounds that the system in the United States is (1) highly wasteful of blood, resulting in chronic acute shortages; (2) administratively inefficient because of the large bureaucracy that it requires; (3) more expensive (the price of blood is five to fifteen times higher); and (4) more dangerous, because there is a greater risk of disease and death from contaminated blood.[27] In short, a cost-benefit analysis shows that it is better not to have a market for blood.

Other Values in Cost-Benefit Analysis

Cost-benefit analysis is offered as a method that is itself value-free and applies only the values that people express in the market. Critics charge, however, that the method is heavily value-laden since the values of the analyst cannot be excluded entirely.[28] First, the analyst must choose the range of alternatives to be considered, and some may be deliberately excluded or inadvertently overlooked because of the analyst's values. Cost-benefit analysis requires the analyst to determine what constitutes a cost and a benefit. Loud outdoor music at rock concerts, for example, is a benefit to fans of that kind of music, but it is a cost to others who are forced to endure the noise. Whose values will determine whether the music is a cost or a benefit? Analysts must further decide what is to count as a *consequence* of a particular course of action. Should the costs and benefits of various packaging materials be calculated only up to the time that the product reaches consumers, for example, or should the calculations continue to include the costs of disposing of the materials? If better packaging encourages people to eat more fast food to the detriment of their health, should this also be included as a consequence in the analysis? In economic terms, the question is, to what extent should "spillover effects" or externalities be considered? And the answer to this question will be decided to some extent by the analyst's values. Finally, how far into the future should consequences be calculated? Applying cost-benefit analysis presupposes some commitment to a time frame for calculating the consequences of alternatives for future generations.

Defenders of cost-benefit analysis reply that any theory is "value laden," and an advantage of cost-benefit analysis is that it makes its value commitments explicit, so that they can be "flagged" and properly taken into account. The validity of any particular cost-benefit analysis depends, moreover, on the objectivity of the people who conduct it. And we must also have an understanding of the proper role of cost-benefit analysis in public decision making. It is not intended to be the sole means for arriving at the choices we make as a society. Efficiency in the allocation of resources is not our only value. The key question is, what matters should be turned over to the analysts? And this question cannot itself be decided by a cost-benefit analysis.

Conclusion

Utilitarianism is a powerful and widely accepted ethical theory that has special relevance to problems in business. Not only does it enable us to justify many of the obligations of individuals and corporations, such as to refrain from bribery in the case of Lockheed in Japan, but the principle of utility, as we will see in subsequent chapters, provides a strong foundation for various rights and also for our most deeply held views about justice. Utilitarianism fits in easily, moreover, with the emphasis on results in business decision making.

Act-utilitarianism provides a relatively straightforward decision procedure for determining the best course of action in any given situation: Make a list of all the available alternatives, follow the consequences of each one as far into the future as possible, and select the alternative with the greatest balance of pleasure over pain for everyone. Most of the ethical obligations of people in business are expressed in terms of codes of conduct for employees and the responsibility of a company toward employees, competitors, consumers, and the public at large. This framework of rules and generally accepted practices can be grounded by rule-utilitarianism. We will find in this book that utilitarianism, either in its act- or rule-utilitarian form, is relevant to most of the topics considered. Utility arguments occur in just about every chapter, and they provide a relatively firm and coherent basis for business ethics.

CASE 2.2   Declining Sales at Supravac

Supravac faces an unusual problem: The company's only product, a home vacuum cleaner, is so well-made that it lasts a lifetime. Some Supervacs have even been handed down from one generation to another.[29] As a result, the company has few repeat customers and must depend on the limited number of first-time buyers. Sales have been declining for several years now, and George Evans, the president of Supravac, wonders how long he can keep the company's plants, with about 400 workers, in full operation. Lately, he has developed an idea that just might work, and so he convenes a meeting with Charlie Smith, the director of production, and Margaret Lange, the chief financial officer, to discuss it.

Evans: Studies I've read indicate that repeat buyers are the key to success in the appliance industry, but we don't have many because our product is so durable. I've worked out the figures, and if our customers bought a vacuum cleaner about every eight years, we could sell enough to keep everyone employed.

Lange: But people aren't going to throw away a perfectly good vacuum cleaner merely because. . . .

Evans: That's the point. We've gotta make Supravacs that don't last forever. We pride ourselves on quality, but it's quality that's killing us. Now, my idea is to change the design so it will wear out eventually.

Smith: But that's called planned obsolescence, and it's ripping off the customer.

Evans: It's true that our customers will pay more overall, but they will be very happy with our vacuum cleaners for eight years or so, and by then they won't even remember when they bought it. If they don't know they're paying more, what's the problem? Besides, if we don't do this, we'll have to cut our work force by half. And I just can't do that to people who have been here their whole working lives. As I see it, it's a question of who loses, the public or our own employees.

Smith: Have you figured out how to change the design or what it will cost? From a production point of view, it's not simple to make a product fail in a fixed period of time. We'd have to redesign it using different materials. R&D costs alone would be at least $3 million, and it would take three years or more to get into actual production. This would keep our work force employed until then, but with that amount of money, we might even be able to develop a totally different product to sell.

Lange: There are some financial implications here, too. I would have to write the R&D costs off against current earnings, and that would depress our dividends and our stock price for a while. Plus, we're not going to realize any gain from this for at least eleven years from now, or eight years after going into production. You may be benefiting stockholders in the future, but they'll take a hit in the short run.

Evans: But don't forget, we're stockholders too, and our pension fund consists mostly of Supravac stock, which we're all depending on for retirement. So looking at the long run and at everyone concerned, I think my plan is the best alternative. If not, what do you suggest?

CASE 2.3   Exporting Pollution

As an assistant to the vice president of environmental affairs at Americhem, Rebecca Wright relishes the opportunity to apply her training in public policy analysis to the complex and emotion-laden issues that her company faces.[30] Rebecca is convinced that cost-benefit analysis, her speciality, provides a rational decision-making tool that cuts through personal feelings and lays bare the hard economic realities. Still, she was startled by the draft of a memo that her boss, Jim Donnelly, shared with her. The logic of Jim's argument seems impeccable, but the conclusions are troubling—and Rebecca is sure that the document would create a furor if it were ever made public. Jim is preparing the memo for an upcoming decision on the location for a new chemical plant. The main problem is that atmospheric pollutants from the plant, while mostly harmless, would produce a persistent haze; and one of the particles that would be released into the atmosphere is also known to cause liver cancer in a very small portion of the people exposed. Sitting down at her desk to write a response, Rebecca reads again the section of the memo that she had circled with her pen.

> From an environmental point of view, the case for locating the new plant in a third world country is overwhelming. These reasons are especially compelling in my estimation:
>
> (1) The harm of pollution, and hence its cost, increases in proportion to the amount of already existing pollution. Adding pollutants to a highly polluted environment does more harm than the same amount added to a relatively unpolluted environment. For this reason, much of the third world is not efficiently utilized as a depository of industrial wastes, and only the high cost of transporting wastes prevents a more efficient utilization of this resource.
>
> (2) The cost of health-impairing pollution is a function of the forgone earnings of those who are disabled or who die as a result. The cost of pollution will be least, therefore, in the country with the lowest wages. Any transfer of pollution from a high-wage, first world country to a low-wage, third world country will produce a net benefit.
>
> (3) The risk of liver cancer from this plant's emissions has been estimated at one-in-a-million in the United States, and the resulting cancer deaths would occur mostly among the elderly. The risk posed by the new plant will obviously be much less in a country where people die young from other causes and where few will live long enough to incur liver cancer from any source. Overall, the people of any third world country might prefer the jobs that our plant will provide if the only drawback is a form of cancer that they are very unlikely to incur.
>
> (4) The cost of visibility-impairing pollution will be greater in a country where people are willing to spend more for good visibility. The demand for clear skies—which affects the aesthetics of the environment and not people's health—has very high income elasticity, and so the wealthy will pay more than the poor to live away from factory smoke, for example. Since the cost of anything is determined by how

much people are willing to pay in a market, the cost of visibility-impairing pollution in a first world country will be higher than the same amount of pollution in a third world country. Thus, people in the United States might prefer clear skies over the benefits of our plant, but people elsewhere might choose differently.

NOTES

1. The most complete source of information on this case is ROBERT SHAPLEN, "Annals of Crime: The Lockheed Incident," *The New Yorker*, 23 January 1978, 48–74; and 30 January 1978, 74–91. Kotchian's own reflections are contained in A. CARL KOTCHIAN, "The Payoff: Lockheed's 70-Day Mission to Tokyo," *Saturday Review*, 9 July 1977, 7–12. This article is adapted from a memoir, *Lockheed Sales Mission: Seventy Days in Tokyo*, published in Japan. Two case studies are "A Japanese Bribe," in MANUEL G. VELASQUEZ, *Business Ethics: Concepts and Cases*, 3rd ed.(Englewood Cliffs, NJ: Prentice Hall, 1992), 207–9; and "Selling the Lockheed TriStar," in MILTON SNOEYENBOS, ROBERT ALMEDER, and JAMES HUMBER, eds. *Business Ethics: Corporate Values and Society* (Buffalo: Prometheus Books, 1983), 138–44.

2. KOTCHIAN, "The Payoff," 11.

3. KOTCHIAN, "The Payoff," 10.

4. KOTCHIAN, "The Payoff," 12.

5. For the distinctions between bribery, kickbacks, and extortion, see MICHAEL PHILLIPS, "Bribery," *Ethics*, 94 (1984), 621–36; THOMAS L. CARSON, "Bribery, Extortion, and the 'Foreign Corrupt Practices Act'," *Philosophy and Public Affairs*, 14 (1985), 66–90; JOHN DANLEY, "Towards a Theory of Bribery," *Business and Professional Ethics Journal*, 2 (1983), 19–39; and KENDALL D'ANDRADE, JR., "Bribery," *Journal of Business Ethics*, 4 (1985), 239–48. A comprehensive study is NEIL JACOBY, PETER NEHEMKIS, and RICHARD EELLS, *Bribery and Extortion in World Business: A Study of Corporate Political Payments Abroad* (New York: Macmillan, 1977).

6. Although the payments were legal under U.S. law at the time, Lockheed was found guilty in 1979 of four counts of fraud and four counts of making misleading statements for deducting payments from their taxes as "marketing cost" in violation of Section 162C of the Internal Revenue Code.

7. W. D. ROSS, *The Right and the Good* (Oxford: Oxford University Press, 1930), 21.

8. For a thorough examination of the distinction, see H. J. McCLOSKEY, "Ross and the Concept of Prima Facie Duty," *Australasian Journal of Philosophy*, 41 (1964), 336–45.

9. For a brief account of the historical origins of utilitarianism, see ANTHONY QUINTON, *Utilitarian Ethics* (New York: St. Martin's Press, 1973).

10. This view is attributed to Mill in J. O. URMSON, "The Interpretation of the Moral Philosophy of J. S. Mill," *The Philosophical Quarterly*, 3 (1953), 33–39. For criticism of Urmson's interpretation, see J. D. MABBOTT, "Interpretations of Mill's *Utilitarianism*," *The Philosophical Quarterly*, 6 (1956), 115–20; and MAURICE MANDELBAUM, "Two Moot Issues in Mill's *Utilitarianism*," in J. B. SCHNEEWIND, ed., *Mill: A Collection of Critical Essays* (Garden City, NY: Anchor Books, 1968), 206–33.

11. This formulation of RU follows that given by David Lyons for what he calls ideal rule-utilitarianism. DAVID LYONS, *Forms and Limits of Utilitarianism* (Oxford: Oxford University Press, 1965), 140. There is considerable controversy over the correct formulation of RU and the relation between AU, RU, and another principle usually called utilitarian generalization. In addition to the discussion in LYONS, *Forms and Limits of Utilitarianism*, see MARCUS G. SINGER, *Generalization in Ethics* (New York: Knopf, 1961), chap. 7; JAN NARVESON, *Morality and Utility* (Baltimore: Johns Hopkins University Press, 1967), 129–40; and R. B. BRANDT, *A Theory of the Good and the Right* (Oxford: Oxford University Press, 1979), 278–85. Early discussions of the distinction between AU and RU are R. F. HARROD, "Utilitarianism Revised," *Mind*, 45 (1936), 137–56; JONATHAN HARRISON, "Utilitarianism, Universalization, and Our Duty to Be Just," *Proceedings of the Aristotelian Society*, 53 (1952–53), 105–34; J.J.C. SMART, "Extreme and Restricted Utilitarianism," *The Philosophical Quarterly*, 6 (1956), 344–54. Perhaps the most ambitious attempt to formulate an adequate statement of RU is R. B. BRANDT, "Toward a Credible Form of Utilitarianism," in HECTOR NERI CASTANEDA and GEORGE NAKHNIKIAN, eds., *Morality and the Language of Conduct* (Detroit: Wayne State University Press, 1963), 107–43. Criticism of Brandt is contained in ALAN DONAGAN, "Is There a Credible Form of Utilitarianism?" in MICHAEL BAYLES, ed., *Contemporary Utilitarianism* (Garden City, NY: Anchor Books, 1968), 187–202. Brandt's fullest statement of a

roughly rule-utilitarian position that he calls "a pluralistic welfare-maximizing moral system" is in *A Theory of the Good and the Right*.

12. Some philosophers hold that there is no difference between the two formulations. See LYONS, *Forms and Limits of Utilitarianism*, chap. 3. Also, R. M. HARE, *Freedom and Reason* (Oxford: Oxford University Press, 1963), 130–36; and ALAN F. GIBBARD, "Rule-Utilitarianism: Merely an Illusory Alternative?" *Australasian Journal of Philosophy*, 43 (1965), 211–20.

13. See, for example, LIONEL ROBBINS, *An Essay on the Nature and Significance of Economic Science* (London: Macmillan, 1932), 140; and KENNETH ARROW, *Social Choice and Individual Values*, 2nd ed. (New York: Wiley, 1963), 9.

14. A defense of interpersonal comparisons of utility by a prominent economist is I.M.D. LITTLE, *A Critique of Welfare Economics*, 2nd ed. (Oxford: Oxford University Press, 1957), chap. 4. For attempts to develop a means for interpersonal comparisons, see JOHN C. HARSANYI, "Cardinal Welfare, Individualistic Ethics, and Interpersonal Comparisons of Utility," *Journal of Political Economy*, 63 (1955), 309–21; reprinted in *Essays in Ethics, Social Behaviour, and Scientific Explanation* (Dordrecht: Reidel, 1976). And ILMAR WALDNER, "The Empirical Meaningfulness of Interpersonal Utility Comparisons," *The Journal of Philosophy*, 70 (1972), 87–103.

15. Cited in SHAPLEN, "The Lockheed Incident."

16. For an authoritative exposition, see E. J. MISHAN, *Cost-Benefit Analysis* (New York: Praeger, 1976).

17. MICHAEL S. BARAM, "Cost-Benefit Analysis: An Inadequate Basis for Health, Safety, and Environmental Regulatory Decision Making," *Ecological Law Quarterly*, 8 (1980), 473.

18. See M. W. JONES-LEE, *The Value of Life: An Economic Analysis* (Chicago: University of Chicago Press, 1976). Also, MICHAEL D. BAYLES, "The Price of Life," *Ethics*, 89 (1978), 20–34. For trenchant criticism of these methods, see STEVEN E. RHOADS, "How Much Should We Spend to Save a Life?" in RHOADS, ed., *Valuing Life: Public Policy Dilemmas* (Boulder, CO: Westview Press, 1980), 285–311.

19. PETER PASSELL, "How Much for a Life? Try $3 to $5 Million," *New York Times*, 29 January 1995, D3.

20. PASSELL, "How Much for a Life?"

21. These points are made by STEVEN KELMAN, "Cost-Benefit Analysis: An Ethical Critique," *Regulation*, January–February 1981, 33–40.

22. ROSEMARY TONG, *Ethics in Public Policy Analysis* (Englewood Cliffs, NJ: Prentice Hall, 1986), 20.

23. MARK SAGOFF, "At the Shrine of Our Lady of Fatima, or Why Political Questions Are Not All Economic," *Arizona Law Review*, 23 (1981), 1283–98.

24. KELMAN, "Cost-Benefit Analysis: An Ethical Critique," 39.

25. RICHARD M. TITMUSS, *The Gift Relationship: From Human Blood to Social Policy* (London: Allen & Unwin, 1971).

26. PETER SINGER, "Rights and the Market," in JOHN ARTHUR and WILLIAM H. SHAW, eds., *Justice and Economic Distribution* (Englewood Cliffs, NJ: Prentice Hall, 1978), 213.

27. TITMUSS, *The Gift Relationship*, 246.

28. See ALASDAIR MACINTYRE, "Utilitarianism and Cost-Benefit Analysis: An Essay on the Relevance of Moral Philosophy to Bureaucratic Theory," in KENNETH SAYRE, ed., *Values in the Electric Power Industry* (Notre Dame: University of Notre Dame Press, 1977), 217–37.

29. This case is adapted from JAMES A. HEELY and ROY L. NEREESIAN, "The Case of Planned Obsolescence," *Management Accounting*, February 1994, 67–68.

30. This case is based on a memo written by Lawrence Summers, then chief economist at the World Bank. See "Let Them Eat Pollution," *The Economist*, 8 February 1992, 66.

3

Kantian Ethics, Rights, and Virtue

CASE 3.1   Big Brother at Procter & Gamble

In early August 1991, a former employee of Procter and Gamble telephoned *Wall Street Journal* reporter Alecia Swasy at her Pittsburgh office to report some disturbing news.[1] "The cops want to know what I told you about P&G," he said. This twenty-year veteran of the company had just been grilled for an hour by an investigator for the Cincinnati fraud squad. The investigator, Gary Armstrong, who also happened to work part-time as a security officer for P&G, had records of the ex-manager's recent long-distance calls, including some to Swasy.

Alecia Swasy had apparently angered CEO Edward Artz with two news stories about troubles at P&G that the company was not ready to reveal. An article in the *Wall Street Journal* on Monday, June 10, reported that B. Jurgen Hintz, executive vice president and heir apparent as CEO, had been forced to resign over difficulties in the food and beverage division. The next day, on Tuesday, June 11, a long article on the division's woes quoted "current and former P&G managers" as saying that the company might sell certain product lines, including Citrus Hill orange juice, Crisco shortening, and Fisher nuts. Swasy believes that Artz had deliberately lied to her when she tried to confirm the story of Hintz's departure in a telephone conversation on Saturday, and that he tried to sabotage the *Journal* by allowing the news to be released to the rival *New York Times* and the Cincinnati newspapers in time for the Sunday editions while the PR department continued to deny the story to Swasy.

Immediately after the two articles appeared in the *Wall Street Journal*, Artz ordered a search of P&G's own phone records to determine the source of the leaks

51

to the press. When this investigation failed to uncover any culprits, the company filed a complaint with the Hamilton County prosecutor's office, which promptly opened a grand jury investigation. The grand jury then issued several subpoenas calling for Cincinnati Bell to search its records for all calls in the 513 and 606 area codes, which cover southern Ohio and northern Kentucky, and to identify all telephone calls to Alecia Swasy's home or office and all fax transmissions to the newspaper's Pittsburgh office between March 1 and June 15. The search combed the records of 803,849 home and business telephone lines from which users had placed more than 40 million long-distance calls.

P&G contended that it filed the complaint because of "significant and ongoing leaks of our confidential business data, plans and strategies," which included not only leaks to the news media but leaks to competitors as well. The legal basis for the grand jury probe was provided by a 1967 Ohio law that makes it a crime to give away "articles representing trade secrets" and a 1974 Ohio law that prohibits employees from disclosing "confidential information" without the permission of the employer. However, reporters are generally protected by the First Amendment right of freedom of the press, and Ohio, Pennsylvania, and twenty-four other states have so-called "shield laws" that protect the identities of reporters' confidential sources. Information about an executive's forced departure is scarcely a trade secret on a par with the formula for Crest toothpaste, and the use of the phrase "articles representing trade secrets" has been interpreted in the Ohio courts to mean documents like photographs and blueprints, not word-of-mouth news. Any law that limits First Amendment rights must define the kind of speech prohibited and demonstrate a compelling need, but the 1974 law does not specify what constitutes confidential information nor the conditions under which it is protected. Thus, some legal experts doubt the law's constitutionality. P&G denied that any reporter's First Amendment rights were being violated: "No news media outlet is being asked to turn over any names or any information. The investigation is focused on individuals who may be violating the law."

The response to P&G's role in the investigation was quick and angry. The Cincinnati chapter of the Society of Professional Journalists wrote in a letter to CEO Artz: "The misguided action Procter & Gamble is taking threatens to trample the First Amendment and obviously reflects more concern in identifying a possible leak within the company rather than protecting any trade secrets. . . . Your complaint has prompted a prosecutorial and police fishing expedition that amounts to censorship before the fact and could lead to further abuse of the First Amendment by other companies also disgruntled by news media coverage." An editorial in the *Wall Street Journal* asked "What possessed P&G?" and questioned the legality by saying, "We understand that P&G swings a big stick in Cincinnati, of course, and maybe the local law can, like Pampers, be stretched to cover the leak. It is not funny, though, to the folks being hassled by the cops." The sharpest criticism came from William Safire, the *New York Times* columnist, who objected to Edward Artz's contention that P&G's mistakes are not "an issue of ethics." Safire concluded a column entitled "At P&G: It Sinks" with the words: "It's not enough to say, 'our leak hunt backfired, so excuse us'; the maker of Tide and Ivory can only come clean by showing its publics, and tomorrow's business leaders, that it understands that abuse of power and invasion of privacy are no mere errors of judgment, regrettably inappropriate—but are unethical, bad, improper, wrong."

In the end, no charges were filed against any individual, and the company continued to deny any wrongdoing. A spokesperson for P&G asserted that the press "has the right to pursue information, but we have the right to protect proprietary information." Fraud squad investigator Gary Armstrong later went to work for Procter & Gamble full-time.

INTRODUCTION

The critics of Procter & Gamble's heavy-handed investigation did not cite any harmful consequences beyond the chilling effect it might have had on employees and members of the press. They complained instead about the abuse of power and invasion of privacy. In particular, P&G was charged with violating certain *rights*—the right of the reporters to search out newsworthy information and the right of ordinary citizens not to have their telephone records searched. Violations of rights can have very serious consequences, especially if they become common, and so we should be alarmed by any occurrences. Consequences aside, however, there is something objectionable about a company snooping on its own employees and using law enforcement officials for company purposes.

This chapter examines two approaches to ethics that do not appeal to consequences. One of these is the most prominent deontological theory, namely Kantian ethics; the other approach is virtue ethics, which is most commonly associated with the name of Aristotle. Rights also figure prominently in our thinking about ethical issues, but rights do not themselves constitute a theory of ethics. A right is instead a moral concept like ought, so judgments about it need to be justified by some ethical theory. Although utilitarians have offered a foundation for rights, the concept has been thought to pose a stumbling block for any teleological theory, since rights seem to be independent of consequences. So deontological theories, such as Kantian ethics, have been considered more promising candidates for justifying the rights that we have. Before we can examine the justification of rights, though, we need to understand Kant's theory of ethics.

KANT'S ETHICAL THEORY

Immanuel Kant (1724–1804) wrote his famous ethical treatise *Foundations of the Metaphysics of Morals* (1785) before the rise of English utilitarianism, but he was well acquainted with the idea of founding morality on the feelings of pleasure and pain, rather than on reason. Accordingly, Kant set out to restore reason to what he regarded as its rightful place in our moral life. Specifically, he attempted to show that there are some things that we ought to do and others that we ought not to do merely by virtue of being rational. Moral obligation thus has nothing to do with consequences, in Kant's view, but arises solely from a moral law that is binding on all rational beings.

The main features of the ethical theory presented in the *Foundations* can be illustrated by considering one of Kant's own examples:

> . . . [A] man finds himself forced by need to borrow money. He well knows that he will not be able to repay it, but he also sees that nothing will be loaned him if he does not firmly promise to repay it at a certain time. He desires to make such a promise, but he has enough conscience to ask himself whether it is not improper and opposed to duty to relieve his distress in such a way.

What (morally) ought this man to do? A teleological theory would have us answer this question by determining the consequences of each alternative course of action. Making a promise that he knows he cannot keep might enable the man to extricate himself from his immediate troubles, but more likely the long-term consequences of being in debt and losing the trust of others would outweigh any possible gain. No rule that would make such an action morally right could possibly be justified, moreover, by the consequences of everyone's acting in that way. According to both act- and rule-utilitarianism, therefore, the man probably ought to refrain from making the untruthful promise.

Kant regarded all such appeals to consequences as morally irrelevant. As a deontologist, he held that the duty to tell the truth when making promises arises from a rule that ought to be followed without regard for consequences. Even if the man could do more good by borrowing money under false pretenses—by using it to pay for an operation that would save a person's life, for example—the action would still be wrong. Kant denied, furthermore, that any consequence, such as pleasure, could be good. In a deontological theory, duty rather than good is the fundamental moral category. As a result, the only thing that can be good without qualification, according to Kant, is what he called a *good will*, performing an action solely because it is our duty.

The Problem of Knowing Which Rules to Follow

The main difficulty of deontological theories that include a list of absolute moral rules is the lack of any convincing answer to the question, How do we know that these are the rules we should follow? Kant attempted to answer this question by seizing on a difference between the moral and nonmoral senses of the word *ought*. Consider the following examples:

1. If you want to improve your serve, then you ought to take lessons from a tennis pro.
2. If you want to lower your cholesterol level, then you ought to eat less red meat.

Kant called these *hypothetical imperatives*, because they tell us to do something only on the condition that we have the relevant desire. They have the form If you want _____, then do _____. If we do not care about improving our serve, though, or lowering our cholesterol level, then there is nothing that we *ought* to do. In neither case does the use of the word *ought* express a moral obligation.

Kant characterized moral rules as imperatives that express what we ought to do *categorically* rather than hypothetically. That is, they are uses of the word *ought* that tell us what to do regardless of our desires. Imperatives that command categorically are of the form Do _____ (period). Thus, we cannot evade the force of the moral rule Tell the truth merely by saying, for example, "But I don't care about being trusted." The question of how we can know which rules to follow was posed by Kant, then, as follows: How is it possible for there to be imperatives that command categorically; that is, that command us to perform actions no matter what desires we happen to have? His answer is that they follow from a principle, called the *categorical imperative*, which he believed every rational being must accept.

Kant's own turgid statement of the categorical imperative is

> *Act only according to that maxim by which you can at the same time will that it should become a universal law.*

Rendered into more comprehensible English, Kant's principle is, act only on rules (or maxims) that you would be willing to see everyone follow.[2] The categorical imperative suggests a rather remarkable "thought experiment" to be performed whenever we deliberate about what to do. Suppose, for example, that every time we accept a rule for our own conduct, that very same rule would be imposed, by some miracle, on everybody. Under such conditions, are there some rules that we, as rational beings, simply could not accept (that is, will to become universal law)?

Let us see how this would apply to Kant's example. If the man were to obtain the loan under false pretenses, the rule on which he would be acting would be something like, Whenever you need a loan, make a promise to repay the money, even if you know that you cannot do so. Although such a rule could easily be acted on by one person, the effect of its being made a rule for everyone—that is, of becoming a universal law—would be, in Kant's view, self-defeating. No one would believe anyone else, and the result would be that the words "I promise to do such-and-such" would lose their meaning.

Kant has sometimes been accused of being a "closet utilitarian" by slipping in an appeal to consequences. To Kant's own way of thinking, however, the objection to the rule just stated is not that everyone's following it would lead to undesirable consequences but that everyone's following it describes an impossible state of affairs. Willing that everyone act on this rule is analogous to a person making plans to vacation in two places, say Acapulco and Aspen, *at the same time.* Both are desirable vacation spots, but willing the metaphysical impossibility of being in two places at once is not something that can be done by a rational person.

Regardless of whether Kant is successful in his attempt to show how it is possible for some imperatives to command categorically and not merely hypothetically, many philosophers still find a kernel of truth in Kant's principle of the categorical imperative, which they express as the claim that all moral judgments must be *universalizable.* That is, if we say that an act is right for one person, then we are committed to saying that it is right for all other relevantly similar persons in relevantly similar circumstances. By the same token, if an act is wrong for other people, then it is wrong for any one person unless there is some difference that justifies making an exception. This *principle of universalizability* expresses the simple point that, as a matter of logic, we must be consistent in the judgments we make.

The Principle of Universalizability

The principle of universalizability has immense implications for moral reasoning. First, it counters the natural temptation to make exceptions for ourselves or to apply a double standard. Consider a job applicant who exaggerates a bit on a résumé but is incensed to discover, after being hired, that the company misrepresented the opportunity for advancement. The person is being inconsistent to hold that it is all right for him to lie to others but wrong for anyone else to lie to him, or that there is nothing wrong with lying if it is necessary to get a job, but companies ought to be completely truthful in their dealings with potential employees. An effective move in a moral argument is to challenge people who hold such positions to cite some morally relevant difference. What is so special about you specifically or job applicants in general? If they can give no acceptable answer, then they are forced by the laws of logic to give up one or the other of the inconsistent judgments.

Second, the universalizability principle can be viewed as underlying the common question, "What if everyone did that?"[3] The consequences of a few people cheating on their taxes, for example, are negligible. If everyone were to cheat, however, the results would be disastrous. The force of "What if everyone did that?" is to get people to see that since it would be undesirable for everyone to cheat, no one ought to do so. This pattern of ethical reasoning involves an appeal to consequences, but it differs from standard forms of utilitarianism in that the consequences are hypothetical rather than actual. That is, whether anyone else actually cheats is irrelevant to the question "What if everyone did that?" The fact that the results would be disastrous *if everyone did* is sufficient to entail the conclusion that cheating is wrong.[4]

Although this kernel of truth in Kant's categorical imperative is of great importance, it is too limited to serve as the basis for a complete ethical theory.[5] First, people accused of wrongdoing can insist that significant differences exist between their actions and those of others. Of course it would be wrong if everyone were to cheat on their taxes, but my case is different, a tax evader might say; it would be okay for everyone to do exactly what I am doing. Second, the principle of universalizability is incapable of refuting fanatics who would be content for everyone to act as they do. R. M. Hare asks us to consider the case of a Nazi who is so convinced of the rightness of the ideal of a pure Aryan race that even evidence proving him to be a Jew does not change his mind. Most people are unlikely to accept such repugnant consequences. But as long as there are fanatics who are willing for everyone else to act in the same way, their positions—no matter how immoral—cannot be refuted by appealing merely to the principle of universalizability.

RESPECT FOR PERSONS

The *Foundations* contains a second formulation of the categorical imperative, which Kant expressed as follows:

> *Act so that you treat humanity, whether in your own person or in that of another, always as an end and never as a means only.*

These words are usually interpreted to mean that we should respect other people (and ourselves!) as human beings. The kind of respect that Kant had in mind is compatible with achieving our ends by enlisting the aid of other people. We use shop clerks and taxi drivers, for example, as a means for achieving our ends, and the owners of a business use employees as a means for achieving their ends. What is ruled out by Kant's principle, however, is treating people *only* as a means, so that they are no different, in our view, from mere "things."

The moral importance of human beings is not unique to Kant's theory, of course. Virtually all systems of ethics require that we respect other persons. The distinctiveness of Kant's contribution lies in his view of what it means to be a human being and what we are respecting when we have respect for persons. For utilitarians, human beings are creatures capable of enjoying pleasure, and so we are morally obligated to produce as much pleasure as possible, taking into consideration the pleasure of everyone alike. Kant holds, by contrast, that the morally significant feature of human beings is not their capacity for enjoying pleasure but their *rationality*. Lower animals are capable of enjoying pleasure, too; what distinguishes human beings, for Kant, is their capacity for using reason. To respect persons, therefore, is to respect them as rational creatures.

Rationality is what gives persons a greater moral value than anything else in creation, including pleasure. Indeed, rational beings are the only things that ultimately have value, according to Kant; other things have value only because we place a value on them as means to our ends. Books, music, fine food, travel, and the company of friends, for example, have value as a result of our enjoyment of them. Apart from rational beings who want them and act to obtain them, they have no value at all. Kant expressed this point by saying that their value is *conditional*. The only thing that has *unconditional* value and is an end in itself is that which gives value to other things; namely, human beings. In Kant's own words:

> Now, I say, man and, in general, every rational being exists as an end in himself and not merely as a means to be arbitrarily used by this or that will. In all his actions, whether they are directed to himself or to other rational beings, he must always be regarded at the same time as an end.

From this follows the second formulation of the categorical imperative.

Our account of the second formulation is not complete, however, without an explanation of how Kant understood reason. Reason, in Kant's view, is what enables human beings to act freely. Every event in nature other than the actions of human beings is rigidly determined by antecedents. The ringing of a doorbell, for example, follows inevitably once the button is pushed. Human beings are exempt, however, from the determinism that prevails in the rest of the natural world. We alone have a free will. Thus, we are free to push a doorbell button—or not to push it, as we choose. Freedom of this kind is possible, according to Kant, because we are able to create the rules that govern our conduct. His conception of rationality can be expressed roughly by saying that we are rule-making beings. This idea of acting on rules of our own devising is also conveyed by the term *autonomy*, which is derived from two Greek words meaning "self" and "law." To be autonomous is quite literally to be a lawgiver to oneself, or self-governing. A rational being, therefore, is a being who is autonomous. To respect other people, then, is to respect their capacity for acting freely; that is, their autonomy.

Strengths and Weaknesses of the Principle

The principle of respect for persons has some significant strengths and weaknesses. The main weakness is that it does not lend itself to a precise method for decision making. Certainly, slavery and gross exploitation of labor are forbidden by the principle, but utilitarianism judges these practices to be immoral as well. Respect for persons is likely to yield different results, though, in cases where utilitarians would sacrifice the interests of a few individuals to increase the overall welfare of society. Kant's principle lays a greater stress on the welfare of every person, thereby providing greater protection for the claims of individuals over those of society at large. However, it does not tell us where to draw the line.

For example, any company that claims to treat its employees with respect must assure them of reasonable job security. Lifetime employment is a frequently cited feature of Japanese management. Job security involves a certain loss of efficiency, though, since companies are less able to adapt to changing conditions, and the cost is borne by consumers in higher prices or by the employees themselves in lower wages. If job security increases unemployment, it protects those workers who already have a job while harming those who are unemployed. Respect for persons supports *some* level of job security, then, but it provides little help in managing the inevitable trade-offs. Utilitarianism, although perhaps too ready to sacrifice the interests of individuals, is better suited to this task.

Respect for persons is also likely to yield different results in cases where the welfare of individuals comes into conflict with their freedom to choose. In matters of occupational health and safety, for example, utilitarians tend to favor government regulations to protect workers. An alternative that is more compatible with Kant's principle is to inform workers of the dangers and allow *them* to decide whether to assume the risk. Regulation, according to some critics, is *paternalistic;* that is, it treats workers as a parent treats a child. It is demeaning, they contend, for bureaucrats in Washington to tell workers what conditions they can work under, even if the regulation is for their own good. Utilitarians argue in reply that a lack of regulation leaves workers vulnerable to exploitation by employers, so that outlawing unsafe working conditions shows greater respect for workers as persons than leaving the choice to them. Regulation is justified, they say, because workers cannot effectively exercise individual choice in this case.

Conclusion

Despite shortcomings, Kant's ethical theory yields at least two important results. The principles of universalizability and respect for persons, although not sufficient for deciding all questions of ethics, are still important avenues of ethical reasoning that serve as valuable correctives to the utilitarian approach. Kantianism also provides a strong foundation for rights, which is another part of morality.

THE CONCEPT OF A RIGHT

Rights play an important role in business ethics—and, indeed, in virtually all moral issues. Both employers and employees are commonly regarded as having certain rights. Employers have the right to conduct business as they see fit, to make decisions about hiring and promotion, and to be protected against unfair forms of competition. Employees have the right to organize and engage in collective bargaining and to be protected against discrimination and hazardous working conditions. Consumers and the general public also have rights in such matters as marketing and advertising, product safety, and the protection of the environment.

Beyond business, the debate over abortion, the use of life-support systems, access to medical care, and discrimination in housing and education all involve the rights of different parties. Each side in the abortion debate, for example, appeals to a supposed right: the right to life of the fetus or the right of a woman to choose whether to bear a child. There is growing support for the recognition of the right of the terminally ill to choose to die, the right of people to a minimal level of health care, and so on. Many of our constitutional protections in the Bill of Rights arouse controversy. Does the First Amendment right of free speech, for example, protect obscenity or flag burning?

The introduction of rights into the discussion of ethical issues is often confusing. First, the term *rights* is used in many different ways, so that the concept of a right and the various kinds of rights must be carefully distinguished. Second, many rights come into conflict. The right of an employee to leave his or her employer and join a competitor conflicts with the legitimate right of employers to protect trade secrets, for example, so that some balancing is required. Third, because of the moral significance that we attach to rights, there is a tendency to stretch the concept in ways that dilute its meaning. For example, the rights to receive adequate food, clothing, and medical care, mentioned in the Universal Declaration of Human Rights, are perhaps better described as political goals rather than rights. Finally, there can be disagreement over the very existence of a right. Whether employees have a right to due process in discharge decisions, for example, is a subject of dispute. For all these reasons, the claim of a right is frequently the beginning of an ethical debate rather than the end.

The Nature and Value of Rights

The concept of a right can be explained by imagining a company that treats employees fairly but does not recognize due process as a right.[6] In this company, employees are dismissed only for good reasons after a thorough and impartial hearing, but there is no contract, statute, or other provision establishing a right of due process for all employees. Something is still missing, since the fair treatment that the employees enjoy results solely from the company's voluntary acceptance of certain personnel policies. If the company were ever to change these policies, then employees dismissed without due process would have no recourse. Contrast this with a company in which due process is established as a right. Employees in this company have something that was lacking in the previous company. They have an independent basis for challenging a decision by the company to dismiss them. They have something to stand on; namely, their rights.

Rights can be understood, therefore, as *entitlements.*[7] To have rights is to be entitled to act on our own or to be treated by others in certain ways without asking permission of anyone or being dependent on other people's goodwill. Rights entitle us to make claims on other people either to refrain from interfering in what we do or to contribute actively to our well-being—not as beggars, who can only entreat others to be generous, but as creditors, who can demand what is owed to them. This explanation of rights in terms of entitlements runs the risk of circularity (after all, what is an entitlement but something we have a right to?), but it is sufficiently illuminating to serve as a beginning of our examination.

Some Distinctions between Rights

A distinction needs to be made at the outset between legal rights and moral rights. *Legal rights* are rights that are recognized and enforced as part of a legal system. In the United States, these consist primarily of the rights set forth in the Constitution, including the Bill of Rights, and those created by acts of Congress and state legislatures. *Moral rights,* by contrast, are rights that do not depend on the existence of a legal system. They are rights that we (morally) *ought* to have, regardless of whether they are explicitly recognized by law. Moral rights derive their force not from being part of a legal system but from more general ethical rules and principles.

Some rights are *specific* in that they involve identifiable individuals. In law, these are called *in personam* rights. A major source of specific, or *in personam,* rights is contracts, since these ubiquitous instruments create a set of mutual rights as well as duties for the individuals who are parties to them. Other rights are *general,* or *in rem,* rights, since they involve claims against everyone, or humanity in general. Thus, the right of free speech belongs to everyone, and the obligation to enforce this right rests with the whole community.

Another common distinction exists between *negative* and *positive* rights. Generally, negative rights are correlated with obligations on the part of others to refrain from acting in certain ways; that is, to act negatively by not interfering with our own freedom of action. Positive rights, by contrast, impose obligations on other people to provide us with some good or service and thereby to act positively on our behalf.[8] The right to property, for example, is largely a negative right, since no one else is obligated to provide us with property, but everyone has an obligation not to use or take our property without permission. The rights mentioned in the Bill of Rights are negative rights insofar as they serve to limit the extent to which government can encroach on the sphere of individual liberty. Some of the rights enumerated in the Universal Declaration of Human Rights, however, such as a right to an adequate standard of living and to adequate health care, are positive rights. Implementation of these rights requires extensive action by the state to ensure that basic goods and services are available.

THE FOUNDATION OF RIGHTS

With this examination of the concept of a right now complete, let us turn to the more difficult and controversial matter of the foundation of rights. Are rights fundamental moral categories with their own source of support? Or are rights part of some more general ethical theory, such as utilitarianism or Kantian ethics? We begin by considering the natural rights tradition, which offers a historically influential account of rights separate from these other possible grounds.

Natural Rights Theory

One prominent foundation for rights focuses on what are called *natural* rights or, more recently, *human* rights. Rights of this kind, which are prominent in historical documents, are rights that belong to all persons purely by virtue of their being human.[9] They are characterized by two main features: *universality* and *unconditionality*. Universality means that they are possessed by *all* persons, without regard for race, sex, nationality, or any specific circumstances of birth or present condition. Unconditionality means that natural or human rights do not depend on any particular practices or institutions in society. The right of U.S. citizens to vote, for example, depends on the specific form of government and the election laws of this country and so cannot be a natural, or human, right. The unconditionality of rights also means that there is nothing we can do to relinquish them or to deprive ourselves or others of them. This feature of natural, or human, rights is what is usually meant by the term "inalienable."[10]

The idea of natural rights has a long and distinguished history going back to the ancient Greeks, who held that there is a "higher" law which applies to all persons everywhere and serves as a standard for evaluating the laws of states.[11] Both Roman law and the medieval church adopted this idea and developed it into a comprehensive legal theory. Perhaps the most influential natural rights theory, though, is that presented by John Locke (1633–1704) in his famous *Second Treatise of Government* (1690).[12]

Locke began with the supposition of a state of nature, which is the condition of human beings in the absence of any government. The idea is to imagine what life would be like if there were no government, and then to justify the establishment of a political state to remedy the defects of the state of nature. Locke held that human beings have rights, even in the state of nature, and that the justification for uniting into a state is to protect these rights. The most important natural right for Locke is the right to property, which he justified in the following way:

> God, who has given the world to men in common, has also given them reason to make use of it to the best advantage of life and convenience. The earth and all that is therein is given to men for the support and comfort of their being. And though all the fruits it naturally produces and beasts it feeds belong to mankind in common . . . ; yet being given for the use of men, there must of necessity be a means to appropriate them some way or other before they can be of any use or at all beneficial to any particular man.

The means by which people are able to take goods out of the common storehouse of nature and make them their own is by the use of labor, which is also a form of property. "Every man has property in his own person," according to Locke, and so "The labor of his body and the work of his hands . . . are properly his."

Locke's theory of natural rights represents a significant advance over the traditional natural law theory in at least two respects. First, it clearly distinguishes between a right as an entitlement and right action, which are run together in Greek and medieval theories. Rights, in particular, are protections against the encroachment of the state in certain spheres of our lives, so that individuals have moral standing as persons independent of their role as citizens. Second, the particular rights listed by Locke, especially the right to property, are precisely those required for the operation of a free market. Thus, Locke's theory is important in the rise of modern capitalism.

However, natural rights theory, in its traditional form or the version offered by Locke, fails to provide a wholly satisfactory basis for the full range of rights in our modern society. A number of contemporary philosophers have attempted to resurrect the notion of natural rights with only limited success.[13]

Utility and Rights

Any attempt to found rights on utility might seem to be doomed from the start, since a standard objection against utilitarianism is that the theory is incapable of accounting for rights. The major stumbling block for the utilitarian theory is that rights often serve to protect individual interests against claims based on general welfare. For example, the right of due process entitles employees to a fair hearing *even if more good could be achieved by firing employees without one.* Similarly, the right of free speech protects unpopular and dangerous opinions that society might be better off without. A tough-minded utilitarian such as Bentham can respond by simply holding that we have a right to due process and free speech only insofar as respecting these rights usually has good consequences, but if more utility can be achieved in certain instances by denying them, then these rights no longer provide us with any protection. Mill's writings suggest a different kind of response, however.[14] The ultimate test of a system of morality, for Mill as for Bentham, is whether it maximizes utility. But the greatest amount of utility is apt to be achieved, in Mill's view, not by *direct* pursuit—that is, by selecting in each instance the action that has the best outcome—but *indirectly,* by developing practices and institutions that lead people to act in socially beneficial ways. In contemporary terms, Mill was a rule- rather than an act-utilitarian.

The main reason for the superiority of the indirect pursuit of utility or rule-utilitarianism is that we do not know all the consequences of our actions, so that attempts to achieve the utilitarian optimum directly, by using act-utilitarian reasoning, occasionally backfire. Rights facilitate the indirect pursuit of utility in these kinds of situations where (1) substantial considerations of human welfare are at stake, and (2) the connection between right action and the consequences for human welfare are difficult to see and we are strongly tempted to act in the wrong way. Since claims of rights have a stronger moral force than mere rules of obligation, people are induced by them to disregard utilitarian considerations and act on the basis of rights—thereby achieving the greatest good from the utilitarian point of view.

Mill's analysis neatly fits the right of free speech. At first glance, it is difficult to understand how a utilitarian could justify unbridled liberty for inflammatory racist diatribes or sordid pornographic works. The principle of utility would seem to support some restrictions on the expression of socially undesirable views. Mill contends, however, in his famous defense of free speech in Chapter 2 of *On Liberty,* that by denying a right to free speech we run the risk of suppressing the truth along with error, and to suppose that we can distinguish between the two is to make an assumption of infallibility. History is full of examples of the persecution of people holding unpopular opinions, including Socrates, Jesus, Galileo, and Gandhi. Even the expression of false beliefs ought to be allowed, since by public discussion their falsity is all the more clearly revealed. Also, the absence of a right of free speech creates an atmosphere in which thinkers are afraid to challenge prevailing orthodoxies and to entertain new and unfamiliar ideas. "The greatest harm done," Mill said, "is to those who are not heretics and whose whole mental development is cramped, and their reason cowed, by the fear of heresy."

The justification for a right to free speech, then, is that once we start restricting people's expression, we lose much of the benefit of the open exchange of ideas. The utilitarian optimum would be to permit only beneficial speech, while suppressing speech that is socially undesirable; but this ideal is unattainable. And since the utility of suppressing unpopular views is often immediate and evident, while the utility of permitting them distant and speculative, there is a great temptation to deny freedom of speech. Giving free speech the status of a right, therefore, serves to keep us from being shortsighted and acting precipitously.

Mill's theory provides a plausible utilitarian foundation for rights. In order to justify them, he found it necessary to abandon the direct pursuit of utility in favor of pursuing utility indirectly. That is, Mill held that we should disregard all consequences and consider only rights and the other rules that make up our system of morality.[15] Still, the justification that Mill offers for various rights is very strong, and it is certainly wrong to charge that utilitarianism is incapable of accounting for rights.

A Kantian Foundation for Rights

Kant himself did not give a great deal of attention to rights, but subsequent philosophers in the Kantian tradition have developed a number of justifications based on the concepts of rational agency and respect for persons.

Kant observed that rights are distinguished by the fact that we are justified in using coercion to enforce them.[16] He defined a right, accordingly, as a "moral capacity to bind others."[17] Rights are divided by Kant into innate and acquired. Innate rights are those that belong to everyone "by nature, independently of any juridical act"; that is, any explicit human convention. These are what other writers call natural, or human, rights. Acquired rights, by contrast, depend on some human convention or "juridical act."

Innate rights are founded by Kant on his conception of humans as rational agents; that is, as beings who are capable of acting autonomously. In order to be agents of this kind, it is necessary for us to be free from limitations imposed by the will of others. Complete freedom is impossible, however, since one person can be free only if others are constrained in some way. We are free to speak, for example, only if everyone else is prevented from interfering. Being rational, autonomous agents requires, therefore, that we be justified in placing restrictions on what others can do, which is to say that we have rights.

Our rights must be in accord with universal law, however. That is, we have rights that justify our limiting the freedom of others only to the extent that others have these same rights to limit us. (This is the requirement of universality contained in the first formulation of the categorical imperative.) It follows that there is only one fundamental innate right, according to Kant, and that is the right to be free from the constraint of the will of others insofar as this is compatible with a similar freedom for all. From this fundamental right follow several subsidiary rights, including the right to equal treatment, equality of opportunity, and the ownership of property.

One criticism of the Kantian foundation for rights is that the fundamental right it supports—namely, the right to freedom—is excessively narrow.[18] In particular, Kant argues primarily for negative rights to noninterference and not for positive rights to welfare. A further difficulty is that Kantian theory provides few resources for determining what rights we do have. Without a doubt, slavery and torture are wrong because they violate the minimal conditions for rational action or dignity and respect. But the minimal conditions in other instances are less clear. Exactly how much freedom and well-being must we have to be rational, or autonomous, agents? Kantian rights theorists are often vague on whether rights are minimal conditions for rational action or dignity and respect, or whether they are maximal conditions. If they are minimal conditions, then their theories run the risk of justifying too little. But if rights are maximal conditions, then these theorists are in danger of justifying too much, since full autonomy and human dignity are ideals that go beyond the obligations that can reasonably be imposed on people.

VIRTUE ETHICS

Despite their differences, utilitarian and Kantian ethics both address the question, What actions are right? Virtue ethics asks instead, What kind of person should we be? Moral character rather than right action is fundamental in this ethical tradition, which originated with the ancient Greeks and received its fullest expression in Aristotle's *Nicomachean Ethics*. The role of ethics according to Aristotle is to enable us to lead successful, rewarding lives—the kind of lives that we would call "the good life." The good life in Aristotle's sense is possible only for virtuous persons—that is, persons who develop the traits of character that we call the virtues. Aristotle not only made the case for the necessity of virtue for good living but also described particular virtues in illuminating detail.

The Greek view of ethics as a guide to the good life has been overshadowed in Western thought by the Judeo-Christian heritage with its emphasis on obedience to God's will. When morality is conceived of as following divine rules like the Ten Commandments or the dictates of reason in the way proposed by Kant, then the test of a moral person lies in the actions performed, and character is important only for its role in producing right actions. However, some ethical theorists have attempted to revitalize the Greek tradition, either out of despair over the possibility of justifying ultimate moral principles, such as Kant's categorical imperative, or from the conviction that understanding ethics in terms of character yields better insights about the moral life.[19] If utilitarianism and Kantian ethics—which are theories about what actions are right—are ultimately unsatisfactory, then perhaps we should give virtue ethics a second chance. Or perhaps virtue ethics is simply better than these as an ethical theory.

A complete theory of virtue ethics must do three things. First, it must explain what is a virtue. That is, the concept of a virtue needs to be defined. Second, it must offer some list of the virtues—and a list of their corresponding vices. Finally, the theory must offer some justification of that list and explain how we decide what are virtues and vices. Honesty, for example, is likely to be on any list of the virtues. But what is it about honesty that makes it a virtue? How could we defend honesty as a virtue to someone who disagreed?

What Is a Virtue?

Defining virtue has proven to be difficult, and philosophers are by no means agreed.[20] Aristotle described virtue as a character trait that manifests itself in habitual action. Honesty, for example, cannot consist in telling the truth once; it is rather the trait of a person who tells the truth as a general practice. Only after observing people over a period of time can we determine whether they are honest. A virtue also results from something within a person rather than occurring by chance. An honest person can be relied on to tell the truth; and we can say, "I know she is telling the truth *because* she is honest." Honesty is similar in this respect to the solubility of a sugar cube. We cannot see the solubility but only the fact that sugar cubes always dissolve in water; yet we attribute the solubility to the physical properties of sugar cubes and say that the cube dissolved *because* sugar is soluble. Honesty and solubility are both (unobservable) dispositions that serve to explain what is observable.

    This account is incomplete, however, because it does not distinguish virtue from other dispositions, such as the disposition to eat when hungry or the disposition of a carpenter to cut square corners. Mere feelings, like hunger, are not virtues, according to Aristotle, in part because virtues are *acquired* traits. A person must become honest through proper upbringing. A virtue is also something that we actually *practice.* A skilled carpenter may know how to cut square corners but need not do so, but honesty is not simply a matter of knowing how to tell the truth. Honesty, in other words, is not merely a skill that a person possesses but an inclination to act. For these reasons, Aristotle classified virtue as a *state* of character, which is different from a feeling or a skill. Finally, a virtue is something that we *admire* in a person; a virtue is an excellence of some kind that is worth having for its own sake. A skill like carpentry is useful for building a house, for example, but not everyone need be a carpenter. Honesty, by contrast, is a trait that everyone needs for a good life.

    A complete definition of virtue must be more encompassing yet, because a compassionate person, for example, must have certain kinds of feelings at the distress of others and also the capacity for sound, reasoned judgments in coming to their aid. Virtue, for Aristotle, is integrally related to what he calls *practical wisdom*, which may be described roughly as the whole of what a person needs in order to live well. Being wise about how to live involves more than having certain character traits, but being practically wise and being of good moral character are ultimately inseparable. Although the problems of defining virtue are important in a complete theory of virtue ethics, the idea of virtue as a trait of character that is essential for leading a successful life is sufficient for our purposes.

A List of the Virtues

Most lists of the virtues contain few surprises. Such traits as benevolence, compassion, courage, courtesy, dependability, friendliness, honesty, loyalty, moderation, self-control, and toleration are most often mentioned. Aristotle also considered both pride and shame to be virtues on the grounds that we should be proud of our genuine accomplishments (but not arrogant) and properly shamed by our failings.

More significantly, Aristotle lists justice among the virtues. A virtuous person not only has a sense of fair treatment but can determine what constitutes fairness. The conception of justice as a virtue led Aristotle to develop a useful classification of kinds of justice and a complex theory of justice that is discussed in the next chapter.

Defending the Virtues

Defending any list of the virtues requires a consideration of the contribution that each character trait makes to a good life. In particular, the virtues are those traits that everyone needs for the good life no matter their specific situation. Thus, courage is a good thing for anyone to have, because perseverance in the face of dangers will improve our chances of getting whatever it is we want. Similarly, Aristotle's defense of moderation as a virtue hinges on the insight that a person given to excess will be incapable of effective action toward any end. Honesty, too, is a trait that serves everyone well because it creates trust, without which we could not work cooperatively with others. The character traits that make for a good gardener or for excellence in academics, by contrast, are good for some people to have but are not necessary for everyone.

In defending a life of virtues, we cannot consider merely their contribution to some end, however; we must also inquire into the end itself. If our conception of a successful life is amassing great power and wealth, for example, then would not ruthlessness be a virtue? A successful life of crime or lechery requires the character of a Fagin or a Don Juan, but we scarcely consider their traits to be virtues—or Fagin and Don Juan to be virtuous characters. The end of life—that at which we all aim, according to Aristotle—is *happiness*, and Aristotle would claim that no despot or criminal or lecher can be happy, no matter how successful such a person may be in these pursuits. Defending any lists of virtue requires, therefore, that some content be given to the idea of a good life. What is the good life, the end for which the virtues are needed? Only by answering that question can we determine what character traits are means to that end.

The virtues, moreover, are not merely means to happiness but are themselves constituents of it. That is, happiness does not consist solely of what we get in life but also includes who we are. A mother or a father, for example, cannot get the joy that comes from being a parent without actually having the traits that make one a good parent. Similarly, Aristotle would agree with Plato that anyone who became the kind of person who could be a successful despot would thereby become incapable of being happy because that person's personality would be disordered in the process.

To summarize, defending a list of the virtues requires both that we determine the character traits that are essential to a good life and that we give some content to the idea of a good life itself. Virtue ethics necessarily presupposes a view about human nature and the purpose of life. It needs some context, in other words. This point is worth stressing because the possibility of applying virtue ethics to business depends on a context that includes some conception of the nature and purpose of business.

Virtue Ethics in Business

Virtue ethics could be applied to business directly by holding that the virtues of a good businessperson are the same as those of a good person (period). Insofar as business is a part of life, why should the virtues of successful living not apply to this realm as well? However, businesspeople face situations that are peculiar to business, and so they may need certain business-related character traits. Some virtues of everyday life, moreover, are not wholly applicable to business. Any manager should be caring, for example, but a concern for employee welfare can go only so far when a layoff is unavoidable. Honesty, too, is a virtue in business, but a certain amount of bluffing or concealment is accepted in negotiations. Regardless of whether the ethics of business is different from that of everyday life, we need to show that virtue ethics is relevant to business by determining the character traits that make for a good businessperson.

Applying virtue ethics to business would require us, first, to determine the end at which business activity aims. If the purpose of business is merely to utilize resources efficiently, as economists claim, or to make as much money as possible—as Gordon ("Greed is good!") Gekko said in the 1987 movie *Wall Street*—then we get one set of virtues. Robert C. Solomon, who has developed a virtue ethics–based view in his book *Ethics and Excellence*, argues that mere wealth creation is not the purpose of business. According to Solomon:

> The bottom line of the Aristotelean approach to business ethics is that we have to get away from "bottom line" thinking and conceive of business as an essential part of the good life, living well, getting along with others, having a sense of self-respect, and being part of something one can be proud of.[21]

Theories like utilitarianism and Kantian ethics, with their emphasis on right action, suggest that business is an individual activity for personal gain and that ethics is a constraint on what we can do. Thus, a farmer is free to sell corn that he has raised to anyone who is willing to buy it, but the farmer ought not give short weight or conceal any rotten corn. Solomon contends instead that individuals are embedded in communities and that business is essentially a communal activity in which people work together for a common good. Happiness is still the end of business as it is of life, and success in business is a matter of attaining happiness. For individuals this means achieving a good life that includes rewarding, fulfilling work; and excellence for a corporation consists in making the good life possible for everyone in society.

Solomon finds that the character traits that lead to success in life also enable us to work together in economic production. Thus, he argues that:

> . . . such notions as "honest advertising" and "truth in lending" are not simply legal impositions upon business life nor are they saintly ideals that are unrealistic for people in business. They are rather the preconditions of business and, as such, the essential virtues for any business dealing.[22]

Honesty in business is not necessarily the same as honesty is other spheres of life, however. A person selling a house, for example, may rightly conceal the minimum price at which she would settle, in the hope that a buyer will bid higher; so too may she conceal the fact that she is eager to sell the house quickly, since this information would give the buyer an advantage. To conceal unseen termite damage, however, is a form of dishonesty that is generally illegal. The ethics of negotiation permits some concealment that would be unacceptable between family members or friends, but the differences may be accounted for by the purposes of the different activities. If the purpose of negotiation is to arrive at a fair price, then the concealment of certain matters may actually conduce to this end. Thus, the buyer and seller of a house are more likely to arrive at a fair price if the buyer is not aware of the seller's eagerness. Whether any given character trait is a virtue in business, then, is to be determined by the purpose of business and by the extent to which that trait contributed to that purpose.

Strengths and Weaknesses of Virtue Ethics

The main strengths of virtue ethics derive from a better fit with our own moral experience. In particular, an ethical theory that emphasizes character over the rules of right conduct is better suited to explain the following.

1. How we actually think about decisions.   Although utilitarianism and Kantian ethics provide universal moral principles that can be applied to specific cases, the proponents of a virtue ethics approach respond that people generally do not reason that way. The response of most people to a complex ethical dilemma is to ask what they feel comfortable with or what a person they admire would do. Codes of professional ethics generally offer abstract principles and sometimes specific rules; but they also stress that a professional should be a person of integrity, and this conception of the character of a professional may be a more effective guide than principles and rules. Furthermore, the moral education that we provide for children does not consist merely of telling them which actions are right and wrong but, more importantly, of shaping their character. Our concern with shaping character springs mainly from the belief that a disposition to do the right thing is more important than merely knowing what is right. According to Aristotle, doing the right thing should be so ingrained that we do not even have to think about it. Ideally, morality should be something that we do not think about at all—but merely do out of habit.

2. The importance of relations in morality.   A second strength of a virtue ethics approach is that a concern for universal principles seems to leave out the role that personal relations play in morality. Utilitarianism and Kantian ethics would have us treat the interests of everyone impartially, but, in fact, we consider the interests of family members, friends, and members of a local community to be of greater moral importance. Insofar as virtue ethics views individuals as embedded in a community and holds that a web of close relationships is essential for a good life, it is better able, so its proponents claim, to give an account of the importance of relations in morality. A concern for the virtues also echoes some themes in feminist ethics, which models ethics on family relations in which love and caring are central.[23] Since business activity consists so much of roles and relationships, in which such concepts as loyalty and trust figure prominently, then perhaps an ethics of virtue is more relevant to the experience of people in the workplace.

Virtue ethics also has some well-known weakness that afflict both Aristotle's theory and modern attempts to restore the Aristotelean tradition.

1. Incompleteness. For all its importance, a virtuous character can take us only so far in dealing with genuine ethical dilemmas. Some dilemmas involve the limits of rules—such as, when not revealing information becomes a lie—or conflicts between rules. If telling the truth will do great harm to a person, for example, then we are forced to choose between the rules Tell the truth and Avoid harm. Merely relying on the virtues of honesty and compassion does not give us much guidance in such situations, although some writers offer lengthy and subtle descriptions of particular virtues. There are also some difficult ethical situations to which the virtues do not readily apply. Decisions about whether to bribe a foreign official or to require drug testing of employees or to give preference to minorities in hiring involve complex considerations of people's rights and the demands of justice, which are not easily reduced to the character traits that we call virtues.

Utilitarianism and Kantian ethics also have difficulty with ethical dilemmas, precisely because they force us to make difficult choices. However, these theories face up to the need to resolve ethical dilemmas and attempt to provide some means. Their primary purpose is to enable us to deal with complex moral issues and to make difficult choices. Some virtue ethics theorists respond that the importance of dilemmas or quandaries in ethics has been overstated and that questions of rights and justice should not be the central concerns of ethics.[24] Although these are important matters for some people, ethical theory should deal instead with the more mundane problems of everyday life that affect us all.

2. Conflicting Interests. Happiness, according to Aristotle, is possible for anyone who becomes a certain kind of person. Being a successful person in life is, in this respect, like being a good poet: If only we all cultivate our poetic abilities, then we can all become good poets together. In assuming that we can all achieve happiness through a life of virtue, Aristotle is often accused of overlooking the fact that our interests often conflict. Insofar as our goals in life include possessing goods that are in limited supply, then not everyone can be successful. Maybe everyone could be a good poet, but not everyone could be fabulously rich. Consequently, a major task of traditional ethical theory is to manage conflict and to enable us to live in peace with one another. This view of morality is also congenial to economic theory because the market provides a mechanism for moderating conflict and enabling self-interested individuals to interact in ways that benefit all. One response of virtue ethics theorists is to play down the problem of conflicting interests and to insist that morality is more a matter of living cooperatively in communities than of moderating conflict. It is true that business is about cooperation; but it is also about power and curbing the abuse of power, and virtue ethics has little to say about that.

The idea of virtue in business is not hopelessly out of place. There are character traits that not only lead to success in business but elevate the tone of business, and the world of business contains leaders and ordinary workers with exemplary character. No ethical theory neglects the virtues entirely, however; both utilitarianism and Kantian ethics consider character to be important in leading us to perform right actions. The distinguishing feature of virtue ethics is its insistence that being of certain character and not performing right actions is central to morality. Although this view fits some features of our moral experience, it fares less well with others. Ultimately, the choice lies between two different conceptions of what we expect of an ethical theory. If we expect an ethical theory to help us solve the really hard and complex problems of life, then an ethics of right action may be more helpful. If, on the other hand, we are more concerned with living our daily life in a community with others, then perhaps an ethics of character is more appropriate.

Conclusion

This concludes our discussion of the three major theories of ethics considered in this book, along with the foundation they provide for rights. As theories about the ultimate justification of our moral judgments (that is, about what makes right actions right), they are very different. To the extent that they suggest patterns of moral reasoning, however, they are not wholly incompatible. For example, a utilitarian can also accept the principle of universalizability and even combine it with the principle of utility to form a hybrid ethical system.[25] Utilitarians no less than Kantians consider the principle of respect for persons and the concepts of dignity and autonomy as essential elements of morality, although they offer different reasons for their importance. And all three theories agree that certain virtues are important to have, although only virtue ethics makes being virtuous the essential element in leading a moral life. Our treatment of ethical theory would not be complete, however, without a consideration of one remaining concept—namely, justice—which is the subject of the next chapter.

CASE 3.2   Clean Hands in a Dirty Business

Even with her newly minted MBA, Janet Moore was having no luck in finding that dream job in the marketing department of a spirited, on-the-move company. Now, almost any job looked attractive, but so far no one had called her back for a second interview. Employers were all looking for people with experience, but that requires getting a job first. Just as she began to lose hope, Janet bumped into Karen, who had been two years ahead of her in college. Karen, too, was looking for a job, but in the meantime she was employed by a firm that was planning to add another marketing specialist. Janet was familiar with Karen's employer from a case study that she researched for an MBA marketing course. But what she learned appalled her.

    The company, Union Tobacco, Inc., is the major U.S. manufacturer of snuff, and her case study examined how this once-staid company had managed to attract new customers to a product that had long ago saturated its traditional market.[26] Before 1970, almost all users of snuff—which is a form of tobacco that is sucked rather than chewed—were older men. The usual form of snuff is unattractive to nonusers because of the rough tobacco taste, the unpleasant feel of loose tobacco particles in the mouth, and the high nicotine content, which makes many first-time users ill. Snuff, to put it mildly, is a hard sell.

The company devised a product development and marketing campaign that a federal government report labeled a "graduation strategy." Two new lines were developed, a low-nicotine snuff in a tea-bag-like pouch with a mint flavor that has proved to be popular with young boys and a step-up product with slightly more nicotine, a cherry flavor, and a coarse cut that avoids the unpleasantness of tobacco floating in the mouth. Both products are advertised heavily in youth-oriented magazines with the slogan "Easy to use, anywhere, anytime," and free samples are liberally distributed at fairs, rodeos, and car races around the country.

The strategy has worked to perfection. Youngsters who start on the low-nicotine mint- and cherry-flavored products soon graduate to the company's two stronger, best-selling brands. Within two decades, the market for snuff tripled to about seven million users, of which one to two million are between the ages of 12 and 17. The average age of first use is now estimated to be 9½ years old. Janet also reported in her case study that snuff users are more than four times more likely to develop cancers of the mouth generally and fifty times more likely to develop specific cancers of the gum and inner-cheek lining. Several suits had been filed by the parents of teenagers who had developed mouth cancers, and tooth loss and gum lesions have also been widely reported, even in relatively new users.

Karen admitted that she was aware of all this but encouraged Janet to join her anyway. "You wouldn't believe some of the truly awful marketing ploys that I have been able to scuttle," she said. "Unless people like you and me get involved, these products will be marketed by people who don't care one bit about the little kids who are getting hooked on snuff. Believe me, it's disgusting work. I don't like to tell people what I do, and I sometimes look at myself in the mirror and ask what has become of the idealism I had starting out. But there will always be someone to do this job, and I feel that I have made a difference. If you join me, then the two of us together can slow things down and avoid the worst excesses, and maybe we'll even save a few lives. Plus, you can get some experience and be in a better position to move on."

Janet admitted to herself that Karen had a strong argument. Maybe she was being too squeamish and self-centered, just trying to keep her own hands clean. Maybe she could do others some good and help herself at the same time by taking the job. But then again. . . .

CASE 3.3   An Auditor's Dilemma

Sorting through a stack of invoices, Alison Lloyd's attention was drawn to one from Ace Glass Company. Her responsibility as the new internal auditor for Gem Packing is to verify all expenditures, and she knew that Ace had already been paid for the June delivery of the jars that are used for Gem's jams and jellies. On closer inspection, she noticed that the invoice was for deliveries in July and August that had not yet been made. Today was only June 10. Alison recalled approving several other invoices lately that seemed to be misdated, but the amounts were small compared with the $130,000 that Gem spends each month for glass jars. I had better check this out with purchasing, she thought.

Over lunch, Greg Berg, the head of purchasing, explains the system to her. The jam and jelly division operates under an incentive plan whereby the division manager and the heads of the four main units—sales, production, distribution, and purchasing—receive substantial bonuses for meeting their quota in pre-tax profits for the fiscal year, which ends on June 30. The bonuses are about one-half of annual salary and constitute one-third of the managers' total compensation. In addition, meeting quota is weighted heavily in evaluations, and missing even once is considered to be a death blow to the career of an aspiring executive at Gem. So the pressure on these managers is intense. On the other hand, there is nothing to be gained from exceeding a quota. An exceptionally good year is likely to be rewarded with an even higher quota the next year, since quotas are generally set at corporate headquarters by adding 5 percent to the previous year's results.

Greg continues to explain that several years ago, after the quota had been safely met, the jam and jelly division began prepaying as many expenses as possible—not only for glass jars but for advertising costs, trucking charges, and some commodities, such as sugar. The practice has continued to grow, and sales also helps out by delaying orders until the next fiscal year or by falsifying delivery dates when a shipment has already gone out. "Regular suppliers like Ace Glass know how we work," Greg says, "and they sent the invoices for July and August at my request." He predicts that Alison will begin seeing more irregular invoices as the fiscal year winds down. "Making quota gets easier each year," Greg observes, "because the division gets an ever increasing head start, but the problem of finding ways to avoid going too far over quota has become a real nightmare." Greg is not sure, but he thinks that other divisions are doing the same thing. "I don't think corporate has caught on yet," he says. "But they created the system, and they've been happy with the results so far. If they're too dumb to figure out how we're achieving them, that's their problem."

Alison recalls that upon becoming a member of the Institute of Internal Auditors, she agreed to abide by the IIA code of ethics. This code requires members to exercise "honesty, objectivity, and diligence" in the performance of their duties, but also to be loyal to the employer. However, loyalty does not include being a party to any "illegal or improper activity." As an internal auditor, she is also responsible for evaluating the adequacy and effectiveness of the company's system of financial control. But what is the harm of shuffling a little paper around? she thinks. Nobody is getting hurt, and it all works out in the end.

NOTES

1. The information in this case is taken from: ALICIA SWASY, *Soap Opera: The Inside Story of Procter & Gamble* (New York: Touchstone, 1994); "Procter & Gamble Calls In the Law To Track News Leak," *Wall Street Journal*, 12 August 1991, A1, A4; "P&G Says Inquiry on Leak to Journal Was Done Properly," *Wall Street Journal*, 13 August 1991, A3; "What Possessed P&G," *Wall Street Journal*, 13 August 1991,

A16; "No Charges Are Expected in P&G Affair," *Wall Street Journal*, 14 August 1991, A3; MARK FITZGER-ALD, "Cops Investigate News Leak," *Editor & Publisher*, 17 August 1991, 9, 39; "P&G Won't Bring Criminal Charges as a Result of Probe," *Wall Street Journal*, 19 August 1991, A3, A5; WILLIAM SAFIRE, "At P&G: It Sinks," *New York Times*, 5 September 1991, A25; "P&G Looks for a News Leak," *ABA Journal*, November 1991, 32; "Biggest Business Goofs of 1991," *Fortune*, 13 January 1992, 80–83.

2. As might be expected, there is considerable controversy over the exact interpretation of Kant's principle. A very good starting point for those unfamiliar with the *Foundations* is FRED FELDMAN, *Introductory Ethics* (Englewood Cliffs, NJ: Prentice Hall, 1978), 97–134. Reprinted in CHRISTINA HOFF SOMMERS, ed., *Right and Wrong: Basic Readings in Ethics* (San Diego: Harcourt Brace Jovanovich, 1986), 18–43. A helpful commentary on the *Foundations* is ROBERT PAUL WOLFF, *The Autonomy of Reason* (New York: Harper & Row, 1973). For a full-length study of the categorical imperative, see ONORA NELL, *Acting on Principle: An Essay on Kantian Ethics* (New York: Columbia University Press, 1975).

3. For a discussion of the logical force of this question, see COLIN STRANG, "What If Everyone Did That?" *Durham University Journal*, 53 (1960), 5–10. This article is widely reprinted. One source is SOMMERS, *Right and Wrong*, 51–62.

4. For Marcus G. Singer, this is the generalization argument, which utilizes the generalization principle but also requires the support of a utilitarian principle that he calls the principle of consequences. See MARCUS G. SINGER, *Generalization in Ethics* (New York: Knopf, 1961), chap. 4.

5. An ambitious attempt to develop the principle of universalizability into a complete ethical theory is ALAN GEWIRTH, *Reason and Morality* (Chicago: University of Chicago Press, 1978).

6. This method of explaining rights is derived from JOEL FEINBERG, "The Nature and Value of Rights," *The Journal of Value Inquiry*, 4 (1970), 243–57. Reprinted in JOEL FEINBERG, *Rights, Justice, and the Bounds of Liberty* (Princeton: Princeton University Press, 1980), 143–55, and in DAVID LYONS, ed., *Rights* (Belmont, CA: Wadsworth, 1979), 78–91.

7. This term is used in H. J. MCCLOSKEY, "Rights," *The Philosophical Quarterly*, 15 (1965), 115–27, and also in RICHARD A. WASSERSTROM, "Rights, Human Rights, and Racial Discrimination," *The Journal of Philosophy*, 61 (1964), 628–41. This latter article is reprinted in LYONS, *Rights*, 46–57. For a useful survey of different accounts, see REX MARTIN and JAMES W. NICKEL, "Recent Work on the Concept of Rights," *American Philosophical Quarterly*, 17 (1980), 165–80.

8. Closely related is a distinction between negative and positive liberty. A poor man is free (in a negative sense) to buy a loaf of bread, for example, as long as no one stands in his way, but he is not free (in a positive sense) unless he has the means to buy the bread. Compare these two senses in the case of "fee for service" medical care, which secures free *choice*, and socialized medicine, which provides free *access*. Which system of medical care is more "free"? The classic discussion of this distinction is ISAIAH BERLIN, "Two Concepts of Liberty," in *Four Essays on Liberty* (Oxford: Oxford University Press, 1969), 118–72.

9. Among the many works describing natural or human rights are: MAURICE CRANSTON, *What Are Human Rights?* (New York: Basic Books, 1963); B. MAYO, "What Are Human Rights?" in D. D. RAPHAEL, ed., *Political Theory and the Rights of Man* (Bloomington: Indiana University Press, 1967), 68–80; D. D. RAPHAEL, "Human Rights, Old and New," in RAPHAEL, *Political Theory and the Rights of Man*, 54–67; MAURICE CRANSTON, "Human Rights, Real and Supposed," in RAPHAEL, *Political Theory and the Rights of Man*, 43–53; FEINBERG, *Social Philosophy*, 84–97; and A. I. MELDEN, *Rights and Persons* (Berkeley and Los Angeles: University of California Press, 1977), 166–69.

10. See STUART M. BROWN, JR., "Inalienable Rights," *The Philosophical Review*, 64 (1955), 192–211; and B. A. RICHARDS, "Inalienable Rights: Recent Criticism and Old Doctrine," *Philosophy and Phenomenological Research*, 29 (1969), 391–404.

11. A good survey of the early history of natural rights is RICHARD TUCK, *Natural Rights Theories: Their Origin and Development* (Cambridge: Cambridge University Press, 1979).

12. Locke's theory of natural rights is the subject of great controversy. Two articles that provide a good introduction are W. VON LEYDEN, "John Locke and Natural Law," *Philosophy*, 21 (1956), 23–35; and WILLIAM J. WAINWRIGHT, "Natural Rights," *American Philosophical Quarterly*, 4 (1967), 79–84. The thesis that Locke was not a natural rights theorist is developed in LEO STRAUSS, *Natural Right and History* (Chicago: University of Chicago Press, 1953). One response is CHARLES H. MONSON, JR., "Locke and His Interpreters," *Political Studies*, 6 (1958), 120–35.

13. For a survey, see TIBOR R. MACHAN, "Some Recent Work in Human Rights Theory," *American Philosophical Quarterly*, 17 (1980), 103–15. Two important articles are MARGARET MACDONALD, "Natural Rights," *Proceedings of the Aristotelian Society*, 47 (1947–1948), reprinted in A. I. MELDEN, ed., *Human*

Rights (Belmont, CA: Wadsworth, 1970), 40–60; and H. L. A. HART, "Are There Any Natural Rights?" *The Philosophical Review*, 64 (1955), 175–91, also reprinted in MELDEN, *Human Rights*, 61–75.

14. The account that follows is one developed by DAVID LYONS in several articles, most notably "Human Rights and the General Welfare," *Philosophy and Public Affairs*, 6 (1977), 113–29; but see also "Mill's Theory of Morality," *Noûs*, 10 (1976), 101–20; "Mill's Theory of Justice," in A. I. GOLDMAN and J. KIM, eds., *Values and Morals: Essays in Honor of William Frankena, Charles Stevenson, and Richard Brandt* (Dordrecht: Reidel, 1978), 1–20; and "Benevolence and Justice in Mill," in HARLAN B. MILLER and WILLIAM H. WILLIAMS, eds., *The Limits of Utilitarianism* (Minneapolis: University of Minnesota Press, 1982), 42–70. Lyons is doubtful, however, of the account presented in these articles. See "Utility and Rights" in J. ROLAND PENNOCK and JOHN W. CHAPMAN, eds., *Ethics, Economics and the Law* (New York: New York University Press, 1982), 107–38, reprinted in JEREMY WALDRON, ed., *Theories of Rights* (Oxford: Oxford University Press, 1984), 110–36. Criticism of Lyons is contained in ALAN GEWIRTH, "Can Utilitarianism Justify Any Moral Rights?" in PENNOCK and CHAPMAN, *Ethics, Economics and the Law*, 158–93, reprinted in GEWIRTH, *Human Rights* (Chicago: University of Chicago Press, 1982), 143–62.

15. LYONS, "Utility and Rights," 134.

16. An examination of Kant's account of rights, on which the following discussion is largely based, is BRUCE AUNE, *Kant's Theory of Morals* (Princeton: Princeton University Press, 1979), 141–52.

17. IMMANUEL KANT, *The Metaphysical Elements of Justice: Part I of the Metaphysics of Morals*, trans. JOHN LADD (Indianapolis: Bobbs-Merrill, 1965), 37.

18. See AUNE, *Kant's Theory of Morals*, 151.

19. An influential article that renewed interest in virtue ethics is G.E.M. ANSCOMBE, "Modern Moral Philosophy," *Philosophy*, 33 (1958), 1–19. Perhaps the strongest recent case for an ethics of virtue is ALASDAIR MACINTYRE, *After Virtue*, 2nd ed. (Notre Dame: Notre Dame University Press, 1984).

20. For recent analyses of the virtues, see PHILIPPA FOOT, *Virtues and Vices and Other Essays in Moral Philosophy* (Berkeley: University of California Press, 1978); PETER T. GEACH, *The Virtues* (Cambridge: Cambridge University Press, 1977); GREGORY E. PENCE, "Recent Work on the Virtues," *American Philosophical Quarterly*, 21 (1984), 281–97; JAMES D. WALLACE, *Virtues and Vices* (Ithaca: Cornell University Press, 1978); G. H. VON WRIGHT, *The Varieties of Goodness* (London: Routledge & Kegan Paul, 1963).

21. ROBERT C. SOLOMON, *Ethics and Excellence: Cooperation and Integrity in Business* (New York: Oxford University Press, 1992), 104.

22. SOLOMON, *Ethics and Excellence*, 209.

23. Two books influential in defining feminist ethics are: CAROL GILLIGAN, *In a Different Voice: Psychological Theory and Women's Development* (Cambridge: Harvard University Press, 1982); and NEL NODDINGS, *Caring: A Feminine Approach to Ethics and Moral Education* (Berkeley: University of California Press, 1984). A good survey is ROSEMARY TONG, *Feminine and Feminist Ethics* (Belmont, CA: Wadsworth, 1993).

24. This point is made in EDMUND L. PINCOFFS, *Quandaries and Virtues: Against Reductionism in Ethics* (Lawrence: University of Kansas Press, 1986).

25. This is proposed by R. M. HARE in *Moral Thinking: Its Levels, Method and Point* (Oxford: Oxford University Press, 1981).

26. Material for this case is taken from ALIX M. FREEDMAN, "How a Tobacco Giant Doctors Snuff Brands to Boost Their 'Kick'," *Wall Street Journal*, 26 October 1994, A1, A6; and PHILIP J. HILTS, "Snuff Makers Are Accused of a Scheme to Lure Young," *New York Times*, 27 April 1995, A13.

4

Justice and the Market System

CASE 4.1   Green Giant Runs for the Border

To generations of consumers, the image of the Jolly Green Giant with his trusty side-kick Little Sprout has symbolized the convenience and dependability of frozen vegetables from America's agricultural heartlands.[1] The Ho, Ho, Ho of this genial figure is now being heard increasingly from the fields of Mexico, however, where Green Giant's production has been shifted in recent years. And Pillsbury, the owner of Green Giant, was itself the victim of a 1989 hostile takeover by Grand Metropolitan, PLC, a British food, liquor, and retailing concern, whose other properties include Burger King, Pearl Vision Centers, and Häagen-Dazs ice cream. The Jolly Green Giant, it turns out, is not an American but a citizen of the world with no fixed home.

The idea that companies like Green Giant are part of the American economy and will stay put, providing jobs for local residents and benefits for communities, is deeply ingrained. The citizens of Watsonville, California, were shaken, then, when Green Giant, which once employed more than 1,000 people in plants that packaged frozen broccoli and cauliflower, began laying off workers and hiring new employees at a facility in Irapuato, Mexico. Today, Green Giant employs fewer than 150 people in Watsonville and over 850 in Irapuato, and in California as a whole, roughly one-half of all frozen-food processing firms have gone South, taking over 16,000 jobs with them. An estimated 40 percent of all frozen vegetables sold in the United States is now imported from Mexico.

The economic benefits for Green Giant's move to Mexico are immense. The wages of plant workers in Watsonville averaged $7.50 per hour or about $15,600 annually. Their counterparts in Irapuato receive $4.50 a day for an annual income of around $1,400. Even after other costs are counted, Green Giant is estimated to save $13,224 per worker by moving jobs to Mexico. With fringe benefits that raise the pay by almost 60 percent, Green Giant's wages are slightly above the local rate, and unsuccessful union organizers have had to admit that the company's workers are quite content. Still, their income allows them only a very minimal standard of living and falls short of the guarantee in the Mexican constitution of a minimum wage sufficient to support a wife and children. Many of the unemployed in California are legal immigrants who came in search of economic opportunity and now find that American companies are going to Mexico for the same reason. The irony of the situation is understood by one worker who remarked: "The company is going away to get rich. Just like we did."

Forces other than the immediate gain are behind Green Giant's move to Mexico. Pillsbury planned the phaseout of production in California as part of a futile effort to avoid the takeover by Grand Met. The company realized that their customers in the East could be served more cheaply by growing and packaging vegetables in Mexico and the Midwest and that a failure to capitalize on this savings would only make them more vulnerable to a hostile raider. Remaining independent requires that managers take advantage of every opportunity for increasing profit, because other managers are always ready to step in and reap the benefit themselves. Furthermore, in an age of worldwide competition, other countries are forming their own trading blocs and allowing their companies to move production into low-wage areas. As Robert Reich observes: "Today, corporate decisions about production and location are driven by the dictates of global competition, not by national allegiance. . . . The global manager who fails to take advantage of global opportunities will lose profits and market share to global managers who do."[2]

Green Giant's move imposed great hardships on those workers who have few job skills. The average laid-off worker has been described as a forty-five-year-old Hispanic woman with no high school diploma and fourteen years' experience at the single task of trimming broccoli. An expanding economy, sparked in part by an increased demand for American products in Mexico, will create new jobs for other workers, but few of these jobs will be filled by the workers laid off by Green Giant. The transfer of low-wage jobs to Mexico might increase the job prospects of American workers as a whole, but the gain of some workers will come at a painful cost to others. American consumers also gain as cheaper vegetables imported from Mexico stretch everyone's pocketbook. Spending a dollar less for broccoli is as good as a dollar raise in salary, but that is little consolation for the newly unemployed.

The job gains in Mexico benefit the new hires at Green Giant, which is known locally as *Gigante Verde;* and the Mexican economy as a whole receives a needed boost, not only from the foreign investment but also from the exposure to more advanced technology. The move of Green Giant and countless other American companies to Mexico increases the competitiveness of both countries in the global economy, but the benefit to Mexican citizens also comes at a price. The conversion of vast acreage to vegetables for the American table increases the price of beans and corn, which are the staples of the local diet. The Green Giant facility in Irapuato pumps more than half a million gallons of well water each day, and the water table, which used to be between 30 and 60 feet, is now over 450 feet. Few local residents can afford to drill wells that deep, and so most are forced to rely on the heavily polluted Guanajuato River. The use of well water to process vegetables protects American consumers from contaminants in the river but increases the health hazards for the citizens of Irapuato.

American companies are not required to observe U.S. standards for worker health and safety and for protection of the environment, and the applicable Mexican standards are generally much lower and weakly enforced. Although Green Giant claims to operate by the same standards on both sides of the border, the record of many other companies is not as clean. In *maquiladora* plants, which receive special tax treatment, sweatshop conditions are know to prevail, and toxic wastes— which, by law, should be shipped back to the United States for proper disposal —now pollute the Rio Grande.

Green Giant did not merely walk away from the problems in Watsonville. The company gave some severance pay to the displaced workers and provided them with resources for retraining and job relocation. The federal government also contributed half a million dollars to the effort, which bore some fruit, although in 1991 the unemployment rate in Watsonville approached 15 percent. For twenty-five years, Green Giant was a good corporate citizen, paying taxes and supporting a variety of community services. So what does the company owe the community now that it is leaving? After summing up the gains and losses to all the different groups affected by Green Giant's move, the plant manager in Irapuato concluded: "Is it right or wrong? I can't tell you. But it's the way the world is going."

INTRODUCTION

Justice, like rights, is an important moral concept with a wide range of applications. We use it to evaluate not only the actions of individuals but also social, legal, political, and economic practices and institutions. Although the word *just* is sometimes used interchangeably with *right* and *good,* it generally has a more restricted meaning that is closer to *fair.* Questions of justice often arise when there is something to distribute. If there is a shortage of organ donors, for example, we ask, what is a just, or fair, way of deciding who gets a transplant? And if there is a burden, such as taxes, we want to make sure that everyone bears a fair share. Justice is also concerned with the righting of wrongs. It requires, for example, that a criminal be punished for a crime and that the punishment fit the crime by being neither too lenient nor too severe. To treat people justly is to give them what they deserve, which is sometimes the opposite of generosity and compassion. Indeed, we often speak of tempering justice with mercy.

The concept of justice is relevant to business ethics primarily in the distribution of benefits and burdens in situations like the move of Green Giant to Mexico. Economic transformations often involve an overall improvement of welfare that is unevenly distributed, so that some groups pay a price while others reap the rewards. Is the resulting distribution just, and if not, is there anything that is owed to the losers? Justice is also at issue when a wrong has been done and we want to know what can be done to make amends. Justice requires that something be done to compensate the victims of discrimination or defective products or industrial accidents. Since justice is also an important concept in evaluating institutions and various forms of social organization, we can also ask about the justice of the economic system in which business activity takes place.

In succeeding sections, four theories of justice are examined; namely, Aristotle's principle of proportionate equality, the utilitarian theory, and the prominent contemporary theories of John Rawls and Robert Nozick. One important kind of justice is economic justice, and a system of free markets is both criticized and defended on grounds of justice. This chapter includes, therefore, a discussion of the justification of the market system.

ARISTOTLE'S ANALYSIS OF JUSTICE

The first thorough analysis of the concept of justice is still the best. Aristotle observed in Book V of the *Nicomachean Ethics* that the word *justice* has a double meaning. In one sense it applies to the whole of virtue. A just or morally upright person is one who always does what is morally right and obeys the law. Justice in this sense is called *universal justice* by Aristotle. The other sense of justice, which he called *particular justice,* is concerned with virtue in specific situations. More precisely, particular justice consists in taking only a proper share of some good. An unjust person is thus a grasping person who takes too much wealth, honor, or other benefit that society offers, or a shirker who refuses to bear a fair share of some burden. Aristotle divided particular justice into:

1. **Distributive justice,** which deals with the distribution of benefits and burdens.
2. **Compensatory justice,** which is a matter of compensating persons for wrongs done to them.
3. **Retributive justice,** which involves the punishment of wrongdoers.

Both compensatory and retributive justice are concerned with correcting wrongs. Generally, compensating the victims is the just way of correcting wrongs in private dealings, such as losses resulting from accidents and the failure to fulfill contracts, whereas retribution—that is, punishment—is the just response to criminal acts, such as assault or theft.[3]

Questions about distributive justice arise mostly in the evaluation of our social, political, and economic institutions, where the benefits and burdens of engaging in cooperative activities must be spread over a group. In some instances, a just distribution is one in which each person shares equally; but in others, unequal sharing is just if the inequality is in accord with some principle of distribution. Thus, in a graduated income tax system, ability to pay and not equal shares is the principle for distributing the burden. Generally, distributive justice is *comparative*, in that it considers not the absolute amount of benefits and burdens of each person but each person's amount relative to that of others.[4] Whether income is justly distributed, for example, cannot be determined by looking only at the income of one person but requires us, in addition, to compare the income of all people in a society.

The rationale of compensatory justice is that an accident caused by negligence, for example, upsets an initial moral equilibrium by making a person worse off in some way. By paying compensation, however, the condition of the victim can be returned to what it was before the accident, thereby restoring the moral equilibrium. Similarly, a person who commits a crime upsets a moral equilibrium by making someone else worse off. The restoration of the moral equilibrium in cases of this kind is achieved by a punishment that "fits the crime." Both compensatory and retributive justice are *noncomparative*. The amount of compensation owed to the victim of an accident or the punishment due a criminal is determined by the features of each case and not by a comparison with other cases.

Just Procedures and Just Outcomes

A useful distinction not discussed by Aristotle is that between just *procedures* and just *outcomes*.[5] In cases of distributive justice, we can distinguish between the procedures used to distribute goods and the outcome of those procedures; that is, the actual distribution achieved. A similar distinction can be made between the procedures for conducting trials, for example, and the outcomes of trials. If we know what outcomes are just in certain kinds of situations, then just procedures are those that produce or are likely to produce just outcomes. Thus, an effective method for dividing a cake among a group consists of allowing one person to cut it into the appropriate number of slices with the stipulation that that person take the last piece. Assuming that an equal division of the cake is just, a just distribution will be achieved, since cutting the cake into equal slices is the only way the person with the knife is assured of getting at least as much cake as anyone else. Similarly, just outcomes in criminal trials are those in which the guilty are convicted and the innocent are set free. The complex procedures for trials are those that generally serve to produce those results.

John Rawls further distinguishes perfect and imperfect procedural justice. Perfect procedural justice always produces a just outcome, whereas imperfect procedural justice does so only to some extent. The method of having the person who slices the cake take the last piece is an example of the former (assuming, of course, a steady hand), and trial by jury is an example of the latter.[6] In some situations, which John Rawls calls "pure procedural justice," there is no independent criterion of a just outcome; a just outcome is, instead, whatever results from following a given procedure.[7] Gambling provides a good example. As long as the rules of wagering are strictly observed, any distribution of a betting pool that results is just. Sometimes there are good reasons to follow proven procedures even when they are imperfect and fail occasionally. Trial by jury, for example, is not a perfect procedure, but any alternative is worse. So unless we are willing to accept the verdicts of juries—even when the outcome is the conviction of an innocent person or the exoneration of a guilty one—the result is likely to be even more unjust outcomes.

Aristotle on Distributive Justice

Aristotle observed in the *Politics* that, "All men think justice to be a sort of equality," but what sort of equality justice is remains a source of controversy to the present day.[8] The extreme egalitarian position that everyone should be treated exactly alike has found few advocates, and most who call themselves egalitarians are concerned only to deny that certain differences ought to be taken into account.[9] A more moderate egalitarianism contends that we ought to treat like cases alike. That is, any difference in the treatment of like cases requires a moral justification.

Aristotle expressed the idea of treating like cases alike in an arithmetical equation that represents justice as an equality of ratios.[10] Let us suppose that two people, A and B, each receive some share of a good, P. Any difference in their relative shares must be justified by some relevant difference, Q. Thus, a difference in pay, P, is justified if there is a difference in some other factor, Q, that justifies the difference in P—such as the fact that one person worked more hours or was more productive. Aristotle added the further condition that the difference in each person's share of the good must be *proportional* to the difference in their share of the relevant difference. If one person worked twice as many hours as another, then the pay should be exactly twice as much—no more and no less. Aristotle's principle of distributive justice can be stated in the following manner.[11]

$$\frac{\text{A's share of P}}{\text{B's share of P}} = \frac{\text{A's share of Q}}{\text{B's share of Q}}$$

This account of Aristotle's principle of distributive justice is obviously not complete until the content of both P and Q are fully specified. What are the goods in question? What features justify different shares of these goods? Among the goods distributed in any society are material goods—such as food, clothing, and housing—and income and wealth, which enable the people to purchase material goods. There are many nonmaterial goods, including economic power, participation in the political process, and access to the courts, which are also distributed in some manner. Finally, Aristotle counted honor as a good, thereby recognizing that society distributes status and other intangibles. This multiplicity of goods has led philosophers to speak of many different kinds of justice, such as economic justice, legal justice, political justice, and social justice. It is unclear whether Aristotle's principle is intended to be an account of all these or only some.

Justifying Features

Among the many different justifying features that have been proposed are ability, effort, accomplishment, contribution, and need.[12] In setting wages, for example, an employer might award higher pay to workers who have greater training and experience or greater talent (*ability*); to workers who apply themselves more diligently, perhaps overcoming obstacles or making great sacrifices (*effort*); to workers who have produced more or performed notable feats (*accomplishment*) or who provide more valued services (*contribution*); or, finally, to workers who have large families to support or who, for other reasons, have greater *need.*

Each of these justifying features has some merits and some defects. Ability alone is not a suitable criterion since it rewards workers with great ability who exert little effort and consequently do not accomplish much. The criterion of effort rewards people with less ability who must try harder to make the same contribution. We also use different justifying features in different contexts. Thus, ability is an appropriate criterion for selecting budding tennis players for a training program, whereas invitations to a tournament ought to be based on accomplishment. The socialist slogan, From each according to his abilities, to each according to his needs holds that different criteria are relevant to determining what a person ought to contribute to society and what a person ought to receive in return. Finally, more than one criterion may be relevant to a single decision. College scholarships, for example, are often awarded on the basis of a combination of ability, effort, achievement, contribution, and need. Disagreements are possible, therefore, over the relevant justifying features and their relative weight.

In a competitive labor market, wages are determined by none of the features listed above but by supply and demand. Is Aristotle's principle applicable to the determination of wages in a capitalist economy? Some argue that it is not. The distribution of income, these philosophers contend, is an outcome of a system of pure procedural justice. That is, the economy is a kind of game played according to certain rules, and as long as the rules are followed, any distribution of economic goods that results is just. (This is roughly the view of Robert Nozick, which is examined later in this chapter.) Another answer, however, is that the distribution of income by means of a competitive labor market is an example of imperfect procedural justice. Under capitalism, wages ought to be distributed in proportion to contribution, which is to say, productivity, and a competitive labor market is a procedure that achieves this outcome, albeit imperfectly.

A final difficulty is that the arithmetical form of Aristotle's principle suggests more precision than is possible. If Q is quantifiable (the number of hours worked, for example), then it is possible to say that A worked twice as many hours as B and hence ought to be paid twice as much. There is no reason, however, for insisting on strict ratios. A pay scale with higher wages for overtime might result in A's being paid *more* than twice as much; and a system in which workers are paid a bonus for exceeding a production quota might result in A's being paid more than B but *less* than twice as much. Some relevant differences are not quantifiable in ways that permit meaningful ratios. Education, for example, is a legitimate criterion for evaluating job applicants, and, other things being equal, an employer is justified in selecting an applicant with a 4.0 average over one with an average of 2.0. It does not follow, however, that the 4.0 applicant is twice as able and ought to be paid twice as much. And many relevant differences are simply incapable of being quantified and hence cannot be expressed in ratios at all. On what scale, for example, can we compute people's needs?

Conclusion

Despite these difficulties, Aristotle's principle of distributive justice contains much of value. The main shortcoming of the theory is that it is a purely *formal* principle; that is, the statement of the principle contains variables with no specified content. Aristotle's principle lays down a logical requirement of consistency and thus provides a necessary condition for distributive justice but not a sufficient condition. A sufficient condition could be provided only by a principle that fully specifies, among other things, the relevant features that justify different treatment. The value of the principle lies chiefly in its insistence that different treatment be justified by citing relevant differences and that difference in treatment be in proportion to these differences.

UTILITY AND JUSTICE

Justice, along with rights, is commonly regarded as a stumbling block for utilitarianism. One problem that distributive justice poses for utilitarianism has already been discussed. It is that the principle of utility seems to favor any redistribution that increases the total amount of utility, without regard for how it is distributed. Thus, in the following three distribution schemes, I and II are morally indistinguishable, as judged by the total amount of utility; and III is preferable to both I and II, despite the apparent inequality.

I		II		III	
A	10	A	14	A	16
B	10	B	8	B	9
C	10	C	8	C	7
	30		30		32

We have seen, however, that justice does not require complete equality. In Aristotle's principle of justice, certain departures from I are justified *if* there are morally relevant differences between A, B, and C. So it might be that II and III are more just than I and that III is the most just distribution of all. This would be the case if A were more talented and hard-working, for example, and hence deserved more. The possibility of justified inequalities provides no defense for utilitarianism, however, because it might also be the case that there are no relevant differences between A, B, and C, so that the inequality is unjustified.

The problem that justice poses for utilitarianism, then, is not merely that the theory seems to place no value on equality but that it seems to make no allowance for justified claims for unequal treatment.

Bentham's Theory of Justice

Utilitarians generally respond that any conflict between utility and justice is only apparent and that utilitarianism, properly understood, is capable of providing a wholly adequate foundation for our judgments about what is just and what is unjust.[13] One position taken by Bentham and his followers consists of the assertion that the principle of utility, consistently applied, results in outcomes that fit with our ordinary views about justice. A society with the greatest amount of utility, in other words, is also a just society, as justice is commonly understood.[14] The concepts of equality and desert, however, are not part of the meaning of utility; rather, the connection between them is purely a matter of fact, and if utility should ever conflict with equality or desert, the latter would have to give way. Utilitarians such as Bentham believe that conflicts of this kind rarely if ever occur, though.[15]

The Arguments for Convergence

The main argument used by utilitarians to account for the convergence of utility and justice is that a system of maximizing utility has a tendency toward equality in distribution because of the phenomenon of *diminishing marginal utility*.[16] A basic tenet of economics is that the amount of utility we receive from a good decreases as the amount of the good increases. The first cookie in a box, for example, gives us much pleasure, especially if we are hungry; the second cookie, less so; and by the time we reach the last cookie, we are likely to be so full that it gives us no pleasure at all. The marginal utility of income is similar. We use the first few dollars we earn to satisfy our most basic needs and our strongest desires, with a great increase in utility. Succeeding dollars satisfy lesser felt needs and more ephemeral desires, and so they bring us correspondingly less utility. Each additional (marginal) dollar of a person's income, therefore, "buys" less utility than the one before it. A utilitarian decision maker with a dollar to give away would thus produce a greater amount of utility by giving it to a poor person than to a rich one. Similarly, practices and institutions that redistribute wealth from the rich to the poor, thereby moving a society toward greater equality, at the same time increase utility.

Although this argument is plausible, it has proven difficult in practice to verify the effect of income redistribution on the amount of utility—mainly because of the problem of measurement. Some economists argue that the marginal utility of income increases and decreases in stages, so that a person coming into great wealth might suddenly have a burning desire for a yacht and French Impressionist paintings, which he did not have before.[17] Further, some inequality increases utility. A stock argument for putting money in the hands of the wealthy is that they will put it to more productive use than the poor and thereby increase the wealth of the whole society. The tendency of utilitarianism toward equality is offset, therefore, by a countertendency toward inequality, and the optimal level of equality (or inequality) is not easily determined. An additional complication is that diminishing marginal utility constitutes a powerful argument for satisfying the basic needs of all members of society, but it is less persuasive as an argument for equality once everyone attains a certain minimal level of welfare—that is, the wealthier a society becomes, the greater the inequality permitted by the principle of utility (as long as the basic needs of everyone are met).

A second argument for the convergence of utility and justice is that a system for maximizing utility also tends to reward people according to desert. The reason why it is considered just to distribute goods in proportion to ability, effort, accomplishment, or contribution is that doing so encourages people to develop their abilities, exert greater effort, accomplish more, and perform more valued services—all of which promote the welfare of society. We do not reward all abilities or efforts, for example, but only those that contribute to human well-being, and we do the same with accomplishments and contributions. The social benefit of these criteria can be obtained, moreover, only in a stable social order in which people are treated according to their deserts *consistently*. A company that discriminates against women, for example, is unlikely to motivate female employees to develop their abilities and put forth their best efforts; it is also not likely to attract the best female applicants. A utilitarian objection to discrimination of all kinds, then, is that it reduces the overall level of utility.

Mill's Theory of Justice

Mill's position on the connection between justice and utility is, at first glance, different from that of Bentham. Although Bentham held that the standards of equality and desert are conceptually distinct from the utilitarian principle, Mill contended that they are involved "in the very meaning of Utility."

Mill's argument can be sketched as follows. One sense of equality, which is expressed in Aristotle's principle of justice, is a presumptive right of equal treatment that requires any inequalities in treatment to be justified. In Mill's words, "All persons are deemed to have a *right* to equality of treatment, except when some recognised social expediency requires the reverse." Mill characterized impartiality, which is a part of justice closely related to equality, as an obligation not to be swayed by irrelevant considerations in treating others. And this obligation, in turn, is part of "the more general obligation of giving to every one his right." Mill's argument, in short, is that justice includes treating people according to their rights unless utility dictates otherwise, and that this obligation of justice is implicit in the meaning of the utilitarian principle.

Mill further supported his argument by noting that equality is incapable of providing a complete account of justice and must be supplemented by another criterion of just action, such as utility. On the question of whether justice requires paying workers on the basis of effort or productivity, there are two conflicting considerations. From the point of view of what individuals deserve, wages ought to be determined by effort, since productivity is often due to accidents of birth over which an individual has little control. Productivity is the appropriate criterion, however, from the point of view of society, which is paying for the labor of individuals. The principle of treating workers equally is compatible with either criterion and so cannot be used to decide between them; only another principle of justice can settle the question.[18]

Mill thus held that equality is a part of the meaning of utility—all the while contending that it can be overridden by considerations of utility. "Each person maintains," Mill wrote, "that equality is a dictate of justice, except where he thinks that expediency requires inequality." This position is not contradictory, as some have argued.[19] But it does make equality superfluous. The meaning of Treat people equally except where utility requires unequal treatment can be fully expressed by the simple Treat people as utility requires.

Mill did not succeed, then, in showing that equality and desert are involved in "the very meaning of Utility," and his position, in the end, is little different from Bentham's. The arguments for the convergence of justice and utility have some plausibility, however, and so it may be possible for utilitarianism to provide a foundation for justice after all, despite the skepticism of many philosophers. One of these skeptics is John Rawls, who offers a highly influential egalitarian theory of justice as an alternative to utilitarianism.

THE EGALITARIAN THEORY OF JOHN RAWLS

In *A Theory of Justice* (1971), the contemporary American philosopher John Rawls argues for two principles that he thinks express our considered views about justice. Although his arguments and the principles themselves are rather complex, the basic outlines of his theory, which were first presented in a 1958 article, "Justice as Fairness," are relatively easy to understand.[20]

Rawls's aim is to give an account of justice that embodies a Kantian conception of equality. His objection to utilitarianism, as we have already seen, is that it does not give adequate attention to the way in which utility is distributed among different individuals. "Utilitarianism," Rawls charges, "does not take seriously the difference between persons."[21] As an alternative to the utilitarian ideal of a society with the highest level of welfare, Rawls proposes a society that recognizes its members as free and equal moral persons, a concept he attributes to Kant.[22] For Rawls, questions of justice arise primarily when free and equal persons attempt to advance their own interests and come into conflict with others pursuing their self-interests.

The key to a well-ordered society is the creation of institutions that enable individuals with conflicting ends to interact in mutually beneficial ways. The principles of justice assist in this effort by assigning rights and duties in the basic institutions of society and distributing the benefits and burdens of mutual cooperation.[23] The focus of Rawls's theory, then, is on *social* justice; that is, on a conception of justice that is suited to a well-ordered society. Once we have determined what constitutes a just society, however, we can then apply the results to questions of justice in the political, legal, and economic spheres.

Rawls's Method

Rawls begins by asking us to imagine a situation in which free and equal persons, concerned to advance their own interests, attempt to arrive at unanimous agreement on principles that will serve as the basis for constructing the major institutions of society. He does not assume that these individuals already have some conception of the principles of justice and that their task is to come to an agreement about what these principles are. Rather, he describes persons in this imaginary situation as self-interested agents, who evaluate principles according to whether they help or hinder them in achieving their ends. These people favor principles that enable them to get more of what they want and oppose principles that hinder them. Thus, Rawls's theory is based on the notion of pure procedural justice; that is, any principles on which everyone would agree are for that reason just—no matter what their content.[24] He assumes, moreover, that the people he is describing are rational in the sense that they conceive ends and act purposefully to achieve them and that they are willing to cooperate with others when this is possible and to abide by any agreements made.[25]

The approach taken by Rawls in *A Theory of Justice* is similar to the traditional contract theories of Hobbes, Locke, Rousseau, and Kant. The underlying assumption of most contract theories, including Rawls's, is that if individuals in some hypothetical precontract situation would unanimously accept certain terms for governing their relations, then those terms are just and all people have an obligation to abide by them. Crucial to any contract theory is a description of the precontract situation, which is called the state of nature by Hobbes, Locke, and others and the *original position* by Rawls. A distinctive feature of the original position, as described by Rawls, is the *veil of ignorance*.[26] The individuals who are asked to agree on the principles of justice must do so without knowing many facts about themselves and their situation. They do not know their social status or class, their natural assets or abilities, their intelligence or physical strength, their race or sex, or even their own conception of the good life. However, they have enough general knowledge about human psychology, social organization, political affairs, and the like to make informed choices about the principles of justice.

The purpose of the veil of ignorance is to ensure that agreement is possible. Rawls conceives of the process as a "bargaining game," in which people are free to offer proposals of their own and to reject those of others until unanimity is achieved.[27] If people in the original position know too much about themselves and how proposed principles would affect them personally, they might become deadlocked and prefer no agreement to one that puts them at a disadvantage. Behind the veil of ignorance, they are forced to be impartial and to view proposed principles from the perspective of all persons at once. Without any knowledge of their race or sex, for example, they are unlikely to advocate or support discriminatory principles, since they could be among the victims of discrimination. Certainly, no one could rationally choose a system of slavery without knowing who would be the masters and who, the slaves.

The Principles of Justice

Now, what principles would rational, self-interested persons freely agree to in a position of equality behind a veil of ignorance? Rawls thinks that there are two, which he states as follows:

1. Each person is to have an equal right to the most extensive total system of basic liberties compatible with a similar system of liberty for all.

2. Social and economic inequalities are to be arranged so that they are both:
   a. to the greatest benefit of the least advantaged, and
   b. attached to offices and positions open to all under conditions of fair equality of opportunity.[28]

The two principles are arranged by Rawls in order of priority. The task of ensuring that everyone has basic rights (the first principle) ought to be completed before any inequalities based on the second principle are permitted.[29] Further, liberty ought not to be traded for welfare; that is, no one following these principles would give up liberties for the sake of an increase in welfare.

The Reasoning Behind the Two Principles

The reasoning behind the first principle is that an equal share of whatever goods are available is the most that any person could reasonably expect, given the requirement of unanimous agreement.[30] No one would voluntarily accept less than an equal share if it were possible to share equally, since to do so would make that person comparatively worse off. Also, no one would be able to get more than an equal share by pressing for some special advantage, since someone else would have to agree to receive less than an equal share; and that, we have already seen, no one would voluntarily do. Like the person who cuts the cake knowing that he will get the last piece, persons in the original position would opt for equal shares.

The second principle recognizes, however, that there are conditions under which rational, self-interested persons would make an exception to the first principle and accept less than an equal share of some primary goods. One such condition is that everyone would be better off with the inequality than without it.[31] If it is possible to increase the total amount of income, for example, but not possible to distribute it equally, then the resulting distribution is still just, according to Rawls, as long as the extra income is distributed in such a way that everyone benefits from the inequality.

To illustrate, consider the following distribution schemes:

I		II		III		IV	
A	10	A	14	A	16	A	14
B	10	B	8	B	9	B	11
C	10	C	8	C	7	C	11
	30		30		32		36

We have already seen that from the utilitarian point of view, I and II are morally indistinguishable; and III is superior to both I and II, despite the inequality, because of the increase in the total amount of utility. For Rawls, however, people in the original position would prefer I over II, since two people, B and C, are worse off in II. For the same reason, they would reject III, despite the greater amount of utility, since B and C are still worse off than they are in I. However, IV would be unanimously favored by people in the original position over I, because everyone is better off.

The Difference Principle and Equal Opportunity

In principle 2(a), commonly known as the *difference principle*, Rawls states another condition under which persons in the original position would be willing to accept inequalities. The condition is not that everyone be better off but that the *least-advantaged person* be better off.[32] What Rawls has in mind here is that in every distribution there is a worst-off person—although this is not necessarily the same person in each possible scheme. For example:

IV	V	VI	VII
A 14	A 14	A 12	A 10
B 11	B 12	B 10	B 12
C 11	C 10	C 14	C 14
36	36	36	36

The least-advantaged person in V, VI, and VII is C, B, and A, respectively. In V, VI, and VII, at least one person is better off than in IV. Still, IV is preferable, according to Rawls, since the worst-off persons, namely B and C, are better off than the worst-off person in each of V, VI, and VII. (A person in the original position would also choose IV over I, II, or III for the reason that the worst-off person in IV is still better off than the worst-off person in I, II and III.)

The difference principle accounts for our intuitive judgment that it would be wrong to enslave a portion of society even if the result were a vast increase in the total amount of utility. At the same time, it bars even the smallest sacrifice on the part of the least-advantaged person, no matter how great the increase in welfare to the rest of society. The difference principle is also compatible with a redistribution that considerably worsens the condition of people not too far above the least-advantaged person, as long as it improves the condition of the person at the bottom, even if only slightly. Thus, although protecting the least advantaged from a worsening of their position, Rawls's theory provides no corresponding protection to the more advantaged members of society.

Principle 2(b), the principle of equal opportunity, is similar to the view that careers should be open to all on the basis of talent. Whether a person gets a certain job, for example, ought to be determined by competence in that line of work and not by skin color, family connections, or any other irrelevant characteristic. From the moral point of view, these characteristics are no more relevant to the distribution of income and wealth than a person's sex or race.[33] In a just society, therefore, every effort should be made to eliminate differences that result from the accidents of birth and social conditions, in order to give people roughly equal prospects to fill positions in society. Thus, the principle of equal opportunity would lead to a heavy inheritance tax, child-care support, comprehensive free education, training programs for the unskilled, and effective measures to prevent discrimination. Natural differences that cannot be eliminated ought to be regarded, Rawls says, as "a common asset," to be used for the benefit of everyone.[34]

The Maximin Rule

Rawls's argument for the difference principle is that under conditions of uncertainty, a rational person would "play it safe" and choose the alternative in which the worst possible outcome is still better than the worst possible outcome of any other alternative. His argument thus employs a rule of rational choice drawn from game theory known as "maximin," which holds that it is rational to *maxi*mize the *mini*mum outcome in choosing between different alternatives.[35] This is a rational rule to follow when, as Rawls says, your place will be determined by your worst enemy.

Whether Rawls's theory is superior to utilitarianism depends in large part on his success in defending maximin as a rule of rational choice.[36] Persons who have to choose principles behind a veil of ignorance might well "play it safe" and give exclusive priority to improving the condition of a representative "least-advantaged" person out of fear that they might be that person. But why is it not also rational for them to opt for a principle of maximizing average utility, especially if they have a propensity for risk?[37] By choosing the principle of maximum average utility, the chances of being better off are greater than under Rawls's principles. Further, they just might be one of the best-off people in the society that results.

Conclusion

Ultimately, the justification for Rawls's theory of justice is its congruence with our most deeply held beliefs about justice. Some of the consequences of the two principles fit better than those of utilitarianism, others do not fit as well. Although Rawls's list of basic liberties is relatively uncontroversial, he provides no priority among them when not all basic liberties can be realized or when they come into conflict with one another. There are other liberties, moreover, that might be added to the list, and Rawls provides no justification for excluding them. In addition, the priority of liberties over other primary goods is criticized for reflecting the bias of a well-to-do society whose material needs are already satisfied.[38] People in a struggling third world country might prefer to sacrifice some liberties in order to improve their standard of living.

UTILITY AND THE MARKET SYSTEM

In a capitalist economy, such as we have in the United States, major decisions about what goods and services to produce, how to manufacture and sell them, and so on, are made primarily through the impersonal forces of supply and demand in the marketplace. The principal aim of business firms in this system is to maximize the return on investment, or to make a profit. Although the market system operates largely without any explicit consideration of what is right or just, it does not follow that the system itself lacks an ethical justification. Indeed, we value our capitalist economy and hold it to be superior to other forms of economic organization, not only because of its ability to provide an abundance of goods and services at low prices but also because *we believe it to be morally justified.*

The market system is characterized by three main features: (1) *private ownership* of resources and the goods and services produced in an economy; (2) *voluntary exchange*, in which individuals are free to enter into mutually advantageous trades; and (3) the *profit motive*, whereby people engage in trading solely to advance their own well-being. In the market system described by Adam Smith and other classical economic theorists, individuals trade with each other, giving up things they own in exchange for other things they need or want. The motive of these economic actors is to improve their lives. This simple picture of the market is considerably complicated by neoclassical economics, in which the firm is the major unit of analysis. Business organizations of various kinds mobilize the productive resources of society, including labor, and transform them into goods and services to be sold in a mass market. Corporations are owned by tens of thousands or millions of shareholders. Still, all three features are present in the description of the market system offered by neoclassical economists.

The arguments justifying the market system can be conveniently reduced to two: a utilitarian argument that a market system produces the highest possible level of welfare for society and a rights-based argument that a market system best protects our liberty, especially with respect to private property.[39] The first of these is derived from Adam Smith and his notion of an invisible hand that leads self-seeking individuals to promote a collective good. The second argument originated with John Locke's defense of property as a fundamental right, which today is generally advanced by conservative economists and libertarians. The utilitarian argument is examined in this section, and the rights-based argument is considered in the one following.

Adam Smith's "Invisible Hand"

Adam Smith (1723–1790) is generally regarded as the founder of modern economics, and his major work, *An Inquiry into the Nature and Causes of the Wealth of Nations,* published in 1776, is a landmark in the history of Western thought. One of Smith's key insights is the importance of trading in an economy. A central problem for any economic system is how to enlist the aid of others in satisfying our basic needs. Trading solves this problem by appealing to other people in terms of their own advantage. According to Smith:

> . . . [M]an has almost constant occasion for the help of his brethren, and it is in vain for him to expect it from their benevolence only. He will be more likely to prevail if he can interest their self-love in his favour, and shew them that it is for their own advantage to do for him what he requires of them. Whoever offers to another a bargain of any kind, proposes to do this. Give me that which I want, and you shall have this which you want, is the meaning of every such offer; and it is in this manner that we obtain from one another the far greater part of those good offices which we stand in need of. It is not from the benevolence of the butcher, the brewer, or the baker, that we expect our dinner, but from their regard to their own interest. We address ourselves, not to their humanity but to their self-love, and never talk to them of our own necessities but of their advantages.

If two people want the same thing, conflict is inevitable; but if they want different things, and each person has what the other wants, then a trade is to the advantage of both. Trading is an instance, therefore, of mutually advantageous cooperation. And whenever a trade takes place voluntarily, we can be sure that both parties believe themselves to be better off (or, at least, not worse off), since, by assumption, no one willingly consents to being worse off.

In an economy built on free trade, the same beneficial effects occur. Laborers, in search of the highest possible wages, put their efforts and skill to the most productive use. Buyers seeking to purchase needed goods and services at the lowest possible price force sellers to compete with each other by making the most efficient use of the available resources and keeping prices at the lowest possible level. The resulting benefit to society as a whole is due not to any concern with the well-being of others but solely to the pursuit of self-interest. By seeking only personal gain, each individual is, according to a famous passage in *The Wealth of Nations,* "led by an invisible hand to promote an end which was no part of his intention." He continued, "Nor is it always the worse for the society that it was no part of it. By pursuing his own interest he frequently promotes that of the society more effectually than when he really intends to promote it."

The invisible hand argument was developed further by the successors of Adam Smith. Using refined mathematical techniques, economic theorists are able to demonstrate that in a free market, individuals will continue to trade up to a point of equilibrium where no further mutually advantageous trades are possible. Thus, a system of free trades results in maximum efficiency. The details of this argument can be found in virtually any introductory economics textbook.[40]

Problems with the "Invisible Hand" Argument

There are many problems with the utilitarian argument in both the invisible-hand version offered by Adam Smith and the more technical formulation of modern economic theory. First, the argument, strictly speaking, does not prove that free markets maximize *utility;* only that they are *efficient,* which is to say that they produce the greatest amount of output for the least amount of input. It stands to reason that a more productive economy has a higher level of utility, since more goods and services are available. But the connection is not assured unless the economy produces the goods and services that people want and manufactures and distributes them in ways that meet these needs.

Second, the argument that free markets are efficient presupposes *perfect competition.* This condition is satisfied when there are many buyers and sellers who are free to enter or leave the market at will and a large supply of relatively homogeneous products that buyers will readily substitute one for another. In addition, each buyer and seller must have complete knowledge of the goods and services available, including prices. In a market with these features, no firm is able to charge more than its competitors, since customers will purchase the competitors' products instead. Also, in the long run, the profit in one industry can be no higher than that in any other, since newcomers will enter the field and offer products at lower prices until the rate of profit is reduced to a common level.

Competition in actual markets is always imperfect to some degree. One reason is the existence of monopolies and oligopolies, in which one or a few firms dominate a market and exert an undue influence on prices. Competition is also reduced when there are barriers to market entry, when products are strongly differentiated, when some firms have information that others lack (about new manufacturing processes, for example), and when consumers lack important information. Competition is also reduced by *transaction costs;* that is, the expense required for buyers and sellers to find each other and come to an agreement. Great expense is involved, for example, merely in making and enforcing contracts, so that manufacturers with superior resources have a decided advantage in dealing with consumers about such matters as sales agreements and warranties.

Third, the argument that free markets are efficient makes certain assumptions about human behavior. It assumes, in particular, that the individuals who engage in economic activity are fully rational and act to maximize their own utility.[41] This construct, commonly called *economic man,* is faulty for at least two reasons. One is that people lack the ability to make all the calculations required to act effectively in their own interests. Consequently, they are unable to act as rational utility maximizers even when they are motivated to do so. The other reason is that human motivation is much more complex than the simple view of economic theory. People often give money to the poor or return a lost wallet, for example, with no expectation of gain. Altruism and moral commitment play a prominent role in our economic life, along with self-interest, and yet economic theory gives them scant regard.[42]

Also, firms do not always act in the ways predicted by economic theory. Because of limitations on the ability of human beings to acquire and process the amount of information needed for corporate decision making, managers have what is described as *bounded rationality.* To compensate for these limitations, business organizations develop rules and procedures for decision making that substitute for the direct pursuit of profit. Also, firms do not necessarily seek optimal outcomes, as economists assume, but, in the view of some organizational theorists, they settle for merely adequate solutions to pressing problems through a process known as *satisficing.* The immediate aim of firms, according to these theorists, is to achieve an *internal* efficiency; which is to say, the well-being of the firm, rather than *external* efficiency in the marketplace.[43]

Fourth, the invisible hand argument disregards the possibility of spillover effects or *externalities.* It assumes that all costs of production are reflected in the prices of goods and services and are not passed on to others. An externality is present when the manufacturer of a product is permitted to pollute a stream, for example, thereby imposing a cost on businesses downstream and depriving people of the opportunity to fish and swim in the stream. Other examples of externalities in present-day markets include inefficient use of natural resources (automobile drivers do not pay the full cost of the gasoline they use), occupational injuries, and accidents from defective products.

The task of dealing with externalities falls mainly to governments, which have many means at their disposal.[44] Polluters can be forced to internalize the costs of production, for example, by regulations that prohibit certain polluting activities (the use of soft coal, for example), set standards for pollution emissions, create tax incentives for installing pollution control devices or switching to less polluting technologies, and so on. Some free market theorists have proposed solutions to the problem of externalities that make use of market mechanisms. Allowing firms that exceed pollution standards to "sell" the rights to pollute to those whose emissions violate the standards is one example.

A fifth and final objection to the "invisible hand" argument concerns the problem of *collective choice.*[45] In a market system, choices that must be made for a whole society—a transportation policy, for example—are made by aggregating a large number of individual choices. Instead of leaving to a central planner a decision about whether to build more roads or more airports, we allow individuals to decide for themselves whether to drive a car or to take an airplane to their destination, and through a multitude of such individual decisions, we arrive at a collective choice. The underlying assumption is that if each individual makes rational choices—that is, choices that maximize his or her own welfare—then the collective choice that results will also be rational and maximize the welfare of society as a whole.

The Problem of Public Goods

The validity of the assumption about collective choice is open to question, most notably, in the case of *public goods.* A market economy has a well-known bias in favor of private over public consumption; that is, the production of goods that can be owned and used by one person as opposed to goods that can be enjoyed by all.[46] Automobiles are an example of a private good. Roads, by contrast, are a public good in that their use by one person does not exclude their use by others. As a result of this bias in favor of private consumption, people spend large sums on their own cars but little to build and maintain a system of roads. Public parks, a free education system, public health programs, and police and fire protection are all examples of public goods that are relatively underfunded in an otherwise affluent society.[47]

The reason for this bias is simple: There is no profit in public goods. Since they cannot be packaged and sold like toothpaste, there is no easy way to charge for them. And although some people are willing to pay for the pleasure of a public park, for example, others, who cannot be excluded from enjoying the park as well, will be *free riders;* that is, they will take advantage of the opportunity to use a public good without paying for it. Indeed, if we assume a world of rational economic agents who always act in their own interest, then everyone would be a free rider, given the chance. To act otherwise would be irrational.[48] Consequently, public goods are ignored by the market and left for governments to provide, usually in a grudging manner. As the economist Joan Robinson has observed:

> When you come to think of it, what can easily be charged for and what cannot, is just a technical accident. Some things, such as drainage and street lighting, are so obviously necessary that a modicum is provided in spite of the fact that payment has to be collected through the rates, but it is only the most glaring necessities that are met

in this way, together with some traditional amenities, like flower-beds in the parks, that are felt to be necessary to municipal self-respect.[49]

The Prisoner's Dilemma

The assumption that rational individual choices always result in rational collective choices is also brought into question by another problem illustrated by the well-known *prisoner's dilemma*.[50] Suppose that two guilty suspects have been apprehended by the police and placed in separate cells where they cannot communicate. Unfortunately, the police have only enough evidence to convict them both on a minor charge. If neither one confesses, therefore, they will receive a light sentence of one year each. The police offer each prisoner the opportunity of going free if he confesses and the other does not. The evidence provided by the suspect who confesses will then enable the police to convict the other suspect of a charge carrying a sentence of twenty years. If they both confess, however, they will each receive a sentence of five years. A matrix of the four possible outcomes is represented in Figure 4.1.

Obviously, the best possible outcome—one year for each prisoner—is obtained when both do not confess. Neither one can afford to seek this outcome by not confessing, however, since he faces a twenty-year sentence if the other does not act in the same way. Confessing, with the prospect of five years in prison or going scot-free, is clearly the preferable alternative. The rational choice for both prisoners, therefore, is to confess. But by doing so, they end up with the second-best outcome and are unable to reach the optimal solution to their problem.

The dilemma in this case would not be solved merely by allowing the prisoners to communicate, since the rational strategy for each prisoner in that case would be to agree not to confess and then turn around and break the agreement by confessing. The prisoner's dilemma is thus like the free-rider problem discussed earlier. If each prisoner has the opportunity to take advantage of the other's cooperation without paying a price, then it is rational to do so.[51] The true lesson of the prisoner's dilemma is that to reach the best possible outcome, each must be *assured* of the other's cooperation. The prisoner's dilemma is thus an assurance problem.[52] It shows that a rational collective choice can be made under certain circumstances only if each person in a system of cooperative behavior can be convinced that others will act in the same way.

| | | **Prisoner B** | |
		Confess	*Not confess*
Prisoner A	*Confess*	A: 5 years B: 5 years	A: 0 years B: 20 years
	Not confess	A: 20 years B: 0 years	A: 1 year B: 1 year

Figure 4-1   The Prisoner's Dilemma

The prisoner's dilemma is not an idle intellectual puzzle. Many real-life situations involve elements of this problem.[53] Consider the following example. The factories located around a lake are polluting the water at such a rate that within a few years none will be able to use the water and they will all be forced to shut down or relocate. The optimal solution would be for each factory to install a water-purification system or take other steps to reduce the amount of pollution. It would not be rational for any one factory or even a few to make the investment required, however, since the improvement in the quality of the water would be minimal and their investment wasted. Without assurance that all will bear the expense of limiting the amount of pollution, each factory will continue to pollute the lake and everyone will lose in the end. The most rational decision for each factory individually will thus result in a disastrous collective decision.

The usual solution to prisoner's dilemma cases—along with those involving externalities and public goods—is government action. By ordering all the factories around the lake to reduce the amount of pollution and backing up that order with force, a government could assure each factory owner that the others will bear their share of the burden. As a result, they could achieve an end that they all desire but could not seek without this assurance. Regulation of this kind is not necessarily incompatible with the operation of a free market. Thomas C. Schelling points out that voluntarism versus coercion is a false dichotomy because coercion can enable firms to do what they want to do but could not do voluntarily.[54] Firms are not always averse to internalizing costs and providing public goods, Schelling observes, as long as they are not penalized more than their competitors.[55] This condition can also be secured by government regulation.

Conclusion

We have seen that the utilitarian argument for the market system, expressed primarily in Adam Smith's famous invisible hand metaphor, has a number of significant problems. These do not show that free markets are unjustified but only that they have limitations, or shortcomings. The proper response, therefore, is not to scrap the market system but to find ways of correcting the problems and helping markets to achieve the goal of providing for our well-being. With an understanding of the problems of the utilitarian argument, we are in a better position to adopt measures that enable the market system to operate in a morally justified manner.

THE LIBERTARIAN JUSTIFICATION OF THE MARKET SYSTEM

Present-day libertarians are the intellectual successors to the laissez-faire tradition in economics. The distinctive feature of the libertarian philosophy is a commitment to individual liberty, conceived in the Lockean sense of a right to own property and to live as much as possible free from the interference of others. Two of the most prominent exponents of libertarianism are the Austrian-born economist Friedrich von

Hayek and the American economist Milton Friedman, both of whom are strong defenders of the classical free market as the economic system that most fully supports their conception of individual liberty. The fullest statement of libertarianism by a contemporary philosopher is Robert Nozick's *Anarchy, State, and Utopia,* published in 1974.[56] The discussion that follows is mainly concerned, therefore, with the theory of justice that Nozick calls the entitlement theory.

Nozick's Entitlement Theory

The principles of justice in Nozick's theory differ from the principle of utility and Rawls's principles in two major respects. First, they are *historical* principles as opposed to nonhistorical or *end-state* principles.[57] Historical principles, he explains, take into account the process by which a distribution came about, whereas end-state principles evaluate a distribution with regard to certain structural features at a given time. Second, the principles of justice in both utilitarianism and Rawls's theory are *patterned.*[58] A principle is patterned if it specifies some feature in a particular distribution and evaluates the distribution according to the presence or absence of that feature. Any principle of the form Distribute according to _____, such as Distribute according to IQ scores, is a patterned principle. Both Aristotle's principle and the principle of utility are patterned principles, as is the socialist formula From each according to his abilities, to each according to his needs. Rawls's two principles might appear at first glance to be nonpatterned because he allows a process of bargaining to determine the principles of justice, but once these are determined, no agreement is just unless the result is a distribution that conforms to the pattern in the principles.[59]

Nozick thinks that any acceptable principle of justice must be nonpatterned because any particular pattern of distribution can be achieved and maintained only by violating the right to liberty. Upholding the right to liberty, in turn, upsets any particular pattern of justice. He argues for this point by asking us to consider a case in which there is a perfectly just distribution, as judged by some desired pattern, and also perfect freedom. Now suppose that a famous athlete—Nozick suggests Wilt Chamberlain—will play only if he is paid an additional twenty-five cents for each ticket sold and that many people are so excited to see Wilt Chamberlain play that they will cheerfully pay the extra twenty-five cents for the privilege. Both Wilt Chamberlain and the fans are within their rights to act as they do, but at the end of the season, if one million people pay to see him play, then Wilt Chamberlain will have an additional income of $250,000, which is presumably more than he would be entitled to on a patterned principle of justice. By exercising their right to liberty, though, Wilt Chamberlain and the fans have upset the just distribution that formerly prevailed. In order to maintain the patterned distribution, it would be necessary to restrict the freedom of Wilt Chamberlain or the fans in some way, such as prohibiting the extra payment or taxing away the excess.

Nozick has observed:

> The general point illustrated by the Wilt Chamberlain example . . . is that no end-state principle or distributional patterned principle of justice can be continuously

realized without continuous interference with people's lives. Any favored pattern would be transformed into one unfavored by the principle, by people choosing to act in various ways; for example, by people exchanging goods and services with other people, or giving things to other people, things the transferrers are entitled to under the favored distributional pattern. To maintain a pattern one must either continually interfere to stop people from transferring resources as they wish to, or continually (or periodically) interfere to take from some person the resources that others for some reason chose to transfer to them.[60]

The entitlement theory can be stated very simply. A distribution is just, Nozick says, "if everyone is entitled to the holdings they possess."[61] Whether we are entitled to certain holdings is determined by tracing their history. Most of what we possess comes from others through transfers, such as purchases and gifts. Thus, we might own a piece of land because we bought it from someone, who in turn bought it from someone else, and so on. Proceeding backward in this fashion, we ultimately reach the original settler who did not acquire it through a transfer but by clearing the land and tilling it. As long as each transfer was just and the original acquisition was just, then our present holding is just. "Whatever arises from a just situation by just steps is itself just," Nozick writes.[62] In his theory, then, particular distributions are just not because they conform to some pattern (equality or social utility, for example) but solely because of antecedent events.

Just Transfer and Original Acquisition

Nozick's theory requires at least two principles: a principle of just transfer and a principle of just original acquisition. Since holdings can be unjustly appropriated by force or fraud, a third principle, a principle of rectification, is also necessary, in order to correct injustices by restoring holdings to the rightful owners. If we rightfully possess some holding—a piece of land, for example, either by transfer or original acquisition—then we are free to use or dispose of it as we wish. We have a right, in other words, to sell it to whomever we please at whatever price that person is willing to pay, or we can choose to give it away. As long as the exchange is purely voluntary, with no force or fraud, the resulting redistribution is just. Any attempt to prevent people from engaging in voluntary exchanges in order to secure a particular distribution is a violation of liberty, according to the entitlement theory.

A world consisting only of just acquisitions and just transfers would be just, according to Nozick, no matter what the pattern of distribution. Some people, through hard work, shrewd trades, or plain good luck, would most likely amass great wealth, while others, through indolence, misjudgment, or bad luck, would probably end up in poverty. However, the rich in such a world would have no obligation to aid the poor,[63] nor would it be just to coerce them into doing so. Each person's share would be determined largely through his or her choices and those of others. Nozick suggests that the entitlement theory can be expressed in the form of a patterned theory of justice as follows:

> From each according to what he chooses to do, to each according to what he makes for himself (perhaps with the contracted aid of others) and what others choose to

do for him and choose to give him of what they've been given previously (under this maxim) and haven't yet expended or transferred.[64]

Or more simply: *From each as they choose, to each as they are chosen.*

Justice and Free Markets

A market system with only the absolute minimum of government intervention would be just, in Nozick's theory, as long as the principles of just acquisition and just transfer are satisfied. The reason is that a system in which we have complete freedom to acquire property and engage in mutually advantageous trades (without violating the rights of another person, of course) is one in which our own rights are most fully protected. To critics who fear that unregulated markets would lead to great disparities between rich and poor and a lowering of the overall welfare of society, Nozick has a reply. The point of justice is not to promote human well-being or to achieve a state of equality; it is to protect our rights. Since a market system does this better than any other form of economic organization, it is just.

Difficulties with Nozick's Theory

The main difficulty with Nozick's theory is the lack of argument for the key assumption that liberty, conceived as the unhindered exercise of property rights, is a paramount value. First, there are rights, such as a right to a minimal level of welfare, that some consider to be at least as important as the rights of property owners. Yet, in Nozick's view, it would be unjust to provide for the well-being of the members of society if doing so involved forcing the well-to-do against their will to aid the poor. Taxation for this purpose, according to Nozick, is on a par with forced labor.[65] What is the justification, though, for allowing the poor to starve merely to protect the rich against being coerced in this way?

Second, Nozick seems to overlook the point that not all restrictions of liberty are due to interference by the state. By exercising their property rights, people sometimes effectively restrict the choices of others. Suppose that Wilt Chamberlain uses his wealth to buy the only factory in town and immediately cuts all wages. Libertarians hold that it would be an unjustified violation of property rights for the state to tax an individual $500, say, to finance a social security system; but according to Nozick, the liberty of the workers in the factory is not restricted by Wilt Chamberlain's action even if they are deprived by the same amount. James P. Sterba asks:

> But how can requiring a person to pay $500 into a social security program, under threat of greater financial loss, infringe upon the person's liberty when requiring a person to take a job that pays $500 less, under threat of greater financial loss, does not infringe upon the person's liberty? Surely, it would seem that if one requirement restricts a person's liberty, the other will also.[66]

Third, justice in transfers and original acquisition depends on conditions that are scarcely ever satisfied in the actual world. Transfers are just, according to Nozick, if each person is entitled to the holdings he or she possesses. The present distribution of holdings is heavily determined, however, by forced takings—fraud, theft, wars, and the like. And the original acquisition of much of the earth's land and resources scarcely left "enough, and as good" for others. Correcting such injustices is a task for the principle of rectification, which is applied by attempting to predict what would have happened had the injustice not occurred and then enforcing the result. Although isolated injustices can be rectified in this manner,[67] what is the possibility of determining the course of events if American Indians had not been deprived of their land, slavery had never occurred, and so on?[68] An adequate theory of justice should be capable of leading us from an unjust world to one a little more just, a test that Nozick's theory fails.

Conclusion

In this chapter, we have examined four theories of justice; namely, those of Aristotle, Mill, Rawls, and Nozick. The purpose of these theories is primarily to provide a means for evaluating existing and proposed institutional arrangements. They are intended, in other words, to be applied not to relatively small-scale decisions, such as pay increases in an office, but rather to larger questions—about the way in which wages are determined in an economy, for example. We should not be concerned, therefore, if these four theories of justice have little immediate practical use. They come into play mainly when we seek to justify our social, political, and economic forms of organization.

On the question of the organization of our economic system, utilitarianism and libertarianism both support a system of free markets.[69] Insofar as the market system promotes utility *and* protects rights, it is doubly justified, so to speak. Some proponents of free markets employ both justifications. The two are not wholly compatible, however, and in practice we often face trade-offs between utility or welfare on the one hand and liberty or property rights on the other. When such situations occur, the holders of these two justifications are forced to choose between them. Typically, libertarians cast their lot with unregulated markets, whereas utilitarians favor limited regulation to correct what they see as market failures.

CASE 4.2   What's Fair?

Scenario: A crisis in the Middle East has severely restricted world oil supplies and dramatically raised the price of gasoline in the United States. The price at the pump is currently $5 per gallon and could rise to $8 or more. The rich have been relatively unaffected, but the poor are being forced to spend more on gasoline or to purchase less. An ethicist and an economist discuss the best way to handle the shortage in order to be fair to everyone concerned.

> *Ethicist:* Although a free market generally sets prices fairly, a sudden shortage presents an exception. The market solution for shortages is to allow

the price to rise to the equilibrium point where demand equals supply. When gasoline reaches this price, there will be no long lines at service stations, but that will be because only the rich will be able to afford to buy it. This method of distributing gasoline is effective because it does not require any administration, but it is *unfair* for the reason that it imposes an undue burden on the poor and exacerbates the unequal distribution of goods.

Economist: I agree that sudden shortages cause painful readjustments and that the rich will consume an increasingly disproportionate share of the available supply of any good, whether it be gasoline or caviar. But the problem is the unequal distribution of income and wealth, not the way in which the market distributes scarce resources. There are great disparities in the distribution of all goods, with the rich getting more of everything; but if these disparities are unfair, then the only way to correct them—and to make the world a fairer place—is to take money from the rich and give it to the poor. Blaming the market as a method of distribution is misguided. Besides, what other method would you propose?

Ethicist: Why, *rationing*, of course. During World War II, rationing was used with great success to ensure that the meager supplies of gasoline, sugar, meat, and a few other basics were distributed equally. Coupons were distributed to each family according to their size, and no one could purchase any rationed commodity without a coupon. This method is not only fair but very practical—because it avoids the long lines that often afflict socialist countries, where people "pay" for scarce goods with their time and patience.

Economist: I don't dispute that rationing can be very effective, but let's not confuse effectiveness with justice. You admit that a market distribution is more effective because a system of rationing requires some administration. So I assume that you believe that the outcome of a rationing system for scarce goods is more just than the outcome of a free market, and that this increase in justice offsets the administrative costs of using coupons. That is, we should accept some loss of practicality for the sake of greater justice.

Ethicist: That's true.

Economist: With regard to justice, let me ask you one more question. If rationing is used in this case, would it be more just to allow coupons to be bought and sold on a market, so that people who don't need all of the gasoline that they are allowed could trade unused coupons with people who want more? Or would justice require that the coupons could be used only by the persons to whom they are issued?

Ethicist: If coupons are a right to purchase a certain amount of gasoline that is granted to the holder, then people's liberty would be infringed if they were prevented from trading coupons. The poor, in particular, would welcome the opportunity to sell their coupons in order to satisfy more pressing needs and would be resentful if the opportunity were denied.

Besides, it would be very difficult to administer a system that prevented people from trading coupons—or the goods themselves, which amounts to the same thing. So fairness and practicality each requires that a free market be allowed in coupons—once they are issued equally to everyone, of course.

Economist: But in that case, the distribution produced by a rationing system will be no different from the distribution produced by a free market in gasoline, except for the added administrative costs of issuing and collecting coupons. If the price of gasoline would rise to $8 per gallon without rationing and we want to keep the price at $5 per gallon, then a coupon that entitles the holder to purchase one gallon of gasoline for $5 is itself worth $3. Giving every citizen twenty coupons per month is the equivalent of giving them $60 in cash, which they could spend on gasoline—or on bread and milk if they choose to trade their coupons. Since this $60 is money in people's pockets to spend as they wish, the price of gasoline, for all practical purposes, is $8 per gallon. The rich who want more than twenty gallons of gasoline per month will buy coupons from the poor and consume exactly the same amount that they would in a free market. The only difference is that under a system of rationing each gallon of gasoline is purchased with $5 in real currency and $3 in the form of a coupon. And, of course, we have to add the cost of administering the system.

Ethicist: You have made me see that a system of rationing is like imposing a $3-per-gallon tax that is returned to the consumer in the form of a coupon. But at least that $3 does not go to the gasoline producer as a windfall profit. So rationing is still a fairer system after all.

Economist: If we consider increased profit to the producer to be unfair—and we can debate that question later—then we can tax it away by imposing a $3-per-gallon windfall profit tax on the producer and still leave the distribution of gasoline to a free market. If we do this, a question of distribution remains, namely how to distribute the revenue from this new tax. Distributing tax revenue, moreover, is a job for government, not the marketplace, and government can decide on grounds of fairness to help the poor. But such an outcome would promote fairness by altering the distribution of income and wealth, which, as I said before, is the only way to make the world a fairer place.

Ethicist: Well, at least we agree on the end to be achieved if not the means.

CASE 4.3   Executive Compensation

The news that Michael D. Eisner received $203 million in 1993 for his efforts on behalf of the Walt Disney Company was greeted with a predictable outcry about runaway executive pay. How could anyone be worth that much in any just economic system? Eisner's earnings reached that astronomical figure by a one-time exercise of accumulated stock options. In 1994, the highest paid executive received a paltry $25.9 million in salary, bonus, and long-term compensation, and Eisner ranked only 16th on that year's list of top-paid chief executives with a total package of $10.6 million.[70] The dollar value of executive compensation is difficult to gauge because of uncertainty in the pricing of stock options, and the ranking of executives varies from year to year as some executives exercise stock options and others defer them. Still, the average total compensation of CEOs in 1994 at 371 companies surveyed by *Business Week* was more than $2.8 million, and 25 executives each received more than $10 million.

Aside from the dollar amount of executive compensation, critics note that CEOs tend to receive their fat paychecks regardless of their company's performance. Louis V. Gerstner was rewarded with a 34 percent increase in his 1994 salary and bonus for raising the stock of IBM over 30 percent; but the CEO of AT&T, Robert E. Allen, received an even higher increase of 38 percent despite a drop of 4.3 percent in the price of Ma Bell's stock.[71] And some executives are compensated handsomely even as they order massive layoffs that create misery for many hardworking employees. One study found that compensation for the CEO rose in 1993 at 27 of the 30 companies with the largest staff reductions over a three-year period.[72] In 1993, Sears Roebuck increased by 198 percent the compensation of a CEO who presided over the elimination of 50,000 jobs.

By any measure, the CEOs of U.S. firms are well compensated. But are they overcompensated, as many contend? If Michael Eisner's $203 million is too much, how much is just right? How should executive pay be determined? One answer is that we should use the same standards for CEOs that are generally applied to lower-level managers and other employees; namely, the degree of responsibility involved, the knowledge, skill, and effort required, and success in meeting certain goals. A CEO's compensation should be higher for those who run larger companies and companies that face greater problems or risks. The reward for turning around a troubled giant like IBM should be greater than that for attending to everyday business at a heavily regulated utility, for example. Most of all, an executive should be rewarded for doing well, which may be reflected not only in the price of the stock but by desired changes, such as improving customer relations or a company's environmental record. The demands on a CEO are heavy and the talents needed are in short supply, so high pay for the very best executives is to be expected.

That CEOs are paid more than most workers is no surprise. But how much more should they be paid? And what should their pay be compared with? Derek Bok, the former president of Harvard University, notes that he headed a very large and complex organization for twenty years with relatively modest compensation. Bok further observes that average CEO pay is two to three times the average in industrial nations, and some American CEOs are paid ten to twelve times their counterparts in Japan and Europe. "Are American CEOs ten or twelve, or even two or three times better?" he asks.[73] The average CEO in Japan and Europe earns ten to twelve times as much as the average manufacturing employee; in the United States the comparable figure is twenty-five,[74] and among Fortune 500 companies, CEOs earn more than one hundred times the salary of the average employee.

Graef Crystal, a persistent critic of executive compensation, is less concerned about the amount of CEO pay than the lack of linkage to the usual standards.[75] Although sports and entertainment figures negotiate multimillion-dollar contracts, Crystal finds that at least 70 percent of those amounts can be explained by purely economic considerations. Thus, a star pitcher who negotiates a $10 million contract can usually be expected to produce at least $7 million in extra revenue for the team owner. Crystal's studies have never been able to account for more than 40 percent of CEO pay by such factors as company size, performance, business risk, government regulation, industry type, and location. Crystal concludes that the pay of top executives is highly arbitrary, with some CEOs receiving two to three times what his model indicates as "rational." The problem, according to Crystal, is that boards of directors, who hire the CEO, are not very good negotiators. Unlike team owners and movie producers, board members have little idea of what the talent they are buying is really worth. After a bad season, a highly paid sports star may receive much less the next year; this seldom happens with CEOs.

Another answer to the question of how executive pay should be determined looks to the benefit that attracting and motivating good talent can bring to the American economy. If high compensation succeeds in placing the most competent people in positions of business leadership, then everyone benefits. According to this view, companies bid against each other for the best among the available pool of managerial talent and that it may be worth $10 million to a company to hire the most capable person whose success may result in profits many times that amount. Compensation packages are also designed with a mixture of base pay, bonuses, and stock options in order to align the CEO's interests with those of the corporation. Some critics scoff at the idea that the people of CEO caliber have to be coaxed with multimillion dollar salaries to take the reins of a company and would not give the job their full attention without huge bonuses.

These objections are beside the point, however, if the need for high pay is not to attract a CEO from the pool of existing candidates but to attract the best to the field of management. If some other occupations, such as law and finance, attract the cream of the crop by their high pay, then American business and the whole of society will be deprived of their potential contribution. Michael C. Jensen and Kevin J. Murphy suggest that critics of executive pay should at least ask the right question: "Are current levels of CEO compensation high enough to attract the best and brightest individuals to careers in corporate management?" The answer, they say, is probably not.[76] If CEOs were paid for performance—which most people believe to be fair—then some would receive far more compensation than they currently do, and some would receive far less or be booted out the door. Why don't boards act in this way? One reason, according to Jensen and Murphy, is the public perception that executives are already overpaid. When boards are afraid to pay high performers what they are really worth because of popular pressure, then they also are reluctant to punish poor performers. The result is a level of compensation that fails to attract the best people to management and keeps mediocre people in place. If Jensen and Murphy are right, then widespread concern about the justice of executive compensation is itself part of the problem.

NOTES

1. Material for this case is taken from KATHERINE ELLISON, "The Two Valleys of the Green Giant," *West Magazine, San Jose Mercury News*, 16 June 1991, 6–11.

2. ROBERT B. REICH, "Who Is Them?" *Harvard Business Review*, March–April 1991, 77–78.

3. Aristotle makes the distinction between compensatory and retributive justice in terms of voluntary and involuntary relations. A contract is a voluntary arrangement between two people, whereas the victim of an assault enters into the relation involuntarily. Many commentators have found this a rather awkward way of making the distinction.

4. The distinction between comparative and noncomparative justice is discussed in JOEL FEINBERG, "Comparative Justice," *The Philosophical Review*, 83 (1974), 297–338. Reprinted in JOEL FEINBERG, *Rights, Justice, and the Bounds of Liberty* (Princeton: Princeton University Press, 1980), 265–306. See also JOEL FEINBERG, *Social Philosophy* (Englewood Cliffs, NJ: Prentice Hall, 1973), 98–99.

5. The distinction is discussed in BRIAN BARRY, *Political Argument* (London: Routledge & Kegan Paul, 1965), 97–100. See also FEINBERG, *Social Philosophy*, 117–19.

6. JOHN RAWLS, *A Theory of Justice* (Cambridge: Harvard University Press, 1971), 85–86.

7. RAWLS, *A Theory of Justice*, 86.

8. For a discussion of the connection, see GREGORY VLASTOS, "Justice and Equality," in RICHARD B. BRANDT, ed., *Social Justice* (Englewood Cliffs, NJ: Prentice Hall, 1962), 31–72.

9. For a discussion of egalitarianism, see S. I. BENN and R. S. PETERS, *Social Principles and the Democratic State* (London: Allen & Unwin, 1959), chap. 5. Also, H. J. McCLOSKEY, "Egalitarianism, Equality, and Justice," *Australasian Journal of Philosophy*, 44 (1966), 50–69.

10. For a discussion of Aristotle's principle, see HANS KELSEN, "Aristotle's Doctrine of Justice," in KELSEN, *What is Justice* (Berkeley and Los Angeles: University of California Press, 1957), 117–36; and RENFORD BAMBROUGH, "Aristotle on Justice," in BAMBROUGH, ed., *New Essays on Plato and Aristotle* (London: Routledge & Kegan Paul, 1965), 159–74.

11. Taken from WILLIAM K. FRANKENA, "Some Beliefs about Justice," in JOHN BRICKE, ed., *Freedom and Morality* (Lawrence: University of Kansas, 1976), 56.

12. For a discussion of this list, see NICHOLAS RESCHER, *Distributive Justice* (Indianapolis: Bobbs-Merrill, 1966), chap. 4.

13. For a discussion of utilitarian responses, see D. C. EMMONS, "Justice Reassessed," *American Philosophical Quarterly*, 4 (1967), 144–51.

14. For an account of Bentham's theory of justice, see HUGO A. BEDAU, "Justice and Classical Utilitarianism," in CARL J. FRIEDRICH and JOHN W. CHAPMAN, eds., *Justice* (New York: Atherton Press, 1963), 284–305.

15. Contemporary philosophers who take this position are JAN NARVESON, *Morality and Utility* (Baltimore: Johns Hopkins University Press, 1967), 210–19; ROLF E. SARTORIUS, *Individual Conduct and Social Norms* (Encino, CA: Dickinson, 1975), 130–33; J.J.C. SMART, "Distributive Justice and Utilitarianism," in JOHN ARTHUR and WILLIAM H. SHAW, eds., *Justice and Economic Distribution* (Englewood Cliffs, NJ: Prentice Hall, 1978), 103–15; and R. M. HARE, "Justice and Equality," in ARTHUR and SHAW, *Justice and Economic Distribution*, 116–31. RICHARD B. BRANDT argues for a convergence of justice with his version of utilitarianism as a pluralistic welfare-maximizing moral system in *A Theory of the Good and the Right* (Oxford: Oxford University Press, 1979), chap. 16.

16. A good statement of this argument is given in RICHARD B. BRANDT, *Ethical Theory* (Englewood Cliffs, NJ: Prentice Hall, 1959), 415–19. A more extended discussion is BRANDT, *A Theory of the Good and the Right*, 311–16.

17. On this point, see BRANDT, *Ethical Theory*, 416–17; and C. DYKE, *The Philosophy of Economics* (Englewood Cliffs, NJ: Prentice Hall, 1981), 38–39.

18. Henry Sidgwick discusses the bearing of the principle of equality on wages and reaches a similar conclusion, that the principle must be supplemented by other considerations. See HENRY SIDGWICK, *The Methods of Ethics*, 7th ed. (Chicago: University of Chicago Press, 1907), 285–90.

19. See BEDAU, "Justice and Classical Utilitarianism," 303.

20. A good exposition is ROBERT PAUL WOLFF, *Understanding Rawls: A Reconstruction and Critique of A Theory of Justice* (Princeton: Princeton University Press, 1977). For a critical study, see BRIAN BARRY, *The Liberal Theory of Justice* (Oxford: Oxford University Press, 1973). Among the many collections of arti-

cles are NORMAN DANIELS, ed., *Reading Rawls: Critical Studies of A Theory of Justice* (New York: Basic Books, 1975); and H. GENE BLOCKER and ELIZABETH H. SMITH, eds., *John Rawls's Theory of Social Justice* (Athens: Ohio University Press, 1980).

21. RAWLS, *A Theory of Justice*, 27.

22. See JOHN RAWLS, "A Kantian Conception of Equality," *Cambridge Review*, February 1975, 94.

23. RAWLS, *A Theory of Justice*, 4.

24. RAWLS, *A Theory of Justice*, 136.

25. RAWLS, *A Theory of Justice*, 142–45.

26. RAWLS, *A Theory of Justice*, 136–42.

27. The term "bargaining game" is derived from game theory, which Rawls employs in *A Theory of Justice*. The classic work on game theory is R. D. LUCE and HOWARD RAIFFA, *Games and Decisions* (New York: Wiley, 1957).

28. RAWLS, *A Theory of Justice*, 302.

29. RAWLS, *A Theory of Justice*, 243–51, 541–48.

30. The reasoning behind both principles is discussed in RAWLS, *A Theory of Justice*, 150–61.

31. Rawls's formulation of the second principle in "Justice as Fairness" is, "Inequalities are arbitrary unless it is reasonable to expect that they will work out for everyone's advantage." JOHN RAWLS, "Justice as Fairness," *The Philosophical Review*, 67 (1958), 165. And his initial statement in *A Theory of Justice* is that "social and economic inequalities are to be arranged so that they are both (a) reasonably expected to be to everyone's advantage, and (b) attached to positions and offices open to all." RAWLS, *A Theory of Justice*, 60.

32. The reasons for the shift in the formulation of the difference principle involve rather technical problems concerning the comparison of alternatives. For an explanation, see WOLFF, *Understanding Rawls*, 42–47, 63–65.

33. RAWLS, *A Theory of Justice*, 104.

34. RAWLS, *A Theory of Justice*, 102.

35. RAWLS, *A Theory of Justice*, 152–56. For a full explanation, see LUCE and RAIFFA, *Games and Decisions*, chap. 13.

36. For further objections to the justification of maximin in the original position, see THOMAS NAGEL, "Rawls on Justice," *The Philosophical Review*, 82 (1973), 229–32.

37. Some critics of Rawls argue that a principle of maximum average utility is the only possible choice in the original position. See JOHN C. HARSANYI, "Can the Maximin Principle Serve as a Basis for Morality? A Critique of John Rawls' Theory," *American Political Science Review*, 69 (1975), 594–606. Also, HARSANYI, "Morality and the Theory of Rational Behavior," in AMARTYA SEN and BERNARD WILLIAMS, eds., *Utilitarianism and Beyond* (Cambridge: Cambridge University Press, 39–62).

38. On this problem, see BARRY, *The Liberal Theory of Justice*, 59–82; and H.L.A. HART, "Rawls on Liberty and Its Priority," *University of Chicago Law Review*, 40 (1973), 534–55.

39. A comprehensive survey of the economic and ethical arguments for and against the market system is ALLEN BUCHANAN, *Ethics, Efficiency, and the Market* (Totowa, NJ: Rowman and Littlefield, 1988). See also the collection of essays in GERALD DWORKIN, GORDON BERMANT, and PETER G. BROWN, eds., *Markets and Morals* (Washington, DC: Hemisphere, 1977); and VIRGINIA HELD, ed., *Property, Profits, and Economic Justice* (Belmont, CA: Wadsworth, 1980).

40. A good explanation is contained in DYKE, *Philosophy of Economics*. A more detailed account is presented in A. FELDMAN, *Welfare Economics and Social Choice Theory* (Dordrecht: Martinus Nijhoff, 1980).

41. For a brief discussion of this assumption, see AMARTYA SEN, *On Ethics and Economics* (Oxford: Basil Blackwell, 1987), 10–28.

42. Some economists and behavioral scientists recognize the role of altruism and moral commitment and attempt to incorporate them into economic theory. See, for example, E. S. PHELPS, ed., *Altruism, Morality, and Economic Theory* (New York: Russell Sage Foundation, 1975); HARVEY LEIBENSTEIN, *Beyond Economic Man* (Cambridge: Harvard University Press, 1976); DAVID COLLARD, *Altruism and Economy: A Study in Non-Selfish Economics* (New York: Oxford University Press, 1978); HOWARD MARGOLIS, *Selfishness, Altruism, and Rationality: A Theory of Social Choice* (Cambridge: Cambridge University Press, 1982); AMITAI ETZIONI, *The Moral Dimension: Towards a New Economics* (New York: Free Press, 1988);

and ROBERT H. FRANK, *Passions Within Reason: The Strategic Role of the Emotions* (New York: W. W. Norton, 1988).

43. On the concepts of bounded rationality and satisficing, see HERBERT A. SIMON, *Administrative Behavior: A Study of Decision Making Processes in Administrative Organization*, 3rd ed. (New York: Free Press, 1976), originally published in 1947; JAMES G. MARCH and HERBERT A. SIMON, *Organizations* (New York: Wiley, 1958); and RICHARD M. CYERT and JAMES G. MARCH, *A Behavioral Theory of the Firm* (Englewood Cliffs, NJ: Prentice Hall, 1963).

44. See BUCHANAN, *Ethics, Efficiency, and the Market*, 24–25.

45. For an insightful study of this problem, see AMARTYA SEN, *Collective Choice and Social Welfare* (San Francisco: Holden Day, 1970). Also, KENNETH ARROW, *Social Choice and Individual Values*, 2nd ed. (New York: Wiley, 1963).

46. JOAN ROBINSON, *Economic Philosophy* (London: C. A. Watts, 1962), 132.

47. The disparity between private and public consumption in the United States is the major theme in JOHN KENNETH GALBRAITH, *The Affluent Society* (Boston: Houghton Mifflin, 1958).

48. If everyone attempts to be a free rider, however, then certain kinds of collective choices are impossible unless people are coerced in some way. See MANCUR OLSON, *The Logic of Collective Action* (Cambridge: Harvard University Press, 1965), 44.

49. ROBINSON, *Economic Philosophy*, 132–33.

50. For discussion of the prisoner's dilemma see any book on game theory, such as LUCE and RAIFFA, *Games and Decisions*.

51. This point is made by RUSSELL HARDIN, "Collective Action as an Agreeable n-Person Prisoners' Dilemma," *Behavioral Science*, 16 (1971), 472–79.

52. C. FORD RUNGE, "Institutions and the Free Rider: The Assurance Problem in Collective Action," *Journal of Politics*, 46 (1984), 154–81. Cited in IAN MAITLAND, "The Limits of Business Self-Regulation," *California Management Review*, 27 (Spring 1985), 134.

53. For the empirical significance of the prisoner's dilemma, see ANATOL RAPOPORT and ALBERT M. CHAMMAH, *The Prisoner's Dilemma* (Ann Arbor: University of Michigan Press, 1965); and ROBERT AXELROD, *The Evolution of Cooperation* (New York: Basic Books, 1984).

54. THOMAS C. SCHELLING, "Command and Control," in JAMES W. MCKIE, ed., *Social Responsibility and the Business Predicament* (Washington, DC: The Brookings Institution, 1974), 103–5.

55. SCHELLING, "Command and Control," 103.

56. ROBERT NOZICK, *Anarchy, State, and Utopia* (New York: Basic Books, 1974).

57. NOZICK, *Anarchy, State, and Utopia*, 153–55.

58. NOZICK, *Anarchy, State, and Utopia*, 155–60.

59. NOZICK, *Anarchy, State, and Utopia*, 207–10.

60. NOZICK, *Anarchy, State, and Utopia*, 163.

61. NOZICK, *Anarchy, State, and Utopia*, 151.

62. NOZICK, *Anarchy, State, and Utopia*, 151.

63. Individuals could voluntarily agree with others to contribute to the relief of poverty, in which case an obligation would exist. See NOZICK, *Anarchy, State, and Utopia*, 265–68.

64. NOZICK, *Anarchy, State, and Utopia*, 160.

65. NOZICK, *Anarchy, State, and Utopia*, 169.

66. JAMES P. STERBA, *The Demands of Justice* (Notre Dame: University of Notre Dame Press, 1980), 113.

67. For a discussion of some of the problems, see LAWRENCE DAVIS, "Comments on Nozick's Entitlement Theory," *The Journal of Philosophy*, 73 (1976), 839–42.

68. For one answer, see DAVID LYONS, "The New Indian Claims and Original Rights to Land," *Social Theory and Practice*, 4 (1977), 249–72.

69. Rawls's theory also justifies the market system, although he distinguishes between free markets as a method of allocation and distribution and capitalism as an economic system that includes private ownership. Markets, according to Rawls, can be a feature of either capitalism or socialism, and whether an economic system with free markets is just depends a great deal on other background institutions. See RAWLS, *A Theory of Justice*, 270–74.

70. These figures were taken from "CEO Pay: Ready for Takeoff," *Business Week*, 24 April 1995, 88–119.

71. "Deliver or Else: Pay-for-Performance Is Making an Impact on CEO Paychecks," *Business Week*, 27 March 1995, 36–38.

72. MOLLY BAKER, "I Feel Your Pain? When the CEO Orders Massive Layoffs, Should He Get a Pay Raise?" *Wall Street Journal*, 12 April 1995, A6.

73. "Former Harvard President Slams U.S. Exec Pay," *HR Focus*, December 1994, 11.

74. These figures are derived from data in AMANDA BENNETT, "Managers' Incomes Aren't Worlds Apart," *Wall Street Journal*, 12 October 1992, B1, B5.

75. GRAEF S. CRYSTAL, *In Search of Excess* (New York: W. W. Norton, 1991).

76. MICHAEL C. JENSEN and KEVIN J. MURPHY, "CEO Incentives—It's Not How Much You Pay, But How." *Harvard Business Review*, 68 (May–June 1990), 145.

5

Whistle-Blowing

CASE 5.1 Two Whistle-Blowers

Chuck Atchinson

At the age of forty, Charles (Chuck) Atchinson had achieved a measure of success.[1] His job as a quality control inspector for Brown & Root, a construction company building a nuclear power plant for the Texas Utilities Electric Company, paid more than $1,000 a week. This was enough to provide a comfortable house for his wife and thirteen-year-old daughter, along with new cars, vacation trips, and a bounty of other luxuries. Four years later, the family was six months behind on the rent on a trailer home on a gravel street in Azle, Texas, near Fort Worth. Chuck Atchinson had been fired by Brown & Root and was unable to find work. The house was repossessed, and most of the family's furniture and other possessions had been sold to cover living expenses and mounting legal bills.

   The source of Chuck Atchinson's misfortune was his inability to get his superiors at Brown & Root to observe safety regulations in the construction of the Comanche Peak nuclear power plant being built in Glen Rose, Texas, and to correct a number of potentially dangerous flaws. When his repeated complaints to the company got no response, he brought the situation to the attention of government regulators. Soon after that he was dismissed from his job. Brown & Root justified the dismissal on the grounds of poor performance as a safety inspector, and the company attempted to downplay the credibility of his charges. Around the time that he was testifying to government regulators, he received threatening anonymous telephone calls warning him to keep quiet, and he suspected that he was being followed and his telephone monitored.

Finding a new job was not easy. He worked for a while driving a wrecker, and out of desperation he even gathered cans along the highway for sale as scrap aluminum. After finally landing a job as an inspector at a plant in New Orleans, Chuck Atchinson was on the job for only a week before he was subpoenaed to give further testimony about the Comanche Peak plant. According to his own account, "When I got back, my boss called me in and fired me. He said I was a troublemaker." He was not even given the chance to assume a new job at a power plant in Clinton, Illinois. "Two days before I was to leave," he said, "they called and said they wouldn't take me, because I was a troublemaker. I tried other plants and I found that I was blacklisted."

Chuck Atchinson eventually found stable employment doing quality control work for the aerospace division of the LTV Corporation, and he is finally getting back on his feet financially. But the psychic scars still remain. Especially disturbing to the family was the loss of friends. "The whistle-blower has about the same image as the snitch does," he said. "Everyone thinks you're slime." Still he expresses few regrets for blowing the whistle and asserts that he would do it again if he had to. "I've got absolutely nothing in my hand to show as a physical effect of what I've done, except the losses I've had. But I know I was the cutting edge of the knife that prevented them from getting their license and sent them back to do repairs. I know I did right. And I know I'll always sleep right. I'll sleep like a baby."

Joseph Rose

In the course of his work as an in-house attorney for the Associated Milk Producers Incorporated (AMPI), Joseph Rose became aware of illegal political contributions to the Nixon reelection campaign.[2] He knew that the confidentiality of the attorney-client relation barred him from voluntarily releasing information about past contributions, even if they constituted a criminal conspiracy. At the same time, his legal training told him that his present activity—helping to cover up illegal activity—made him a coconspirator in a crime. He first contacted the president of AMPI, a Wisconsin dairy farmer, and told him that he would not approve certain payments. Warned that he was now as guilty as anyone else, he concluded that there was no point in going to the other executives of AMPI, who were all deeply implicated in the illegal scheme. So he decided that he had to collect the incriminating evidence and present it to the board of directors. In his own words:

> I was never allowed to do that. My attempt [to talk to the board] happened on a weekend during their convention in Minneapolis. Labor Day followed, and then Tuesday I went to work. I found a guard posted at my door; locks had been changed. The general manager demanded to see me. My services had become very, very unsatisfactory. After I was fired, I felt virtually a sense of relief. I was glad to be out of it, and I planned to keep my mouth shut. Then I had a call from one of the lawyers involved in an antitrust case against AMPI. He said, "They are really slandering you—making some very vicious attacks on you." I had indicated to AMPI executives

that if the board would not listen to me, I would go right to the dairy farmers and they obviously felt my career and credibility had to be completely destroyed to protect their own tails.

In the end, AMPI was fined $35,000 and forced to pay $2.9 million in back taxes. Two executives were convicted, and one received a prison sentence. (The other executive died while he was waiting to be sentenced.) Joseph Rose also paid a price in terms of the disruption of his career. Despite the fact that he had been compelled by law to testify before Congress and to the grand jury led by the Watergate special prosecutor, Joseph Rose was regarded by potential employers as someone who had been disloyal and was unreliable as an employee.

Joseph Rose was able to put his life back together. He has been able to establish a successful practice in San Antonio, Texas, and some of his clients come to him because of his reputation for integrity and toughness in the face of adversity. However, the experience has left him with a cynical view of American business.

> . . . [A]ll of the public utterances of corporations and indeed of our own government concerning "courage, integrity, loyalty, honesty, and duty" are nothing but the sheerest hogwash that disappear very rapidly when it comes to the practical application of these concepts by strict definition. The reason that there are very few . . . [whistle-blowers] is that the message is too clearly out in this society that white-collar crime, or nonviolent crime, should be tolerated by the public at large, so long as the conduct brings a profit or a profitable result to the institution committing it. . . .

INTRODUCTION

There have always been informers, or snitches, who reveal information to enrich themselves or to get back at others. However, whistle-blowers like Chuck Atchinson and Joseph Rose are generally conscientious people who expose some wrongdoing, often at great personal risk. The term *whistle-blower* was applied first to government employees who "go public" with complaints of corruption or mismanagement in federal agencies. It is now used in connection with similar activities in the private sector.[3]

As the examples of Chuck Atchinson and Joseph Rose show, whistle-blowers often pay a high price for their acts of dissent. Retaliation is common and can take many forms—from poor evaluations and demotion to outright dismissal. Some employers seek to blacklist whistle-blowers, so that they cannot obtain jobs in the same industry. Many whistle-blowers suffer career disruption and financial hardship resulting from the job dislocation and legal expenses, and there is severe emotional strain on whistle-blowers and their families as co-workers, friends, and neighbors turn against them. Given the high price that whistle-blowers sometimes pay, should people really be encouraged to blow the whistle? Is the exposure of corruption and mismanagement in government and industry the best way to correct these faults? Or are there more effective ways to deal with them without requiring individuals to make heroic personal sacrifices? Should whistle-blowers be protected, and if so, how can this best be done?

In addition to these practical questions, there are more philosophical issues about the ethical justification of whistle-blowing. Do employees have a right to blow the whistle? Although they usually act with the laudable aim of protecting the public by drawing attention to wrongdoing on the part of their organization, whistle-blowers also run the risk of violating genuine obligations that employees owe to employers. Employees have an obligation to do the work that they are assigned, to be loyal to their employer, and generally to work for the interest of the company, not against it. In addition, employees have an obligation to preserve the confidentiality of information acquired in the course of their work, and whistle-blowing sometimes involves the release of this kind of information. Cases of whistle-blowing are so wrenching precisely because they involve very strong conflicting obligations. It is vitally important, therefore, to understand when it is morally permissible to blow the whistle and when whistle-blowing is, perhaps, not justified. Our first task, though, is to develop a definition of whistle-blowing.

WHAT IS WHISTLE-BLOWING?

As a first approximation, whistle-blowing can be defined as the release of information by a member or former member of an organization that is evidence of illegal and/or immoral conduct in the organization or conduct in the organization that is not in the public interest. There are several points to observe in this definition.

First, blowing the whistle is something that can be done only by a member of an organization. It is not whistle-blowing when a witness of a crime notifies the police and testifies in court. It is also not whistle-blowing for a reporter who uncovers some illegal practice in a corporation to expose it in print. Both the witness and the reporter have incriminating information, but they are under no obligation that prevents them from making it public. The situation is different for employees who become aware of illegal or immoral conduct in their own organization. Whistle-blowing, therefore, is an action that takes place *within* an organization.

The difference is due to the fact that an employee is expected to work only as directed, to go through channels, and, especially, to act in all matters for the well-being of the organization. Also, the information involved is typically obtained by an employee in the course of his or her employment, as a part of the job. Such information is usually regarded as confidential, so that an employee has an obligation not to reveal it, especially to the detriment of the employer. To "go public" with information that is damaging to the organization is generally viewed as violating a number of obligations that an employee has as a member of the organization.

Second, there must be information. Merely to dissent publicly with an employer is not in itself to blow the whistle; whistle-blowing necessarily involves the release of nonpublic information. According to Sissela Bok, "The whistleblower assumes that his message will alert listeners to something they do not know, or whose significance they have not grasped because it has been kept secret."[4] A distinction can be made between *blowing the whistle* and *sounding the alarm*. Instead of revealing new facts, as whistle-blowers do, dissenters who take a public stand in opposition to an organization to which they belong can be viewed as trying to arouse public concern, to get people alarmed about facts that are already known.

Third, the information is generally evidence of some significant kind of misconduct on the part of an organization or some of its members. The term *whistle-blowing* is usually reserved for matters of substantial importance. The illegal campaign contributions that AMPI funneled to the Nixon reelection campaign provide a good example, since information about the contributions constituted grounds for legal action against the organization and several executives. An employee could also be said to blow the whistle about other practices that are legal but contrary to the public interest, such as a lobbying effort for maintaining artificially high prices for milk products. Information of this kind could alert the public and aid consumers and other interest groups in counteracting the lobbying effort, for example. However, merely exposing incompetent or self-serving management or leaking information to influence the course of events is not commonly counted as whistle-blowing. Lacking in these kinds of cases is a serious wrong that could be averted or rectified by whistle-blowing.

Fourth, the information must be released outside normal channels of communication. In most organizations, employees are instructed to report instances of illegal or improper conduct to their immediate superiors, and other means often exist for employees to register their concerns. Some corporations have an announced policy of encouraging employees to submit any suspicions of misconduct in writing to the CEO, with an assurance of confidentiality. Others have a designated official—often called an *ombudsman*—for handling employee complaints. Whistle-blowing does not necessarily involve "going public" and revealing information outside the organization. There can be *internal* as well as *external* whistle-blowing. However, an employee who follows established procedures for reporting wrongdoing is not a whistle-blower. Joseph Rose, by contrast, saw that it would be futile to confront the executives of AMPI with his evidence of their illegal campaign contributions and decided to go over their heads to the board of directors, thereby blowing the whistle.

A definition of whistle-blowing also needs to take into account *to whom* the whistle is blown. In both internal and external whistle-blowing, the information must be revealed in ways that can reasonably be expected to bring about a desired change. Merely passing on information about wrongdoing to a third party does not necessarily constitute whistle-blowing. Chuck Atchinson testified before a regulatory agency, for example, and Joseph Rose testified before a committee of Congress and the Watergate grand jury. Going to the press is often effective because the information ultimately reaches the appropriate authorities. Reporting to a credit-rating agency that a person faces bankruptcy, by contrast, would not usually be an instance of whistle-blowing but of ordinary snitching.

Fifth, the release of information must be something that is done voluntarily, as opposed to being legally required, although the distinction is not always clear. Joseph Rose did not volunteer his evidence of illegal campaign contributions outside the organization, for example; he had to be subpoenaed and legally forced to testify. And some of Chuck Atchinson's testimony was also the result of court orders.

One thing that confuses the distinction is that whistle-blowers are often required by law to reveal information, but the call to testify comes only after they volunteer that they have incriminating evidence. However, in a state supreme court case, *Petermann* v. *International Brotherhood of Teamsters*, a treasurer for a union had no desire to be a whistle-blower, but he refused to perjure himself before a California state legislative body as he had been ordered to do by his employer.[5] Although Petermann acted with considerable courage, it is not clear whether he should be called a whistle-blower, since he had little choice under the circumstances.

A sixth point is that whistle-blowing must be undertaken as a moral protest; that is, the motive must be to correct some wrong and not to seek revenge or personal advancement. This is not to deny that a person with incriminating evidence could conceivably be justified in coming forth, whatever the motive. People "go public" for all sorts of reasons—a common one being fear of their own legal liability—and by doing so, they often benefit society. Still, it is useful to draw a line between the genuine whistle-blower and corporate malcontents and intriguers. Because the motives of whistle-blowers are often misperceived in the organization, employees considering the act must carefully examine their own motivation.

Putting all these points together, a more adequate (but unfortunately long-winded) definition of whistle-blowing is as follows: Whistle-blowing is the voluntary release of nonpublic information, as a moral protest, by a member or former member of an organization outside the normal channels of communication to an appropriate audience about illegal and/or immoral conduct in the organization or conduct in the organization that is opposed in some significant way to the public interest.

With a definition of whistle-blowing out of the way, we can now proceed to the central question of the conditions for justified whistle-blowing. Can this act ever be justified?

THE JUSTIFICATION OF WHISTLE-BLOWING

The ethical justification of whistle-blowing might seem to be obvious in view of the laudable public service that whistle-blowers provide—often at great personal risk. However, whistle-blowing has the potential to do great harm to both individuals and organizations.

This view is given vigorous expression in a widely cited passage from a 1971 speech by James M. Roche, who was chairman of the board of General Motors Corporation at the time:

> Some critics are now busy eroding another support of free enterprise—the loyalty of a management team, with its unifying values of cooperative work. Some of the enemies of business now encourage an employee to be disloyal to the enterprise. They want to create suspicion and disharmony, and pry into the proprietary interests of the business. However this is labelled—industrial espionage, whistle blowing, or professional responsibility—it is another tactic for spreading disunity and creating conflict.[6]

A more temperate statement along the same lines is given by Sissela Bok:

> Furthermore, the whistleblower hopes to stop the game; but since he is neither referee nor coach, and since he blows the whistle on his own team, his act is seen as a violation of loyalty. In holding his position, he has assumed certain obligations to his colleagues and clients. He may even have subscribed to a loyalty oath or a promise of confidentiality. Loyalty to colleagues and to clients comes to be pitted against loyalty to the public interest, to those who may be injured unless the revelation is made.[7]

As these remarks indicate, the main stumbling block in justifying whistle-blowing is the duty of loyalty that employees have to the organization of which they are a part. The public service that whistle-blowers provide has to be weighed against the disruptive effect that the disclosure of information has on bonds of loyalty. Does a person in a position to blow the whistle have a greater obligation to the public or to the organization? Where does the greater loyalty lie?

That we have an obligation to the public is relatively unproblematic; it is the obligation to prevent serious harm to others whenever this is within our power. An obligation of loyalty to an organization is more complex, involving, as it does, questions about the basis of such an obligation and the concept of loyalty itself. What does an employee owe an employer, and, more to the point, does the employment relation deprive an employee of a right to reveal information about wrongdoing in the organization? In order to answer these questions, let us begin with a commonly used argument against the right of an employee to blow the whistle.

The Loyal Agent Argument

According to one argument, an employee is an *agent* of an employer.[8] An agent is a person who is engaged to act in the interests of another person (called a *principal*) and is authorized to act on that person's behalf. This relation is typical of professionals, such as lawyers and accountants, who are called upon to use their skills in the service of a client. Employees are also considered to be agents of an employer in that they are hired to work for the benefit of the employer. Specifically, an employee, as an agent, has an obligation to work as directed, to protect confidential information, and, above all, to be loyal. All these are seemingly violated when an employee blows the whistle.

The loyal agent argument receives considerable support from the law, where the concept of agency and the obligations of agents are well developed. Although our concern is with the *moral* status of employees, the law of agency is a rich source of relevant insights about the employment relation.[9] According to one standard book on the subject, "an agent is a person who is authorised to act for a principal and has agreed so to act, and who has power to affect the legal relations of his principal with a third party."[10] Agents are employed to carry out tasks that principals are not willing or able to carry out for themselves. Thus, we hire a lawyer to represent us in legal matters, where we lack the expertise to do the job properly.

The main obligation of an agent is to act in the interest of the principal. We expect a lawyer, for example, to act as we would ourselves, if only we had the same ability. This obligation is expressed in the *Second Restatement of Agency* as follows: ". . . an agent is subject to a duty to his principal to act solely for the benefit of the principal in all matters connected with his agency."[11] The ethical basis of the duty of agents is a contractual obligation or an understood agreement to act in the interests of another person. Lawyers agree for a fee to represent clients, and employees are similarly hired with the understanding that they will work for the benefit of an employer.

At first glance, a whistle-blower is a disloyal agent who backs out of an agreement that is an essential part of the employer-employee relation. A whistle-blowing employee, according to the loyal agent argument, is like a lawyer who sells out a client—clearly a violation of the legal profession's code of ethics. Closer examination reveals that the argument is not as strong as it appears. Athough employees have an obligation of loyalty that is not shared by a person outside the organization, the obligation is not without its limits. Whistle-blowing is not something to be done without adequate justification, but at the same time, it is not something that can never be justified.

First, the law of agency does not impose an absolute obligation on employees to do whatever they are told. Rather, an agent has an obligation, in the words of the *Second Restatement*, to obey all *reasonable* directives of the principal. This is interpreted to exclude illegal or immoral acts; that is, employees are not obligated as agents to do anything illegal or immoral—even if specifically instructed by a superior to do so. Questions can arise, of course, about the legal and moral status of specific acts. Is an agent free to disobey an order to do something that is suspect but not clearly illegal or immoral, for example? Borderline cases are unavoidable, but in situations where a crime is being committed or people are exposed to the risk of serious injury and even death, the law of agency is clear: An employee has no obligation to obey.

The law of agency further excludes an obligation to keep confidential any information about the commission of a crime. Section 395 of the *Second Restatement of Agency* reads in part: "An agent is privileged to reveal information confidentially acquired . . . in the protection of a superior interest of himself or a third person." The *Restatement* does not define what is meant by a "superior interest" except to note that there is no duty of confidentiality when the information is about the commission of a crime. ". . . [I]f the confidential information is to the effect that the principal is committing or is about to commit a crime, the agent is under no duty not to reveal it."[12] Protecting oneself from legal liability can reasonably be held to be a "superior interest," as can preventing some serious harm to others.

Second, the obligations of an agent are confined to the needs of the relation. In order for a lawyer to represent a client adequately, it is necessary to impose a strong obligation of loyalty, but the obligation of loyalty required for employees to do their job adequately is less stringent. The obligation of agents to follow orders exactly stems, in part, from the fact that they may be binding the principal to a contract or exposing the principal to tort liability. The duty of confidentiality is justified by the legitimate right of an employer to maintain the secrecy of certain vital information. Thus, a quality control inspector, such as Chuck Atchinson, has an obligation to perform his work as directed so that nuclear power plants are built safely, and he has an obligation of confidentiality since certain information could benefit a competitor. These obligations are essential to a quality control inspector's job.

Employees are hired for limited purposes, however. As Alex Michalos points out, a person who has agreed to sell life insurance policies on commission is committed to performing *that* activity as a loyal agent. "It would be ludicrous," he continues, "to assume that the agent has also committed himself to painting houses, washing dogs, or doing anything else that happened to give his principal pleasure."[13] Similarly, a quality control inspector is not hired to overlook defects, falsify records, or do anything else that would permit a dangerous plant to go into operation. Information about irregularities in safety matters is also not the kind that the employer has a right to keep confidential, since it is not necessary to the normal operation of the business of constructing nuclear power plants.

To conclude, the loyal agent argument does not serve to show that whistle-blowing can never be justified. The obligations that employees have as agents of an organization are of great moral importance, but they do have limits. Specifically, the agency relation does not require employees to engage in illegal or immoral activities or to give over their whole life to an employer.

The Meaning of Loyalty

The concept of loyalty itself raises some questions. One is whether whistle-blowing is always an act of disloyalty or whether it can sometimes be done out of loyalty to the organization. The answer depends, in part, on what we mean by the term *loyalty*. If loyalty means merely following orders and not "rocking the boat," then whistle-blowers are disloyal employees. But loyalty can also be defined as a commitment to the true interests or goals of the organization, in which case whistle-blowers are often very loyal employees. Thus, whistle-blowing is not necessarily incompatible with loyalty, and, indeed, in some circumstances, loyalty may require employees to blow the whistle on wrongdoing in their own organization.

All too often, the mistake of the whistle-blower lies not in being disloyal to the organization as such but in breaking a relation of trust with a few key members of an organization or with associates and immediate superiors. Insofar as an employee has a duty of loyalty, though, it cannot be merely to follow orders or to go along with others. Loyalty means serving the interests and goals of an organization, which can sometimes lead to divided loyalties and uncertainties about what is best for an organization.

Some evidence for the claim that whistle-blowers are often loyal—perhaps even too loyal—to the organizations they serve is provided by Myron Glazer, a sociologist who interviewed fifty-five whistle-blowers in depth. One of his findings is that:

> Virtually all of the ethical resisters . . . had long histories of successful employment. They were not alienated or politically active members of movements advocating ma-

jor changes in society. On the contrary, they began as firm believers in their organizations, convinced that if they took a grievance to superiors, there would be an appropriate response. This naiveté led them into a series of damaging traps. They found that their earlier service and dedication provided them with little protection against charges of undermining organizational morale and effectiveness.[14]

The irony of this finding is that whistle-blowers are often loyal employees who take the first steps toward whistle-blowing in the belief that they are doing their job and acting in the best interests of the company. This is true of Joseph Rose, who has written:

> I never set out to be a whistle-blower; I merely tried to alert the appropriate officials at AMPI to the misconduct I became aware of—I felt that was my duty as AMPI's in-house counsel. Even though AMPI fired me abruptly for attempting to discharge my duty . . . , my personal set of ethics dictated that I attempt to shield the company because of the unsettled question of our attorney-client relationship. If I was a whistle-blower, I became one reluctantly.[15]

As further evidence that the relation between whistle-blowing and loyalty is far more complex than it first appears, the economist Albert O. Hirschman argues in a book entitled *Exit, Voice, and Loyalty* that members of organizations and people who deal with organizations, such as customers of a firm, can respond to dissatisfaction either by leaving the organization and having no further dealings with it (exit) or by speaking up and making the dissatisfaction known in the hope of bringing about change (voice). Loyalty is a factor that keeps people from exiting an organization; but, at the same time, it activates the voice option. According to Hirschman:

> . . . the likelihood of voice increases with the degree of loyalty. In addition, the two factors are far from independent. A member with a considerable attachment to a product or organization will often search for ways to make himself influential, especially when the organization moves in what he believes is the wrong direction; conversely, a member who wields (or thinks he wields) considerable power in an organization and is therefore convinced that he can get it "back on the track" is likely to develop a strong affection for the organization in which he is powerful.[16]

On Hirschman's analysis, exit is a more extreme form of dissent than voice, but business firms do not usually regard an employee's departure as a form of disloyalty. In fact, whistle-blowers are often treated in ways designed to get them to leave voluntarily. It may benefit an organization in the short run to get rid of troublemakers, but Hirschman argues that in the long run, encouraging employees to use the exit option will harm the organization by depriving it of those people who can bring about healthy change.

> As a result of loyalty, these potentially most influential customers and members will stay on longer than they would ordinarily, in the hope or, rather, reasoned expectation that improvement or reform can be achieved "from within." Thus loyalty, far from being irrational, can serve the socially useful purpose of preventing deterioration from becoming cumulative, as it so often does when there is no barrier to exit.[17]

A further complication is the fact that employees typically have a number of loyalties, both inside and outside an organization, which can come into conflict. This point is well made by Daniel Ellsberg, the Defense Department employee who finally decided to disclose the so-called Pentagon Papers to the press.

> I think the principle of "company loyalty," as emphasized in the indoctrination within any bureaucratic structure, governmental or private, has come to sum up the notion of loyalty for many people. This is not a healthy situation, because the loyalty that a democracy requires to function is a somewhat varied set of loyalties which includes loyalty to one's fellow citizens, and certainly loyalty to the Constitution and to the broader institutions of the country. Obviously, these loyalties can come into conflict, and merely mentioning the word "loyalty" doesn't dissolve those dilemmas that one faces.[18]

Even if we limit loyalty to a specific employer, such as a government agency or a corporation, questions about what loyalty means still arise. The Code of Ethics for Government Service, for example, contains the following instruction for federal employees: "Put loyalty to the highest moral principles and to country above loyalty to persons, party, or government department." This lofty statement is a prescription for confusion when employees of an administration or an agency are called upon to be team players.

THE CONDITIONS FOR JUSTIFIED WHISTLE-BLOWING

The following are some questions that should be considered in deciding whether to blow the whistle in a specific case.[19]

Is the situation of sufficient moral importance to justify whistle-blowing? A coverup of lethal side effects in a newly marketed drug, for example, is an appropriate situation for disclosure because people's lives are at stake. But situations are not always this clear. Is whistle-blowing warranted if the side effects are not lethal or debilitating but capable of causing temporary discomfort or pain? What if the drug is the most effective treatment for a serious medical problem, so that the harm of the side effect is outweighed by the benefit of using the drug? We need to ask, in such a case, how serious is the potential harm compared with the benefit of the drug and the trouble that would be caused by blowing the whistle? The less serious the harm, the less appropriate it is to blow the whistle.

In addition to the moral importance of the situation, consideration should also be given to the extent to which harm is a direct and predictable result of the activity that the whistle-blower is protesting. For example, a toy that might be hazardous under unusual circumstances warrants whistle-blowing less than one that poses a risk under all conditions. Sissela Bok contends that the harm should also be imminent. According to her, an alarm can be sounded about defects in a rapid-transit system that is already in operation or is about to go into operation, but an alarm should not be sounded about defects in a system that is still on the drawing boards and is far from being operational.[20]

   Do you have all the facts and have you properly understood their significance?   Whistle-blowing usually involves very serious charges that can cause irreparable harm if they turn out to be unfounded or misinterpreted. A potential whistle-blower, therefore, has a strong obligation to the people who are charged with wrongdoing to make sure that the charges are well-founded. The whistle-blower should also have as much documentation and other corroboration as possible. A whistle-blower's case is stronger when the evidence consists of verifiable facts and not merely hunches or rumors. Since whistle-blowing cases often end up in court, the proof should also be strong enough to stand up under scrutiny. The support for the charges need not be overwhelming, but it should meet the ordinary legal standard of a preponderance of evidence.

   Employees often have access to only some of the facts of a case and are liable, as a result, to form false or misleading impressions. Would-be whistle-blowers must be careful, therefore, not to jump to conclusions about matters that higher-level managers, with a fuller knowledge of the situation, are in a better position to judge. Typically, employees have only one kind of expertise, so they are not able to make an accurate judgment when different kinds of knowledge are needed.

   Have all internal channels and steps short of whistle-blowing been exhausted?   Whistle-blowing should be a last rather than a first resort. It is justified only when there are no morally preferable alternatives. The alternatives available to employees depend to a great extent on the provisions an organization makes for dissent, but virtually every organization requires employees to take up any matter of concern with an immediate superior before proceeding further—unless that person is part of the problem. Courts will generally not consider a complaint unless all possible appeals within an organization have been exhausted. Some progressive corporations have recognized the value of dissent in bringing problems to light and have set up procedures that allow employees to express their concern through internal channels. Steps of this kind reduce the need for whistle-blowing and the risks that external whistle-blowers take. It is possible to justify not using internal channels, however, when the whole organization is so mired in the wrongdoing that there is little chance that using them would succeed.

   Another justification for "going public" before exhausting internal channels is if there is a need for a quick response and internal whistle-blowing would be too slow and uncertain. Two engineers at Morton Thiokol expressed concern to their superiors about the effects of low temperature on the O-rings on the booster rockets for the *Challenger* spacecraft, but their warning never reached the officials at NASA who were responsible for making the decision to go ahead with the launch. The engineers spoke out after the *Challenger* explosion—for which they were disciplined by Morton Thiokol—but their whistle-blowing was too late to avert the disaster. To be effective, they would have had to blow the whistle before the decision was made to launch the spacecraft. This would have required them to go outside the company and contact the officials at NASA directly.

What is the best way to blow the whistle? Once a decision is made to "go public," a host of other questions have to be answered. To whom should the information be revealed? How much information should be revealed? Should the information be revealed anonymously or accompanied by the identity of the whistle-blower? Often an anonymous complaint to a regulatory body, such as the Environmental Protection Agency or the Securities and Exchange Commission, is sufficient to spark an investigation. The situation might also be handled by contacting the FBI or a local prosecuting attorney or by leaking information to the local press. The less information that is revealed, the less likely an employee is to violate any duty of confidentiality. Employees can also reduce conflicts by waiting until they leave an organization to blow the whistle.

Whistle-blowing is also more likely to be effective when an employee presents the charge in an objective and responsible manner. It is especially important that a whistle-blower stick to the important issues and refrain from conducting crusades or making personal attacks on the persons involved. Organizations often seek to discredit whistle-blowers by picturing them as disgruntled misfits or crazy radicals; intemperate, wide-ranging attacks undermine the whistle-blower's own credibility. Many whistle-blowers recommend developing a clear plan of action. Do not blow the whistle impulsively, they advise, but think out each step and anticipate the possible consequences.[21]

What is my responsibility in view of my role in the organization? The justification for blowing the whistle depends not only on the wrongdoing of others but also on the particular role that a whistle-blower occupies in an organization. Thus, an employee is more justified in blowing the whistle—and may even have an obligation to do so—when the wrongdoing concerns matters over which the employee has direct responsibility. Chuck Atchinson, for example, was not merely an employee of Brown & Root; he was a quality control inspector, and so the irregularities in the construction of the nuclear power plant involved matters that were part of his job. A company such as Brown & Root employs quality control inspectors in order to be sure that nuclear power plants are built to certain standards of safety. The welfare of the company and the public alike depend on people such as Chuck Atchinson doing their job conscientiously. In order to operate a nuclear power plant, moreover, a company must file an application under oath with the Nuclear Regulatory Commission (NRC), and it is a criminal offense for any employee to participate knowingly in the submission of an application that contains false information. Had Chuck Atchinson been called upon to verify that the work on the plant had been performed according to specifications, he would have faced the choice of refusing or becoming an accomplice in a crime.

When an employee is a professional, the question of whether to blow the whistle must be considered in the context of professional ethics. Professionals, such as lawyers, accountants, and engineers, have a greater obligation to blow the whistle under some circumstances and are restricted or prohibited from whistle-blowing under others. For example, Joseph Rose, the staff lawyer for the Associated Milk Producers Incorporated, realized that he had an obligation as a lawyer for AMPI to seek to recover the missing funds, which is an obligation that an employee in a different position would not necessarily have. Yet, at the same time, he planned after leaving his position to keep quiet about what he knew, because he had also discharged his legal responsibility by informing his superiors. In addition, he had to be careful about violating the guarantee of confidentiality inherent in the lawyer-client relation. His situation was thus substantially different from that of other employees at AMPI.

What are the chances for success?   Insofar as whistle-blowing is justified because of some good to the public, it is important to blow the whistle only when there is a reasonable chance of achieving that good. Whistle-blowing may be unsuccessful for many reasons. Sometimes the fault lies with the whistle-blower, who fails to make a case that attracts widespread concern or to devise an effective plan of action; other times it is simply that the organization is too powerful or the public not sufficiently responsive.

IS THERE A RIGHT TO BLOW THE WHISTLE?

Even though whistle-blowing can be justified in some situations, the sad fact remains that courageous employees who perform a valuable public service are often subjected to harsh retaliation. Our reaction when this occurs is, "There ought to be a law!" and, indeed, many have been proposed in Congress and various state legislatures.[22] Few have passed, however, and there are some strong arguments against providing legal protection for whistle-blowers. In this section we will examine the debate over the moral justification of laws to protect whistle-blowers against retaliation. It will be useful, first, to survey the existing legal protection.

Existing Legal Protection

Retaliation against federal employees who report instances of waste and corruption in government is prohibited by the Civil Service Reform Act of 1978, which also set up the Merit System Protection Board (MSPB) to receive and act on complaints of retaliation.[23] The provisions of this act were strengthened by the Whistleblower Protection Act of 1989, which designates the Office of Special Counsel as the recipient of whistle-blower reports, although federal workers are still protected if they disclose information about waste or corruption to "any person."

Some protection for whistle-blowers in both the public and private sectors exists in the antiretaliation provisions of various pieces of federal legislation. The National Labor Relations Act of 1935 (NLRA) forbids employers to retaliate against any employee who files a charge with the National Labor Relations Board (NLRB). Title VII of the 1964 Civil Rights Act protects employees who file a charge of discrimination, participate in an investigation or proceeding connected with a charge, or oppose an activity of a company that the employee believes is discriminatory. The Occupational Safety and Health Act of 1970 also prohibits retaliation against any employee who files a complaint with the Occupational Safety and Health Administration or testifies in a proceeding. Other federal acts with antiretaliatory provisions are the Surface Mining Act, the Railway Safety Act, the Surface Transportation Safety Act, the Safe Drinking Water Act, the Toxic Substance Control Act, the Clear Air Act, the Water Pollution Control Act, the Energy Reorganization Act, and the Solid Waste Disposal Act.

Perhaps the most effective federal statute for protecting whistle-blowers is the once-moribund Federal False Claims Act of 1863 (amended 1986). This act was originally passed by Congress to curb fraud during the post–Civil War reconstuction period by allowing private citizens who blow the whistle on government contractors to share in the financial recovery. The False Claims Act has been updated to encourage employees of defense industry contractors to report any fraud that they observe by entitling whistle-blowers to receive between 15 and 30 percent of the funds recovered in any suit.[24] The largest settlement to date was made to Douglas D. Keith, a former employee of United Technologies Corporation, who received $22.5 million of the $150 million that the company paid the government to settle a suit over billing practices in the building of helicopters for the Pentagon in the 1980s.[25]

More than thirty-five states have passed laws designed to protect whistle-blowers. Most of these apply only to government employees, but a few—Michigan's Whistle Blowers Protection Act, for example—extend more widely. Most of these state statutes specify the procedures that a whistle-blower must follow to receive protection and place requirements on the persons to whom the information is disclosed and on the kind of information that the whistle-blower discloses. Another source of protection for whistle-blowers is state court decisions limiting the traditional right of employers to fire at will. These decisions protect workers against retaliation for many reasons besides whistle-blowing, but they also leave some whistle-blowers unprotected. A further discussion of the issues in this kind of protection is contained in Chapter 10, "Unjust Dismissal."

The Arguments against Whistle-Blower Protection

There are many problems with drafting legislation for protecting whistle-blowers. First, a law recognizing whistle-blowing as a right is open to abuse. Whistle-blowing might be used by disgruntled employees to protest company decisions or to get back at their employers. Employees might also find an excuse to blow the whistle in order to cover up their own incompetence or inadequate performance. Alan F. Westin notes, "Forbidding an employer to dismiss or discipline an employee who protests against illegal or improper conduct by management invites employees to take out 'antidismissal insurance' by lodging a whistle-blowing complaint."[26]

Second, legislation to protect whistle-blowers would encroach on the traditional right of employers to conduct business as they see fit and would add another layer of regulation to the existing legal restraints on business, thereby making it more difficult for managers to run a company efficiently. The courts would be called upon to review and possibly reverse a great many personnel decisions. And the likely increase in employee litigation could also, according to Westin, "create an informer ethos at work that would threaten the spirit of cooperation and trust on which sound working relationships depend."[27]

Third, if whistle-blowing were protected by law, what should be the legal remedy for employees who are unjustly dismissed? Reinstatement in the workplace, which is the usual remedy in union contract grievance procedures, may not be feasible in the case of employees who are perceived as being disloyal. As an alternative to reinstatement, though, whistle-blowers could be offered a monetary settlement to compensate them for the losses suffered by being wrongly dismissed. An award could be arrived at by negotiation or arbitration, or it could result by allowing dismissed employees to sue for tort damages.

The Arguments for Whistle-Blower Protection

The main argument in defense of a law to protect whistle-blowers is a utilitarian one that rests on the contribution whistle-blowers make to society. There is a direct benefit in having instances of illegal corporate conduct, gross waste and mismanagement, and dangers to the public brought to light. This benefit can be achieved, the argument goes, only if whistle-blowers are encouraged to come forward and make their information known. Ralph Nader makes the further point that allowing employees greater freedom to speak out makes it easier to enforce existing laws and to bring about desirable changes in corporate behavior. He has observed:

> Corporate employees are among the first to know about industrial dumping of mercury or fluoride sludge into waterways, defectively designed automobiles, or undisclosed adverse effects of prescription drugs and pesticides. They are the first to grasp the technical capabilities to prevent existing product or pollution hazards. But they are very often the last to speak out, much less to refuse to be recruited for acts of corporate or governmental negligence or predation. Staying silent in the face of a professional duty has direct impact on the level of consumer and environmental hazards.[28]

These benefits must be balanced against the undeniable harm that a greater incidence of whistle-blowing would have on business firms. Insofar as companies are less efficient—either because of the greater regulation or the loss of loyalty within organizations—a right to blow the whistle is not justified on utilitarian grounds.

A second argument for providing legal protection for whistle-blowers appeals to the First Amendment right of freedom of speech. A distinction needs to be made, though, between the appeal to freedom of speech as a legal argument and as a moral argument. Our rights under the Constitution protect us for the most part only against acts of government and not against those of private employers. Consequently, the freedom of speech that we have as a matter of legal right does not necessarily prevent corporations from retaliating against whistle-blowers, although it does confer some protection on government employees who speak out as citizens.

A teacher in Illinois, for example, wrote a letter to the editor of a local newspaper criticizing the school board for favoring athletics at the expense of the academic program. The teacher, named Marvin Pickering, was fired on the grounds that writing the letter was "detrimental to the efficient operation and administration of the schools of the district." Pickering charged in reply that writing the letter was an exercise of the First Amendment right of free speech that cannot be denied citizens just because they are government employees. The U.S. Supreme Court agreed with Pickering and thereby established whistle-blower protection for government employees.[29] The Court, in a 1978 decision, *Holodnak* v. *Avco Corporation*, extended the precedent set by *Pickering* to private employers who do extensive work for the federal government.[30] The Supreme Court further refined the *Pickering* precedent fifteen years later in *Connick* v. *Myers*. In this case, the court ruled that the "speech" in question—which consisted of distributing a questionnaire to protest a personnel matter—did not address a matter of "public concern" sufficient to override the interest of the employer in maintaining control and efficiency in the workplace.[31]

Although the First Amendment right of free speech cannot be used as a *legal* argument for holding that whistle-blowing is a protected activity in the private sector, it can still be maintained that there is a *moral* right to freedom of speech and that (morally) there ought to be a law extending this right to whistle-blowers.[32] At least one writer has urged that we recognize a right that is broader than merely freedom of speech—namely, a right to follow one's own conscience. Whistle-blowers are often led to speak out not by a desire to serve the public good but to do what they feel is morally required of them. "Thus," this writer concludes, "the interests that weigh in favor of providing legal protection to the external whistleblower are not those embodied in an employee's obligation to society, but rather those embodied in his interest as an individual to act in accordance with the dictates of conscience."[33]

DEVELOPING A COMPANY WHISTLE-BLOWING POLICY

Companies have many incentives to develop a whistle-blowing policy.[34] No company is immune from wrongdoing, and an effective policy on whistle-blowing enables a company to deal with misconduct internally, thereby preventing embarrassing public disclosure. For a policy to be effective, however, employees must be assured that their reports will be taken seriously—which means that an investigation will be conducted and appropriate action taken. More importantly, employees must feel confident that they will not suffer any retaliation.

Benefits and Dangers of a Policy

Although companies might prefer to ignore some wrongdoing and to continue profitable but questionable practices, they can also benefit from learning about problems early and taking corrective action before the problems become public.

The lack of a policy will not prevent whistle-blowing by a company's employees, and the increasing public acceptance of whistle-blowing combined with expanded legal protection makes whistle-blowing all the more likely. The aftermath of a whistle-blowing incident also creates problems that are best avoided. In particular, dismissing whistle-blowers with legitimate complaints sends the wrong signal to other employees, and yet allowing whistle-blowers to remain in the workplace may cause tension and strife. These equally undesirable alternatives can be avoided by eliminating the need for any employee to go outside of the normal channels of communication. An effective whistle-blowing policy can have the added benefit of affirming a company's commitment to good ethics and creating an ethical corporate climate.

Whistle-blowing policies also benefit employees by providing them with a channel of communication for responding to perceived wrongdoing in the organization. Employees are likely to welcome an opportunity to express their legitimate concerns without the risk of going public with damaging information. Whistle-blowing policies involve some dangers, however. Encouraging employees to report on each other can create an environment of mistrust and intimidation, especially if people feel vulnerable to the possibility of false accusations.

Components of a Whistle-Blowing Policy

A well-designed whistle-blowing policy should include the following components.

1. An effectively communicated statement of responsibility.   Employees should understand that they have a responsibility to report all concerns about serious unethical or illegal conduct through the appropriate internal channels.

2. A clearly defined procedure for reporting.   A procedure should be established that allows employees to report their concerns in a confidential manner. The procedure should specify the persons to whom reports are to be made and the proper form, and employees should be made aware of the procedure. Some companies use an ethics "hotline" that allows employees to make a report by calling an 800 number; other companies insist that reports be made to a person's immediate superior unless that person is involved in the suspected wrongdoing. Multiple means of reporting concerns and the choice of anonymous reporting are available in some companies with whistle-blowing policies.

3. Well-trained personnel to receive and investigate reports.   The success of a whistle-blowing policy depends heavily on the skill of the personnel who receive and investigate the reports from employees. Especially critical is the ability to maintain confidentiality and to conduct a fair and thorough investigation. For these reasons, the personnel should be well-trained and have sufficient authority within the organization, and the program should be evaluated periodically for effectiveness.

4. A commitment to take appropriate action.   Employees must be assured that their reports of suspected wrongdoing will not be ignored or misused. Not only should the purposes of a whistle-blowing policy be effectively communicated to all employees, but the company must assure employees by both word and deed that their reports will be used only for these purposes. The best policies also stipulate that reporting employees will be informed about the outcome of an investigation and the action taken.

5. A guarantee against retaliation.   By far the most critical component in any whistle-blowing policy is the assurance that employees will not suffer retaliation for making reports in good faith. Retaliation can be prevented, however, only if the importance of the policy is effectively communicated to everyone in the organization and there is a credible commitment to the policy's success by top management. Companies must be on guard, of course, for employees who might abuse an ethics "hotline" or other reporting mechanisms for personal ends, but a fair and thorough investigation should reveal the facts of the case apart from the reporting employee's motives.

A whistle-blowing policy by itself will neither protect an organization from wrongdoing nor prevent whistle-blowing outside of prescribed channels. A poorly designed or implemented policy also runs the risk of doing more harm than good. Still, a policy with regard to whistle-blowing is worth considering by any company that is committed to ethical conduct.

Conclusion

Whether to blow the whistle on misconduct in an organization is the most difficult decision that some people ever have to make. The decision is wrenching personally because the stakes are so high. The lives of Chuck Atchinson and Joseph Rose were irreparably damaged, and yet many whistle-blowers say that they could not have lived with themselves if they had stayed silent. The decision is also difficult ethically, since whistle-blowing involves a conflict between two competing duties: to protect the public and to be loyal to an organization. And although loyalty is not always overriding, as the loyal agent argument holds, neither is it inconsequential. Deciding between these duties often requires that an employee exercise very careful judgment.

The one certain conclusion of this chapter is that whistle-blowing is ethically permissible under certain carefully specified conditions. (Whether it can ever be ethically required is a different question that seldom arises. Everyone has an obligation not to be a part of illegal and immoral activity, but exposing it at great risk to oneself is usually regarded as beyond what duty requires.) Blowing the whistle is only one response that an employee can make to corporate misconduct, however, and the act of whistle-blowing itself can take many different forms. So in addition to *whether* to become a whistle-blower, employees are faced with the further question of *how* to blow the whistle in a justified manner.

Finally, it is evident that employees who are justified in blowing the whistle ought not to suffer retaliation. What ought to be done to protect whistle-blowers from this fate is less clear. A plausible case can be made for legislation in this area, but the difficulty is drafting laws that achieve the desired result without interfering unduly in the legitimate conduct of business.

CASE 5.2   A Whistle-Blower Accepts a "Deal"

As the head of corporate audit for a major pharmaceutical company, I was involved in the lengthy approval process that the Food and Drug Administration requires before a new drug can be brought to market.[35] The reviewer for the FDA was asking some tough questions about the data supporting our application to market a new drug. Although I managed to answer the reviewer's questions to his apparent satisfaction, doubts were beginning to form in my own mind about the reliability of the data I was defending. So I instructed my staff to get me photocopies of the original research reports as soon as possible.

The photocopies provided evidence of "double books." The raw data in the original reports were entirely different from the data in our FDA application and showed the new drug failing every required test. I had heard rumors of other questionable conduct by the project director, and I suspected that he was implicated in the falsification of the data, although I had no proof for any accusations. I rejected the idea of blowing the whistle on the company by telling everything to the FDA and decided instead to follow the procedure outlined in the company's own whistle-blowing policy. Accordingly, I prepared a report stating only the facts that I could document, and I sent it to the next highest level above the person involved, which in this situation was the legal department of the corporation.

My internal whistle-blowing prompted a quick response. I was summoned to meet with the board of directors, which had a team of lawyers from an outside firm present. The original research reports had apparently been destroyed, but there was no question about the authenticity of the photocopies that I still retained because the raw data was accompanied by the researchers' signatures and the dates of entry. After friendly but close questioning, the board of directors offered me a "deal." They would give me all of the resources that I needed to get the drug approved by the FDA, but they promised that the drug would never be marketed. The board intended to correct the problems within the company (and the project director soon resigned), but they wanted to avoid the embarrassment of public exposure. Their plan was to request that approval of the drug be withdrawn afterward by telling the FDA that mistakes had been made in the marketing projections. I accepted the deal and succeeded in getting the drug approved. The board kept their word, and ten years later the drug is still not on the market.

After my "deal" with the board, other changes were made. Corporate policy was revised so that I no longer had ready access to company records. The FDA has the authority to conduct "surprise" audits at any time, and the policy had been to allow my office to mimic FDA audits, so that the company would always be "FDA-ready." Under the new policy, audits must be prearranged with the department involved, and the department can stop an audit and reschedule it at any point. Finally, the department is allowed to review the audit report before it is submitted. To my knowledge, there has been no repetition of the events ten years ago, but my ability to uncover such misconduct has been severely limited. Oftentimes I wonder whether I should have accepted that "deal."

CASE 5.3 Better Late than Never?

Seven years ago, Rockland International adopted a whistle-blowing policy that requires employees to report any suspicions of unethical or illegal conduct. During that time, Ken Dryden had investigated many cases, but the thick folder on his desk presented him with his greatest challenge yet. As he thumbed through it once more, he reflected on the pledge that was the cornerstone of Rockland's policy: "No employee will suffer any adverse personnel action as a result of making a report in compliance with this policy, and the company will seek, as far as possible, to ensure that employees are protected against other forms of retaliation." He wondered now whether this guarantee could be kept.

The problem began when Ken followed up on a call to Rockland's 800 number "hotline" by seeking further information from the employee, Art Holmes. Art was a top-notch purchasing agent, who was usually cheerful and outgoing, but the prospect of impending layoffs had affected him along with many others in the company. He suspected—rightly as it turned out—that his job was slated for elimination.

Ken was surprised to be presented with photocopies of dozens of canceled checks and invoices that Art had meticulously gathered. A comparison of the invoices with shipments received revealed convincingly that payments had been made for goods not delivered, and the authorization for the checks was made in every case by the head of the purchasing department. The head of the department at first denied any knowledge of the discrepancy and then claimed that he allowed the payment for undelivered goods because he wanted to keep a good supplier afloat during troubled times. Eventually he broke down and admitted that he had arranged a kickback scheme with the supplier in which the two shared the amounts overpaid. The details of the kickback scheme—and Art's role in uncovering it—soon became known throughout the company. The head of purchasing made restitution to the company and hastily resigned.

So far, it would appear that the whistle-blowing policy was working as intended: Art suspected wrongdoing, documented his suspicions, and reported them to the appropriate office. What bothered Ken, however, was the fact that the checks and invoices in the photocopies were more than a year old. He surmised that Art had surreptitiously photocopied the evidence as a form of "insurance" and, now that he feared being laid off, was seeking the protective cover provided by the whistle-blowing policy. Art vehemently denied such motives and contended that he feared retaliation from the wrongdoer, who was his immediate boss. Now that he had less to lose, he felt safer in doing his duty according to the company's own policy. "Better late than never," he quipped.

If Art is let go, Ken thought to himself, then a lot of people in the company will attribute it to his whistle-blowing, and everything that we have done to build trust at Rockland will go up in smoke. On the other hand, if employees get the idea that they can get job insurance by collecting evidence to present at an opportune time, then the policy will fail to encourage timely reporting of wrongdoing, and terminating anyone will become impossible. Closing the folder, he reminded himself that he not only had to make a decision in this case, but he also needed to learn how this mess had arisen and what could have been done to prevent it.

NOTES

1. The material for this case is taken from N. R. KLEINFIELD, "The Whistle Blowers' Morning After," *New York Times*, 9 November 1986, sec. 3, p. 1.

2. Material for this case is taken from MYRON GLAZER, "Ten Whistleblowers and How They Fared," *The Hastings Center Report*, 13 (December 1983), 33–41; and from ALAN F. WESTIN, ed., *Whistle Blowing! Loyalty and Dissent in the Corporation* (New York: McGraw-Hill, 1981), 31–38.

3. For a discussion of the etymology of the word, see WILLIAM SAFIRE, *Safire's Political Dictionary*, 3rd ed. (New York: Random House, 1978), 790.

4. SISSELA BOK, "Whistleblowing and Professional Responsibility," in TOM L. BEAUCHAMP and NORMAN E. BOWIE, eds., *Ethical Theory and Business*, 4th ed. (Englewood Cliffs, NJ: Prentice Hall, 1993), 308.

5. *Petermann v. International Brotherhood of Teamsters*, 174 Cal. App. 2d 184, 344, P. 2d 25 (1959). This case is discussed further in the chapter on unjust dismissal, since Petermann was fired for testifying.

6. JAMES M. ROCHE, "The Competitive System to Work, to Preserve, and to Protect," *Vital Speeches of the Day*, May 1971, 445.

7. BOK, "Whistleblowing and Professional Responsibility," 307.

8. One form of this argument is examined in ALEX C. MICHALOS, *A Pragmatic Approach to Business Ethics* (Thousand Oaks, CA: Sage Publications, 1995) 44–53.

9. The concept of agency is not confined to law but occurs in economics (especially the theory of the firm) and organizational theory. For a useful collection of articles exploring the ethical relevance of agency theory, see NORMAN E. BOWIE and R. EDWARD FREEMAN, eds., *Ethics and Agency Theory* (New York: Oxford University Press, 1992).

10. R. POWELL, *The Law of Agency* (London: Pitman and Sons, 1965), 7.

11. *Second Restatement of Agency*, Sec. 387. A Restatement is not a statute passed by a legislature but a summary of the law in a given area, written by legal scholars, which is often cited in court opinions. Other important Restatements are those on contracts and torts.

12. *Second Restatement of Agency*, Sec. 358, Comment f.

13. MICHALOS, *A Pragmatic Approach to Business Ethics*, 51.

14. MYRON PERETZ GLAZER and PENINA MIGDAL GLAZER, "Whistleblowing," *Psychology Today*, August 1986, 39. See also MYRON PERETZ GLAZER and PENINA MIGDAL GLAZER, *The Whistle-Blowers: Exposing Corruption in Government and Industry* (New York: Basic Books, 1989).

15. WESTIN, *Whistle Blowing!* 36.

16. ALBERT O. HIRSCHMAN, *Exit, Voice, and Loyalty* (Cambridge: Harvard University Press, 1970), 77.

17. HIRSCHMAN, *Exit, Voice, and Loyalty*, 79.

18. CHARLES PETERS and TAYLOR BRANCH, *Blowing the Whistle: Dissent in the Public Interest* (New York: Praeger, 1972), 269.

19. For similar lists, see RICHARD T. DeGEORGE, *Business Ethics*, 4th ed. (Englewood Cliffs, NJ: Prentice Hall, 1995), 231–38; GENE G. JAMES, "Whistle Blowing: Its Moral Justification," in W. MICHAEL HOFFMAN and ROBERT E. FREDERICK, eds., *Business Ethics: Readings and Cases in Corporate Morality*, 3rd ed. (New York: McGraw-Hill, 1995), 290–301.

20. BOK, "Whistleblowing and Professional Responsibility," 307.

21. For a more thorough discussion of the practical aspects of whistle-blowing, see PETER RAVEN-HANSEN, "Dos and Don'ts for Whistleblowers: Planning for Trouble," *Technology Review*, 83 (May 1980), 34–44.

22. See MARTIN H. MALIN, "Protecting the Whistle-blower from Retaliatory Discharge," *Journal of Law Reform*, 16 (Winter 1983), 277–318; DOUGLAS MASSENGILL and DONALD J. PETERSEN, "Whistleblowing: Protected Activity or Not?" *Employee Relations Law Journal*, 15 (Summer 1989), 49–56; and ELLETA SANGREY CALLAHAN and TERRY MOREHEAD DWORKIN, "Internal Whistleblowing: Protecting the Interests of the Employee, the Organization, and Society," *American Business Law Journal*, 37 (1991), 267–308.

23. Two studies of the MSPB in 1980 and 1983 showed that it had done little to encourage employees to report waste and corruption or to prevent retaliation against those who did. See ROSEMARY CHALK, "Making the World Safe for Whistleblowers," *Technology Review*, 91 (January 1988), 55.

24. See ELLETA SANGREY CALLAHAN and TERRY MOREHEAD DWORKIN, "Do Good and Get Rich: Financial Incentives for Whistleblowing under the False Claims Act," *Villanova Law Review*, 37 (1992), 273–336.

25. CALVIN SIMS, "Trying to Mute the Whistle-Blowers," *New York Times*, 11 April 1984, C1, C3.

26. WESTIN, *Whistle Blowing!* 134.

27. WESTIN, *Whistle Blowing!* 136. The points in this paragraph are made by WESTIN.

28. RALPH NADER, PETER J. PETAKAS, and KATE BLACKWELL, eds., *Whistle Blowing: The Report of the Conference on Professional Responsibility* (New York: Grossman, 1972), 4.

29. *Pickering* v. *Board of Education*, 391 U.S. 563 (1968).

30. *Holodnak* v. *Avco Corporation*, 423 U.S. 892 (1975). In other Supreme Court decisions, the right to speak out on matters of public concern was upheld in cases involving a police officer, a firefighter, and a public health nurse. *Muller* v. *Conlisk*, 429 F. 2d 901 (7th Cir. 1970). *Dendor* v. *Board of Fire and Police Commissioners*, 11 Ill. App. 3d 582, 297 N.E. 2d 316 (1973). *Rafferty* v. *Philadelphia Psychiatric Center*, 356 F. Supp. 500 (E.D.Pa. 1973).

31. *Connick* v. *Myers*, 461 U.S. 138 (1983).

32. This is advocated by PATRICIA H. WERHANE, "Individual Rights in Business," in TOM REGAN, ed., *Just Business: New Introductory Essays in Business Ethics* (New York: Random House, 1984), 114–18.

33. MALIN, "Protecting the Whistleblower from Retaliatory Discharge," 309.

34. For discussions of whistle-blowing policies, see TIM BARNETT, "Why *Your* Company Should Have a Whistleblowing Policy," *SAM Advanced Management Journal*, 57 (1992), 37–42; and MARCIA P. MICELI and JANET P. NEAR, *Blowing the Whistle: The Organizational and Legal Implications for Companies and Employees* (New York: Lexington Books, 1992), chap. 7.

35. This case is based on an experience reported to Professor John T. Delaney, University of Iowa. Some details have been changed. Used with the permission of Professor Delaney.

6

Trade Secrets and Conflict of Interest

CASE 6.1   The Aggressive Ad Agency

Rob Lebow was used to aggressive advertising agencies. As director of corporate communications for Microsoft Corporation, the giant computer software producer located in Redmond, Washington, Lebow helped to administer the company's $10 million advertising budget. So when it was announced in the fall of 1987 that Microsoft was conducting an agency review, putting its business up for grabs, he was prepared for a flood of calls and letters. One particular piece of mail that caught his eye was a specially prepared flier from a small agency in Boston named Rossin Greenberg Seronick & Hill (RGS&H).

Under the leadership of its president, Neal Hill, this five-year-old advertising agency had accounts totaling $26 million and a growth rate of 65 percent for the past year. Although its business was concentrated in New England, RGS&H was attempting to become a national force by going after high-tech industries. As part of this strategy, the agency recruited two talented people who had worked on an account for the Lotus Corporation at another firm. Jamie Mambro and Jay Williams, who were creative supervisors at Leonard Monahan Saabye in Providence, Rhode Island, joined RGS&H on November 2.

A few days later, Neal Hill read a news story in a trade publication about the agency review by the Lotus rival. Since Microsoft's new spreadsheet program, Excel, was competing directly against Lotus 1-2-3, the industry leader, this seemed to be an ideal opportunity for RGS&H.

The flier was sent by Neal Hill on November 20, after two previous letters and several telephone calls elicited no response from Microsoft. Included in the flier was a round-trip airline ticket from Seattle to Boston and an invitation that read in part:

> You probably haven't thought about talking to an agency in Boston. . . But, since we know your competition's plans, isn't it worth taking a flier? . . . You see, the reason we know so much about Lotus is that some of our newest employees just spent the past year and a half working on the Lotus business at another agency. So they are intimately acquainted with Lotus' thoughts about Microsoft—and their plans to deal with the introduction of Excel.

In order to do an effective job for a client, advertising agencies must be provided with a certain amount of confidential information that would be of value to competitors. Many companies include a confidentiality clause in their contracts with advertising agencies, and Lotus had such an agreement with its agency, Leonard Monahan Saabye. Even in the absence of a confidentiality clause, however, advertising agencies generally recognize an obligation to preserve the confidentiality of sensitive information.

On the other hand, offering the experience of employees who have handled similar accounts is an accepted practice in the advertising industry. As the president of one firm observed, "There's a thin line between experience and firsthand recent knowledge." But, he continued, "I can't imagine a new-business presentation in which the agency didn't introduce people who worked on the prospect's kind of business."[1]

Rob Lebow was left to wonder, was Neal Hill at RGS&H offering Microsoft the experience of two employees who had worked on the Lotus account, or was he offering to sell confidential information? In either event, what should he do?

If the new employees at RGS&H had information about Lotus's advertising strategy for countering the introduction of Excel, this could be of considerable value to Microsoft. Anticipating the moves of rivals is often critical to the success of a campaign. However, moving even a part of Microsoft's business to another agency—especially to a small, untested agency like RGS&H—would surely attract the attention of Lotus. And in the rumor-filled world of advertising, the presence of two employees who formerly worked on a Lotus account would not go unnoticed. Therefore, any information that RGS&H had might be "too hot to touch."

Rob Lebow recognized that he could decline the offer in different ways. He could merely ignore the flier, or he could return it with the reply "Thanks but no thanks." Another possibility was to forward the flier to Lotus. Even the rumor that Microsoft had communicated with RGS&H could be damaging to the company, and so being open with Lotus would provide some protection. However, Lotus has a reputation within the industry of being quick to sue, and considerable harm could be done to RGS&H—and to the two new employees, Jamie Mambro and Jay Williams, who might be unaware of the offer made in the flier.

Thus, any decision that Rob Lebow made was bound to have significant ethical, legal, and practical implications.

INTRODUCTION

It is not surprising that corporations such as Microsoft and Lotus attempt to protect themselves against the loss of trade secrets and to utilize what they can learn about their competitors. Information is a valuable business asset that generally provides companies with a significant advantage over competitors who lack it. We need to ask, however, what rights do companies have in maintaining the secrecy of valuable information? And what corresponding obligations do employees have not to disclose company trade secrets to outsiders or use them for their own advantage? Because companies also seek to learn about each other through competitor intelligence gathering, the ethics of such activities is also a critical issue.

There is considerable justification for holding that companies have some rights with respect to trade secrets and other intellectual property, such as patents, copyrights, and trademarks. In general, employees have an obligation of confidentiality not to disclose or use information acquired during their employment. On the other hand, employees have the right to change jobs or to start up a business of their own using some of the skill and knowledge they have acquired while working for a former employer. Furthermore, companies have a right to use their own employees' skill and knowledge that have been legitimately acquired elsewhere and to gather legitimate competitor intelligence.

Trade secrets, then, pose a complex set of problems about the rights and obligations of companies possessing valuable information as well as the rights and obligations of employees and competitors. The courts have long struggled with these problems without much success. Even what information constitutes a trade secret is a source of contention.

A rough definition of a trade secret is that it is information which is used in the conduct of a business and is not commonly known by others. Section 757 of the *Restatement of Torts* defines a trade secret as follows:

> A trade secret may consist of any formula, pattern, device or compilation of information which is used in one's business, and which gives him an opportunity to obtain an advantage over competitors who do not know or use it.

Examples of trade secrets include the ingredients or chemical composition of a product, the design of a machine, the details of a manufacturing process, methods of quality control, results of marketing surveys, financial projections, and lists of customers and suppliers.

A distinction is made in the *Restatement* between trade secrets and confidential business information. The latter is information concerning specific matters, such as the salary of an employee, which is kept secret but not actually used to manufacture anything or provide a service. The amount of a specific bid is also not a trade secret, but the procedure of a company for calculating bids might be. A former employee who is knowledgeable about the bidding procedure of a company, for example, might be able to use that information to enter lower bids.

The *Restatement* admits that an exact definition is not possible, but it lists six factors that can be used to determine what information is protectable as a trade secret. These are

> (1) the extent to which the information is known outside his business; (2) the extent to which it is known by employees and others involved in his business; (3) the extent of measures taken by him to guard the secrecy of the information; (4) the value of the information to him and his competitors; (5) the amount of effort or money expended by him in developing the information; (6) the ease or difficulty with which the information could be properly acquired or duplicated by others.

There are three major arguments for trade secret protection. One argument views trade secrets as a kind of *property* and attempts to apply common-law principles of property rights to them. In the second argument, cases involving trade secrets are considered in terms of the right to compete and the principles of *fair competition*. The third argument holds that employees who disclose trade secrets to others or who use them for their own gain violate an obligation of *confidentiality* that is part of the employer-employee relation.

TRADE SECRETS AS PROPERTY

Imagine a lone inventor who, after years of hard work, develops an improved process for manufacturing a common product and builds a factory to turn out the product using the new process. Even if the innovations are not sufficiently original to be patentable, we can accept that he owns the results of his creative efforts, at least to the extent that it would be wrong for a worker in the factory to disclose the details of the manufacturing process to a competitor, especially if the employee had been sworn to secrecy.[2]

Trade secrets, along with patents, copyrights, and trademarks, are commonly regarded in the law as intellectual property that can be said to belong to an owner. Patents, copyrights, and trademarks, in particular, are like tangible property in that the owner has a right of exclusive use and the right to sell, license, or otherwise assign ownership to others. This right does not depend on keeping the information secret. Ownership of a trade secret, by contrast, does not confer a right of exclusive use but only a right not to have the secret misappropriated or wrongfully acquired by others. And once the information is widely known, it ceases to be a protectable trade secret. All forms of intellectual property are unlike tangible property, however, in that they are not inherently exclusive; that is, their use by one person does not preclude their use by another.

The question of who owns what becomes more complicated if the inventor is himself employed by a manufacturer of the product in question. As long as he gets his ideas while performing unrelated work for his employer, however, and conducts the experiments on his own time using his own materials and facilities, then it seems only right that he be recognized as the sole owner of the improved manufacturing process and be permitted—perhaps after leaving his present employer—to sell the secrets of the process to another manufacturer or to go into business for himself. If, on the other hand, he is hired as an inventor to develop improved methods of manufacture or if he does his creative work on his employer's time with the resources of his employer, then some or all the rights of ownership could reasonably be claimed to belong to the employer.

The *Wexler* Case

The case *Wexler* v. *Greenberg* is instructive in this regard. Alvin Greenberg was employed as chief chemist for the Buckingham Wax Company, which manufactured floor cleaners, polishes, and other maintenance materials. One of his tasks as chief chemist was to analyze the products of competitors and to use the results to develop new formulas. After eight years with the company, Greenberg left to join Brite Products, which had previously purchased exclusively from Buckingham. With the formulas that Greenberg had developed while working for Buckingham, Brite was able to dispense with Buckingham as a supplier and become a manufacturer itself, whereupon Buckingham sued to prevent Greenberg and his new employer from using the formulas, on the grounds that they were trade secrets which Greenberg had misappropriated.

According to the decision in this landmark case, an employer has the burden of showing two things: "(1) a legally protectable trade secret; and (2) a legal basis, either a covenant or a confidential relationship, upon which to predicate relief."[3] Information is protectable as a trade secret, in other words, only as long as it meets certain conditions, one of which is that it is genuinely a secret. Furthermore, the owner of a trade secret is protected against the use of this information by others only when it is disclosed by an employee in violation of an obligation of confidentiality, for example, or when a competitor obtains it by theft, bribery, industrial espionage, or some other impermissible means.

In overturning a lower court ruling which held that Greenberg had an obligation of confidentiality not to disclose the formulas, the Supreme Court of Pennsylvania ruled in favor of Greenberg, citing the fact that the supposed trade secrets had not been disclosed to Greenberg by his employer but had been developed by Greenberg himself.

> The usual situation involving misappropriation of trade secrets in violation of a confidential relationship is one in which an employer *discloses to his employee* a preexisting trade secret (one already developed or formulated) so that the employee may duly perform his work. . . . It is then that a pledge of secrecy is impliedly extracted from the employee, a pledge which he carries with him even beyond the ties of his employment relationship. Since it is conceptually impossible, however, to elicit an implied pledge of secrecy from the sole act of an employee turning over to his employer a trade secret which he, the employee, has developed, as occurred in the present case, the appellees must show a different manner in which the present

circumstances support the permanent cloak of confidence cast upon Greenberg. . . .

The formulas, moreover, were not significant discoveries on Greenberg's part but were merely the result of routine applications of Greenberg's skill as a chemist. As such, they were, in the court's view, the kinds of technical knowledge that any employee acquires by virtue of being employed. Even though the formulas are trade secrets, which the Buckingham Wax Company is permitted to use, they properly belong to Greenberg, who has a right to use them in his work for a new employer. Society also makes an investment in the development of information; it is not the exclusive property of an individual or a firm. Because patentable ideas and other innovations are generally built on foundations that have been laid by others, even companies that have spent a great deal for research cannot claim sole right of ownership.

Sources of Property Rights

One source for the argument that patentable ideas, trade secrets, and the like are a form of property is the Lockean view that we own the results of our own labor.[4] Patent and copyright laws are based in part on the premise that inventors and writers who work with their minds and turn out such products as blueprints and novels should have the same right of ownership that is accorded to creators of more tangible objects. Insofar as intellectual property is created by individuals who have been hired by a company for that purpose and paid for their labor, then it follows, in the Lockean view, that the company is the rightful owner. Just as the products made on an assembly line belong to the company and not to the workers who make them, so too do inventions made by people who are hired to invent. The company has paid them for their efforts and provided them with the wherewithal to do their work.

In addition, there are good utilitarian reasons for holding that companies have property rights to certain kinds of information. First, society generally benefits from the willingness of companies to innovate, but without the legal protection provided by patent and trade secret laws, companies would have less incentive to make the costly investments in research and development that innovation requires. Second, patent and copyright laws encourage a free flow of information, which leads to additional benefits. Patent holders are granted a period of seventeen years in which to capitalize on their discoveries; but even during the period of the patent, others can use the information in their research and perhaps make new discoveries.

The existence of legal protection for trade secrets, patents, and other forms of intellectual property also has its drawbacks. A patent confers a legal monopoly for a fixed number of years, which raises the price that the public pays for the products of patent holders during that time. Trade secrets permit a monopoly to exist as long as a company succeeds in keeping key information out of the hands of competitors. Since there is no requirement that patents be used, a company could conceivably patent a large number of processes and products that rival its own and thereby prevent competitors from using them.[5] And the owner of copyrighted material can prevent the wide dissemination of important information either by denying permission to print it or by charging an exorbitant price.

These drawbacks can be minimized by the optimal trade-off between the advantages and disadvantages of providing legal protection for patents, trade secrets, and the like. This trade-off is achieved, in part, by the limits on what can be patented or copyrighted or protected as a trade secret. Other means for achieving the optimal trade-off include placing expiration dates on patents and copyrights and defining what constitutes infringements of patents and copyrights. Thus, the Copyright Act of 1976 includes a provision for "fair use" that permits short quotations in reviews, criticism, and news reports.

Clarifying the Ownership of Ideas

Many companies attempt to clarify the ownership of patentable ideas by requiring employees to sign an agreement turning over all patent rights to the employer. Such agreements are morally objectionable, however, when they give companies a claim on discoveries that are outside the scope of an employee's responsibilities and make no use of the employer's facilities and resources.[6] Courts in the United States have often invalidated agreements that force employees to give up the rights to inventions that properly belong to them. The law in most of the other industrialized countries of the world provides for sharing the rights to employee inventions or providing additional compensation to employees, especially for highly profitable discoveries.[7]

The ownership of ideas is a difficult area, precisely because the contributions of employers and employees are so difficult to disentangle. Arguably, the law in the United States has tended to favor the more powerful party, namely, employers. Contracts or other agreements that spell out in detail the rights of employers and employees are clearly preferable to ambiguous divisions that often land in the courts. These arrangements must be fair to all concerned, however, and granting employees a greater share of the rewards might be a more just solution—and also one that benefits corporations in the long run, by motivating and retaining talented researchers.

FAIR COMPETITION

The second argument holds that companies are put at an unfair competitive disadvantage when information they have expended resources in developing or gathering can be used without cost by their competitors. Even when the information is not easily classifiable as property and there is no contract barring disclosure or use of the information, it may still be protected on grounds of fairness in trade.

In *Wexler* v. *Greenberg*, the court considered not only who owns the formulas that Greenberg developed for the Buckingham Wax Company but also whether placing restrictions on Greenberg's use of the formulas in his work for another company unfairly deprived him of a right to compete with his former employer. According to the decision in *Wexler:*

> . . . any form of post-employment restraint reduces the economic mobility of employees and limits their personal freedom to pursue a preferred course of livelihood. The employee's bargaining position is weakened because he is potentially shackled by the acquisition of alleged trade secrets; and thus, paradoxically, he is restrained because of his increased expertise, from advancing further in the industry in which he is most productive. Moreover . . . society suffers because competition is diminished by slackening the dissemination of ideas, processes and methods.

The problem of trade secrets, in the view of the court, is one of accommodating the rights of both parties: "the right of a businessman to be protected against unfair competition stemming from the usurpation of his trade secrets and the right of an individual to the unhampered pursuit of the occupations and livelihoods for which he is best suited."

A good illustration of the fair competition argument is provided by a 1918 case in which the Associated Press complained that a news service was rewriting its stories and selling them to newspapers in competition with the Associated Press.[8] The defendant, International News Service, argued in reply that although the specific wording of a news story can be regarded as a form of property, like a literary work, which belongs to the writer, the content itself cannot belong to anyone. Further, there is no contract between the parties that International News Service had breached. In the words of Justice Louis D. Brandeis:

> An essential element of individual property is the legal right to exclude others from enjoying it. . . . But the fact that a product of the mind has cost its producer money and labor, and has a value for which others are willing to pay, is not sufficient to insure to it this legal attribute of property. The general rule of law is, that the noblest of human productions—knowledge, truths ascertained, conceptions, and ideas—become, after voluntary communication to others, free as the air to common use.

In this view, information that cannot be patented or copyrighted has the same legal status as trade secrets, so that a plaintiff must show that there is a breach of contract or some other wrongful means of acquisition. Accordingly, Brandeis continued:

> The means by which the International News Service obtains news gathered by the Associated Press is . . . clearly unobjectionable. It is taken from papers bought in the open market or from bulletins publicly posted. No breach of contract, or of trust and neither fraud nor force, are involved. The manner of use is likewise unobjectionable. No reference is made by word or act to the Associated Press. . . . Neither the International News Service nor its subscribers is gaining or seeking to gain in its business a benefit from the reputation of the Associated Press. They are merely using its product without making compensation. That, they have a legal right to do; because the product is not property, and they do not stand in any relation to the Associated Press, either of contract or trust, which otherwise precludes such use.

A majority of the justices of the Supreme Court sided with the Associated Press, however, arguing that the case should be decided not on grounds of property rights or breach of contract but on considerations of fair competition. Although the public may make unrestricted use of the information contained in news stories, the two parties were direct competitors in a business in which the major stock in trade is news, a product that requires the resources and efforts of a news-gathering organization. In selling news stories based on dispatches from the Associated Press, the International News Service was, in the words of the majority opinion, "endeavouring to reap where it has not sown, and . . . appropriating to itself the harvest of those who have sown." The opinion further held:

> We need spend no time, however, upon the general question of property in news matter at common law, or the application of the Copyright Act, since it seems to us the case must turn upon the question of unfair competition in business. . . . The underlying principle is much the same as that which lies at the base of the equitable theory of consideration in the law of trusts—that he who has fairly paid the price should have the beneficial use of the property. It is no answer to say that complainant spends its money for that which is too fugitive or evanescent to be the subject of property. That might . . . furnish an answer in a common-law controversy. But in a court of equity, where the question is one of unfair competition, if that which complainant has acquired fairly at substantial cost may be sold fairly at substantial profit, a competitor who is misappropriating it for the purpose of disposing of it to his own profit and to the disadvantage of complainant cannot be heard to say that it is too fugitive and evanescent to be regarded as property. It has all the attributes of property necessary for determining that a misappropriation of it by a competitor is unfair competition because contrary to good conscience.

Noncompetition Agreements

Because of the difficulty of imposing legal restraints on employees after they leave, many companies require employees to sign a noncompetition agreement when they are hired. These agreements typically restrict an employee from working for a competitor for a certain period of time or within a given geographical territory after leaving a company. Agreements not to compete are a common feature of the sale of a business, and the courts have generally not hesitated to enforce them.

But there is little justification for restricting employees in this way. Noncompetition agreements are almost entirely for the benefit of the employer and inflict a burden on employees that is out of proportion to any gain. At least twelve states consider them so unfair that they are prohibited entirely.[9] Where noncompetition agreements are permitted by law, the courts have generally imposed a number of tests to determine whether they are justified.[10] These tests are that the restrictions contained in an agreement: (1) must serve to protect legitimate business interests, (2) must not be greater than that which is required for the protection of these legitimate interests, (3) must not impose an undue hardship on the ability of an employee to secure gainful employment, and (4) must not be injurious to the public. Legitimate business interests include the protection of proprietary information or customer relations, but the purpose of an agreement cannot be merely to protect an employer against competition.

In determining whether restrictions are greater than those required to protect the legitimate interests of an employer, three factors are important. These are the time period specified, the geographical area, and the kind of work that is excluded. The value of trade secrets is reduced over time, so that a noncompetition agreement designed to protect trade secrets can justifiably restrain an employee only during the time that they have value. Without a time limit on an agreement, an employee could be prevented from working for a competitor even after former proprietary information becomes common knowledge. Similarly, an employer with a legitimate interest in protecting the customers it serves in New York City, for example, might be justified in preventing a sales representative from working for a competitor in that area but not elsewhere.

Noncompetition agreements that specify the kind of work too broadly also run the risk of hampering an employee unduly. In one case, a woman in Georgia signed a contract with an employment agency in which she agreed not to work in any capacity for a period of one year for any competitor within a twenty-five-mile radius. The Supreme Court of Georgia ruled that the time period and the area were reasonable but that the phrase "in any capacity" was unreasonably broad, since it would bar her from doing any work for a competitor and not merely the work that she had done for her former employer.[11] Generally, agreements prohibiting employees from working on a particular project or soliciting specific clients, for example, are less likely to be objectionable than vague restrictions such as writing computer programs or selling insurance.

THE CONFIDENTIALITY ARGUMENT

The third argument—that employees who disclose trade secrets to others or use them themselves are guilty of violating an obligation of confidentiality—is based on the view that employees agree as a condition of employment to become agents of an employer and be bound by the duty that agents have to preserve the confidentiality of certain information.[12] Section 395 of the *Restatement of Agency* states that an agent has an obligation:

> . . . not to use or to communicate information confidentially given him by the principal or acquired by him during the course of or on account of his agency . . . to the injury of the principal, on his own account or on behalf of another . . . unless the information is a matter of general knowledge.

The obligation of confidentiality does not end with the employment relation but continues to exist after an employee leaves one job for another. And employees who sign an explicit confidentiality agreement may be bound by more stringent contractual obligations than those contained in the agency relation.

Companies can also have an obligation of confidentiality that prohibits them from misappropriating trade secrets. A company that inveigles trade secrets from another company under the guise of negotiating a license agreement or a merger, for example, might be charged with a violation of trade secret law, since the process of negotiation creates a relation of confidentiality. (They might also be charged with failing to negotiate in good faith.) It is also not uncommon for companies to reject ideas brought to them by outsiders, only to adopt them later as their own. The courts have ruled in many such instances that inventors and others have a right to expect that their ideas will be received in confidence and not misappropriated.

The argument for an obligation of confidentiality provides strong support for the right of employers to trade secret protection, but it too has a number of shortcomings. It assumes, for example, that the information was received from the employer and was not, as in the case of Alvin Greenberg, developed by the employee. And the obligation of confidentiality is also limited by the right of employees to use their skill and knowledge in the pursuit of a trade or occupation.

Confidentiality Agreements

Many employees sign a confidentiality agreement which creates an explicit contractual obligation that is often more stringent than the obligation of confidentiality that employees ordinarily have as agents. Although confidentiality agreements have some advantages for both employers and employees, they are open to the same objections as agreements to assign patent rights to employers and to refrain from postemployment competition. Since they are usually required as a condition of employment, employees are effectively coerced into giving up rights to which they might otherwise be entitled.

By relying on an enforceable obligation of confidentiality, companies often place unnecessary restraints on employee mobility and career prospects. Michael S. Baram contends that litigation rarely preserves either the secrecy of company information or the liberty of employees and that both of these are better served by more sophisticated management.[13] Among the policies he suggests are improving security procedures in the workplace; securing the legal protection of patents, copyrights, and trademarks whenever possible; segmenting information so that fewer people know the full scope of a trade secret; limiting information to those with a need to know; and using increased pensions and postemployment consulting contracts to keep employees from taking competitive employment.

In addition, the incentive for employees to leave with valuable trade secrets can be reduced by greater recognition of employees for their contributions. Not infrequently, employees go to a competitor or set up a business of their own because of a feeling that they have not been fairly treated. Baram concludes that the key to protecting trade secrets lies in improved employee relations, in which both employers and employees respect the rights of the other and take their obligations seriously. And a key element in improving employee relations is an ethical climate of fair play. Employers might find that treating employees fairly provides more protection for trade secrets than relying on the law.

COMPETITOR INTELLIGENCE GATHERING

Not all use of a company's trade secrets and other confidential business information is unethical or illegal. The systematic collection and analysis of competitor intelligence has become an accepted practice in the corporate world, and companies that do not avail themselves of this valuable tool may find themselves at a disadvantage. This is especially true in a global environment where some of America's competitors have long-established and highly efficient intelligence units.

Computers have greatly facilitated competitor intelligence gathering, first, by making immense volumes of information available in open-access databases and, second, by enabling companies to store and sort through the information they have compiled. Much of the information used for intelligence purposes is publicly available from news sources, trade publications, court records, regulatory filings, and presentations at industry meetings, and some is also obtained from employees' own contacts with customers, suppliers, and even competitors themselves. The challenge is to piece the information together so that conclusions can be drawn.

Although competitor intelligence gathering has shed its unsavory, cloak-and-dagger image, it still has ethical and legal limits that companies ignore at their peril. Unethical collection practices often lead to costly litigation in which the outcome is uncertain because of confusion in the law. A lack of ethics in competitor intelligence gathering also creates a climate of mistrust that hampers normal business activity and forces companies to adopt costly defensive measures. Most importantly, companies that routinely cross ethical boundaries in gaining competitor intelligence can scarcely expect others to respect their own trade secrets and confidential business information. The importance of ethics in competitor intelligence gathering has led some companies to adopt policies that give employees firm guidelines on acceptable practices and also set the tone for practices within their industries. Not only can a well-designed policy protect a company from the consequences of unethical intelligence gathering, but it can also enable a company to gain the maximum benefit from ethically acquired information by making the ethical and legal limits known to all employees.

The ethical and legal limits on competitor intelligence gathering are generally concerned with the *methods* used to acquire the information.[14] The importance of the method of acquisition is due to the point that trade secrets are protected, according to the *Wexler* decision, only if there is a legal basis "upon which to predicate relief," which means that some *duty* has been breached. The duties in question are most often breached by using improper methods to acquire information from a competitor. Thus, a company that carelessly allows a trade secret to become known has no right to prevent competitors from using it. Companies do have a right, however, to prevent the use of a trade secret that is sold by an employee, for example, or stolen by a competitor, because theft is present in both cases and there is a duty not to steal. The unethical methods for gathering competitor intelligence can be grouped under four headings, each of which involves a breach of a particular duty.

1. Theft and receipt of unsolicited information.   Theft of information, either by an employee or an outsider, is obviously an improper method for acquiring information because of the violation of *property rights* that it involves. Examples of employee theft include freely offering information to competitors to take revenge, selling it for monetary reasons, and taking it to a new job in order to advance one's career. Companies that receive the information, for whatever reason it is offered, are receiving, in effect, stolen property. More controversial, however, are cases in which an employee inadvertently leaves a document where it can be seen or taken by a competitor or carelessly discloses information in casual conversation. Suppose that a competitor's bid on an important project is accidentally enclosed along with the specifications that are sent by the customer. Would it be ethical to use that knowledge in preparing one's own bid? Or does the information still belong to the competitor?

2. Misrepresentation.   To gain information under false pretenses is a form of deception that violates a duty to be *honest* in all dealings. Posing as a customer to obtain information from a competitor, for example, is an act of dishonesty. Other devious practices include asking consulting firms to solicit information from competitors under the guise of doing a study of the industry and getting friendly customers to make phony requests for bids from competitors, which might contain confidential technical information about the bidder's products. Since useful bits of information are sometimes picked up during job interviews with a competitor's employees, some companies have advertised and conducted interviews for positions that do not exist, in the hope that some applicants would inadvertently reveal trade secrets of their present employer.[15]

3. Improper influence.   The employment relation is built on *trust,* and to induce an employee to reveal information through bribery or some other means is to exert an improper influence that undermines that trust. An employee who accepts a bribe and turns over a company's secrets has broken a bond with the employer, but the company that offers the bribe has obtained those secrets by inducing that break. Improper influence can be exerted not only by bribery but also by promising or holding out the possibility of a job or some other opportunity. Offering to purchase from a supplier in return for a competitor's price list would be an example of improper influence. More direct would be plying a competitor's employee with drinks in order to make that person less discrete.

4. Covert surveillance.   Some methods for obtaining information intrude in ways that companies have not anticipated and taken steps to prevent. These can be said to violate a company's right to privacy. Employees who talk about confidential matters in a public place, for example, can have no expectation of privacy; but planting hidden microphones in a competitor's place of business is a form of espionage that intrudes into an area that is regarded as private. Virtually all of the high-tech gadgetry that government intelligence agencies use to spy on enemies abroad is available for competitor intelligence gathering at home. Whether corporations have a right to privacy is controversial, but if covert surveillance were to become an accepted practice, companies would be forced to take costly defensive measures. Respecting a company's reasonable expectations of privacy, then, is in everyone's best interests.

CONFLICT OF INTEREST

In April 1984, a reporter for the *Wall Street Journal* was fired for violating the newspaper's policy on conflict of interest. The firing occurred after R. Foster Winans, a contributor to the influential stock market column "Heard on the Street," admitted to his employer and investigators from the Securities and Exchange Commission (SEC) that he conspired over a four-month period, beginning in October 1983, with two stockbrokers at Kidder, Peabody & Company, to trade on the basis of advance information about the content of the column. Since the publicity generated by "Heard on the Street" often caused short-run price swings, Mr. Winans and his co-conspirators were able to make a profit of $690,000 by buying stock or call options when a column contained favorable news about a stock and by selling short or buying put options when the news was unfavorable.

Just as employees have an obligation to respect trade secrets and confidential business information generally, they also have an obligation to avoid *conflict of interest* of the kind illustrated by the Winans case. Virtually all corporate codes of ethics address conflict of interest, since it interferes with the ability of employees to act in the best interests of an employer. The acceptance of gifts or lavish entertainment from suppliers, for example, is generally prohibited or strictly limited for the simple reason that the judgment of employees is apt to be compromised. Company codes usually contain guidelines on investing in customers, suppliers, and competitors of an employee's firm for the same reason.

Prohibitions on conflict of interest cannot be so extensive, however, as to prevent employees from pursuing unrelated business opportunities, taking part in community and political affairs, and generally acting as they see fit in matters outside the scope of their employment. One problem with conflict of interest is in drawing a line between legitimate and illegitimate activities of employees in the pursuit of their personal interests. A further problem is the large gray area that surrounds conflict-of-interest situations. Perhaps no other ethical concept in business is so elusive and subject to dispute. Many people charged with conflict of interest see nothing wrong with their behavior. It is important, therefore, to define the concept clearly and to understand the different kinds of conflict of interest.

What Is Conflict of Interest?

The case of R. Foster Winans involved a personal interest that came into conflict with the interests of his employer, the *Wall Street Journal*. It would be inaccurate, however, to define a conflict of interest as merely a clash between conflicting or competing interests. A report prepared for the Twentieth Century Fund Steering Committee on Conflict of Interest in the Securities Markets asserts, for example, that the term *conflict of interest* denotes "a situation in which two or more interests are legitimately present and competing or conflicting."[16] This definition is too broad, since it could be extended to cover virtually every business relation. In the relation between buyer and seller, for example, each party strives to advance his or her own interest at the expense of the other, but neither party faces a conflict of interest as the term is commonly understood.[17]

Although the Twentieth Century Fund report (mistakenly) describes the relation between buyer and seller as a conflict of interest, it further notes that conflict of interest arises in the securities market—which is the concern of the report—when a person or an institution operates as a fiduciary with an obligation to a client.

> It is important to distinguish the relation between fiduciary and client from that between ordinary buyer and seller. A used car salesman has much narrower obligations to his customers than a fiduciary has to his client. Of course, sellers have obligations of truthfulness—for example, the used car dealer has a duty not to set back the odometer—and in some situations sellers may have special duties, such as when a buyer relies upon a seller to select an article for particular use. But except for such limited duties, neither party is obligated to serve the other's interests.[18]

The key to understanding conflict of interest is in the last sentence. The conflict in a conflict of interest is not merely a conflict between conflicting interests, although conflicting interests are involved. The conflict occurs when a personal interest comes into conflict with an obligation to serve the interests of another. More precisely, we can say that a conflict of interest is a conflict that occurs when a personal interest interferes with a person's acting so as to promote the interests of another *when the person has an obligation to act in that other person's interest.* This obligation is stronger than the obligation merely to avoid harming a person and can arise only when the two persons are in a special relation, such as employer and employee.

Specifically, the kind of obligation described in this definition is that which characterizes an agency relation, in which one person (an agent) agrees to act on behalf of another (the principal) and to be subject to that person's control. This fact explains why conflict of interest is most often encountered by professionals—lawyers, doctors, and accountants, for example—and among fiduciaries, such as executors and trustees. Employees of business firms are also in an agency relation in that they have a general obligation to serve the interests of an employer.

An important feature of an agency relation is its open-endedness. An agent is obligated to perform not merely this or that act but, in the words of the *Second Restatement of Agency,* "to act solely for the benefit of the principal *in all matters concerned with his agency.*"[19] The duties of an agent are not determined solely by a list of moral rules but by the nature of the interests to be served. This open-ended character of the agency relation explains why it is a conflict of interest for an agent to acquire *any* interest that is contrary to that of a principal, since the kinds of situations in which an agent might be called upon to act in the interest of another are not easily anticipated.

To complete the definition of conflict of interest, some account should also be given to a personal interest. Roughly, a person has an interest in something when the person stands to gain a benefit or an advantage from that thing. "Having an interest" is not the same as "taking an interest." A person can take an interest in someone else's interest, especially when that person is a family member or a close associate. In that case, however, the benefit or advantage accrues to someone else—

although the person taking an interest in the well-being of another might also gain in some way. The benefit or advantage is usually restricted to a financial gain of some kind and should be limited to something tangible. Merely satisfying a desire, for example, would not seem to be enough, for otherwise a lawyer who detests a client and secretly hopes that the client will be convicted would face a conflict of interest, as would a lawyer who prefers to play golf instead of spending the time adequately representing a client. The benefit or advantage would also have to be substantial enough to interfere significantly with a person's performance of an obligation.

SOME RELEVANT DISTINCTIONS

All instances of conflict of interest are morally suspect, but some are more serious than others. In their rules on conflict of interest, company codes of ethics and codes for professionals, such as lawyers and accountants, contain a number of relevant distinctions that can aid us in understanding the concept of conflict of interest.

Actual and Potential Conflict of Interest

There is a distinction between *actual* and *potential* conflict of interest.[20] A conflict is actual when a personal interest leads a person to act against the interests of an employer or another person whose interests the person is obligated to serve. A situation constitutes a potential conflict of interest when there is the possibility that a person will fail to fulfill an obligation to act in the interests of another, even though the person has not yet done so.[21]

R. Foster Winans was clearly in an actual conflict-of-interest situation by virtue of the fact that he engaged in stock trading based on information that was to appear in forthcoming columns. All reporters face a potential conflict of interest, though, in writing stories that could have an impact on their own financial holdings. Many newspapers avoid such potential conflict of interest by prohibiting reporters from writing about companies in which they have stock or from buying stock in a company immediately before or after writing an article about it. A policy of this kind serves the dual purpose of removing the temptation for reporters to compromise their standards and assuring readers of the journalistic integrity of the reporting in the newspaper.

Obviously, the categories of actual and potential conflict of interest involve subjective elements. A dedicated reporter might honestly claim that he or she is able to write objectively about events that could adversely affect his or her personal interests. Merely having these interests creates a potential conflict of interest, but determining whether an actual conflict of interest exists would require us to make a judgment about the reporter's objectivity. Similarly, whether an interest creates a potential conflict depends on the strength of the influence it exerts on a person. Owning a small amount of stock in a company, for example, is unlikely to influence anyone's conduct, and so most employers do not impose an absolute prohibition on investments. More often they place a dollar limit on outside financial interests, or else they require a disclosure of stock ownership so that the potential for conflict of interest can be evaluated in each case.

Personal and Impersonal Conflict of Interest

A second distinction can be made between *personal* and *impersonal* conflict of interest. The definition developed in the preceding section is phrased in terms of a personal interest that comes into conflict with the interests of another. A conflict can also arise when a person is obligated to act in the interests of two different persons or organizations whose interests conflict. Thus, a lawyer who represents two clients with conflicting interests may not stand to gain personally from favoring one or the other, and yet, according to Rule 1.7(a) of the American Bar Association's "Model Rules of Professional Conduct," such an arrangement constitutes a conflict of interest.[22] A lawyer who has a personal interest that conflicts with the interests of a client has a personal conflict of interest, whereas a lawyer who represents two clients with conflicting interests faces an impersonal conflict of interest.

It is necessary to qualify the category of an impersonal conflict of interest to avoid cases of the following kind. Lawyers are regarded in the law not only as agents of a client but also as agents of the court. In this dual role, a lawyer might find that delaying a trial unnecessarily, for example, would be to the advantage of a client but doing so would be an abuse of the court system and, hence, a violation of the lawyer's duty to the court. Public accountants face a similar conflict as a result of being simultaneously agents of the companies being audited and public servants who have an obligation to ensure the integrity of financial information. It seems inappropriate to speak of such cases as involving conflict of interest, since doing so generally implies that a person has done something wrong. The conflicts in these cases, however, involve systematic features of situations that professionals such as lawyers and accountants individually cannot alter. We can avoid labeling cases of this kind conflict of interest by excluding from the definition conflicts that arise from systematic features of situations that are not easily altered. These kinds of conflicts present difficult moral dilemmas for individuals, however, and they need to be addressed in the structure and codes of ethics of the professions in question.

Individual and Organizational Conflict

Third, conflict of interest can be either *individual* or *organizational.* In the agency relation, the agent is typically a person acting in the interests of a principal, which may be another person or an organization; however, organizations can be agents as well and hence parties to conflicts of interest. Many large accounting firms, for example, provide management services to companies they also audit, and there is great concern in the profession that this dual function endangers the independence and objectivity of accountants—even when the work is done by different divisions of a firm.[23] Advertising agencies whose clients have competing products face a similar kind of conflict of interest. And investment banking houses have also been accused of conflict of interest for financing takeovers of companies with which they have had long-standing relations. Further, large law firms face the possibility of conflicts of interest when they have clients with competing interests—even when the work is done by different lawyers in the firm.

For an accountant to provide management services to a company that he or she also audits—or for an individual ad person, banker, or lawyer to accept clients with conflicting interests—is a clear conflict of interest. But why should it be a conflict when these functions are performed by different persons in different departments of a firm? The answer is that an accounting firm, for example, also has an interest that is shared by every member of the organization, and the interests of the firm can affect decisions about individual clients. When management services are more lucrative than auditing, for example, firms may have an incentive to concentrate on them to the detriment of other functions. They may also be tempted to conduct audits in ways that favor the clients to whom they provide management services.

Similarly, the creative work for competing advertising accounts is generally done by independent groups, but there is an incentive to commit greater resources and talent to more valuable accounts. In addition, when an organization such as an advertising agency takes on a client, there is an organizational commitment of loyalty that goes beyond merely delivering agreed-upon services. For an organization to work for and against a client at the same time is incompatible with this kind of organizational commitment. In addition, advertising campaigns involve sensitive information about product development and marketing strategies that is not easily kept confidential. Banking houses and large law firms encounter similar challenges to their ability to serve the interests of all clients to the fullest.

Organizations, then, can encounter conflicts of interest that are genuinely organizational in nature and not merely an instance of individuals within an organization facing a conflict of interest. This fact raises no difficulty for the definition that has been developed, since organizations as well as individuals can be agents and can have organizational obligations and interests that are not necessarily the same as those of the individuals who compose an organization. They can also have obligations to serve the interests of two or more parties with conflicting interests, so that the distinction between personal and impersonal conflict of interest applies to organizations as well. Organizational conflict of interest can be accommodated in the definition merely by expanding the term *person* to include organizations.

THE KINDS OF CONFLICT OF INTEREST

The concept of conflict of interest is complex in that it covers several distinct moral failings that are often run together. It is important to separate them, though, in order to have a full understanding both of the definition of conflict of interest and of the reasons that it is morally wrong for a person to be in a conflict-of-interest situation. Briefly, there are four kinds of conflict of interest: (1) exercising biased judgment, (2) engaging in direct competition, (3) misusing a position, and (4) violating confidentiality. Each of these calls for some explanation.

Biased Judgment

The exercise of judgment is characteristic of professionals, such as lawyers, accountants, and engineers, whose stock in trade is a body of specialized knowledge that is used in the service of clients. Not only are professionals paid for using this knowledge to make judgments for the benefit of others but part of the value of their services lies in the confidence that can be placed in a professional's judgment. Accountants do not merely examine a company's financial statement, for example, they also attest to the accuracy of that statement and to its compliance with generally accepted accounting principles, or GAAP. The National Society of Professional Engineers' *Code of Ethics for Engineers* stipulates that engineers shall not submit plans or specifications that are unsafe or not in conformity with accepted engineering standards.[24] So an engineer's signature on a blueprint is also a warrant of its quality.

Judgment is not exclusively a feature of professional work, however. Most employees are called upon to exercise some judgment in the performance of their jobs. Purchasing agents, for example, often have considerable latitude in choosing among various suppliers of a given product. The judgment of purchasing agents in all matters, however, should be used to make decisions that are in the best interests of the employing firm. For a purchasing agent to accept a bribe or kickback in return for placing an order constitutes a clear conflict of interest.

The reason is simple. Bribes and kickbacks are usually intended to induce an employee to grant some favor for a supplier at the expense of the employer. Other factors that could influence the judgment of an employee include outside business interests, such as stock or other investments in companies that have a business relation with the employee's company as a competitor, supplier, or customer or that are possible targets for merger or acquisition. Conflict of interest also occurs when an employee is in a position to make decisions that affect family members, relatives, or close associates. A purchasing agent would be in a conflict-of-interest situation if one of the suppliers submitting a bid were owned by a brother-in-law, for example, since there is a personal interest that is liable to influence the judgment of the purchasing agent in selecting the best bid.

Whether it is a potential conflict of interest for a purchasing agent to accept a gift from a supplier who expects favorable treatment in the future is less clear. An answer to this question depends largely on the value of the gift, the circumstances under which it is offered, the practice within the industry, and whether the gift violates any law. The code of ethics of a large bank, for example, states that employees should not accept gifts where the purpose is "to exert influence in connection with a transaction either before or after that transaction is discussed or consummated. Gifts, for any other purposes, should be limited to those of nominal value." "Gifts of nominal value," the code continues, "generally should be limited to standard advertising items displaying a supplier's logo." A maximum value of twenty-five dollars is suggested as a guideline.

Direct Competition

For an employee to engage in direct competition with his or her employer is a conflict of interest. One reason, of course, is that an employee's judgment is apt to be impaired by having another interest. In addition, the quality of the employee's work might be reduced by the time and effort devoted to other activities. Unlike other kinds of outside business interests, however, direct competition is generally prohibited by companies even when it is disclosed and there is no danger of impaired judgment or diminished work performance. Consider this case, which is taken from a policy statement issued by the Xerox Corporation:

> The wife of a Xerox tech rep inherits money. They decide it would be profitable to open a copy shop with her money and in her name in a suburban city. The territory they choose is different from his. However, there are several other copy shops and an XRC [Xerox Resource Center] in the vicinity. She leases equipment and supplies from Xerox on standard terms. After working hours, he helps his wife reduce costs by maintaining her equipment himself without pay. He also helps out occasionally on weekends. His job performance at Xerox remains as satisfactory as before. One of the nearby competitive shops, also a lessee of Xerox equipment, writes to his manager complaining that the employee's wife is getting free Xerox service and assistance.

The conflict of interest in this case consists mainly in the fact that the employee's investment and work outside of his employment at Xerox place him in direct competition with the company. The territory is different from his own, and so he would never have to make decisions on the job that could be influenced by his wife's business. And the outside interest has no effect on the quality of his work for Xerox. Still, on the assumption that the husband benefits from his wife's business venture, he is competing directly with his employer, since Xerox operates an XRC in the area.

In addition, by maintaining the equipment in his wife's shop himself, the employee harms the company by depriving it of the potential for additional business. It would be a conflict of interest for the tech rep to do service for any copy shop using equipment of any make, as long as he is employed by Xerox. His skill as a technician, which is in part the result of company training, belongs in a sense to the company, and he would be free to exercise these skills only upon leaving the employment of Xerox. And finally, the employee is indirectly harming the interests of Xerox by upsetting the relations between the company and other lessees of Xerox equipment.

Misuse of Position

Misuse of position constitutes a third kind of conflict of interest. One of the charges against R. Foster Winans was that he misused his position as a *Wall Street Journal* reporter to enrich himself, in violation of a provision in the newspaper's code of ethics that reads as follows:

It is not enough to be incorruptible and act with honest motives. It is equally important to use good judgment and conduct one's outside activities so that no one—management, our editors, an SEC investigator with power of subpoena, or a political critic of the company—has any grounds for even raising the suspicion that an employee misused a position with the company.[25]

Or consider the hypothetical case of a bank manager who, in the course of arranging home improvement loans, makes it a point to ask customers whether they have lined up a contractor. She casually drops the name of her brother who operates a general contracting business and mentions that a number of bank customers have been very satisfied with the work of his company.

The bank manager's mention of her brother is clearly improper if she misuses her power to grant or deny a loan to induce customers to use him as a contractor. A conflict of interest is still present, though, even if she does not allow her personal interest to have any effect on the decisions she makes on behalf of her employer. There is no conflict between the interests of the manager and those of the bank, and the bank is not harmed in any significant way. Still, the manager has taken the opportunity to advance her personal interests while acting in her capacity as an official of the bank. Holding a position with a company or other organization gives a person powers and opportunities that would not be available otherwise, and an employee has an obligation not to use these powers and opportunities for personal gain.

Extortion also constitutes a misuse of position. Unlike bribery, with which it is often confused, extortion does not involve the use of a payment of some kind to influence the judgment of an employee. Rather, extortion in a business setting occurs when a person with decision-making power for a company demands a payment from another party as a condition for making a decision favorable to that party. For example, a purchasing agent who threatens a supplier with a loss of business unless the supplier agrees to give a kickback to the purchasing agent is engaging in extortion. Extorting money from a supplier in this way is a conflict of interest, even if the company is not directly harmed, since the purchasing agent is violating an obligation to act in the position solely for the interests of the employer.

Violation of Confidentiality

Finally, violating confidentiality constitutes, under certain circumstances, a conflict of interest. The duty of lawyers, accountants, and other professionals, for example, precludes the use of information acquired in confidence from a client to advance personal interests—even if the interests of the client are unaffected. Similarly, because a director of a company is privy to much information, it would be wrong to use it for personal gain or other business interests.

The case of R. Foster Winans also illustrates a conflict of interest involving a breach of confidentiality. A reporter with information prior to publication who attempts to capitalize on the expected results is using that information for his or her own personal gain. Specifically, the courts found Mr. Winans guilty of *misappropriat-*

ing confidential information that properly belonged to his employer. In the Supreme Court decision affirming the conviction of Mr. Winans, Justice Byron White observed:

> Confidential business information has long been recognized as property. "Confidential information acquired or compiled by a corporation in the course and conduct of its business is a species of property to which the corporation has the exclusive right and benefit. . . ."[26]

Justice White further noted:

> The District Court found, and the Court of Appeals agreed, that Winans had knowingly breached a duty of confidentiality by misappropriating prepublication information regarding the timing and the contents of the "Heard" columns, information that had been gained in the course of his employment under the understanding that it would not be revealed in advance of publication and that, if it were, he would report it to his employer.

THE ETHICS OF INSIDER TRADING

Although the conduct of R. Foster Winans illustrates several different kinds of conflict of interest, he was prosecuted by the SEC for *insider trading*. In violating the conflict-of-interest provisions of his employer's code of ethics, the main victim was the *Wall Street Journal* itself. Insider trading, by contrast, is commonly viewed as a crime against other investors and the public at large. What constitutes insider trading, however, and why it ought to be illegal are the subjects of much dispute. Many financial markets have fewer restrictions on insider trading, and some economists argue that our laws prohibiting insider trading ought to be relaxed. What, then, is really wrong with insider trading?

The Definition of Insider Trading

Insider trading is commonly defined as trading in the stock of publicly held corporations on the basis of material, nonpublic information. In a landmark 1968 decision, executives of Texas Gulf Sulphur Company were found guilty of insider trading for investing heavily in their own company's stock after learning of the discovery of rich copper ore deposits in Canada.[27] The principle established in the *Texas Gulf Sulphur* case is that corporate insiders must refrain from trading on information that significantly affects stock price until it becomes public knowledge. The rule for corporate insiders is: Reveal or refrain!

Much of the uncertainty in the law on insider trading revolves around the relation of the trader to the source of the information. Corporate executives are definitely "insiders," but some "outsiders" have also been charged with insider trading. Among such outsiders have been a printer who was able to identify the targets of several takeovers from legal documents that were being prepared; a financial analyst who uncovered a huge fraud at a high-flying firm and advised his clients to sell;

a stockbroker who was tipped off by a client who was the nephew by marriage of the president of company and who learned about the sale of the business through a chain of family gossip; and a psychiatrist who was treating the wife of a financier who was attempting to take over a major bank.[28] The first two traders were eventually found innocent of insider trading; the latter two were found guilty (although the stockbroker case was later reversed in part). From these cases a legal definition of insider trading is slowly emerging.

The key points are that a person who trades on material, nonpublic information is engaging in insider trading when: (1) the trader has violated some legal duty to a corporation and its shareholders; or (2) the source of the information has such a legal duty and the trader knows that the source is violating that duty. Thus, the printer and the stock analyst had no relation to the corporations in question and so had no duty to refrain from using the information that they had acquired. The stockbroker and the psychiatrist, however, knew or should have known that they were obtaining inside information indirectly from high-level executives who had a duty to keep the information confidential. The corresponding rule for outsiders is: Don't trade on information that is revealed in violation of a trust. Both rules are imprecise, however, and leave many cases unresolved.

The Arguments against Insider Trading

The difficulty of defining insider trading is due to disagreement over the moral wrong involved. Two main rationales are used in support of a law against insider trading. One is based on *property rights* and holds that those who trade on material, nonpublic information are essentially stealing property that belongs to the corporation. The second rationale is based on *fairness* and holds that traders who use inside information have an unfair advantage over other investors and that, as a result, the stock market is not a level playing field. These two rationales lead to different definitions, one narrow, the other broad. On the property rights or "misappropriation" theory, only corporate insiders or outsiders who bribe, steal, or otherwise wrongfully acquire corporate secrets can be guilty of insider trading. The fairness argument is broader and applies to anyone who trades on material, nonpublic information no matter how it is acquired.

Inside Information as Property

One difficulty in using the property rights or misappropriation argument is determining who owns the information in question. The main basis for recognizing a property right in trade secrets and confidential business information is the investment that companies make in acquiring information and the competitive value that some information has. Not all insider information fits this description, however. Advance knowledge of better-than-expected earnings would be an example. The information still has value in stock trading, even if the corporation does not use it for that purpose; and so it might be held that any information that an employee gains in the course of employment belongs to the employer. This position is too broad, though, since an employee is unlikely to be accused of stealing company property by using knowledge of the next day's earning report for any purpose other than stock trading.

A second difficulty with the property rights argument is that if companies own certain information, then they could give their own employees permission to use it, or they could sell the information to favored investors or even trade on it themselves to buy back stock. Giving employees permission to trade on insider information could be an inexpensive form of extra compensation that further encourages employees to develop valuable information for the firm. Such an arrangement would also have some drawbacks; for example, investors might be less willing to buy the stock of a company that allowed insider trading because of the disadvantage to outsiders. What is morally objectionable about insider trading, according to its critics, though, is not the misappropriation of a company's information but the harm done to the investing public. So the violation of property rights in insider trading cannot be the sole reason for prohibiting it. Let us turn, then, to the second argument against insider trading, namely the argument from fairness.

The Fairness Argument

Fairness in the stock market does not require that all traders have the same information. Indeed, trades will take place only if the buyers and sellers of a stock have different information that leads them to different conclusions about the stock's worth. It is only fair, moreover, that a shrewd investor who has spent great time and money studying the prospects of a company should be able to exploit that advantage. Otherwise there would be no incentive to seek out new information. What is objectionable about using inside information is that other traders are barred from obtaining it no matter how diligent they may be. The information is unavailable not for lack of effort but for lack of access. Poker also pits card players with unequal skill and knowledge without being unfair, but a game played with a marked deck gives some players an unfair advantage over others. By analogy, then, insider trading is like playing poker with a marked deck.

The analogy may be flawed, however. Perhaps a more appropriate analogy is the seller of a home who fails to reveal hidden structural damage. One principle of stock market regulation is that both buyers and sellers of stock should have sufficient information to make rational choices. Thus, companies must publish annual reports and disclose important developments in a timely manner. A CEO who hides bad news from the investing public, for example, can be sued for fraud. Good news, such as an oil find, need not be announced until a company has time to buy the drilling rights, and so on; but to trade on that information before it is public knowledge might also be described as a kind of fraud.

Insider trading is generally prosecuted under SEC Rule 10b-5, which merely prohibits fraud in securities transactions. In fraudulent transactions, one party, such as the buyer of the house with structural damage, is wrongfully harmed for lack of knowledge that the other party concealed. So too—according to the fairness argument—are the ignorant parties to insider-trading transactions wrongfully harmed.

The main weakness of the fairness argument is determining what information ought to be revealed in a transaction. The reason for requiring a homeowner to disclose hidden structural damage is that doing so makes for a more efficient housing market. In the absence of such a requirement, potential home buyers would pay less because they are not sure what they are getting, or they would invest in costly home inspections. Similarly—the argument goes—requiring insiders to reveal before trading makes the stock market more efficient.

The trouble with such a claim, some economists argue, is that the stock market would be more efficient *without* a law against insider trading.[29] If insider trading were permitted, they claim, information would be registered in the market more quickly and at less cost than the alternative of leaving the task to research by stock analysts. The main beneficiaries of a law against insider trading, critics continue, are not individual investors but market professionals who can pick up news "on the street" and act on it quickly. Some economists argue further that a law against insider trading preserves the illusion that there is a level playing field and that individual investors have a chance against market professionals.

Economic arguments about market efficiency look only at the cost of registering information in the market and not at possible adverse consequences of legalized insider trading, which are many. Among such consequences is the effect on the treatment of information in a firm. Employees whose interest is in information that they can use in the stock market may be less concerned with information that is useful to the employer; and the company itself might attempt to tailor its release of information for maximum benefit to insiders. More importantly, the opportunity to engage in insider trading might undermine the relation of trust that is essential for business organizations.[30] A prohibition on insider trading frees employers of a corporation to do what they are supposed to be doing—namely, working for the interests of the shareholders—not seeking ways to advance their own interests.

The debate over the ethics of insider trading is not easily settled. Whether insider trading is unethical and ought to be illegal turns on many of the moral considerations at issue in conflict of interest, but the integrity of our financial markets and the moral fabric of business are also at stake.

Conclusion

Like whistle-blowing, trade secrets and conflict of interest involve a delicate balancing of the rights and interests of employers and employees, as well as the public at large. Especially in the case of trade secret protection, we see how different kinds of arguments—for property rights, fair competition, and a duty of confidentiality—underlie the law in this area and support our views about what is morally right. For the most part, the language of rights and the obligations of agents have dominated our discussion, although utilitarian considerations about the harm and benefit of protecting trade secrets have been introduced. In the next chapter we examine another right, namely, the right of employees to privacy in the workplace, in which strongly utilitarian and Kantian arguments are used to explain the concept of employee privacy and provide a foundation for it. Unlike trade secrets and conflict of interest, privacy is an area where the law has yet to develop very far, and so we can focus mainly on ethical issues.

CASE 6.2   Three Trade Secret Disputes

Spies in the Sky

Taking aerial photographs of a competitor's plant under construction is illegal according to a landmark U.S. Supreme Court decision.[31] The victim in this case, Du Pont, took every precaution in the construction of a new plant to keep the layout of the facility away from prying eyes in order to protect their secret, unpatented process for manufacturing methanol. But a competitor hired a photographer to take aerial photographs of the plant before the roof of the building was in place. When the photographer refused to reveal the name of the client, Du Pont sued— and won. However, a competitor intelligence firm, Research Source, Inc., of Newark, Delaware, provides clients with aerial photographs that are publicly available from government sources, such as the U.S. Geological Survey.[32] Small portions of these photographs can be blown up to show revealing details of companies' manufacturing facilities. This service is apparently legal. The difference seems to be this: It is wrong to gain the information for oneself by using intrusive means, but once the same information enters the public domain there is no prohibition against its use. Does this make sense?

Mouldings, Inc.

Mouldings, Inc., was the brainchild of a mother-daughter team with a taste for molded desserts.[33] When friends and neighbors in Salt Lake City, Utah, showed enthusiasm for their idea of chocolate and gelatin desserts in the shape of teddy bears, the two entrepreneurs, Dee and Tammy McBride, launched a line of plastic molds that eventually included other animals and seasonal symbols, such as Christmas trees and Halloween pumpkins. The most popular filling for the molds, they discovered, was a dessert made from Kellogg's Rice Krispies, and so they proposed a joint promotion to the giant cereal company. When Kellogg expressed an interest, the two women sent some sample molds and a price list. They heard nothing more until a letter arrived informing them that a contract had been awarded to another manufacturer. A few months later, the side panels of Kellogg's Rice Krispies boxes offered five molds called "Shapesters," with holiday motifs for molding Rice Krispies Treats. Mouldings, Inc., sued, charging not only that Kellogg had stolen their idea but that the promotion caused them to lose more than $50,000 by confusing their customers, who assumed that Kellogg was offering the McBrides' product at a discount. Kellogg countersued on the grounds that Mouldings, Inc., had infringed on the Rice Krispies trademark in recipes that were distributed to the customers of their molds.

Spaghetti Wars

When Hunt-Wesson Foods, Inc., decided to introduce a prepared spaghetti sauce, the company recognized the need for a unique product if they were to make a dent in the 65 percent market share held by Ragu, Inc.[34] Extensive marketing research revealed an unmet consumer demand for a thicker sauce, which Hunt-Wesson food technicians were able to achieve by experimenting with a longer cooking process. Marketing research also confirmed the effectiveness of the slogan "Extra Thick and Zesty," which Hunt-Wesson finally adopted. Just before the launch of a national campaign, Ragu introduced its own new product, "Ragu Extra Thick and Zesty" spaghetti sauce. The sauce did not employ any new cooking process but was thickened with starches, a fact that was not clearly disclosed on the label. Ragu also used a similar image of a sauce being ladled over a steaming plate of spaghetti. Hunt-Wesson sued Ragu for confusing consumers by appropriating the results of the company's own marketing research. Ragu claims that the idea of a thicker sauce and the slogan "Extra Thick and Zesty" are not original enough to prevent their use by a competitor and that the introduction of a new sauce to keep market share is simply good business strategy.

CASE 6.3   The Conflict of an Insurance Broker

I work for an insurance brokerage firm, Ashton & Ashton (A&A), which is hired by clients to obtain the best insurance coverage for their needs.[35] To do this, we evaluate a client's situation, keep informed about insurance providers, negotiate on the client's behalf, and present a proposal to the client for approval. Our compensation comes primarily from a commission that is paid by the client as part of the premium. The commission is a percentage of the premium amount, and the industry average for commissions is between 10 and 15 percent. A secondary source of compensation is a contingency payment that is made annually by insurance providers; the amount of this payment is based on the volume of business during the past year.

One of our clients, a world-class museum in a major American city, has been served for years by Haverford Insurance Company. Haverford is a financially sound insurer that has provided the museum with reliable coverage at reasonable prices and has gone out of its way on many occasions to be accommodating. Haverford has also built good relations with A&A by allowing a 17 percent commission—a fact that is not generally known by the clients. When the museum's liability insurance policy was up for renewal, A&A was asked to obtain competitive proposals from likely insurers. We obtained quotations from four comparable insurance companies with annual premiums that ranged between $90,000 and $110,000. A fifth, unsolicited proposal was sent by a small, financially shaky insurance company named Reliable. The annual premium quoted by Reliable was $60,000.

There is no question but that the museum is best served by continuing with Haverford, and our responsibility as an insurance broker is to place clients with financially sound insurers who will be able to honor all claims. The museum has a very tight operating budget, however, and funding from public and private sources is always unpredictable. As a result, the museum is forced to be extremely frugal in its spending and has always chosen the lowest bid for any service without regard for quality. The dilemma I faced, then, was: Do I present the Reliable bid to the museum? If I do, they will almost certainly accept it given their priority of saving money. Since the market indicates that the value of the needed policy is around $100,000, the Reliable proposal is definitely an attempt to "low-ball" the competition, and the company would probably raise the premium in future years. Is this honest competition? And if not, should A&A go along with it? Allowing a client to accept a low-ball bid might also jeopardize our relations with the reputable insurers who submitted honest proposals in good faith. If relations with Reliable are not successful, the museum is apt to blame us for not doing our job, which is not merely to pass along proposals but to evaluate them for suitability.

On the other hand, A&A will receive a higher commission and a larger contingency payment at the end of the year if the museum is presented with only the four solicited proposals and never learns of the Reliable bid. Because of our financial stake in the outcome, however, do we face a conflict of interest? Could we be accused of choosing a course of action that benefits us, even though in reality the client is also better served?

NOTES

1. CLEVELAND HORTON, "Ethics at Issue in Lotus Case," *Advertising Age*, 21 December 1987, 6.
2. These are essentially the facts in the classic case *Peabody* v. *Norfolk*, 98 Mass. 452 (1868).
3. *Wexler* v. *Greenberg*, 160 A. 2d 430 (1960).
4. For a discussion of the Lockean view as well as the utilitarian argument discussed below, see EDWIN C. HETTINGER, "Justifying Intellectual Property," *Philosophy and Public Affairs*, 18 (1989), 36–51.
5. This point is made by ROBERT E. FREDERICK and MILTON SNOEYENBOS, "Trade Secrets, Patents, and Morality," in *Business Ethics* (Buffalo: Prometheus Books, 1983), 165–66.
6. For a discussion of the ethical issues, see MARK MICHAEL, "Patent Rights and Better Mousetraps," *Business and Professional Ethics Journal*, 3 (1983), 13–23.
7. For a summary of the law in other countries, see STANLEY H. LIEBERSTEIN, *Who Owns What Is in Your Head?* (New York: Hawthorn Books, 1979), 225–32.
8. *International News Service* v. *Associated Press*, 248 U.S. 215 (1918).
9. See KEVIN MCMANUS, "Who Owns Your Brain?" *Forbes*, 6 June 1983, 178.
10. See HARLAN M. BLAKE, "Employee Covenants Not to Compete," *Harvard Law Review*, 73 (1960), 625–91.
11. *Dunn* v. *Frank Miller Associates, Inc.*, 237 Ga. 266 (1976). The case is cited by LIEBERSTEIN, *Who Owns What Is In Your Head?* 50–51.
12. All employees are regarded in law as agents, at least while acting within the scope of their assigned responsibilities, but their specific obligations, including those with respect to confidentiality, are determined by the amount of trust placed in them and any understandings, such as company policies or professional ethics.
13. MICHAEL S. BARAM, "Trade Secrets: What Price Loyalty?" *Harvard Business Review*, 46 (November–December 1968), 66–74.
14. LYNN SHARP PAINE, "Corporate Policy and the Ethics of Competitor Intelligence Gathering," *Journal of Business Ethics*, 10 (1991), 423–36.
15. Much of the material in this paragraph and the one following is contained in STEVEN FLAX, "How to Snoop on Your Competitors," *Fortune*, 14 May 1984, 28–33.

16. *Abuse on Wall Street: Conflicts of Interest in the Securities Markets* (Westport, CT: Quorum Books, 1980), 4.

17. Norman E. Bowie has also characterized a conflict of interest as the presence of conflicting legitimate interests with the further stipulation that only one of the interests can be fulfilled as opposed to "competing interests," which permit the balancing and partial satisfaction of different interests. NORMAN E. BOWIE, *Business Ethics* (Englewood Cliffs, NJ: Prentice Hall, 1982), 103. BOWIE continues to hold this view in a more recent paper, "Accountants, Full Disclosure, and Conflicts of Interest," *Business and Professional Ethics Journal*, 5, nos. 3–4, 59–73.

18. *Abuse on Wall Street*, 5.

19. *Second Restatement of Agency*, Sec. 385. Emphasis added.

20. This distinction is made in THOMAS M. GARRETT and RICHARD J. KLONOSKY, *Business Ethics*, 2nd ed. (Englewood Cliffs, NJ: Prentice Hall, 1986), 55; and in MANUAL G. VELASQUEZ, *Business Ethics: Concepts and Cases*, 3rd ed. (Englewood Cliffs, NJ: Prentice Hall, 1992), 377–78.

21. MICHAEL DAVIS, in "Conflict of Interest," *Business and Professional Ethics Journal*, 1 (1982), 17–27, makes a threefold distinction between actual, latent, and potential conflicts of interest. Latent conflict of interest involves conflict situations that can reasonably be foreseen, whereas potential conflict of interest involves conflict situations that cannot reasonably be foreseen.

22. The rule reads: "A lawyer shall not represent a client if the representation of that client will be directly adverse to another client unless: (1) the lawyer reasonably believes the representation will not adversely affect the relationship with the other client; and (2) each client consents after consultation."

23. See ABRAHAM J. BRILOFF, "Do Management Services Endanger Independence and Objectivity?" *CPA Journal*, 57 (August 1987), 22–29.

24. National Society of Professional Engineers, *Code of Ethics for Engineers*, 1987, III, 2(b).

25. "Media Policies Vary on Preventing Employees and Others from Profiting on Knowledge of Future Business Stories," *Wall Street Journal*, 2 March 1984, A12.

26. *Carpenter et al. v. U.S.*, 484 U.S. 19 (1987).

27. *SEC v. Texas Gulf Sulphur*, 401 F. 2d 833 (2d Cir. 1968).

28. *Chiarella v. U.S.*, 445 U.S. 222 (1980); *Dirks v. SEC*, 463 U.S. 646 (1983); *U.S. v. Chestman*, 903 F. 2d 75 (1990), 947 F. 2d 551 (1991); *U.S. v. Willis*, 737 F. Supp. 269 (1990).

29. HENRY MANNE, *Insider Trading and the Stock Market* (New York: Free Press, 1966).

30. This point is argued in JENNIFER MOORE, "What Is Really Unethical about Insider Trading?" *Journal of Business Ethics*, 9 (1990), 171–82.

31. *E.I. du Pont de Nemours & Co. v. Christopher*, 431 F. 2nd 1012 (5th Cir. 1970).

32. EDWARD PARKER, "Learn from the Masters of Competitive Intelligence: The Fighters," *Success*, 41 (April 1994), 37–38.

33. Material for this case is taken from NIKHIL DEOGUN, "Small Firms Sue, Charging Theft of Ideas," *Wall Street Journal*, 25 August 1993, B1.

34. *Hunt-Wesson Foods, Inc. v. Ragu Foods, Inc.*, 627 F. 2d 919 (9th Cir. 1980).

35. This case is based on actual events, but the names of the companies have been disguised. The case was prepared by Michael Streett under the supervision of Professor John R. Boatright. Copyright 1995 by John R. Boatright.

7

Privacy in the Workplace

CASE 7.1   Ford Meter Box

In 1989, the Ford Meter Box Company adopted a policy of hiring only nonsmokers. Smoking had already been banned on the job by the Wabash, Indiana, manufacturer, but employees hired prior to the date of the policy's adoption were permitted to continue smoking away from the plant on their own time. However, newly hired employees were told that they could not smoke at all—anyplace, anytime. Janice Bone, a part-time clerk and a smoker, refrained from smoking at work and was unaffected by the new hiring policy . . . until she applied for a vacant full-time position. The job change would make her a "new hire," subject to the policy. To get the job she would have to give up smoking entirely. Janice Bone agreed to quit and got the job, but a drug test routinely administered to all new employees after six weeks of service, revealed the presence of nicotine. Subsequently, Ford Meter Box terminated her employment.

Ford Meter Box is not alone in adopting a policy to hire only nonsmokers. An estimated 20 percent of employers give some preference to nonsmoking applicants,[1] and many provide some inducements for employees to stop smoking or impose penalties on those who continue to smoke. Turner Broadcasting is perhaps the best-known company that refuses to hire smokers, although previously hired smokers are permitted to smoke at work in designated areas. Employers' interest in their employees' smoking habits stem largely from the extra cost that smoking imposes. A study by Texas Instruments, Inc., found that the cost of a smoker's health care was 50 percent greater than that of a nonsmoker,[2] and a study by Du Pont in the late

161

1980s showed that smokers cost the company an additional $960 each in medical bills and days lost from work. Instead of forbidding employees to smoke, however, Texas Instruments charges employees an extra $10 a month in their health insurance premiums for each family member, including the employee, who smokes.

Critics of smoking bans and extra charges worry that employers will soon turn their attention to other unhealthy lifestyles and attempt to regulate employees' weight or alcohol consumption and dangerous hobbies, such as mountain climbing or bungee jumping. Employers' options are being limited, however, by state laws that protect employees in their pursuit of legal, off-duty activities. The new laws have been promoted by an unusual alliance between the tobacco industry lobby and the American Civil Liberties Union, each of which claims to be protecting employees' privacy and "right to choose."

INTRODUCTION

Early in the century, the Ford Motor Company set up a "Sociological Department" in order to make sure that workers, in Henry Ford's words, were leading "clean, sober, and industrious" lives.[3] Company inspectors checked bank accounts to keep Ford employees from squandering their munificent five-dollars-a-day wages. They visited employees' living quarters to see that they were neat and healthful, and they interviewed wives and acquaintances about the handling of finances, church attendance, daily diet, drinking habits, and a host of other matters. Workers who failed to live up to Henry Ford's standards of personal conduct were dismissed.

Employers today would scarcely dare to intrude so openly into the private lives of their employees, but they possess less obvious means for acquiring the information sought by Ford's teams of snooping inspectors—and some information that Henry Ford could not have imagined! Among the tools available to present-day employers are quick and inexpensive drug tests, polygraph machines and pencil-and-paper tests for assessing honesty and other personality traits of employees, extensive computer networks for storing and retrieving information about employees, and sophisticated telecommunication systems and concealed cameras and microphones for supervising employees' work activities. In addition, employers can now do genetic testing to screen employees for genes that make them more vulnerable to chemicals in the workplace.

Although privacy is a cherished value, we recognize that we must give some personal information to others. We volunteer a great many details of our lives to employers, and businesses know a great deal about us as consumers. Still, there are limits beyond which business, government, and others are not entitled to go.

One way of protecting workers from abuses of corporate power is by recognizing an employee's right to privacy. Concern about employee privacy is a relatively recent occurrence. However, a 1979 public-opinion survey conducted by Louis Harris for the Sentry Insurance Company revealed that three out of four respondents believe that privacy should be regarded as a fundamental right akin to life, liberty, and the pursuit of happiness and that half of them fear that American corporations do not adequately safeguard the personal information they gather on individuals.[4] More than 90 percent of those who responded said that they favored safeguards to prevent the disclosure of personnel and medical files to outsiders. A law granting employees access to the information collected about them was favored by 70 percent, and 62 percent wanted Congress to pass a law regulating the kind of information that corporations may collect about individuals.

Reasons for Concern about Employee Privacy

Privacy has become a major issue in government and business in recent years for many reasons. One is simply the vast amount of personal information that is collected by government agencies. The need to protect this information became especially acute after the passage of the Freedom of Information Act (FOIA) in 1966. Intended by Congress to make government more accountable for its actions, the act had the unforeseen consequence of compromising the confidentiality of information about private individuals. The Privacy Act of 1974 was designed in large part to resolve the conflict between government accountability and individual privacy. So great were the problems that Congress created the Privacy Protection Study Commission to investigate and make recommendations about further action. The National Labor Relations Board has long faced a similar problem with union demands for access to personnel files and other employee records. Unions claim that they need the information in order to engage in fair collective bargaining, but allowing unions to have unlimited access to this information without consent violates the employees' right of privacy.[5]

Government is not the only collector of information. Great amounts of data are required by corporations for the hiring and placement of workers, for the evaluation of their performance, and for the administration of fringe benefit packages, including health insurance and pensions. Private employers also need to compile personal information about race, sex, age, and handicap status in order to document compliance with the law on discrimination, and the law on workers' compensation and occupational health and safety requires employers to maintain extensive medical records. Alan F. Westin, an expert on privacy issues, observes that greater concern with employee rights in matters of discrimination and occupational health and safety has had the ironic effect of creating greater dangers to employees' right of privacy.[6]

Monitoring the work of employees is an essential part of the supervisory role of management, and new technologies enable employers to watch more closely than ever before, especially when the work is done on telephones or computer terminals. Supervisors can eavesdrop on the telephone conversations of employees, for example, and call up on their own screens the input and output as it appears on the terminals of the operators.[7] Hidden cameras and microphones can also be used to observe workers without their knowledge. A computer record can be made of the number of telephone calls, their duration, and their destination. And the number of keystrokes made by a data processor, the number of errors and corrections made, and the amount of time spent away from the desk can also be recorded for use by management. Even the activities of truck drivers can be monitored by a small computerized device attached to a vehicle that registers speed, shifting, and the time spent idling or stopped.

Companies claim that they are forced to increase the monitoring of employees with these new technologies as a result of the changing nature of work. More complex and dangerous manufacturing processes require a greater degree of oversight by employers. And the electronic systems for executing financial transactions and transferring funds used by banks and securities firms have a great potential for misuse and costly errors. In addition, employers are increasingly concerned about the use of drugs by workers and the high cost of employee theft, including the stealing of trade secrets. Employers also claim to be acting on a moral and a legal obligation to provide a safe workplace in which employees are free from the risk of being injured by drug-impaired co-workers.[8]

Ethical questions about employee privacy are unavoidable, since obtaining and using personal information about employees and monitoring their work performance is essential for the conduct of business. But employees also have a legitimate interest in maintaining a private life that is free from unwarranted intrusion by employers and in preventing employers from using personal information against them. Finding the right balance between the rights of employers and employees in matters of privacy is not a simple task. A set of guidelines or a company code on privacy must address an immense number of different questions. Before we make the attempt to find a balance between these competing rights, though, it is necessary for us to inquire into the meaning of privacy as an ethical concept.

THE CONCEPT OF EMPLOYEE PRIVACY

A definition of privacy has proven to be very elusive. After two years of study, the members of the Privacy Protection Study Commission were still not able to agree on one. Much of the difficulty is due to the diverse nature of the many different situations in which claims of a right of privacy are made. Even the narrower concept of employee privacy is applied in such dissimilar circumstances that it is not easy to find a common thread running through them.

History of the Concept

As a legal concept, privacy dates only from the late nineteenth century. There is no mention of privacy in the original Constitution or the Bill of Rights. Although a number of rights related to privacy have long been recognized in American law, they have generally been expressed in terms of freedom of thought and expression, the right of private property, protection from "unreasonable searches and seizures," and other constitutional guarantees. The first sustained discussion of privacy occurred in an 1890 article in the *Harvard Law Review* written by two young attorneys, Samuel Warren and Louis Brandeis (who later became a famed Justice of the Supreme Court).[9]

The theory of privacy presented by Warren and Brandeis was slow to gain acceptance. It was rejected by the courts in a number of cases around the turn of the century in which the names and pictures of prominent persons were used to advertise products. The public uproar over one of these cases prompted the New York legislature to enact a law prohibiting the commercial use of a person's name or likeness without permission.[10] Gradually, most states followed the lead of New York in granting persons a right to be free of certain kinds of intrusion into their private life. But it was not until 1965 that the Supreme Court declared privacy to be a constitutionally protected right. The decision came in *Griswold* v. *Connecticut*, which concerned the right of married couples to be free of state interference in the use of contraceptives.[11]

Some philosophers and legal theorists have argued that the concept of privacy does not introduce any new rights into the law but merely expresses several traditional rights in a new way. Consequently, our legal system already contains the resources to protect individuals against these wrongs without creating a distinct right of privacy.[12] For example, disclosing embarassing facts about a person or intruding into their solitude might be described as inflicting mental distress; and the publication of false accusations could be said to constitute libel or defamation of character. What, these critics ask, does the concept of privacy add to other, better established rights?

The Warren and Brandeis Definition

The literature contains many attempts to elucidate privacy as an independent right that is not reducible to any other commonly recognized right. Three definitions in particular merit examination. One, which derives from Warren and Brandeis and finds expression in *Griswold* v. *Connecticut*, holds that privacy is the right to be left alone. Warren and Brandeis were concerned mainly with the publication of idle gossip in sensation-seeking newspapers. The aim of privacy laws, they thought, should be to protect "the privacy of private life" from unwanted publicity, and their proposals all deal with limits on the publication of information about the private lives of individuals. In his celebrated dissenting opinion in *Olmstead* v. *United States*, a 1928 case concerning the constitutionality of telephone wiretapping, Brandeis wrote that the right of privacy is "the right to be let alone—the most comprehensive of rights and the right most valued by civilized men."[13]

A similar view of privacy was expressed by the majority in *Griswold*. Laws governing the use of contraceptives intrude into an area of the lives of individuals where they have a right to be left alone. Justice William J. Brennan expressed the view in a subsequent birth control case that:

> If the right to privacy means anything, it is the right of the individual, married or single, to be free from unwarranted government invasion into matters so fundamentally affecting a person as the decision whether to bear or beget a child.[14]

Many critics have pointed out that the phrase "to be left alone" is overly broad.[15] Individuals have a right "to be left alone" in matters of religion and politics, for example, but legal restrictions on religious practices, such as snake handling, or on political activities, such as the making of political contributions, do not involve violations of privacy. At the same time, the Warren and Brandeis definition is too narrow, since some violations of privacy occur in situations where there is no right to be left alone. Workers have no right to be free of supervision, for example, even though it can be claimed that their privacy is invaded by the use of hidden cameras to monitor their activity secretly.

These objections, in the view of critics, are merely symptoms of a deeper source of error in the Warren and Brandeis definition, which is the confusion of privacy with liberty. These examples show that a loss of liberty is neither a necessary nor a sufficient condition for a loss of privacy. Perhaps greater clarity is achieved by limiting the concept of privacy to matters involving information and not stretching the concept to include all manner of intrusions into our private lives. This suggests that smoking policies like that of the Ford Meter Box Company are better analyzed as limitations of liberty rather than invasions of privacy.

Privacy as Control over Personal Information

This suggestion is reflected in a second definition in which privacy is expressed in terms of control over information about ourselves.[16] The following definition by Alan F. Westin is typical: "Privacy is the claim of individuals . . . to determine for themselves when, how, and to what extent information about them is communicated to others."[17] This definition is open to the same charge: that it is at once too broad and too narrow. Richard B. Parker observes, "Not every loss or gain of control over information about ourselves is a gain or loss of privacy."[18] Furthermore, all definitions of privacy as exercising control flounder on the fact that individuals can relinquish their own privacy by voluntarily divulging all sorts of intimate details themselves.[19] There is a loss of privacy under such circumstances but not a loss of control. Therefore, privacy cannot be identified with control.

A More Adequate Definition

A third, more adequate definition of privacy holds that a person is in a state of privacy when certain facts about that person are not known by others. W. A. Parent in an important 1983 article, "Privacy, Morality, and the Law," defines privacy as "the condition of not having undocumented personal knowledge about one possessed by others."[20] By the phrase "personal knowledge," Parent does not mean all information about ourselves but only those facts "which most individuals in a given society at any given time do not want widely known."[21] It is necessary that the definition be restricted to *undocumented* personal information, since some facts that individuals commonly seek to conceal are a matter of public record and can be known without prying into their private lives. A person does not suffer a loss of privacy, for example, when a conviction for a crime becomes known to others, since court records are public documents. Similarly, there is no loss of privacy when an easily observable fact, such as a person's baldness, is known to others, even though the person is sensitive about it and prefers that others not be aware of it.

In the remaining discussion, the concept of privacy is limited to matters involving information and, in particular, to the access of others to undocumented personal information, as described by Parent. The two other definitions—as a right to be left alone and to have control over information about ourselves—confuse privacy with other values. The Parent definition, we will discover, encompasses all the situations in which a threat to employee privacy is charged. Having gained some understanding of the concept of privacy, we can now turn to the question of why privacy is a value.

THE VALUE OF PRIVACY

Why do we value privacy so highly and hold that it ought to be protected as an employee right? Certainly, we desire to have a sphere of our life in which others do not possess certain information about us. But the mere fact that we have this desire does not entail that we have a right of privacy. Nor does it tell us how far a right of privacy extends. Some arguments are needed, therefore, to establish the value of privacy and the claim that we have a right to it.

Most of the arguments developed by philosophers and legal theorists fall into one of two categories. One category consists of utilitarian arguments that appeal to consequences, and the second is Kantian arguments that link privacy to being a person or having respect for persons. To a great extent, these two different kinds of arguments express a few key insights about privacy in slightly different ways.

Utilitarian Arguments

One of the consequences cited by utilitarians is that great harm is done to individuals when inaccurate or incomplete information collected by an employer is used as the basis for making important personnel decisions. The lives of many employees have been tragically disrupted by groundless accusations in their personnel record, for example, and the results of improperly administered polygraph and drug tests. Even factual information that ought not to be in an employee's file, such as the record of an arrest without a conviction, can cause needless harm. And the harm from these kinds of practices is more likely to occur and to be repeated when employees are unable to examine their files and challenge the information (or misinformation) in them.

A drawback to this argument is that it rests on an unproved assumption that could turn out to be false. It assumes that on balance more harm than good will result when employers amass files of personal information, use polygraph machines, conduct drug tests, and so on. Whatever harm is done to employees by invading their privacy has to be balanced, in a utilitarian calculation, against the undeniable benefits that these practices produce for both employers and employees.

Furthermore, the argument considers only the possible harmful consequences of privacy invasions. However, some practices, such as observing workers with hidden cameras and eavesdropping on business conducted over the telephone, are generally considered to be morally objectionable in themselves, regardless of their consequences. Honest workers, for example, have nothing to fear from surveillance that is designed to protect against employee theft, and indeed the use of hidden cameras in a warehouse can even benefit those who are honest by reducing the possibility of false accusations. Still, workers have a right to complain that secret surveillance of their activities on the job violates the right of privacy. It is the fact that they are subjected to constant observation and not the possible consequences of being observed that is morally objectionable.

This objection is avoided by more sophisticated utilitarian arguments that do not locate the harmful consequences solely in the harm that occurs when information is misused. According to these arguments, a certain amount of privacy is necessary for the enjoyment of some activities, so that invasions of privacy change the character of our experiences and deprive us of the opportunity for gaining pleasure from them. Monitoring and surveillance in the workplace, for example, affect job satisfaction and the sense of dignity and self-worth of all workers. They send a message to employees that they are not trusted and respected as human beings, and the predictable result is a feeling of resentment and a decline in the satisfaction of performing a job.

An illustration of this point is provided by a truck driver with forty years experience with the Safeway Company who reports that he used to love his job because "you were on your own—no one was looking over your shoulder. You felt like a human being." After the company installed a computerized monitoring device on his truck, he decided to take early retirement. He complains, "They push you around, spy on you. There's no trust, no respect anymore." And a directory-assistance operator reported, "I've worked all those years before monitoring. Why don't they trust me now? I will continue to be a good worker, but I won't do any more than necessary now."[22]

Some writers argue that privacy is of value because of the role it plays in developing and maintaining a healthy sense of personal identity. According to Alan F. Westin, privacy enables us to relax in public settings, release pent-up emotions, and reflect on our experiences as they occur—all of which are essential for our mental well-being. A lack of privacy can result in mental stress and even a nervous breakdown.[23] Another common argument appeals to the importance of privacy in promoting a high degree of individuality and freedom of action among the members of a society. Critics of these arguments object, however, that there is little evidence that privacy has the benefits claimed for it or that the predicted harm would follow from limiting people's privacy.[24] Many societies function very well with less room for solitude than our own, and the experiences of human beings in prisons and detention camps are cited by critics to refute these arguments.

Kantian Arguments

Two Kantian themes that figure prominently in defense of a right to privacy are those of autonomy and respect for persons. Stanley I. Benn, for example, notes that utilitarian arguments for a right of privacy are not able to show what is morally wrong when a person is secretly observed without any actual harm being done. "But respect for persons," Benn claims, "will sustain an objection even to secret watching, which may do no actual harm at all." He continues:

> Covert observation—spying—is objectionable because it deliberately deceives a person about his world, thwarting . . . his attempts to make a rational choice. One cannot be said to respect a man . . . if one knowingly and deliberately alters his conditions of action, concealing the fact from him.[25]

Benn's argument thus appeals to both Kantian themes by arguing that invading a person's privacy violates the principle of respect for persons *and* prevents a person from making a rational choice as an autonomous being.

Hyman Gross argues in a similar vein that what is morally objectionable about being observed unawares through a hidden camera or having personal information in a data bank is that a person loses control over how he or she appears to others.[26] If people form incomplete or misleading impressions of us that we have no opportunity to correct, then we are denied the possibility of autonomous or self-directed activity, which is a characteristic of human beings. Hence, invasions of privacy diminish an essential condition for being human.

In a very influential discussion, Charles Fried argues that privacy is of value because it provides a "rational context" for some of our most significant ends, such as love, friendship, trust, and respect, so that invasions of privacy destroy our very integrity as a person.[27] The reason that privacy is essential for respect, love, trust, and so on is that these are intimate relations, and intimacy is created by the sharing of personal information about ourselves that is not known by other people. In a society without privacy, we could not share information with other people (because they would already know it), and hence we could not establish intimate relations with them. Thus, monitoring, in Fried's view, "destroys the possibility of bestowing the gift of intimacy, and makes impossible the essential dimension of love and friendship."[28] Similarly, trust cannot exist where there is monitoring or surveillance, since trust is the expectation that others will behave in a certain way without the need to check up on them.

The arguments of Benn, Gross, Fried, and others seize upon important insights about the value of privacy, but many critics have found flaws in the details of their arguments. Jeffrey H. Reiman, for one, objects that it is too strong to assert that *all* instances of watching a person unawares result in deceiving a person and depriving that person of a free choice. Otherwise, we would be violating a person's right of privacy by observing him or her strolling down a street or riding a bus.[29] Intimate relations such as love and friendship do not consist solely in the sharing of information but involve, as one writer says, "the sharing of one's total self—one's experiences, aspirations, weaknesses, and values."[30] Consequently, these relations can exist and even flourish in the absence of an exclusive sharing of information.

A Third Kind of Argument

Several philosophers have suggested that the key to a more satisfactory theory of privacy can be constructed by understanding the way in which individuals are socialized in our culture.[31] Privacy, in the view of these philosophers, is neither a necessary means for realizing certain ends nor conceptually a part of these ends. Nevertheless, we are trained from early childhood to believe that certain things are shameful (for example, public nudity) and others strictly our own business (such as annual income). There is no intrinsic reason why our body or our financial affairs should be regarded as private matters. People at different times and places have been socialized differently with regard to what belongs to the sphere of the private, and might even be better off if we had been socialized differently. Still, we have been socialized in a certain way. And in our culture, certain beliefs about what ought to be private play an important role in the process by which a newborn child develops into a person and by which we continue to maintain a conception of ourselves as persons. In the words of Jeffrey H. Reiman:

> Privacy is an essential part of the complex social practice by means of which the social group recognizes—and communicates to the individual—that his existence is his own. And this is a precondition of personhood. To be a person, an individual must recognize not just his actual capacity to shape his destiny by his choices. He must also recognize that he has an exclusive moral right to shape his destiny. And this in turn presupposes that he believes that the concrete reality which he is, and through which his destiny is realized, belongs to him in a moral sense.[32]

This argument is broadly utilitarian. The consequences that it appeals to, however, are not the simple pleasures and pains of classical utilitarianism or even the notions of mental health and personal growth and fulfillment of more sophisticated utilitarian arguments. The argument goes deeper by appealing to the importance of privacy for personhood, which is a concept that is more commonly used by Kantian theorists. Unlike Kantian arguments, though, this one recognizes that privacy is not necessary for all people in all times and places but is merely a value specific to our late-twentieth-century Western culture. There are societies that function very well with less privacy than we are accustomed to; however, given the role privacy plays in our socialization process, a certain amount is needed for us to develop as persons and have a sense of dignity and well-being.

Both utilitarian and Kantian arguments point to a key insight: that privacy is important in some way to dignity and well-being. They claim too much, however; privacy is not absolutely essential to either one, except insofar as we have come to depend on it. For better or worse, privacy has become an important value in our culture, and now that it has, it needs to be maintained. Privacy is like the luxury that soon becomes a necessity, but "necessary luxuries" are not less valuable just because we could formerly get by without them. The justification of privacy just offered is thus the most adequate one we have.

JUSTIFYING A RIGHT OF EMPLOYEE PRIVACY

The arguments in the preceding section show that privacy is of sufficient value that it ought to be protected. There are many instances, however, in which other persons and organizations are fully justified in having personal information about us and thereby in intruding into our private lives. The task of justifying a right of employee privacy, then, consists not only in demonstrating the value of privacy but also in determining which intrusions into the private lives of employees are justified and which are not.[33]

A number of different issues must be addressed in developing the case for a right of privacy in employment—and in formulating a company privacy protection plan or a law on employee privacy. Among these are:

1. The kind of information that is collected.
2. The use to which the information is put.
3. The persons within a company who have access to the information.
4. The disclosure of the information to persons outside the company.
5. The means used to gain the information.
6. The steps taken to ensure the accuracy and completeness of the information.
7. The access that employees have to information about themselves.

The Purpose for Gathering Information

The first three issues are closely related, since the justification for an employer's possessing any particular kind of information depends, at least in part, on the purpose for which the information is gathered. Some information is simply of no conceivable use in company decision making and constitutes a gratuitous invasion of employee privacy. It is more often the case, however, that an employer has a need or interest that provides some justification for intruding into the private lives of employees. An invasion of employee privacy is justified, however, only when the information is used for the intended purpose by the individuals who are responsible for making the relevant decisions.

Companies are generally justified in maintaining medical records on employees in order to administer benefit plans, for example, and to monitor occupational health and safety. If these are the purposes for which a company gathers this kind of information, then it follows that: (1) only medical information that is essential for these purposes can be justifiably collected; (2) only those persons who are responsible for administering the benefit plans or monitoring the health and safety of employees are justified in having access to the information; and (3) these persons must use the information only for the intended purposes. There are three corresponding ways in which employees' right of privacy can be violated. These are when: (1) personal information is gathered without a sufficient justifying purpose; (2) it is known by persons who are not in a position that is related to the justifying purpose; and (3) persons who are in such a position use the information for other, illegitimate purposes.

Obviously, the notion of a justifying purpose plays a critical role in determining the exact scope of the right of privacy in employment. There is considerable room for disagreement on the questions of whether any given purpose is a legitimate one for a business firm to pursue, whether a certain kind of information is essential for the pursuit of a particular purpose, and whether the information is in fact being used for the intended purpose. Companies have an interest and, indeed, an obligation to ensure that employees are capable of performing physically demanding work and are not subjected to undue risk, for example. The purposes for which Henry Ford created the Sociological Department, however, went beyond this concern to include a paternalistic regard for the general welfare of his employees, which is not a legitimate purpose. Even to the extent that the work of the inspectors from the Ford Motor Company was justified by a legitimate purpose, there could still be an objection to the excessive amount of information they sought. Information about the handling of finances, church attendance, and eating and drinking habits is more than the company needs to know.

Determining the purpose for which information is being used can raise difficult questions about intentions. A controversy was sparked in 1980, for example, when it became publicly known that the Du Pont Company was routinely screening black applicants at a plant in New Jersey for signs of sickle cell anemia. The company asserted that the purpose for conducting the screening was to protect black workers, since carriers of the disease, who are mostly black, were thought to be more vulnerable to certain chemicals used at the plant. Such a purpose is arguably legitimate, but some critics of Du Pont charged that the company was actually using genetic screening for another purpose, namely to prevent liability suits and to avoid having to protect workers from dangerous chemicals.[34]

Resolving Disagreements about Purpose

Is there any way in which the notion of a justifying purpose can be clarified so that such disagreements can be resolved? One possibility is to specify the conditions necessary for a business to conduct normal operations. In order to do this, a company must be able to assess the suitability of applicants for employment, supervise their work-related behavior, administer fringe benefit plans, and so on. In addition, employers must be left free to acquire the information necessary for complying with legal requirements about taxes, social security, discrimination, health and safety, and the like. As a result, employers are justified in asking potential employees about their educational background, past employment, and so on, but not, for example, about their marital status, since this information is not necessary in order to make a decision about hiring. Once employees are hired, a company may have a need to inquire about marital status in order to determine eligibility for medical benefits, but only if the employee in question chooses to participate in a medical insurance plan.

And even then, this information should be used only for the purpose of determining eligibility for medical benefits.

Joseph R. DesJardins suggests that questions about the extent of the right of privacy in the workplace can be settled by appealing to a contract model of the employer-employee relation.[35] Viewing employment as a contractual relation between an employer and an employee provides a basis for granting a set of rights to both parties, since the validity of contracts requires that certain conditions be satisfied. Contracts are valid, first, only if they are free of force and fraud. As a result, an employer has a right to require applicants to provide enough information to make an informed decision about hiring and to submit to tests for measuring relevant aptitudes and skills. Once hired, employees have an obligation to permit employers to monitor work performance, for example, and to gather whatever information is necessary to maintain an ongoing contractual relation.

Second, valid contracts also require mutual voluntary consent, so a contract model of employment would not permit employers to collect information without the knowledge and permission of the employees affected. Covert searches, surveillance by hidden cameras, the use of private investigators, and so on would be incompatible with the view of employment as a contractual relation. Similarly, objections could be raised to employer demands that employees either submit to drug tests and interrogation with a polygraph machine or be dismissed, because an employee has little choice but to comply. Union contracts in which employees are able to exercise effective choice often contain provisions prohibiting such practices.

Disclosure to Outsiders

The fourth issue—concerning the disclosure of personal information to persons outside a company—arises because of the practice, once very common, of employers sharing the content of personnel files with landlords, lending agencies, subsequent employers, and other inquiring persons without the consent of the employees involved. Even when there is a legitimate purpose that would justify these various parties having the information, it can be argued that an employer has no right to provide it, since the employer is justified in collecting and using information only for purposes connected with the employer-employee relation. What is morally objectionable about an employer's disclosing personal information to an outside party, in other words, is not necessarily that the outside party is not justified in having it but that the employer has no justification for giving it to them.

Thus, medical records collected by a former employer ought not to be passed along to a subsequent employer without the employee's consent. The former employer presumably had a purpose that justified the gathering of that information, and the new employer might also have a similar purpose in gathering the same information. The justification in the case of the former employer, however, is related to *that* employment relation, and the information gathered can be justifiably used only for purposes connected with it. The subsequent employer, although perhaps justified in gathering the same information, must proceed in the same way as the former employer.

This argument points up an important difference between personal information and other kinds of corporate records. Databases of various kinds are generally regarded as resources that are *owned* by a company. Ownership, however, generally entails an exclusive and unrestricted right of access and control, which employers do not have with respect to personal information. A mailing list, for example, is a kind of property that a company can use in any way it pleases, with no restrictions. Medical records, by contrast, can be compiled by a company only for a specific purpose, and any use unrelated to this purpose is prohibited. The fact that employers bear a burden of proof for justifying the collection and use of personal information shows that the notion of ownership is inappropriate in this case.[36]

It is also not appropriate to describe the information in personnel files as belonging to employees either, since they relinquish some rights to it by virtue of entering into the employment relation. Neither an employer nor an employee, therefore, can be said to own the information in a company's personnel files. Such information is simply not property in the usual sense, unlike other kinds of data gathered by corporations. It is necessary, therefore, to develop a conceptual model for personal information other than that of ownership.

The Means Used to Gather Information

Justifying the means used to gather information, which is the fifth issue, involves a different set of considerations. Use of certain means may violate an employee's right of privacy, even when the information gathered is of a kind that an employer is fully justified in possessing. Examples of impermissible means are polygraph testing and pretext interviews. (Pretext interviews are inquiries made under false pretenses, as when an employer seeks information from an applicant's family while posing as a market researcher.) Even if employers are justified in asking certain questions on a job application, they are not, for that reason, justified in using a polygraph machine or a pretext interview to verify the accuracy of a person's responses.

A major consideration in evaluating the means used to gather information is whether less intrusive means are available. In general, less intrusive means are morally preferable to those that are more intrusive. Employers are justified in seeking information about drug use by employees in the workplace, for example, but such means as searches of lockers and desks, hidden cameras in restrooms, random drug tests, and the like are not justified when sufficient information could be gathered by less intrusive means, such as closer observation of work performance and testing only for cause. (Some means are not justified, of course, even if less intrusive means are not available. Hidden cameras and random drug tests are possible examples.)

What makes some means more intrusive than others depends on several factors. Such practices as conducting strip searches and watching while a urine sample is produced involve an affront to human dignity. An objection to constant monitoring, personality tests, and the use of polygraph machines is that they collect more information than is necessary and that they collect it indiscriminately.

Honesty tests, for example, often inquire into personal habits and interests, family relations, and sexual adjustment—matters that are extraneous to the ostensible purpose.[37] Improperly administered polygraph tests can easily become "fishing expeditions," which result in the revelation of information that an employer is not justified in having.

Another reason why some practices such as monitoring and surveillance by hidden cameras and polygraph testing are unusually intrusive is that they deprive persons of an opportunity to exercise control over how they appear to others, which is essential for being an autonomous individual. An employee who is unaware of being observed, for example, might be unwittingly led to reveal facts that he or she would otherwise keep from others. George J. Brenkert argues, very perceptively, that since a polygraph machine measures physical characteristics such as breathing rate, perspiration, and blood pressure over which we have little or no control, it "circumvents the person" and undercuts the "way by which we define ourselves as autonomous persons."[38] As a person, we can shape how we appear to others and create an identity for ourselves. A machine that registers our involuntary responses denies us the power to do that.

Accuracy, Completeness, and Access

The last two issues are concerned primarily with matters of fairness. If the information in personnel files and other corporate databases is going to be used to make critical decisions about wage increases, promotions, discipline, and even termination of employment, then it is only fair that the information be as accurate and complete as possible and that employees have access to their personnel files so that they can challenge the contents or at least seek to protect themselves from adverse treatment based on the information in them.

Employers who maintain inaccurate or incomplete files and deny employees access to them are not invading the privacy of their employees, as the concept of privacy is commonly defined. What is at issue is not the possession of personal information by an employer but its use in ways that are unfair to employees. The right that employers violate is a right of fair treatment, which is not the same as a right of privacy. Still, since these are issues involved in the handling of personal information, they must be considered in devising policies or laws dealing with employee privacy.

Another objection to drug tests and polygraph machines is their unreliability. A number of factors, including the use of prescription drugs and careless laboratory work, can result in false positives, especially in simpler, less expensive drug tests. Polygraph machines are inherently unreliable, since they register only bodily responses and not the mental experience that triggers them. An investigator might conclude that a subject is lying when the responses recorded by the machine are actually due to a different kind of association. One study, in which 14 polygraphers were asked to evaluate the charts of 207 criminal suspects, found that 50 percent of the experts thought that innocent suspects gave deceptive answers and 36 percent of them considered the guilty suspects to be telling the truth.[39] After a review of the studies to date, the U.S. Office of Technology Assessment concluded in 1983 that polygraph testing was useless for screening in preemployment contexts.[40]

Conclusion

In summary, determining the exact limits of the right of employees to privacy in the workplace requires that we address a number of issues. Questions about four of these issues—those concerning the kind of information collected, the use to which it is put, and the persons both inside and outside the company who have access to it—can be answered largely by appealing to the notion of a legitimate purpose. The issue of the means used to gain information involves different questions about whether some means are inherently objectionable and whether others are objectionable because less intrusive means are available. Finally, the remaining issues involve the fair treatment of employees, which is not, strictly speaking, part of a right of privacy but is still related to the handling of personal information.

CASE 7.2   Three Challenges to Employee Privacy

Dating at Wal-Mart[41]

The company's position is crystal-clear: "Wal-Mart strongly believes and supports the 'family unit'." For this reason, the handbook that all newly hired employees must read and sign stipulates, "A dating relation between a married associate with another associate, other than his or her own spouse, is not consistent with this belief and is prohibited." This policy was designed in part to maintain businesslike relations among employees and to avoid the turmoil that extramarital affairs can cause in the workplace. An added, and perhaps not unintended, benefit of the policy is to reinforce the wholesome, down-home image that Wal-Mart carefully fosters. The policy was challenged, however, when the manager of a Wal-Mart store in Johnstown, New York, discovered that two sales associates—one a twenty-year-old single man and the other a twenty-three-year old woman who was married but separated from her husband—were dating. The romantic tie between the two came to the manager's attention when the woman was served with custody papers at the store. The manager immediately fired them both. The woman could not remember reading the no-dating rule in the handbook but expressed her disagreement nonetheless. "I felt it was my personal life," she said.

Integrity by the Numbers

If only potential thieves, embezzlers, and otherwise dishonest workers could be identified in advance! This is the appeal of integrity tests, which are sold by a handful of publishers and administered to an estimated five million job applicants annually. Use of the pencil-and-paper tests has been spurred by the banning of mechanical polygraph testing in 1988 and by the reluctance of former employers to reveal any but the most basic information for fear of litigation. The tests inquire into the applicant's past behavior, responses to hypothetical situations, and attitudes that are thought to be associated with integrity. Among the intimate details explored are family background, health habits, sexual practices, religious beliefs, and emotional stability. The tests are commonly graded by the publisher and the results reported to the employer on a scale of risk from high to low. Employers are free to use the results in any way they wish. Some use them to exclude marginally qualified candidates who pose a high degree of risk; others exclude otherwise well-qualified candidates who fall below a certain score. Studies by the congressional Office of Technology Assessment and the American Psychological Association have found that some tests have moderate predictive value but that others are virtually worthless. One of the major publishers boasts of accuracy 85 percent of the time. Even so, large numbers of honest people are denied jobs and suffer a stigma because of faulty testing, and a few rogues slip through. Ironically, the highly honest may be among the most frequent victims since they are more forthcoming in their answers. Some critics have charged that no one can pass an integrity test without a little dishonesty. The use of integrity tests also assumes that people are honest or not and ignores the role of the work environment in promoting honesty—or dishonesty. Some employees steal when they believe that they are being cheated or abused, for example, and so employers bear some responsibility for the level of honesty. One benefit of integrity tests, therefore, may be to enable employers to recruit a work force that will tolerate shabby treatment without retaliating.

Is E-Mail Private?

A reporter in the Moscow bureau of the *Los Angeles Times* guessed the passwords of his colleagues and read their e-mail, thereby gaining an advantage in office politics. He was disciplined.[42] Two women who worked for Nissan, training dealers in the use of the company's e-mail system, were fired after their supervisor overrode the passwords and read exchanges with the dealers they were training. The messages contained some sexually suggestive banter along with comments by the women disparaging the supervisor's own sexual prowess.[43] Did the reporter or the supervisor do anything unethical? A letter sent to a colleague by U.S. mail would be considered private, as would (perhaps) a sealed envelope delivered through a company's own mail system. E-mail messages are accessible only with a password known to the user, so they are also like letters stored in a locked desk drawer. The desk may belong to the company but not the contents. On the other hand, e-mail messages are also like notes posted on a company-owned bulletin board, since the technology is provided to the employee. Employers claim a right to monitor employee's messages to ensure that the system is not being misused. Company computers have been used to arrange drug deals, to operate office betting pools, and to engage in racial and sexual harassment. Some privacy experts contend that employers have a right to read employees' e-mail if they announce the policy in advance; others believe that reading electronic messages is always wrong, even if employees are put on notice.

NOTES

1. "Company Policies Could Give Smokers Their Day in Court," *HRfocus*, 69 (August 1991), 1.

2. "If You Light Up on Sunday, Don't Come in on Monday," *Business Week*, 26 August 1991, 70.

3. For information on the Sociological Department, see ROBERT LACEY, *Ford: The Men and the Machine* (Boston: Little, Brown, 1986), 117–25.

4. See AL NOEL, "Privacy: A Sign of Our Times," *Personnel Administrator*, 26 (March 1981), 59–62.

5. For a discussion of this problem, see KARL J. DUFF and ERIC T. JOHNSON, "A Renewed Employee Right to Privacy," *Labor Law Journal*, 34 (1983), 747–62.

6. ALAN F. WESTIN, "The Problem of Privacy Still Troubles Management," *Fortune*, 4 June 1979, 120–26. See also JOYCE ASHER GILDEA, "Safety and Privacy: Are They Compatible?" *Personnel Administrator*, 27 (February 1982), 80–83.

7. These new technologies are described in GARY T. MARX and SANFORD SHERIZEN, "Monitoring on the Job: How to Protect Privacy as Well as Property," *Technology Review*, 89 (November–December 1986), 63–72. See also GARY T. MARX, "The New Surveillance," *Technology Review*, 88 (May–June 1985), 42–48.

8. See JOHN C. NORTH, "The Responsibility of Employers for the Actions of Their Employees: Negligent Hiring Theory of Liability," *Chicago-Kent Law Review*, 53 (1977), 717–30; and MARIAN M. EXTEJT and WILLIAM N. BOCKANIC, "Theories of Negligent Hiring and Failure to Fire," *Business and Professional Ethics Journal*, 8 (Winter 1989), 21–34.

9. SAMUEL WARREN and LOUIS D. BRANDEIS, "The Right to Privacy," *Harvard Law Review*, 4 (1890), 193–220. Two earlier discussions are in JAMES FITZJAMES STEPHEN, *Liberty, Equality, and Fraternity* (New York: Henry Holt & Co., 1873), and E. L. GODKIN, "Rights of the Citizen, Part IV—To His Own Reputation," *Scribner's Magazine*, 8 (1890), 58–67.

10. The case is *Robertson* v. *Rochester Folding Box Co.*, 171 N.Y. 538 (1902).

11. *Griswold* v. *Connecticut*, 381 U.S. 479 (1965).

12. WILLIAM L. PROSSER, "Privacy," *California Law Review*, 48 (1960), 389. Other writers who argue that privacy is a complex of rights are FREDERICK DAVIS, "What Do We Mean by 'Right to Privacy'?" *South Dakota Law Review*, 4 (1959), 1–24; and JUDITH J. THOMSON, "The Right to Privacy," *Philosophy and Public Affairs*, 4 (1975), 295–315. For criticism of Prosser, see EDWARD J. BLOUSTEIN, "Privacy as an Aspect of Human Dignity: An Answer to Dean Prosser," *New York University Law Review*, 39 (1964), 962–1007.

13. *Olmstead* v. *United States*, 277 U.S. 438 (1928).

14. *Eisenstadt* v. *Baird*, 405 U.S. 438 (1972).

15. See W. A. PARENT, "Privacy, Morality, and the Law," *Philosophy and Public Affairs*, 12 (1983), 269–88; H. J. MCCLOSKEY, "Privacy and the Right to Privacy," *Philosophy*, 55 (1980), 17–38; and JOSEPH R. DESJARDINS, "Privacy in Employment," in GERTRUDE EZORSKY, ed., *Moral Rights in the Workplace* (Albany: State University of New York Press, 1987), 127–39.

16. See CHARLES F. FRIED, *An Anatomy of Values* (Cambridge: Harvard University Press, 1970), 141; RICHARD A. WASSERSTROM, "Privacy," in WASSERSTROM, ed., *Today's Moral Problems*, 2nd ed. (New York: Macmillan, 1979), 393; ELIZABETH L. BEARDSLEY, "Privacy: Autonomy and Selective Disclosure," in J. ROLAND PENNOCK and JOHN W. CHAPMAN, eds., *Privacy* (New York: Atherton Press, 1971), 65; and ARTHUR MILLER, *The Assault on Privacy* (Ann Arbor: University of Michigan Press, 1971), 25.

17. ALAN F. WESTIN, *Privacy and Freedom* (New York: Atheneum, 1967), 7.

18. RICHARD B. PARKER, "A Definition of Privacy," *Rutgers Law Review*, 27 (1974), 279.

19. This point is made by PARENT, "Privacy, Morality, and the Law," 273.

20. PARENT, "Privacy, Morality, and the Law," 269.

21. PARENT, "Privacy, Morality, and the Law," 269–70.

22. Both of these cases are contained in MARX and SHERIZEN, "Monitoring on the Job," 67.

23. WESTIN, *Privacy and Freedom*, 31–42.

24. For criticisms of these arguments, see MCCLOSKY, "Privacy and the Right to Privacy," 34–35; and PARENT, "Privacy, Morality, and the Law," 275–76.

25. STANLEY I. BENN, "Privacy, Freedom, and Respect for Persons," in PENNOCK and CHAPMAN, *Privacy*, 10–11.

26. HYMAN GROSS, "Privacy and Autonomy," in PENNOCK and CHAPMAN, *Privacy*, 174.

27. Fried, *An Anatomy of Values*, 9. A similar account is given in James Rachels, "Why Privacy Is Important," *Philosophy and Public Affairs*, 4 (Summer 1975), 295–333.

28. Fried, *An Anatomy of Values*, 148.

29. See Jeffrey H. Reiman, "Privacy, Intimacy, and Personhood," *Philosophy and Public Affairs*, 6 (1976), 26–44.

30. Parent, "Privacy, Morality, and the Law," 275. A similar point is expressed by Reiman, "Privacy, Intimacy, and Personhood," 33.

31. Arguments of this kind are presented in Wasserstrom, "Privacy," and Reiman, "Privacy, Intimacy, and Personhood."

32. Reiman, "Privacy, Intimacy, and Personhood," 39.

33. This point is made by Parent, "Privacy, Morality, and the Law," 280. Much of the argument in this section is derived from Parent's analysis of wrongful invasion of privacy.

34. See Thomas H. Murray, "Thinking the Unthinkable about Genetic Screening," *Across the Board*, 20 (June 1983), 34–39.

35. DesJardins, "Privacy in Employment."

36. This point is made by Donald Harris, "A Matter of Privacy," *Personnel*, 64 (February 1987), 38.

37. See Anne E. Libbin, Susan R. Mendelssohn, and Dennis P. Duffy, "The Right to Privacy, Part 5: Employee Medical and Honesty Testing," *Personnel*, 65 (November 1988), 47.

38. George J. Brenkert, "Privacy, Polygraphs and Work," *Business and Professional Ethics Journal*, 1 (1981), 30.

39. David T. Lykken, "Polygraphic Interrogation," *Nature*, 23 February 1984, 681.

40. "Scientific Validity of Polygraph Testing: A Research Review and Evaluation," Technical Memorandum OTA-TM-H-15 (Washington, DC: Office of Technology Assessment, November 1983).

41. Material for this case is taken from Jacques Steinberg, "At Wal-Mart, Workers who Dated Lose Jobs," *New York Times*, 14 July 1993, A16.

42. Calvin Sims, "Reporter Disciplined for Reading His Co-workers' Electronic Mail," *New York Times*, 6 December 1993, B9.

43. Glenn Rifkin, "Do Employees Have a Right to Electronic Privacy," *New York Times*, 8 December 1991, sec. 3, p. 8.

8

Discrimination and Affirmative Action

CASE 8.1   Clara Watson

Clara Watson felt fortunate in 1976 to be one of the few blacks ever employed as a teller by the Fort Worth Bank and Trust. Her ambition, though, was to become a supervisor in charge of other tellers at the bank, despite the fact that only one other black person had ever held this position.[1] She applied to be a supervisor on four separate occasions, and each time she was denied the position. The bank claimed that all promotion decisions were based strictly on evaluations of fitness for the job and that race was not a factor in filling any of the vacancies for which Clara Watson applied. However, a study showed that during a four-year period, white supervisors at the bank hired 14.8 percent of the white applicants and only 3.5 percent of the black applicants. The same supervisors rated black employees 10 points lower than white employees on a scale used for annual salary evaluations. As a result, blacks were promoted more slowly from one salary grade to another and earned less. In 1981, Clara Watson left the bank, but not before she went to the Equal Employment Opportunity Commission and filed a charge of racial discrimination.

INTRODUCTION

Before the civil rights movement of the 1960s, it was unlikely that Clara Watson would have been hired even as a teller by the bank, much less as a supervisor. Rigid segregation in American society confined blacks mostly to menial labor and prevented their entry into jobs traditionally held by whites. This kind of discrimination is now against the law. Although the barriers have fallen in one area after another, however, the advancement of blacks into more desirable occupations is still hampered by subtle forms of discrimination that are difficult to confirm. How can it be determined, for example, whether Clara Watson was a victim of discrimination or simply less qualified than the whites who were promoted ahead of her? Is the statistical underrepresentation of blacks employed at the bank sufficient evidence to charge the bank with discrimination? These are difficult questions that separate cases such as that of Clara Watson from blatant discrimination.

Many racial and ethnic groups have been subject to discrimination, and the treatment of women by American business constitutes another prominent form of discrimination. Discrimination is not simply a matter of the number of women, blacks, and other groups who are hired by an employer. In the early 1970s, for example, more than one half of the employees of American Telephone & Telegraph Company (AT&T) were women, and racial minorities constituted more than 10 percent of the AT&T work force.[2] Women employees were largely concentrated in low-paying clerical and telephone operator jobs, however; and blacks, Hispanics, and members of other racial minorities were employed chiefly in unskilled job categories, such as maintenance workers and janitors. As a result, AT&T was charged with discriminating against women and racial minorities by using sex and race as factors in making job assignments. Eventually, the company agreed to increase the representation of these groups in job categories from which they had previously been excluded.

This chapter is concerned primarily with the ethical arguments against discrimination in employment. Because of the controversial nature of these issues, it will be helpful to begin with a definition of discrimination in employment and to discuss some of the forms it can take.

WHAT IS DISCRIMINATION?

The term *discrimination* describes a large number of wrongful acts in employment, housing, education, medical care, and other important areas of public life. Although discrimination in each of these areas takes different forms, what they have in common is that a person is deprived of some benefit or opportunity because of membership in some group toward which there is substantial prejudice. Discrimination in employment, which is our concern here, generally arises from the decisions employers make about hiring, promotion, pay, fringe benefits, and the other terms and conditions of employment that directly affect the economic interests of employees. There is nothing unjust about such decisions as long as they are made for reasons that are reasonably job-related, but singling out a person for adverse treatment merely because of that person's race or sex is generally an act of discrimination.

Although discrimination is a form of unequal treatment, not all unequal treatment is discrimination. An employer who shows favoritism in deciding on promotions, for example, is guilty of violating the principle of equality in dealing with employees but not necessarily of discriminating against them. Two further elements are necessary. First, discrimination involves decisions that directly affect the employment status of individuals or the terms and conditions of their employment; that is, discrimination occurs in what are generally regarded as *personnel* decisions, such as those involving hiring and firing, promotion, pay, advancement opportunities, and the like. Second, the unequal treatment results from prejudice or some other morally unjustified attitude against members of the group to which an individual belongs. In cases of discrimination, individuals are not treated on the basis of individual merit but on the basis of membership in a group.

The 1964 Civil Rights Act

These two elements can be observed in Title VII of the 1964 Civil Rights Act. Section 703(a) reads as follows:

> It shall be an unlawful employment practice for an employer—(1) to fail or refuse to hire or to discharge any individual, or otherwise to discriminate against any individual with respect to his compensation, terms, conditions, or privileges of employment, because of such individual's race, color, religion, sex, or national origin; or (2) to limit, segregate, or classify his employees or applicants for employment in any way which would deprive or tend to deprive any individual of employment opportunities or otherwise adversely affect his status as an employee, because of such individual's race, color, religion, sex, or national origin.[3]

Notice that Title VII first describes the kinds of employment decisions that are governed by the statute and then lists five factors—race, color, religion, sex, and national origin—that employers are not legally permitted to take into consideration. These factors define groups that are called in law *protected classes.* In subsequent legislation, Congress extended the list of protected classes in order to prevent discrimination against older people (Age Discrimination in Employment Act of 1967), the handicapped (Rehabilitation Act of 1973 and the Americans with Disabilities Act of 1990), and pregnant women (Pregnancy Discrimination Act of 1978).

The prejudice involved in discrimination is of several different kinds. One kind of prejudice behind much racial and ethnic discrimination consists of strong feelings of antipathy and intolerance. Some prejudice is based not on strong feelings but on misunderstandings, such as stereotypes about women, older workers, and the handicapped. Finally, some prejudice is due primarily to economic considerations. Employers are sometimes deterred from hiring pregnant women, older workers, and the handicapped merely because of the higher cost.

Among the questions to be addressed in defining discrimination is whether there must be an *intent* to discriminate. A charge of discrimination requires that the adverse treatment of a person be related in some way to membership in a certain group, but what is the nature of this relation? Section 703(a) of Title VII states that it is illegal for an employer to make decisions about hiring, discharge, compensation, and so on because of an individual's race, color, sex, religion, or national origin. The crucial phrase "because of" is not explained in the law, however.

One kind of discrimination occurs when there is an express intent to treat the members of certain groups differently. Thus, an employer who refuses to receive applications from blacks or has a policy of hiring blacks only for certain jobs would be guilty of discrimination of this kind. It would be discriminatory in a similar way for an employer to seek a "competent, experienced woman" for a secretarial position or a "recent college graduate" for an opening in sales. Such wording implies that sex and age will be considered in decisions about hiring.

In some cases, employers defend themselves against charges of discrimination by arguing that race, sex, or some other characteristic is relevant to the job. Although admitting an intent to treat their employees and applicants differently on the basis of some characteristic, these employers maintain that they are motivated not by racism or sexism or some other kind of prejudice but purely by business considerations. Some situations of this kind are relatively uncontroversial. Obviously, Catholic priests and Jewish rabbis must be of the religion that they serve. A woman's college could justifiably have a preference for a female president.

Section 703(e) of Title VII allows exceptions for sex, religion, and national origin when these are a "bona fide occupational qualification [BFOQ] reasonably necessary to the normal operation of that particular business or enterprise." Race and color are not included in Section 703(e) as a BFOQ and thus cannot be used legally to make distinctions for purposes of employment. The courts have interpreted the BFOQ exception very narrowly, so that employers must show that the qualification is absolutely essential for the conduct of business and not merely useful. Airlines are legally permitted to force pilots to stop flying at the age of sixty for safety reasons, but a federal appeals court rejected an airline's argument against male flight attendants on the grounds that the job of reassuring anxious passengers and giving courteous personalized service not only could be performed by men but were peripheral to Pan Am's main business of transporting passengers safely.[4]

One of the few cases in which the Supreme Court has held sex to be a BFOQ concerned a rule adopted by the Alabama Board of Corrections excluding women from positions in a maximum-security male prison requiring close contact with the inmates.[5] The majority opinion argued, first, that women employees are likely to be the victims of sexual assaults in a prison characterized by "rampant violence" and a "jungle atmosphere." Second, the likelihood of sexual assaults would reduce the ability of a woman to maintain order in the prison, which is the main function of a prison employee. The presence of women in a male prison poses a threat, therefore, "not only to the victim of the assault but also to the basic control of the penitentiary and protection of its inmates and other security personnel."

Several members of the Court disagreed. It is not clear, they said, that women are exposed to significantly greater risk of attack than men who are employed in the same positions at the prison. And even if a job is more dangerous for some individuals than others, it is less discriminatory to allow individuals to decide voluntarily the degree of risk to assume rather than bar those at greater risk. Also, Justice Thurgood Marshall observed, "It is women who are made to pay the price in lost job opportunities for the threat of depraved conduct by male prison inmates." A better solution, perhaps, would be to make the workplace safer for women instead of limiting their employment opportunities because of the threatened conduct of others.

Disparate Treatment and Disparate Impact

Employment policies that do not explicitly involve classifying employees by race, sex, or other impermissible characteristics can still serve to exclude members of these groups in disproportionate numbers. In interpreting Title VII, the courts have generally held that employers are guilty of discrimination in the absence of any intent *when the effects are the same as if there had been an intent to discriminate*. Discrimination is thus not solely a matter of intention but also of consequences. A distinction is made in law between *disparate treatment*, which is discrimination of the first kind, involving an express intention, and *disparate impact*, which is discrimination of the second kind.

A landmark case in discrimination law that illustrates the distinction between disparate treatment and disparate impact is *Griggs* v. *Duke Power Company*.[6] Before the passage of Title VII of the Civil Rights Act of 1964, Duke Power Company openly practiced discrimination against blacks. At the Dan River Plant in Draper, North Carolina, blacks were employed only in the labor department, which was the lowest paying of the five operating divisions. In order to comply with Title VII, the company revised its hiring and promotion policies in 1965 so as to eliminate distinctions between blacks and whites. All applicants for jobs in any department except labor were now required to have a high school diploma and pass two standardized tests, the Wonderlic Personnel Test, which is designed to measure general intelligence, and the Bennett Mechanical Comprehension Test.

Thirteen black employees in the labor department brought suit against Duke Power Company, contending that the education and test requirements were discriminatory for two reasons. First, according to the 1960 census, 34 percent of white males in North Carolina had graduated from high school compared with only 12 percent for black males. The requirement of a high school diploma, therefore, served to exclude black applicants in proportionately greater numbers than white applicants. Second, the passing scores on the two standardized tests were set by the company at the national median of high school graduates, with the result that 58 percent of whites taking the test passed, whereas only 6 percent of the blacks succeeded in doing so. Again, a requirement imposed by the company had a disproportionate impact on blacks applying for employment.

The difference between blacks and whites in the percentages graduating from high school and the performance of the two groups on the standardized tests is largely attributable to the segregated school system in the state. Thus, the requirements, although ostensibly colorblind, served to perpetuate the effects of discrimination in schooling. Chief Justice Warren Burger asserted in the majority opinion that "practices, procedures, and tests neutral on their face, and even neutral in terms of intent, cannot be maintained if they operate to 'freeze' the status quo of prior discriminatory employment practices." Duke Power Company responded to the charge of discrimination by holding that Title VII does not require employers to treat workers without regard for qualifications. The requirement of a minimal educational attainment is reasonable, and intelligence and aptitude tests are specifically sanctioned by Section 703(h) of the Civil Rights Act. This section authorizes the use of "any professionally developed ability test" that is not "designed, intended, or used to discriminate because of race."

The position of the Supreme Court is that neither requirement had been shown by the company to be related to successful job performance. According to the majority opinion:

> On the record before us, neither the high school completion requirement nor the general intelligence test is shown to bear a demonstrable relationship to successful performance of the jobs for which it was used. . . . The evidence, however, shows that employees who have not completed high school or taken the tests have continued to perform satisfactorily and make progress in departments for which the high school and test criteria are now used. The promotion record of present employees who would not be able to meet the new criteria thus suggests the possibility that the requirements may not be needed even for the limited purpose of preserving the avowed policy of advancement within the company. . . .

The decision in *Griggs* v. *Duke Power Company* interprets Title VII as prohibiting employment practices that involve no intent to discriminate (disparate treatment) but still operate to exclude members of protected classes unnecessarily (disparate impact). Companies are free to hire and promote workers on the basis of defensible requirements. But in the words of the Court: "The touchstone is business necessity. If an employment practice which operates to exclude Negroes cannot be shown to be related to job performance, the practice is prohibited." Moreover, the burden of proof in showing business necessity rests on the employer.[7]

The Forms of Discrimination

A definition cannot answer all the difficult questions about discrimination in the workplace, and some further clarification is necessary for understanding each form of discrimination.

1. Discrimination on the basis of sex. In the interpretation of Title VII, sex discrimination is discrimination based on the fact that a person is male or female and not on sex-related matters, such as sexual orientation or marital status. Although some local governments have passed laws barring discrimination in employment and other matters against homosexuals, discrimination of this kind is not covered by the Civil Rights Act of 1964. Employers are permitted by Title VII to treat married and single employees differently as long as no distinction is made between men and women. An employer can give a preference in hiring to married applicants, for example, but it would be discriminatory to prefer married men and single women in filling jobs. Because of uncertainty over the legality of discrimination against pregnant women Congress passed the Pregnancy Discrimination Act in

1978, which amends the phrase in Title VII "because of sex" to include decisions made on the basis of "pregnancy, childbirth, or related medical conditions." Sexual harassment has also been ruled by the courts to constitute a form of sex discrimination. These matters are treated in the following chapter.

2. Religious Discrimination.   Religious discrimination is substantially different from discrimination based on race or sex. There are instances, to be sure, of religious discrimination in which employers refuse to hire or promote individuals simply because of prejudice against members of certain religious groups, such as Catholics and Jews. Most charges of religious discrimination in employment, however, involve conflicts between the religious beliefs and practices of employees and workplace rules and routines. Employees sometimes request revised work schedules for Sabbath observance or time off to observe religious holidays. Members of some religious groups have special dress or grooming requirements, such as a yarmulke for Jewish men and a turban and a beard for Sikh men.[8] Some employees have religious objections to performing certain kinds of work or to submitting to medical examinations; others request prayer breaks and special foods in the company cafeteria.

Religious discrimination also involves the violation of a right not to be adversely affected because of the religious beliefs and practices of employers or other employees. For example, a Texas woman who was an atheist resigned her job at a savings and loan association in order to avoid compulsory monthly staff meetings that began with a religious service.[9] Aggressive proselytizing on the job has occurred in many companies. There are a growing number of "Christian" companies that attempt to do business according to certain principles and to impose these principles on their employees. What makes these conflicts different from racial and sexual discrimination is that employees are not being treated differently because of their religion. The problem is quite the opposite: They are being treated like everyone else *when they have a right to be treated differently because of their religion or lack of one.*

In 1972, Congress amended Title VII by adding Section 701(j), which states that there is no religious discrimination if "an employer demonstrates that he is unable to reasonably accommodate an employee's or prospective employee's religious observance or practice without undue hardship on the conduct of the employer's business." As a result of this amendment, the bulk of the court cases involving charges of religious discrimination raise questions about what constitutes "reasonable accommodation" and "undue hardship." In addition, the courts have held that religious objections can be dismissed by an employer when they interfere with employee safety.

3. National Origin Discrimination.   National origin discrimination overlaps discrimination based on race, color, and, to some extent, religion. It is conceptually distinct, however, since an employer could have employment policies that exclude Mexican immigrants but not other Hispanics, or Vietnamese but not other Asians. It is not discriminatory under Title VII for an employer to require U.S. citizenship as a condition for hiring or promotion as long as the requirement is reasonably job-related and is not a pretext for excluding members of some nationality group. Similarly, an employer is permitted by Title VII to impose a requirement that employees be fluent in English, even if it excludes recent immigrants, as long as the requirement is dictated by legitimate business reasons and is uniformly applied.

A curious unresolved question is whether there can be national origin discrimination against American nationals. As more businesses in the United States come under the control of Japanese and European parent companies, there is a growing tendency for them to draw plant supervisors and higher level managers from their own countries. Is this discrimination on the basis of national origin against Americans by foreigners?

4. Age Discrimination. Age discrimination results largely from the benefits that employers perceive in shunting older employees aside to make room for younger employees who often have more up-to-date skills and innovative ideas. Younger employees are also less expensive to employ, since older employees generally have higher salaries and make more extensive use of fringe benefits. Youth is sometimes preferred by employers for marketing reasons. Three employees in their fifties were dismissed by I. Magnin Department Stores in 1978, for example, as part of what they claimed was a new strategy by the company to appeal to younger shoppers.[10]

The Age Discrimination in Employment Act (ADEA), passed by Congress in 1967, follows the form of Title VII in prohibiting employers from discriminating in the hiring, promotion, discharge, compensation, or other terms and conditions of employment because of age. Exceptions to the ADEA are permitted when age is a bona fide occupational qualification and in cases where a company has a bona fide seniority system. Highly paid corporate executives are also generally excluded from protection under the ADEA.

5. Discrimination against the Handicapped. In many respects, discrimination against the handicapped is like religious discrimination rather than discrimination on the basis of race or sex. Employing the handicapped often requires that they be treated differently in order to compensate for their disabilities. And it may be argued that employers ought to be willing to make reasonable accommodations for the impairments or disabilities of the handicapped just as they are obligated to make reasonable accommodations for the religious beliefs of their employees.

Conclusion

This section has been concerned with defining discrimination. Although some personnel decisions are obviously discriminatory, others are more subtle and even controversial. Moreover, employers are permitted to treat protected groups differently (except those based on race and color) if there is sufficient reason. Gender-based classifications can be justified by law, for example, for jobs in which sex is a BFOQ. And policies with a disparate impact are legal if they serve a legitimate business purpose (the "business necessity" test). The burden that businesses can be justifiably expected to bear also varies for different kinds of discrimination. Employers are required by law to go to great lengths to accommodate pregnant women and the handicapped, for example, but employees' religious beliefs are to be accommodated only if the cost is minimal. As our discussion shows, what constitutes discrimination is not always easy to determine.

ETHICAL ARGUMENTS AGAINST DISCRIMINATION

That discrimination is wrong can be shown by a variety of arguments. There are, first, straightforward utilitarian arguments that cite the ways discrimination harms individuals, business firms, and society as a whole. A second kind of argument appeals to the Kantian notions of human dignity and respect for persons. Arguments of a third kind are based on various principles of justice. Any one of these arguments is sufficient to establish the point, but it is still worthwhile to examine them all, since each brings out some important aspects of the problem of discrimination.

The Utilitarian Argument

One standard utilitarian argument favored by economists is that discrimination creates an economically inefficient matching of people to jobs. The productivity of individual businesses and the economy as a whole is best served by choosing the most qualified applicant to fill any particular position. When applicants are evaluated on the basis of characteristics, such as race and sex, that are not job-related, productivity suffers. Similarly, it is economically disadvantageous for employees to discriminate by refusing to work with blacks or women and for customers to discriminate by refusing to patronize minority-owned businesses.

There are a number of difficulties with this argument. First, not all forms of discrimination produce economic inefficiencies. This is especially true of religious discrimination and discrimination against the handicapped, where complying with the law imposes some cost. It is often cheaper for employers to dismiss employees with troublesome religious beliefs and practices and to avoid hiring handicapped people who have special needs. Second, it is not clear that even racial and sexual discrimination are always inefficient. Under the assumptions of classical economic theory, employers who discriminate on the basis of race or sex are expressing a "taste for discrimination," which they pay for by imposing a higher cost on themselves.[11] For example, when a more productive black applicant is passed over by an employer who prefers to hire whites merely because of race, the output of that employer will be lower. The difference is a cost that the employer is presumably willing to assume in order to satisfy a preference for a white work force. In a free market, then, employers with a "taste for discrimination" are liable to be driven out of business, and discrimination should be reduced over time.[12] This theoretical result is not always borne out in practice, and economics have offered a variety of explanations for the discrepancy.[13]

Another utilitarian argument focuses on the harm that discrimination does to the welfare of society as a whole by perpetuating the effects of racism and sexism. When racial discrimination in employment is combined with discrimination in education, housing, medical care, and other areas of life, the result is poverty with all its attendant social ills. Sexism too serves to disadvantage women as a group and create social problems. Employers who discriminate on the basis of race and sex thus impose an external cost on society. An externality is also imposed when employers attempt to cut costs by refusing to hire the handicapped; the savings to employers may be more than offset by the cost to the handicapped themselves and to the society that is forced to care for them.

Kantian Arguments

From a nonconsequentialist point of view, discrimination can be shown to be wrong by appealing to the Kantian notions of human dignity and respect for persons. This is especially true of discrimination based on contempt or enmity for racial minorities or women. Discrimination of this kind typically involves a racist or sexist attitude that denies individuals in these groups the status of fully developed human beings who deserve to be treated as the equal of others. The victims of racial and sexual discrimination are not merely disadvantaged by being forced to settle for less desirable jobs and lower pay. They are also deprived of a fundamental moral right to be treated with dignity and respect.

This moral right is also denied when individuals are treated on the basis of group characteristics rather than individual merit. Much of the discrimination against women, older workers, and the handicapped does not result from the belief that they are less deserving of respect and equal treatment. It results instead from the stereotypes that lead employers to overlook significant differences among individuals. Stereotypes, which are a part of racism and sexism, clearly result in a denial of dignity and respect. But stereotyping by its very nature is morally objectionable since it leads employers to treat individuals only as members of groups.

Arguments Based on Justice

Perhaps the strongest arguments against discrimination are those that appeal to some principle of justice. Fundamental to many principles of justice is the requirement that we be able to justify our treatment of other people by giving good reasons, but to discriminate is to treat people differently when there is no good reason for doing so. According to Aristotle's principle of justice as proportional equality—that like cases should be treated alike, and unlike cases should be treated differently in proportion to the relevant differences—discrimination is unjust because characteristics such as race and sex are generally irrelevant to the performance of a job. Even when the differences between individuals constitute genuinely job-related characteristics, the difference in pay, for example, should still be in proportion to that difference.

The contract theory of John Rawls provides the basis for yet another argument against discrimination. One of the principles that would be adopted in the original position is described by Rawls as follows: "Social and economic inequalities are to be arranged so that they are . . . attached to offices and positions open to all under conditions of fair equality of opportunity."[14] Even if it were to the advantage of everyone to exclude some groups from certain positions, such a denial of opportunity could not be justified because individuals would be deprived of an important human good, namely the opportunity for self-development.

AVOIDING DISCRIMINATION

Being a truly nondiscriminatory employer is not an easy task. In addition to good-faith compliance with the law, employers must be aware of some subtle and surprising sources of discrimination. This section discusses what is involved in pursuing a policy of nondiscrimination by examining three basic steps in the hiring and promotion process: analyzing the job to be performed, recruiting applicants, and assessing the applicants for suitability.

Job Analysis

In order to ensure that decisions on hiring and promotion consider only job-related characteristics and result in finding the best person for the job, it is necessary to conduct a *job analysis*. A job analysis consists of two parts: (1) an accurate *job description* that details the activities or responsibilities involved in a position, and (2) a *job specification* listing the qualifications required to perform the job as described. Virtually every job in any present-day corporation has been analyzed in this way, since job analysis is a standard management tool for organizing work and appraising performance.

Because a job description focuses on the specific activities or responsibilities of a position rather than on the people who have traditionally held it, certain kinds of work are less likely to be stereotyped as belonging to one group or another. Even when the qualifications for a job favor one sex over another, a job description that lists only the qualifications will not serve to exclude the members of the other sex who meet them. And since the qualifications must be related to the description, it is easier to determine whether they are really needed for the satisfactory performance of a job. A job analysis need not be confined to traditional job categories. If a job is unnecessarily identified with one sex or another, it can be redesigned, perhaps by combining the activities of one or more other jobs, so that the newly created job is attractive to both men and women. Jobs can also be narrowed so as to avoid excluding some groups unnecessarily. A desk job that involves some moving and lifting can be redesigned to exclude these tasks in order to accommodate the handicapped.

Recruitment and Selection

After a job analysis is done, a company is faced with the task of recruiting applicants in a nondiscriminatory manner. An obvious first step is to make sure that information about an opening is widely disseminated, especially to nontraditional groups.

Employers who are serious about not discriminating will place listings of job opportunities with minority publications and educational institutions and employment agencies serving minorities. Also, applications from members of nontraditional groups are more likely to be received if significant numbers of minorities and women are involved in the company's recruitment effort and if a number of nontraditional applicants are hired at one time.[15]

After a sufficient number of applicants have been recruited, the next task is to select the person who is best suited to fill the job. Discrimination can enter into this stage of hiring in many different ways. The selection process itself, which often includes a battery of tests and rounds of interviews, can be discouraging for many nontraditional applicants. Employers can address this problem by simplifying the application procedure or providing instruction on how to proceed. Small differences in treatment can also make racial minorities and women feel uncomfortable. A company can further reduce the barriers to nontraditional applicants by reducing the number of promotion lines and increasing their flexibility so that minorities and women have more opportunities for advancement.

Objective Tests and Subjective Evaluations

Two other important sources of discrimination in both the hiring and the promotion process are objective tests and subjective evaluations formed on the basis of personal interviews or the recommendations of supervisors. Three kinds of objective tests are commonly used to make decisions on hiring and promotion: (1) tests that measure specific knowledge and skills, such as those needed to be a bookkeeper or a typist; (2) tests that measure intelligence and general aptitude for performing certain kinds of work; and (3) tests that attempt to gauge an applicant's suitability for employment generally and the extent to which an applicant will fit into a specific work environment.

Objective tests of these kinds are permissible under Title VII of the 1964 Civil Rights Act as long as they are not used as a cover for discrimination. One condition laid down in *Griggs* v. *Duke Power Company*, however, is that a test not unnecessarily exclude a disproportionate number of members of protected classes, which is to say that it should not have disparate impact. A second condition is that a test be *validated*; that is, an employer must be able to show that a test for any given job is a reliable predictor of successful performance in that job. The two tests administered by Duke Power Company, the Wonderlic Personnel Test and the Bennett Mechanical Comprehension Test, are professionally prepared instruments that presumably provide an accurate measure of general intelligence and mechanical ability, respectively. What the company failed to prove, however, is that passing scores on these tests are closely correlated with successful job performance. They failed, in other words, to validate the tests that they used.

The Supreme Court has held employers to very high standards of proof in validating tests. It is not sufficient merely to show that employees who successfully perform a certain job also attain high scores on any given test. An employer must be able to show, further, that applicants with lower scores would not be capable of performing just as well. A biased test that results in the exclusion of a substantial percentage of blacks or women, for example, might still be a reliable predictor of successful performance for those who pass but not a reliable predictor of the lack of success of those who fail the test. Further, comparing the scores of employees who are currently performing a job successfully with the scores of inexperienced applicants is not sufficient proof of the reliability of a test. In order to draw a significant conclusion, it would be necessary to know how the current job holders would have scored on the test before they were hired.[16]

Objective tests are ethically and legally permissible, then, as long as they do not have disparate impact and are validated. Do the same two conditions apply to subjective evaluations based on personal interviews or the recommendations of supervisors? On the one hand, evaluations of this kind are made by experienced employees who are well acquainted with the job to be filled and have an opportunity to assess qualities in an applicant that do not lend themselves to objective testing. On the other hand, the evaluations of interviewers and supervisors are apt to be influenced by irrelevant factors, such as a person's appearance or manner, and by conscious or unconscious prejudice. This is especially true when the evaluator is not well trained for the task.

The Clara Watson Case

The first opportunity for the Supreme Court to decide on the conditions for an acceptable subjective evaluation system came in 1988 with the suit of Clara Watson against the Fort Worth Bank and Trust Company, which opened this chapter. The statistical evidence of discrimination was not in dispute, and so the principal issue in this case is not whether the procedures used by the bank had disparate impact (they did) but whether the fact that they involved subjective evaluations rather than objective tests made a difference in the interpretation of Title VII. A related issue is whether the requirement of validation, which applies to objective tests, should be extended to subjective evaluations.

The Fort Worth Bank and Trust Company used three common types of subjective evaluation procedures: interviews, rating scales, and experience requirements. Rating scales differ from interviews in that they record evaluations derived from observations made over a long period of time while an employee is actively at work. Typically, an evaluator is asked to rank an employee on a numerical scale with respect to certain qualities, such as drive and dependability. Experience requirements involve an inventory of specific jobs performed that provide a basis on which to make judgments about future performance.

The American Psychological Association (APA) submitted an amicus curiae, or "friend of the court," brief in the Watson case in order to support the claim that these three types of subjective evaluation procedures are capable of validation.[17] Each procedure is open to bias. The most common bias in interviews and rating scales is the "halo effect," in which a single trait exercises an inordinate influence on an evaluator. Closely related to the halo effect is stereotyping, in which assumptions about members of certain groups influence an evaluator. Interviewers are also subject to the "similar-to-me" phenomenon, in which they are inclined to be more favorable to people who have the same traits as themselves. Among the problems with rating scales are the tendencies of evaluators to place persons toward the center of a scale, thereby avoiding the extremes, and to be lenient, scoring most people favorably. The APA brief also cites considerable evidence to show that scores on rating scales are affected by racial factors.

All these biases can be avoided by subjective evaluation procedures that are designed and carried out according to the APA's *Standards for Educational and Psychological Testing* and the *Principles for the Validation and Use of Personnel Selection Procedures*. The key in each type of procedure is to relate it to a thorough analysis of the job to be filled. The interview should be carefully structured with questions designed to elicit information that is relevant only to the qualifications and performance criteria of the job. The traits on the rating scale and the kinds of experience used as experience requirements should be similarly selected. As much as possible, the results of evaluation procedures should reflect the personal characteristics of the person being evaluated and not the person doing the evaluating, so that differences between evaluators is kept to a minimum. And interviewers, supervisors, and other persons involved in the process should be thoroughly trained in performing their roles in the hiring and promotion process.

The APA brief faults Fort Worth Bank and Trust for failing to meet the generally accepted standards for subjective evaluation procedures and for the lack of any validation of the procedures used. Interviews were conducted by only one person, a white male, and there is no evidence that the questions were carefully designed with job-related qualifications in mind. No job analysis was done in order to guide the selection of questions in the interview and the traits on the rating scale. Moreover, the traits on the rating scale were vaguely defined and not clearly related to job performance. The supervisors who performed the ratings were not specifically trained for that task, and no steps were taken to avoid the effect that race is known to have on the results of rating scales. Finally, it would be impossible without a job analysis of the position to determine what prior experience would enable her superiors to judge the success of Clara Watson in that position.

In a 8–0 decision, the Supreme Court found in favor of Clara Watson and established that the theory of disparate impact applied to subjective evaluation procedures as well as to objective tests of the kind at issue in *Griggs*.

AFFIRMATIVE ACTION

After the passage of the 1964 Civil Rights Act, employers scrutinized their hiring and promotion practices and attempted to eliminate sources of discrimination. Even the best efforts of companies did not always succeed in increasing the advancement opportunities of women and racial minorities, however. In 1974, at a plant operated by the Kaiser Aluminum Company in Grammercy, Louisiana, for example, only five skilled craft workers (out of 273) were black. Kaiser had long sought out qualified black workers, but few met the requirement of five years of prior craft experience, in part because of the traditional exclusion of blacks from craft unions. In an effort to meet this problem, Kaiser Aluminum and the local union, the United Steelworkers of America, developed an innovative program to train the company's own employees to become skilled craft workers. The plan set up a training program that admitted blacks and whites in equal numbers based on seniority until the proportion of blacks in the skilled craft category equaled the percentage of blacks in the area work force, which was approximately 39 percent.

In 1978, Santa Clara County in California undertook a similar effort. According to the 1970 census, women constituted 36.4 percent of local workers. Only 22.4 percent of county employees were women, and these were concentrated in two areas: paraprofessionals (90 percent female) and office and clerical workers (75.9 percent female). Out of 238 skilled craft workers, not one was a woman. In order to correct these imbalances, the county board adopted an Equal Employment Opportunity Policy that set broad goals and objectives for hiring and promotion in each agency. Specifically, the policy stated:

> It is the goal of the County and Transit District to attain a work force which includes in all occupational fields and at all employment levels, minorities, women and handicapped persons in numbers consistent with the ratio of these groups in the area work force.

To carry out the board's policy, the Santa Clara Transportation Agency, the agency responsible for road maintenance in the county, developed a detailed plan for increasing the percentages of women and minorities in job categories where they were underrepresented.

The programs adopted by Kaiser Aluminum and Santa Clara County are examples of *affirmative action*. The idea behind affirmative action is that merely ceasing to discriminate is not enough. Employers, if they choose to do so, ought to be permitted to take more active steps to ensure a balanced work force, including plans that give preference to job applicants on the basis of race or sex. In response to the plan at Kaiser Aluminum, however, a white employee, Brian Weber, sued both the company and his own union.[18] Weber had insufficient seniority to be admitted as a white trainee, even though he had worked longer at the Kaiser plant than any of the blacks who were selected. He charged, therefore, that he himself was a victim of discrimination in violation of Title VII of the 1964 Civil Rights Act.

A suit also arose as a result of the plan adopted by the Transportation Agency of Santa Clara County when a white male, Paul Johnson, was passed over for promotion and the job went to a woman.[19] In December 1979, Paul Johnson and Diane Joyce applied along with ten other employees for promotion to the position of dispatcher for the road division of the transportation agency. Dispatchers, who assign road crews, equipment, and materials for road maintenance and keep records of the work done, are classified as skilled craft workers. Applicants for the position were required to have four years of dispatch or road maintenance experience with Santa Clara County. The eligible candidates were interviewed by two different boards. The first board, using a numerical scale, rated Johnson slightly above Joyce

(75 to 73), and the second board, although rating both candidates "highly qualified," also recommended Johnson over Joyce. The director of the agency was authorized to select any eligible candidate, however, and in order to implement the affirmative action plan, he gave the nod to Joyce. Johnson, like Weber, believed himself to be a victim of discrimination and sued.

Another kind of affirmative action plan that has been challenged in the courts is a "set-aside" provision for minority contractors. The Public Works in Employment Act, passed by Congress in 1977, required that at least 10 percent of the funds granted to state and local governments for construction be set aside for "minority business enterprise." Some municipalities have enacted similar legislation. The city of Richmond, Virginia, for example, adopted a Minority Business Utilization Plan that required recipients of city construction contracts to subcontract at least 30 percent of the dollar amount of each contract to minority-owned businesses. Some white contractors have charged that set-aside provisions are an illegal form of discrimination.[20]

In *Weber* v. *Kaiser Aluminum* and *Johnson* v. *Transportation Agency*, the Supreme Court held that the affirmative action plans in question were not discriminatory under Title VII. Both Brian Weber and Paul Johnson thus lost their suits. After approving set-asides for minority-owned contractors in a 1980 decision, *Fullilove* v. *Klutznick*, the Court cast all such programs into doubt in *City of Richmond* v. *J. A. Croson* (1989) and subsequently *Adarand* v. *Peña* (1995).

Although the goal of eliminating discrimination in employment has generally been accepted in business, people are still divided over the appropriate means. Advocates of affirmative action argue that special programs are required as a matter of "simple justice." Victims of discrimination, they say, deserve some advantage. Preferential treatment is necessary to ensure equality of opportunity. Opponents counter that if it is unjust to discriminate against racial minorities and women on account of their race or sex, then it is similarly unjust to give them preference for the same reason. People who are passed over in favor of a black or a woman are victims of discrimination in reverse. Who is right in this debate?

THE COMPENSATION ARGUMENT

One argument for giving preferential treatment to members of certain groups is that it is owed to them as *compensation* for the injustice done by discrimination directed against them personally or against other members of a group to which they belong. The root idea in this argument derives from Aristotle's discussion in Book V of the *Nicomachean Ethics*, in which he distinguished between justice in the distribution of goods (distributive justice) and justice where one person has wrongfully inflicted some harm on another (corrective justice). In the latter case, justice requires that the wrong be corrected by providing compensation. For example, if A, while driving carelessly, crashes into B's new car, then B suffers a loss that is A's fault. An injustice has been done. It can be corrected, though, if A compensates B for the amount of the loss, say the cost of repairs plus any inconvenience. Similarly, if A has a right not to be discriminated against and B discriminates, thereby harming A unjustifiably, then it is only just that B compensate A to correct the harm done.

Aristotle's analysis perfectly fits the situation, for example, of an employer who has been found guilty of discriminating against women or racial minorities by assigning them to lower paying jobs and bypassing them in promotions. The law in such cases is guided by the dictum No right without a remedy, which is to say that a person cannot be said to have a right unless there is also some means of correcting a violation of that right. If we have a right not to be discriminated against, then the courts should be able to provide some remedy when that right is violated. The remedy is often to require the employer to pay the victims the difference between what they actually earned and what they would have earned had no discrimination taken place and to advance them to the positions that they would have attained.

Critics of affirmative action charge that not all affirmative action plans are justified by the compensation argument. First, the individuals who are given preferential treatment are often not the same as those who are victims of discrimination. Affirmative action plans almost always single out persons as members of a group that has suffered discrimination without requiring any evidence that the persons themselves have been victimized in any way. A person may be a member of a disadvantaged group and yet lead a rather privileged life, relatively free of the effects of discrimination.

Defenders of affirmative action respond that racial and sexual discrimination has subtle psychological effects despite the profound changes that have taken place in our society, and racial and sexual discrimination affects all members of that group to some degree. Bernard R. Boxill observes that the critics' objection involves a non sequitur. From the premise that better-qualified blacks or women are less deserving of compensation than some who have been more severely handicapped by discrimination, we cannot conclude that no compensation is owed. "Because I have lost only one leg," he argues, "I may be less deserving of compensation than another who has lost two legs, but it does not follow that I deserve no compensation at all."[21] Nor does it follow, according to Boxill, that victims of discrimination who succeed in overcoming the harm done to them are any less deserving of compensation than those who are unable to succeed to the same degree.[22]

This response still does not answer the question, Why should preference not be given to those who most deserve compensation, the people who have most suffered the effects of racial discrimination and who are consequently among the least qualified? One reply is that giving preference in hiring is only one way of compensating individuals for past discrimination, and it is a way that is of greater help to those who are better qualified for the jobs available. Those who have been more disadvantaged by discrimination may be less able to benefit from affirmative action and may derive greater benefit from other forms of help, such as job-training programs.

A defender of affirmative action can also argue that claims of compensatory justice must be balanced against another principle of justice, the principle that hiring should be done on the basis of competence.[23] Giving preference to the best qualified of those who are deserving of compensation, according to this argument, is the best way of accommodating these two conflicting principles. Another argument cites the practical difficulty of evaluating each case to determine the extent to which an individual has been harmed by discrimination and hence deserves compensation. Giving preference to members of groups without regard for the particulars of individual cases, therefore, is a matter of administrative convenience.[24]

A second objection to the compensation argument is that in affirmative action the burden of providing compensation often falls on individuals who are not themselves guilty of acts of discrimination. In the competition for admission into colleges and universities and for hiring and promotion in jobs, it is largely white males who are asked to pay the price of correcting injustices that are not of their making. Critics ask, why should a few white males bear such a disproportionate burden?

One answer to this question is that white males, even when they are not themselves guilty of discrimination, are still the beneficiaries of discrimination that has occurred and thus are merely being asked to give back some ill-gotten gain. This response does not fully meet the critics' point, however. Even if all white males have benefited to some degree, it still needs to be shown that what is given up by the few white males who are passed over when preference is given to others is equal to the benefit they have obtained by living in a discriminatory society. Furthermore, it would still seem to be unjust to place the full burden in such an arbitrary manner on a few when so many other members of society have also benefited from discrimination.[25]

A second answer to the critics' question is that white males are typically asked not to give up gains they have already made but to forgo a future benefit to which no one has an undisputed right.[26] Brian Weber and Paul Johnson, for example, were not deprived of any gains they had made but only of an opportunity for advancement. Although this is a real loss, neither one had a right to be selected but only a right not to be discriminated against in the selection process. If the compensation argument is correct, then those who were selected *deserved* the advantage given by their race or sex and hence no discrimination took place. (Ironically, the opportunity for Brian Weber to receive on-the-job training for a skilled craft position would not have existed had Kaiser Aluminum not adopted an affirmative action plan in order to hire more blacks.) Still, if the job prospects of white males are substantially reduced by affirmative action, then they have suffered a loss. And there is surely some limit on the amount of compensation any individual or group of individuals can justifiably be required to pay.

Accordingly, the courts have laid down three conditions for permissible affirmative action plans to protect those adversely affected by them. They are (1) that a plan does not create an absolute bar to the advancement of any group, (2) that the plan does not unnecessarily trammel the rights of others, and (3) that it be temporary. The training program in the Weber case was open to black and to white workers in equal numbers. Although Brian Weber failed to gain admittance to the first class, his seniority would have assured him a place eventually. In addition, he had other opportunities for realizing his ambition of becoming a skilled craft worker. Finally, the training program was scheduled to terminate when the proportion of black craft workers reached 39 percent, the percentage of blacks in the local work force.

EQUALITY ARGUMENTS

We noted in Chapter 4 that, according to Aristotle, justice is a kind of equality. Whether affirmative action is just, therefore, can be decided, perhaps, by the principle that people ought to be treated equally or treated as equals. Two quite different concepts of equality are relevant to the debate over affirmative action, however. These are *equality of opportunity* and *equality of treatment.*

Justice, in the first interpretation of equality, requires that everyone have an equal opportunity to succeed in life and that no one be held back by arbitrarily imposed restraints or barriers. Better enforcement of the laws against discrimination can help to equalize the opportunities for everyone, but the effects of past discrimination also need to be neutralized in some way.

President Lyndon B. Johnson expressed the argument graphically in a 1965 speech on an executive order requiring every federal contractor to be an "equal opportunity employer":

> Imagine a hundred yard dash in which one of the two runners has his legs shackled together. He has progressed 10 yards, while the unshackled runner has gone 50 yards. How do they rectify the situation? Do they merely remove the shackles and allow the race to proceed? Then they could say that "equal opportunity" now prevailed. But one of the runners would still be forty yards ahead of the other. Would it not be the better part of justice to allow the previously shackled runner to make-up the forty yard gap; or to start the race all over again? That would be affirmative action towards equality.[27]

The equal opportunity argument addresses not only the harm done to individuals from past discrimination but also the barriers posed by discrimination in present-day society. Many fully qualified blacks and women have not been disadvantaged by past discrimination but are still at a competitive disadvantage because of lingering racism and sexism on the part of employers. Giving preferential treatment may be necessary under such circumstances simply to ensure that people are considered equally. Whether this is true depends, in part, on what we mean by equal opportunity.

The Meaning of Equal Opportunity

What does equal opportunity mean? To say that every child born today has an equal opportunity to become a surgeon, for example, has two distinct senses. One interpretation is that each child initially has an equal chance in the same way that every ticket holder is equally likely to win the lottery. The other is that the means for pursuing the career of a surgeon are open to all. Following Douglas Rae in his book *Inequalities*, let us call these two possibilities the *prospect-regarding* and the *means-*

regarding interpretations of the concept of equal opportunity.[28] Prospect-regarding equality aims at eliminating *all* factors affecting the distribution of goods in a society except for mere chance. Means-regarding equality, by contrast, is compatible with considerable inequality of prospects. The only requirement for equality of opportunity in this latter interpretation is that the results reflect only differences in personal attributes and not differences in the means available to persons.

Equality of prospects is an ideal of egalitarians who want to minimize the role of "accidents" of birth on people's success in life. Just as our race or sex should have no bearing on what we are able to achieve, so too should it not matter whether we are born into wealth or poverty or whether we are born with certain mental or physical endowments. There are a number of difficulties with interpeting equal opportunity as equality of prospects. First, because people begin life with vastly different prospects, steps would have to be taken to equalize these prospects. Achieving an equality of prospects would entail considerable remedial education and a reallocation of resources to schools with disadvantaged students. Second, how are we to know when unequal prospects have been offset? One way might be to look at equality of outcomes, but equality of prospects need not result in equal outcomes if people make different choices. So there must be some way of determining when prospects are equal without looking at the outcomes.

The interpretation of equal opportunity as equality of means entails that rewards should be distributed on the basis of some relevant criteria. Artificial barriers to advancement, such as racial or sexual characteristics, are irrelevant and should be removed, but justice does not require the removal of inequalities in prospects resulting from differences in a person's various physical and mental characteristics. Equal opportunity, on this view, means a chance to compete under fair conditions.

One difficulty with this interpretation is that it requires only that all discrimination cease; it does nothing to address President Johnson's concern about the head start provided by discrimination in the past. A further difficulty is that the conditions for fair competition are highly suspect. What is commonly called talent is largely the acquisition of the expertise and skills provided by education and certified through formal procedures. If access to education or certification is affected by racial or sexual discrimination, then we can scarcely be said to have equal access to the means for achieving success in life.

Some defenders of affirmative action have argued that the goal ought to be not equal opportunity but equal treatment. This concept, too, is ambiguous, with two distinct senses. Ronald Dworkin points out that when we say that certain white males have been denied a right to equal treatment, we might have in mind two different rights.[29]

> The first is the right to *equal treatment*, which is the right to an equal distribution of some opportunity or resource or burden. . . . The second is the right to *treatment as an equal*, which is the right, not to receive the same distribution of some burden or benefit, but to be treated with the same respect and concern as anyone else.[30]

The right to equal treatment in the sense of a right to receive an equal share applies only to a few things, such as the right that each person's vote shall count equally. In the distribution of most things, it is a right to the same respect and concern that is at stake. Affirmative action is objectionable, then, only if the alleged victims are not treated as equals.

Dworkin argues that any selection process advantages some people and disadvantages others. Admitting students to medical school on the basis of academic preparation, for example, serves to exclude some applicants. Such a selection process is justified, however, by a social good that outweighs any harm done to those who are turned away. Affirmative action plans are adopted to serve an important social good, namely overcoming the effects of racisim. In so doing, it must be recognized that some white applicants who are denied admission to medical school would be admitted in the absence of a plan. As long as the interests of these unsuccessful applicants are taken into consideration with the same respect and concern as those of others in adopting rules for medical school admission that best meet the needs of society; and as long as these rules are applied impartially, showing the same respect and concert to every applicant, then no one has cause to complain. Everyone has been treated as an equal.

This argument is open to a serious objection.[31] In Dworkin's interpretation, the right to equal treatment is the right to equal respect and concern as rational calculations are made about the social good. According to Robert L. Simon, "So understood, the right to treatment as an equal looks suspiciously like the utilitarian requirement that everyone count for one and only one in computing social benefits and burdens."[32] Simon suggests that placing more emphasis on *respect* for other persons rather than on *concern* that their welfare be given equal weight would make affirmative action programs less compatible with equal treatment interpreted as treatment as an equal.

The conclusion to be drawn from the discussion in this section is that the concept of equal opportunity is too vague and ambiguous to provide conclusive support for any particular position on the justification of affirmative action. Those who favor preferential treatment programs and those who oppose them can find a meaning of "equal opportunity" to fit their particular position. Equality of treatment, by contrast, provides a more solid basis for affirmative action. This principle demands, however, that we think carefully about the reasons for affirmative action and make sure that the goals to be achieved are worthwhile and cannot be attained by means that do not involve taking race or sex into account.

UTILITARIAN ARGUMENTS

Unlike the two previous arguments for affirmative action, arguments based on utility do not hold that programs of preferential treatment are morally *required* as a matter of justice but that we are morally *permitted* to use them as means for attacking pressing social problems. Utilitarian arguments stress that preferential treatment programs are necessary to eradicate lingering racial and sexual discrimination and to accelerate the pace of integrating certain groups into the mainstream of American society. The underlying assumption of these arguments is that racism and sexism are deeply embedded in the major social, political, and economic institutions of our society and in people's attitudes, expectations, and perceptions about social realities. If this assumption is correct, then antidiscrimination legislation addresses only the surface manifestations of racism and sexism and does not penetrate to the root causes. Action must be taken to change the institutions of society and the ways people think about themselves and their world. Otherwise, the goal of a discrimination-free society will come only slowly, if at all.

Preferential treatment programs serve to combat the effects of discrimination, first, by making more jobs available to racial minorities, women, and others through lowering the stated qualifications and formal accreditation required for hiring and promotion. Opportunities for groups subject to discrimination are further increased by breaking down stereotypes in the eyes of employers and the rest of society and by creating role models for people who would not otherwise consider certain lines of work. The long history of sexual and racial stereotyping of jobs in this country has hampered the acceptance of women and members of some racial minorities into desirable positions in our society, and this history has also affected the very people who were excluded by limiting their career aspirations. Finally, affirmative action increases opportunities by heightening awareness about discrimination and changing the hiring and promotion process. When business firms make a commitment to achieve a certain racial and sexual mix in their work force with established goals, the officials responsible for hiring and promoting employees cannot help but be sensitive to the issue of discrimination in every decision they make.

Affirmative action also provides a direct economic benefit to corporations themselves by increasing the pool of job applicants and generally improving community relations. Discrimination introduces inefficiency into the job market by excluding whole groups of people on the basis of race or sex, some of whom are highly qualified. The result is that people in these groups tend to be "underutilized" in jobs that do not make full use of their abilities and training, and employers are deprived of the best possible work force. The following statement by an executive of Monsanto Corporation testifies to the benefit that affirmative action can have for employers: "We have been utilizing affirmative action plans for over 20 years. We were brought into it kicking and screaming. But over the past 20 years we've learned that there's a reservoir of talent out there, of minorities and women that we hadn't been using before. We found that it works."[33]

Some Problems with Affirmative Action

Affirmative action has some significant undesirable consequences that must be balanced against the undeniable utilitarian benefits of preferential treatment programs. Three arguments in particular are commonly used by opponents of affirmative action. These are (1) that affirmative action involves hiring and promoting less qualified people and lowering the quality of the work force, (2) that it is damaging to the self-esteem of employees who are favored because of race or sex, and (3) that it produces race consciousness, which promotes rather than fights discrimination. Let us examine these in turn.

The Quality Argument

The first argument—the quality argument—can be expressed in the following way. The most qualified person for a position has no need for special consideration. Therefore, a person who is given preference on the basis of race or sex cannot be the most qualified person and cannot perform as well in a job as someone who is more qualified. The result is a decline in the quality of goods and services, which has an adverse affect on the whole of society.

A supporter of affirmative action can question, first, how much quality is given up. Preferential treatment does not involve the hiring or promotion of people who are *un*qualified but who are (at worst) *less* qualified to some degree. And the degree can be so slight as to be of no significance. Many jobs require only minimal qualifications and can readily be mastered by persons of normal abilities. Even occupations requiring considerable ability and expertise involve many tasks that can be satisfactorily performed by people who are not the best available. In many instances, "qualified" means "already trained," which brands as unqualified those people who are capable of being fully competent with some training.

Also, whether a person is qualified for a certain job depends on how qualifications are recognized or determined. Conventional measures, such as standardized tests and academic record, are often criticized for containing a bias against women and racial minorities. The credentials used to certify competence in various fields, such as licenses, certificates, union cards, diplomas, and the like, have been accused of containing a similar bias. More complications emerge when we ask, what are the relevant qualifications for the performance of any given job? It is sometimes argued, for example, that a black police officer can be more effective in a black community and that an applicant's race is, therefore, a legitimate consideration in the hiring of a police force.[34] In education, a largely male college faculty may not provide a learning environment that is as beneficial to women students as one with a substantial number of female professors.

The Injury Done by Affirmative Action

A second utilitarian argument against affirmative action is that it injures the very people it is designed to help. The effect of hiring and promoting blacks and women because of their race or sex is to draw attention to their lack of qualifications and create an impression that they could not succeed on their own. Another effect of affirmative action is to reduce the respect of society for the many hard-won achievements of blacks and women and to undermine their own confidence and self-esteem. The stigma attached by preferential treatment may even have the unintended consequence of impeding racial integration if qualified minority applicants avoid jobs where race is a factor in selection.

This is an argument to be taken seriously. It rests, however, on the questionable assumption that programs of preferential treatment have not significantly helped some people. Insofar as affirmative action has boosted some racial minorities and women into higher-level positions of prestige and responsibility, there is bound to be an increase in their pride and self-respect as well as their financial well-being. Success in life is often unearned, but there is little evidence that the beneficiaries of good fortune are psychologically damaged by it. Manuel Velasquez observes, "For centuries white males have been the beneficiaries of racial and sexual discrimination without apparent loss of their self-esteem." [35]

The third and final utilitarian argument against preferential treatment programs is that they increase rather than decrease the importance of race and other factors in American society. If the ideal of an equal society is one in which no one is treated differently because of color, ethnic origin, religion, or any other irrelevant factor, then preferential treatment defeats this ideal by heightening our consciousness of these differences. To some critics of affirmative action, all uses of racial, ethnic, and religious classifications are abhorrent and ultimately destructive of the fabric of a society.

One response by proponents of affirmative action is that the use of racial classifications is a temporary expedient, necessary only to eradicate racism before we can realize the ideal of an equal society. Justice Harry Blackmun wrote in an opinion:

> I suspect that it would be impossible to arrange an affirmative action program in a racially neutral way and have it successful. To ask that this be so is to demand the impossible. In order to get beyond racism, we must first take account of race. There is no other way. And in order to treat some persons equally, we must treat them differently.[36]

The Supreme Court has long held that distinctions based on race and ethnic origin are "by their very nature odious to a free people whose institutions are founded upon the doctrine of equality."[37] Nevertheless, they are permissible when the conditions warrant their use.

Others argue that there is nothing inherently wrong with race consciousness and the awareness of sexual, religious, ethnic, and other differences. What makes any of these wrong is their use to degrade and oppress people with certain characteristics. There is a great difference between the racial distinctions that were an essential element of the institution of slavery, for example, and the race consciousness that is a part of the present-day attack on racism. Any utilitarian analysis of affirmative action must take into account the history of racial minorities and women in this country and the present-day social realities. All things considered, the race consciousness engendered by affirmative action may be socially beneficial.

Conclusion

The ethical issues surrounding discrimination and affirmative action are very problematical. Rights figure prominently in these issues—both the rights of people who have been victimized by discrimination and the rights of people who now bear the burden of correcting past wrongs. Considerations of justice also play a role. Justice requires that people who have been wronged be compensated in some way and that all people be treated equally, but the concepts of just compensation and of equal opportunity or equal treatment are subject to differing interpretations. Finally, arguments based on utility provide strong support for antidiscrimination and affirmative action policies, although the benefits of any given policy must be weighed against the harms with uncertain results. The ideal of a nondiscriminatory society is clear, but the pathway to it is strewn with formidable obstacles.

CASE 8.2   The Alaskan Salmon Cannery

You have been sent from the head office of a large food-packing company to a salmon cannery in Alaska with instructions to investigate charges of discrimination that have been made by a group of nonwhite workers.[38] Your assignment is especially critical in view of the fact that the protesting cannery workers have threatened to bring a lawsuit against the company for its alleged discriminatory hiring and promotion practices.

This company-owned salmon cannery on a remote section of the Alaskan coast operates for only a few months each year during the salmon run. The entire work force must be transported to the unpopulated location and housed in specially constructed barracks. There are two kinds of jobs at the cannery: unskilled jobs on the cannery line and both skilled and unskilled noncannery jobs. The cannery workers, who are mostly Filipino and Native American, prepare the fish and pack it into four-ounce cans. Afterward, the cans are sealed and the fish is cooked under carefully controlled conditions. The Filipino workers are recruited through an agreement with a major labor union, whereas the Native Americans live in villages near the cannery. The noncannery employees are mostly skilled and include machinists, engineers, carpenters, cooks, bookkeepers, and office workers. A few noncannery jobs are classified as unskilled; examples of these are kitchen help, table servers, janitors, laundry workers, night watchmen, and deckhands.

The nonwhite cannery workers have complained that the unskilled noncannery jobs generally pay more than similar unskilled cannery jobs and are filled almost entirely by whites. The existence of two classes of unskilled workers, one consisting mainly of lower-paid nonwhites and another consisting largely of higher-paid whites, is prima facie evidence, they claim, of disparate impact. As a result, the company can be legally required in court to show that the selection criteria for both kinds of jobs are reasonably necessary for the operation of the business. (This is called the "business necessity" test.) The cannery workers also charge that certain employment practices prevent them from filling unskilled noncannery jobs. These include: nepotism, a preference for rehiring previous employees, not posting notices of openings at the cannery, and an English proficiency requirement. Finally, the two classes of unskilled workers are housed separately and rarely mingle.

The managers you talk to admit the truth of the workers' complaints but differ in their interpretation of the facts. There is no discrimination, they contend, because the unskilled noncannery workers are recruited from the company's base of operations in the Pacific Northwest, and the racial composition of the unskilled noncannery category is roughly equal to the racial composition in that region of the country and also to the composition of the people who apply for the jobs. "It is a mistake," one manager says, "to compare the two unskilled job categories at the cannery and conclude that there is a statistical imbalance. The proper comparison is with the available work force for temporary labor in the Pacific Northwest. And there we compare very favorably."

Upon returning to company headquarters, you consult with a staff lawyer about the situation. She tells you that the courts have indeed held disparate impact to be determined by comparing the racial or sexual composition of an employer's work force to the composition of the available, qualified pool of applicants in the local area. The fact that workers must be recruited elsewhere and transported to the work site makes this case unusual, she admits. "If the workers succeed in bringing suit," she continues, "we might still win using some untested legal arguments. We could argue, for example, that the workers need to show more than a racial imbalance in the work force; that they need to show that our employment practices are responsible for that imbalance. That would be very difficult for them to do, but the requirement is a reasonable one. Otherwise every employer could be brought into court to justify their practices as a matter of business necessity merely because of a statistical imbalance, and this could force employers to adopt strict quotas in order to avoid baseless suits, which is not what Congress intended in passing the Civil Rights Act."

Having heard from all sides in this dispute, you now sit down at your desk and begin drawing up a list of recommendations.

CASE 8.3 The Walkout at Wilton's

News of the walkout greeted Sam Hilton as he settled into his office chair on Monday morning. As the Director of Human Resources for Wilton's Department Stores, he prided himself on the company's progressive personnel relations, but a policy that he thought a success was backfiring on him. Eight of the twenty drivers in the Wilton's warehouse were sitting in their trucks in the parking lot, refusing to enter the warehouse building where the merchandise is loaded.

The walkout occurred when the drivers learned that Roy Stone had returned to work from a six-month medical leave of absence. A year ago, Roy revealed to his supervisor, who had demanded an explanation for repeated requests to take time off for doctors' appointments, that he had ARC or AIDS-related complex. ARC is a less severe condition than AIDS that is caused by the Human Immunodeficiency Virus (HIV), which is also responsible for AIDS, and about 50 percent of ARC patients eventually develop AIDS. Although Roy had insisted that his revelation remain absolutely confidential, the supervisor felt compelled to explain the situation to his own superior, and within weeks the information had spread to Roy's co-workers. A few were sympathetic, but others avoided him; derogatory comments began appearing on bulletin boards and bathroom walls; and some employees avoided using the sinks and toilets in the warehouse building.

Sam had been preparing a company policy statement on AIDS and decided that now was the time to act. The Vocational Rehabilitation Act of 1973 and the 1990 Americans with Disabilities Act, which became effective in 1992, protect employees with handicaps and disabilities from discrimination. Whether AIDS would be considered a disability by the courts was uncertain, but many companies were already preparing themselves for the difficult challenges that the inevitable rise of AIDS would create. Relying on the most up-to-date information from the U.S. Centers for Disease Control, which indicates that AIDS cannot be transmitted through ordinary casual contact, Sam and his staff completed the draft of an AIDS policy statement that sought to protect the rights of everyone in the organization. One provision of the policy statement says: "Wilton's recognizes that employees who have or may be perceived as having AIDS may wish to continue in their normal work activities as long as their physical condition allows them to do so. No difference in treatment should be accorded these individuals so long as they are able to meet work standards and so long as medical evidence indicates that their condition is not a threat to themselves or others."[39] In addition, the policy states that the company will make reasonable accommodation for AIDS-infected employees to the extent that they would for any handicapped or disabled employee, and that the confidentiality of all medical information provided to the responsible company officials will be preserved. After the adoption of the policy, Roy Stone requested and received a medical leave of absence, a benefit to which all employees are entitled for a maximum of one year.

After six months, Roy felt strong enough to return to work full-time, although by this time he had developed AIDS, a fact that he shared with the company doctor. He requested a position on the loading dock instead of the work as a driver that he had done previously. Sam and his staff met with all employees in the warehouse to prepare them for Roy's return. Through presentations and pamphlets, the employees were informed that HIV could be transmitted only through the sharing of bodily fluids such as occurs in sexual intercourse and the sharing of needles. Employees in the ordinary course of work are at virtually no risk.

The Monday of Roy's return did not go smoothly. In addition to the walkout of the eight drivers, several employees were threatening a lawsuit under a provision in their labor contract that obligates the company to take reasonable steps to assure the health and safety of all employees. The supervisor of the warehouse, who reported the walkout to Sam, tells him, "These guys aren't troublemakers. They're really scared about breathing the same air and touching what he's touched. They don't believe that everything is known about AIDS, and they don't want to be guinea pigs for the company's sake, not when they have wives and children to protect. One guy who just got married and really needs this job was crying hysterically this morning."

As the news sank in, Sam thought that maybe the AIDS policy was a mistake, or maybe it could have been handled better. At any rate, he had to go out now and speak with the warehouse personnel again. But what should he say to them? And what should he say to Roy?

NOTES

1. Material in the case is taken from "Bias Lawsuit May Have Wide Impact," *New York Times*, 18 January 1988, sec. 1, p. 10; and from *Clara Watson v. Fort Worth Bank and Trust*, 487 U.S. 977 (1988).

2. The information on AT&T is taken from EARL A. MOLANDER, "Affirmative Action at AT&T," in *Responsive Capitalism: Case Studies in Corporate Conduct* (New York: McGraw-Hill, 1980), 56–70.

3. 42 U.S.C. 2000e-2.

4. *Diaz v. Pan American World Airways, Inc.*, 442 F. 2d 385 (1971).

5. *Dothard v. Rawlinson*, 433 U.S. 321 (1977).

6. *Griggs v. Duke Power Company*, 401 U.S. 424 (1970). Some material is also taken from a case prepared by NANCY BLANPIED and TOM L. BEAUCHAMP, in TOM L. BEAUCHAMP and NORMAN E. BOWIE, eds., *Ethical Theory and Business*, 3rd ed. (Englewood Cliffs, NJ: Prentice Hall, 1988), 383–85.

7. The precedent of *Griggs* was altered by several subsequent court decisions, most notably *Wards Cove Packing Co. v. Antonio*, 490 U.S. 642 (1988), which made it more difficult for employees to sue for discrimination. A 1991 civil rights bill largely restored the interpretation of *Griggs* that had prevailed before.

8. For a discussion of these and other problems, see JAMES G. FRIERSON, "Religion in the Workplace," *Personnel Journal*, 67 (July 1988), 60–67; and DOUGLAS MASSENGILL and DONALD J. PETERSEN, "Job Requirements and Religious Practices: Conflict and Accommodation," *Labor Law Journal*, 39 (July 1988), 402–10.

9. *Young v. Southwestern S & L Association*, 509 F. 2d 140 (5th Cir. 1975).

10. TONY MAURO, "Age Bias Charges: Increasing Problem," *Nation's Business* (April 1983), 46.

11. This analysis and the phrase "taste for discrimination" are due to GARY S. BECKER, *The Economics of Discrimination*, 2nd ed. (Chicago: University of Chicago Press, 1971).

12. This point is also made in MILTON FRIEDMAN, *Capitalism and Freedom* (Chicago: University of Chicago Press, 1962), 109–10. Ironically, Friedman uses the analysis to argue *against* legislation curbing discrimination on the grounds that competition alone is sufficient to bring discrimination to an end.

13. See KENNETH J. ARROW, "The Theory of Discrimination," in ORELY ASHENFELTER and ALBERT REES, eds., *Discrimination in Labor Markets* (Princeton: Princeton University Press, 1973), 3–33; LESTER C. THUROW, *Generating Inequality* (New York: Basic Books, 1975); DENNIS J. AIGNER and GLEN G. CAIN, "Statistical Theories of Discrimination in Labor Markets," *Industrial and Labor Relations Review*, 30 (1977), 175–87; and BARBARA R. BERGMANN and WILLIAM DARITY, JR., "Social Relations, Productivity, and Employer Discrimination," *Monthly Labor Review*, 104 (April 1982), 47–49.

14. JOHN RAWLS, *A Theory of Justice* (Cambridge: Harvard University Press, 1971), 83.

15. ROSABETH MOSS KANTER in *Men and Women of the Corporation* (New York: Basic Books, 1977), chap. 8, proposes "batch" promotions of two or more individuals from excluded groups so that they can support each other and break down barriers.

16. These points are made in *Albemarle Paper Company v. Moody*, 422 U.S. 405 (1975).

17. "In the Supreme Court of the United States: *Clara Watson v. Fort Worth Bank and Trust*," *American Psychologist*, 43 (1988), 1019–28. See also an accompanying explanation by DONALD N. BERSOFF, "Should Subjective Employment Devices Be Scrutinized? It's Elementary, My Dear Ms. Watson," *American Psychologist*, 43 (1988), 1016–18.

18. *United Steelworkers and Kaiser Aluminum v. Weber*, 443 U.S. 193 (1979).

19. *Johnson v. Transportation Agency, Santa Clara County*, 480 U.S. 616 (1987).

20. The landmark cases are *Fullilove v. Klutznick*, 448 U.S. 448 (1980); *City of Richmond v. J. A. Croson Company*, 488 U.S. 469 (1989); and *Adarand v. Peña*, 115 S. Ct. 896 (1995).

21. BERNARD R. BOXILL, "The Morality of Preferential Hiring," *Philosophy and Public Affairs*, 7 (1978), 247.

22. BOXILL, "The Morality of Preferential Hiring," 248.

23. For a defense of this principle, see ALAN H. GOLDMAN, "Justice and Hiring by Competence," *American Philosophical Quarterly*, 14 (1977), 17–26.

24. For an argument of this kind, see JAMES NICKEL, "Classification by Race in Compensatory Programs," *Ethics*, 84 (1974), 147–48.

25. These points are made by GEORGE SHER, "Preferential Hiring," in TOM REGAN, ed., *Just Business: New Introductory Essays in Business Ethics* (New York: Random House, 1984), 48.

26. Boxill, "The Morality of Preferential Hiring," 266.

27. Quoted in Lewis D. Solomon and Judith S. Heeter, "Affirmative Action in Higher Education: Towards a Rationale for Preference," *Notre Dame Lawyer*, 52 (October 1976), 67.

28. Douglas Rae, *Inequalities* (Cambridge: Harvard University Press, 1981), 66–68.

29. Ronald Dworkin, *Taking Rights Seriously* (Cambridge: Harvard University Press, 1978), 223–39; and Dworkin, *A Matter of Principle* (Cambridge: Harvard University Press, 1985), 293–331.

30. Dworkin, *Taking Rights Seriously*, 227.

31. For criticism of Dworkin's argument see Robert L. Simon, "Individual Rights and 'Benign' Discrimination," *Ethics*, 90 (1979), 88–97.

32. Simon, "Individual Rights and 'Benign' Discrimination," 91.

33. Quoted in Peter Perl, "Rulings Provide Hiring Direction: Employers Welcome Move," *The Washington Post*, 3 July 1986, A1. Cited by Tom L. Beauchamp, "The Justification of Goals and Quotas in Hiring," in Beauchamp and Bowie, *Ethical Theory and Business*, 355.

34. The example and much that follows is taken from Alan Wertheimer, "Jobs, Qualifications, and Preferences," *Ethics*, 94 (1983), 99–112. A different kind of argument for the relevance of race as a qualification is presented by Michael Davis, "Race as Merit," *Mind*, 42 (1983), 347–67. For a criticism of the kind of argument presented by Wertheimer, see Robert K. Fullinwider, *The Reverse Discrimination Controversy: A Moral and Legal Analysis* (Totowa, NJ: Rowman Littlefield, 1980) 78–86; and Alan H. Goldman, *Justice and Reverse Discrimination* (Princeton: Princeton University Press, 1979), 167–68.

35. Manuel G. Velasquez, *Business Ethics: Concepts and Cases*, 3rd ed. (Englewood Cliffs, NJ: Prentice Hall, 1992), 355.

36. *Regents of the University of California* v. *Bakke*, 438 U.S. 265 (1978).

37. *Hirabayashi* v. *United States*, 320 U.S. 81 (1943).

38. This case is adapted from *Wards Cove Packing Co., Inc., et al.* v. *Antonio*, 490 U.S. 642 (1988).

39. Adapted from a proposed AIDS policy statement in Rose Knotts and J. Lynn Johnson, "AIDS in the Workplace: The Pandemic Firms Want to Ignore," *Business Horizons*, July–August 1993, 5–9.

9

Women and Family Issues

Lois Robinson was a first-class welder at Florida-based Jacksonville Shipyards, Inc. (JSI).[1] Women in any skilled craft job are a rarity in the largely men's world of shipbuilding and repair. JSI records show that fewer than 5 percent of shipyard workers between 1980 and 1987 were female, and no woman had ever held a supervisory or executive position at the company. Starting out as a third-class welder in 1977, Lois Robinson had steadily increased her skill so that she was the equal of any male welder. Still, she never quite fit in at JSI, which has been characterized as "a boys club," where a woman could be admitted only as a sex object. She could not be accepted merely as a good welder.

None of Lois Robinson's co-workers or supervisors had ever solicited her for sex, nor had any of them offered some benefit for her sexual favors or threatened to retaliate if she refused. Lois Robinson was occasionally ridiculed, as when one co-worker handed her a pornographic magazine while those around laughed at her response, or when another co-worker passed around a picture of a nude woman with long blond hair and a whip. (Because she has long blond hair and uses a welding tool known as a whip, she thought that the picture was being displayed to humiliate her.) It was not these incidents that infuriated her, however; it was rather the pervasive presence of calendars, magazines, pictures, graffiti, and other visual displays of nude women that she found intolerable.

The workplace was plastered with pinup calendars from suppliers that featured nude or partially clad women in sexually submissive poses, often with breasts and genital areas exposed. The suppliers' calendars were distributed by JSI to its employees with permission to display them wherever they pleased. Employees were required to get permission to post any other material in the workplace—and permission was denied in some instances for requests to post material of a commercial or political nature—but pictures of nude women from magazines or other sources were displayed with the full knowledge of management, from the president of JSI down. The pictures observed by Lois Robinson included one with a woman's pubic area exposed and a meat spatula pressed against it and another of a nude woman in full-frontal view and the words "USDA Choice." A drawing on a dartboard pictured a woman's breast with the nipple as the bull's eye. Lois Robinson also became aware that the sexually suggestive comments increased when her male coworkers noticed that she had seen one of the pornographic pictures. Although crude sexual jokes were sometimes told in her presence, she was often warned to "take cover" or leave so that the men could exchange jokes out of her hearing.

In January 1985, Lois Robinson complained to JSI management about the visual displays. Afterward, the pictures became more numerous and more graphic and the number of sexually suggestive comments to her and the other women increased. The complaints to her supervisors were apparently passed to higher levels of management, and a few pictures were removed only to be replaced by others. Some of the pictures to which she objected were in the shipfitter's trailer, where she and other workers reported to receive instructions, and she sometimes entered the trailer to check on paperwork. One day the words "Men Only" appeared on the door of the trailer, and though the sign was soon painted over, the words could still be observed. One supervisor pointed out that the company had no policy against the posting of pictures and claimed that the men had a constitutional right to do so. The supervisor's superior declined to order the pictures removed. Another supervisor suggested that Ms. Robinson "was spending too much time attending to the pictures and not enough time attending to her job."

As a federal contractor (JSI performed repairs on ships for the U.S. Navy), the company is obligated by presidential order to be nondiscriminatory and to have an affirmative action plan. In 1980, JSI adopted a policy entitled "Equal Employment Opportunity." The policy stated in part:

> . . . we should all be sensitive to the kind of conduct which is personally offensive to others. Abusing the dignity of anyone through ethnic, sexist, or racist slurs, suggestive remarks, physical advances or intimidation, sexual or otherwise, is not the kind of conduct that can be tolerated.

The policy asked that any violations be reported to the Equal Employment Opportunity (EEO) coordinator at the facility. The policy was not generally known to the supervisors at the shipyards, nor was it incorporated in the standard JSI rule book. The supervisors received no training on how to deal with reports of sexual harassment or other problems, and the name of the EEO coordinator was not given in the policy and was not widely known to employees in the company. In any event, the experience of Lois Robinson was not likely to encourage any victim of harassment to make a report to anyone at JSI.

On September 2, 1986, Lois Robinson filed a suit against Jacksonville Shipyards, Inc., for sexual harassment. In the suit she cited the pervasive presence of sexually explicit pictures, the sexually suggestive and humiliating comments of her male co-workers, and the "Men Only" sign on the shipfitter's trailer.

INTRODUCTION

Women populate the American workplace. According to 1990 data, women hold 46 percent of the jobs in this country, and the figure is expected to rise to 50 percent by the end of the century. A closer look, however, reveals that women are more highly represented in traditionally female job categories, which carry less pay, prestige, and potential for promotion. The result is a "pay gap" between men and women, which has narrowed in recent years, but women still receive only 71 cents for every dollar earned by a man. Although women have entered the ranks of management in greater numbers, a 1994 *Wall Street Journal* study of the 200 largest U.S. firms found that women held only a quarter of all management positions and that these were mainly at lower levels.[2] Women constituted a mere 5 percent of the vice presidents surveyed, and the number of women presidents, CEOs, and board directors was exceedingly small. A "glass ceiling" appears to exist in corporate America, preventing the promotion of women beyond a certain level.

In addition to the pay gap and the glass ceiling, women experience other adversities in the workplace from which men are largely spared. Women who enter male-dominated lines of work are often made to feel unwelcome, either because their presence breaks accepted routines or because of attitudes about women's roles. Sexual stereotypes about women's commitment to work or their capacity for leadership also interfere with their advancement up the corporate ladder. In addition, women are compelled to deal with the complications of sexual attraction in the workplace, which range from office romances to sexual harassment. Although sexual harassment is thought by some to be merely unwanted sexual interest, it is viewed by others to be an abuse of power and an assertion of existing power relations by men over women.

Finally, women more than men face the challenges of combining full-time work with family obligations. Two-thirds of men in the work force have wives who also work, thus creating so-called two-earner families; and more than half of all employed women have children under the age of six. Although responsibility for children in two earner families could be shared fifty-fifty, this is seldom the case. The sociologist Arlie Hochschild has called work at home "the second shift," and she notes that it constitutes roughly an extra month of twenty-four-hour days each year. Working this second shift takes its toll on women who attempt to balance the conflicting demands, and some women drop out of the work force for varying periods of time in order to fulfill family obligations. Many companies have responded to the problems of working mothers and two-earner families by a set of family-friendly programs that include maternity leaves, flexible working hours, and child-care centers.

This chapter examines three issues that affect mainly women in the workplace. These are sexual harassment as a form of sex discrimination, comparable worth as a solution for the problem of the pay gap, and the family-friendly programs that help employees balance the demands of family and work life.

SEXUAL HARASSMENT

Improper sexual conduct in the workplace—which includes lewd and suggestive comments, touching and fondling, persistent attention, and requests for sexual favors—has long been a problem for women, and occasionally men. All too often, such sexual harassment has been regarded by employers as a personal matter beyond their control, or as an unavoidable part of male–female relations. However, increased attention to the problem and developments in the law have made employers aware of their responsibilities—and women, of their rights!

That sexual harassment is morally wrong is not in dispute. The main questions are: What is sexual harassment? How serious is the problem? And who is responsible for preventing it? A further, legal question is whether sexual harassment is prohibited by the 1964 Civil Rights Act. Although Title VII does not mention sexual harassment, the courts have ruled that it is a form of discrimination and, hence, an illegal employment practice.

What Is Sexual Harassment?

Surveys of employee attitudes reveal substantial agreement on some of the activities that constitute sexual harassment, and differences on others. In particular, most of the respondents in a 1980 poll conducted by *Harvard Business Review* and *Redbook* magazine consistently rated a supervisor's behavior as more serious than the same action by a co-worker, thereby recognizing that sexual harassment is mainly an issue of power.[3] Barbara A. Gutek has found that more than 90 percent of both men and women consider socializing or sexual activity as a job requirement to be sexual harassment. However, 84 percent of the women surveyed, but only 59 percent of the men, identified "sexual touching" as sexual harassment.[4] In general, women are more likely than men to label the same activity as sexual harassment.

In 1980, the Equal Employment Opportunity Commission (EEOC) issued guidelines on sexual harassment that included the following definition:

> Unwelcome sexual advances, requests for sexual favors, and other verbal or physical conduct of a sexual nature constitute sexual harassment when (1) submission to such conduct is made either explicitly or implicitly a term or condition of an individual's employment, (2) submission to or rejection of such conduct by an individual is used as the basis for employment decisions affecting such individual, or (3) such conduct has the purpose or effect of unreasonably interfering with an individual's work performance or creating an intimidating, hostile, or offensive working environment.

This definition makes a distinction between two kinds of harassment. One is *quid pro quo* harassment, in which a superior, who is usually a man, uses his power to grant or deny employment benefits to exact sexual favors from a subordinate, who is usually a woman. The other kind is *hostile working environment* harassment, in which the sexual nature of the conduct of co-workers and others causes a woman (or a man) to be very uncomfortable. What constitutes discomfort is not easy to specify, but the judge in the *Jacksonville Shipyards* case ruled that the display of pinup calendars and pornographic pictures constitutes an unrelenting "visual assault on the sensibilities of female workers" and that such a situation constitutes sexual harassment under the "hostile working environment" provision. In reaching its decision, the court relied on testimony about sexual (and racial) stereotyping. Stereotyping is likely to occur when members of a group are few in number and when members of another group are in power. The stereotypes in sexual harassment cases are those that prevail outside the workplace, where some men view women as sex objects. The conditions for stereotyping thus permit "sex role spillover," in which women's roles outside of employment "spill over" or become central in an environment where other roles, such as the job to be performed, ought to be the only ones relevant.[5] A good welder who is also a husband and father can be treated on the job only as a good welder, whereas a woman like Lois Robinson cannot escape the stereotypes that the men bring with them to the workplace. She cannot be, in their eyes, only a good welder. Stereotyping becomes more prevalent when there are "priming" elements, such as pictures that create a stimulus for harassing treatment. One effect of stereotyping is selective interpretation, whereby complaints may be perceived in accord with a stereotype, such as that women are "overly emotional." The failure of Lois Robinson's supervisors to take her complaints seriously may have been due that effect.

The decision in the *Jacksonville Shipyards* case upheld the EEOC view that a hostile working environment constitutes sexual harassment under Title VII. Even when there is no demand for sexual favors, conditions in a workplace can produce a form of stress that interferes with a person's ability to work and erodes that person's sense of well-being. Not only does a visual display of pornographic pictures produce stress, but the need to be diligent to avoid the next incident may induce more stress; and the feeling that their complaints will not produce any change further compounds the stress that harassed women have.

Whether a work environment is hostile or offensive is not easily determined. Much depends on the attitudes of the employees involved and the response of management to employee concerns. The two situations described in Case 9.2, for example, are debatable. The manager of the Dairy Mart store was not subjected to harassing treatment by particular persons, nor was she exposed to the contents of the magazines in question; she merely objected to the fact that the magazines were being sold in her store. The readers of the magazine were customers, not Dairy Mart employees, and she would have no further contact with the readers after they left the store. Unlike the women at Stroh Brewery, she did not blame any actual harassing treatment on fellow employees who were influenced by the objectionable material. Both Dairy Mart and Stroh Brewery were responding to demonstrable consumer interest in the kinds of material that some employees found offensive.

Sexual Harassment as a Form of Sex Discrimination

Title VII of the 1964 Civil Rights Act and other legislation protects women against many forms of discrimination. The Equal Pay Act of 1963 forbids an employer to offer different wages to men and women who perform the same or substantially similar work unless the difference is based on some valid factor other than sex, such as seniority or productivity. Unlike race and color, sex can be a bona fide occupational qualification (BFOQ). Many of the problems about what constitutes sexual discrimination arise in cases where a person's sex can arguably be taken into consideration, such as in hiring guards for a male prison. In some other cases, sex is not a BFOQ, but the stated qualifications serve to exclude virtually all women. Examples are tests for police officers and firefighters that require considerable strength and endurance. Whether the qualifications are discriminatory depends largely on whether they are absolutely necessary for the performance of the job.

Does the Title VII prohibition against discrimination because of sex protect women who are pregnant? Congress passed the Pregnancy Discrimination Act in 1978 in order to resolve this question. The main impetus came from a case in which a woman challenged a policy at General Electric Company forcing her to take unpaid maternity leave with the loss of all fringe benefits.[6] After a miscarriage, the woman suffered a further medical problem unrelated to the pregnancy. Since she lost all fringe benefits because of her pregnancy, the company refused to cover the cost of the unrelated medical problem. The Supreme Court ruled that the policy at General Electric did not constitute sexual discrimination under Title VII but challenged Congress, if it disagreed, to clarify whether the law on sexual discrimination covers pregnancy. Congress accepted the challenge and declared it did.

The Pregnancy Discrimination Act amends the phrase in Title VII "because of sex" to include decisions made on the basis of "pregnancy, childbirth, or related medical conditions." The act mainly affects fringe benefits of two kinds: hospital and major medical plans and policies on temporary disability and sick leave. All such plans and policies are required by the act to treat pregnancy as any other condition. Employers are not required to grant maternity leaves or pay for the medical care associated with pregnancy. But if they allow an employee with a broken leg, for example, to have a paid leave of absence or they pay for the cost of a broken leg under the company's medical plan, then a woman's pregnancy must be treated in exactly the same way. Men are also protected by the Pregnancy Discrimination Act in that the medical coverage for the pregnant wife of a male employee must be the same as that provided for the husband of a female employee.[7]

Quid pro quo harassment clearly violates the Title VII provision that men and women should not be treated differently in their "compensation, terms, conditions, or privileges of employment." A woman who is promised a promotion or a raise—or threatened with demotion, termination, or loss of pay—based on whether she submits to the sexual demands of her boss is being held to a different standard, merely because of her sex.

Some observers contend that quid pro quo harassment, while unfortunate, is not sexual discrimination but merely a wrongful act committed by one employee against another. It is not uncommon for workers of both sexes to encounter personal problems on the job, and harassment, in this view, is one of these personal problems. However, Catharine A. MacKinnon has argued that sexual harassment in the workplace is more than "personal"; it has a connection to "the female condition as a whole."

> As a practice, sexual harassment singles out a gender-defined group, women, for special treatment in a way which adversely affects and burdens their status as employees. Sexual harassment limits women in a way men are not limited. It deprives them of opportunities that are available to male employees without sexual conditions. In so doing, it creates two employment standards: one for women that includes sexual requirements, one for men that does not.[8]

Initially, the courts were reluctant to recognize sexual harassment as discrimination unless a woman suffered some economic loss, such as a reduction in pay or the loss of her job. If this position is accepted, however, then any amount of harassment is legal as long as the woman's employment status is not affected. In 1981, though, a court held that sexual harassment is illegal even when there is no economic loss. No woman, the court declared, should be forced to endure the psychological trauma of a sexually intimidating workplace as a condition of employment.[9] Finally, in *Meritor Savings Bank* v. *Vinson* (1986), the U.S. Supreme Court declared that "without question" both quid pro quo harassment and hostile working environment harassment constitute sexual discrimination under Title VII.[10]

Hostile working environment harassment is both more pervasive and more difficult to prove. Studies have shown that quid pro quo harassment is relatively rare, but in surveys about one-third of working women (33 percent) report incidents of sexual remarks and jokes and around a fourth cite staring and suggestive leers (27 percent) and unwanted sexual touching (24 percent).[11] Not all of this conduct is considered to be sexual harassment, however, even by the women who report it. Removing all sexual conduct from the workplace, moreover, is impractical—and, perhaps, even undesirable. Still, a line must be drawn somewhere.

One possibility is a *reasonable person* standard, whereby conduct that is offensive to a person of average sensibilities would be impermissible. However, one court has rejected this approach on the grounds that it "tends to be male-biased and tends to systematically ignore the experiences of women." This court has proposed, instead, a *reasonable woman* standard, which requires that the alleged harassment be judged from the recipient's point of view.[12]

In *Meritor*, the Court also considered the question of an employer's responsibility for harassment by a supervisor or co-worker. Although Mechelle Vinson charged that her supervisor, Sidney Taylor, made repeated sexual advances and raped her on several occasions, she did not report this to anyone at the bank or use the bank's formal complaint procedure. The bank held that it was not responsible, therefore, because of the lack of knowledge. The Supreme Court disagreed, however, and held that an employer has a responsibility to ensure that the workplace is free of sexual harassment.

Even if a woman need not show economic harm as a result of harassing conduct, need she at least show psychological harm? Theresa Harris's employer made disparaging comments about women, suggested that she negotiate a raise at a local motel, publicly announced (falsely) that she had slept with a client to get an account, and required her to retrieve change from his pant pocket. The employer claimed that he was only joking. A lower court found that the employer, the president of a Nashville-based truck-leasing company, was "a vulgar man" but contended that his behavior was not so egregious as to seriously affect her "psychological well-being."[13] In *Harris* v. *Forklift Systems, Inc.*, the U.S. Supreme Court ruled that no psychological harm needs to be shown as long as a reasonable person would find the conduct offensive.[14] In the words of one observer, "You don't have to have a nervous breakdown, but one joke does not make a case."[15] The highest court had an opportunity in the *Harris* case to affirm the reasonable *woman* standard, but the justices relied instead on the reasonable *person* standard.

Preventing Sexual Harassment

Although sexual harassment is usually committed by one employee against another, employers bear both a legal and an ethical obligation to prevent harassment and to act decisively when it occurs. Harassment is more likely to occur when management has not prescribed clear policies and procedures with regard to conduct of a sexual nature. Employers who display an insufficient concern (a "head-in-the-sand" attitude) or have inadequate procedures for detecting harassment in the workplace bear some responsibility for individuals' harassing conduct. In addition, companies cannot fully evade responsibility by blaming the victim for not reporting sexual harassment in accord with established procedures. The way in which employers respond to claims of sexual harassment sends a powerful message about the seriousness with which management takes it own policies and procedures. The legal duty of an employer also extends to harassment by nonemployees, such as customers or clients.

Aside from the law—including the cost of litigating and paying settlements—employers have strong financial incentives to avoid sexual harassment. Tolerating sexual harassment can result in hidden costs to companies. A 1988 study of 160 Fortune 500 companies calculated that sexual harassment costs an average company with about 24,000 employees a stunning $6.7 million.[16] This figure does not include litigation and settlement costs but merely the losses that result from absenteeism, low morale, and employee turnover. According to the study, productivity suffers when women are forced to waste time avoiding uncomfortable situations or to endure the stress of coping with them. The stress induced by sexual harassment leads to health problems, loss of self-confidence, and a lack of commitment, all of which may reduce career prospects and deprive employers of valuable talent. Women who have been harassed are more likely to seek transfers or to quit, thereby increasing the cost of employee training.

Most corporations have recognized the cost of sexual harassment and accepted their responsibility to prevent it by establishing programs to deal with sexual harassment on the job. The major features of these programs are (1) developing a firm policy against harassment; (2) communicating this policy to all employees and providing training, where necessary, to secure compliance; (3) setting up a procedure for reporting violations and investigating all complaints thoroughly and fairly; and (4) taking appropriate action against the offenders.

1. A sexual harassment policy.   The first step in a corporate program to eliminate sexual harassment is a firm statement from a high level in the organization that certain conduct will not be tolerated. The policy statement should not only convey the serious intent of management but also describe the kinds of actions that constitute sexual harassment. A good policy should educate as well as warn.

2. Communicating the policy.   No policy can be effective unless it is effectively communicated to the members of the organization, and effective communication is not merely a matter of making the policy known but of gaining understanding and acceptance of the policy. Many corporations include sexual harassment awareness in their initial training and ongoing education programs, often utilizing videos of situations and simulation games to heighten employee sensitivity to the issues.

3. Setting up procedures.   A complete policy should include a well-publicized procedure for handling incidents of sexual harassment with assurances of nonretaliation against an accuser. Employees should be informed of the procedure to follow in making a complaint, including the specific person or office to which complaints should be made, and preferably offered several alternatives for making complaints. In addition, those who handle complaints should be aware of the procedure they should follow. The policy should assure all parties—the accuser as well as the accused—of confidentiality. The investigation itself should seek to ascertain all the relevant facts and to observe the rules of due process, especially in view of the harm that could result from false accusations. Although companies should have a formal complaint procedure, some also make use of an informal process through which a situation may be resolved to the victim's satisfaction. An informal procedure is well suited for less serious, infrequent incidents among peers where there is some misunderstanding or insensitivity; it is inappropriate for repeat offenses with multiple victims and for harassment by a victim's superior.

4. Taking Appropriate Action.   Any disciplinary action—which may include a reprimand, job transfer, demotion, pay reduction, loss of a bonus, or termination—should aim, at a minimum, to deter the offender and perhaps to deter others in the organization (although the deterrent effect on others will depend on publicizing the penalty). Because the victims of harassment may have suffered some job loss or been deprived of some opportunities, a proper resolution may also include compensating the victims for any harm done.

CASE 9.2   Sexual Harassment or Business as Usual?

Selling *Playboy* at Dairy Mart

Dolores Stanley, a thirty-three-year-old church-going mother of three, was promoted in 1990 to the position of manager of a Dairy Mart store in rural Toronto, Ohio, after ten years with the convenience store chain. One of her first acts as a manager was to remove all "adult" magazines, including *Playboy* and *Penthouse*, from behind the counter, where they were displayed in opaque plastic wrappers. Her Dairy Mart superiors insisted that the magazines be put back on display in the store, saying that it was not the company's role to censor their customers' reading. Dolores Stanley replied that she could not participate in the selling of material that was offensive to her personally and degrading for all women. Forcing her to sell the magazines constituted sexual harassment, she claimed.

The Swedish Bikini Team

In a TV ad for Old Milwaukee beer, the scantily clad Swedish Bikini Team descends by parachute into the campsite of several awed young males. The voiceover to the women's bump-and-grind routine is "It just doesn't get any better than this." Things got a lot worse for five women employees of Stroh Brewery, the maker of Old Milwaukee beer, who claim that their harassment by fellow male employees was encouraged by the company's advertising. The Stroh executives conceded that the women had been subjected to lewd comments and displays of pornographic pictures but pointed to the company's own sexual harassment policy as evidence that such conduct is not condoned. They labeled as "preposterous" the claim that the Swedish Bikini Team ads contributed in any way to the harassment.[17] The women argued that "these ads tell Stroh's male employees that women are stupid, panting playthings."[18] One woman said of the men in her office, "When they are getting feedback from the top of the company that women are bimbos and that's OK, that's why I'm getting treated the way I'm getting treated."[19] Shortly after the women filed suit, the Swedish Bikini Team was featured in *Playboy* magazine.

COMPARABLE WORTH

In 1981, a strike was called by a union representing about half of the 4,000 municipal workers in San Jose, California. One issue in the strike was the union's insistence
that the city spend $3.2 million over four years to upgrade the salaries of nonman-
agement employees in female-dominated jobs. A study recently conducted by the
city with the aid of a national consulting firm revealed considerable differences in
salary between men and women in comparable positions. Using a point-factor evaluation system, with points being assigned for knowledge, problem solving, accountability, and working conditions, the study showed that Senior Chemists, for
example, (501 points) received $29,094 annually, while the salary for the compara-
ble female-dominated job of Senior Librarian (496 points) was $23,348. The male-
dominated job category of Painter (173 points) was held by the study to be
comparable to that of Secretary (177 points), but the pay for painters and secretaries was $24,518 and $17,784 respectively. The nine-day strike ended after the city
council pledged to spend $1.45 million over two years to upgrade salaries in the low-
est-paid female-dominated positions and to bargain in good faith in subsequent
years to close the wage gap further. Mayor Janet Gray Hayes hailed the settlement as
"the first giant step toward fairness in the workplace for women."

The situation in San Jose is remarkable only for the response of the city to
the problem of the undervaluing of jobs held predominantly by women. It is well
documented that women earn less than men. The figure at the end of 1989 was that
the median income for women was 68 percent of the earnings for men. This earnings gap has been relatively constant over the past fifty years with the difference in
pay between men and women dipping in recent years before rising again. In 1939,
women who were employed full-time, year-round earned 63.6 percent of the wages
of men who were similarly employed, and this figure remained above 63 percent
during the middle of the 1950s. In 1972, the earnings of women as a percentage of
men's fell to a record low of 56.6, and by 1981 the figure had risen only to 59.2
percent.

Women are not the only group with lower earnings. The income of racial
minorities is also substantially less than that of whites. With increasing access to education and the elimination of discrimination in hiring and promotion, though,
black men have made significant economic gains. In 1959, the mean salary of black
men was 71 percent of the earnings of the average white man. Ten years later the figure had risen to 75 percent, and by 1975 the percentage had increased to 85. Conventional remedies for discrimination have thus proven effective in reducing wage
differences between blacks and whites but not those between men and women. As a
result, advocates of women's rights have sought out new means of attacking this
form of discrimination.

The Principle of Comparable Worth

The means chosen is the principle of *comparable worth*. This principle holds that dissimilar jobs can still be compared with respect to certain features and that jobs
which are similar with respect to these features ought to be paid the same. The job

of a secretary, for example, is quite different from that of a painter, but if it can be shown that the two jobs require a similar degree of skill and effort, then secretaries and painters should be paid at the same rate. Expressed in this way, the principle of comparable worth provides a method for setting wages that is an alternative to market forces operating according to the laws of supply and demand.

On the standard economic view, wages are determined largely by the contribution workers make to *productivity*. More technically, the pay of any given worker is a function of the net addition that worker makes to the revenues of the employer. The value of a job, then, on the economic view, is what the work of an employee is worth to an employer, and this value is measured largely by the price a worker can command in the marketplace. In a competitive labor market in which the workers are free to move from one job to another and employers are forced to compete for their services, the laws of supply and demand will result in a state of equilibrium in which the wages of workers match their productivity.

Advocates of the principle of comparable worth hold the view that compensation ought to be based on *job content*. This is typically done by a process known as job evaluation, which measures and compares the features of a job for which a worker ought to be compensated. The general features considered in most job evaluation systems are skill, effort, responsibility, and working conditions. Each job is assigned a certain number of points from a range for each feature; these points are added together to arrive at a total; different jobs are then ranked according to their total number of points. Compensation is based on these rankings so that jobs with the same number of points are paid the same and jobs with more points carry higher rates of pay.

The use of job evaluations to set wages is a familiar practice in American business. Since the 1920s, companies have employed methods for measuring the content of jobs in order to provide a rational means for setting wages where market forces alone are inadequate for the task. While the laws of supply and demand determine the overall level of wages for different kinds of work, they are not suited for making fine distinctions between the multitude of jobs in large organizations, especially where the productivity of individual workers is difficult to measure. This method also gives managers a great deal of control over decisions about wages and the deployment of labor, which is especially valuable in dealing with a unionized work force.

Job evaluation studies are used extensively in the public sector, since governments are largely insulated from market forces. In order to attract and retain competent personnel and to maintain equity among different jobs, civil service systems on the local, state, and federal levels evaluate the content of jobs and set wages according to the value of comparable jobs in the private sector. Prior to the study of nonmanagement workers in San Jose, for example, the city conducted a job evaluation of salaried managers in the municipal government. The purpose was merely to ensure that all salaries were competitive in order to prevent other cities in the area from luring managers away with offers of higher pay. Washington, which was the first state to conduct a comparable worth study to determine the extent of discrimination against women, had been required since 1960 to pay workers the prevailing "market rate," which was determined by an elaborate salary survey of state jobs and jobs in business and industry. No attempt was made to compare every state job with jobs in the private sector. Rather, the compensation for a few "benchmark" jobs was set by determining the wages which work of that kind would command in a competitive market, and the pay for other state jobs was set by comparing them with the "benchmark" jobs.

Two Versions of the Principle

There are two different versions of the principle of comparable worth. In one version, the value of a job is determined by features of the work performed—by the content of the job, in other words, as opposed to supply and demand. Unlike the value of other goods, then, the value of labor is not the same as the market price, and the possibility exists that the wages resulting from market forces undervalue (or in some cases overvalue) the work performed. The principle of comparable worth, in this version, is offered as a morally preferable alternative to the market, especially when the market price does not accurately reflect the value of the work performed.

A second version of the principle of comparable worth does not maintain that there is a concept of value other than the price that a worker can command in a competitive market. Because of discrimination, however, the wages that are actually paid to some workers are not the same as what they would be paid if there were no discrimination. Since the skill and effort required to perform a job are largely the features that enable workers to command a certain price for their labor in a free market, a comparison of jobs according to their content provides a means for determining whether discrimination exists and what wages would be without the presence of discrimination. In this version, comparable worth is a method for detecting discrimination in the labor market and correcting it. It is not an alternative to the market but an adjunct that frees the market from the distorting force of discrimination.

The difference between the two versions of the principle of comparable worth can be expressed in the language of rights. The first version claims that each worker has a right to be paid according to the content of the job performed and that this right is violated when one worker is paid less than another for performing comparable work, whatever the reason for the difference in pay. The right involved in the second version is simply the right not to be discriminated against in the setting of wages, that is, the right not to be paid lower wages simply because the work is performed predominantly by persons of a certain sex or race. The principle "equal pay for comparable work," in this version, is thus a means for protecting an already existing right rather than the creation of a new right.

In order to justify the principle of comparable worth in the first version, it is necessary to demonstrate that the only morally relevant features for setting wages are those which concern the character of the work performed and that all other differences, such as those resulting from the forces of supply and demand, are morally irrelevant. This is by no means an easy task. The justification of the second version of the principle is much easier. A defender need only show that the market has operated in a discriminatory manner and that setting wages on the basis of job content is better suited than any other means for a nondiscriminatory labor market. Since the second version is what most advocates intend, it is the one considered in the remainder of this discussion.

The Equal Pay Act and Title VII

The principle of comparable worth ("equal pay for comparable work") is not the same as the principle embodied in the Equal Pay Act of 1963 (EPA). Passed by Congress as an amendment to the Fair Labor Standards Act, the EPA prohibits an employer from paying men and women in the same establishment different wages for jobs that require "equal skill, effort, and responsibility," and that are performed under the same conditions. Exceptions are allowed by the act for differences due to any factor other than sex, such as seniority, a merit system, and compensation based on productivity. As interpreted by the courts, the EPA applies to employees who perform substantially the same but not necessarily identical work.[20] The principle embodied in the EPA can be expressed, therefore, as "equal pay for the *same* work" rather than "equal pay for *comparable* work."

While Title VII of the 1964 Civil Rights Act provides more extensive protection against wage discrimination than the EPA, the courts have not ruled that the failure of employers to pay equal wages for work of comparable worth is a violation of Title VII. The issue was raised in a suit filed by a woman, Alberta Gunther, and three co-workers who were employed as jail matrons in Washington County, Oregon. Since the matrons were responsible for fewer inmates than male guards and performed some clerical duties that were not shared by their male counterparts, the jobs were held by the courts to be dissimilar. Consequently, there was no violation of the EPA. Still, the women argued that the difference in pay was the result of intentional discrimination on the basis of sex. In support of their argument they cited a county-commissioned study that evaluated the job of jail matron at 95 percent of the market value of the guards' job. While the male guards received the full recommended wages, the women were paid only 70 percent of theirs. As a result, the women earned one-third less than the men. In a 5–4 decision, the Supreme Court ruled that Alberta Gunther and her co-workers could sue under Title VII for equal pay for work that is comparable to but not substantially the same as that performed by men. The decision emphasized, however, that the matrons' suit was "not based on the controversial concept of 'comparable worth'," but that they "seek to prove by direct evidence, that their wages were depressed because of *intentional sex discrimination.*"[21]

Are Wage Differences Due to Discrimination?

One important issue in the debate over comparable worth is whether the difference in earnings between men and women is due to discrimination or whether it results from the impersonal workings of the labor market. If discrimination is not the cause of the earnings gap, then there is no substance to the claim that women are being unfairly compensated for the work they do and hence there is no need to adopt remedial measures, such as a system of compensation based on the principle of comparable worth. Of course, a comparable worth system could still be advanced as a morally preferable method of setting wages (the first version of the principle) or as a pragmatic step toward reducing the disparity in earnings between the sexes as a socially desirable goal.

The main evidence for discrimination in compensation is statistical. Unfortunately, the statistical evidence—which indisputably documents the existence of an earnings gap between men and women—is explainable in a variety of ways, not all of which point to discrimination as the culprit. One reason why men earn more is that they work more hours, and so a distinction has to be made between income (the amount actually received in a paycheck) and wages (the amount earned for each hour worked). Earnings also increase with experience, and women, who voluntarily leave the work force more often to raise a family and pursue other interests, have a shorter work history on the average than men. When comparisons are made between male and female workers with the same number of years of experience or between never married women and men, the wage gap narrows, though not by much. By 1980, women who had never married, for example, still earned only 65 percent as much as men their own age.

Success also depends on a willingness to acquire an education and specialized training, to accept positions of greater responsibility, to relocate when necessary, and to make other sacrifices. These are examples of what economists call *human capital*, which is the amount of resources invested in order to increase the productivity of individual workers. If men "invest" more in themselves and thereby increase their value to employers, then they can rightly expect to be paid more. It can be objected, however, that insofar as women leave the work force more often and are less willing to do what is necessary to build a career, their choices simply reflect the lower return that their investment in human capital brings in a job market that discriminates against them. The result is a "chicken-and-egg" question: Do women earn less because they have less human capital, or do women rationally choose to invest less in themselves because of low pay?

By far the most significant factor in explaining the lower wages of women is the segregation of jobs according to sex. Women are crowded into traditionally female occupations that are not highly valued by the market in the first place, and the large number of women competing for jobs further depresses wages. Of the 553 occupations listed in the 1970 census, 310 were 80 percent or more male-dominated, while women held 80 percent or more of the jobs in 50 of the occupations. Further, 70 percent of men and 54 percent of women were in occupations where workers of their own sex held more than 70 percent of the jobs. And 25 percent of women workers were employed in occupations that were 95 percent female.

Experts are sharply divided on whether women are forced into traditionally female occupations because they are the only jobs available or whether they freely choose them because of a preference for certain kinds of work. Advocates of the latter view cite gender differences in the factors that contribute to job satisfaction. According to some studies, women are willing to sacrifice some income for clean, safe, comfortable work, and they place more value than men on interpersonal relations, the opportunity to serve others, and the intrinsic interest of a job.[22] As a result, some of the gap between the earnings of men and women may be due to the higher wages employers must offer to induce workers (who are predominantly men) to perform less desirable work, while women compete among themselves for more attractive jobs.

If the explanation of the pay gap is that women are confined by discrimination to female-dominated jobs, then one solution is to remove the barriers to the advancement of women into traditionally male lines of work by more rigorous enforcement of Title VII. This is an alternative to comparable worth known as *realignment*, which involves reducing the extent of job segregation according to sex. In the view of many experts, however, realignment does not address the source of the problem, which can be succinctly stated as follows:

> Women are paid less because they are in women's jobs, and women's jobs are paid less because they are done by women. The reason is that women's work—in fact, virtually anything done by women—is characterized as less valuable.[23]

As an illustration, the formerly male-dominated job of bank teller has been largely taken over by women. The result has not been an increase in the opportunities of women for higher pay but a decrease in the relative earning power (as well as the prestige) of this kind of work. If the undervaluing of work done by women is a significant factor in explaining why men earn more, then comparable worth is likely to be a more effective strategy than realignment.

To summarize this portion of the discussion, some of the differences in male and female earnings are due to the choices women make. These are (perhaps) the result of inherent differences between men and women, and certainly they result from social forces that operate outside the job market. Many structural features of the job market also play a role. Among these are differences between industries and firms within an industry, regional differences, age distribution in the work force, unionization, and a host of other variables that have not been adequately studied. Whatever residual amount is left unaccounted for by these factors is due to discrimination against women. The only conclusion to emerge consistently from the many studies on the question, though, is that we do not know how much that residual amount is.

Measuring Job Content

A second issue in the comparable worth debate is whether it is possible to measure job content in such a way that the resulting comparisons are meaningful and reliable. Some critics use the analogy of comparing apples and oranges to support their contention that no significant comparison can be made between extremely dissimilar jobs. Other opponents of comparable worth argue that job evaluations are not wholly objective and are potentially discriminatory. The evaluator must use judgment, first, in determining the features to be taken into account and their relative weight and, second, in deciding the number of points to assign for each feature in evaluating a job. And studies have shown that there is considerable variation in the results obtained by different evaluators. There is a tendency, for example, for the judgment of an evaluator to reflect the prevailing status and pay of the jobs being evaluated, with the result that the evaluation simply ratifies the existing practices of an employer. This is a problem known as "policy capturing."

A study of comparable worth conducted by the National Academy of Sciences for the Equal Employment Opportunity Commission also cites the problem that the judgment of evaluators may also introduce a systematic bias against women.[24] The potential for introducing bias is vividly illustrated by an evaluation of the job of bindery workers in the U.S. Government Printing Office.[25] Not only did the evaluator assign women fewer points for performing work with the same features (lifting heavy objects and handling confidential material, for example), but the skill and effort required for the work done by women was consistently underestimated. The evaluator gave no points to the women for stitching bindings, for example, since sewing is a skill possessed by most women! The response of supporters of comparable worth is that there are carefully designed, generally reliable techniques for conducting job evaluations that are not open to the critics' charge. The reasons that some workers deserve to be paid more than others refer to factors that are inherent in all jobs. The high pay of truck drivers is deserved because of the long grueling hours and the heavy responsibility of hauling valuable cargo. But nursing is also exhausting work on which the lives of patients often depend. So these two jobs have much in common despite the obvious differences.

The reliability of a comparable worth study depends on how it is conducted. Experts in the field recommend that a committee of employees be formed, so that the choice of factors and the assignment of weights are done by people who are thoroughly familiar with the jobs being evaluated. In the San Jose study, the city's personnel department distributed questionnaires to employees in order to gather firsthand information on each job. After interviews with approximately 20 percent of the respondents, detailed job descriptions were written, and a committee was formed to study and evaluate every job. This committee consisted of an equal number of men and women, and before a decision was made, seven of the ten members had to agree on the number of points to be assigned for each factor. Furthermore, the factors used and their weight can be validated by applying a job evaluation system only to white males, where discrimination is not present, and comparing actual earnings with those predicted by system.

The Effect on the Labor Market

A third issue in the debate is the charge of many opponents of comparable worth that ignoring market forces will undermine the ability of the market to price and allocate labor in an efficient manner, with a resultant lowering of productivity. One beneficial effect of market forces, for example, is to provide incentives for workers to leave crowded areas with low-productivity jobs for which there is a declining demand and to prepare themselves for more productive work in newer areas where the demand is greater. Paying workers on the basis of job content will remove this valuable incentive. The introduction of comparable worth, moreover, is likely to be accompanied by a complex administrative structure that will increase the hand of government in business decision making and further impair productivity.

A major difficulty with arguments based on the virtues of a free market is that they assume that wages are now set in an efficient manner by the workings of an impersonal economy, when in fact the actual wage setting practices of employers are highly arbitrary and discriminatory. The issues in this dispute are highly complex and form the basis for competing theories in labor economics. In opposition to mainline economists who hold that wages are determined largely by human capital in a competitive market, a growing number of economists, commonly known as "institutionalists," stress the importance of structural features of labor markets and features that are peculiar to specific industries.[26]

One of these structural features is the existence of *internal* labor markets. Most jobs are filled by the transfer or promotion of workers already employed, so the practices and relationships within a firm, including collective bargaining agreements, play a much more important role than the supply of labor on the outside. In addition, some jobs involve unique firm-specific tasks for which employees receive extensive on-the-job training. In the absence of an external market for these jobs, wages cannot be set by the laws of supply and demand, and other means must be used. Institutionalists further cite the existence of *dual* labor markets. Alongside a primary market consisting of "good" jobs, with high status and pay, fringe benefits, and advancement opportunities, there exists a secondary market of low-paying, dead-end, "bad" jobs. The primary market is largely the preserve of white males, while women and minorities are heavily represented in the secondary market.

Institutionalist theories of labor markets suggest strategies for reducing discrimination that are quite different from those of the standard economic view. Instead of encouraging women to prepare themselves for entering male-dominated lines of work (the market solution), it may be more effective to scrutinize the personnel practices of firms and especially the ways in which employees are selected in the internal market for on-the-job training and other opportunities. If the dual market theory is correct, then discrimination is likely to persist unless more "good" jobs are created and upward mobility from "bad" jobs is increased. Compensation systems based on the principle of comparable worth can serve to enhance both of these strategies.

The Issue of Cost

A fourth and final issue in the debate is the cost of implementing a system of compensation based on comparable worth. In addition to the indirect cost of reduced efficiency, there is also the direct cost of raising the wages of women (and some men) in undervalued jobs. Faced with the need to meet the increased payroll cost, employers may be led to increase prices, thus producing inflation, or to lower the wages of the men (and a few women) in predominantly male lines of work. The $1.45 million committed by the city of San Jose to implement comparable worth over two years was still considerably short of the union's estimate of $5.4 million over four years. The Minnesota legislature set aside $21.8 million to be spent in

1983–84 to eliminate about half of the wage gap that was estimated to be due to discrimination against women among the 9,000 state employees. In 1984, Iowa began the first phase of a comparable worth plan at a cost of $10 million. Estimates of the cost, both direct and indirect, of eliminating wage discrimination nationwide range between $2 billion and $150 billion.

The National Academy of Sciences report concludes that "because of the complexity of market processes, actions intended to have one result may well turn out to have other, even perverse, consequences."[27] One of these unintended consequences might be to harm the women who are supposed to be the beneficiaries. This is because another way for employers to reduce their payroll costs is by increasing capital investment so as to cut down on the number of workers in less productive jobs. And the workers thrown out of jobs will tend to be women with less training and experience. According to one writer, "Nine secretaries working at word processors might become more cost-effective than twelve secretaries working at typewriters."[28] The nine secretaries who are still employed will benefit by higher wages, but the other three will lose.

Advocates of comparable worth respond that the estimates of cost and predictions of unintended consequences are overstated. Helen Remick and Ronnie J. Steinberg point out that:

> . . . the assumption underlying these estimates is that *all* wage discrimination in *all* work organizations is going to be rectified all at once and tomorrow. . . . Most legal reforms that impact upon the labor market have been implemented in stages: either the scope of coverage is initially restricted and gradually expanded to cover a larger proportion of employees over time, or the legal standard is introduced in steps.[29]

Furthermore, if increased pay is owed to women in undervalued jobs as a matter of right, then justice requires that society be willing to bear the burden, no matter what the cost. With regard to the impact on the employment of women, evidence one way or the other is scarce, since comparable worth has not been extensively implemented in the United States. The only available evidence comes from the experience of Australia. Between 1969 and 1975, a system of comparable worth was adopted in stages. In the decade of the 1970s, the ratio of women's earnings to those of men rose from 65 percent to 86 percent. Experts who have studied the Australian experience agree that the economic impact has been slight. One study reports that while the number of women employed continued to rise, due to an expanding economy, the rate was one-third less than it would have been otherwise, and the unemployment among women increased by 0.5 percent.[30] These consequences, while not insignificant, fall short of the dire predictions made before Australia adopted a comparable worth system.

Conclusion

The comparable worth debate teaches many valuable lessons. It shows us, first, the importance of an accurate understanding of the problem at hand. The existence of a wage gap is a fact, but a great deal of careful analysis is necessary to determine whether the differences in pay are due to discrimination or other causes. Second, the debate forces us to address a fundamental issue in any economic system, namely how should wages be determined? What is a just wage? One version of the comparable worth principle challenges the basic tenet of our economic system, that our labor is worth what it can command in the marketplace. The content of a job and not supply and demand, its advocates say, should determine what we receive. Even if we accept the version of the principle that seeks to use comparable worth as a remedy for discrimination in the market, we still have to ask, is this the best solution to the problem? Insofar as the wage gap is due to discrimination, it ought to be eliminated. About this there can be no dispute. But many strategies have been proposed for dealing with the problem, and more, perhaps, will be developed. Each solution involves a host of factors that need to be considered before we settle on any one.

CASE 9.3   The Mommy Track

Memo

From: Robert C. Begley, President and CEO

To: Maria L. Mendoza, Vice President for Human Resources

Your innovative programs to recruit and promote women in every department of our company have surpassed all expectations. Our recent listing among the top ten of the best companies for working women is a tribute to your dedication and management skill. After studying some recent figures on turnover among the managers in the company and the demographics of those in higher-level positions, however, I see some problems, and I would like your response to some ideas I have for addressing these problems.

First, despite our nationally recognized family-friendly environment, the turnover rate among women managers continues to be two and one-half times the rate for men, which is little different from the experience of other companies. I need not remind you that every employee who leaves is money out the window because of the need to train their replacements. As a result, the cost of employing women in our company is greater than the cost of employing men. Second, we have a higher percentage of women executives than most companies, but a majority of them, more than 60 percent, have no children, while 95 percent of male executives do. This suggests to me that although the overall numbers look good, we have not been successful in enabling women with children to reach the executive ranks.

Both of these problems might be due to the family-friendly programs of which we are so proud. We encourage women to take advantage of extended leaves, flexible scheduling, and flextime, and we have permitted some women to share jobs and to work at home through telecommuting. The result has been that women managers have been pleased with the work environment, but too many may have been content to stay at the lower and middle layers of management and not strive for the highest positions. Some women managers are the equal of their male colleagues and are future COO, CFO, and even CEO material. They will be held back in their progress toward these ranks, however, if they take time out or fail to get critical experience.

These thoughts were inspired by reading an article in the *Harvard Business Review* by Felice Schwartz, the founder and president of Catalyst, a research organization that works with business to improve the situation of women.[31] In this article, "Management Women and the New Fact of Life," she identifies two types of women managers in corporations: "career-and-family women," who are "willing to trade some career growth and compensation for freedom from the constant pressure to work long hours," and high-potential "career-primary women," who put their careers first and are willing to make whatever sacrifices are required to reach the top. Ms. Schwartz recommends that women in this latter group be identified early and given the same opportunities as men to gain experience and develop skills. They should also be asked to travel and relocate and to work the same long hours as their male colleagues.

In this vein, I have been considering whether we should recognize two tracks, a "fast track" and a so-called "mommy track." Should we explain to women in management positions the realities of what it takes to get ahead and the consequences of using "family-friendly" programs? We are already doing what Ms. Schwartz recommends to enable "career-and-family" women to balance conflicting demands. But are we shortchanging "career-primary" women or women who ought to be encouraged in this direction? I recognize some of the objections to a two-track approach.[32] Ms. Schwartz has been widely criticized for giving male executives a ready excuse to put most women in a second-class, nonpromotable category and for giving women only two inflexible alternatives that preclude shifting gears at different points in a career. Her proposals have also been charged with placing full responsibility for child rearing on women and trying to keep traditional patterns of promotion.

Still, I think we ought to consider the problems raised above seriously. Please give me the benefit of your thoughts as soon as possible.

FAMILY AND WORK

The increasing prevalence of single parents and two-earner couples with children has led many American companies to assess the impact of this development on their own business and to develop programs that ease the demands on their employees. Traditional attitudes are still present in the American workplace, however, as evidenced by the following two comments. First, from a woman office manager with a working husband and four children:

> When you punch a time clock, your children don't exist. You don't go to the supervisor and tell him that you must go home to care for a sick or injured child. You punch out in the face of many complaints; you will not be paid for the time; and if you do this too often, you will be looking for another job. Things are changing slowly. But when you get down into most companies' production lines, the script still says, "If you want to work, be here and you will get paid."[33]

The second statement comes from a lawyer on the staff of a high-tech manufacturing company who has a working wife and a two-year-old daughter.

> I left private practice and entered the corporate world, in part, to get more control over my life so that I could spend more time with my family. . . . [When the babysitter has a crisis in her own life] we have to decide who can take the morning off . . . or who can take the baby to the office and for how long. . . . Many friends tell me that their companies are not receptive to the idea of fathers who want to take time off to go to the school-appointed pediatrician. The "that's women's work" attitude persists.[34]

This traditional attitude is changing in response to new realities. Companies that were once reluctant to hire women now find that they have little choice. In addition to antidiscrimination legislation, which provides legal protection for women, the demographics of the work force make the employment of women a practical necessity. An estimated two-thirds of the entrants into the work force for the rest of the century will be women, and about three-fourths of them will have children during some portion of their working career.[35] The cost to employers of ignoring the family burdens of their employees includes lost productivity due to stress, the loss of the investment in training when experienced workers leave, and the failure to attract the best talent in the first place. Many companies are discovering that a family-friendly environment is good business and have developed a range of programs that enable employees to balance family and work life.

Further impetus for change has come from the Family and Medical Leave Act (FMLA), which became effective in August 1993. The FMLA requires companies with fifty or more employees to allow employees up to twelve weeks of unpaid leave for the birth or adoption of a child or for the serious illness or injury of a family member, with the guarantee of the same or an equivalent job upon the employee's return and continued medical benefits. Passage of the FMLA was vigorously opposed by many American businesses, despite the fact that the United States was the last major industrial country to provide some form of maternity leave, and many employers have failed to abide fully by the bill's provisions.[36] The main concern of opponents is the cost of unpaid leave, especially for small companies, but studies suggest that permitting leaves for childbirth is statistically less costly than the alternative of recruiting and training a replacement.[37] Whether employees will still be set back in their careers if they take advantage of the FMLA and other family-friendly programs is also a source of concern for employees and employers alike.

The Problems Facing Employees

The advancement of women in the workplace has been impeded by at least three different factors. First is the unalterable biological function of motherhood; and as Felice Schwartz observes, "Maternity is not simply childbirth but a continuum that begins with an awareness of the ticking of the biological clock, proceeds to the anticipation of motherhood, includes pregnancy, childbirth, physical recuperation, psychological adjustment, and continues on to nursing, bonding, and child rearing." Second, the responsibility of running a household—the "second shift" in Arlie Hochschild's phrase— falls primarily on women in our society, so that women, more than men, find it difficult to be both a parent and a full-time worker. Third are the stereotypes about why women work and what they want in a job. Even women who are fully committed to a career are often assumed to be working temporarily, until the time comes for motherhood; or, if they have a family, they are frequently thought to be less committed than a man because of their dual role. As a result, they are often passed over for promotion or denied the experiences that would lead to advancement.

Motherhood can be accommodated—and historically has been accommodated—by women leaving and reentering the work force. The role of homemaker can be similarly accommodated when women accept less demanding jobs that allow flexibility and do not disrupt family life. Such accommodation rules out "fast track" jobs that involve long hours, unpredictable schedules, and a willingness to relocate. The drawback to such solutions is that women pay a price in career advancement and earning potential. Much of the pay gap is due to interruptions in women's work histories, which are incompatible with the expectations for promotion in most companies. Traditionally, careers have been built with a single employer in a slow, steady rise to the top, and to reenter the work force after an absence is often to start the ascent over again.

Both men and women find it difficult to balance family and work life when emergencies arise, as when a family member suffers a serious illness or is injured in an accident. As the American population ages, caring for the elderly will impose a greater burden on whole families. One specialist on aging predicts, "In the coming years, elder care will have a greater impact on the workplace than child care."[38] Whereas child care generally affects working people in the early years of a career, the responsibility of caring for elder parents usually falls during people's peak working years, with a significant impact on both employers and employees.

Maternity and home responsibilities thus impose a cost, and until recently, this cost has been borne mostly by women themselves. Viewed from an employer's perspective, retaining women in management positions and allowing them to advance is possible only if employers assume some portion of this cost. This is the reality that prompted Felice Schwartz to make a controversial statement in her *Harvard Business Review* article "Management Women and the New Facts of Life." "The cost of employing women in management is greater," she announced, "than the cost of employing men."[39] She immediately added, however, that we must draw the right conclusions from this fact.

First, some of the cost of employing women arises from corporate practices that serve little useful purpose and can be easily altered. "Business as usual" in American corporations reflects to some extent a past era in which men worked and women stayed home. That managers should work from eight o'clock to five and always be present in an office, for example, is a work pattern that was made possible by nonworking wives; but modern communications makes flexible working hours and telecommuting possible. Changes like these can reduce costs overall and benefit both women and employers. Other corporate practices result from male perceptions and expectations that are now counterproductive. Schwartz cites as an example the masculine conception of a career as "either an unbroken series of promotions and advancements toward CEOdom or stagnation and disappointment."[40] Women bring similarly counterproductive perceptions and expectations to the workplace as a result of social conditioning. As the socialization of both men and women changes, corporations have an opportunity to change those practices that have arisen from the differing perceptions and expectations of both men and women.

Second, much of the cost involved in employing women in management positions is offset by the value that they bring to an employer. Some of the cost of employing women cannot be cut merely by changing corporate practices, but women constitute a valuable resource that employers cannot afford to neglect. Family-friendly programs that enable women to remain employed and advance involve an unavoidable cost to employers, but the money may be well spent when one considers the alternatives. In addition to the cost of recruiting and retraining when women leave, employers incur a cost when they do not compete for the best talent available. Employers who want to hire from the top 10 percent of college graduates or MBAs, now find that about half of the people in this select group are women, and that proportion is likely to increase.

Third, limited career opportunities constitutes a form of discrimination that reduces women's choice and their freedom of action. Both men and women are concerned about the impact of work on family life and would prefer employment that enables them to balance family and work more successfully. In one study, 60 percent of employees described the effect on family life as very important in deciding to take a job, and 46 percent cited family-friendly policies as a very important factor in their decision.[41] The strain of balancing family and work life takes a toll on all employees and affects other family members. Among the results of family-friendly programs could be improvements in family well-being and a corresponding reduction in poverty, crime, and other social ills. Aside from considerations of cost, there are substantial moral reasons, rooted in freedom of choice and individual and social welfare, for changing corporate practices that pose problems for employees with families.

Evaluating Family-Friendly Programs

Family-friendly programs take a variety of forms, and companies vary in the mix of programs that they adopt. In general, the programs fall into three groups: (1) resource and assistance programs, such as providing child care, giving guidance about care of the elderly, and counseling employees with family problems; (2) programs for emergencies and occasional needs, such as sick-child care, leaves for childbirth and adoption that go beyond legal requirements, and financial aid for family emergencies; and (3) programs involving flexible working arrangements, including flexible hours, temporary part-time status, working at home by means of telecommuting, and job sharing (in which two people fill a single full-time job together).

Although a few companies have highly commended programs and consistently rank in lists of America's most family-friendly companies, the evidence suggests that most companies have yet to take effective steps.[42] The Families and Work Institute, which publishes *The Corporate Reference Guide*, a benchmarking guide for companies with family-friendly programs, has developed a three-stage classification. Companies at Stage I have several policies but no comprehensive program; at Stage II, companies have developed their policies into a coordinated program; and Stage III companies have begun to change the corporate culture. In the 1991 edition of *The Corporate Reference Guide*, only four companies were identified as being at Stage III.

Employers face a number of problems in becoming family-friendly. Resource and assistance programs are relatively easy to establish, but programs that require changes in work patterns often impose hardships. Allowing a key member of a project to take an extended leave of absence or keeping a job open for an employee on leave may be difficult. Flexible working arrangements may not be suitable for jobs that demand an employee's presence during certain hours or that require the coordination of several employees' schedules. Job sharing may be resisted by clients, for example, who want a single person to handle their business. Employers are also concerned about employee abuse of family-friendly policies and fear that voluntary policies might come to be perceived as entitlements for which they could be sued.[43] Family-friendly policies are apt to be resented by single employees and others without family obligations (see Case 9.4). In addition, the Family and Medical Leave Act of 1993 leaves open questions about what illnesses qualify, who counts as a family member, and what constitutes a calendar year.

Family-friendly programs also create some uncertainties and dangers for employees. Employees who exercise their rights under the FMLA or who take advantage of flextime or other company benefits run the risk of alienating some superiors or of being considered uncommitted. In organizations that have not made changes in the culture, family-friendly policies are often utilized only by women, and the women who utilize them may be identified as being on the "mommy track." Much of the critical reaction to Felice Schwartz's article, "Management Women and the New Facts of Life" (see Case 9.3), was due to the fear that without changes in the corporate culture, her proposals for enabling women to balance family and work life would result in two classes of female employees. Evidence that such a development is already taking place is provided by a study which finds that companies with the best family-friendly programs have some of the worst records for promoting women.[44] This study confirms the suspicion of many women managers that taking advantage of family benefits is dangerous to their careers, and it suggests that programs which concentrate on training and succession planning are more effective in boosting women into top management positions.

Conclusion

Major structural changes in the economy, such as the entry of women into the work force and the rise of the two-earner family, involve costs that must be distributed in some way and require accommodation by both employers and employees. However, the need to balance family and work life raises issues beyond the distribution of costs and the means of accommodation. The central ethical issues are the freedom of employees, men and women alike, to integrate work into a satisfying whole life and the interest of society in minimizing the ills that result when work affects the quality of family life. The political response to these issues has consisted mainly in the enactment of the Family and Medical Leave Act. American corporations have also responded to these issues by developing family-friendly programs, which benefit both employers and their employees. The evaluation of these programs suggests that they cannot be fully effective until significant changes are made in corporate cultures. Until family-friendly programs are perceived as benefits for both men and women and as a normal part of corporate routine, they will fail to address the issues of family and work.

CASE 9.4   Is Family-Friendly Always Fair?

Martha Franklin had never seen Bill so angry. It was past seven-thirty on a Friday evening, and both were tired from a long day. The November sales report had been due at four o'clock, but Martha's assistant, Janet, had taken the last two days off to be with her ten-year-old daughter, who had undergone emergency surgery to remove an abdominal obstruction. Martha had attempted to pull the figures together herself but was slowed by her unfamiliarity with the new computerized sales-reporting system. As the regional sales director, the report was her responsibility, but she generally relied on others to generate the numbers. Just before lunch, she asked Bill Stevens, one of three district sales managers, to help out until the job was finished. As he dropped the completed report on her desk, he slumped down in a chair and began to complain, calmly at first and then with increasing agitation.

"Don't get me wrong," he said. "I'm willing to do my part, and it's great that Janet was able to spend this time with her daughter. Many employers are not as caring as we are here. But every time someone in this office gets time off to care for a family member, one of us single people takes up the slack. I feel that I'm doing my own job and a bit of everyone else's. If you recall, I spent half the day on Thanksgiving straightening out a billing problem for Frank, so that he wouldn't have to disrupt his family's plans. Many people in the office jealously guard their time, leaving at five sharp in order to attend a son's Little League game or get their children to a birthday party.

"This is a very family-friendly place. But what about those of us without families? It's as if we're expected to be married to the company. No one considers that we have a life to lead too. Also, no one wanted to be transferred to the office in Omaha, but Susan was selected to go because she had no family to relocate. She's been transferred three times while most people with families have managed to stay put. And most of the fringe benefits are for families, so we lose out yet again. We've got a great child-care center but no workout room. It's unfair. This company is discriminating against single people and childless couples, and a lot of us are beginning to resent the unequal treatment."

As Martha heard Bill out, she sympathized with his complaints and wondered what could be done. She supported the family-friendly programs for which the company had received national recognition. Was Bill describing the inevitable trade-off, or could the company treat everyone fairly and yet differently?

NOTES

1. Material for this case is taken from *Lois Robinson* v. *Jacksonville Shipyards, Inc.*, No. 86-927-Civ-J-12 (1991).
2. ROCHELLE SHARPE, "Women Make Strides, but Men Stay Firmly in Top Company Jobs," *Wall Street Journal*, 29 March 1994, A1.
3. ELIZA G. C. COLLINS and TIMOTHY B. BLODGETT, "Sexual Harassment: Some See It . . . Some Won't," *Harvard Business Review*, 59 (March–April 1981), 76–95.
4. BARBARA A. GUTEK, *Sex and the Workplace* (San Francisco: Jossey-Bass, 1985), 43–44.
5. The expert witness in *Robinson* v. *Jacksonville Shipyards, Inc.* who made this point was Susan Fiske. The term "sex role spillover" was developed by VERONICA F. NIEVA and BARBARA A. GUTEK, *Women and Work: A Psychological Perspective* (New York: Praeger, 1981).
6. *General Electric Co.* v. *Gilbert*, 419 U.S. 125 (1976).
7. *Newport News Shipbuilding and Dry Dock Co.* v. *EEOC*, 462 U.S. 669 (1983). For a discussion, see MICHAEL A. MASS, "The Pregnancy Discrimination Act: Protecting Men from Pregnancy-Based Discrimination," *Employee Relations Law Journal*, 9 (1983), 240–50.
8. CATHARINE A. MACKINNON, *Sexual Harassment of Working Women* (New Haven: Yale University Press, 1979), 193.
9. *Bundy* v. *Jackson*, 641 F. 2d 934 (D.C. Cir. 1981).
10. *Meritor Savings Bank* v. *Vinson*, 477 U.S. 57 (1986).
11. ROBERT C. FORD and FRANK McLAUGHLIN, "Sexual Harassment at Work: What Is the Problem?" *Akron Business and Economic Review*, 20 (Winter 1988), 79–92.
12. *Ellison* v. *Brady*, 924 F. 2d 872 (1991). See also HOWARD A. SIMON, "*Ellison* v. *Brady*: A 'Reasonable Woman' Standard for Sexual Harassment," *Employee Relations Law Journal*, 17 (Summer 1991), 71–80.
13. LINDA GREENHOUSE, "High Court to Decide Burden of Accusers in Harassment Cases," *New York Times*, 2 March 1993, A1.
14. *Harris* v. *Forklift Systems, Inc.*, 114 S.Ct. 57 (1986).
15. BARBARA PRESLEY NOBLE, "Little Discord on Harassment Ruling," *New York Times*, 13 November 1993, sec. 5, p. 25.
16. The study by Freada Kelin is reported in SUSAN CRAWFORD, "A Wink Here, a Leer There: It's Costly," *New York Times*, 28 March 1993, sec. 5, p. 17.
17. "Battling the Bimbo Factor," *Time*, 28 November 1991, 70.
18. "Battling the Bimbo Factor," 70.
19. MARTHA T. MOORE, "Taste Test: Debate Brews over Selling Beer with Sex," *USA Today*, 15 November 1991, 1B.
20. The landmark case is *Schultz* v. *Wheaton Glass Company*, 21 F. 2d 259 (3d Cir. 1970), *cert. denied* 398 U.S. 905 (1970).
21. *Gunther* v. *County of Washington*, 452 U.S 967 (1981).
22. See, for example, GUISEPPI A. FORGIONNE and VIVIAN E. PETERS, "Differences in Job Motivation and Satisfaction among Male and Female Managers," *Human Relations*, 35 (1982), 101–18.
23. SHARON TOFFEY SHEPELA and ANN T. VIVIANO, "Some Psychological Factors Affecting Job Segregation and Wages," in HELEN REMICK, ed., *Comparable Worth and Wage Discrimination* (Philadelphia: Temple University Press, 1984), 47.
24. DONALD J. TREIMAN and HEIDI I. HARTMANN, eds., *Women, Work, and Wages: Equal Pay for Jobs of Equal Value* (Washington, D.C.: National Academy Press, 1981).
25. *Thompson* v. *Boyle*, 499 F. Supp. 1147 (D.D.C. 1980).

26. See P. B. DOERINGER and M. J. PIORE, *Internal Labor Markets and Manpower Analysis* (Lexington, MA: D. C. Heath, 1971); and FRANCINE BLAU, *Equal Pay in the Office* (Lexington, MA: Lexington Press, 1978).

27. TREIMAN and HARTMANN, *Women, Work, and Wages*, 65–66.

28. MICHAEL EVAN GOLD, *A Dialogue on Comparable Worth* (Ithaca, NY: ILR Press, 1983), 55.

29. HELEN REMICK and RONNIE J. STEINBERG, "Technical Possibilities and Political Realities: Concluding Remarks," in REMICK, *Comparable Worth and Wage Discrimination*, 290.

30. ROBERT G. GREGORY and ROBERT C. DUNCAN, "Segmented Labor Market Theories and the Australian Experience of Equal Pay for Women," *Journal of Post Keynesian Economics*, 3 (1981), 403–28.

31. FELICIA SCHWARTZ, "Management Women and the New Facts of Life," *Harvard Business Review* (January–February 1989), 65–76.

32. "The Mommy Track," *Business Week*, 20 March 1989, 126–34; and reader response in "Is the Mommy Track a Blessing—Or a Betrayal?" *Business Week*, 15 May 1989, 98–99.

33. *Work and Family Policies: The New Strategic Plan* (New York: The Conference Board, 1990), 13.

34. *Work and Family Policies,* 13.

35. BARBARA PRESLEY NOBLE, "The Family Leave Bargain," *New York Times*, 7 February 1993, sec. 3, p. 25.

36. SUE SHELLENBARGER, "Many Employers Flout Family and Medical Leave Law," *Wall Street Journal*, 26 July 1994, B1, B7.

37. NOBLE, "The Family Leave Bargain."

38. SUE SHELLENBARGER, "The Aging of America Is Making 'Elder Care' a Big Workplace Issue," *Wall Street Journal*, 16 February 1994, A1.

39. SCHWARTZ, "Management Women and the New Facts of Life," 65.

40. SCHWARTZ, "Management Women and the New Facts of Life," 67.

41. CHARLENE MARMER SOLOMON, "Work/Family's Failing Grade: Why Today's Initiatives Aren't Enough," *Personnel Journal*, May 1994, 82.

42. SUE SHELLENBARGER, "If You Want a Firm That's Family Friendly the List Is Very Short," *Wall Street Journal*, 6 September 1995, B1.

43. SUE SHELLENBARGER, "How Accommodating Workers' Lives Can Be a Business Liability," *Wall Street Journal*, 4 January 1995, B1.

44. ROCHELLE SHARPE, "Family Friendly Firms Don't Always Promote Females," *Wall Street Journal*, 29 March 1994, B1, B5.

10

Unjust Dismissal

CASE 10.1   The Firing of Robert Greeley

On May 22, 1987, Robert Greeley was abruptly dismissed from his job as a laborer at Miami Valley Maintenance Contractors, Inc., in Hamilton, Ohio.[1] This was a blow not only to the thirty-year-old, recently divorced father of two young children but also to his ex-wife, who was relying on this job for child support payments. Three weeks prior, a county court judge had ordered that Mr. Greeley's employer withhold the payments from his paycheck as permitted under Ohio law. But his bosses at Miami Valley Maintenance Contractors decided that the bookkeeping involved was too much trouble. Firing him was much easier.

Divorced fathers often fail to make court-ordered child support payments, and judges and legislators have few means for making deadbeat fathers pay. To address this problem, the U.S. Congress enacted the Child Support Enforcement Amendments of 1984, which require states to provide income withholding as a means of collecting payments. The federal law also mandates that states make provisions for fining employers who refuse to withhold such payments. The Ohio General Assembly complied with this federal law by passing legislation the following year. An employer who violates the Ohio law is subject to a $500 fine. Miami Valley Maintenance Contractors readily admitted that they fired Mr. Greeley to avoid complying with the Ohio law, and they did not contest the $500 fine. The company contended, however, that Robert Greeley, who was not a union member under a contract, was an at-will employee. Accordingly, he could leave his employment at any time, for any reason, and his employers could terminate him with the same ease. The law in some states prohibits employers from firing for certain kinds of reasons—such as for refusing to break the law or for serving on a jury—because permitting them to do so conflicts with important matters of public policy. However, Ohio was, at the time, a strict employment-at-will state. Employers could hire and fire at will, with virtually no legal restrictions. In 1986, for example, the state Supreme Court upheld the firing of a Toledo-area chemist who reported illegal dumping of toxic wastes, even though the employer was eventually found guilty and fined $10 million by the Ohio Environmental Protection Agency. By comparison, Mr. Greeley's employer got off cheaply: They had to pay a paltry $500 fine for the privilege of firing him.

INTRODUCTION

At first glance, there is nothing remarkable about this case. In the United States, employers are generally regarded as having the right to make decisions about hiring, promotion, and discharge, as well as wages, job assignments, and other conditions of work. Employees have a corresponding right to accept or refuse work on the terms offered and to negotiate for more favorable terms. But in the absence of a contract that spells out the conditions under which employment can be terminated, employees can be legally dismissed for any reason—or for no reason at all.

The moral and legal basis for this particular assignment of rights for employers and employees is a doctrine known as *employment at will.* Employment, according to this doctrine, is an "at-will" relation that comes into existence when two parties willingly enter into an agreement, and the relation continues to exist only as long as both parties will that it do so. Employers and employees both have the right to enter into any mutually agreeable arrangement without outside interference. Each party is also free to end an arrangement at any time without violating the rights of the other, as long as doing so is in accord with the terms that they have agreed on. Employment at will is a common-law doctrine long embodied in American labor practice. The first explicit statement that employment is an at-will relation occurred in an 1877 work by H. G. Wood entitled *A Treatise on the Law of Master and Servant.*[2] The doctrine was first given legal force by an 1884 Tennessee Supreme Court decision in the case *Paine* v. *Western & A.R.R.* In an often quoted sentence, the court declared, "All may dismiss their employee(s) at will, be they many or few, for good cause, for no cause, or even for a cause morally wrong."[3] Other state courts followed the example of Tennessee, as did the U.S. Supreme Court, so that shortly after the turn of the century, the doctrine of employment at will was firmly established in American law.

A typical decision from the turn of the century is *Lochner* v. *New York* (1905).[4] At issue in this case was an 1897 New York statute limiting the work of bakers to ten hours a day and sixty hours a week. The law was intended to protect the health of bakers, which was being undermined by the long, exhausting hours that they were required to work. This piece of protective legislation was struck down, however, on the grounds that it violated the right of bakers and bakery owners alike to contract on mutually agreeable terms. According to the majority opinion, "the freedom of master and employee to contract with each other in relation to their employment . . . cannot be prohibited or interfered with, without violating the Federal Constitution." More specifically, the Court ruled that the law violated the due process clause of the Fourteenth Amendment, which stipulates that no state shall "deprive any person of life, liberty, or property, without due process of law."

The reasoning of *Lochner* was embraced in a long series of decisions extending into the 1930s, striking down worker protection legislation and minimum wage laws as similar violations of the due process clause. But in the changed climate of the Depression and the New Deal, the Court abruptly reversed itself, for reasons that are described later in this chapter. The doctrine of employment at will, however, remained firmly entrenched, and it has been only in the past thirty years that some state courts have begun to make exceptions to it.

The task of this chapter is to examine the justification of this doctrine in order to determine the rights that employees have against unjust dismissal and other adverse treatment at the hands of employers. Three arguments are commonly used to justify employment at will. One argument holds that the doctrine is entailed by the rights of property owners; the second argument appeals to the notion of freedom of contract; and the third argument is based on considerations of efficiency. Each of these arguments upholds certain rights of employers, but they can also be used to make a strong case for the rights of employees and to provide greater protection from unjust dismissal than the prevailing legal interpretation of employment at will.

PROPERTY RIGHTS AND EMPLOYMENT AT WILL

One argument for employment at will—the property rights argument—begins with the assumption that both employers and employees have property of some kind. The owner of a factory, for example, owns the machinery and raw materials for the manufacture of a product, along with a certain amount of money for wages. The only resource lacking is labor for operating the machinery and turning the raw materials into a finished product. Labor, or more precisely the productivity of labor, thus has an economic value and can be said to be a kind of "property" that is "owned" by the worker. Employment can be described, therefore, as an exchange of a worker's productive power for the wages that are given out in return by the factory owner.

In this exchange, both parties are free to exercise the rights of property ownership. The owner of the factory is free to utilize the productive resources of the factory and to pay out money as wages in any way that workers are willing to accept. And the workers are free to accept work under the conditions and at the wages offered or to seek work elsewhere on more favorable terms. It follows that any restriction on the kinds of agreements that employers and employees can make is a violation of the property rights of one or both parties. Just as consumers are under no obligation to continue buying a product, employers are free to stop "buying" the labor of an employee. Although the loss of a job may create some hardship for the person dismissed, no rights are violated.

The historical roots of the property rights argument are contained in John Locke's idea that there is a *natural* right to property, by which he meant a morally fundamental right that exists apart from any particular legal system. Accepting the biblical belief that God gave the bounty of the earth to all persons in common for the purposes of life, Locke went on to observe that we can make use of this bounty only by appropriating it and making it our own. The fruit of a tree cannot nourish us, for example, until we pluck and eat it; but when one person eats a piece of fruit, that person deprives another of its use. Locke's argument for property as a natural right is based, therefore, on the role that property, including labor, plays in satisfying human needs.

How Important Are Property Rights?

The property rights argument seems to confer a right on the owners of businesses to hire and fire at will. All rights are limited, however, for the simple reason that they inevitably come into conflict with each other and with important societal interests. Government is permitted under the Constitution to place legal restrictions on the use of property as long as "due process" is observed. The doctrine of employment at will is supported by the property rights argument, then, only when it is further assumed that the right to property is of such importance that it takes precedence over all other competing values.

This was the view of the Supreme Court in the decisions of the *Lochner* era, when considerations of adequate pay, worker health and safety, the right to organize, and the like were held to be of little account. The *Lochner* era came to an end in 1937 with the decision in *West Coast Hotel* v. *Parrish*, which upheld the constitutionality of a Washington State law setting a minimum wage for women and children.[5] In the majority opinion, Chief Justice Charles Evans Hughes observed that:

> . . . the Constitution does not recognize an absolute and uncontrollable liberty. Liberty in each of its phases has its history and connotation. But the liberty safeguarded is liberty in a social organization which requires the protection of law against the evils which menace the health, safety, morals and welfare of the people.

He continued:

> In dealing with the relation of employer and employed, the legislature has necessarily a wide field of discretion in order that there may be suitable protection of health and safety, and that peace and good order may be promoted through regulations designed to insure wholesome conditions of work and freedom from oppression.[6]

Problems with Locke's Theory

A further objection to an unlimited right to property can be constructed using Locke's own premises. Property rights are fundamental in Locke's political theory because of the role they play in satisfying our basic needs and securing liberty. It can be argued, however, that instead of serving these Lockean ends, the doctrine of employment at will has the opposite effect: namely, the impoverishment of a substantial portion of society and their subjugation to the will of others. Philip J. Levine has observed, for example:

> The notion of an absolute right to property, although originally conceived of as the basis of liberty, has resulted in the subjugation of the working class. It has allowed employers to exercise dominion over their employees, without any corresponding protection of the employee's interests. This freedom from governmental restraint has enabled employers to place unconscionable conditions on employment.
>
> The seriousness of the situation is compounded by the importance of employment to the individual employee. The essential elements of his life are all dependent on his ability to derive income. His job is the basis of his position in society, and, therefore, may be the most meaningful form of wealth he possesses.[7]

If this argument is correct, then something has gone seriously wrong. The explanation, according to C. B. Macpherson, is to be found in two factors, neither of which was anticipated by Locke. One is a change in the conception of property.

> As late as the 17th century, it was quite usual for writers to use the word in what seems to us an extraordinarily wide sense. John Locke repeatedly and explicitly defined men's properties as their lives, liberties, and estates. . . . One's own person, one's capacities, one's rights and liberties were regarded as individual property. They were even more important than individual property in material things and revenues, partly because they were seen as the source and justification of individual material property.
>
> That broad meaning of property was lost in the measure that modern societies became fully market societies. Property soon came to have only the narrower meaning it generally has today: property in material things or revenues.[8]

The second factor is the unequal distribution of property that prevails in modern society. A certain amount of inequality is justified by Locke insofar as it reflects the differing efforts of individuals. What Locke failed to anticipate is that those who have only their labor to "sell" accelerate the process of transferring the wealth of society to those who are in a position to employ them. As a result of these two factors, Macpherson has claimed:

> Those who have to pay for access to the means of using their capacities and exerting their energies, and pay by making over to others both the control of their capacities and some of the product of their energies—those people are denied equality in the use and development and enjoyment of their own capacities. And in a modern market society, that amounts to most people. . . .[9]

Property Rights and Democracy

In holding that property rights enable individuals to be free and equal members of a state, Locke failed to recognize another aspect of property rights, pointed out in a classic essay, "Property and Sovereignty," by Morris R. Cohen. Property makes it possible for individuals to be citizens in a democracy, in Locke's view, by providing them with a base of individual power that enables them to stand up against the sovereign power of the state. Without a right to the means for making a living by developing and exercising our own capacities, human beings would be in the position of supplicants who receive the necessities of life as gifts from the state. What Cohen observed is that property gives individuals not only power against the state but also power against each other. The owner of property has not only a right to the exclusive use of some material thing but also a means for gaining control over fellow human beings. Property itself thus constitutes a kind of sovereignty in addition to that of the state.

According to Cohen:

> The extent of the power over the life of others which the legal order confers on those called owners is not fully appreciated by those who think of the law as merely protecting men in their possession. Property law does more. It determines what men shall acquire. Thus, protecting the property rights of a landlord means giving him the right to collect rent, protecting the property of a railroad or a public-service corporation means giving it the right to make certain charges. . . .
>
> From this point of view it can readily be seen that when a court rules that a gas company is entitled to a return of 6 per cent on its investment, it is not merely protecting property already possessed, it is also determining that a portion of the future social produce shall under certain conditions go to that company. Thus not only medieval landlords but the owners of all revenue-producing property are in fact granted by the law certain powers to tax the future social product. When to this power of taxation there is added the power to command the services of large numbers who are not economically independent, we have the essence of what historically has constituted political sovereignty.[10]

Because of the many problems with Locke's theory, there is ample reason to limit property rights—and with them the doctrine of employment at will—by recognizing counterbalancing rights of employees in the employment relation. If the justification for property rights is the securing of liberty, and if these rights, when applied to the employment relation, fail to do that, then we are no longer justified in holding property rights as absolute.

Property Rights in a Job

For some philosophers and legal theorists, the problem lies not with the notion of property rights but with the limited way property is conceived. Employees, according to Locke, have property in their own labor, but it is argued that they also have property rights in a job and in the education and special skills that they put at the service of an employer. If employees have property rights of this kind, then the right of an employer to dismiss "at will," instead of being a right entailed by the employer's property rights, should be viewed as a violation of the property rights of an *employee*. The property rights argument can thus be turned on its head to undermine rather than to support the doctrine of employment at will. Before jumping to this conclusion, however, it is necessary to defend the claim that employees can be said to have property rights in a job.[11]

Consider the case of Robert Sindermann, who had been a teacher for ten years with the Texas state college system, rising to the position of professor of government and social science at Odessa Junior College. After four years in this position, he was not offered a contract for the next academic year. The reason cited by the college's board of regents was Sindermann's "insubordination." But no specific reasons were given, and his request for a hearing to challenge the dismissal was refused by the regents. During the past academic year, however, Sindermann had served as president of the Texas Junior College Teachers Association, and in this capacity he left the classroom on several occasions to testify before committees of the Texas State Legislature. His name also appeared in a newspaper advertisement that was highly critical of the board of regents.

In the resulting lawsuit, *Perry* v. *Sindermann*, Sindermann claimed that in addition to violating his right to freedom of speech, the board of regents had violated his rights under the Fourteenth Amendment by depriving him of property without due process of law.[12] Since the college did not have a tenure system, Sindermann had no contractual guarantee of continued employment. The college had nevertheless given assurances that any faculty member with seven or more years of service "may expect to continue in his academic position unless adequate cause for dismissal is demonstrated in a fair hearing, following established procedures of due process." Sindermann contended that this promise of continued employment constitutes property, so that he was at least entitled to a hearing of the charges against him.

What Is Property?

A crucial issue in evaluating Sindermann's claim is, what is property? As Morris R. Cohen noted, "Any one who frees himself from the crudest materialism readily recognizes that as a legal term 'property' denotes not material things but certain rights."[13] In a famous passage, R. H. Tawney wrote:

> Property is the most ambiguous of categories. It covers a multitude of rights which have nothing in common except that they are exercised by persons and enforced by the State. Apart from these formal characteristics, they vary indefinitely in economic character, in social effect, and in moral justification. They may be conditional like the grant of patent rights, or absolute like the ownership of ground rents, terminable like copyright, or permanent like a freehold, as comprehensive as sovereignty or as restricted as an easement, as intimate and personal as the ownership of clothes and books, or as remote and intangible as shares in a gold mine or rubber plantation.[14]

The economic assets of most employees do not consist of land, machines, and the like, which are commonly thought of as productive property. Rather, they consist in the possession of an education and certain specialized skills, which are often certified by a diploma or a license of some kind. The most valuable economic asset of a medical doctor is likely to be the MD degree and the license from a state, which permit the doctor to practice. Charles A. Reich has observed that government bestows many entitlements and that these are steadily taking the place of more traditional forms of property.[15] Unless we recognize that the wealth of many employees consists in their education, skills, and government entitlements, these valuable assets will not be protected as well as traditional forms of property.

In *Perry* v. *Sindermann*, the Supreme Court ruled for the first time that a job is a form of property for purposes of the Fourteenth Amendment, so that Sindermann and employees in a similar situation are entitled by the due process clause to a fair hearing. In the majority opinion, Justice Potter Stewart, wrote:

> We have made it clear . . . that "property" interests subject to procedural due process protection are not limited by a few rigid, technical forms. Rather, "property" denotes a broad range of interests that are secured by "existing rules or understandings." A person's interest in a benefit is a "property" interest for due process purposes if there are such rules or mutually explicit understandings that support his claim of entitlement to the benefit and that he may invoke at a hearing.

There are some legal obstacles, however, to the claim that the due process clause applies to cases of private employment where an employee is dismissed without a just cause or a fair hearing. *Perry* v. *Sindermann* and similar cases have involved only government and not private employment. The due process clause protects an individual only when deprivation of property occurs by the action of a state, not by a private employer. Furthermore, there must be some basis other than the Constitution for asserting that a property right exists. The Supreme Court has clearly stated that the Constitution does not create property rights but merely extends "various procedural safeguards" to protect them.[16]

Still, a powerful moral argument can be constructed to support the claim that employees such as Sindermann have interests in a job that (morally) ought to be protected. If we accept such an argument, then these moral rights of employees must be weighed against the property rights that have traditionally been accorded to the owners of a business. The right of employees to be protected from unjust dismissal cannot be denied merely by appealing to the property rights of corporations. Employees have property rights, too, and these are just as deserving of protection as the property rights of employers.

THE FREEDOM OF CONTRACT ARGUMENT

Employment can be viewed as a contractual arrangement between employers and employees. This arrangement arises in some instances from an *explicit* contract, a legal document signed by both parties, in which a business firm states the terms under which it is willing to hire a person and that person signifies by his or her acceptance a willingness to work under those terms. Union employees are typically covered by a companywide contract that is agreed to by both the management of a company and the union rank and file. In the absence of an explicit contract, we can still understand the employment relation as involving an *implicit* contract insofar as the conditions of employment are understood and tacitly accepted by both parties.

To place a limit, then, on the kinds of agreements that can be made between an employee and an employer is to limit the right of contract of both parties. Just as it would be a violation of rights to force an employee to remain in a job, so it would be a violation of rights to prevent an employer from terminating an employee who voluntarily entered into an at-will employment relation. This was the reasoning of the Supreme Court in *Lochner*. A more explicit statement of employment at will as a consequence of freedom of contract occurs in a decision upholding the right of an employer to fire an employee for belonging to a labor organization. The majority opinion in this case, *Adair* v. *United States* (1907), held:

> . . . [I]t is not within the functions of government—at least in the absence of contract between the parties—to compel any person, in the course of his business and against his will, to accept or retain the personal services of another, or to compel any person, against his will to perform personal services for another. The right of a person to sell his labor upon such terms as he deems proper is, in its essence, the same as the right of the purchaser of labor to prescribe the conditions upon which he will accept such labor from the person offering to sell it. So the right of the employee to quit the service of the employer for whatever reason is the same as the right of the employer, for whatever reason, to dispense with the services of such employee. . . . In all such particulars the employer and the employee have equality of right, and any legislation that disturbs that equality is an arbitrary interference with the liberty of contract which no government can legally justify in a free land.[17]

In another case the Court held, "This right is as essential to the laborer as to the capitalist, to the poor as to the rich; for the vast majority of persons have no other honest way to begin to acquire property, save by working for money."[18]

The Philosophical Basis for Freedom of Contract

In the British and American legal traditions, the philosophical basis for the freedom of contract argument, as for the property rights argument, derives from John Locke, who considered the exercise of property rights to be only one part of a more general freedom of action. On the Continent, however, the philosophical basis for freedom of contract derives not from Locke but from Immanuel Kant and his concept of autonomy.

The Kantian argument can be sketched briefly as follows. Autonomy involves the capacity and opportunity to make meaningful choices about matters that bear most significantly on our lives. That is, we are autonomous insofar as it is *we* who make the important decisions affecting our lives and not *others*. An essential part of acting autonomously in this sense is the possibility of making mutually binding voluntary agreements. Therefore, autonomy entails freedom of contract.

Use of the freedom of contract argument to support the doctrine of employment at will is problematic because of the immense difference in bargaining power that usually prevails between employers and employees. Bargaining almost always takes place between parties of different strengths, and the stronger side usually gains at the expense of the weaker. The outcome need not be unjust for this reason. But is there some point at which employers ought not to be permitted to take advantage of their superior bargaining position? The decision in *Lochner* v. *New York* denied that there was any morally significant difference in bargaining strength between bakery workers and their employers. The majority opinion held, "There is no contention that bakers as a class are not equal in intelligence and capacity to men in other trades . . . or that they are not able to assert their rights and care for themselves without the protecting arm of the state."

As mentioned earlier, the *Lochner* era came to an end in 1937 with the decision in *West Coast Hotel* v. *Parrish*. Chief Justice Hughes, who delivered the majority opinion, cited "an additional and compelling consideration which recent economic experience has brought into a strong light." This consideration is the "exploitation of a class of workers who are in an unequal position with respect to bargaining power and are thus relatively defenseless against the denial of a living wage." The doctrine of employment at will cannot be justified by a right to freedom of contract, according to Chief Justice Hughes, when the result is to deprive employees of the ability to protect their most vital interests. This decision was followed by a series of federal and state worker protection laws that addressed the most serious abuses of employment at will.

Restrictions on Freedom of Contract

Freedom of contract, like the right to property, is not absolute. Outside the employer-employee relation, there are a number of moral and legal limits on the right of individuals to enter into contractual relations. Children and people who are mentally incompetent cannot be parties to a contract, for example. Contracts can be invalidated by showing that they were made under duress or under threats of harm or that they involve misrepresentation or fraud. And the courts sometimes refuse to recognize contracts that exploit people's inexperience or ignorance.

The reason for these restrictions is that contracts are valid only when they are made with the genuine consent of both parties. Children and the retarded and insane, for example, do not have the mental or emotional capacity to understand the terms of a contract. Hence, they are not able to give their consent in a meaningful way. A person who is coerced into accepting the terms of a contract through the use of intimidation or force "consents" only in a very artificial sense of the term, since the person lacks any significant degree of choice. And when a contract is secured by misrepresentation or fraud—as is the case when a buyer of a house is not told about hidden structural defects or termite damage—the victim's "consent" is also not consent in the full meaning of the term, since the person lacks full knowledge of what is being agreed to.[19] These restrictions are compatible with, and indeed even required by, Locke's conception of freedom.

The same restrictions on freedom of contract are justified when freedom of contract is based on Kant's conception of autonomy. Children and the mentally incompetent lack the capacity for autonomous action to a sufficient degree. And when a person is coerced into agreeing to the terms of a contract—whether it be by physical compulsion or deception of some kind—that person cannot be said to be acting autonomously. Autonomy, along with Lockean freedom, requires that our consent be voluntarily given.

An Autonomy Argument

Although autonomy can be used to support freedom of contract—and with it the doctrine of employment at will—the same concept can also serve as the basis for an argument *against* employment at will.[20] A sketch of the argument is as follows.

If people are to have autonomy, then they must have not only the capacity for autonomous action but also an acceptable range of alternatives from which to choose. What makes us autonomous is not the mere fact that we are able to make a choice, no matter what the alternatives are. A meaningful account of autonomy must also consider the number and desirability of alternatives available to us. When we choose to do one thing and not another, the alternatives are largely fixed by a social, political, and economic order over which we have little control. A student who wants to become a doctor, for example, cannot merely *choose* to do so. For some, a career in medicine is not a viable alternative. The student may be limited by his or her own abilities and education in comparison with those who are also competing for entry into a medical school. Once trained, a doctor must practice within a system of medical care that is constrained by the resources available, by the demand for services, and by the priorities of the society.

Some people have more alternatives from which to choose than others. A person with few skills and limited resources might "choose" to accept menial, exhausting, and dangerous work at low pay when the alternative is no work at all. But the choices these people make are scarcely the ones they would *like* to make. They would like to be able to choose from a more desirable list of alternatives. To some extent the degree of freedom of choice each of us has is a matter of our own endowments, but it is also due to forces outside ourselves. Complete freedom of choice, in the sense that we are free to make any choice we please from an unlimited list of alternatives, is an unrealistic ideal. And this cannot be what autonomy requires. At the other extreme, it would be absurd to say that slaves are free simply because they can choose to obey their master or accept the consequences. There must be some point between these two extremes where we are justified in saying that a person is acting autonomously.

Once we recognize that the autonomy of a person cannot be separated from the alternatives available to that person, it becomes obvious that employment cannot be analyzed merely as a contractual arrangement between two parties. Any agreement between an employer and an employee takes place in a larger setting that profoundly influences the relative bargaining strength of the two parties and consequently the outcome of their negotiations. Among people with relatively equal bargaining strength with respect to employment, there might be no need for any restrictions on the agreements that are made. But this is seldom the case. To require employees to negotiate a contract with regard to the terms of their employment under conditions of decidedly unequal bargaining strength, then, is not to enhance their autonomy but to diminish it.

How should the employment relation be constructed in a society that values and wishes to advance the autonomy of its members? Adina Schwartz suggests, "A crucial implication is that respecting people as autonomous is not equivalent, as commonly assumed, to leaving them as free as possible from social influences. Instead, a society respects all its members as autonomous to the extent that it assists them in leading a certain kind of life."[21] A kind of life that embodies a realistic view of autonomy, according to Schwartz, is one that allows for "shaping one's circumstances by planning rationally to achieve some over-all conception of one's goals" and "shaping one's goals by rationally criticizing and changing one's over-all conception."[22] In short, a society fosters autonomy to the extent that it makes it possible for people to decide for themselves how they want to live and enables them to implement their decisions effectively.

Conclusion

The two arguments for freedom of contract discussed in this section lead to the same conclusion. Whether the right of employers and employees to contract freely is based on a Lockean conception of freedom or a Kantian conception of autonomy, certain conditions must be satisfied in order for the resulting agreements to be just. There is ample room for controversy over what these conditions are. But to the extent that the necessary conditions are not satisfied, the doctrine of employment at will cannot be supported by the freedom of contract argument.

EFFICIENCY AND EMPLOYMENT AT WILL

 The third argument for employment at will is a utilitarian one that relies not on property rights or the freedom of contract but on the importance of this doctrine for the efficient operation of business. The success of any business enterprise depends on the efficient use of all resources, including the resource of labor. For this reason, employers are generally accorded considerable leeway to determine the number of workers needed, to select the best workers available, to assign them to the jobs for which they are best suited, and to discipline and dismiss workers who perform inadequately. The intrusion of factors other than the most efficient allocation of resources into business decision making can only impair efficiency, according to this argument, and thereby harm everyone concerned. Furthermore, legal limitations on the commonly accepted prerogatives of employers puts legislatures and courts in the position of making vital business decisions.

Although employment at will has undeniable benefits, most of these go to employers. A utilitarian justification does not allow us to look merely at the consequences of this doctrine for employers but requires that we also consider the consequences for workers and for the whole of society. One of the objections made by Chief Justice Hughes in *West Coast Hotel* v. *Parrish* is that the exploitation of workers which the doctrine of employment at will makes possible is "not only detrimental to their health and well-being but casts a direct burden for their support upon the community. What these workers lose in wages the taxpayers are called upon to pay." When the benefits to employers are balanced against the cost to workers and the other members of society, it may be that employment at will is not an efficient but a very inefficient way of using human resources.

The case of Dr. Grace Pierce is instructive here. As an employee of the Ortho Pharmaceutical Corporation, she was forced to resign after she refused to proceed with tests of a new drug containing what she considered to be a dangerously high level of saccharin. In remanding the case for trial, an appeals court judge ruled that there was a clear and well-defined public policy at issue. Members of the public have a right to be protected against the testing of potentially unsafe drugs, and the public interest is not served by allowing the company to pressure Dr. Pierce to act against her best professional judgment. The trial judge stated that it may be that:

> . . . public policy will develop to a degree that professionals, even though employees at will, will be permitted to resist what they consider to be a professionally unsound and unethical decision without fear of demotion or discharge.

Dr. Pierce eventually lost her case in the New Jersey Supreme Court, however.[23]

Robert Greeley won his case, and with the decision in *Greeley* v. *Miami Valley Contractors, Inc.*, Ohio joined the growing list of states that recognize a public policy exception to the doctrine of employment at will. Ensuring that the children of divorced parents are properly supported is an important matter of public policy, and the means devised by the Ohio state legislature—namely, ordering employers to withhold child support payments from a parent's paycheck—is a reasonable means of achieving a policy objective. Allowing employers to ignore a court order merely by paying a small fine would undermine the child support enforcement mechanism created by the state legislature. The state legislature established a policy, and the state supreme courts justices said, "It is our job to enforce, not frustrate, that policy."

The efficiency argument, then, not only provides some grounds for justifying employment at will but also justifies some limitations for reasons of public policy. Merely admitting that there are some limits, however, does not enable us to determine exactly what these limits are. There are still some good reasons for proceeding cautiously in this area. These are well expressed by the appeals judge in *Pierce* v. *Ortho Pharmaceutical Corporation*:

> We note that a public policy exception would represent a departure from the well-settled common law employment-at-will rule. If such a departure is to be made, care is required in order to insure that the reasons underlying the rule will not be undermined. Most notably in this regard, the employer's legitimate interests in conducting his business and employing and in retaining the best personnel available cannot be unjustifiably impaired. Thus, it cannot change the present rule which holds that just or good cause for the discharge of an employee at will or the giving of reasons therefore are not required. In addition the exception must guard against

a potential flood of unwarranted disputes and litigation that might result from such a doctrine, based on vague notions of public policy. Hence, if there is to be such an exception to the at-will employment rule, it must be tightly circumscribed so as to apply only in cases involving truly significant matters of clear and well-defined public policy and substantial violations thereof. If it is to be established at all, its development must be on a case-to-case basis.

What are some of the "truly significant matters of clear and well-defined public policy" that justify making exceptions to the doctrine of employment at will? First, employees ought not to be subject to demotion, discipline, or discharge for refusing to violate the law. If anything is contrary to public policy, it is a doctrine that permits employers to use the threat of dismissal to force an employee to commit illegal acts. In a 1959 California case, *Petermann* v. *International Brotherhood of Teamsters*, Petermann, the business manager for a local of the Teamsters union, was fired by the union after he refused an order to commit perjury before an investigative committee of the state legislature.[24] The California Court of Appeals held that in order to make the law against perjury effective, some restriction had to be placed on an employer's right of discharge. Another employee was dismissed for being away from work to serve on a jury.[25] Although jury duty is a legal obligation for the persons selected, the court in Oregon did not find that the employer was prevented by any statute from dismissing the employee. Nevertheless, the court ruled in favor of the employee on the grounds that the discharge was for "a socially undesirable motive" that tended to "thwart" the jury system.

Second, employers ought not to prevent employees from receiving the full benefit of their legal rights and entitlements relating to employment. The legislation creating many employee rights include antiretaliation provisions, so there is no need for the courts to create a separate public policy exception. Thus, the National Labor Relations Act and the Occupational Safety and Health Act, among others, not only forbid retaliation but provide for legal remedies. In many instances, employees have been dismissed for filing workers' compensation claims for benefits that are guaranteed as a matter of right for injuries suffered on the job. In one such case, the court ruled: "When an employee is discharged solely for exercising a statutorily conferred right, an exception to the general rule [of employment at will] must be recognized."[26]

Aside from public policy, the courts have made exceptions under two other conditions. One is the existence of an *implied contract* and the other is the presence of *bad faith and malice*.

An Implied Contract to Continued Employment

In some instances, prospective employees are given assurances in job interviews that dismissal is only for cause, that attempts are made to work through any problems before the company resorts to dismissal, and that due process is followed in all cases. These assurances are conveyed in other instances by employee manuals, policy statements, personnel guidelines and procedures, and other company documents. The claim that an implied contract exists as a result of different kinds of assurances makes an appeal not to a utilitarian justification based on public policy but to the law of contracts. Employee suits have not always been successful, however, as witness the following case.

Walton L. Weiner was hired away from his job at Prentice Hall with promises of secure employment.[27] He was told in a preemployment interview that it was the policy at McGraw-Hill not to dismiss an employee without just cause, and the company's personnel handbook contained a procedure for help in overcoming any problem with an employee's performance. When he was summarily fired after eight years at McGraw-Hill, without just cause and without following the prescribed procedure, he sued his employer for breach of contract. However, the court ruled against Weiner's claim that the company's verbal and written assurances constituted an implied contract. The personnel handbook, for example, was not itself a contract, since it did not spell out the terms of employment, such as salary and duration, and it could be modified at any time by the company. In a dissenting opinion, however, one judge asserted:

> . . . I cannot agree that an employee handbook on personnel policies and procedures is a corporate illusion, "full of sound . . . signifying nothing."
>
> The application form presented to the employee which required his signature prior to the employment, stated that employment would be subject to handbook rules. An employee should be able to rely thereon, perhaps to his detriment. The employer should be estopped from acting other than with respect thereto.

In two Michigan cases that were decided together, *Toussaint* v. *Blue Cross and Blue Shield of Michigan* and *Ebling* v. *Masco Corporation*, the plaintiffs were given assurances of job security by their employers as long as they performed satisfactorily.[28] Charles Toussaint testified that he was told by his employer that he would be with the company until the mandatory retirement age of 65 "as long as I did my job." The supervisory manual at Blue Cross and Blue Shield stipulated that employees could be dismissed only for just cause and that specific disciplinary proceedings were to be used. The court found that his supervisor, in asking him to resign, had not observed these provisions in the manual. Furthermore, the court held:

> While an employer need not establish personnel policies or practices, where an employer chooses to establish such policies and practices and makes them known to its employees, the employment relation is presumably enhanced.
>
> The employer secures an orderly, cooperative and loyal work force, and the employee the peace of mind associated with job security and the conviction that he will be treated fairly.

Walter Ebling was given similar assurances of job security at the Masco Corporation as long as he performed satisfactorily, and he testified that he was told that he could be discharged only for just cause and after a review of the case by the company's executive vice president. Ebling claimed that he was discharged merely to prevent him from exercising a stock option that had greatly appreciated in value. The Michigan Supreme Court held that the oral assurances and the company manual create a commitment on the part of the employer with regard to the terms of employment and thus constitute an implied contract.

Bad Faith and Malice

Even without an implied contract, a commonly accepted principle in business is acting in good faith. This concept is applied widely as both a moral and a legal requirement in collective bargaining, contract negotiations, consumer relations, and indeed virtually all commercial dealings. The Uniform Commercial Code, for example, requires that all sales be in good faith, which is defined as "honesty in fact and the observance of reasonable commercial standards of fair dealing in trade." And the UCC also holds that an "unconscionable" sales contract is unenforceable. Although the same requirements have not commonly been applied by the courts to the employment relation, there are good moral reasons for doing so.

An example of conspicuous *bad* faith is the case of a twenty-five-year veteran employee of the National Cash Register Company, named Fortune, who was dismissed the next business day after he had secured an order for $5 million worth of equipment to be delivered over the next four years. The court found that the dismissal was motivated by a desire to deprive Fortune of the very substantial commission he would receive as the equipment was sold. The Massachusetts court held that Fortune had an implied contract with his employers and stated that:

> . . . in every contract there is an implied covenant that neither party shall do anything which will have the effect of destroying or injuring the right of the other party to receive the fruits of the contract, which means that in every contract there exists an implied covenant of good faith and fair dealing.[29]

A California court issued a similar ruling in the case of *Cleary* v. *American Airlines*.[30] Cleary claimed that his dismissal, after eighteen years of satisfactory service, was based on a false accusation of work rule violations and was not in accord with the company's personnel policies. In agreeing with Cleary, the court held that the dismissal was contrary to the "implied-in-law covenant of good faith and fair dealing contained in all covenants." At about the same time, a court in New York ruled in favor of an employee who was fired after thirteen years of service for no reason except to deprive him of his pension benefits, which would be vested in two more years.[31] Although New York State law had no provision for wrongful discharge, the court held that the employer's action "smacks of the unconscionable."

Conclusion

This discussion of unjust dismissal is of vital importance for all employees and not just those unfortunate enough to be fired without cause. The reason is that the pivotal doctrine of employment at will pervades the whole employer-employee relation. To be an at-will employee is to be at all times subject to the power of an employer to grant or deny something that is essential for our well-being, namely, a job. The alternative is not necessarily a lifetime guarantee of employment but an assurance that we will be treated fairly.

Employment at will is, fortunately, an idea whose time is past, although it still retains a strong hold in the laws of many states. The main supports, historically, have been property rights and the right of contract, which we have examined in depth. These arguments have been rebutted not by denying these rights but by showing their limits. In particular, the imbalance that exists between employer and employee makes a mockery of the idea that the rights of both are being preserved. When employers can dismiss at will, legitimate property rights of employees and the right of employees to contract freely are severely eroded.

The present-day debate revolves mainly around utilitarian issues.[32] To what extent is the welfare of society advanced by preserving or limiting the traditional prerogatives of employers? Employers typically favor employment at will not because they want to fire without cause but because they would rather avoid the need to account for their personnel decisions in court and face the possibility of stiff punitive awards. Even advocates of greater employee protection recognize the dangers of the courts becoming too deeply involved in business decison making.

CASE 10.2   Waiving the Right to Sue

Seven years ago, David Parker thought that he made the right decision. He now realizes that it was the biggest mistake of his life, and he hopes that it can be undone. But the decision, in any event, was a tough one.

At the time, the company was reducing its work force because of declining sales, and a group of dismissed employees had filed a class action suit, alleging that they were terminated in violation of the procedures in the company's own personnel handbook. Previously, the company had been sued by disgruntled former employees for wrongful discharge on a variety of grounds. Although no suit had been successful, the cost of defending the company in court, not to mention the cost in management's time, was substantial. In order to protect the company against employee suits, an offer was made to all senior-level employees: If they would waive their right to sue the company in the event of termination, then the company would guarantee them an enhanced severance package. Dismissed employees regularly receive six months' pay with no continued benefits; employees who signed a waiver releasing the company from any other claims would receive full pay and all benefits for one year. The company emphasized the significance of signing and encouraged employees to take their time and to consult with an attorney. No pressure was placed on anyone to sign the waiver, and employees were assured that the fact that they did or did not sign would not be used in any decision to terminate employment.

David Parker finally decided to sign the waiver. Without consulting an attorney, he concluded that if he were laid off, the enhanced severance package would enable him to maintain his present standard of living until he found a new job, and it would soften the blow of a job loss on his wife and children. He never doubted his ability to land a new job fairly quickly. Fortunately, he kept his job through those turbulent times, but now, seven years later, he found himself dismissed at the age of fifty-eight in yet another round of cutbacks. This time, however, finding a new job had proven difficult, and he was still unemployed.

Although his position was officially eliminated, the major responsibilities were assumed by a thirty-eight-year-old woman, whom he had trained as his assistant. Five other employees, all over the age of forty, were terminated at the same time and also found their jobs turned over to younger colleagues. After consulting with a lawyer, a decision was made to sue the company for violation of the Age Discrimination in Employment Act of 1967, which protects employees over the age of forty from dismissal solely on the grounds of age. The six employees, including David Parker, held that the company had no reason to believe that they were any less capable than the employees who remained. The lawyer thought that they had a good chance of prevailing in court, but the waivers posed a problem. Two of the other five employees had also signed waivers not to sue the company; two had joined the company within the past five years and had not been asked to sign; and one refused to sign a waiver seven years ago. The only hope for those who signed a waiver, the lawyer explained, is that the court will hold they were improperly obtained by the company. They could argue that because of the unequal bargaining power between employers and employees, their consent was not wholly voluntary. And even if they knew what they were signing at the time, they could not anticipate their situation in the future, so asking them to sign away their rights like that is unfair.

CASE 10.3   A "State-of-the-Art" Termination

Monday had been the most humiliating day of Bill Collin's life. Rumors of downsizing had been swirling for months, and every computer analyst in Bill's department knew that the ax would fall on some of them. Bets had even been taken on who would stay and who would go. When the news was finally delivered, Bill was not surprised. He also understood the necessity of reducing the computer support staff in view of the merger that had made many jobs redundant, and he felt confident that he would find a new job fairly quickly. What upset him was the manner in which he had been terminated.

Bill arrived in the office at eight o'clock sharp to find a memo on his desk about a nine-thirty meeting at a hotel one block away. Since this site was often used for training sessions, he gave the notice little thought. Bill decided to arrive a few minutes early in order to chat with colleagues, but he found himself being ushered quickly into a small conference room where three other people from his department were already seated. His greeting to them was cut short by a fourth person whom Bill had never seen before. The stranger explained that he was a consultant from an outplacement firm that had been engaged to deliver the bad news and to outline the benefits the company was providing for them. Once he started talking, Bill felt relieved: The package of benefits was greater than he had dared hope. All employees would receive full salary for six months plus pay for accrued vacation time; medical insurance and pension contribution would be continued during this period; and the outplacement firm would provide career counseling and a placement service that included secretarial assistance, photocopying and fax service, and office space. The consultant assured the four longtime employees that the company appreciated their years of service and wanted to proceed in a caring manner. It was for this reason that they hired the best consulting firm in the business, one that had a reputation for a "state-of-the-art" termination process.

Bill's relief was jolted by what came next. The consultant informed the four that they were not to return to their office or to set foot inside the corporate office building again; nor were they to attempt to contact anyone still working for the company. (At this point, Bill suddenly realized that he had no idea how many employees might be in other four-person groups being dismissed at the same time.) The contents of their desks would be boxed and delivered to their homes; directories of their computer files would be provided, and requests for any personal material would be honored after a careful review of their contents to make sure that no proprietary information was included. The consultant assured them that all passwords had already been changed, including the password for remote access. Finally, they were instructed not to remain at the hotel but to proceed to a service exit where prepaid taxis were stationed to take them home.

Bill regretted not being able to say goodbye to friends in the office. He would have liked some advance warning in order to finish up several projects that he had initiated and to clear out his own belongings. The manner in which he had been terminated was compassionate up to a point, Bill admitted, but it showed that the company did not trust him. A few days later, Bill understood the company's position better when he read an article in a business magazine that detailed the sabotage that had been committed by terminated employees who had continued access to their employer's computer system. Some disgruntled workers had destroyed files and done other mischief when they were allowed to return to their offices after being informed of their termination. One clever computer expert had previously planted a virtually undetectable virus that remained dormant until he gained access long enough through a co-worker's terminal to activate it. The advice that companies were receiving from consulting firms that specialize in termination was: Be compassionate, but also protect yourself. Good advice, Bill thought, but the humiliation was still fresh in his mind.

NOTES

1. *Greeley* v. *Miami Valley Maintenance Contractors, Inc.*, 49 Ohio St. 3d 228 (1990); 551 N.E. 2d 981 (1990).

2. H.G. Wood, *A Treatise on the Law of Master and Servant* (Albany: John D. Parsons, Jr., 1877), 134. Cited in Patricia H. Werhane, *Persons, Rights, and Corporations* (Englewood Cliffs, NJ: Prentice Hall, 1985), 82.

3. *Paine* v. *Western & A.R.R.*, 81 Tenn. 507, 519–20 (1884).

4. 198 U.S. 45, 25 S.Ct. 539 (1905).

5. *West Coast Hotel* v. *Parrish*, 300 U.S. 379 (1937).

6. In a landmark decision, *Nebbia* v. *New York*, 291 U.S. 502 (1934), the Supreme Court had previously ruled that states have the power to regulate business—and thereby limit the property rights of owners—for the sake of the public welfare. The decision in *West Coast Hotel* thus extends the precedent of *Nebbia*, which concerned the setting of prices, to matters of employment.

7. PHILIP J. LEVINE, "Towards a Property Right in Employment," *Buffalo Law Review*, 22 (1973), 1084.

8. C. B. MACPHERSON, "Human Rights as Property Rights," *Dissent*, 24 (Winter 1977), 72.

9. MACPHERSON, "Human Rights as Property Rights," 74.

10. MORRIS R. COHEN, "Property and Sovereignty," in *Law and the Social Order* (New York: Harcourt, Brace & Co., 1933), 47.

11. For discussions of a job as property, see BARBARA A. LEE, "Something Akin to a Property Right: Protections for Employee Job Security," *Business and Professional Ethics Journal*, 8 (Fall 1989), 63–81; and WILLIAM B. GOULD, IV, "The Idea of the Job as Property in Contemporary America: The Legal and Collective Bargaining Framework," *Brigham Young Law Review* (1986), 885–918.

12. *Perry et al. v. Sindermann*, 408 U.S. 593 (1971). See also *Arnett v. Kennedy*, 416 U.S. 134 (1974); *Cleveland Board of Education v. Loudermill*, 470 U.S. 532 (1985); and *Foley v. Interactive Data Corporation*, 47 Cal. 3rd 654, 254 Cal. Rptr. 211 (1988).

13. COHEN, "Property and Sovereignty," 45.

14. R. H. TAWNEY, *The Acquisitive Society* (New York: Harcourt, Brace & World, 1920), 53–54.

15. CHARLES A. REICH, "The New Property," *Yale Law Review*, 73 (1964), 733.

16. *Leis v. Flynt*, 439 U.S. 438 (1979). There is at least one writer, though, who believes that the due process clause when combined with all the protective legislation that applies to private employment can be interpreted to make interests in a job a form of property so that employees can be protected against unjust discharge. See CORNELIUS J. PECK, "Unjust Discharges from Employment: A Necessary Change in the Law," *Ohio State Law Journal*, 40 (1979), 1–49. This view remains untested in the courts, however.

17. *Adair v. United States*, 208 U.S. 161, 28 S.Ct. 277 (1907).

18. *Coppage v. Kansas*, 26 U.S. 1, 35 S.Ct. 240 (1914).

19. For a discussion of these restrictions, see ANTHONY T. KRONMAN, "Contract Law and Distributive Justice," *Yale Law Journal*, 89 (1980), 472–97.

20. The argument developed here is largely derived from ADINA SCHWARTZ, "Autonomy in the Workplace," in TOM REGAN, ed., *Just Business: New Introductory Essay in Business Ethics* (New York: Random House, 1984), 129–66.

21. SCHWARTZ, "Autonomy in the Workplace," 151.

22. SCHWARTZ, "Autonomy in the Workplace," 150.

23. *Pierce v. Ortho Pharmaceutical*, 84 N.J. 58, 417 A. 2d 505 (1980).

24. *Petermann v. International Brotherhood of Teamsters*, 174 Cal. App. 2d 184, 344 P. 2d 25 (1959).

25. *Nees v. Hocks*, 272 Or. 210, 536 P. 2d 512 (1975).

26. *Frampton v. Central Indiana Gas Company*, 260 Ind. 249, 297 N.E. 2d 425 (1973). In addition, see *Kelsay v. Motorola*, 74 Ill. 2d 172, 384 N.E. 2d 353 (1978); *Sventko v. Kroger Co.*, 69 Mich. App. 644, 245 N.W. 2d 151 (1976).

27. *Weiner v. McGraw-Hill*, 83 A.D. 2d 810 (1981).

28. *Toussaint v. Blue Cross and Blue Shield of Michigan* and *Ebling v. Masco Corporation*, 408 Mich. 579, 272 N.W. 2d 880 (1980).

29. *Fortune v. National Cash Register Company*, 364 N.E. 2d 1251 (1977).

30. *Cleary v. American Airlines*, 168 Cal. Rptr. 722 (1980).

31. *Savodnick v. Korvettes, Inc.*, 488 F. Supp. 822 (1980).

32. One exception is provided by RICHARD A. EPSTEIN, who argues for retaining contract theory as a basis for the employee relation. See "In Defense of Contract at Will," *The University of Chicago Law Review*, 51 (1984), 947–82.

11

Ethical Issues in Advertising

CASE 11.1   Volvo's "Bear Foot" Misstep

The television ad showed a monster truck riding atop the roofs of cars lined up in its path.[1] The truck, named "Bear Foot" because of its oversized, six-foot tires, crushed every car but one—a Volvo station wagon. The scene of devastation around the still-standing Volvo vividly illustrated the company's advertising message of strength and safety. The TV and print ads both appeared in October 1990 and received immediate critical acclaim for their effectiveness. The monster truck campaign was quickly dropped, however, amid charges of deceptive advertising. The idea for the ad came from a monster truck rally in Vermont in which a Volvo was the only survivor of a similar stunt. In recreating the scene at a Texas arena, the production crew employed by the advertising agency Scali, McCabe, Sloves reinforced the roof of the Volvo with lumber and steel and partially sawed through the roof supports of the other cars. When word leaked out, the attorney general of Texas began an investigation that confirmed the rigging and led to a lawsuit for consumer fraud. Volvo quickly settled the suit by running corrective ads and by reimbursing the state of Texas for the cost of the investigation and the legal fees incurred. Scali, McCabe, Sloves also resigned its Volvo account, which generated $40 million a year in revenues.

In apologizing for the ads, Volvo insisted that the company was unaware of the rigged demonstration but defended the rigging all the same. The reasons for the alterations to the cars, the company explained, were to enable the production crew to conduct the demonstration and to film it safely and to allow the Volvo to withstand the repeated runs of the monster truck that were required for filming. The claim being made was not false: Volvo engineers had determined that the roof could withstand the weight of a five-ton monster truck. The mistake was not revealing to consumers that the ad was not an actual demonstration but a dramatization of the event in Vermont.

This was not the first time that Volvo and Scali, McCabe, Sloves had been criticized for questionable ads. A year prior, an ad was produced that showed a large truck perched atop a Volvo with the tag line "How well does your car stand up to heavy traffic?" This ad was similar to one from the 1970s showing a Volvo withstanding the weight of six other Volvos stacked one on top of another. In both ads, the Volvo on the bottom was supported by jacks. The reason for the jacks, according to the company, was that the ads were intended to show only the strength of the main body; no claim was being made about the tires and suspension system, which, in any event, could not withstand such a load. The tires would blow out and the supension system would collapse.

INTRODUCTION

Advertising pervades our lives. It is impossible to read a newspaper or magazine, watch a television show, or travel the streets of our cities without being bombarded by commercial messages. Although some ads may be irritating or offensive, the better efforts of Madison Avenue provide a certain amount of entertainment. We also derive benefit from information about products and from the boost that advertising gives to the economy as a whole. On the other side of the fence, companies with products or services to sell regard advertising as a valuable, indeed indispensable marketing tool. Approximately 2 percent of the gross national product is currently devoted to advertising. So whether we like it or not, advertising is a large and essential part of the American way of doing business.

A typical definition of advertising, from a marketing text, is that it is "a paid form of nonpersonal communication about an organization and/or its products that is transmitted to a target audience through a mass medium."[2] So defined, advertising is only one kind of promotional activity. The others are *publicity* (press releases and other public relations efforts that do not involve the purchase of air time or space in the mass media), *sales promotion* (contests, coupons, free samples, and so on, which are not, strictly speaking, forms of communication), and *personal selling* by shop clerks and telephone solicitors (which, of course, is not impersonal and also does not take place through a mass medium). Although most advertising is for a product or a service, some of it is devoted to enhancing the image of a corporation or advancing some issue or cause. Thus, a distinction is commonly made between product advertising on the one hand and corporate or advocacy advertising on the other.[3]

Advertising is widely criticized. Exaggerated claims and outright falsehoods are the most obvious targets for complaints, followed closely by the lack of taste, irritating repetition, and offensive character of many ads. More recently, questions have been raised about the morality of specific kinds of advertising, such as advertising for alcohol and tobacco products, and the extensive advertising aimed at children. Particular ads are also faulted for their use of excessive sex or violence or for presenting negative stereotypes of certain groups, such as blacks, American workers, and the elderly.[4]

More subtle are the complaints of some critics about the role advertising plays in creating a culture of consumerism. Advertising encourages people not only to buy more and more but also to believe that their most basic needs and desires can be satisfied by things that can be bought. The goals and aspirations of consumers thus come to be defined in materialistic terms. Christopher Lasch claims, for example, that advertising "serves not so much to advertise products as to promote consumption as a way of life."[5] Also part of a consumer culture is the extension of a "market mentality" into all aspects of life.

Some economists charge that advertising is wasteful and inefficient. In their view, advertising is a largely nonproductive activity that stifles competition and leads to monopoly conditions. A few economists also charge that advertising appeals to the emotions and manipulates the needs and desires of consumers, even to the extent of creating wants, thereby hindering the ability of consumers to make rational choices.

Finally, there is great concern about the potential of advertising for behavior control. In 1957, Vance Packard frightened Americans with his best-selling book *The Hidden Persuaders*, which revealed how advertisers were turning to motivational research to discover the subconscious factors that influence human action. A pioneer in this area, Dr. Ernest Dichter, declared in 1941 that advertising agencies were "one of the most advanced laboratories in psychology" and that a successful advertiser "manipulates human motivations and desires and develops a need for goods with which the public has at one time been unfamiliar—perhaps even undesirous of purchasing."[6] The key to success in advertising, according to Dr. Dichter, is to appeal to feelings "deep in the psychological recesses of the mind" and to discover the right psychological "hook."[7]

These objections to advertising have led to calls for regulation. However, both government regulation and voluntary self-regulation involve a number of substantial ethical issues. Among them are questions about whether regulation hampers competition by preventing price comparisons and keeping rivals out of the market (which is the opposite of the economists' argument that unregulated advertising is anticompetitive) and about whether government regulation of advertising violates the First Amendment right of free speech. Deceptive advertising is subject to control by the Federal Trade Commission (FTC), but many questions still arise about the definition of deception in advertising and about the burden of proof an advertiser has for claims made in an ad.

This chapter examines the ethical objections to advertising and, in particular, the arguments that advertising is wasteful and inefficient and that it uses unacceptable means of persuasion and control. The problem of defining deceptive advertising is also considered, along with the issues involved in regulating advertising.

THE ECONOMIC ANALYSIS OF ADVERTISING

An analysis of the economic impact of advertising is relevant to the ethics of advertising for two reasons. First, from a utilitarian point of view, it is necessary to take into account the effect of advertising on the welfare of society as a whole. If advertising is a waste of resources and an anticompetitive practice, as some economists claim, then there are strong utilitarian grounds for opposing it. Second, if a free market economy is justified on utilitarian or other grounds, then advertising is morally objectionable to the extent that it interferes with the efficient operation of a free market. For both utilitarians and advocates of free market capitalism, then, economic analysis has a bearing on the question of whether advertising is morally justified.

Unfortunately, there is sharp disagreement among economists on the effects of advertising. Many defenders of advertising regard it as an important source of information for market transactions and a legitimate form of nonprice competition. In spite of considerable research, no resolution of the controversy seems to be near. Still, we can examine the arguments on both sides and make some tentative judgments. The overall conclusion to be drawn is that although advertising has some economic benefits in a free market economy, there are limits to the amount and kind of morally permissible advertising.

The Charge That Advertising Is Wasteful

The charge that advertising is wasteful is based on the assumption that advertising adds nothing to the value of consumer products and diverts resources from the production of more valuable goods and services. The money spent on advertising, according to critics, does not result in any new products people can consume; it is used only to persuade people to consume products already available, many of which they do not need and would otherwise not desire. Since the value of a product, in economic terms, resides in its ability to satisfy people's needs and desires, more value could be created by eliminating advertising and using those resources, which are now wasted, on things that could provide more satisfaction.

Advertising automobiles, for example, does not improve their quality or safety. Without the extra cost of advertising, cars could be sold more cheaply or else made better for the same price. Or the money saved by not advertising automobiles could be used to purchase other consumer goods or applied to pressing social problems, such as poverty and education. Even greater savings would be realized if people were not persuaded by advertising to buy higher priced luxury cars with more power than they can use.

Especially wasteful are defensive advertising strategies designed to maintain or enlarge a company's market share. Strategies of this kind often seek to foster brand loyalty by creating illusory differences between products. Many smokers are fiercely loyal to a particular brand of cigarettes, for example, even though blind tests reveal that they often cannot tell one brand from another. Not only are smokers deceived into believing that their favorite brand is superior in some way to the others, but the cost of the advertising that makes this deception possible is passed along to them in the form of higher prices.

Defenses to the Charge of Wastefulness

Defenders of advertising reply to this charge by arguing that the assumption of the critics is flawed. A product cannot satisfy a need or a desire until it is purchased by a consumer, and advertising facilitates the process of consumer choice by providing information. Through advertising, the argument goes, buyers of automobiles, for example, are given the information they need to find the model that best suits them; and with better-informed consumers, manufacturers are able to offer consumers a larger number of models with options that more closely fit consumer tastes. The result is an increase in the satisfaction of the needs and desires of consumers and hence an increase in the value of products.

Critics respond that the informational content of advertising is minimal and not really a benefit to consumers. Much automobile advertising, for example, consists of nonrational appeals to a desire for status or the thrill of driving fast. The small amount of information provided by such advertising typically reinforces these appeals by stressing luxury features or the power of the engine. Rarely do advertisements for automobiles offer information that permits consumers to make cost comparisons of different makes or judgments about their relative safety. The amount of information in advertisements, moreover, could be conveyed to consumers by much more economical means.

Even advertising designed to foster brand loyalty is defended by some economists. Although some of the differences between brands are illusory, brand identification makes significant product differentiation possible, with the result that consumers have more choices. Brand loyalty also facilitates mass-merchandizing, which lowers the per unit cost of goods, thereby benefiting consumers with lower prices. Consumers who are satisfied from past experience with a certain brand save time while shopping and avoid the risk of experiencing dissatisfaction with unknown brands. To the objection that smokers often cannot taste the difference between brands of cigarettes, defenders reply that smokers who prefer one brand to another are buying a certain image in addition to the taste. And as long as this image satisfies a desire, it too contributes to the value of the product.

A noted defender of advertising, the economist Phillip Nelson, argues that the amount of advertising for brand-name products is itself a kind of information.[8] The best-selling brands, he argues, are the ones consumers are generally satisfied with and purchase repeatedly. Because these brands are best-sellers, the manufacturers have an incentive to advertise them more heavily. The reason is that, other things being equal, each dollar spent advertising a product that consumers are more likely to buy will bring a greater return than a dollar spent advertising a less popular product. "Simply put," Nelson says, "it pays to advertise winners. It does not pay to advertise losers. In consequence, the brands that are advertised the most heavily are more likely to be winners."[9] A consumer can pick out the best products, therefore, by looking for those with the most advertising.

This argument assumes that being a best-selling product is, first, an indicator of value and, second, a cause and not an effect of heavy advertising. The best-seller list, for example, is not a reliable guide for book lovers. The reason is that a best seller is apt to cater to mass tastes, whereas book lovers tend to prefer books with more limited appeal. In books, tastes differ widely, and where this is true, advertising will not indicate value. Where people want the same things from a product, though, a history of repeat purchases is generally significant. Possible exceptions are cases involving indistinguishable products, such as soaps and detergents, where heavy advertising is more likely to be a cause of their popularity rather than vice versa. A long list of advertising failures shows that no amount of advertising can sell a poor product. However, the amount of advertising is also a reflection of the resources that companies have available. A large, profitable company with an inferior product can afford to spend more on advertising than a small, struggling company with a superior product. Thus, advertising can be used to give large, successful companies a competitive edge.

Advertising is further defended on the grounds that even if some resources are wasted, the overall effect is to create an expanding market with more plentiful and cheaper consumer goods and an increasing number of higher-paying jobs. There is no guarantee, moreover, that the resources currently devoted to advertising would be utilized more efficiently for other purposes, especially in a surplus economy. Finally, since advertising is only one of many methods of marketing, it is likely that some of the money saved by cutting back on advertising would still be spent on other marketing methods, some of which are less efficient than advertising.[10]

The Charge That Advertising Is Inefficient

The basis of the second charge—that advertising interferes with the efficient operation of a free market—is that advertising enables large firms with well-established, brand-name products to create and maintain monopoly conditions.[11] Massive advertising campaigns by industry leaders serve not only to protect their market share but also to prevent the entry of new and smaller firms into the market. Brand loyalty and artificial product differentiation, which advertising makes possible, tend toward the same end.

In 1970, for example, the Federal Trade Commission issued a report, *Influence of Market Structure on Profit Performance of Food Manufacturing Companies*, accusing the major cereal manufacturers of monopolizing the ready-to-eat breakfast cereal market, in part by the extensive use of advertising.[12] The advertising budgets of the "Big Four"—Kellogg, General Mills, General Foods, and Quaker Oats—which had 91 percent of the market, averaged 18 percent of annual sales, according to the report. (The average for the food industry is 5.3 percent.)[13] Such a high proportion of advertising to sales could not be justified, the FTC claimed, by the return on the amount spent and was designed to keep competitors out of the market. Similarly, the proliferation of new brands by these companies (150 between 1950 and 1970) had the intended effect of stifling competition by outsiders.

Heavy advertising obviously raises the price of products, since the cost is passed along to the consumer. The FTC estimated, for example, that the price of ready-to-eat cereals would be between 15 and 25 percent lower with more reasonable levels of advertising. In addition, the effect of monopoly is to reduce competition, so that manufacturers are able to raise prices above what fully competitive market conditions would allow. Advertising also encourages nonprice competition, thus enabling the members of the Big Four to compete with each other by increasing their advertising budgets rather than reducing prices. Possible savings to consumers, then, are diverted to other uses.

Defenses to the Charge of Inefficiency

The defenders of advertising hold that advertising does not promote monopoly but in fact fosters competition.[14] If the critics are right, then there should be a positive correlation between the extent of monopoly and the amount of advertising as a percentage of sales and a negative correlation with the rate of product turnover. That is, firms in more concentrated industries should devote a higher proportion of revenues to advertising and introduce fewer new products. But no such patterns have been found. Further, advertising facilitates rather than bars market entry, according to the defenders, since it enables firms to inform the public about new products. Some evidence for this view is provided by studies showing that new products are more intensively advertised than old ones.

In addition, there is some theoretical and empirical support for the conclusion that advertising has the effect of lowering prices instead of raising them. Theoretically, advertising should lower prices by reducing the per unit cost of products (because of increased volume) and the sales cost (that is, the cost of making a sale to a customer). Prices should also fall when advertising enables consumers to make price comparisons. The strongest support for this latter proposition comes from a well-known study by the economist Lee Bentham, who found that prices for eye examinations and eyeglasses in states that regulated advertising were almost double those in states with fewer restrictions.[15] Similar results have been obtained from studies of the prescription drug industry.[16]

Finally, defenders reply to the charge that advertising encourages nonprice competition by pointing out that there are many legitimate forms of competition. Instead of reducing prices, for example, manufacturers can offer a higher quality product at the same price—or spend more on advertising. Under competitive conditions, therefore, the decision to lower prices, raise quality, or advertise would be determined by whatever strategy produces the greatest profit. The market, therefore, encourages advertising only as long as it promotes efficiency, and firms that engage in inefficient advertising will be penalized with lower profits. The economist Yale Brozen also argues that if a shared monopoly existed in the cereal industry, as the FTC claimed, then the major firms would be expected to cut advertising in order to raise profits. So the high level of advertising by the Big Four reflects vigorous competition.[17]

Conclusion

In conclusion, the defenders have sufficiently strong arguments for maintaining that advertising has a legitimate role to play in a free market economy, especially when ads contain substantial information that enables consumers to make rational economic choices. The information-providing function of advertising is a weak foundation for building a justification, though, since advertising is a relatively inefficient means for providing consumers with information. Moreover, only ads that are primarily informative, such as classified ads in the newspaper or entries in the yellow pages, could be justified by such an argument. Of course, no advertising that is justified in this way could be deceptive or misleading.

However, providing consumers with information is not the purpose of advertising; it is, rather, to stimulate consumer demand. Although increased consumer demand provides benefits, such as more choices and lower prices, the major beneficiary is still the businesses that advertise. A drawback, therefore, is that the defenders' case is built on the benefits of advertising to consumers and the public at large, but decisions about advertising are made by companies with a view to their own welfare. There is some reason to question whether the welfare of consumers is always well served by such an arrangement. Certainly, benefit to consumers is not the driving force behind advertising, and there is an element of duplicity in arguments for advertising that (misleadingly) suggest that it is all done with the consumer in mind.

At bottom, the economic arguments justifying advertising are utilitarian in character; they appeal to the contribution advertising supposedly makes to the welfare of all members of society. If this is, indeed, the justification of advertising, then it can plausibly be maintained that, on balance, advertising does more good than harm and that the advertising we now have is better than no advertising at all. A utilitarian would insist, however, that advertising be done in a way that best promotes the well-being of society as a whole, and *that* would entail a very different kind of advertising than we have at present.

PERSUASION AND BEHAVIOR CONTROL

Vance Packard's revelations in *The Hidden Persuaders* were disturbing forty years ago because of the possibility that advertisers have means of influence that we are powerless to resist. It is now fashionable to scoff at extreme claims about the potential of advertising for behavior control. We know that advertising and propaganda—advertising's political cousin—have limited power to change people's basic attitudes. Still, there is evidence that the techniques of modern advertising are reasonably successful in playing on natural human desires for security, acceptance, self-esteem, and the like so as to influence consumer choices. Constant exposure to advertising in general is bound to have some cumulative psychological effect in creating a consumer society.

Although there is no consensus on the extent of the power of advertising to persuade, there is no disputing the fact that this power is substantial. The major difference between critics of advertising and defenders is whether there is anything morally objectionable about the use of this power. What, if anything, is wrong with using the methods of Madison Avenue to bring about changes in consumer behavior? There are two closely related answers to this question. One is given primarily by economists and the other, by philosophers. Both of these answers contend that certain kinds of advertising cross the boundary between legitimate persuasion and unacceptable forms of behavior control.

The Dependence Effect

The economist John Kenneth Galbraith coined the term *dependence effect* to describe the fact that present-day industrial production is concerned not merely with turning out goods to satisfy the wants of consumers but also with creating the wants themselves. He has written:

> As a society becomes increasingly affluent, wants are increasingly created by the process by which they are satisfied. This may operate passively. Increases in consumption . . . act by suggestion or emulation to create wants. Or producers may proceed actively to create wants through advertising and salesmanship. Wants thus come to depend on output.[18]

The dependence effect, in turn, is a consequence of the increasingly planned nature of the American economy. New products with a proven consumer demand, such as a pain reliever, require advertising only for the purpose of competing with products already available. But the introduction of an unfamiliar product, such as (at one time) mouthwash, must be preceded by a campaign designed to ensure a receptive market. People who never before worried about "bad breath" now need to be made to feel that they have a problem that only gargling with mouthwash will solve.

The main significance of the dependence effect lies in the challenge it poses to a fundamental tenet of economic theory, which is that production is justified because it satisfies consumer demand. The defense offered by corporate leaders when they are criticized for applying their immense resources to seemingly nonessential consumer goods while ignoring pressing needs is, "We only give the public what it wants." These words are a hollow, self-serving excuse if, as Galbraith and others claim, these same corporations have a good deal to do with determining what the public wants. David Braybrooke has written, for example:

> The automobile companies have shaped the public's ideas about safety, and hence the wants related to safety: negatively, by suppressing information about the dangers of the cars that they produce; and positively, by extolling speed, and selling cars on

the basis of power. Half a century of dilation on speed, power, and thrills have fostered and intensified wants that now seem questionable to many; and those who have the wants, without now questioning them, might be brought to revise them by perceiving the interested part that the automobile companies have played in instilling them.[19]

More technically, economic theory presupposes: (1) that the value of goods arises from their role in satisfying the needs and desires of consumers, and (2) that consumers themselves are the best judges of what will best satisfy their needs and desires. (This latter assumption is known as the principle of consumer sovereignty.) It follows that the optimal satisfaction of everyone's needs and desires will be achieved by allowing individuals to express their preferences in a free market. Producers of goods, therefore, do not need to ask whether people would be better off with more books and fewer television sets, since this question is best answered by the free choices of individual consumers.

Galbraith contends that there is a flaw in this argument:

> If the individual's wants are to be urgent they must be original with himself. They cannot be urgent if they must be contrived for him. And above all they must not be contrived by the process of production by which they are satisfied. For this means that the whole case for the urgency of production, based on the urgency of wants, falls to the ground. One cannot defend production as satisfying wants if that production creates the wants. . . . Production only fills a void that it has itself created.[20]

Furthermore, if Galbraith is right about the dependence effect, one cannot argue for the production of more goods on the grounds that the members of society will be better off. "The higher level of production," Galbraith says, "has, merely, a higher level of want creation, necessitating a higher level of want satisfaction."[21]

The significance of the dependence effect is not confined wholly to economic theory. The creation of wants, aided by advertising, is responsible for a conspicuous feature of American society, in Galbraith's view; namely, the imbalance between the private production of consumer goods and the level of public services. When advertising instills a strong desire for products that can be packaged and sold for a profit by a business firm but not for services—such as road maintenance, recreational areas, public health, police protection, and education—that are typically provided by government, the inevitable result is an abundance of the former and a dearth of the latter.

What Wants Are Worth Satisfying?

Galbraith's criticism of advertising has not gone unchallenged. The dependence effect, in Galbraith's formulation, involves a distinction between wants that originate in a person and those that are created by outside forces. F. A. von Hayek has pointed out that almost all wants beyond the most primitive needs for food, shelter, and sex are the result of cultural influences.[22] Thus, desires for art, music, and literature are no less *created* than desires for any consumer product. The creation of the former desires, moreover, is due in part to efforts by painters, composers, and novelists to earn a living. It is a complete non sequitur, therefore, to hold that wants that are created by the forces that also satisfy them are less urgent or important for that reason.

The point that Galbraith is trying to make is that some wants are more worth satisfying than others. What Hayek convincingly demonstrates is that the worth of a want cannot depend on its *source*—that is, on whether it originates within a person or is created by outside forces. A distinction between wants of greater and lesser worth, therefore, cannot be made in the way Galbraith proposes. It may still be possible, however, to rescue Galbraith's point—and with it, his criticism of advertising—by drawing the distinction in another way.

If some wants are more worth satisfying than others, then we need a criterion for making such a distinction. One such criterion is whether a desire is *rational*. Rationality is often described as a matter of the suitability of a desire for achieving some end or purpose. Consider, for example, the desires that advertising creates for expensive brands of liquor or designer clothing by appealing to people's yearning for status. Any clear-headed person should see the absurdity of thinking that status could be achieved merely by what one drinks or wears. A defender of advertising can reply that people do not really believe (irrationally) that they are "buying" status in making certain consumer purchases. Rather, advertising has succeeded in surrounding some products with an aura of status, so that people derive a certain satisfaction from purchasing and using those products.

Consumer behavior suggests, however, that people really do make certain purchases because they want status and that they recognize subconsciously the irrationality of some of their desires. Vance Packard reported that in the 1950s people expressed reluctance to buy small cars because they were less safe. Research showed that a process of rationalization was taking place. What worried people was not physical safety but psychological safety; they feared that small cars would make them look small in the eyes of neighbors.[23] People wanted large cars for reasons of status but disguised their true motivation as a concern for safety. Today, many ads for luxury cars stress safety so that buyers can assure themselves of the rationality of their decisions, even though status is uppermost in their minds. (The headline of one ad asks, "How important is the elegance of Chrysler Fifth Avenue if it can't protect you in an emergency?")

Rational Persuasion

The main concern of philosophers with advertising is whether the influence it exerts on consumers is consistent with a respect for personal freedom or autonomy. Persuasion is a broad category that ranges from the laudable (such as guidance by parents and teachers) to the sinister (psychoactive drugs, psychosurgery, and torture, for example). Advertising does not involve such extreme methods, of course. Still, advertising that cynically exploits deep-seated emotions or short-circuits logical thought processes can be criticized on the ground that it wrongfully deprives people of a certain amount of freedom in the making of consumer choices.

An advertising technique that might be faulted for this reason is subliminal communication. There is a story, possibly apocryphal, of an experiment in which a movie theater in New Jersey boosted sales of ice cream by flashing split-second messages on the screen during the regular showing of a film.[24] Several other studies have reported a decrease in shoplifting in department stores when exhortations against stealing were mixed with the background music being piped over speakers.[25] A related form of unconscious, if not subliminal, communication is the conspicuous placement of brand-name products in movies, a practice known as *product placement*.[26]

Although many people believe that subliminal communication is a commonly used technique in advertising,[27] there is little evidence to establish either its frequency or its effectiveness.[28] It might seem scarcely worth exploring the ethical issues in subliminal communication, therefore, except for the help it provides in understanding the concept of rational persuasion, which is relevant to the ethical evaluation of advertising generally.

What Is Wrong with Subliminal Ads?

The ethical argument against the use of subliminal communication in advertising—assuming that it is effective in influencing consumer behavior—is quite simple. Richard T. DeGeorge expressed it in the following way:

> Subliminal advertising is manipulative because it acts on us without our knowledge, and hence without our consent. If an ad appears on TV, we can tune it out or change stations if we do not want to be subject to it. If an ad appears in a magazine, we are not forced to look at it. In either case, if we do choose to look and listen, we can consciously evaluate what we see and hear. We can, if we wish, take a critical stance toward the advertisement. All of this is impossible with subliminal advertising, because we are unaware that we are being subjected to the message. The advertiser is imposing his message on us without our knowledge and consent.[29]

A similar argument can be made against product placement. Because moviegoers are unaware that advertising is being directed at them, they may not be prepared to evaluate it critically. Ads in newspapers and magazines and on television are clearly identified as such, so that we can separate them from news, entertainment, and other elements and treat them accordingly. Plugs in movies, under the guise of entertainment, catch us unawares, without our critical faculties at work, so to speak. We are not able to subject them to the same scrutiny as other ads because we do not recognize them for what they are.[30]

In both of these arguments, the main complaint is that certain advertising techniques—namely, subliminal communication and product placement—do not allow people to use their capacity for critical evaluation. The significance of this capacity lies in the role that it plays in freedom of choice. In the view of many philosophers, a choice is free to the extent that a person makes it on the basis of reasons that are considered by that person to be good reasons for acting. Freedom, in this view, is compatible with persuasion, but only as long as the techniques used do not undermine the ability of people to evaluate reasons for or against a course of action.

One kind of persuasion that enables people to evaluate reasons is rational argument. Advertising does not compare favorably with the dialogues of Plato as a model of reasoned discourse, but there is some argumentation in advertising, especially in the print media. Ads that cite good reasons for buying a product (by showing its uses, for example) or preferring one product over another (such as low cost or better quality) make a rational appeal to consumers and permit them to evaluate the reasons and decide for themselves. Ads of this kind may still be objectionable on other grounds, however. The claim that a low-tar cigarette is safer than other brands, for example, accompanied by data to back it up, makes a rational appeal to health-conscious smokers. But as long as ads are truthful and do not mislead—that is, as long as they contain respectable arguments—they cannot be faulted for depriving consumers of freedom. What makes an ad misleading is, of course, a critical issue. An ad can be deceptive for leaving out certain information, and some critics charge that ads that make an implied health claim for a patently unhealthy product are inherently deceptive. (These matters are discussed in the next section.)

Most attempts at persuasion, including those that involve rational argument, make some emotional or other nonrational appeal. A suitor is unlikely to win the heart of his beloved with logical arguments alone; a romantic setting with candlelight and soft music improves the chances of success. Courtroom lawyers do not rely solely on strong legal arguments to win cases but also on their ability to play on the feelings of jurors.[31] Similarly, good advertising appeals on many levels; it is aesthetically pleasing, intellectually stimulating, and often humorous or heartwarming. In all these examples, both rational and nonrational elements are combined for greater effect than could be achieved by using one element alone. In none of them, however, is a person necessarily being deprived of freedom of choice.

Persuasion and Freedom of Choice

What kind of persuasion, then, would deprive a person of freedom of choice? One possibility put forth by several philosophers is that it is nonrational persuasion that a person could not reasonably be expected to resist.[32] This is a very promising approach, but more needs to be said about what constitutes nonrational persuasion and what a person can reasonably be expected to resist. The dividing line between rational and nonrational persuasion is not easy to draw and may turn out in the end to presuppose some account of rational desire. A person may be rationally persuaded by ads that demonstrate the effectiveness of a brand of deodorant, for example. But does the ad make a rational appeal if the desire for a deodorant itself rests on an irrational association with social acceptability or sexual attractiveness?

Even more difficult, though, is drawing the line between resistible and irresistible influences. Stanley I. Benn holds that one test is whether people can be aware of what is happening to them.[33] By this test, he suggests, subliminal communication is probably objectionable because it operates subconsciously. Other possibilities include political propaganda in a closed society that suppresses all contrary views and advertising directed at children, who have not formed the capacity for critical judgment. Beyond these obvious cases, however, the test is not specific enough to be useful. How much do people have to be able to know, for example, about what is happening to them?

For the test suggested by Benn to be accepted, more psychological research would have to be done into the effects of advertising and other forms of mass communication in order to say with any assurance what people can and cannot resist. We would also need a better understanding of the motivation for choices that are generally considered to be free.[34] If, as psychologists such as B. F. Skinner maintain, our choices are the result of operant conditioning, then freedom is an illusion and the reasons that we give are mere rationalizations. Even if this extreme position is mistaken, probably more of our choices are shaped by outside forces than we would like to admit.

Finally, it may be that an adequate criterion must consider the *ends* for which techniques of persuasion are used and not merely the techniques themselves, considered as *means*. Public health programs employing slick Madison Avenue campaigns, for example, are not usually thought to be objectionable. But if ads to induce people to smoke and antismoking ads both employ the same nonrational techniques of persuasion—including some that people cannot reasonably be expected to resist—then the moral difference between them cannot be solely a matter of the morality of the means. Although some techniques, such as subliminal communication, may be morally unacceptable means no matter how worthy the end, most of the techniques of advertisers can be put to morally acceptable uses so that the morality of advertising depends, at least in part, on the ends for which certain techniques are used.

Conclusion

The concerns of economists and philosophers—the former with the creation of wants and the latter with the threat to freedom or autonomy—pose significant challenges to the morality of advertising. Although sweeping charges against advertising as a general practice are unwarranted, there is still an undeniable potential for behavior control that requires advertisers to act in a responsible manner. The major difficulty is finding a precise way of determining what constitutes responsible use of the persuasive power of advertising. Benn's proposal that advertising is morally objectionable when it uses nonrational forms of persuasion that we are unable to resist is sufficient to rule out certain kinds of ads and raise questions about others. However, this criterion is concerned with the ability of people to resist the effects of individual ads but not the barrage of commercial messages that we encounter every day. Even if all ads are resistible individually, it does not follow that even the most rational of us can remain unaffected by the sheer volume of ads around us.

CASE 11.2   Is It Deceptive to . . . ?

- An ad claims that a children's cereal contains less sugar than an apple. The cereal is 40 percent sugar, and its calories have little nutritional value, whereas an apple contains many nutrients that the cereal lacks.

- A reformulated gasoline is advertised as a "breakthrough in technology" that provides the "highest performance." A rival has used the same process for more than ten years and produces gasoline that is just as good. The company claims that "highest performance" means "the highest performance of which the engine is capable" and does not imply that the gasoline is better than the competitor's.

- Airfares are often advertised for one-way travel, but this price is available only with a round-trip purchase. The advertised airfare also omits applicable airport taxes. The round-trip condition and the possibility of taxes are revealed in small print elsewhere in the ad.

- An ad for a brand of disposable diapers shows a handful of dirt and proclaims, "Ninety days ago this was a disposable diaper." The ad does not reveal that the diaper is recyclable only if the plastic liner is removed, and that no facilities exist in most metropolitan areas to recycle the product.

- A popular fashion magazine produces a separate advertising supplement (called an "outsert") that is packaged with copies of the magazines. The supplement, commissioned by a cosmetic company, uses the magazine's typeface and layout with photographs by the magazine's contributing photographers; but the copy is written by an ad agency instead of the magazine's editorial staff.

DECEPTIVE ADVERTISING

Whether an ad is deceptive is not easy to determine. The main source of the difficulty is the concept of deception itself, which does not have a clear, settled meaning. As a first approximation, something is deceptive if it has a tendency to deceive. In this definition, the deceptiveness of an ad does not depend solely on the truth or falsity of the claims made in it but also on the impact the ad has on the people who see or hear it. It is possible for advertising to contain false claims without being deceptive and for advertising to be deceptive without containing any false claims.

A patently false claim—for a hair restorer, for example—might not actually deceive anyone or even have the potential to do so. Furthermore, there are other advertising claims that are false if taken literally but are commonly regarded as harmless exaggerations or bits of puffery.[35] Every razor blade, for example, gives the closest, most comfortable shave; every tire, the smoothest, safest ride; and every pain reliever, the quickest, gentlest relief. Few people are deceived by such hyperbole—or, apparently, bothered by the logical inconsistency of two different brands both being the safest or the gentlest. Even if no one is deceived, however, it does not follow that such claims are not objectionable for other reasons, such as the debasement of the language.

Similarly, we are not misled by the claims that Avis tries harder (the latest version is "We're trying harder than ever") or that Gallo releases no wine before its time. Expressions such as these are usually regarded not as serious claims to truth but as suggestive rhetorical devices. Some ad copy, furthermore, has no determinate meaning at all and cannot be characterized as either true or false. Examples are pointless comparisons, such as claims that a cleaner is new and improved or 50 percent more effective, and inane jingles such as "Things go better with Coke" and "Chevrolet—the Heartbeat of America."

Some writers even defend the literal falsehoods and meaningless babble of advertising as legitimate and even socially desirable. Perhaps the best known of these defenders is Theodore Levitt, who compares advertising to poetry:

> Like advertising, poetry's purpose is to influence an audience; to affect its perceptions and sensibilities; perhaps even to change its mind. . . . [P]oetry's intent is to convince and seduce. In the service of that intent, it employs without guilt or fear of criticism all the arcane tools of distortion that the literary mind can devise. Keats does not offer a truthful engineering description of his Grecian urn. He offers, instead, . . . a lyrical, exaggerated, distorted, and palpably false description. And he is thoroughly applauded for it, as are all other artists, in whatever medium, who do precisely this same thing successfully.
>
> Commerce, it can be said without apology, takes essentially the same liberties with reality and literality as the artist, except that commerce calls its creations advertising. . . . As with art, the purpose is to influence the audience by creating illusions, symbols, and implications that promise more than pure functionality. . . .[36]

In order to see that true claims can still be deceptive, consider an ad for Anacin that prompted a complaint by the FTC in 1973. The ad asserted that Anacin has a unique pain-killing formula that is superior to all other nonprescription analgesics. Anacin is composed of two active ingredients, aspirin (400 milligrams) and caffeine (32.5 milligrams), but the sole pain-relieving component is aspirin. Aspirin itself is unique—if indeed it makes any sense to describe a chemical compound in this way—and at the time, aspirin was superior to any other pain reliever available without a prescription. Therefore, it is literally true that Anacin contains a unique and superior pain-killing formula: aspirin. The impression that the ad conveyed, however, was that only Anacin has this superior pain-relieving ingredient (false) and that consequently Anacin itself is superior to competing brands of analgesics containing aspirin (also false).

The basis of the FTC complaint, therefore, was not that the claims made for Anacin are literally false but that they gave rise to, or were likely to give rise to, false beliefs in the minds of consumers. Ads for Anacin also claimed that it causes less frequent side effects. The position of the FTC is that the deceptiveness of this claim does not depend solely on whether it is true or false but also on whether the manufacturer, American Home Products, had sufficient evidence to back it up. That is, unsupported claims that turn out to be true are still deceptive, since, in the words of the court, "a consumer is entitled to assume that the appropriate verification has been performed." Even if Anacin does cause less frequent side effects, the consumer is deceived by being led to believe that there is evidence for the claim when there is not. In order to make comparative claims of superiority that are nondeceptive, drug companies have a responsibility to conduct scientifically valid clinical studies.

Whether a claim is deceptive, therefore, depends, in some cases, on the strength of the evidence for it. Even if claims are true and supported by some evidence, they are still deceptive if the amount of evidence is less than consumers, viewing an ad, would reasonably be led to expect. Consequently, the resolution of some disputes over the deceptiveness of a claim in an ad depend ultimately on the judgment of experts in scientific methodology.

A More Precise Definition of Deception

The rough definition of deception that has been developed so far is not adequate, either for increasing our understanding of the ethical issues in deceptive advertising or for enforcing a legal prohibition against it. Unfortunately, the FTC has yet to offer a precise legal definition, and none of the attempts by marketing theorists and others to define deception in advertising has been entirely successful.

A frequently cited definition, offered by David M. Gardner, is as follows:

> If an advertisement (or advertising campaign) leaves the consumer with an impressions(s) and/or belief(s) different from what would normally be expected if the consumer had reasonable knowledge, and that impression(s) and/or belief(s) is factually untrue or potentially misleading, then deception is said to exist.[37]

In this definition, deception occurs if after being exposed to an ad a consumer has impressions or beliefs that do not constitute reasonable knowledge and those impressions or beliefs are false or misleading.[38] A number of objections can be raised against this definition.

First, an ad is not deceptive merely for failing to ensure that a consumer has reasonable knowledge.[39] Otherwise, a person who believes that brushing every day eliminates the need for occasional visits to the dentist would be deceived by a toothpaste ad that (truthfully) promoted the benefits of daily brushing without suggesting in the least that users could skip regular dental checkups. Yet, in Gardner's definition such an ad would be deceptive, since the belief that the person is left with is different from that which the person would be expected to have if the person had reasonable knowledge and the belief is false.

Second, the definition counts any ad as deceptive that leaves a person with unreasonable knowledge without regard for whether the fault lies with the ad or with the person. Ivan Preston recounts the story of an irate customer who failed to catch the joke in an ad for a novelty beer, Olde Frothingslosh, that proclaimed it to be the only beer with the foam on the bottom.[40] The customer was dissuaded from taking legal action by a lawyer who pointed out that the FTC does not consider an ad to be deceptive if it fools only a few extremely gullible people. That is, in deciding whether an ad is deceptive, the FTC considers *who* would be misled by an ad. Would it be misleading to any reasonable consumer or only to one who is extremely ignorant?

Consider, for example, whether it is deceptive for Clairol to advertise a dye that will "color hair permanently."[41] Most people know that hair grows, and so only a few, rather ignorant people are likely to be duped into believing that dyeing will never again be necessary. It is even less likely that many people would mistake a slogan used at one time for Ipana toothpaste—"the Smile of Beauty"—for a claim that the product straightens crooked teeth.[42] Both of these cases date from the 1940s, at which time a very literal-minded FTC generally enforced an ignorant-consumer standard. Accordingly, these ads were found by the commission to be deceptive. Similar rulings would probably not be made today.

However, the FTC was called upon recently to make a ruling in a case against the Ford Motor Company in which data on a mileage test were accompanied by the following qualification:

> You yourself might actually average less, or for that matter more. Because mileage varies according to maintenance, equipment, total weight, driving habits and road conditions. And no two drivers, even cars, are exactly the same.[43]

Would a reasonably intelligent, well-informed person reading this carefully qualified claim conclude that the data given in the advertisement described the mileage for an *average* driver? The FTC, employing the more restrictive reasonable-consumer standard, decided that it did and asked Ford for substantiation.

Third, there is the problem of what constitutes reasonable knowledge. Presumably this means the knowledge that is needed to make rational consumer choices. That is, the false impressions or beliefs conveyed by an ad must be "material" in the sense that they are likely to affect people's purchasing decisions to their detriment. An ad that gives people mistaken information about geography or literature is not for that reason alone deceptive. However, the knowledge needed for making rational consumer choices is an uncertain standard for determining whether deception exists. People always have less-than-perfect information, and no amount of advertising can clear away all the false impressions and beliefs that they have or, for that matter, avoid creating new ones. Gardner's definition cannot be used to determine whether an ad is deceptive, therefore, without specifying some standard of reasonable knowledge.

Patching Up the Definition

Several suggestions have been made for patching up this analysis of deception. One possible response to the first objection is to say that deception occurs only if the false impressions or beliefs are in some way *caused* by the ad in question.[44] But this is too strong. An ad would probably be considered deceptive if it reinforced or took advantage of an already existing false belief. An attempt might be made to overcome the second objection by specifying that the consumers in question are intelligent, knowledgeable adults; that is, the rational-consumer standard could be built right into the definition. Thomas L. Carson, Richard E. Wokutch, and James E. Cox, Jr., point out that this is inadequate, since the resulting definition does not apply to deceptive advertising to children. They have proposed instead the following definition of deception:

> An advertisement is deceptive if it causes a significant percentage of potential consumers (i.e., those at whom it is directed or whose consumption behavior is likely to be influenced by it) to have false beliefs about the product.[45]

What constitutes a "significant percentage" remains to be specified, but this is not a serious problem. More crucial is the fact that this definition employs a causal analysis of deception, which has already been shown to be inadequate. Furthermore, any false belief about a product that is caused by an ad is sufficient, according to the revised definition, to make it deceptive. Both definitions, therefore, are vulnerable to the third objection.

In order to see the problem more fully, consider health claims in food advertising. The word *natural*, which usually means the absence of artificial ingredients, evokes images of wholesomeness in the minds of consumers. Yet many food products advertised as natural contain unhealthy concentrations of fat and sugar and are deficient in vitamins and minerals.[46] In response to concerns about refined sugar, some manufacturers are switching to more natural-sounding brown sugar and honey, despite the fact that from a nutritional point of view all sugar provides the same empty calories. The makers of some brands of peanut butter advertise their products as cholesterol free even though cholesterol is present only in animal fats, so no brand of peanut butter contains any cholesterol.

Is it deceptive for food advertising to make use of terms such as *natural, sugar free,* and *no cholesterol?* In Gardner's definition, the answer to this question depends on what people with reasonable knowledge know, a matter that is by no means easy to determine.[47] In the revised definition, the answer depends only on whether the use of these terms causes a substantial percentage of potential consumers to have false beliefs about the product. Again, allowance needs to be made for ads that do not create but merely take advantage of the false beliefs of consumers, and the false beliefs need to be limited to those relevant to consumer choice.

A Final Definition

The root of the problem is that deception in advertising is a normative concept. Consequently, it cannot be adequately expressed by purely factual definitions of the kind considered so far. A more satisfactory definition, therefore, is the following:

> Deception occurs when a false belief, which an advertisement either creates or takes advantage of, substantially interferes with the ability of people to make rational consumer choices.

Advertising is not intended to produce knowledgeable consumers, and so it should not be faulted for every failure to do so. Also, not every false belief is of such importance that consumers should be protected from it. But there is still a certain standard of rational consumer behavior, and advertising is deceptive when it achieves its effect by false beliefs that prevent consumers from attaining this standard.

In this definition, deception in advertising is one form of illegitimate persuasion of the kind examined in the previous section. The objection to subliminal advertising and some other persuasive techniques is that they keep people from being able to evaluate the reasons for or against a course of action, thereby depriving them of a certain amount of freedom. Outright lies in advertising, along with more subtle deceptive claims, similarly constitute morally objectionable forms of behavior control.

One shortcoming of this definition is that the concept of a rational consumer choice is left undefined. Any definition of deception is unavoidably normative, however, which is to say that deception must be defined in terms of some other concept that embodies a standard of right and wrong. We have already seen that a purely factual definition cannot work. Any adequate definition, therefore, will contain at least one undefined normative term. The virtue of this definition is that it shows the relation between the ethical objections to behavior control, discussed in the last section, and deception, the subject of this section.

Whether an ad *substantially interferes* with the ability of people to make rational consumer choices assumes some view of what choices they would make if they were not influenced by an ad. Advertisers have no responsibility to ensure that people make rational consumer choices. But when their ads lead people to make choices they would not have made otherwise, they bear some responsibility. Since the aim of advertising is precisely to change (or reinforce) behavior so that people make different choices than they would otherwise, advertisers almost always bear this responsibility. Advertising is laudable to the extent that is enables consumers to make rational choices, but it is objectionable when the result is to interfere with this ability. Not all interference warrants the same degree of concern, however, and the notion of substantial interference sets a threshold beyond which advertising ought not to go.

At least two factors are relevant to the notion of substantial interference. One is the ability of consumers to protect themselves and make rational choices despite advertising that creates or takes advantage of false beliefs. Thus, claims that are easily verified or not taken seriously by consumers are not necessarily deceptive. The second factor is the seriousness of the choice that consumers make. False beliefs that affect the choices we make about our health or financial affairs are of greater concern than false beliefs that bear on inconsequential purchases. Claims in life insurance advertising, for example, ought to be held to a higher standard than those for chewing gum.

Both of these factors can be observed in two cases involving the Campbell Soup Company. Campbell ran afoul of the FTC in 1970 when they ran television ads showing a bowl of vegetable soup chock-full of solids.[48] This effect was achieved by placing clear-glass marbles on the bottom of the bowl to hold the solids near the surface. How does this case differ from one in which clear-plastic cubes are used instead of real ice in ads for cold drinks? In each case, false beliefs are created in consumers' minds. The false beliefs that viewers have about the contents of a glass of iced tea as a result of using plastic cubes have no bearing on a decision to purchase the product (an iced-tea mix, for example), whereas a decision to purchase a can of Campbell's vegetable soup can definitely be influenced by the false belief created by the glass marbles. Consumers who buy the soup in the belief that the bowl at home will look like the one in the ad will be disappointed, but not the consumers who buy the iced tea mix. The ads have the potential, therefore, to interfere in the ability of consumers to make rational choices.

In 1991, the Campbell Soup Company was charged again by the FTC for ads stressing the low-fat, low-cholesterol content of some of its soups and linking these qualities to a reduced risk of heart disease.[49] The soups in question have reduced amounts of fat and cholesterol, but the ads failed to mention that they are high in sodium, which increases the risk of some forms of heart disease. In the FTC's judgment, Campbell was implying that their soups could be part of a diet that reduces heart disease, while at the same time refusing to tell consumers how much sodium the soups contain or that salt should be avoided by people concerned about heart disease. Consumers who are unaware of the salt content of canned soups might purchase Campbell products as part of a diet aimed at reducing the risk of heart disease. In so doing, they would be better off buying these products than high-salt soups that are also high in fat and cholesterol. But health-conscious consumers who are aware of the salt content might well make different, more rational consumer purchases instead.

Although these ads may not directly cause consumers to have false beliefs about certain Campbell products, the campaign depends for its success on consumer ignorance about the salt content of its soups and the link between salt and heart disease and thus takes advantage of this ignorance. Whether Campbell would have an obligation to reveal the sodium content of its soups if it did not make health claims is debatable, but having made claims designed to lead people concerned about heart disease to buy their products, Campbell definitely has such an obligation. (Campbell eventually agreed to reveal the sodium content in ads for soups with more than 500 milligrams of sodium in an eight-ounce serving.)[50] The health claims made on behalf of some Campbell soups also involve the two factors that are a part of *substantial interference*. The salt content of a soup, unlike the amount of vegetable solids, cannot be easily verified by consumers, and the decisions consumers make to protect their health are of great importance. Accordingly, the FTC rigorously scrutinizes health claims in ads and holds them to a higher standard.

Conclusion

The evaluation of advertising in this chapter proceeds on several levels. Charges that advertising is inefficient and manipulative are concerned primarily with advertising as a general practice or with certain advertising techniques. The charge of deception in advertising is directed, by contrast, at the content of specific advertisements and, in particular, the claims made or implied by them. One principle for evaluating advertising is utilitarian. Are we better or worse off with advertising? Does advertising as a practice or do individual ads promote or diminish the welfare of society as a whole? Both manipulative and deceptive advertising are objectionable, according to utilitarianism, for the reason that they harm consumers.

A second principle, which ties together the latter two charges, is one based on the Kantian theme of rationality. Consumers ought to be free to make choices that best satisfy their desires. The process of creating desires, which Galbraith calls the dependence effect, can be objected to not only because it prevents the realization of our other desires (a utilitarian reason) but also because it interferes with our ability to act on rational desires (a Kantian reason). The concept of deception, we have seen, assumes that consumers ought to be free to make rational consumer choices. Although advertisers may have no obligation to ensure that we make such choices, they have a negative duty not to create or take advantage of false beliefs that interfere significantly with our ability to make rational consumer choices.

CASE 11.3   Does Nike Ad Step out of Bounds?

Nike, Inc. is pushing the limits of taste and coherence with a new advertising campaign starring Dennis Hopper, a cult-hero of American cinema who is proving to be a controversial choice as pitchman.[51] The campaign for Air Veer cross-training shoes has touched a nerve with advocates for the mentally ill, who say such ads trivialize mental disorders by using stereotypes. The campaign also has reignited a debate on Madison Avenue about the purpose of advertising: Is it to entertain or to sell? And can it do both?

In the new campaign, Mr. Hopper portrays the ultimate football fanatic: an ex-referee so obsessed with the game and the athletes that he has turned into, well, Dennis Hopper. The actor is known for playing violent and eccentric characters. In the commercials, he rants about the athletes in frenetic performances. Created by Nike agency Wieden & Kennedy, of Portland, Oregon, the spots include real-life footage of Troy Aikman, Barry Sanders, and Bruce Smith. But the real star is Mr. Hopper, whose over-the-top performance includes twitches, tics, and manic laughter that to some viewers clearly add up to a mentally ill man.

In one sidewalk scene, Mr. Hopper faces the camera and rhapsodizes about Barry Sanders's moves on the field. "He does things on the field that make your eyes go all crazy!" Mr. Hopper says excitedly. "Sometimes I still see him when I sleep," he confides, adding, "And I don't sleep that much." In another spot, Mr. Hopper sneaks into the Buffalo Bills' locker room and removes Bruce Smith's Nike shoe from his locker. He even takes a deep whiff. "You know what Bruce would do if he found me messing with this shoe?" he asks, a look of fear on his face. "Bad things, man, bad things."

"What is the point in feeding upon the constant notion that people who have a mental illness are, as this ad seems to imply, paranoid or out of control?" asks Shadrach Stanleigh, spokesman for the National Stigma Clearinghouse, a watchdog group that monitors advertising and media for stereotypes of mental illness. "The implication is they are the outcasts of society who can't be trusted to do anything." In 1991, the National Stigma Clearinghouse protested a Nike print ad that said, "Your mother and father told you repeatedly, crazy people talk to themselves. . . . And finally you realized, only a madman doesn't listen." The group also objected to a billboard that labeled one of its shoes "Multiple Personalities."

Agency founder Dan Wieden defends the campaign. "The job of commercials is to wake people up and make them think differently and entertain them in the process," he says. "The role isn't to be politically correct. It's to be provocative." "The responsibility of the advertiser is to develop a relationship with the audience, and a complex one," he says. "I don't know why advertising has to be restricted to jingles and superficiality."

Some observers like the ads but disapprove of them anyway. *Advertising Age* columnist Bob Garfield, who says the spots make him laugh, also believes Mr. Hopper's performance isn't an "appropriate characterization for a national TV commercial." "It isn't a question of political correctness," Mr. Garfield says. "Advertisers have a special obligation to observe the golden rule. No one asks to see a TV commercial. It just comes barging in. Advertising has to take special care not to be offensive or exploitative because it is completely unsolicited."

NOTES

1. Material for this case is from BARRY MEIER, "For this Pounding, Volvo Had Help," *New York Times*, 6 November 1990, D1, D17; KIM FOLZ, "Scali Quits Volvo Account, Citing Faked Commercial," *New York Times*, 14 November 1990, D1; KRYSTAL MILLER and JACQUELINE MITCHELL, "Car Marketers Test Gray Area of Truth in Advertising," *Wall Street Journal*, 19 November 1990, B1, B6.

2. WILLIAM M. PRIDE and O. C. FERRELL, *Marketing: Basic Concepts and Decisions*, 4th ed. (Boston: Houghton Mifflin, 1985), 332.

3. See H. L. DARLING, "How Companies Are Using Corporate Advertising," *Public Relations Journal*, 31 (November 1975), 26–29; W. S. SACHS, "Corporate Advertising: Ends, Means, Problems," *Public Relations Journal*, 37 (November 1981), 14–17; and S. PRAKASH SETHI, "Institutional/Image Advertising and Idea/Issue Advertising as Marketing Tools: Some Public Policy Issues," *Journal of Marketing*, 47 (January 1983), 68–78.

4. See, for example, RONALD HUMPHREY and HOWARD SCHUMAN, "The Portrayal of Blacks in Magazine Advertisements: 1950–1982," *Public Opinion Quarterly*, 48 (1984), 551–63; JAMES U. MCNEAL, "Advertising's Disparagement of American Workers," *Business Horizons* (January–February 1983), 7–12; and BRIAN KVASNICKA, BARBARA BEYMER, and RICHARD M. PERLOFF, "Portrayals of the Elderly in Magazine Advertisements," *Journalism Quarterly*, 59 (1982), 656–58.

5. CHRISTOPHER LASCH, *The Culture of Narcissism* (New York: W. W. Norton, 1978), 72.

6. VANCE PACKARD, *The Hidden Persuaders* (New York: David McKay, 1957), 20–21.

7. PACKARD, *The Hidden Persuaders*, 25.

8. See PHILLIP NELSON, "Advertising and Ethics," in RICHARD T. DEGEORGE and JOSEPH A. PILCHER, eds., *Ethics, Free Enterprise, and Public Policy* (New York: Oxford University Press, 1978), 187–98.

9. NELSON, "Advertising and Ethics," 190.

10. These points are made in JULES BACKMAN, "Is Advertising Wasteful?" *Journal of Marketing*, 32 (January 1968), 2–8.

11. The foremost advocates of this view are EDWARD CHAMBERLAIN, *The Theory of Monopolistic Competition* (Cambridge: Harvard University Press, 1933); NICHOLAS H. KALDOR, "The Economic Aspects of Advertising," *The Review of Economic Studies*, 18 (1950–51), 1–27; and WILLIAM S. COMANOR and THOMAS A. WILSON, *Advertising and Market Power* (Cambridge: Harvard University Press, 1975).

12. Material on this case is taken from EARL A. MOLANDER, "Marketing Ready-to-Eat Breakfast Cereals at the Kellogg Company," in *Responsive Capitalism: Case Studies in Corporate Social Responsibility* (New York: McGraw-Hill, 1980), 128–43.

13. DONALD TULL and LYNN KAHLE, *Marketing Management* (New York: Macmillan, 1990), 498.

14. The main defenders of advertising against the charge of being an anticompetitive practice are LESTER G. TELSER and YALE BROZEN. See TELSER, "Advertising and Competition," *Journal of Political Economy*, 72 (1964), 537–62; "Some Aspects of the Economics of Advertising," *Journal of Business* (April 1968), 166–73; and BROZEN, "Advertising, the Consumer and Inflation," in JOHN S. WRIGHT and JOHN E. MERTES, eds., *Advertising's Role in Society* (St. Paul, MN: West, 1974), 86–92. For a survey of the literature, see JAMES M. FERGUSON, *Advertising and Competition: Theory and Measurement* (Cambridge: Ballinger, 1974).

15. LEE BENTHAM, "The Effect of Advertising on the Price of Eyeglasses," *Journal of Law and Economics*, 15

(1972), 337–52. See also ROBERT L. STEINER, "Does Advertising Lower Consumer Prices?" *Journal of Marketing*, 37 (October 1973), 19–26.

16. See KEITH B. LEFFLER, "Persuasion or Information? The Economics of Prescription Drug Advertising," *Journal of Law and Economics*, 24 (1981), 45–74.

17. BROZEN, "Advertising, the Consumer and Inflation," 90. One defect in this argument is that advertising currently enjoys a preferential tax status, so that it is more profitable for firms to advertise than to cut prices. In order for free market forces to allocate resources efficiently, advertising would have to be treated like any other expenditure for tax purposes, a move that manufacturers and the advertising industry vigorously oppose.

18. JOHN KENNETH GALBRAITH, *The Affluent Society* (New York: Houghton Mifflin, 1958), 128.

19. DAVID BRAYBROOKE, "Skepticism of Wants, and Certain Subversive Effects of Corporations on American Values," in SIDNEY HOOK, ed., *Human Values and Economic Policy* (New York: New York University Press, 1967), 229.

20. GALBRAITH, *The Affluent Society*, 124–25.

21. GALBRAITH, *The Affluent Society*, 128.

22. F. A. VON HAYEK, "The *Non Sequitur* of the 'Dependence Effect,'" *Southern Economic Journal*, 27 (April 1961), 346–48. Similar points are made in THEODORE LEVITT, "The Morality (?) of Advertising," *Harvard Business Review*, 48 (July–August 1970), 84–92.

23. PACKARD, *The Hidden Persuaders*, 110.

24. Cited in PACKARD, *The Hidden Persuaders*, 35.

25. For one example, see "Secret Voices: Messages That Manipulate," *Time*, 10 September 1979, 71.

26. See MICHAEL SCHUDSON, *Advertising, The Uneasy Persuasion: Its Dubious Impact on Society* (New York: Basic Books, 1984), 102–3.

27. See RALPH NORMAN HABER, "Public Attitudes Regarding Subliminal Advertising," *Public Opinion Quarterly*, 23 (1959), 291–93; and ERIC J. ZANOT, J. DAVID PINCUS, and E. JOSEPH LAMP, "Public Perceptions of Subliminal Advertising," *Journal of Advertising*, 12 (1983), 39–45.

28. A researcher who claims to find evidence for both the frequency and effectiveness of subliminal advertising is WILSON BRIAN KEY, who has written three books, *Subliminal Seduction* (Englewood Cliffs, NJ: Prentice Hall, 1974); *Media Sexploitation* (Englewood Cliffs, NJ: Prentice Hall, 1976); and *The Clam-Plate Orgy and Other Subliminal Techniques for Manipulating Your Behavior* (Englewood Cliffs, NJ: Prentice Hall, 1980). A generally negative appraisal of the effectiveness of the technique is offered in N. F. DIXON, *Subliminal Perception* (London: McGraw-Hill, 1971). For evidence specifically on advertising, see STEPHEN G. GEORGE and LUTHER B. JENNINGS, "Effect of Subliminal Stimuli on Consumer Behavior: Negative Evidence," *Perceptual and Motor Skills*, 41 (1975), 847–54; DEL I. HAWKINS, "The Effects of Subliminal Stimulation on Drive Level and Brand Preference," *Journal of Marketing Research*, 8, (1970) 322–26; and TIMOTHY E. MOORE, "Subliminal Advertising: What You See Is What You Get," *Journal of Marketing*, 46 (Spring 1982), 38–47.

29. RICHARD T. DEGEORGE, *Business Ethics*, 4th ed. (Englewood Cliffs, NJ: Prentice Hall, 1995), 262.

30. This is not the only ground for objecting to product placement. Critics also cite the element of deception and the corrupting effect of product placement on the artistic integrity of movies.

31. Although this practice is generally accepted as legitimate persuasion, an interesting issue is posed by the increasing use of market research in jury selection and the formation of legal strategy. If lawyers start adopting the techniques of advertisers, then they could open themselves up to many of the same criticisms. See SCOTT M. SMITH, "Marketing Research and Corporate Litigation . . . Where Is the Balance of Ethical Justice?" *Journal of Business Ethics*, 3 (1984), 185–94.

32. This criterion is advanced by STANLEY I. BENN, "Freedom and Persuasion," *Australasian Journal of Philosophy*, 45 (1967), 267.

33. BENN, "Freedom and Persuasion," 269.

34. This point is made in ALAN H. GOLDMAN, "Ethical Issues in Advertising," in TOM REGAN, ed., *Just Business: New Introductory Essays in Business Ethics* (New York: Random House, 1984) 251.

35. For a thorough study of puffery, see IVAN L. PRESTON, *The Great American Blow-Up: Puffery in Advertising and Selling* (Madison: University of Wisconsin Press, 1975).

36. LEVITT, "The Morality (?) of Advertising," 85.

37. DAVID M. GARDNER, "Deception in Advertising: A Conceptual Approach," *Journal of Marketing*, 39 (January 1975), 40–46.

38. This definition is open to several different interpretations. See THOMAS L. CARSON, RICHARD E. WOKUTCH, and JAMES E. COX, JR., "An Ethical Analysis of Deception in Advertising," *Journal of Business Ethics*, 4 (1985), 103, note 6.

39. This point is made in CARSON, WOKUTCH, and COX, "An Ethical Analysis of Deception in Advertising," 94–95.

40. IVAN L. PRESTON, "Reasonable or Ignorant Consumer? How the FTC Decides," *Journal of Consumer Affairs*, 8 (1974), 132.

41. *Gelb* v. *FTC*, 144 F. 2d 580 (2d Cir. 1944).

42. 47 FTC 162 (1949).

43. Cited in JAMES C. MILLER, "Why FTC Curbs Are Needed," *Advertising Age*, March 22, 1982, 83.

44. CARSON, WOKUTCH, and COX respond in this way. They assert, "in order to count as deceptive an ad must be the cause of one's misinformation or lack of reasonable knowledge." "An Ethical Analysis of Deception in Advertising," 95.

45. CARSON, WOKUTCH, and COX, "An Ethical Analysis of Deception in Advertising," 96.

46. See BONNIE LIEBMAN, "Nouveau Junk Food: Consumers Swallow the Back-to-Nature Bunk," *Business and Society Review*, 51 (Fall 1984), 47–51.

47. Gardner is aware of this problem and proposes a solution as part of a technique for measuring deception. Using what he calls the normative belief technique, "adequately informed consumers," which he defines as those who have the opportunity to acquire extensive information about a product, agree on an "optimal" set of functional attributes for a product. Research can then reveal the extent to which the beliefs of a wide range of consumers deviate from the beliefs of adequately informed consumers regarding the set of functional attributes. This technique does not solve the problem, however, since everything still depends on how much "adequately informed consumers" know—and also on what is an acceptable deviation—which is presumably determined, again, by "adequately informed consumers." See GARDNER, "Deception in Advertising," 44–45.

48. *Campbell Soup*, 77 FTC 664 (1970).

49. See JEANNE SADDLER, "Campbell Soup Will Change Ads to Settle Charges," *Wall Street Journal*, 9 April 1991, B6.

50. "F.T.C. in Accord with Campbell," *New York Times*, 10 April 1991, sec. 4, p. 4.

51. LAURA BIRD, "Critics Cry Foul at Nike Spots with Actor," *Wall Street Journal*, 16 December 1993, B12. Reprinted by permission of the *Wall Street Journal*. Copyright 1993 Dow Jones & Company, Inc. All rights reserved worldwide.

12

Marketing and Product Safety

CASE 12.1   Dow Corning's Breast Implants

On May 15, 1995, Dow Corning Corporation filed for federal bankruptcy protection.[1] Founded in 1943 as a joint venture of Dow Chemical Company and Corning Glass Works (later changed to Corning, Inc.), Dow Corning had prospered by making lubricants, sealants, electrical insulators, and other products from silicone. One product, however, silicone breast implants, now threatened to destroy the company.

During the 1980s, as an estimated two million women received silicone breast implants, thousands of women began to experience severe headaches, unexplained rashes, pain in the joints and muscles, weight loss, and extreme fatigue. The women and their doctors were baffled, until a common thread began to emerge: the presence of silicone. The implants themselves often caused a painful hardening of the surrounding tissues, known as capsular contracture. The semiliquid filling in the implants was suspected of bleeding through the pouchlike outer covering, and some women's implants ruptured, releasing silicone that eventually lodged in the liver, spleen, and other internal organs. A variety of autoimmune diseases—in which the body attacks its own tissue as if it were a foreign object—were believed by doctors to result from the bleeding and ruptured implants.

In December 1991, Dow Corning was found guilty in a San Francisco court of manufacturing a defective product and of fraudulently concealing evidence of safety problems. The jury awarded the woman in the case, Mariann Hopkins, $7.3 million (a figure that was upheld on appeal). Dow Corning repeated its contention that scientific evidence showed the implants to be safe, and the company denounced the verdict as a politicization of the issue. At the time, the Food and Drug Administration (FDA) was deciding whether to continue the unrestricted use of breast implants. Before 1976, medical devices of all kinds were unregulated, but a law was passed that year by Congress requiring manufacturers to prove the safety of their products. In April 1992, the FDA ruled that sufficient proof had not been provided, and breast implants were ordered off the market (except for special cases of reconstructive surgery, which were to be closely monitored).

More suits followed, and in April 1994, Dow Corning agreed to contribute $2 billion to a $4.23 billion global settlement fund for women around the world who claimed to suffer because of breast implants. At the time of Dow Corning's bankruptcy filing, 410,000 women had submitted claims for compensation from the fund, and the company faced between 5,000 and 15,000 suits from women who elected not to join the settlement. The bankruptcy filing put the global settlement fund and all unsettled suits in jeopardy. The two parent corporations, Dow Chemical and Corning, had to write off their $374 million investment in the joint venture.

Dow Corning introduced the first version of a breast implant in 1963 for use in reconstructive surgery for breast cancer victims following a mastectomy. The prototype had been developed by Dr. Thomas D. Cronin, a surgeon at Baylor University in Texas. Dow Corning performed no tests on the safety of the implant prior to the introduction, relying instead on a limited study done by Dr. Cronin on dogs. However, the company believed silicone to be biologically inert on the basis of other animal studies and experience with a few other silicone medical devices. In 1964, Dow Corning commissioned an independent laboratory to do a study on the safety of the medical-grade silicone used in all implants. Researchers discovered that silicone injected into dogs caused "persistent, chronic inflammation," but the results were dismissed by Dow Corning officials as a typical foreign body reaction that is not specific to silicone. A 1969 study revealed that injected silicone eventually lodged in the vital organs of test animals, but this result too was not regarded as significant since the company did not advocate the injection of silicone directly into the body.

In 1975, Dow Corning introduced a new type of breast implant that was softer and more pliable. This second-generation version was the result of a crash program in response to the entry of competitors into the market, several of which were aided by ex-employees who built on Dow Corning's existing technology. These upstart companies reduced Dow Corning's market share to 35 percent by providing plastic surgeons with an implant that produced a more natural look and feel. The fact that the newer implants were also suited for breast enlargement and not merely reconstructive surgery fueled an increase in purely cosmetic uses. Within four months the redesigned breast implant was ready to demonstrate to plastic surgeons and full production was achieved by September. No additional testing was done for the new product, even though the changed design used a more liquid form of silicone. Some Dow Corning scientists voiced concerns that greater silicone bleed through the outer covering was possible and constituted an unknown risk. These fears were confirmed when the samples displayed to plastic surgeons became oily to the touch and stained the velvet showcases that were used. Sales personnel were instructed to change the sample often and to wipe them before they were presented to the surgeons.

In news articles based on internal company documents, Dow Corning was charged with conducting inadequate research and with suppressing memos and research reports that questioned the safety of breast implants. One indignant salesperson wrote that selling possibly defective implants "has to rank right up there with the Pinto gas tank." Another person in marketing reported that he had assured a group of doctors "with crossed fingers" that Dow Corning had safety studies underway. A *New York Times* columnist described Dow Corning as "a company adrift without a moral compass." One of many cartoons in the press showed a Dow Corning representative explaining to a group of women, "We're testing breast implants on you to see if they're safe for guinea pigs."

Several recent studies involving large populations of women over extended periods of time have found no increase in autoimmune diseases or any other illnesses among women with implants. Some doctors question whether the health problems of women with implants are due to silicone, since a certain number of women in any population will develop autoimmune diseases. The prestigious *New England Journal of Medicine*, which published one of the studies, questioned the need for the FDA's decision to pull breast implants from the market. If breast implants eventually prove to be safe, this fact will not satisfy critics who fault Dow Corning for going ahead with the product without having sufficient evidence. Nor will it save Dow Corning from its current financial crisis. Ironically, in no year did breast implants account for more than 1 percent of Dow Corning's profits.

INTRODUCTION

Ethical issues in marketing are not confined to product safety. Virtually all aspects of marketing—from the development of new products to pricing, promotion, and sales—raise ethical questions for which there are no easy answers. This chapter begins with an examination of two competing theories on the role of marketing, in an attempt to develop a framework for understanding the justification of marketing and the basis for the ethical obligations of people engaged in marketing activities. Among the questions that an adequate theory must answer are, What specific rights do buyers and sellers have in market transactions? And what role should the needs and desires of consumers play in making marketing decisions? The rise of the consumer movement since the 1960s has brought these questions to the forefront of public discussion and has forced American corporations to address them as never before.

This theoretical discussion is followed by a brief look at some of the major problem areas in marketing ethics. These include problems in packaging and labeling, the use of deceptive and manipulative sales techniques, and anticompetitive practices, such as price fixing and price discrimination. Of course, these areas of marketing are heavily regulated, so that many unethical marketing practices are specifically prohibited by law. We need to look, therefore, at the ethical justification for consumer protection legislation and other legal restrictions on marketing activities.

Of the many ethical issues involved in product safety, none is more controversial than the responsibility of manufacturers to compensate people who suffer some financial loss or physical injury as a result of defective products. Many observers believe that recent changes in product liability law tip the balance too heavily in favor of consumers and impose an unfair burden on corporations. However, liability suits are an important source of protection for consumers. Not only does the prospect of having to pay compensation for product-related accidents provide a strong incentive for manufacturers to protect consumers against injury, but if accidents do occur, compensating the victims is usually the only way to rectify the wrong that has been done. The remainder of this chapter is devoted, therefore, to examining three rival theories concerning the responsibility of manufacturers for product safety.

ETHICAL ISSUES IN MARKETING

Marketing, according to one often cited definition, "consists of the performance of business activities that direct the flow of goods and services from producer to consumer or user."[2] Within this broad characterization, there are a number of distinct functions, including product development, distribution, pricing, promotion, and sales. Although many of the activities of marketers are relatively free of ethical problems, others have drawn extensive criticism and spawned, in some instances, organized consumer opposition that challenges the prevailing philosophy of marketing in American corporations.

Consumerism and the Marketing Concept

Beginning in the early sixties, the public was stirred to action by books such as *Silent Spring*, by Rachel Carson,[3] which detailed the disastrous effects of pesticides on the environment; Jessica Mitford's scathing critique of sales practices in the funeral industry, *The American Way of Death*;[4] and perhaps the best known of all, *Unsafe at Any Speed*, by Ralph Nader, which criticized General Motors for a callous disregard of safety, especially in the design of the Chevrolet Corvair.[5]

Many politicians at the local, state, and national levels championed the consumer movement, including President John F. Kennedy, who in 1962 proclaimed a four-point bill of rights for consumers: the right to safety, the right to be informed, the right to choose, and the right to be heard. The result of this political backing was a period of legislative activity that saw passage of the Fair Packaging and Labeling Act (1966), Truth-in-Lending Act (1968), Child Protection and Toy Safety Act (1969), Consumer Product Safety Act (1972), and the Magnuson-Moss Warranty Act (1975). The media also seized on consumerism and spread it with front-page coverage of graphic events, such as grocery store boycotts by enraged shoppers.

The consumer movement arose in spite of the fact that business has long operated with a marketing approach that focuses on consumer satisfaction. The guiding principle in marketing, commonly called the *marketing concept*, stresses that in order to succeed, producers need to begin with an understanding of the needs and desires of consumers and proceed from there to develop and deliver the appropriate goods and services.[6] All the activities of a firm must be integrated into the effort of satisfying consumers, and this effort must be ongoing to ensure that consumers remain satisfied long after the sale.

Ironically, the main targets of consumerism were not small behind-the-times companies but the largest and most progressive corporations that had most fully implemented the marketing concept. This fact prompted *Business Week* to observe that "In the broadest sense, consumerism can be defined as the bankruptcy of what business schools have been calling the 'marketing concept.' "[7] Peter F. Drucker used even stronger language, describing consumerism as "the shame of the total marketing concept."[8] In the view of such critics, the marketing concept itself is faulty and in need of replacement.[9]

Defenders of the marketing concept respond that the goals of consumerism are achieved by making the consumer central to all marketing decisions. There is no need for producers to recognize an expanded list of consumer rights, since it is in their own interest to pay close attention to what consumers want. As long as they obey the law, corporations can continue to operate with only one object in mind, to make a profit, since producers can make a profit only by understanding and satisfying the needs and desires of consumers. Flouting consumer rights is a sure prescription for business failure.

Consumer Rights

Some of the disagreements between marketers and their critics are due to different understandings of the rights of consumers. Traditionally, producers, as sellers, are regarded as having the following rights in a free market system:

1. The right to make decisions regarding the products offered for sale, such as their design and style.
2. The right to set the price for products and all other terms of sale, including warranties.
3. The right to determine how products will be made available to consumers (that is, the right to make decisions about distribution).
4. The right to promote products in any way that they choose, including the use of any truthful advertising message.

These rights are limited by the usual rules of fair market exchanges. Thus, products must be as represented; producers must live up to the terms of the sales agreement; and advertising and other information about products must not be deceptive. Except for these restrictions, however, producers are free to operate pretty much as they please.

Consumers, on the other hand, are traditionally recognized as having only the right not to buy a product that is offered for sale. The opportunity for consumers to satisfy their needs and desires is thus restricted to a "veto" option. If the goods that consumers want are provided by producers, then all is well, but the rights of consumers are not violated if producers fail for any reason to provide consumers with goods they desire. Moreover, the burden of protecting the interests of consumers falls primarily on consumers themselves. In particular, they have the responsibility for acquiring the information needed to make rational choices. The number one rule in market exchanges is thus caveat emptor, or buyer beware.

The consumer movement holds that the right not to buy provides inadequate opportunities for consumers to satisfy their needs and desires. Also, the burden of protecting their own interests is too heavy for consumers to bear, especially in view of the unequal relation between buyers and sellers in present-day markets. In a "David and Goliath" struggle, with giant corporations wielding the immense power of modern marketing tools, individual consumers, armed only with a veto option and limited knowledge, have little chance. Consumer advocates contend, therefore, that the rights outlined by President Kennedy need to be added to the list of the rights of buyers. These rights include:

1. The right to be protected from harmful products.
2. The right to be provided with adequate information about products.
3. The right to be offered a choice that includes the products that consumers truly want.
4. The right to have a voice in the making of major marketing decisions.

The first two of these rights are now embodied to some extent in consumer protection legislation. The Consumer Product Safety Act, for example, created an independent regulatory body, the Consumer Product Safety Commission, which has the power to issue standards, require warnings, and even ban dangerous products entirely. The Fair Packaging and Labeling Act requires that containers disclose the ingredients of the product, the amount, and other pertinent information, including nutritional content in the case of food. The Magnuson-Moss Warranty Act specifies the information and the minimum conditions that must be included in a full warranty and requires that all warranties be written in comprehensible language. The latter two rights, especially the right to a voice, have not been addressed by the law and remain unrealized goals of the consumer movement.

Packaging and Labeling

Some problems of the right to be informed are revealed by a closer look at the law on packaging and labeling. Consumers need a certain amount of information to make rational choices, and often this information is not easily obtained. A consumer buying apples, for example, can easily check their condition and compare them with other fruit on display. But consider the plight of a consumer comparing two brands of canned apple pie filling or attempting to determine the value of a frozen apple pie in a sealed, opaque cardboard box. Without information on the label, consumers have no practical means for determining the quantity of apples in the filling or the size of the frozen pie. They also cannot easily determine the ingredients used, the nutritional content, or the length of time the product has been sitting on the grocer's shelf or in the freezer case. Health-conscious consumers are especially disadvantaged by the welter of claims about low fat and salt content and the unregulated use of words like *light* and *healthy*. Certainly, the more information consumers have, the better they can protect themselves in the marketplace. The ethical question, though, is, how much information is a manufacturer obligated to provide? And to what extent are consumers responsible for informing themselves about the products for sale?

The Fair Packaging and Labeling Act was passed by Congress in 1966 with the aim of enabling consumers to make meaningful value comparisons. Specifically, the act requires that each package list the identity of the product; the name and location of the manufacturer, packer, or distributor; the net quantity; and, as appropriate, the number of servings, applications, and so on. There are detailed requirements for many specific kinds of products in the Fair Packaging and Labeling Act and other statutes. In order to enable consumers to compare food products and to evaluate health information, Congress passed the Nutrition Labeling and Education Act (NLEA) in 1990. This act requires that the labels on packaged food products sold after May 1994 contain information about fat, cholesterol, salt, carbohydrates, and certain other ingredients expressed by weight and as a percentage of the recommended daily diet in a standardized serving size. The total number of calories and the number of calories from fat must also be listed along with the percentage of the recommended daily intake of certain vitamins and minerals. In addition, the NLEA lists the health claims that are permissible and defines such terms as *low fat, light, less* or *reduced*, and *healthy*.

Prior to 1994, food manufacturers were able to manipulate the information on labels. The amount of fat or salt could be reduced, for example, merely by decreasing the listed serving size. A product labeled "light" could contain a substantial amount of fat and derive proportionately more of its calories from fat. The health benefits of low fat or salt and high fiber or calcium content for cancer, heart disease, hypertension, and osteoporosis were commonly touted. Regulations in the NLEA apply, however, only to packaged foods and not to meat or restaurant menus, and similar rules have been strongly resisted by the meat and restaurant industries.

Manufacturers offer a number of reasons for not providing more information. A detailed listing of amounts of ingredients might jeopardize recipes that are trade secrets; listing the kind of fat would prevent them from switching ingredients to take advantage of changes in the relative prices of, say, soybean and palm oil; product dating is often misunderstood by consumers, who reject older products that are still good; and packaging has to be designed with many considerations in mind in addition to revealing the contents. It must be easy to fill, protect goods in transit, prevent spoilage, and so on. Therefore, the objectives of the Fair Packaging and Labeling Act and the Nutrition Labeling and Education Act, manufacturers argue, need to be balanced against a number of practical constraints.

Pricing

The question of how much information sellers are obligated to provide arises not only in packaging and labeling but also in pricing. The proliferation of products at different prices makes it difficult for consumers to compare even those from the same manufacturer. Price codes that can be understood only by sales personnel put consumers at a disadvantage. The use of a universal product code (UPC) that can be machine read has raised concern about the accuracy of posted prices, and some retailers attempt to reduce costs by not marking prices on individual packages. As a result, some local and state governments now require retailers to mark the price on each product, and the FTC has investigated the accuracy of the price posted on products. The A&P grocery store chain, for example, entered into an agreement with the FTC to reduce the number of discrepancies between the posted price and the price charged at the checkout counter to an "acceptable level."[10] With improvements in scanning and greater consumer acceptance, this issue has largely died away.

Also, some products have hidden costs. The price of tires, for example, often excludes mounting, balancing, extended warranties, and other extras, which are often mentioned to consumers after a decision has been made to buy (a sales technique know as "low-balling"). Consumers cannot compare two air conditioners without knowing the cost of operating them, since a cheaper but less efficient air conditioner can cost more in the long run. Manufacturers of electrical household appliances are now required by law, therefore, to disclose the amount of energy used in a year and the range of energy consumption for products of the same kind. Similarly, lightbulbs must list the average life and the amount of light produced. Comparisons are facilitated by standard units for measuring the relevant factors. Thus, tires are required by federal law to be graded with a tread-wear index and an A, B, or C rating for traction, and insulating materials have an R-value that enables consumers to compare different grades of insulation.

The Obligation to Provide Information

What is the justification for the Fair Packaging and Labeling Act, the Nutrition Labeling and Education Act, and various statutes governing price displays, disclosure of hidden costs, and standardized units of measurement? Consumer protection legislation of this kind seems, at first glance, to run counter to classical economic theory. In a free market system, buyers bear the primary burden of informing themselves about the products offered for sale. Generally, sellers are not obligated to provide complete information but only to avoid misrepresentation, although buyers are entitled to rely on any representations that are made and to make minimal assumptions about the quality of goods and their suitability. These are referred to in law as implied warranties of merchantability and fitness for use. However, beyond the obligations to be truthful and fulfill warranties, both expressed and implied, caveat emptor is the rule of the marketplace.

An alternative rule that underlies much consumer protection legislation is that manufacturers have an obligation to provide relevant information that consumers cannot reasonably obtain for themselves. The rationale for abandoning caveat emptor is that in a modern industrial economy, with technologically advanced products that are developed, manufactured, and marketed with all the expertise at the command of large corporations, it is impossible for consumers to acquire sufficient information to protect themselves in the marketplace. A division of the burden on buyers and sellers that might have been appropriate to an earlier age is impractical, therefore, under present-day economic conditions. Because manufacturers already have the information or, at least access to it, and because they make the key decisions regarding product development, packaging and labeling, and so on, it is more cost-effective to place the burden of providing information on them.

Deceptive and Manipulative Marketing Practices

Deception in marketing is similar to deception in advertising, discussed in the previous chapter. Roughly, marketing practices are deceptive when consumers are led to hold false beliefs about a product. Examples of some common deceptive pricing and sales practices are markdowns from a "suggested retail price" for products that are seldom if ever sold at that price, "cents off" labeling and "introductory offers" that incorrectly purport to offer a savings, and bogus clearance sales in which inferior goods are brought in especially for the sale. In these cases, consumers are led to believe that the prices represent a substantial reduction when, in fact, they do not. Packaging and labeling are deceptive when the size or shape of a container, a picture or description, or the use of terms such as *economy size* and *new and improved* mislead consumers in some significant way. Warranties that cannot be easily understood by the average consumer are also deceptive. And, of course, advertising provides fertile ground for deceiving consumers.

Manipulation is generally distinguished from deception, in that it typically involves no false or misleading claims. Instead, it consists of taking advantage of consumer psychology to make a sale. More precisely, manipulation is noncoercively shaping the alternatives open to people or their perception of those alternatives so that they are effectively deprived of a choice.[11] Examples of harmless forms of manipulation with full disclosure (and hence no deception) include multiple pricing, such as "3 for $1" and "buy two, get one free," and odd-even pricing, $2.99 instead of $3.00. When customers are accustomed to paying a certain price for a product, such as a candy bar, manufacturers often reduce the amount in order to maintain the same price, a practice known as customary pricing. Customary pricing can also be deceptive, however, when consumers fail to notice the change. In 1991, the size of one popular brand of tuna, for example, was reduced without any fanfare from the industry standard of 6½ ounces to 6⅛ ounces, a nearly invisible 5.8 percent price increase.[12]

A more objectionable form of manipulation is "bait and switch," a generally illegal practice in which a customer is lured into a store by an advertisement for a low-cost item and then sold a higher priced version. If the low-cost item is not available, then deception has been used, but often the "bait" is available but of such low quality that customers are easily "switched" to a higher priced product. "Bait and switch" is manipulative not only because consumers are tricked into entering the store but because they enter in a frame of mind to buy as a result of the apparent bargain in the "bait." Having already decided to buy and not merely look, they are more receptive to a sales pitch for a different product.

Manipulation can also take place, with or without deception, by people who are skilled in using high-pressure sales techniques. The sales force of one encyclopedia company used deception to gain entry to the homes of prospects by claiming to be conducting advertising research (the questionnaires were thrown away afterward). Another company offered to place a set of encyclopedias "free" provided the family bought a yearly supplement for a certain number of years at a price that exceeded the cost of the encyclopedia set alone. Although the companies involved have agreed to stop using these deceptive practices, subtle psychological manipulation is not easily regulated and still persists. Some groups of people are more vulnerable to manipulation than others, most notably children and the poor.[13] Special care needs to be taken, therefore, in marketing aimed at those groups.

The moral case against deceptive and manipulative marketing needs little explanation, since it rests on the requirement that markets be free of force and fraud. The difficult ethical questions in this area concern the definition of deception and manipulation and the dividing line between acceptable and unacceptable marketing practices. Virtually all companies that market to children, for example, concede the special vulnerability of this group but vigorously deny that their own marketing practices are deceptive or manipulative. Personal selling requires an understanding of consumer psychology and skill in using persuasive techniques. When does effective selling, however, cross the line and become ethically objectionable manipulation?

For drawing the line on deceptive marketing practices, we can use the definition of deception developed in the preceding chapter on advertising. Deception involves creating or taking advantage of false beliefs that significantly interfere with the ability of consumers to make rational choices. The same notion of rational choice can be used to distinguish between effective selling and manipulation. Successful sales personnel are often adept at "sizing up" customers' preferences, for example, and steering them toward suitable goods. Such an understanding of consumer psychology still leaves consumers free to make a rational choice in a way that "bait and switch" does not. In the latter case, consumers who are unaware of what is happening to them are led to make choices they would not make otherwise.

Marketing Research

Some of the objections to deceptive and manipulative marketing practices apply to the area of marketing research, which also raises questions about privacy of the kind discussed in Chapter 7. Corporations engage in a great amount of systematic information gathering about consumers to aid them in developing new products and planning marketing strategies. Data are collected using all the techniques of social science research, including in-depth surveys, field studies, and controlled laboratory experiments.

One set of problems for marketing research conducted by outside agencies concerns the relation between researchers and clients, including integrity in undertaking research assignments and honesty in interpreting data and presenting results.[14] Another set concerns the treatment of research subjects or respondents. These include manipulating persons into participating in research projects, deceiving them about the purpose of a study, and invading their privacy by the use, for example, of one-way mirrors during interviews.[15] An especially blatant form of misconduct in marketing research is the use of surveys and other research tools to make a sales pitch or to generate a list of sales prospects. This is a practice known as *sugging*, from the acronym for selling under the guise of marketing research.

A further threat to privacy comes from the use of research data in the growing field of database marketing, in which retailers, through credit card records and information derived from universal product codes, are able to construct detailed profiles of individual customers and develop tailor-made products or marketing offers. It is no longer necessary to have a mainframe computer for these kinds of tasks; a small desktop PC will do. In April 1990, Lotus Development Corporation announced that it would market a compact disk, called *Lotus Marketplace: Households*, containing the names, addresses, demographic data, and information on the purchasing habits of 120 million Americans, thus giving small businesses with PCs access to the same computerized information large corporations have long used. The announcement aroused a storm of protest about the invasion of consumers' privacy, however, and the project was shelved.[16] Although marketing research is a legitimate activity for marketers, care must be taken to ensure that surveys and other instruments are not used to deceive or manipulate test subjects or consumers generally. And safeguards are needed to protect the privacy of all concerned.

ANTICOMPETITIVE MARKETING PRACTICES

Most of the unethical marketing practices that come under the heading of being anticompetitive are also illegal as a result of the major antitrust statutes; namely, the Sherman Act (1890), the Clayton Act (1914), the Federal Trade Commission Act (1914), and the Robinson-Patman Act (1936). Many states also have antitrust statutes that prohibit the same practices. Our task, therefore, is largely to understand the ethical arguments for prohibiting certain anticompetitive marketing practices and to note some questions about these arguments.

The major anticompetitive marketing practices are

1. Price-fixing. Price-fixing is an agreement among two or more companies operating in the same market to sell goods at a set price. Such an agreement is contrary to the usual practice, whereby prices are set in a free market by arm's-length transactions. Most commonly, price-fixing is *horizontal*, among different sellers at the same level of distribution, but price-fixing can also be *vertical*, when it occurs between buyers and sellers at different levels. An agreement between the manufacturer, a wholesaler, and retailers in transactions involving the same goods is an example. Price-fixing occurs not only when there is an explicit agreement among competitors to charge similar prices but also when the same result is achieved by other means. Among these are the exchange of price information among competitors, a tacit agreement to follow an industry standard (parallel-pricing) or the lead of a dominant seller (price leadership), and a situation in which one company effectively controls the prices of competitors (administered price). Market allocation, in which competitors agree not to compete in certain geographical areas or to seek the business of certain buyers or agree to limit their volume, is also a form of price-fixing.

2. Resale price maintenance.   This is a practice whereby products are sold on the condition that they be resold at a price fixed by the manufacturer or distributor. Resale price maintenance is thus a form of vertical price-fixing, as described above. There are various reasons for imposing resale price maintenance on retailers, including fostering a prestige image, enabling a larger number of retailers to carry a product, and providing an adequate margin for promotion or service. As a form of price-fixing, resale price maintenance prevents prices from being set by the forces of a competitive market.

3. Price discrimination.   Sellers engage in price discrimination when they charge different prices or offer different terms of sale for goods of the same kind to different buyers. Often this occurs when buyers are located in different geographical regions or vary in size or their access to other sellers. Thus, a seller who gives a discount to large buyers solely by virtue of their size is guilty of discriminating against small buyers.

4. Reciprocal dealing, tying arrangements, and exclusive dealing.   Reciprocal dealing involves a sale in which the seller is required to buy something in return, as when an office supply firm agrees to buy a computer system only on the condition that the computer firm agrees to purchase supplies from the office supply firm. A tying arrangement exists when one product is sold on the condition that the buyer purchase another product as well. An example of a tying arrangement is an automotive supply firm that requires as a condition for selling tires to a service station that the buyer also purchase batteries from the seller. In an exclusive dealing agreement, a seller provides a product—a brand of sportswear, for example—on the condition that the buyer not handle competing brands.

The law on anticompetitive practices is extremely complex and makes numerous exceptions. Some of these practices are strictly illegal—such as price-fixing, market allocation, and tying arrangements (so-called per se violations)—but sellers can defend themselves against a charge of price discrimination, for example, by showing that the difference in price is justified as a cost of doing business, as a good-faith attempt to meet competition, or as a promotional discount that is available to all similar buyers. Also, legal restrictions on resale price agreements can be skirted by the right of any company not to do business with another. Thus, the law permits a manufacturer to "punish" a retailer for selling below a suggested retail price simply by refusing to sell to that retailer (a tactic known as *Colgating* after a court case vindicating the Colgate Company),[17] although care must be taken that the action does not constitute a concerted effort by two or more manufacturers to retaliate.[18] For a fuller discussion of the law on these practices, consult any standard business law text.

The overall ethical objection to these practices is that they are not fair forms of competition. In particular, anticompetitive practices distort prices by preventing the market from serving as a mechanism for setting prices fairly. The question "What is a fair price?" has long been debated without any satisfactory answer. However, a price arrived at by mutual agreement under competitive conditions at arm's length is generally considered to be fair. Classical economic theory assumes that competitive markets are characterized by a number of buyers and sellers who are free to enter or leave the market at any time and by largely undifferentiated products that buyers are willing to substitute one for another. Under such conditions, the forces of supply and demand ensure not only that resources are used efficiently (the greatest output for the least input) but that goods are fairly priced.

A more specific objection to horizontal price-fixing is that it leads to monopoly. Where there is a single seller of a product, the forces of supply and demand no longer work and the monopolist is free to manipulate the supply to obtain a higher price than could be achieved under conditions of perfect competition. The primary objective of antitrust legislation, therefore, is to prevent the formation of monopolies, which are clearly incompatible with the operation of a free market. Horizontal price-fixing in its many forms and market allocation permit the creation of monopoly conditions, despite the existence of many sellers, since they act in concert and thus become, in effect, one. If the leading manufacturers of electrical supplies, for example, meet in hotel rooms and agree on prices, then they act as a single seller, thereby creating an artificial monopoly.[19] An agreement to allocate markets achieves the same result, since each seller becomes a monopolist in a certain geographical area or among a select group of buyers.

The main argument against price discrimination and other so-called "predatory" practices is not that they *constitute* monopolies in the manner of price-fixing but that they *facilitate* the creation of monopolies by enabling sellers to eliminate competition. Even when monopoly is not the result, price discrimination enables stronger sellers to inflict harm on weaker competitors and thereby gain an additional advantage. Generally, the lower prices offered to some buyers in cases of price discrimination are based not on any competitive advantage but on the sheer size that enables the company to endure a loss that cannot be endured by others. The immediate aim is not to gain some good for the company but to inflict harm on competitors.

A number of early cases were prosecuted under the provision in the Sherman Act against restraint of trade in interstate commerce. If a large national oil company, for example, is permitted to offer lower prices in a few geographical regions, thereby forcing smaller, local companies out of business, then the large company is left in a monopoly position and can raise prices at will to recoup the losses from underselling. This, of course, was a favored tactic of the Standard Oil Company, which around the turn of the century achieved and maintained control over more than 80 percent of the nation's refining capacity.[20] About the same time, the American Tobacco Company attempted to achieve a monopoly by selling their brands at less than cost in local markets to drive out competitors.[21] Price discrimination can be practiced not only by sellers but also by large buyers. The law that specifically forbids price discrimination, the Robinson-Patman Act, prevents large buyers, such as chain stores, from demanding and receiving preferential treatment from manufacturers and wholesalers to the detriment of smaller buyers.

Opinion is sharply divided on whether price discrimination actually lessens competition and whether it should be prevented.[22] Price is a legitimate competitive tool that enables firms to take advantage of efficiencies of scale and to respond flexibly to differences in market conditions. It is difficult to distinguish between predatory pricing that attempts to clobber the competition and honest efforts to offer greater value in an attempt to gain market share, albeit at the expense of competitors. Moreover, some economists argue that predatory pricing is generally not advantageous even in the long run because would-be monopolists cannot ordinarily recoup the losses of undercutting the competition.[23]

The remaining practices—resale price maintenance, reciprocal dealing, tying arrangements, and exclusive dealing—are objectionable for the reason that they result in market transactions that are less efficient than they would be otherwise. They do not necessarily lead to monopoly, but they still distort the market mechanism for setting prices. The assumption of the courts is that there would be no need for reciprocal dealing, tying arrangements, or exclusive dealing agreements if any of the exchanges involved would be made under perfectly competitive conditions. The need for the automotive supply firm to insist that buyers of tires also purchase batteries would not exist if the batteries represented as great a value as the tires. The fact that a tying arrangement exists is prima facie evidence that service stations would not buy the batteries if they were given the chance to buy the two products separately. Similarly, an exclusive dealing agreement would not be necessary if the retailer would handle only one line of sportswear given the opportunity to choose.

Conclusion

The ethical issues in marketing are extremely diverse. Packaging and labeling is a moral minefield of questions about what information manufacturers have an obligation to provide and consumers a right to expect. Deception and manipulation are major issues in packaging and labeling as well as in pricing, personal selling, and marketing research. Marketing research also raises concerns about consumer privacy, especially in view of the vast amount of information on individuals available to marketers. Finally, the area of anticompetitive practices, which deals primarily with pricing, involves fundamental notions of fair competition as well as highly technical questions about requirements for a free market economy. None of these issues is unique to marketing; they are all discussed elsewhere in this book under other headings. But marketing is an especially rich field for ethical exploration, since the issues are so many and varied.

THEORIES OF PRODUCT LIABILITY

The right of consumers to be protected from harmful products raises innumerable problems for manufacturers. Many products can injure and even kill people, especially if the products are used improperly. Every dangerous product can be made safer at some cost, but is there a limit to the safety improvements that a manufacturer ought to provide? And do manufacturers also have a responsibility to ensure that a product is safe before it is placed on the market? Even if silicone breast implants, for example, are eventually shown to be safe, did Dow Corning fail in a responsibility to conduct the appropriate tests? Three theories are commonly used to determine when a product is defective and what is owed to the victims of accidents caused by defective products.[24] Each of these theories appeals to a different ground for its ethical justification; and as legal doctrines, they each have a different source in the law.

THE DUE CARE THEORY

This theory holds that manufacturers ought to exercise *due care.* Their obligation is to take all reasonable precautions to ensure that products they put on the market are free of defects likely to cause harm. According to this theory, manufacturers are liable for damages only when they fail to carry out this obligation and so are at fault in some way. One ethical justification for this view is the Aristotelian principle of corrective justice: Something is owed by a person who inflicts a wrongful harm upon another. By failing to exercise due care, a manufacturer is acting wrongly and hence ought to pay compensation to anyone who is injured as a result.

The legal expression of this theory is the view in the law of torts that persons are liable for acts of negligence. Negligence is defined in the *Second Restatement of Torts* (Section 282) as "conduct which falls below the standard established by law for the protection of others against unreasonable risk of harm." The usual standard established by law is the care that a "reasonable person" would exercise in a given situation. Accordingly, a reckless driver is negligent (since a reasonable person would not drive recklessly), and the driver can be legally required to pay compensation to the victims of any accident caused by the negligent behavior.[25] In the case of persons with superior skill or knowledge, the standard is higher. A manufacturer can be assumed to know more than the average person about the product and, hence, can be legally required to exercise a greater degree of care.

The standard of due care for manufacturers or other persons involved in the sale of a product to a consumer, including wholesalers and retailers, covers a wide variety of activities. Among them are

1. Design.   The product ought to be designed in accord with government and industry standards to be safe under all foreseeable conditions, including possible misuse by the consumer. A toy with small parts, for example, that a child could choke on, or a toy that could easily be broken by a child to reveal sharp edges is badly designed. Similarly, due care is not taken in the design of a crib or a play pen with slats or other openings in which a child's head could become wedged. Many manufacturers have a design review board, composed of a variety of experts within the company, to evaluate the design of products, and some companies also submit designs to outside consulting firms, such as the Underwriter's Laboratory for electrical products.

2. Materials.   The materials specified in the design should also meet government and industry standards and be of sufficient strength and durability to stand up under all reasonable use. Testing should be done to ensure that the materials withstand ordinary wear and tear and do not weaken with age, stress, extremes of temperature, or other forces. The wiring in an appliance is substandard, for example, if the insulation cracks or peels, posing a risk of electrical shock.

3. Production.   Due care should be taken in fabricating parts to specifications and assembling them correctly, so that parts are not put in the wrong way or left out. Screws, rivets, welds, and other ways of fastening parts should be properly used, and so on. Defects due to faulty construction can be avoided, in part, by giving adequate training to employees and creating conditions that allow them to do their job properly. Fast assembly lines, for example, are an invitation to defects in workmanship.

4. Quality control.   Manufacturers should have a systematic program to inspect products between operations or at the end to ensure that they are of sufficient quality in both materials and construction. Inspections may be done either by trained personnel or by machines. In some programs every product is inspected, whereas in others inspection is done of samples taken at intervals. Records should be maintained of all quality control inspections, and the inspectors themselves should be evaluated for effectiveness.

5. Packaging, labeling, and warnings.   The product should be packaged so as to avoid any damage in transit, and the packaging and handling of perishable food stuffs, for example, should not create any new hazard. Since products often come in packages that prevent customers from making a thorough inspection before purchase, manufacturers have an even greater obligation to ensure the quality of the design, materials, and workmanship. Also, the labels and any inserts should include instructions for correct use and adequate warnings in language easily understood by users. Warnings that enable consumers to understand a hazard are more effective. Thus, a label warning of an electrical shock is better than one that simply warns against touching a part.

6. Notification.   Finally, the manufacturers of some products should have a system of notifying consumers of hazards that only become apparent later. Automobile manufacturers, for example, maintain lists of buyers, who can be notified of recalls by mail; and appliances, electronic equipment, and the like frequently contain cards for a buyer to return, giving the name and address. Some companies have toll-free numbers, so that customers may ask questions. And recalls, warnings, and other safety messages are often conveyed by paid notices in the media.

The Problem of Misuse

One question that arises in the due care theory is whether manufacturers have an obligation to ensure that a product is safe to use as intended or to anticipate all the conditions under which injury could occur. The driver of a 1963 Chevrolet Corvair, for example, was severely injured in a head-on collision when the steering column struck him in the head. In the model of the car he was driving, the steering column was a rigid shaft that extended to the front end of the car, thus forming a spear aimed directly at the driver. Although this design did not cause the accident, the victim claimed that his injuries were greater as a result of it. General Motors contended that its cars were intended to be used for driving on streets and highways and not for colliding with other objects. Consequently, they had no obligation to make them safe for this latter purpose. A U.S. court of appeals held, however, that due care includes "a duty to design the product so that it will fairly meet any emergency of use which can reasonably be anticipated."[26]

This duty also extends to foreseeable misuse by the consumer. The owner's manual for the 1976 Mercury Cougar, for example, explicitly stated that the original equipment Goodyear tires should not be used "for continuous driving over 90 miles per hour."[27] A U.S. court of appeals determined that the tread separation on the right-rear tire of a Cougar being driven in excess of 100 miles per hour was not the result of any flaw in the tire. However, the Ford Motor Company should have known that a car designed for high performance and marketed with an appeal to youthful drivers would occasionally be driven at speeds above the safe operating level of the tires. Accordingly, Ford should have warned owners of the Cougar more effectively or else equipped the car with better tires.

Some courts have held companies responsible not only for foreseeable misuse but also for misuse that is actively encouraged in the marketing of a product.[28] General Motors, for example, marketed the Pontiac Firebird Trans Am by entering specially reinforced models in racing competitions and by featuring the car in crash scenes in "antihero scofflaw" motion pictures. A promotion film that had spliced together stunt scenes from these movies was used for promotions in dealers' showrooms. In a suit brought on behalf of the driver of a 1978 Trans Am who was injured when the car went out of control while traveling more than 100 miles per hour, the court found for the plaintiff by invoking a doctrine of "invited misuse."[29]

What Is Due Care?

The major difficulty with the due care theory is establishing what constitutes due care. Manufacturers have an obligation to take precautions that are more stringent than the "reasonable person" standard, but no means exist for determining exactly how far the obligation of manufacturers extends. The courts have developed a flexible standard derived from Justice Learned Hand's famous formulation of the negligence rule.[30] In this rule, negligence involves the interplay of three factors: (1) the probability of harm, (2) the severity of the harm, and (3) the burden of protecting against the harm. Thus, manufacturers have a greater obligation to protect consumers when injury in an accident is more likely to occur, when the injury is apt to be greater, and when the cost of avoiding injury is relatively minor. These are relevant factors in formulating a standard of due care, but they are not sufficient by themselves to decide every case.

Some standards for design, materials, inspection, packaging, and the like have evolved through long experience and are now incorporated into engineering practice and government regulations. These comprise the minimum standards of due care. However, they also reflect the scientific knowledge and technology at a given time and fail to impose an obligation to guard against hazards that are discovered later. Whether asbestos companies exercised due care, for example, is a case in point.

The manufacture of asbestos products and the instructions for their use in the 1930s later conformed to industry and government standards. The asbestos companies claim that the danger of asbestos exposure was not known until the 1960s, at which time they instituted changes to make handling asbestos safer. (Critics of the asbestos companies maintain that substantial evidence of the dangers of asbestos was available earlier.) This so-called "state-of-the-art" defense—in which a company contends that it exercised due care as defined by the scientific knowledge and technology at the time—was flatly rejected by the New Jersey Supreme Court decision in *Bashada* v. *Johns-Manville Products Corp.* in 1982.[31] The court reasoned that Johns-Manville ought to have made a greater attempt to discover the hazards of asbestos. In the words of the court: "Fairness suggests that manufacturers not be excused from liability because their prior inadequate investment in safety rendered the hazards of their products unknowable."

As a legal doctrine, the due care theory is difficult to apply. The focus of the theory is on the *conduct* of the manufacturer rather than on the *condition* of the product. So the mere fact that a product is defective is not sufficient for holding that a manufacturer has failed in an obligation of due care; some knowledge is needed about specific acts that a manufacturer performed or failed to perform. Lawsuits based on the theory thus require proof of negligence, which the victims of accidents caused by defective products are often not able to provide.

In addition, common law allows for two defenses under the due care theory: contributory negligence and assumption of risk. Just as a manufacturer has an obligation to act responsibly, so too does a consumer. Similarly, if consumers know the dangers posed by a product and use it anyway, then to some extent they assume responsibility for any injury that results. The ethical basis for these defenses is the same Aristotelian principle of compensatory justice that underlies the due care theory. When consumers do not exercise due care in their use of a product, therefore, or when they are fully aware of the hazards of products and use them anyway, the fault for injury falls on them as well as on the manufacturer. For these reasons, the due care theory is rarely used today in product liability cases. There are easier ways for injured consumers to secure compensation.

THE CONTRACTUAL THEORY

A second theory is that the responsibility of manufacturers for harm resulting from defective products is that specified in a sales *contract*. The relation between buyer and seller is viewed in this theory as a contractual relation, which is subject to the terms of a contract, either implicit or explicit. An explicit written or verbal contract is legally enforceable, of course. In the absence of an explicit contract, there are still certain understandings between the two parties that are revealed by their behavior. This fact is recognized by the Uniform Commercial Code (UCC), Section 2-204(1), which states that:

> A contract for sale of goods may be made in any manner sufficient to show agreement, including conduct by both parties which recognizes the existence of such a contract.

One of the usual understandings is that a product is of an acceptable level of quality and fit for the purpose for which it is ordinarily used. These implicit contractual provisions are part of what is described in Section 2-314 of the UCC as an *implied warranty of merchantability*. Manufacturers have both a moral and a legal obligation, therefore, by virtue of their contractual relation, to offer only products free from dangerous defects. A person who buys a new automobile, for example, is entitled to assume that it will perform as expected and that nothing in the design makes it especially hazardous in the event of an accident.

There is also an *implied warranty of fitness* for a particular purpose when the buyer is relying on the seller's expertise in the selection of the product. In addition, an *express warranty* is created, according to Section 2-313 of the UCC, as follows:

> Any affirmation of fact or promise made by the seller to the buyer which relates to the goods and becomes part of the basis of the bargain creates an express warranty that the goods shall conform to the affirmation or promise.

The notion of an affirmation is very broad and includes any description or illustration on a package or any model or demonstration of the product being used in a certain way. Thus, there is an implied warranty of fitness for a particular purpose that a drill bit is safe to use with concrete if the seller knows that is the purpose which the buyer has in mind, and an express warranty exists if drilling concrete is one of the uses listed on the packaging or pictured in any way.

The ethical basis for the contractual theory is fairness in commercial dealings. Agreements to buy or sell a product are fair only when they are entered into freely by the contracting parties. Freedom in such agreements entails, among other things, that both buyers and sellers have adequate information about the product in question. Consumers know that the use of many products involves some danger, and they voluntarily assume the risk when the nature and extent of the hazards are revealed to them. Manufacturers may not take unfair advantage of consumers by exposing them to the risk of harm from hazards that are not disclosed. Selling a product that the manufacturer knows to be dangerous, without informing consumers, is a form of deception, since crucial information is either suppressed or misrepresented. Even when the manufacturer is unaware of a defect, the cost of any accident caused by a defective product still ought to be borne by the manufacturer, since the product was sold with the understanding that it posed no hazards except those already revealed to consumers.

Legal action for compensation based on the contractual theory is generally a suit for breach of contract under contract law. Manufacturers have an obligation to comply with the contractual terms of any sales agreement. And these terms include not only those in any written warranty but also those in all warranties, express or implied.

Objections to the Contractual Theory

One objection to the contractual theory is that the understandings in a sales agreement, which are the basis for implied and express warranties, are not very precise. Whether a product is of an acceptable level of quality or is fit for the purpose for which it is ordinarily used is an extremely vague standard. In practice, the theory leaves consumers with little protection, except for grossly defective products and products for which the manufacturer makes explicit claims that constitute express warranties.

Second, a sales agreement may consist of a written contract with language that sharply limits the right of an injured consumer to be compensated. If buyers and sellers are both free to contract on mutually agreeable terms, then the sales agreement can explicitly disclaim all warranties, express or implied. Section 2-316 of the Uniform Commercial Code provides for the exclusion or modification of an implied warranty of merchantability as long as (1) the buyer's attention is drawn to the fact that no warranty is being given, with expressions such as "with all faults" or "as is"; (2) the buyer has the opportunity to examine the goods; and (3) the defect is one that can be detected on examination. If a consumer signs a contract with limiting language or explicit disclaimers, then, according to the contractual theory, the terms of that contract are binding.

Both of these objections are illustrated in the classic court case in warranty law *Henningsen* v. *Bloomfield Motors, Inc.*[32] Claus Henningsen purchased a new 1955 Plymouth Plaza "6" Club Sedan for use by his wife, Helen. Ten days after taking delivery of the car from a Chrysler dealer in Bloomfield, New Jersey, Mrs. Henningsen was returning home to Keansburg from a trip to Asbury Park, traveling around twenty miles per hour on a smooth road, when she heard a loud noise under the hood and felt something crack. The steering wheel spun in her hands as the car veered sharply to the right and crashed into a brick wall. Mrs. Henningsen was injured and the vehicle was declared a total wreck by the insurer. At the time of the accident, the odometer registered only 468 miles.

In the sales contract signed by Mr. Henningsen, the Chrysler Corporation offered to replace defective parts for ninety days after the sale or until the car had been driven 4,000 miles, whichever occurred first, "if the part is sent to the factory, transportation charges prepaid, and if examination discloses to its satisfaction that the part is defective." The contract further stipulated that the obligation of the manufacturer under this warranty is limited to the replacement of defective parts, which is "in lieu of all other warranties, expressed or implied, and all other obligations or liabilities on its part." By this language, liability for personal injuries was also excluded in the contract.

The question, as framed by the court, is simple:

> In return for the delusive remedy of replacement of defective parts at the factory, the buyer is said to have accepted the exclusion of the maker's liability for personal injuries arising from the breach of warranty, and to have agreed to the elimination of any other express or implied warranty. An instinctively felt sense of justice cries out against such a sharp bargain. But does the doctrine that a person is bound by his signed agreement, in the absence of fraud, stand in the way of any relief?

In giving an answer, the court decided that considerations of justice have greater force than an otherwise valid contract. Furthermore, the main conditions for a valid contract—namely, that the parties have roughly equal bargaining power and are able to determine the relevant facts for themselves—are absent in this case.

First, there is a gross inequality of bargaining power between consumers and manufacturers. Virtually all American cars at the time were sold using a standardized form written by the Automobile Manufacturers Association, which the dealer was prohibited from altering. Due to the lack of competition among manufacturers with respect to warranties, consumers had no choice but to buy a car on the manufacturer's terms—or else do without, which is not a genuine alternative in a society where an automobile is a necessity. Hence, consumers did not have freedom of choice in any significant sense, and manufacturers were not offering consumers what they truly wanted. Consumers would most likely prefer to buy cars with better warranties.

Second, consumers are also at a profound disadvantage in their ability to examine an automobile and determine its fitness for use. They are forced to rely, for the most part, on the expertise of the manufacturer and the dealer to ensure that a car is free of defects. Further, the relevant paragraphs in the contract itself were among the hardest to read, and there was nothing in them to draw the reader's attention. "In fact," the court observed, "a studied and concentrated effort would have to be made to read them."

STRICT LIABILITY

A third theory, now gaining wider acceptance in the courts, holds that manufacturers are responsible for all harm resulting from a dangerously defective product even when due care has been exercised and all contracts observed. In this view, which is known in law as *strict liability,* a manufacturer need not be negligent nor be bound by any implied or express warranty to have responsibility. The mere fact that a product is put into the hands of consumers in a defective condition that poses an unreasonable risk is sufficient for holding the manufacturer liable.

A more precise account of the theory of strict liability is given in Section 402A of the *Second Restatement of Torts* as follows:

1. One who sells any product in a defective condition unreasonably dangerous to the user or consumer or to his property is subject to liability for physical harm thereby caused to the ultimate user or consumer, or to his property, if (a) the seller is engaged in the business of selling such a product, and (b) it is expected to and does reach the user or consumer without substantial change in the condition in which it is sold.
2. The rule stated in Subsection (1) applies although (a) the seller has exercised all possible care in the preparation and sale of his products, and (b) the user or consumer has not bought the product from or entered into any contractual relation with the seller.

The provision of 2(b) addresses an important legal issue in both the due care and the contract theories. Generally, lawsuits under either theory have required that the victim of an accident be in a direct contractual relation with the manufacturer. This relation is known in law as *privity.* Suppose an accident is caused by a defective part that is sold to a manufacturer by a supplier, and the finished product is sold to a wholesaler, who sells it to a retailer. The consumer, under a requirement of privity, can sue only the retailer, who can sue the wholesaler, who in turn can sue the manufacturer, and so on.

The requirement of privity developed as a way of placing reasonable limits on liability, since the consequences of actions extend indefinitely. In a simpler age when goods were often bought directly from the maker, this rule made sense. With the advent of mass production, however, most goods pass through many hands on the way to the ultimate consumer, and the requirement of a direct contractual relation greatly restricts the ability of consumers to collect compensation from manufacturers. In the landmark case *MacPherson* v. *Buick Motor Company* (1916), the New York State Court of Appeals ruled that privity was not necessary when there is negligence.[33] And negligence was present, according to the decision, since the defect in the wooden wheel supplied by another manufacturer should have been detected during the assembly of the car. The Buick Motor Company, in other words, owed a duty of "care and vigilance" to the owner of the car and all others who could be injured as a result of the defective wheel.

The main blow to privity in the contractual theory came in *Baxter* v. *Ford Mo-*

tor Company (1934).[34] The Supreme Court of Washington held that a driver who was injured by flying glass when a pebble struck the windshield had a right to compensation because all Ford cars were advertised as having a Triplex shatterproof glass—"so made that it will not fly or shatter under the hardest impact." One ad continued:

> This is an important safety factor because it eliminates the dangers of flying glass—the cause of most of the injuries in automobile accidents. In these days of crowded, heavy traffic, the use of this Triplex glass is an absolute necessity. Its extra margin of safety is something that every motorist should look for in the purchase of a car—especially where there are women and children.

Because the truth of these claims could not be easily determined by an ordinary person, buyers have a right to rely on representations made by the Ford Motor Company. Hence, the wording of advertisements such as this one creates a warranty, in the view of the court, even without a direct contractual relation. The requirement of privity was also rejected in the *Henningsen* decision.

Strict Liability as a Legal Doctrine

Strict liability as a legal doctrine did not make much headway in the courts until 1963, when the California State Supreme Court ruled in *Greenman* v. *Yuba Power Products*.[35] The relevant facts are that for Christmas 1955, Mr. Greenman's wife gave him a multipurpose power tool, called a Shopsmith, that could be used as a saw, a drill, and a lathe. Two years later, while using the machine as a lathe to make a chalice, the piece of wood he was turning flew out of the machine and struck him on the forehead. Expert witnesses testified that some of the screws used to hold parts of the machine together were too weak to withstand the vibration. As a result, the tailstock was allowed to move, releasing the piece of wood that was being turned on the lathe.

The court declined to consider whether Yuba Power Products was negligent in the design and construction of the Shopsmith or whether it breached any warranties, either express or implied. The only relevant consideration, according to the decision, was the fact that the tool was unsafe to use in the intended way. Specifically, the court held:

> To establish the manufacturer's liability it was sufficient that the plaintiff proved that he was injured using the Shopsmith in a way it was intended to be used as a result of a defect in design and manufacture of which plaintiff was not aware that made the Shopsmith unsafe for its intended use.

Section 402A was formulated a year later in 1964. Since that time, all fifty states and the District of Columbia have adopted the doctrine of strict liability as expressed in the *Second Restatement of Torts*, although it is mixed with elements of the other two theories in many jurisdictions.

The wording of Section 402A raises two questions of definition. What is a "defective condition"? And what does it mean to say that a product is "unreasonably dangerous"? Generally, a product is in a defective condition either when it is unsuitable for use as it is intended to be used or there is some misuse that can reasonably be foreseen and steps are not taken to prevent it. A ladder that cannot withstand the weight of an ordinary user is an example of the first kind of defect; a ladder without a label warning the user against stepping too high is an example of the second. A defect in a product can include a wide range of problems—from poor design and manufacture to inadequate instructions or warnings.

The definition of "unreasonably dangerous" that is offered in a comment on Section 402A is, "The article sold must be dangerous to an extent beyond that which would be contemplated by the ordinary consumer who purchases it, with the ordinary knowledge common to the community as to its characteristics." A product is not unreasonably dangerous, in this definition, merely because it is capable of causing serious injury to a user; otherwise, any power lawn mower would be labeled as such. However, a lawn mower which was so designed that fuel in the tank leaked on a grade, creating a fire hazard, would be unreasonably dangerous, since this is not a possibility that the ordinary user would anticipate.

This definition is inadequate, however, since it implies that a product is not unreasonably dangerous if most consumers are fully aware of the risks it poses. All power lawn mowers are now required by federal law to be equipped with a "kill switch," which stops the engine when the handle is released. Although the danger of removing debris while the blade is in motion or of slipping on a steep hill are obvious to any user, a machine without a "kill switch" is (arguably) unreasonably dangerous.

The Ethical Arguments for Strict Liability

The ethical arguments for strict liability rest on the two distinct grounds of efficiency and equity. One argument is purely utilitarian and justifies strict liability for securing the greatest amount of protection for consumers at the lowest cost. The second argument is that strict liability is the fairest way of distributing the costs involved in the manufacture and use of products.

Both of these arguments recognize that there is a certain cost in attempting to prevent accidents and in dealing with the consequences of accidents that do occur. Preventing accidents requires that manufacturers expend greater resources on product safety. Consumers must also expend resources to avoid accidents by learning how to select safe products and how to use them correctly. Insofar as manufacturers avoid the cost of reducing accidents and turn out defective products, this cost is passed along to consumers who pay for the injuries that result. A manufacturer may save money, for example, by using a cheaper grade of steel in a hammer, but a user who suffers the loss of an eye when the head chips ends up paying instead. When product safety is viewed as a matter of cost, two questions arise: (1) How can the total cost to both manufacturers and consumers be reduced to the lowest possible level? (2) How should the cost be distributed between manufacturers and consumers?

The *efficiency argument* holds, in the words of one advocate, that "responsibility be fixed wherever it will most effectively reduce the hazards to life and health inherent in defective products that reach the market."[36] By this principle, manufacturers ought to bear this responsibility, since they possess greater expertise than consumers about all aspects of product safety. They also make most of the key decisions about how products are designed, constructed, inspected, and so on. By giving manufacturers a powerful incentive to use the advantages of their position to ensure that the products they turn out are free of dangerous defects, strict liability protects consumers at a relatively low cost. The alternatives, which include placing primary responsibility on government and consumers, involve comparatively higher costs.

Further, the activity of manufacturers imposes a cost on society as a result of product-related accidents. The cost of accidents is thus an *externality*, which should be internalized as much as possible in order for the market to operate efficiently. Strict liability, according to the efficiency argument, is an effective means for internalizing the cost of the injuries to consumers that are caused by defective products. Strict liability is also an effective means, insofar as efficiency is achieved by distributing the cost of accidents broadly, since manufacturers are in a position to pass the cost along to consumers in the form of higher prices.

The principle involved in the *equity argument* is expressed by Richard A. Epstein as follows: "the defendant who captures the entire benefit of his own activities should . . . also bear its entire costs."[37] Insofar as manufacturers are the beneficiaries of their profit-making activity, it is only fair, according to this principle, that they be forced to bear the cost—which includes the cost of the injuries to consumers as a result of defective products. Much of the benefit of a manufacturer's activity is shared by consumers, however. But they also share the cost of compensating the victims of accidents through higher prices, and it is also just that they do so insofar as they reap some benefit. The distribution of the cost of compensating the victims of product-related injuries is fair, then, if this cost is distributed among all who benefit in the proportion that they benefit, so that it is not borne disproportionately by accident victims.

The Problem of Fault

The major stumbling block to the acceptance of strict liability is that the theory ignores the element of fault, which is a fundamental condition for owing compensation on the Aristotelian conception of compensatory justice.[38] We all benefit from automotive travel, for example, but we can justly be required to pay only for accidents that are our fault. Any system of liability that makes us pay for the accidents of others is unjust—or so it seems. Similarly, it is unjust to hold manufacturers liable to pay large sums to people who are injured by defective products in the absence of negligence or a contractual obligation to compensate. And it is equally unjust to force consumers indirectly to pay through higher prices the settlements in product liability suits.

The response of some advocates of strict liability is that it is not unjust to require those who are faultless to pay the cost of an activity *if everyone benefits by the use of an alternative method of paying compensation.* After all, the victims of accidents caused by defective products are not necessarily at fault either, and everyone is potentially a victim who deserves to be compensated for injuries received from defective products. Thus, those who "pay" under a system of strict liability are also protected. If a system of strict liability is in fact more efficient than any alternative scheme, then the total cost to society of ensuring that the victims of product-related accidents are compensated is less. This fact alone does not guarantee that the savings will be shared by everyone. But if manufacturers were not held strictly liable for the injuries caused by defective products, then they would take fewer precautions. As a result, everyone would have to spend more, to protect themselves—by taking more care in the selection of products, by using them more carefully, and perhaps by taking out insurance policies—and to make up the losses they suffer in product-related accidents where no one is at fault. In either case, the lower prices that consumers pay for products under a negligence system based on the due care theory would not be sufficient to offset the higher cost of insurance, medical care, and so on.

Under a system of strict liability, consumers give up a right they have in the due care theory—namely, the right not to be forced to contribute to the compensation of accident victims when they (the consumers) are not at fault. Prices are also higher under a strict liability system in order to cover the cost of paying compensation. But consumers gain more than they lose by not being required to spend money protecting themselves and making up their own losses. They also acquire a new right: the right to be compensated for injuries from defective products without regard to fault. Thus, everyone is better off under a strict liability system than under a negligence system.

Critics reject many key assumptions in the two arguments for strict liability. Product liability covers many different kinds of accidents, and the most efficient or equitable system for one kind may not be efficient or equitable for another. Careful studies need to be made of the consequences of competing theories for each kind of accident. Insofar as efficiency and equity are incompatible, decisions must be made about how to handle the efficiency/equity trade-off. Some proposals for reform have recommended strict liability for defects in construction and a negligence system for design defects, for example.[39]

Moreover, the "deep pockets" view, which holds that corporations are able to distribute the burden of strict liability to consumers effortlessly, is not always true. Multimillion-dollar awards in product liability suits and the high cost of insurance premiums place a heavy burden on manufacturers, driving some out of business and hindering the ability of others to compete. The principal beneficiary of the suits is the legal profession. According to a study conducted by the Rand Corporation, for every one dollar received by accident victims in product liability suits, two dollars are spent for legal services.[40] Other complaints of critics are that the threat of liability suits stifles innovation, since new and untested products are more likely to be defective, and that a patchwork of state laws with differing theories and standards creates uncertainty for manufacturers. For these reasons, many business leaders have pressed for uniform product liability laws, upper limits on awards, and other steps to ease the impact of product liability on manufacturers.

Conclusion

Which theory of liability is applied by the courts is of immense importance to manufacturers and consumers. Although this is a matter to be decided, in part, by legal and political considerations, there are also important ethical issues in the debate. The theories rest on different ethical foundations. The due care theory is based on the Aristotelian principle of compensatory justice; the contractual theory, on freedom of contract; and strict liability, largely on utilitarian considerations. Each one embodies something we consider morally fundamental, and yet the three theories are ultimately incompatible. The contractual theory is the least satisfactory because of the power of manufacturers to write warranties and other agreements to their own advantage and to offer them to consumers on a "take it or leave it" basis. The main shortcoming of the due care theory is the difficulty of deciding what constitutes due care and whether it was exercised. Strict liability, despite the absence of fault, is arguably the best theory. It provides a powerful incentive for manufacturers to take extreme precautions and creates a workable legal framework for compensating consumers who are injured by defective products. For strict liability to be just, however, the costs have to be properly distributed, so that they are fair to all parties.

CASE 12.2   The Target Marketing of Cigarettes

Target marketing is taught in business schools as an effective means for increasing sales by tailoring products to the needs and wants of specific consumers. A widely used marketing textbook compares target marketing to using a rifle rather than taking a shotgun approach.[41] This analogy is frighteningly apt, however, when the product is one that kills. As a critic of target marketing by the tobacco industry observed: "When you target for marketing [of cigarettes], you target for death."[42]

The R. J. Reynolds Tobacco Company, a division of RJR Nabisco, was criticized in 1990 for the development of two new cigarette brands that were aimed at narrow market segments. One brand, to be called Uptown, was designed to appeal to blacks, the other, named Dakota, was intended to attract young, blue-collar white women. The introductions of both brands were scuttled by R. J. Reynolds after protests from outraged civil rights groups and women's organizations. The Secretary of Health and Human Services, Dr. Louis W. Sullivan, who is a black physician, charged that Uptown was "deliberately and cynically targeted toward black Americans," and he urged the company to cancel plans to test-market the new brand. "At a time when our people desperately need the message of health promotion," he said, "Uptown's message is more disease, more suffering, and more death for a group already bearing more than its share of smoking-related illness and mortality."

The development of Uptown was based on extensive marketing research. A light menthol flavor was selected because 69 percent of black smokers prefer menthol-flavored cigarettes compared with 27 percent for all smokers. Many blacks open a package from the bottom, and so the cigarettes were to be packed with the filter end pointing down. Researchers discovered that the name Uptown, which evokes images of sophisticated nightlife, drew the most favorable response from blacks in test groups, and the theme of elegance was reinforced by lettering in black and gold, which were chosen instead of the green that is more commonly used for menthol brands. The market testing for Uptown, which was scheduled to begin on February 5, 1990, in Philadelphia, involved print ads in black magazines and newspapers and billboards and point-of-sale displays in black neighborhoods. The target group for Dakota was young white women, 18 to 20 years of age, with a high school education or less, who held an "entry level service or factory job." The profile of the potential Dakota smoker also mentioned that she spent her free time accompanying her boyfriend to tractor pulls and car races. The test marketing for this product was planned for April 1990.

The groups targeted by Uptown and Dakota reflect market realities. As more smokers quit, the tobacco companies can best expand market share by luring customers away from rival brands, and groups with the lowest rate of quitting are more likely prospects. In 1990, 34 percent of adult blacks smoked whereas the rate among the whole adult population was 27 percent. In the period from 1965 to 1987, the number of white smokers declined 28 percent compared with a drop of only 21 percent among blacks. Although more men than women smoke (32 percent versus 27 percent in 1965), the percentage of men who quit smoking (37 percent) during the 1965 to 1987 period was much higher than the figure for women (16 percent). And the decline in smoking among college-educated people was 52 percent, which contrasts sharply with a quit rate of 2 percent for high school dropouts. The data show that the best markets for tobacco products are blacks, women, and the uneducated.

The three largest-selling menthol brands on the market held 53 percent of the black market, attesting to the appeal of menthol-flavored cigarettes among blacks, but R. J. Reynold's product in this market, Salem, ranked behind the other two brands with a market share of only 15 percent. Another menthol brand could increase Reynold's share of the black market. The most popular brand for teenage women was Marlboro, manufactured by rival Philip Morris. R. J. Reynolds could not easily challenge the dominance of this brand among all smokers, but the company apparently thought that many women in that age group did not identify fully with the "Marlboro man" and could be enticed by a cigarette for women only. Thus, the "Dakota woman" was conceived as a feminine counterpart of the "Marlboro man."

The marketing of cigarettes (and alcohol) to blacks is nothing new. Ads for cigarettes contribute between 7 and 10 percent of the advertising revenue in black-oriented publications. Inner-city areas contain more billboards than do suburbs, and more of the billboards in the inner city advertise cigarettes and alcohol. A 1987 survey in St. Louis, for example, revealed that 62 percent of the billboards in predominantly black neighborhoods advertised cigarettes and alcohol compared with 36 percent in white neighborhoods.[43] R. J. Reynolds denies that it is attempting to attract new smokers among blacks and maintains that the company is merely trying to take away business from its competitors. After canceling the test marketing for Uptown, an executive from Reynolds remarked, "Maybe in retrospect we would have been better off not saying we were marketing to blacks. But those were the smokers we were going after, so why shouldn't we be honest about it?"

CASE 12.3 Lotus MarketPlace:Households

In April 1990, the Lotus Development Corporation announced plans for a revolutionary new product.[44] MarketPlace:Households would provide information about 80 million American households that would enable businesses to generate mailing lists for direct marketing. The product was developed jointly with Equifax, Inc., which collects credit information on consumers and provides credit reports and customized mailing lists to client businesses. The distinguishing feature of MarketPlace:Households is that businesses would have information that was formerly contained only in the Equifax mainframe database in a set of compact disks for use on a personal computer. For $695, any business could obtain CD-ROMs with consumers' names, addresses, and purchasing behavior and generate a 5,000-name mailing list with the desired demographic profile using special sorting software. Once a company owns the CD-ROMs and the software, additional lists could be generated at a cost of $400 for each list of 5,000 names.

The announcement of MarketPlace:Households was greeted with loud complaints by groups concerned with consumer privacy. The American Civil Liberties Union charged that the product blurs the line between information that is provided by consumers for obtaining credit and the use of that information for direct marketing. Many privacy advocates contend that people have a right to control the kind of information that they supply to obtain a mortgage or a credit card and that such information should not be used without their consent. When Lotus announced that consumers could have their names deleted from the CD-ROMs, the company was flooded with 30,000 requests. Critics of Lotus were also concerned that the product could be used by unscrupulous businesspersons to fleece consumers with bogus offers. Others raised questions about possible problems due to inaccurate data. Word of MarketPlace:Households spread on computer bulletin boards along with the e-mail address of Lotus CEO Jim Manzi. One irate message to Mr. Manzi read: "If you market this product, it is my sincere hope that you are sued by every person for whom your data is false, with the eventual result that your company goes bankrupt."

Lotus considered concerns about privacy in the development of MarketPlace:Households and engaged a respected privacy expert, Alan F. Westin of Columbia University, to advise the company. All personal information on the CD-ROMs was designed to be inaccessible to the user; only mailing labels in minimum lists of 5,000 names could be generated by the owner of the product. Lotus created a procedure for allowing individuals to request that their names be omitted from the compact disks, although critics pointed out that the names would still be included in CD-ROMs already sold. In addition, MarketPlace:Households would be available only to reputable businesses; the mailing lists generated by the product would be seeded with decoy names so that Lotus would receive copies of items mailed to consumers; and Lotus and Equifax were prepared to take legal action for misuse of the lists. Lotus maintained that MarketPlace:Households merely provides small businesses with the same resources as large corporations that already buy mailing lists from companies like Equifax. Mr. Westin observed: "The aborigines used to believe that to take a picture of a man was to steal his soul. But the bottom line with Lotus MarketPlace is that you'll get a few extra pieces of mail."

NOTES

1. This case is based on material in JOHN A. BYRNE, *Informed Consent* (New York: McGraw-Hill, 1996); ANNE T. LAWRENCE, "Dow Corning and the Silicone Breast Implant Controversy," *Case Research Journal*, 13(4) (1993), 87–112; PHILIP J. HILTS, "Maker Is Depicted as Fighting Tests on Implant Safety," *New York Times*, 13 January 1993, A1; STEVEN FINK, "Dow Corning's Moral Evasions," *New York Times*, 16 February 1992, F13; GINA KOLATA, "Study Finds Nothing to Link Implants with any Diseases," *New York Times*, 16 June 1994, A8.

2. *Marketing Definitions: A Glossary of Marketing Terms* (Chicago: American Marketing Association, 1960), 15.

3. RACHEL CARSON, *Silent Spring* (Boston: Houghton Mifflin, 1962).

4. JESSICA MITFORD, *The American Way of Death* (New York: Simon & Schuster, 1963).

5. RALPH NADER, *Unsafe at Any Speed* (New York: Brossman, 1965).

6. An explanation of the marketing concept can be found in any standard marketing textbook. The origin of the concept is commonly attributed to J. B. MCKITTERICK, "What Is the Marketing Management Concept?" in FRANK M. BASS, ed., *The Frontiers of Marketing Thought and Science* (Chicago: American Marketing Association, 1958), 71–82. See also A. P. FELTON, "Making the Marketing Concept Work," *Harvard Business Review*, 37 (July–August 1959), 55–65.

7. "Business Responds to Consumerism," *Business Week*, 6 September 1969, 95.

8. PETER F. DRUCKER, "The Shame of Marketing," *Marketing/Communications*, August 1969, 60.

9. For further criticism of the marketing concept, see LESLIE M. DAWSON, "The Human Concept: New Philosophy of Business," *Business Horizons*, 12 (December 1969), 29–38; MARTIN L. BELL and C. WILLIAM EMORY, "The Faltering Market Concept," *Journal of Marketing*, 35 (October 1971), 37–42; PHILIP KOTLER, "What Consumerism Means for Marketers," *Harvard Business Review*, 50 (May–June 1972), 48–57; ROGER C. BENNETT and ROBERT G. COOPER, "Beyond the Marketing Concept," *Business Horizons*, 22 (June 1979), 76–83; PETER C. RIESZ, "Revenge of the Marketing Concept," *Business Horizons*, 23 (June 1980), 49–53; LESLIE M. DAWSON, "Marketing for Human Needs," *Business Horizons*, 23 (June 1980), 72–82; ROGER C. BENNETT and ROBERT G. COOPER, "The Misuse of Marketing: An American Tragedy," *Business Horizons*, 24 (November–December 1981), 36–48.

10. *Great A&P Co., Inc.*, 85 FTC. 601 (1975).

11. See TOM L. BEAUCHAMP, "Manipulative Advertising," in TOM L. BEAUCHAMP and NORMAN E. BOWIE, eds., *Ethical Theory and Business*, 4th ed. (Englewood Cliffs, NJ: Prentice Hall, 1993), 475–83.

12. JOHN B. HINGE, "Critics Call Cuts in Package Size Deceptive Move," *Wall Street Journal*, 5 February 1991, B1.

13. Manipulative sales practices that exploit the poor are well documented in DAVID CAPLOVITZ, *The Poor Pay More* (New York: Free Press, 1963) and the report by the National Advisory Commission on Civil Disorders, better known as the Kerner Commission, in 1968. Another study is ALAN R. ANDREASEN, *The Disadvantaged Consumer* (New York: Free Press, 1975).

14. See, for example, LEO BOGART, "The Researcher's Dilemma," *Journal of Marketing*, 26 (January 1962), 6–11; A. B. BLANKENSHIP, "Some Aspects of Ethics in Marketing Research," *Journal of Marketing Research*, 1 (May 1964), 26–31; SHELBY D. HUNT, LAWRENCE B. CHONKO, and JAMES B. WILCOX, "Ethical Problems of Market Researchers," *Journal of Marketing Research*, 21 (1984), 309–24.

15. See ALICE M. TYBOUT and GERALD ZALTMAN, "Ethics in Marketing Research: Their Practical Relevance," *Journal of Marketing Research*, 11 (November 1974), 357–68; KENNETH C. SCHNEIDER, "Subject and Respondent Abuse in Marketing Research," *MSU Business Topics*, Spring 1977, 13–20; and DEL I.

HAWKINS, "The Impact of Sponsor Identification and Direct Disclosure on Respondent Rights on the Quantity and Quality of Mail Survey Data," *Journal of Business*, 52 (1979), 577–90.

16. See JOHN R. WILKE, "Lotus Product Spurs Fears About Privacy," *Wall Street Journal*, 13 November 1990, B1.

17. *United States* v. *Colgate & Company*, 250 U.S. 300 (1919).

18. See, for example, *United States* v. *Parke, Davis, & Co.*, 362 U.S. 29 (1960).

19. There have been two large-scale price-fixing conspiracies in the last half century, one among electrical equipment manufacturers around 1960 and a second among folding-box manufacturers in the late 1970s. On the first, see RICHARD A. SMITH, "The Incredible Electrical Conspiracy," *Fortune*, Part I (April 1961) and Part II (May 1961). An insightful discussion of the factors that lead companies to engage in such conspiracies is JEFFREY SONNENFELD and PAUL R. LAWRENCE, "Why Do Companies Succumb to Price Fixing?" *Harvard Business Review*, 56 (July–August 1978), 145–57.

20. *Standard Oil Company New Jersey* v. *U.S.*, 221 U.S. 1 (1911).

21. *U.S.* v. *American Tobacco Company*, 221 U.S. 106 (1911).

22. See JOHN S. MCGEE, "Predatory Price Cutting: The Standard Oil (N.J.) Case," *Journal of Law and Economics*, 1 (1958), 137–69; PHILIP AREEDA and DONALD F. TURNER, "Predatory Pricing and Related Practices under Section 2 of the Sherman Act," *Harvard Law Review*, 88 (1975), 720–32; and OLIVER E. WILLIAMSON, "Predatory Pricing: A Strategic and Welfare Analysis," *Yale Law Journal*, 87 (1977), 284–340.

23. See B. S. YAMEY, "Predatory Price Cutting: Notes and Comments," *Journal of Law and Economics*, 15 (1972), 129–47.

24. For the sake of simplicity, the discussion in this section focuses only on manufacturers, but a responsibility for product safety extends to wholesalers, distributors, franchisers, and retailers, among others, although their responsibility is generally less than that of manufacturers.

25. The conditions under which a negligent act is a cause of injury to another person (known in law as *proximate* cause) are complicated. See any standard textbook on business law for an explanation.

26. *Larsen* v. *General Motors Corporation*, 391 F. 2d 495 (8th Cir. 1968).

27. *LeBouef* v. *Goodyear Tire and Rubber Co.*, 623 F. 2d 985 (5th Cir. 1980).

28. See ED TIMMERMAN and BRAD REID, "The Doctrine of Invited Misuse: A Societal Response to Marketing Promotion," *Journal of Macromarketing*, 4 (Fall 1984), 40–48.

29. *Commercial National Bank of Little Rock, Guardian of the Estate of Jo Ann Fitzsimmons* v. *General Motors Corporation*, U.S. Dist. Ct. E.D.Ark., No. LR-C-79-168 (1979).

30. *United States* v. *Carroll Towing Co.*, 159 F. 2d 169 (2d Cir. 1947).

31. *Bashada* v. *Johns-Manville Products Corp.*, 90 N.J. 191, 447 A. 2d 539 (1982). The "state-of-the-art" defense has been accepted in other cases. See, for example, *Boatland of Houston, Inc.* v. *Bailey*, 609 S.W. 2d 743 (Tex. 1980). For an overview, see JORDAN H. LEIBMAN, "The Manufacturer's Responsibility to Warn Product Users of Unknowable Dangers," *American Business Law Journal*, 21 (1984), 403–38.

32. *Henningsen* v. *Bloomfield Motors, Inc. and Chrysler Corporation*, 161 A. 2d 69 (1960).

33. *MacPherson* v. *Buick Motor Company*, 217 N.Y. 382 (1916).

34. *Baxter* v. *Ford Motor Co.*, 168 Wash. 456, 12 P. 2d 409 (1932); 179 Wash. 123, 35 P. 2d 1090 (1934).

35. *Greenman* v. *Yuba Power Products*, 59 Cal. 2d 57, 377 P. 2d 897, 27 Cal. Rptr. 697 (1963). The theory was enunciated nineteen years earlier in *Escola* v. *Coca-Cola Bottling Co.*, 24 Cal. 2d 453, 150 P. 2d 436 (1944).

36. *Escola* v. *Coca-Cola Bottling Co.*

37. RICHARD A. EPSTEIN, *Modern Products Liability Law* (Westport, CT: Quorum Books, 1980), 27. Epstein holds, however, that this principle has limited application in product liability cases.

38. GEORGE P. FLETCHER, "Fairness and Utility in Tort Theory," *Harvard Law Review*, 85 (1972), 537–73; RICHARD A. EPSTEIN, "A Theory of Strict Liability," *Journal of Legal Studies*, 2 (1973), 151–204; and JULES L. COLEMAN, "The Morality of Strict Tort Liability," *William and Mary Law Review*, 18 (1976), 259–586. RICHARD POSNER argues that the Aristotelian principle of compensatory justice in a negligence system, correctly understood, is the same as the principle of efficiency that underlies strict liability. See "A Theory of Negligence," *Journal of Legal Studies*, 1 (1972), 29–96; and "The Concept of Corrective Justice in Recent Theories of Tort Law," *Journal of Legal Studies*, 10 (1981), 187–206.

39. This proposal was contained in S. 44, an unsuccessful bill introduced in the 98th Congress.

40. Cited in STEPHEN M. SETTLE and SHARON SPIGELMYER, *Product Liability: A Multibillion-Dollar Dilemma* (New York: American Management Association, 1984), 10.

41. PHILIP KOTLER, *Marketing Management: Analysis, Planning, Implementation, and Control*, 8th ed. (Englewood Cliffs, NJ: Prentice Hall, 1994), 265.

42. ANTHONY RAMIREZ, "New Cigarette Raising Issue of Target Marketing," *New York Times*, 18 February 1990, A28. Other sources used in the preparation of this case are: ANTHONY RAMIREZ, "A Cigarette Campaign Under Fire," *New York Times*, 12 January 1990, D1, D32; PHILIP J. HILTS, "Health Chief Assails Reynolds Co. for Ads That Target Blacks," *New York Times*, 19 January 1990, A1, A13; ANTHONY RAMIREZ, "Reynolds, After Protests, Cancels Cigarette Aimed at Black Smokers," *New York Times*, 20 January 1990, A1, A11.

43. "Media Uproar Over Billboards in Poor Areas," *New York Times*, 1 May 1989, D32.

44. Material for this case is taken from: WILKE, "Lotus Product Spurs Fears about Privacy;" ALAN RADDING, "Lotus Stirs Research Marketplace," *Advertising Age*, 14 January 1991, 21; MICHAEL W. MILLER, "Lotus Likely to Abandon Consumer-Data Project," *Wall Street Journal*, 23 January 1991, B1; and PETER H. LEWIS, "Why the Privacy Issue Will Never Go Away," *New York Times*, 7 April 1991 F4.

13

Occupational Health and Safety

CASE 13.1   The Regulation of Benzene

Benzene is a colorless, vaporous liquid widely used as a solvent in the printing, rubber, paint, and dry-cleaning industries. It is a raw material or an intermediate product in the synthesis of many chemicals and a constituent of many petroleum products. Benzene is also highly toxic. Contact with the skin causes irritation and blistering, and the consequences of breathing benzene vapors in high concentrations include headache, fatigue, dizziness, convulsions, and even death from paralysis of the nervous system. The most serious effects of benzene exposure result from damage to the blood-cell-forming system of the bone marrow. Victims of benzene poisoning experience a variety of blood disorders that often lead to debilitating aplastic anemia and potentially fatal infections. Chronic exposure to high levels of benzene has also been linked to leukemia.

Before the dangers of benzene were known, the exposure of workers was routine. According to a study done in 1939, three printing plants in New York City, employing 350 men, used about fifty thousand gallons of benzene a month, mostly as an ink solvent.[1] The workers were exposed to fumes from open troughs of ink on the printing presses, from accidental spills on the floor, and from ink drying on the paper. Benzene was also used to clean the machines, and workers cleaned themselves with it at the end of the day. An examination of 332 workers found that 130 of them had benzene poisoning in varying degrees, and further tests on a group of 102 workers revealed 22 severe cases, including 6 requiring hospitalization. The use of benzene in printing has long since been discontinued, but it was replaced at first with methanol, also known as wood alcohol, and carbon tetrachloride, both of which damage the central nervous system and internal organs, including the liver and kidneys. Methanol can also produce blindness.

Because of the toxicity of benzene, a permissible exposure limit (PEL) of 10 parts per million (ppm) was set by the Occupational Safety and Health Administration (OSHA), the federal regulatory body created in 1970 to protect Americans from workplace hazards. The assumption that exposure below the level of 10 ppm is safe was challenged in 1977 when a disproportionate number of leukemia deaths occurred at two rubber pliofilm plants in Ohio.[2] On the evidence contained in a report by the National Institute for Occupational Safety and Health (NIOSH), OSHA declared benzene to be a leukemia-causing agent and issued an emergency temporary standard ordering that the PEL for benzene in most work sites be reduced to 1 ppm until a hearing could be conducted on setting a new limit. OSHA was acting under a section of the law that requires the PEL for a known carcinogen (cancer-causing agent) to be set at the lowest technologically feasible level that will not impair the viability of the industries being regulated.

In the resulting uproar, the American Petroleum Institute, a trade association of domestic oil companies, contended that the evidence linking benzene to leukemia was not conclusive and that the exposure standard should take into account the cost of compliance. Previous studies had documented the incidence of leukemia only at exposures above 25 ppm. One study of exposure below 10 ppm, conducted by Dow Chemical Company, found three leukemia deaths in a group of 594 workers, where 0.2 deaths would be expected, but it was impossible to rule out other causes, since the workers who developed leukemia had been exposed to other carcinogens during their careers. OSHA was unable to demonstrate, therefore, that exposure to benzene below the level of 10 ppm had ever caused leukemia.

According to OSHA figures, complying with the 1 ppm standard would require companies to spend approximately $266 million in capital improvements, $187 million to $205 million in first-year operating costs, and $34 million in recurring annual costs. The burden would be least in the rubber industry, where two-thirds of the workers exposed to benzene are employed. The petroleum-refining industry, by contrast, would be required to incur $24 million in capital costs and $600,000 in first year operating expenses. The cost of protecting 300 petroleum refinery workers would be $82,000 each, compared with a cost of only $1,390 per worker in the rubber industry.

INTRODUCTION

No one questions the hazards posed by benzene and the necessity to limit the exposure of workers. Workers have a right to be protected from excessive exposure to toxic chemicals in the workplace. It may be asked, however, whether a reduction to the lowest technologically feasible level is justified, especially in view of the lack of conclusive evidence of the hazards at low levels of exposure. Also, should the cost of complying with the reduced standard be a factor in determining the acceptable level of safety in the workplace?

These are some of the questions that are posed by the benzene case. Questions can also be raised about the right of employees to be given information about the workplace hazards to which they are exposed and their right to refuse to perform dangerous work without fear of dismissal or other reprisals. An especially difficult kind of case is posed by the fact that certain jobs pose a health threat to the fetus of a pregnant woman and to the reproductive capacities of both men and women. Some pregnant women and women of childbearing age are demanding the right to transfer out of jobs thought to pose reproductive hazards. On the other hand, employers who exclude pregnant women or women of childbearing age from certain jobs because of reproductive hazards are open to charges of illegal sexual discrimination, especially when they do not show an equal concern for the reproductive risk to men.

This chapter is concerned with determining how questions about the rights of workers in matters of occupational health and safety ought to be answered. At issue in these questions is not only the obligation of employers with respect to the rights of workers but also the justification for government regulation of the workplace, especially by the Occupational Safety and Health Administration. As a result, many of the questions discussed in this chapter deal with specific regulatory programs and policies, which are the subject of intense controversy.

THE SCOPE OF THE PROBLEM

Many Americans live with the possibility of serious injury and death every working day. For some workers, the threat comes from a major industrial accident, such as the collapse of a mine or a refinery explosion, or from widespread exposure to a hazardous substance, such as asbestos, which is estimated to have caused more than 350,000 cancer deaths since 1940.[3] The greatest toll on the work force is exacted, however, by little-publicized injuries to individual workers, some of which are gradual, such as hearing loss from constant noise or nerve damage from repetitive motions. Some of the leading causes of death, such as heart disease, cancer, and respiratory conditions, are thought to be job-related, although causal connections are often difficult to make. Even stress on the job is now being recognized as a workplace hazard that is responsible for headaches, back and chest pains, stomach ailments, and a variety of emotional disorders.

The Distinction between Health and Safety

Although the term *safety* is often used to encompass all workplace hazards, it is useful to make a distinction between *safety* and *health*.[4] Safety hazards generally involve loss of limbs, burns, broken bones, electrical shocks, cuts, sprains, bruises, and impairment of sight or hearing. These injuries are usually the result of sudden and often violent events involving industrial equipment or the physical environment of the workplace. Examples include coming into contact with moving parts of machinery or electrical lines, getting hit by falling objects or flying debris, chemical spills and explosions, fires, and falls from great heights.

Health hazards are factors in the workplace that cause illnesses and other conditions that develop over a lifetime of exposure. Many diseases associated with specific occupations have long been known. In 1567, Paracelsus identified pneumoconiosis, or black lung disease, in a book entitled *Miners' Sickness and Other Miners' Diseases*. Silicosis, or the "white plague," has traditionally been associated with stone cutters. Other well-known occupational diseases are caisson disease among divers, cataracts in glass blowers, skin cancer among chimney sweeps, and phosphorus poisoning in match makers. Mercury poisoning, once common among felt workers, produces tremors, known as "the hatters' shakes," and delusions and hallucinations that gave rise to the phrase "mad as a hatter."

In the modern workplace, most occupational health problems result from routine exposure to hazardous substances. Among these substances are fine particles, such as asbestos, which causes asbestosis, and cotton dust, which causes byssinosis; heavy metals, such as lead, cadmium, and beryllium; gases, including chlorine, ozone, sulphur dioxide, carbon monoxide, hydrogen sulfide, and hydrogen cyanide, which damage the lungs and often cause neurological problems; solvents, such as benzene, carbon tetrachloride, and carbon disulfide; and certain classes of chemicals, especially phenols, ketones, and epoxies. Pesticides pose a serious threat to agricultural workers and radiation is an occupational hazard to X-ray technicians and workers in the nuclear industry.

Because occupationally related diseases result from long-term exposure and not from identifiable events on the job, employers have generally not been held liable for them, and they have not, until recently, been recognized in workers' compensation programs. The fact that the onset of many diseases occurs years after the initial exposure—thirty or forty years in the case of asbestos—hides the causal connection. The links are further obscured by a multiplicity of causes. The textile industry, for example, claims that byssinosis among its workers results from their own decision to smoke and not from inhaling cotton dust on the job.[5] Lack of knowledge, especially about cancer, adds to the difficulty of establishing causal connections.

Regulation of Occupational Health and Safety

Prior to the passage of the Occupational Safety and Health Act (OSH Act) in 1970, government regulation of occupational health and safety was almost entirely the province of the states. Understaffed and underfunded, the agencies charged with protecting workers in most states were not very effective.[6] Only a small percentage of workers in many states were even under the jurisdiction of regulatory agencies; often, powerful economic interests were able to influence their activities. Because the agencies lacked the resources to set standards for exposure to hazardous substances, they relied heavily on private standard-setting organizations and the industries themselves. The emphasis in most states was on education and training, and prosecutions for violations were rare. State regulatory agencies were also concerned almost exclusively with safety rather than with health.

States still play a major role in occupational health and safety through workers' compensation systems, but in 1970, primary responsibility for the regulation of working conditions passed to the federal government. The "general duty clause" of the OSH Act requires employers "to furnish to each of his employees employment and a place of employment which are free from recognized hazards that are causing or are likely to cause death or serious injury."[7] In addition, employers have a specific duty to comply with all the occupational safety and health standards that OSHA is empowered to make. Employees also have a duty, under Section 5(b), to "comply with occupational safety and health standards and all rules, regulations, and orders issued pursuant to this Act which are applicable to his own actions and conduct." OSHA regulates occupational health and safety primarily by issuing standards, which are commonly enforced by workplace inspections. Examples of standards are permissible exposure limits (PELs) for toxic substances and specifications for equipment and facilities, such as guards on saws and the height and strength of railings.

THE RIGHT TO A SAFE AND HEALTHY WORKPLACE

At first glance, the right of employees to a safe and healthy workplace might seem to be too obvious to need any justification. This right—and the corresponding obligation of employers to provide working conditions free of recognized hazards—appears to follow from a more fundamental right—namely, the right of survival. Patricia H. Werhane writes, for example, "Dangerous working conditions threaten the very existence of employees and cannot be countenanced when they are avoidable." Without this right, she argues, all other rights lose their significance.[8] Some other writers base a right to a safe and healthy workplace on the Kantian ground that persons ought to be treated as ends rather than as means. Mark MacCarthy has described this view as follows:

> People have rights that protect them from others who would enslave them or otherwise use them for their own purposes. In bringing this idea to bear on the problem of occupational safety, many people have thought that workers have an inalienable right to earn their living free from the ravages of job-caused death, disease, and injury.[9]

Congress, in passing the OSH Act granting the right to all employees of a safe and healthy workplace, was apparently relying on a cost-benefit analysis, balancing the cost to industry with the savings to the economy as a whole. Congress, in other words, appears to have been employing essentially utilitarian reasoning. Regardless of the ethical reasoning used, though, workers have an undeniable right not to be injured or killed on the job.

It is not clear, though, what specific protection workers are entitled to or what specific obligations employers have with respect to occupational health and safety. One position, recognized in common law, is that workers have a right to be protected against harm resulting directly from the actions of employers where the employer is at fault in some way. Consider the case of the owner of a drilling company in Los Angeles who had a twenty-three-year-old worker lowered into a thirty-three-foot-deep, eighteen-inch-wide hole that was being dug for an elevator shaft.[10] No test was made of the air at the bottom of the hole, and while he was being lowered, the worker began to have difficulty breathing. Rescue workers were hampered by the lack of shoring, and the worker died before he could be pulled to the surface. The owner of the drilling company was convicted of manslaughter, sentenced to forty-five days in jail, and ordered to pay $12,000 in compensation to the family of the victim. A prosecutor in the Los Angeles County district attorney's office explained the decision to bring criminal charges with the words, "Our opinion is you can't risk somebody's life to save a few bucks. That's the bottom line."

Few people would hesitate to say that the owner of the company in this case violated an employee's rights by recklessly endangering his life. In most workplace accidents, however, employers can defend themselves against the charge of violating the rights of workers with two arguments. One is that their actions were not the *direct cause* of the death or injury, and the other is that the worker *voluntarily assumed the risk*. These defenses are considered in turn.

The Notion of a Direct Cause

Two factors enable employers to deny that their actions are a direct cause of an accident in the workplace.[11] One factor is that industrial accidents are typically caused by a combination of factors, frequently including the actions of workers themselves. When there is such a multiplicity of causes, it is difficult to assign responsibility to any one person.[12] The legal treatment of industrial accidents in the United States incorporates this factor by recognizing two common-law defenses for employers: that a workplace accident was caused in part by (1) lack of care on the part of the employee (the doctrine of "contributory negligence") or by (2) the negligence of co-workers (the "fellow-servant rule"). As long as employers are not negligent in meeting minimal obligations, they are not generally held liable for deaths or injuries resulting from industrial accidents.

The second factor is that it is often not practical to reduce the probability of harm any further. It is reasonable to hold an employer responsible for the incidence of cancer in workers who are exposed to high levels of a known carcinogen, especially when the exposure is avoidable. But a small number of cancer deaths can be statistically predicted to result from very low exposure levels to some widely used chemicals. Is it reasonable to hold employers responsible when workers contract cancer from exposure to carcinogens at levels that are considered to pose only a slight risk? The so-called Delaney amendment, for example, forbids the use of any food additive found to cause cancer.[13] Such an absolute prohibition is practicable for food additives, since substitutes are usually readily available. But when union and public-interest groups petitioned OSHA in 1972 to set zero tolerance levels for ten powerful carcinogens, the agency refused on the ground that workers should be protected from carcinogens "to the maximum extent practicable *consistent with continued use.*"[14] The position of OSHA, apparently, was that it is unreasonable to forgo the benefit of useful chemicals when there are no ready substitutes and the probability of cancer can be kept low by strict controls. This is also the position of philosopher Alan Gewirth, who argues that the right of persons not to have cancer inflicted on them is not absolute. He concluded, "Whether the use of or exposure to some substance should be prohibited should depend on the degree to which it poses the risk of cancer. . . . If the risks are very slight . . . and if no substitutes are available, then use of it may be permitted, subject to stringent safeguards."[15]

The Benzene Case

This issue arose again in 1977 in the benzene case that begins this chapter. The main legal issue faced by the Supreme Court is the authority of the Secretary of Labor under the OSH Act to set standards. An "occupational safety and health standard" is defined in Section 3(8) of the OSH Act as "a standard which requires conditions, or the adoption or use of one or more practices, means, methods, operations, or processes, reasonably necessary or appropriate to provide safe or healthful employment and places of employment." And Section 6(b)(5) states:

> The Secretary, in promulgating standards dealing with toxic materials or harmful physical agents under this subsection, shall set the standard which most adequately assures, to the extent feasible, on the basis of the best available evidence, that no employee will suffer material impairment of health or functional capacity even if such employee has regular exposure to the hazard dealt with by such standard for the period of his working life. Development of standards under this subsection shall be based upon research, demonstrations, experiments, and such other information as may be appropriate. In addition to the attainment of the highest degree of health and safety protection for the employee, other considerations shall be the latest available scientific data in the field, the feasibility of the standards, and experience gained under this and other health and safety laws.

Two specific issues raised by the language of the OSH Act are (1) What is meant by "to the extent feasible"? Should all technologically possible steps be taken? Or should some consideration be given to the economic burden on employers? Should the agency, in determining what is "reasonably necessary and appropriate," also weigh costs and benefits? (2) What amount of evidence is required? To what extent should the agency be required to provide valid scientific studies to prove that a standard addresses a genuine problem and will, in fact, achieve the intended result? On the one hand, the power to set emergency standards on the basis of flimsy evidence that turns out later not to warrant action exposes businesses to the possibility of heavy and unpredictable expenses. On the other hand, adequate scientific research is very costly and time-consuming. Lack of funding for research and the time lag between suspicion and proof that a substance is carcinogenic, for example, could result in the needless deaths of many workers. A high level of proof exposes workers to preventable harm, therefore, but at the price of a possibly unnecessary cost to employers. Where does the balance lie?

A plurality of justices agreed with a lower court opinion that OSHA does not have "unbridled discretion to adopt standards designed to create absolutely risk-free workplaces regardless of the cost." But no consensus was achieved on how the level of risk is to be determined and, in particular, whether OSHA is required to use cost-benefit analysis in setting standards. By a bare majority, though, the Supreme Court struck down the 1-ppm standard because the agency was unable to prove that exposure to benzene below concentrations of 10 ppm is harmful. Ample evidence existed at the time to justify a 10-ppm standard, but little evidence indicated that a lower standard would achieve any additional benefits. The Court's answer to the second question, then, is that a rather high level of proof is needed to impose a highly restrictive standard.

In a subsequent case, however, the Court ruled that OSHA is not required to take cost into account but only technological feasibility. The case, *American Textile Manufacturers Institute Inc.* v. *Raymond J. Donovan, Secretary of Labor*, concerned an established standard for cotton dust, which is the primary cause of byssinosis, or "brown lung," disease. The evidence linking cotton dust to byssinosis was not in dispute, but OSHA relied on cost-benefit studies that the agency itself admitted underestimated the cost of compliance. The reason given for not requiring OSHA to consider costs and benefits is that Congress in passing the OSH Act had already made a cost-benefit analysis.[16] According to the majority opinion:

> Not only does the legislative history confirm that Congress meant "feasible" rather than "cost-benefit" when it used the former term, but it also shows that Congress understood that the Act would create substantial costs for employers, yet intended to impose such costs when necessary to create a safe and healthful working environment. . . . Indeed Congress thought that the *financial costs* of health and safety problems in the workplace were as large as or larger than the *financial costs* of eliminating these problems.

Cost-benefit analysis is the proper instrument for striking a balance on issues of worker health and safety, in other words, but this instrument was used by Congress as a justification for empowering OSHA to set standards without regard for costs. OSHA, therefore, should base its decisions solely on technological feasibility.

As a postscript to the benzene case, OSHA announced in March 1986 a new standard based on subsequent research. The new standard, which took effect in February 1988, set a permissible exposure limit of 1 ppm for an eight-hour workday, with a short-term limit of 5 ppm. By this time, however, improvements in equipment and the monitoring of airborne pollutants required by the Environmental Protection Agency (EPA) had already reduced the level of exposure to benzene close to the 1-ppm standard. Consequently, the initial capital expenditures for meeting the new standard were considerably less than in 1977, ten years earlier, when the controversy first erupted.

The Voluntary Assumption of Risk

A further common-law defense is that employees voluntarily assume the risk inherent in work. Some jobs, such as coal mining, construction, longshoring, and meat-packing, are well-known for their high accident rates, and yet some individuals freely choose these lines of work, even when safer employment is available. The risk itself is sometimes part of the allure, but more often the fact that hazardous jobs offer a wage premium in order to compensate for the greater risk leads workers to prefer them to less hazardous, less well paying jobs. Like people who choose to engage in risky recreational activities, such as mountain climbing, workers in hazardous occupations, according to the argument, knowingly accept the risk in return for benefits that cannot be obtained without it. Injury and even death are part of the price they may have to pay. And except when an employer or a fellow employee is negligent in some way, workers who have chosen to work under dangerous conditions have no one to blame but themselves.

A related argument is that occupational health and safety ought not to be regulated because it interferes with the freedom of individuals to choose the kind of work that they want to perform. Workers who prefer the higher wages of hazardous work ought to be free to accept such employment, and those with a greater aversion to risk ought to be free to choose other kinds of employment or to bargain for more safety, presumably with lower pay. To deny workers this freedom of choice is to treat them as persons incapable of looking after their own welfare.[17] W. Kip Viscusi, who served as a consultant to OSHA during the Reagan administration adds an extra twist by arguing that programs designed to keep workers from being maimed and killed on the job are a form of class oppression. He has written:

> Efforts to promote present risk regulations on the basis that they enhance worker rights are certainly misguided. Uniform standards do not enlarge worker choices; they deprive workers of the opportunity to select the job most appropriate to their own risk preferences. The actual "rights" issue involved is whether those in upper income groups have a right to impose their job risk preferences on the poor.[18]

The argument that employees assume the risk of work can be challenged on several grounds. First, workers need to possess a sufficient amount of information about the hazards involved. They cannot be said to assume the risk of performing dangerous work when they do not know what the risks are. Also, they cannot exercise the right to bargain for safer working conditions without access to the relevant information. Yet, employers have generally been reluctant to notify workers or their bargaining agents of dangerous conditions or to release documents in their possession. Oftentimes, hazards in the workplace are not known by the employer or the employee until after the harm has been done. In order for employers to be relieved of responsibility for injury or death in the workplace, though, it is necessary that employees have adequate information *at the time they make a choice.*

Second, the choice of employees must be truly free. When workers are forced to perform dangerous work for lack of acceptable alternatives, they cannot be said to assume the risk. For many people with few skills and limited mobility in economically depressed areas, the only work available is often in a local slaughter-house or textile mill, where they run great risks. Whether they are coerced into accepting work of this kind is a controversial question. Individuals are free in one sense to accept or decline whatever employment is available, but the alternatives of unemployment or work at poverty-level wages may be so unacceptable that people lack freedom of choice in any significant sense.

Risk and Coercion

In order to determine whether workers assume the risk of employment by their free choice, we need some account of the concept of coercion. A paradigm example is the mugger who says with a gun in hand, "Your money or your life." The "choice" offered by the mugger contains an undesirable set of alternatives that are imposed on the victim by a threat of dire consequences. A standard analysis of coercion that is suggested by this example involves two elements: (1) getting a person to choose an alternative that he or she does not want, and (2) issuing a threat to make the person worse off if he or she does not choose that alternative.

Consider the case of an employer who offers a worker who already holds a satisfactory job higher wages in return for taking on new duties involving a greater amount of risk.[19] The employer's offer is not coercive because there is no threat involved. The worker may welcome the offer, but declining it leaves the worker still in possession of an acceptable position. Is an employer acting like a mugger, however, when the offer of higher pay for more dangerous work is accompanied by the threat of dismissal? Is "Do this hazardous work or be fired!" like or unlike the "choice" offered by the mugger? The question is even more difficult when the only "threat" is not to hire a person. Is it coercive to say, "Accept this dangerous job or stay unemployed!" since the alternative of remaining out of work leaves the person in exactly the same position as before? Remaining unemployed, moreover, is unlike getting fired, in that it is not something that an employer inflicts on a person.

In order to answer these questions, the standard analysis of coercion needs to be supplemented by an account of what it means to issue a threat. A threat involves a stated intention of making a person worse off in some way. To fire a person from a job is usually to make that person worse off, but we would not say that an employer is coercing a worker by threatening dismissal for failure to perform the normal duties of a job. Similarly, we would not say that an employer is making a threat in not hiring a person who refuses to carry out the same normal duties. A person who turns down a job because the office is not provided with air conditioning, for example, is not being made worse off by the employer. So why would we say that a person who chooses to remain unemployed rather than work in a coal mine that lacks adequate ventilation is being coerced?

The answer of some philosophers is that providing employees with air conditioning is not morally required; however, maintaining a safe mine is. Whether a threat is coercive because it would make a person worse off can be determined only if there is some base line that answers the question, worse off compared with what?

Robert Nozick gives an example of an abusive slave owner who offers not to give a slave his daily beating if the slave will perform some disagreeable task the slave owner wants done.[20] Even though the slave might welcome the offer, it is still coercive, since the daily beating involves treating the slave in an immoral manner. For Nozick and others, what is *morally required* is the relevant base line for determining whether a person would be made worse off by a threatened course of action.[21]

It follows from this analysis that coercion is an inherently ethical concept that can be applied only after determining what is morally required in a given situation.[22] As a result, the argument that the assumption of risk by employees relieves employers of responsibility involves circular reasoning. Employers are freed from responsibility for workplace injuries on the ground that workers assume the risk of employment only if they are not coerced into accepting hazardous work. But whether workers are coerced depends on the right of employees to a safe and healthy workplace—and the obligation of employers to provide it.

Conclusion

In conclusion, the right of employees to a safe and healthy workplace cannot be justified merely by appealing to a right not to be injured or killed. The weakness of this argument lies in the difficulty of determining the extent to which employers are *responsible* for the harm that workers suffer as a result of occupational injuries and diseases. The argument applies only to dangers that are directly caused by the actions of employers; however, industrial accidents result from many causes, including the actions of co-workers and the affected workers themselves. The responsibility of employers is also problematical when the probability of harm from their actions is low. Moreover, the responsibility of employers is reduced insofar as employees voluntarily assume the risk inherent in employment. Whether the choice to accept hazardous work is voluntary, though, depends in part on difficult questions about the concept of coercion, which, on one standard analysis, can be applied only after the rights of employees in matters of occupational health and safety have been determined.

CASE 13.2   Whirlpool Corporation

The Whirlpool Corporation operates a plant in Marion, Ohio, for the assembly of household appliances.[23] Components for the appliances are carried throughout the plant by an elaborate system of overhead conveyors. To protect workers from the objects that occasionally fall from the conveyors, a huge wire mesh screen was installed approximately twenty feet above the floor. The screen is attached to an angle-iron frame suspended from the ceiling of the building. Maintenance employees at the plant spend several hours every week retrieving fallen objects from the screen. Their job also includes replacing paper that is spread on the screen to catch dripping grease from the conveyors, and occasionally they do maintenance work on the conveyors themselves. Workers are usually able to stand on the frame to perform these tasks, but occasionally it is necessary to step onto the screen.

In 1973, several workers fell partway through the screen, and one worker fell completely through to the floor of the plant below but survived. Afterward, Whirlpool began replacing the screen with heavier wire mesh, but on June 28, 1974, a maintenance employee fell to his death through a portion of the screen that had not been replaced. The company responded by making additional repairs and forbidding employees to stand on the angle-iron frame or step onto the screen. An alternative method for retrieving objects was devised using hooks.

Two maintenance employees at the Marion plant, Virgil Deemer and Thomas Cornwell, were still not satisfied. On July 7, 1974, they met with the maintenance supervisor at the plant to express their concern about the safety of the screen. At a meeting two days later with the plant safety director, they requested the name, address, and telephone number of a representative in the local office of the Occupational Safety and Health Administration. The safety director warned the men that they "had better stop and think about what they were doing," but he gave them the requested information. Deemer called the OSHA representative later that day to discuss the problem.

When Deemer and Cornwell reported for the night shift at 10:45 P.M. the next day, July 10, they were ordered by the foreman to perform routine maintenance duties above an old section of the screen. They refused, claiming that the work was unsafe; whereupon the foreman ordered the two employees to punch out. In addition to losing wages for the six hours they did not work that night, Deemer and Cornwell received written reprimands, which were placed in their personnel files.

THE RIGHT TO KNOW ABOUT AND REFUSE HAZARDOUS WORK

This case illustrates a cruel dilemma faced by many American workers. If they stay on the job and perform hazardous work, then they risk serious injury and even death. On the other hand, if they refuse to work as directed, then they risk disciplinary action, which can include loss of wages, unfavorable evaluation, demotion, and dismissal. Many people believe that it is unjust for workers to be put into the position of having to choose between safety and their job. Rather, employees ought to be able to refuse orders to perform hazardous work without fear of suffering adverse consequences. Even worse are situations in which workers face hazards of which they are unaware. Kept in the dark about dangers lurking in the workplace, employees have no reason to refuse hazardous work and are unable to take other steps to protect themselves.

Features of the Right to Know and Refuse

The right to refuse hazardous work is different from a right to a safe and healthy workplace. If it is unsafe to work above the old screen, as Deemer and Cornwell contended, then their right to a safe and healthy workplace was violated. A right to refuse hazardous work, however, is only one of several alternatives that workers have for securing the right to a safe and healthy workplace. Victims of racial or sexual discrimination, for example, also suffer a violation of their rights, but it does not follow that they have a right to disobey orders or to walk off the job in an effort to avoid discrimination. Other means are available for ending discrimination and for receiving compensation for the harm done. The same is true for the right to a safe and healthy workplace.

The right to know is actually an aggregation of several rights. Thomas O. McGarity classifies these rights by the correlative duties that they impose on employers. These are (1) the duty to *reveal* information already possessed; (2) the duty to *communicate* information about hazards through labeling, written communications, and training programs; (3) the duty to *seek out* existing information from the scientific literature and other sources; and (4) the duty to *produce* new information (for example, through animal testing) relevant to employee health.[24] Advocates of the right of workers to know need to specify which of these particular rights are included in their claim.

Disagreement also arises over questions about what information workers have a right to know and which workers have a right to know it. In particular, does the information that employers have a duty to reveal include information about the past exposure of workers to hazardous substances? And do employers have a duty to notify past as well as present employees? The issue at stake in these questions is a part of the "right to know" controversy commonly called *worker notification*.

The main argument for denying workers a right to refuse hazardous work is that such a right conflicts with the obligation of employees to obey all reasonable directives from an employer. An order for a worker to perform some especially dangerous task may not be reasonable, however. The foreman in the Whirlpool case, for example, was acting contrary to a company rule forbidding workers to step on the screen. Still, a common-law principle is that employees should obey even an improper order and file a grievance afterward, if a grievance procedure is in place, or seek whatever other recourse is available. The rationale for this principle is that employees may be mistaken about whether an order is proper, and chaos would result if employees could stop work until the question is decided. It is better for workers to obey now and correct any violation of their rights later.

The fatal flaw in this argument is that later may be too late. The right to a safe and healthy workplace, unlike the right not to be discriminated against, can effectively provide protection for workers only if violations of the right are prevented in the first place. Debilitating injury and death cannot be corrected later; neither can workers and their families ever be adequately compensated for a loss of this kind. The right to refuse hazardous work, therefore, is necessary for the existence of the right to a safe and healthy workplace.

The Justification for Refusing Hazardous Work

A right to a safe and healthy workplace is empty unless workers have a right in some circumstances to refuse hazardous work, but there is a tremendous amount of controversy over what these circumstances are. In the *Whirlpool* case, the Supreme Court cited two factors as relevant for justifying a refusal to work. These are (1) that the employee reasonably believes that the working conditions pose an imminent risk of death or serious injury, and (2) that the employee has reason to believe that the risk cannot be avoided by any less disruptive course of action. Employees have a right to refuse hazardous work, in other words, only as a last resort—when it is not possible to bring unsafe working conditions to the attention of the employer or to request an OSHA inspection. Also, the hazards that employees believe to exist must involve a high degree of risk of serious harm. Refusing to work because of a slight chance of minor injury is less likely to be justified. The fact that a number of workers had already fallen through the screen at the Whirlpool plant, for example, and that one had been killed strengthens the claim that the two employees had a right to refuse their foreman's order to step onto it.

The pivotal question, of course, is the proper standard for a reasonable belief. How much evidence should employees be required to have in order to be justified in refusing to work? Or should the relevant standard be the actual existence of a workplace hazard rather than the belief of employees, no matter how reasonable? A minimal requirement, which has been insisted on by the courts, is that employees act in *good faith.* Generally, acting in good faith means that employees have an honest belief that a hazard exists and that their only intention is to protect themselves from the hazard. The "good faith" requirement serves primarily to exclude refusals based on deliberately false charges of unsafe working conditions or on sabotage by employees. Whether a refusal is in good faith does not depend on the reasonableness or correctness of the employees' beliefs about the hazards in the workplace. Thus, employees who refuse an order to fill a tank with a dangerous chemical in the mistaken but sincere belief that a valve is faulty are acting in good faith, but employees who use the same excuse to conduct a work stoppage for other reasons are not acting in good faith, even if it should turn out that the valve is faulty.

Three standards are commonly used for determining whether good faith refusals are justified. One is the *subjective* standard, which requires only that employees have evidence that they sincerely regard as sufficient for their belief that a hazard exists or that most workers in their situation would regard as sufficient. At the opposite extreme is the *objective* standard. This standard requires evidence that experts regard as sufficient to establish the existence of a hazard. In between these two is the *reasonable person* standard, which requires that the evidence be strong enough to persuade a reasonable person that a hazard exists.

The subjective standard provides the greatest protection for worker health and safety. Employees cannot be expected to have full knowledge of the hazards facing them in the workplace. They may not be told what chemicals they are using, for example, or what exposure levels are safe for these chemicals. Safe exposure levels for the chemicals may not even have been scientifically determined. Employees may also not have the means at the moment to measure the levels to which they are exposed. Yet, the objective standard forces employees to bear the consequences if their beliefs about the hazards present in the workplace cannot be substantiated. The reasonable person standard is less exacting, since it requires only that employees exercise reasonable judgment. Still, this standard places a strong burden of proof on workers who have to make a quick assessment under difficult circumstances. A wrong decision can result in the loss of a job or possibly the loss of a worker's life.

On the other hand, the subjective standard allows employees to make decisions that are ordinarily the province of management. Usually management is better informed about hazards in the workplace, along with other aspects of the work to be performed, and so their judgment should generally prevail. To allow workers to shut down production on the basis of unsubstantiated beliefs, and thereby to substitute their uninformed judgment for that of management, is likely to result in many costly mistakes. The subjective standard creates no incentive for workers to be cautious in refusing hazardous work because the cost is borne solely by the company. The reasonable-person standard, therefore, which places a moderate burden of proof on employees, is perhaps the best balance of the competing considerations.

The Justification of a Right to Know

Unlike the right to refuse hazardous work, the right to know about workplace hazards is not necessary for the right to a safe and healthy workplace. This latter right is fully protected as long as employers succeed in ridding the workplace of significant hazards. Some argue that the right to know is still an effective, if not an absolutely essential, means for securing the right to a safe and healthy workplace. Others maintain, however, that the right to know is not dependent for its justification on the right to a safe and healthy workplace; that is, even employees who are adequately protected by their employers against occupational injury and disease still have a right to be told what substances they are handling, what dangers it poses, what precautions to take, and so on.

The most common argument for the right to know is one based on autonomy. This argument begins with the premise that autonomous individuals are those who are able to exercise free choice in matters that affect their welfare most deeply.[25] Sometimes this premise is expressed by saying that autonomous individuals are those who are able to *participate* in decision making about these matters. One matter that profoundly affects the welfare of workers is the amount of risk that they assume in the course of earning a living. Autonomy requires, therefore, that workers be free to avoid hazardous work, if they so choose, or have the opportunity to accept greater risks in return for higher pay, if that is their choice. In order to choose freely, however, or to participate in decision making, it is necessary to possess relevant information. And in the matter of risk assumption, the relevant information includes knowledge of the hazards present in the workplace. Workers can be autonomous, therefore, only if they have a right to know.

In response, employers maintain that they can protect workers from hazards more effectively than workers can themselves without informing workers of the nature of those hazards. Such a paternalistic concern, even when it is sincere and well-founded, is incompatible, however, with a respect for the autonomy of workers. A similar argument is sometimes used to justify paternalism in the doctor-patient relation. For a doctor to conceal information from a patient even in cases where exclusive reliance on the doctor's greater training and experience would result in better medical care is now generally regarded as unjustified. If paternalism is morally unacceptable in the doctor-patient relation, where doctors have an obligation to act in the patient's interest, then it is all the more suspect in the employer-employee relation, where employers have no such obligation.[26]

Although autonomy is a value, it does not follow that employers have an obligation to further it in their dealings with employees. The autonomy of buyers in market transactions is also increased by having more information, but the sellers of a product are not generally required to provide this information except when concealment constitutes fraud.[27] The gain of autonomy for employees must be balanced, moreover, against the not inconsiderable cost to employers of implementing a "right to know" policy in the workplace. In addition to the direct cost of assembling information, attaching warning labels, training workers, and so on, there are also indirect costs. Employees who are aware of the risk they are taking are more likely to demand higher wages or else safer working conditions. They are more likely to avail themselves of workers' compensation benefits and to sue employers over occupational injury and disease. Finally, companies are concerned about the loss of valuable trade secrets that could occur from informing workers about the hazards of certain substances.

An alternative to a right to know policy that respects the autonomy of both parties is to allow bargaining over information. Thomas O. McGarity has described this alternative in the following way:

> Because acquiring information costs money, employees desiring information about workplace risks should be willing to pay the employer (in reduced wages) or someone else to produce or gather the relevant information. A straightforward economic analysis would suggest that employees would be willing to pay for health and safety information up to the point at which the value in wage negotiations of the last piece of information purchased equaled the cost of that additional information.[28]

Although promising in theory, this alternative is not practical. It creates a disincentive for employers, who possess most of the information, to yield any of it without some concession by employees, even when it could be provided at little or no cost. Bargaining is feasible for large unions with expertise in safety matters, but reliance on it would leave members of other unions and nonunionized workers without adequate means of protection. In the absence of a market for information, neither employers nor employees would have a basis for determining the value of information in advance of negotiations. Finally, there are costs associated with using the bargaining process to decide any matter—what economists call "transaction costs"—and these are apt to be quite high in negotiations over safety issues. It is unlikely, therefore, that either autonomy or worker health and safety would be well served by the alternative of bargaining over matters of occupational health and safety.

Utilitarian Arguments for a Right to Know

There are two arguments for the right to know as a means to greater worker health and safety. Both are broadly utilitarian in character. One argument is based on the plausible assumption that workers who are aware of hazards in the workplace will be better equipped to protect themselves. Warning labels or rules requiring protective clothing and respirators are more likely to be effective when workers fully appreciate the nature and extent of the risks they are taking. Also, merely revealing information about hazardous substances in the workplace is not apt to be effective without extensive training in the procedures for handling them safely and responding to accidents. Finally, workers who are aware of the consequences of exposure to hazardous substances will also be more likely to spot symptoms of occupational diseases and seek early treatment.

The second utilitarian argument is offered by economists who hold that overall welfare is best achieved by allowing market forces to determine the level of acceptable risk. In a free market, wages are determined in part by the willingness of workers to accept risks in return for wages. Employers can attract a sufficient supply of workers to perform hazardous work either by spending money to make the workplace safer, thereby reducing the risks, or by increasing wages to compensate workers for the greater risks. The choice is determined by the marginal utility of each kind of investment. Thus, an employer will make the workplace safer up to the point that the last dollar spent equals the increase in wages that would otherwise be required to induce workers to accept the risks. At that point, workers indicate their preference for accepting the remaining risks rather than foregoing a loss of wages in return for a safer workplace.

Unlike the autonomy argument, in which workers bargain over risk information, this argument proposes that workers bargain over the trade-off between risks and wages. In order for a free market to determine this trade-off in a way that achieves overall welfare, it is necessary for workers to have a sufficient amount of information about the hazard in the workplace. Thomas O. McGarity has expressed this point as follows:

> A crucial component of the free market model of wage and risk determination is its assumption that workers are fully informed about the risks that they face as they bargain over wages. To the extent that risks are unknown to employees, they will undervalue overall workplace risks in wage negotiations. The result will be lower wages and an inadequate incentive to employers to install health and safety devices. In addition, to the extent that employees can avoid risks by taking action, uninformed employees will fail to do so. Society will then underinvest in wages and risk prevention, and overall societal wealth will decline. Moreover, a humane society is not likely to require diseased or injured workers to suffer without proper medical attention. In many cases, society will pick up the tab. . . .[29]

Although these two utilitarian arguments provide strong support for the right to know, they are both open to the objection that there might be more efficient means, such as more extensive OSHA regulation, for securing the goal of worker health and safety. Could the resources devoted to complying with a right-to-know law, for example, be better spent on formulating and enforcing more stringent standards on permissible exposure limits and on developing technologies to achieve these standards? And could the cost of producing, gathering, and disseminating information be better borne by a government agency than by individual employers? These are difficult empirical questions for which conclusive evidence is largely lacking.

The Problem of Trade Secrets

One issue that remains to be addressed is the protection of trade secrets. Occasionally, information about the chemical composition of the substances used in industrial processes cannot be disclosed to workers without compromising the ability of a company to maintain a legally protected trade secret. When this is the case, is it justifiable to place limits on the right to know? These two rights—the right of workers to know about the hazards of substances that they use and the right of employers to maintain trade secrets—are not wholly incompatible, however. So it may be possible to implement the right to know in a way that maximizes the amount of information available to workers while at the same time minimizing the risk of exposing trade secrets.

Before limiting the right of employees to know, we need to be sure, first, that a genuine trade secret is involved and that it cannot be protected by any less restrictive means, such as obtaining a patent. Also, employers do not have a right to conceal *all* information connected with a trade secret but only the portion that cannot be revealed without jeopardy. Even when an employer is justified in not disclosing the chemical identity of a critical ingredient in a formula or a process, for example, there may be no justification for not providing workers with information about some of the physical characteristics and special hazards of that ingredient. Finally, information can sometimes be revealed in ways that preserve secrecy. It might be possible, for example, to reveal information about hazardous substances to union representatives or to the employees' own private physicians under a pledge of confidentiality without endangering valuable trade secrets.

The Problem of Reproductive Hazards

Hazardous substances pose a threat not only to workers but to their offspring. Pregnant women who are exposed to certain chemicals in the workplace run an increased risk of spontaneous abortion, miscarriage, and stillbirth, and they are more likely to produce children with birth defects. One common workplace substance that is know to damage the reproductive capacity of women and inflict harm on a fetus in the womb is lead, a fact that caused Johnson Controls, Inc., to consider the problem of lead exposure among its women employees.[30]

Based in Milwaukee, Wisconsin, Johnson Controls is the largest manufacturer of automobile batteries for the United States replacement market. In 1977, the company informed women in the lead battery division of the hazards of lead and asked them to sign a statement that they had been told of the risks of having a child while exposed to lead in the workplace. Between 1979 and 1983, however, eight women with blood lead levels in excess of 30 micrograms per deciliter became pregnant. In response, the company changed its policy in 1982 to exclude fertile women from all jobs where lead is present. Specifically, the policy stated:

> It is [Johnson Controls'] policy that women who are pregnant or who are capable of bearing children will not be placed into jobs involving lead exposure or which could expose them to lead through the exercise of job bidding, bumping, transfer or promotion rights.

The policy defined women "capable of bearing children" as "all women except those whose inability to bear children is medically documented."

In April 1984, a class action suit was filed, charging that Johnson Controls' fetal-protection policy violated the Title VII prohibition against sex discrimination. The policy is discriminatory, the employees complained, because it singled out fertile women for exclusion, when evidence indicates that lead also poses a hazard to the reproductive capacities of men as well. Among the employees suing were a woman who had chosen to be sterilized in order to keep her job, a fifty-year-old divorcé who had been forced to accept a demotion because of the policy, and a man who had requested a leave of absence in order to reduce his blood lead level before becoming a father.

The problem of reproductive hazards puts companies such as Johnson Controls in a very difficult position. On the one hand, fetal protection policies are open to the charge of being discriminatory because they limit the job opportunities of fertile women while ignoring the substantial evidence of risk to men. Employees also claim that the policies are adopted by employers as a quick and cheap alternative to cleaning up the workplace. On the other hand, employers have a responsibility not to inflict harm, and this obligation extends, presumably, to the fetus of a pregnant employee. Asking employees to sign waivers releasing a company from responsibility is no solution, however, because employees cannot waive the right of their future children to sue for prenatal injuries. Employers seem to face a choice, therefore, between discriminating against their female employees and allowing fetuses to be harmed, with potentially ruinous consequences for the company.

The Issue of Who Decides

A number of employers have resolved this dilemma by adopting fetal-protection policies similar to that of Johnson Controls. However, many women are claiming the right to decide for themselves whether to work at jobs that involve reproductive risks. Although they have a strong maternal interest in the health of an unborn child, they are also concerned about their own economic well-being and want to be free to choose the level of risk to themselves and their offspring that they feel is appropriate. Ronald Bayer has observed that these responses to the problem of reproductive hazards involve a reversal of the usual positions of employers and employees:

> Typically, workers and their representatives have pressed management for the most extensive reductions in exposure levels to toxic substances. Further, they have argued that uncertainty requires the most cautious assumptions about the possibility of harmful consequences. Corporations have responded by arguing that a risk-free environment is chimerical and that uncertainty requires a willingness to tolerate lev-

els of exposure that have not been proven harmful. Yet in relation to reproductive hazards, and especially fetal danger, it is labor that has tended to view with some skepticism the data on potential risk. Corporations, on the other hand, have adopted an almost alarmist posture.[31]

This reversal is not hard to understand. Protecting unborn children from harmful chemicals in the workplace and coping with the consequences of occupationally related birth defects involve substantial costs. The struggle between employers and employees is over who will exercise the choice about assuming the risk of reproductive hazards and who will bear the burden of responsibility. Fetal-protection policies are adopted by corporate managers who assume the right to make crucial decisions about how the fetus of an employee will be protected. The cost of these decisions is borne largely by women, however, who find that their economic opportunities are sharply limited. According to estimates by the federal government in 1980, at least 100,000 jobs were closed to women because of fetal-protection policies already in place,[32] and as many as 20 million jobs would be closed if women were excluded from all work involving reproductive hazards.[33] The women most affected by the reduction in the number of jobs available are those with the fewest skills and the least education, who are already near the bottom of the economic ladder. Because they bear the heavy cost, women argue that they should be the ones to make the decisions involved in protecting their own offspring.

Are Women Forced to Undergo Sterilization?

The debate over fetal protection policies takes on a tragic dimension when women undergo sterilization for fear of losing a job. When five women were laid off by the Allied Chemical Company in 1977 because of concern for fetal damage by a substance known as Fluorocarbon 22, two of them underwent surgical sterilization in order to return to work. Shortly afterward, the company determined that Fluorocarbon 22 posed no threat to a developing fetus, so the women's loss of fertility was needless.[34] When the American Cyanamid Company announced the adoption of a fetal protection policy at a plant in Willow Island, West Virginia, in 1978, five women between the ages of 26 and 43 submitted to sterilization in order to retain jobs that involved exposure to lead chromate, an ingredient of paint pigments. Two years later, American Cyanamid stopped producing paint pigments because of a decreased demand for the lead-based product.[35]

Certainly, no person, man or woman, should be put in the position of having to choose between holding a job and being able to bear children unless there is no acceptable alternative. Employers insist that they do not encourage women to take the drastic step of undergoing sterilization. But they also maintain that they have no control over such an intimate decision by employees or women seeking employment and that there is no reason to exclude women who undergo sterilization from jobs involving exposure to reproductive hazards. According to critics of fetal-protection policies, however, companies that exclude fertile women from such jobs effectively force sterilization on those who have no other satisfactory employment opportunities. The problem is one of intentions versus results. Although there is no intention to force women to become sterile, employers create situations that have precisely this result.

Issues in the Charge of Sex Discrimination

Whether employers have a right to adopt fetal-protection policies depends in part on whether excluding fertile women from certain jobs is a form of sex discrimination. The point at issue is not whether women are vulnerable to reproductive hazards (they certainly are) but whether men are vulnerable as well. If they are, then it is discriminatory for employers to adopt a policy that applies only to women and not to men. In order to evaluate the scientific evidence, it is necessary to understand more about the nature of reproductive hazards.

Substances harmful to a fetus are of three kinds. First, there are *fetotoxins*. These are toxic substances that affect a fetus in the same way that they affect an adult, although a fetus, because of the smaller size, may be harmed by exposure to substances below the permissible limits for adults. *Teratogens*, the second kind of substances, interfere with the normal development of the fetus *in utero*. These may pose no danger to a fully developed person outside the womb. Finally, some substances are *mutagens*, which damage genetic material before conception. The effects of fetotoxins, teratogens, and mutagens are similar. They include spontaneous abortion, miscarriage, stillbirth, and congenital defects. Some defects, such as deformities, are visible at birth, whereas others may be latent conditions that manifest themselves later, as in the case of childhood cancers.

Fetotoxins and teratogens (many substances are both) must be transmitted to the fetus through the mother. This can occur, however, when the father is exposed to a hazardous substance in the workplace. Studies show that the nonworking wives of men exposed to lead, beryllium, benzene, vinyl chloride, and anesthetic gases, for example, have higher-than-normal rates of miscarriage. Children of fathers exposed to asbestos and benzene are shown in studies to have a greater incidence of cancer. The most likely explanation for these correlations is that the hazardous substances are brought home on the father's body or on his clothing and other belongings.

The main reproductive hazard to men is posed by mutagenic substances, since these are capable of altering the chromosomal structure of both the ovum and the sperm. Although the mutagenic effect of many suspected substances is not firmly established, some researchers theorize that most teratogens are also mutagens and that there is a strong connection between the three phenomena: teratogenesis, mutagenesis, and carcinogenesis (that is, the development of cancers). The reason is that all three operate on the cellular level by altering the DNA molecule.[36] If these relationships exist, then virtually any substance that poses a reproductive hazard to a woman is also hazardous to the reproductive capacity of a man and ultimately the health of a fetus.

The research on reproductive hazards, although inconclusive, suggests that fetal harm can result when either parent is exposed to hazardous substances. If that is in fact the case, then fetal-protection policies should apply to both sexes. Wendy W. Williams, argues:

> There is simply no basis for resolving doubts about the evidence by applying a policy to women but not to men on the unsubstantiated generalization that the fetus is placed at greatest risk by workplace exposure of the pregnant woman. Indeed, the limited scientific evidence available requires that doubts about the evidence be resolved in favor of an assumption of equal jeopardy.[37]

Fetal-protection policies are also discriminatory if they are applied only to women who occupy traditionally male jobs and not to women in female-dominated lines of work where the hazard is just as great. Some critics charge that fetal protection policies have been used to discriminate by reinforcing job segregation through their selective application to women with jobs in areas formerly dominated by men, while the reproductive risks to other women have been ignored.

American Cyanamid, for example, identified five substances in use at the Willow Island plant as suspected fetotoxins and notified twenty-three women in production jobs that they were exposed to reproductive hazards and would be transferred if they became pregnant. However, the fetal-protection policy was applied only to the nine women who held comparatively high paying jobs in the paint pigments department, which had formerly been reserved for men. Barbara Cantwell, one of the four women who submitted to sterilization in order to retain her job, remarked, "I smelled harassment when the problem was suddenly narrowed to the area where women worked."[38]

Among the women in traditionally female lines of work who are exposed to reproductive hazards are nurses in operating rooms, who have twice as many miscarriages as other women because of anesthetic gases; female X-ray technicians, who are twice as likely to bear defective children; and women who work in dry-cleaning operations, where petroleum-based solvents are used.[39] Yet there has been no movement in the industries employing these women to implement fetal protection policies similar to those in the male-dominated chemical, petroleum, and heavy-manufacturing industries.

Defenses to the Charge of Sex Discrimination

Distinctions based on sex are not always discriminatory. They are morally permissible if they have an adequate justification, and Title VII of the 1964 Civil Rights Act recognizes this by allowing employers two defenses. These are the claims that a sex-based policy serves a proper business purpose (the business necessity defense) and that a person's sex is a bona fide occupational qualification (the BFOQ defense). A bona fide occupational qualification is defined as a qualification "reasonably necessary to the normal operation" of a business. As we saw in Chapter 8 on discrimination, this exception has been narrowly limited by the courts. The business necessity defense is less stringent. Generally, an employer must establish that a policy is needed for achieving a proper business objective in a safe and efficient manner and that the objective cannot reasonably be achieved by less discriminatory means.

The lower courts ruled that the fetal-protection policy adopted by Johnson Controls was permissible under Title VII. The Court of Appeals for the Seventh Circuit held that the policy passed a three-step business necessity defense because the company had established: (1) there is a substantial risk to a fetus, (2) this risk occurs only through women, and (3) there is no less discriminatory alternative. Although not required to do so, the court addressed the question of whether sex is a BFOQ in this case and concluded that it is. The crucial phrase in the BFOQ defense "reasonably necessary for the normal operation" of a business has been interpreted by the courts to include "ethical, legal, and business concerns about the effects of an employer's activities on third parties." Simply put, a qualification is a BFOQ if it is necessary for conducting business without greatly endangering other people. Under this interpretation, the courts had ruled that age was a BFOQ for being an airline flight engineer because the safety of passengers depended on that person's performance.[40] By the same line of reasoning, sex is a BFOQ because a woman working in a battery factory is liable to expose a third party—namely, a fetus—to harm.

The U.S. Supreme Court in a landmark 9–0 decision overruled the lower courts and held Johnson Controls' fetal protection policy to be discriminatory in violation of Title VII. The policy is discriminatory for the reason that it excludes women based only on their childbearing capacity and ignores the risk to men. Thus, the policy does not protect "effectively and equally" the offspring of all employees. Further, the Court ruled that sex is not a BFOQ in this case. All evidence indicates that fertile and even pregnant women are as capable of manufacturing batteries as anyone else. According to the majority opinion, the claim that the safety of third parties ought to be taken into consideration is inapplicable because this exception concerns only the ability of an employee to perform a job in a safe manner, and a fetus, in this case, is not endangered by the manner in which the job is performed. The workers at Johnson Controls, in other words, are not manufacturing batteries in ways that are unsafe for children. "No one can disregard the possibility of injury to future children," the opinion states, but the BFOQ defense "is not so broad that it transforms this deep social concern into an essential aspect of batterymaking."[41]

Remaining Issues

The decision in *Johnson Controls* clearly establishes that fetal-protection policies constitute illegal sex discrimination, and the ruling is a victory for working women. It gives women the right not to have their job opportunities limited because of their ability to conceive and bear children. Still, two important issues remain. One is how to balance this right with the desirable social goal of fetal protection. The other is whether the right established in *Johnson Controls* conflicts with another desirable goal, namely, protecting corporations against liability in the event that a person is harmed before birth from exposure to reproductive hazards in the workplace.

The ruling in *Johnson Controls* does not leave the unborn without protection. In the words of the Court, "Decisions about the welfare of future children must be left to the parents who conceive, bear, support, and raise them rather than to the employers who hire those parents." There is little reason to believe that employees are any less concerned than employers about the well-being of their offspring. Indeed, they have a far more compelling interest. This is not to say that some parents-to-be (both men and women) will not continue to choose work that exposes them to reproductive hazards. However, they, rather than their employer, will be making the crucial decision about the reasonableness of that choice. Employees may decide—all things considered—that the risk is worth the price. Parents also choose where to live with their children, thereby deciding whether they can afford to live farther away from sources of pollution and other hazards. Because parents in our society make choices in other matters that bear on the welfare of their children, why should an exception be made in the case of reproductive hazards? What is unfortunate is that any parents are required to choose between making a living and protecting their children.

Whether the *Johnson Controls* ruling exposes corporations to heavy tort liability is an open question. The view expressed in the majority opinion is that the prospect is "remote at best," provided that employers: (1) fully inform employees of the risks they face and (2) do not act negligently. If employees are to make rational choices in cases of exposure to reproductive hazards, then they must have sufficient information, which employers have an obligation to provide. Employers can protect themselves from suits by cleaning up the workplace and reducing the risk as much as possible. The issue of tort liability, then, is hypothetical but nonetheless important for that reason.

CASE 13.3   Employees as Guinea Pigs

Roger Olson has a lot of sympathy for guinea pigs.[42] The McDonnell Douglas Corporation's material support analyst was among those who volunteered to participate in evacuation drills on a new jetliner model being tested in Long Beach, California. A toe fracture was the worst that had happened in past drills, they were told. But when 410 people surged on command toward exits of the pitch-black MD-11, chaos resulted. Mr. Olson, crashing into a mass of bodies as he slid down the inflatable escape chute, felt his left ankle snap. "I tried to stand up, but I couldn't," he recalls.

During the now-notorious tests last October [1991], fifty people were hurt, including seven with broken bones and one sixty-year-old woman who was left paralyzed, perhaps permanently, from the neck down. The experience has shocked aircraft makers into reconsidering the practice of using people in such testing; McDonnell Douglas and Boeing Company both are clamoring for government permission to use computer simulations in many of the tests.

But the ill-fated drills do raise questions about whether *any* use of employees in product testing—still fairly common among automakers and some other manufacturers and consumer product companies—makes sense. "To just bring people off the production line or the sales staff for product testing is a bad idea," says Mark Rothstein, a University of Houston law professor and specialist in occupational-health and employment law. And employee morale really suffers if there's an accident. Employees "would say things like, 'Hey, did you hear about Harry? He volunteered for a test, and he's in the hospital now.' " Safety issues aside, critics suggest that asking employees to raise their hands for product tests implies subtle pressure. "When it comes time for your promotion, workers will have to believe it will be taken into consideration. And it probably is," says Sidney Wolfe, director of the health research group of Public Citizen, a consumer advocacy group active in workplace-safety issues. And David Stewart, a University of Southern California marketing professor specializing in consumer behavior, believes that in any event workers may be poor test participants, in part because of their lack of objectivity. "They aren't typical of how the average consumer might interact with the product," he says.

However, Bruce Lee, Western regional director for the United Auto Workers, which opposes McDonnell Douglas's new stance against most employee tests, says: "Using employees makes a lot of sense. People who make the products might be able to improve the system they are trying to test." A General Motors Corporation spokesman says GM uses employees "all over the place" for human-factors testing, and Ford Motor Company's human-factors division is responsible for a number of product changes, a Ford spokesman says. It's considered to be "just part of your job," the spokesman says. "We always figure that you're happy to help out the company." In fact, he adds, Ford secretaries are often asked to drive in cross-country testing, because "you don't always want the opinion of engineers."

While some auto-industry testing with employees is rather mundane, contributions to dashboard and seat-belt design can have positive safety implications. Chrysler Corporation's Jeep development team, while leaving the toughest safety tests to dummies and professional test drivers, maintains a database containing names and anatomical descriptions of scores of volunteers who help test various Jeep designs. Tall and short employees are especially prized for testing, although Craig Winn, executive engineer for Jeep development, shrugs off the idea that such individuals might be pressured to participate because of physique. "People really enjoy participating beyond their basic job function," he says. And employees are drawn to the idea that "someone really cares where I think the steering wheel should be."

NOTES

1. MAY MEYERS, et al., "Benzene (benzol) Poisoning in the Rotogravure Printing in New York City," *Journal of Industrial Hygiene and Toxicology* (October 1939), 395–420. The study is cited in JOSEPH A. PAGE and MARY-WIN O'BRIEN, *Bitter Wages* (New York: Grossman, 1973), 37–38.

2. The details in this case are contained in *Industrial Union Dept., AFL-CIO* v. *American Petroleum Institute*, 448 U.S. 607 (1980).

3. The estimate is made in W. J. NICHOLSON, "Failure to Regulate—Asbestos: A Lethal Legacy," U.S. Congress, Committee of Government Operations, 1980.

4. Much of the following description of health and safety problems is adapted from NICHOLAS ASKOUNES ASHFORD, *Crisis in the Workplace: Occupational Disease and Injury* (Cambridge: MIT Press, 1976), chap. 3.

5. For a review of the controversy that discredits the industry claim, see ROBERT H. HALL, "The Truth about Brown Lung," *Business and Society Review*, 40 (Winter 1981), 15–20.

6. For a critical assessment of state efforts, see PAGE and O'BRIEN, *Bitter Wages*, 69–85.

7. Sec. 5(a)(1). This clause is the subject of much legal analysis. See RICHARD S. MORLEY, "The General

Duty Clause of the Occupational Safety and Health Act of 1970," *Harvard Law Review*, 86 (1973), 988–1005.

8. PATRICIA H. WERHANE, *Persons, Rights, and Corporations* (Englewood Cliffs, NJ: Prentice Hall, 1985), 132.

9. MARK MACCARTHY, "A Review of Some Normative and Conceptual Issues in Occupational Safety and Health," *Environmental Affairs*, 9 (1981), 782–83.

10. The case is related in STEPHEN G. MINTER, "Are Prosecutors Stepping in Where OSHA Fears to Tread?" *Occupational Hazards*, 49 (September 1987), 101–2.

11. These two factors are discussed by Alan Gewirth, who cites them as exceptions to his claim that persons have a right not to have cancer inflicted on them by the actions of others. See ALAN GEWIRTH, "Human Rights and the Prevention of Cancer," in *Human Rights: Essays on Justification and Applications* (Chicago: University of Chicago Press, 1982), 181–96. For an evaluation, see ERIC VON MAGNUS, "Rights and Risks," *Journal of Business Ethics*, 2 (February 1983), 23–26.

12. See H. L. A. HART and A. M. HONORE, *Causation in the Law* (Oxford: Oxford University Press, 1959), 64–76.

13. U.S. Code 21, 348(c)(3).

14. *Federal Register*, vol. 39, no. 20 (January 29, 1974), 3758. Emphasis added.

15. GEWIRTH, "Human Rights and the Prevention of Cancer," 189.

16. *American Textile Manufacturers Institute Inc. v. Raymond J. Donovan, Secretary of Labor*, 452 U.S. 490 (1981).

17. For an argument of this kind, see TIBOR R. MACHAN, "Human Rights, Workers' Rights, and the Right to Occupational Safety," in GERTRUDE EZORSKY, ed., *Moral Rights in the Workplace* (Albany: State University of New York Press, 1987), 45–50.

18. W. KIP VISCUSI, *Risk by Choice* (Cambridge: Harvard University Press, 1983), 80.

19. The following argument is adapted from NORMAN DANIELS, "Does OSHA Protect Too Much?" in EZORSKY, *Moral Rights in the Workplace*, 51–60.

20. ROBERT NOZICK, "Coercion," in SIDNEY MORGENBESSER, PATRICK SUPPES, and MORTON WHITE, eds., *Philosophy, Science and Method* (New York: St. Martin's Press, 1969), 440–72.

21. In considering whether a person voluntarily chooses undesirable work when all of the alternatives are even worse as a result of the actions of other people, Nozick says that the answer "depends upon whether these others had the right to act as they did." ROBERT NOZICK, *Anarchy, State, and Utopia* (New York: Basic Books, 1974), 262.

22. Some philosophers have attempted to give a morally neutral analysis of coercion that involves no assumptions about what is morally required. See DAVID ZIMMERMAN, "Coercive Wage Offers," *Philosophy and Public Affairs*, 10 (1981), 121–45.

23. Information on this case is contained in *Whirlpool Corporation v. Marshall*, 445 U.S. 1 (1980).

24. THOMAS O. MCGARITY, "The New OSHA Rules and the Worker's Right to Know," *The Hastings Center Report*, 14 (August 1984), 38–39.

25. For a version of this argument see MCGARITY, "The New OSHA Rules and the Worker's Right to Know." Much of the following discussion of the autonomy argument is adapted from this article.

26. This point is made in RUTH R. FADEN and TOM L. BEAUCHAMP, "The Right to Risk Information and the Right to Refuse Health Hazards in the Workplace," in TOM L. BEAUCHAMP and NORMAN E. BOWIE, eds., *Ethical Theory and Business*, 4th ed. (Englewood Cliffs, NJ: Prentice Hall, 1993), 205.

27. This exception suggests a further argument for the right to know based on fairness. Employers who knowingly place workers at risk are taking unfair advantage of the workers' ignorance. See MCGARITY, "The New OSHA Rules and the Worker's Right to Know," 40.

28. MCGARITY, "The New OSHA Rules and the Worker's Right to Know," 40.

29. MCGARITY, "The New OSHA Rules and the Worker's Right to Know," 41.

30. *United Automobile Workers, et al. v. Johnson Controls, Inc.*, U.S. Supreme Court, No. 89–1215. See also LINDA GREENHOUSE, "Court Backs Right of Women to Jobs with Health Risks," *New York Times*, 21 March 1991, sec. 1, p. 1; and STEPHEN WERMIEL, "Justices Bar 'Fetal Protection' Policies," *Wall Street Journal*, 21 March 1991, B1.

31. RONALD BAYER, "Women, Work, and Reproductive Hazards," *The Hastings Center Report*, 12 (October 1982), 18.

32. WENDY W. WILLIAMS, "Firing the Woman to Protect the Fetus: The Reconciliation of Fetal Protection with Employment Opportunity Goals under Title VII," *The Georgetown Law Journal*, 69 (1981), 647.

33. Equal Employment Opportunity Commission and Office of Federal Contract Compliance Programs, "Interpretive Guidelines on Employment Discrimination and Reproductive Hazards," *Federal Register* (February 1, 1980), 7514.

34. GAIL BRONSON, "Issue of Fetal Damage Stirs Women Workers at Chemical Plants," *Wall Street Journal*, 9 February 1979, A1.

35. "Company and Union in Dispute as Women Undergo Sterilization," *New York Times*, 4 January 1979, sec. 1, p. 1; "4 Women Assert Jobs Were Linked to Sterilization," *New York Times*, 5 January 1979, sec. 1, p. 1; PHILIP SHABECOFF, "Job Threats to Workers' Fertility Emerging as Civil Liberties Issue," *New York Times*, 15 January 1979, sec. 1, p. 1; and BRONSON, "Issue of Fetal Damage Stirs Women Workers at Chemical Plants."

36. See WILLIAMS, "Firing the Woman to Protect the Fetus," 659–60.

37. WILLIAMS, "Firing the Woman to Protect the Fetus," 663.

38. Cited in BRONSON, "Issue of Fetal Damage Stirs Women Workers at Chemical Plants."

39. These examples are cited in LOIS VANDERWAERDT, "Resolving the Conflict between Hazardous Substances in the Workplace and Equal Employment Opportunity," *American Business Law Journal*, 21 (1983), 172–73.

40. *Western Airlines* v. *Criswell*, 472 U.S. 400 (1985).

41. The Supreme Court did not consider the business necessity defense, since only the BFOQ defense was held to be applicable in this case. The reason is that the fetal-protection policy adopted by Johnson Controls was considered by the court to be "facial" discrimination, which is to say that a distinction was made explicitly on the basis of sex, and "facial" discrimination requires the more demanding BFOQ defense rather than the weaker business necessity defense.

42. SONIA L. NAZARIO and ASRA Q. NOMANI, "Use of Staff Guinea Pigs Causes Squeals about Safety of Firms' Product Testing," *Wall Street Journal*, 31 December 1991, B1, B4. Reprinted by permission of *Wall Street Journal*. Copyright 1991 Dow Jones & Company, Inc. All rights reserved worldwide.

14

Corporate Social Responsibility

CASE 14.1   Campbell Soup Company

In 1985, the Campbell Soup Company faced a challenge from an Ohio-based group that was fighting for increased wages and improved living and working conditions for migrant farmworkers.[1] The group, known as the Farm Labor Organizing Committee (FLOC), was threatening to disrupt the annual shareholders' meeting with a demonstration in support of their cause. Since 1979, the company had been the target of a nationwide boycott of its products, instigated by FLOC. Under the dynamic leadership of Baldemar Velasquez, the group gained support for the boycott from the major Protestant and Catholic church organizations in Ohio and from many influential national groups. In July 1983, about one hundred members and supporters of FLOC marched 560 miles from FLOC headquarters in Toledo, Ohio, to the headquarters of the Campbell Soup Company in Camden, New Jersey, to dramatize the boycott and to press their demand for a labor contract.

At the urging of the National Council of Churches, which had been persuaded by FLOC to intervene in the dispute, representatives from the two sides sat down and negotiated an agreement that set up procedures for conducting elections to determine whether the farmworkers wanted to be represented by FLOC. The agreement was signed in May 1985, and the voting took place in September, during the first month of the tomato harvest. The election process broke down, however, amid allegations by FLOC of unfair labor practices, including charges that the growers brought in local laborers on the day of the election and prevented some migrant farmworkers from voting. The possibility now existed that the National Council of

Churches would support the boycott, a move that would generate considerable adverse publicity for Campbell Soup. And FLOC's plan to stage a demonstration at the upcoming shareholders' meeting would create additional bad press.

The plight of the migrant farmworkers is truly deplorable. Many live in crowded camps, without electricity, fresh drinking water, or adequate toilets. Poor nutrition, communicable diseases, and constant exposure to pesticides result in a high infant mortality rate and a life expectancy twenty-five years below the average. FLOC claimed that laborers received an average hourly wage of less than $2.00, although Campbell Soup disputed this figure and insisted they were paid at least the minimum wage of $3.35 an hour. In addition, migrant farmworkers generally lack health insurance and the other benefits that most American workers take for granted.

When the National Labor Relations Act was passed in 1935, giving most workers the right to organize and engage in collective bargaining, farm laborers were deliberately excluded. So the company was under no legal obligation to recognize the existence of FLOC. The migrant farmworkers, moreover, were not Campbell employees but were hired by independent growers, who held contracts with the company to devote a specified number of acres to tomatoes that were sold to the company at a fixed rate. Executives of Campbell Soup did not believe that they had a right to negotiate over the heads of the growers or to dictate to the growers how they should treat their employees.

FLOC decided to launch a campaign against Campbell Soup in the belief that the price the company set for tomatoes did not allow enough profit margin for the growers to increase wages and improve working conditions even if they wanted to. FLOC disregarded the claim that Campbell Soup did not employ the migrant farmworkers, since the company provided seedlings to the growers and dictated how they were to be raised and picked. In response to a strike organized by FLOC in 1978, the company ordered the growers to switch to mechanical harvesters. Thus, the control that Campbell Soup exercised over the growers was greater than that normally exercised by a company over suppliers. The high visibility of the company and its carefully cultivated reputation also made it vulnerable to attack and contributed to FLOC's decision to make Campbell Soup the target of its campaign.

The charge of allowing child labor was one that deeply stung company officials. The basis of the accusation was a 1983 ruling by a federal district court that a pickle grower, who employed workers on a piece-rate basis, had no legal obligation to prevent children from working alongside their parents in the fields, since the workers, in the view of the court, are independent, self-employed contractors.[2] Although Campbell Soup also markets pickles through its Vlasic subsidiary, the company contended that the decision did not apply to tomato pickers, who are paid hourly rates because of the different method of harvesting tomatoes. The company denied, moreover, that it approved of children helping their parents in the tomato fields. In fact, Campbell Soup created the post of Ombudsman for Migrant Affairs in part to promote the availability of day-care facilities and to ensure that children of migrant farmworkers attend classes during the school year.

Campbell Soup took other steps to improve the living conditions of the workers who picked tomatoes. After the passage of an Ohio law upgrading the minimum standards for migrant housing, the duties of the ombudsman were expanded to include inspection of facilities on farms with company contracts. The company also offered to finance half the cost of new housing and to provide low-interest loans for the balance. In addition, a pilot health care project was started.

R. Gordon McGovern, president and CEO of Campbell Soup Company, believed that the company had done all it could reasonably be expected to do. At his urging, Campbell executives refused to budge on FLOC's main demand for union recognition and a labor contract. As the day of the annual meeting approached, however, Mr. McGovern realized that he would soon have to face not only the company's shareholders inside the meeting hall but the protesters from FLOC on the outside.

INTRODUCTION

Although corporations are primarily business organizations, run for the benefit of shareholders, they have a wide-ranging set of responsibilities—to their own employees and customers, to the communities in which they are located, and to society at large. Most corporations recognize these responsibilities and make a serious effort to fulfill them. Often, these responsibilities are set out in formal statements of a company's principles or beliefs. Corporations do not always succeed in fulfilling the responsibilities they acknowledge, however, and disagreements inevitably arise over the responsibilities of corporations in particular situations. What are the responsibilities of Campbell Soup for the welfare of the migrant farmworkers who harvest the tomatoes at farms under contract with the company? Any responsibilities that the company has with respect to this group are in addition to those it has to the growers, its own employees, and Campbell shareholders, among others. What is the proper balance among these different responsibilities?

There are no easy answers to such questions, but some help can be obtained from the theories of corporate social responsibility examined in this chapter. These range from a very restricted position—that corporations have no social responsibility beyond making a profit—to the position that corporations ought to assume a more active role in addressing major social problems. Several preliminary matters must be addressed first, though, beginning with the concept of responsibility itself.

THE MEANING OF CORPORATE SOCIAL RESPONSIBILITY

The concept of corporate social responsibility originated in the 1950s, as American corporations rapidly increased in size and power. And the concept continued to figure prominently in public debate during the sixties and seventies as the nation confronted pressing social problems such as poverty, unemployment, race relations, urban blight, and pollution.[3] Corporate social responsibility became a rallying cry for diverse groups demanding change in American business.

All accounts of corporate social responsibility recognize that business firms have not one but many different kinds of responsibility, including economic and legal responsibilities. Corporations have an *economic* responsibility to produce goods and services and to provide jobs and good wages to the work force while earning a profit. Economic responsibility also includes the obligation to seek out supplies of raw materials, to discover new resources and technological improvements, and to develop new products. By fulfilling these roles, corporations will increase the economic well-being of society and ensure the survival and growth of the organization.

In addition, business firms have certain *legal* responsibilities. One of these is to act as a fiduciary, managing the assets of a corporation in the interests of shareholders and distributing the profits to them as dividends. Corporations also have legal responsibilities to employees, customers, suppliers, and other parties, which are spelled out in the vast body of business law. This body of law is constantly increasing as legislatures, regulatory agencies, and the courts, respond to greater societal expectations and impose new legal obligations on business.

Going Beyond Economic and Legal Responsibilities

The concept of corporate social responsibility is often expressed as the voluntary assumption of responsibilities that go beyond the purely economic and legal responsibilities of business firms.[4] More specifically, social responsibility, according to some accounts, is the selection of corporate goals and the evaluation of outcomes not solely by the criteria of profitability and organizational well-being but by ethical standards or judgments of social desirability. The exercise of social responsibility, in this view, must be consistent with the corporate objective of earning a satisfactory level of profit, but it implies a willingness to forgo a certain measure of profit in order to achieve noneconomic ends.

Archie B. Carroll views social responsibility as a four-stage continuum.[5] Beyond economic and legal responsibilities lie ethical responsibilities, which are "additional behaviors and activities that are not necessarily codified into law but nevertheless are expected of business by society's members."[6] At the far end of the continuum are discretionary responsibilities. These are responsibilities that are not legally required or even demanded by ethics; but corporations accept them in order to meet society's expectations.

In 1971, the Committee for Economic Development issued an influential report that characterized corporate social responsibility in a similar fashion but without an explicit mention of legal responsibilities. The responsibilities of corporations are described in this report as consisting of three concentric circles.

> The *inner circle* includes the clear-cut basic responsibilities for the efficient execution of the economic function—products, jobs, and economic growth.
> The *intermediate circle* encompasses responsibility to exercise this economic func-

tion with a sensitive awareness of changing social values and priorities: for example, with respect to environmental conservation; hiring and relations with employees; and more rigorous expectations of customers for information, fair treatment, and protection from injury.

The *outer circle* outlines newly emerging and still amorphous responsibilities that business should assume to become more broadly involved in actively improving the social environment. Society is beginning to turn to corporations for help with major social problems such as poverty and urban blight. This is not so much because the public considers business singularly responsible for creating these problems, but because it feels large corporations possess considerable resources and skills that could make a critical difference in solving these problems.[7]

A different kind of approach is developed by S. Prakash Sethi. He notes that social responsibility is a relative concept: What is only a vague ideal at one point in time or in one culture may be a definite legal requirement at another point in time or in another culture. One criterion that permits comparisons at different points in time or across cultures is the *legitimacy* of corporate activity. Legitimacy, in turn, is the extent to which this activity meets the expectations of the members of society. In most of the advanced nations of the world, fulfilling traditional economic and legal responsibilities is no longer regarded as sufficient for legitimizing the activity of large corporations. That is, operating efficiently and within the law (which Sethi calls "social obligation") is not enough; corporations are now expected to do more. Corporate social responsibility can thus be defined as "bringing corporate behavior up to a level where it is congruent with the prevailing social norms, values, and expectations of performance."[8]

Examples of Social Responsibility

Although there are some important differences between the accounts of the concept of corporate social responsibility offered by these writers, there is general agreement on the types of corporate activities that show social responsibility. Among these are

1. Choosing to operate on an ethical level that is higher than what the law requires.
2. Making contributions to civic and charitable organizations and nonprofit institutions.
3. Providing benefits for employees and improving the quality of life in the workplace beyond economic and legal requirements.
4. Taking advantage of an economic opportunity that is judged to be less profitable but more socially desirable than some alternatives.
5. Using corporate resources to operate a program that addresses some major social problem.

There are countless examples of activities of these types.[9]

1. Many companies have codes of ethics that are more than rules for employee behavior or public relations devices. The best of them, such as Johnson & Johnson's "Our Credo" and the beliefs of Borg-Warner "To Reach beyond the Minimal," set forth

very high standards of conduct that are consciously applied in the corporate decision-making process.

2. Most corporations practice some form of philanthropy, and the largest often have a company foundation to channel gifts to worthy causes. Although few corporate contributions exceed one percent of pretax profits, the Dayton Hudson Corporation, a Minneapolis-based retailer, has given 5 percent every year since 1946.

3. Virtually all corporations recognize the importance of good employee relations and worker satisfaction, and many have exemplary benefit packages and "quality of work life" (QWL) programs. Lincoln Electric, in Cleveland, Ohio, a maker of welding equipment and supplies, has long been known for worker participation in decision making and for generous bonuses that often equal the base salary. Workers are guaranteed job security after one year, and no one has been laid off since 1949. During slow periods, all employees work fewer hours.

4. Examples of decisions based more on social than economic factors include the following: In 1975, when scientists first suggested that fluorocarbons from aerosol cans were damaging the ozone layer, Johnson Wax voluntarily withdrew all products containing fluorocarbons from the market, years before a ban was issued by the FDA, despite some loss of sales and criticism from other manufacturers. And in the late 1960s, Control Data Corporation decided to tackle the problem of racial tensions by locating a new plant in a predominantly black area of Minneapolis–St. Paul. The CEO of Control Data, William Norris, was willing to wait three years for the new plant to match the productivity of other CDC plants.

5. Many companies have set up programs to address such social problems as hunger (Pillsbury), adult literacy (the B. Dalton bookstore chain), low-income housing (Aetna Life and Casualty), and minority-owned businesses (Control Data). This list, of course, is only a small sampling.

Although these activities are all beyond the economic and legal responsibilities of corporations and may involve some sacrifice of profit, they are not necessarily antithetical to corporate interests and even the long-term profitability of a corporation. Some corporate philanthropy, such as a contribution that makes the community in which a company is located a better place to live and work, results in direct benefits. And the "goodwill" that socially responsible activities create makes it easier for corporations to conduct their business.

It should come as no surprise, then, that some of the most successful corporations are also among the most socially responsible. They are led by executives who see that even the narrow economic and legal responsibilities of corporations cannot be fulfilled without the articulation of noneconomic values to guide corporate decision making and the adoption of nontraditional business activities that satisfy the demands of diverse constituencies.

Social Responsiveness and Social Performance

The concept of social responsibility focuses on specific acts that corporations perform. Another important aspect of corporate responsibility for social concerns is the *responsiveness* of corporations—that is, the ability of corporations to respond in a socially responsible manner to new challenges.[10] William C. Frederick explains that the concept of corporate social responsiveness "refers to the capacity of a corporation to respond to social pressures."[11] The emphasis of corporate social responsiveness, in other words, is on the *process* of responding or the readiness to respond, rather than on the *content* of an actual response. Thus, a socially responsive corporation uses its resources to anticipate social issues and develop policies, programs, and other means of dealing with them. The management of social issues in a socially responsive corporation is integrated into the strategic planning process, instead of being handled as an ad hoc reaction to specific crises.[12]

A shortcoming of the concept of corporate social responsiveness is that it contains no normative standards for the use of the powerful techniques available to corporations for anticipating and dealing with social issues.[13] Corporations threatened by emerging social forces may marshall their immense resources in ways that protect the corporation rather than promote socially desirable change. As a result, some writers have expressed the need for another concept, beyond corporate social responsibility and corporate social responsiveness. Such a concept would also include outcomes—that is, corporations' actual responses to social issues.[14]

Donna Wood has developed a concept of *corporate social performance* that includes all three facets of a corporation's activity with respect to social concerns. Building on the work of Steven L. Wartick and Philip L. Cochran,[15] she defines corporate social performance as:

> A business organization's configuration of principles of social responsibility, processes of social responsiveness, and policies, programs, and observable outcomes as they relate to the firm's societal relationships.[16]

These three elements of principles, process, and outcomes can be used to analyze the performance of a company that responds to environmental concerns about packaging, for example. The *principles* of corporate social responsibility would be those that lead the company to recognize an obligation to change their packaging in order to protect the environment. The *processes* might consist of establishing an office of environmental affairs or working with environmentalists to develop new packaging. And the *outcomes* could include the switch to environmentally responsible packaging and perhaps building facilities to recycle the packaging.

THE CLASSICAL VIEW

By now, the idea that corporations have an obligation to be socially responsible is so widely held, even among business leaders themselves, that it may seem pointless to bring it into question. The movement toward greater corporate social responsibility is not without its critics, however.

Some contend that corporate social responsibility is altogether a pernicious idea. The well-known conservative economist Milton Friedman writes, "Few trends could so thoroughly undermine the very foundations of our free society as the acceptance by corporate officials of a social responsibility other than making as much money for their stockholders as possible."[17] At the other extreme are critics who would like corporations to be more socially responsible but are mistrustful. They consider talk about corporate social responsibility to be a public relations ploy designed to legitimize the role of corporations in present-day American society and to divert attention away from the destructive social consequences of corporate activity.

Even those who are more favorably disposed to the idea have reservations about the ability of corporations, especially as they are currently structured, to respond effectively to social issues. Businesses are single-purpose institutions, conceived, organized, and managed solely in order to engage in economic activity. As such, they lack the resources and the expertise for solving major social problems. And some add that they lack the legitimacy as well. Corporate executives are not elected officials with a mandate from the American people to apply the resources under their control to just any ends that they deem worthwhile.

Furthermore, the idea that corporations should be more socially responsible fails to give adequate ethical guidance to the executives who must decide which causes to pursue and how much to commit to them. This problem is especially acute in view of the fact that all choices involve trade-offs. A program to increase minority employment, for example, might reduce efficiency, thereby keeping the corporation from fulfilling obligations to shareholders and perhaps its other employees, while raising prices for consumers. Or such a program might be adopted at the expense of achieving a greater reduction in the amount of pollution, which creates a conflict with another demand that is made on corporations in the name of social responsibility. Corporations committed to exercising greater social responsibility need more specific moral rules or principles to give them reasons for acting in one way rather than another.

The major alternative to the concept of corporate social responsibility in recent American history is what is often called the *classical view* of corporate social responsibility. This view, which prevailed in the nineteenth century, is still very influential today, especially among economists. It is expressed by James W. McKie in three basic propositions:

1. Economic behavior is separate and distinct from other types of behavior, and business organizations are distinct from other organizations, even though the same individuals may be involved in business and nonbusiness affairs. Business organizations do not serve the same goals as other organizations in a pluralistic society.
2. The primary criteria of business performance are economic efficiency and growth in production of goods and services, including improvements in technology and innovations in goods and services.
3. The primary goal and motivating force for business organizations is profit. The firm attempts to make as large a profit as it can, thereby maintaining its efficiency and taking advantage of available opportunities to innovate and contribute to growth.[18]

On this classical view, corporations should engage in purely economic activity and be judged in purely economic terms. Social concerns are not unimportant, but they should be left to other institutions in society.

Friedman's Statement of the Classical View

Perhaps the best-known exponent of the classical view is Milton Friedman, who writes in *Capitalism and Freedom*:

> The view has been gaining widespread acceptance that corporate officials . . . have a "social responsibility" that goes beyond serving the interest of their stockhold-

ers. . . . This view shows a fundamental misconception of the character and nature of a free economy. In such an economy, there is one and only one social responsibility of business—to use its resources and engage in activities designed to increase its profits so long as it stays within the rules of the game, which is to say, engages in open and free competition, without deception or fraud. . . . It is the responsibility of the rest of us to establish a framework of law such that an individual pursuing his own interest is, to quote Adam Smith . . . , "led by an invisible hand to promote an end which was no part of his intention. Nor is it always the worse for society that it was no part of it. By pursuing his own interest, he frequently promotes that of the society more effectually than when he really intends to promote it. I have never known much good done by those who affected to trade for the public good."[19]

Friedman's main argument for the classical view is that corporate executives, when they are acting in their official capacity and not as private persons, are agents of the stockholders of the corporation. As such, executives of a corporation have an obligation to make decisions in the interests of the stockholders, who are ultimately their employers. He has asked:

> What does it mean to say that the corporate executive has a "social responsibility" in his capacity as businessman? If this statement is not pure rhetoric, it must mean that he is to act in some way that is not in the interest of his employers. For example, that he is to refrain from increasing the price of the product in order to contribute to the social objective of preventing inflation, even though a price increase would be in the best interests of the corporation. Or that he is to make expenditures on reducing pollution beyond the amount that is in the best interests of the corporation or that is required by law in order to contribute to the social objective of improving the environment. Or that, at the expense of corporate profits, he is to hire "hardcore" unemployed instead of better-qualified available workmen to contribute to the social objective of reducing poverty.
>
> In each of these cases, the corporate executive would be spending someone else's money for a general social interest. Insofar as his actions in accord with his "social responsibility" reduce returns to stockholders, he is spending their money. Insofar as his actions raise the price to customers, he is spending the customers' money. Insofar as his actions lower the wages of some employees, he is spending their money.[20]

When corporate executives act in the way Friedman describes, they take on a role of imposing taxes and spending the proceeds that properly belongs only to elected officials. They become, in effect, civil servants with the power to tax, and as civil servants, they ought to be elected through the political process instead of being selected by the stockholders of private business firms.[21]

Some Features of the Classical View

The classical view does not sanction an unrestrained pursuit of profit. Friedman himself acknowledges that business must observe certain essential limitations on permissible conduct, which he describes as the "rules of the game." Presumably, he would also grant the necessity of government with limited powers for setting and enforcing rules. Business activity requires, in other words, a minimal state in order to prevent anticompetitive practices and to enforce the basics of commercial law.

Friedman recognizes, further, that many supposed socially responsible actions are really disguised forms of self-interest. Contributions to schools, hospitals, community organizations, cultural groups, and the like are compatible with the classical view insofar as corporations receive indirect benefits from the contributions. All Friedman asks is that corporations recognize these as effective means for making a profit and not as philanthropic activities.

In addition, holders of the classical view generally admit the legitimacy of three other functions of government that place limits on business activity.[22] First, business activity generates many *externalities*, that is, social harms, such as worker injury, which result indirectly from the operation of business firms. In order to prevent these harms or to correct them after they occur, it is proper for government to act—by requiring safer working conditions, for example, or by taxing employers to fund workers' compensation programs.[23] Second, the operation of a free market economy results in considerable *inequalities* in the distribution of income and wealth. Insofar as it is desirable as a matter of public policy to reduce these inequalities, it is appropriate for government to undertake the task by such means as progressive taxation and redistribution schemes. It is the job of government, in other words, and not business, to manage the equity/efficiency trade-off.[24] Third, free markets are prone to *instability* that manifests itself in inflation, recessions, unemployment, and other economic ills. Individual firms are too small to have much effect on the economy as a whole, and so government must step in and use its powers of taxation, public expenditure, control of the money supply, and the like to make the economy more stable.

The classical view is compatible, then, with some intervention in business activity by government in order to secure the public welfare. The important point to recognize is that the restraints are almost entirely *external*. The primary burden for ensuring that corporations act in a way that is generally beneficial rests on society as a whole, which is charged by Friedman with the task of creating a framework of law that allows business firms to operate solely in their self-interest. The classical theory, therefore, does not permit corporations to *act* in a socially irresponsible manner; it only relieves them of the need to *think* about matters of social responsibility. In a well-ordered society, corporations attend to business while government and other institutions fulfill their proper roles.

CRITICISM OF THE CLASSICAL VIEW

Business activity, in the classical view, is justified partly on the ground that it secures the well-being of society as a whole. The crux of this argument is the efficacy of Adam Smith's invisible hand in harmonizing self-interested behavior to secure an end that is not a part of anyone's intention. The argument also depends on the ability of the rest of society to create the conditions necessary for the invisible hand to operate and to deal with the problems of externalities, inequalities, and instability, without the aid of business. Generally, the classical view is accepted by those who have great faith in free markets, whereas it is rejected by those who are more skeptical. The debate over the workings of the invisible hand cannot be settled here (it is examined at some length in Chapter 4), but there are substantial problems with the classical view.

The Moral Minimum of the Market

First, the classical view does not adequately appreciate the extent to which social responsibility is required by free markets. Holders of this view recognize that a certain level of ethical conduct is necessary for the invisible hand to operate, or indeed for business activity to take place at all. Milton Friedman speaks of the "rules of the game," by which he means "open and free competition, without deception or fraud." And Theodore Levitt, in his article "The Dangers of Social Responsibility," says that, aside from seeking material gain, business has only one responsibility, and that is "to obey the elementary canons of everyday face-to-face civility (honesty, good faith, and so on)."[25] The "rules of the game" and "face-to-face civility" impose not inconsequential contraints on business. Presumably, the prohibition against deception and fraud obligates corporations to deal fairly with employees, customers, and the public and to avoid sharp sales practices, misleading advertising, and the like. Honesty and good faith, moreover, are important elements in the concept of corporate social responsibility.

Several writers find fault with Levitt's concept of social responsibility, in particular. John G. Simon, Charles W. Powers, and Jon P. Gunnemann have argued:

> . . . Levitt presents the reader with a choice between, on the one hand, getting involved in the management of society . . . and, on the other hand, fulfilling the profit-making function. But such a choice excludes another meaning of corporate responsibility: the making of profits in such a way as to minimize social injury. Levitt at no point considers the possibility that business activity may at times injure others and that it may be necessary to regulate the social consequences of one's business activities accordingly.[26]

They appeal in their argument to an important distinction in both law and morality between *negative injunctions* and *affirmative duties*. Although not all corporations have an affirmative duty to take on specific tasks, such as cleaning up the environment, all are under a negative injunction to prevent pollution from occurring and to correct any environmental damage that results from their own activities. For both individuals and corporations, the negative injunction to prevent injury is a moral minimum.

For some holders of the classical view, the minimum level of conduct is what the law requires. If corporations recognize no obligation to adhere to a standard of conduct higher than the legal minimum, however, then they leave themselves open to intervention by outside forces, including pressure from special-interest groups and regulation by government. One of the major reasons advanced for corporations to exercise greater social responsibility is to avoid such external interference. By "internalizing" the expectations of society, corporations retain control over decision making and avoid the costs associated with government regulation. This is a purely self-interested argument, but there are good reasons to believe that the public welfare is also better served when corporations voluntarily adopt a higher level of conduct. Keith Davis has argued, for example:

> This view [that corporations ought to assume greater social responsibility] is . . . consistent with existing political philosophy, which attempts to keep power as decentralized as possible in a democratic system. Further, this view is consistent with organizational theory, which holds that decision making should be kept as near as possible to the point where an operating problem occurs. For these reasons, if the businessman by his own socially responsible behavior can prevent the government from introducing new restrictions, it can be argued that he probably is accomplishing a public good, as well as his own private good.[27]

Power and Responsibility

A second objection is that corporations have become so large and powerful that they are not effectively restrained by market forces and government regulation. Some self-imposed restraint in the form of a voluntary assumption of greater social responsibility is necessary, therefore, for corporate activity to secure the public welfare.

The classical view developed in the nineteenth century when most business firms were small and limited in resources, so that corporate activity posed little threat to the welfare of individuals. Corporations had little need at that time to be concerned with anything besides making a profit. With the rise of corporations to a dominant position in American society, however, has come the need to exercise their immense power responsibly. Keith Davis expressed this point succinctly in the proposition "*social responsibility arises from social power.*"[28] He also cited what he calls the Iron Law of Responsibility: "In the long run, those who do not use power in a manner which society considers responsible will tend to lose it."[29] The need for greater social responsibility by corporations, then, is an inevitable result of their increasing size and influence in American society.

Holders of the classical theory argue in reply that precisely because of the immense power of corporations, it would be dangerous to unleash it from the discipline of the market in order to achieve vaguely defined social goals.[30] Kenneth E. Goodpaster and John B. Matthews, Jr., concede that this is a matter for serious concern but argue in response:

> What seems not to be appreciated is the fact that power affects when it is used as well as when it is not used. A decision by [a corporation] . . . not to exercise its economic influence according to "non-economic" criteria is inevitably a moral decision and just as inevitably affects the community. The issue in the end is not whether corporations (and other organizations) should be "unleashed" to exert moral force in our society but rather how critically and self-consciously they should choose to do so.[31]

A related objection is that business already has enough power, so that the pursuit of social goals by corporations would result in an excessive concentration of power. Such a concentration would threaten the division of power that is required for a pluralistic society and also weaken the effectiveness of other institutions that are better suited for solving social problems.[32] If corporations already have too much power, then it follows that they should not take on any new responsibilities that add to that power. But it also follows that they should be all the more concerned to use the power they have responsibly. Exercising greater social responsibility, moreover, does not always add to the power of corporations, and it is possible for responsible corporate activity to enhance pluralism and strengthen other institutions in society. The support of education by corporations and contributions to civic organizations are obvious examples.

Giving a Helping Hand to Government

Third, the classical view assumes that business provides for the economic well-being of the members of a society, whereas noneconomic goals are best left to government and the other noneconomic institutions of society. In particular, the classical view relies on government, rather than corporations, to deal with the externalities of business activity, considerations of equality, and the task of stabilizing the economy. This sharp distinction between the proper spheres of activity for business and government is justified by utilitarianism on grounds of efficiency. Although certain noneconomic goals are better left to government, it does not follow that corporations have *no* responsibility to provide a helping hand. Corporations have an obligation, for reasons of efficiency, to make whatever contributions are consistent with their role in society as primarily economic institutions.

Corporations cannot attempt to solve every social problem, of course. Some criteria are needed for distinguishing those situations in which corporations have an obligation to pursue noneconomic goals. John G. Simon, Charles W. Powers, and Jon P. Gunnemann, propose the following four criteria:[33]

1. The urgency of the need
2. The proximity of a corporation to the need
3. The capability of a corporation to respond effectively
4. The likelihood that the need will not be met unless a corporation acts

In general, a corporation has an obligation to address social problems that involve more substantial threats to the well-being of large numbers of people, that are close at hand and related in some way to the corporation's activity, that the corporation has the resources and expertise to solve, and that would likely persist without some action by the corporation.

By these criteria, the Campbell Soup Company had a responsibility to help alleviate the plight of migrant farmworkers in Ohio, despite the lack of a direct relation. The need was certainly urgent. Although not located in close geographical proximity, the company occupied a prominent position in the tomato-growing industry, and the actions of the company bore directly on the situation of the farmworkers. Campbell Soup also had the capability of improving the conditions of the migrant laborers, and because of their pivotal role as a large buyer that contracted with many growers, only Campbell was in a position to bring about the three-way agreement that emerged. If Campbell had not acted, then it is unlikely that the need would have been met. Thus, all four of the criteria set out above are met in the Campbell Soup case.

THE "TAXATION" ARGUMENT

The classical view is not based solely on utilitarian considerations of well-being but also on the property rights of shareholders. This latter justification underlies Friedman's argument that managers in exercising corporate social responsibility are spending someone else's money and taking on a role that properly belongs to elected officials. Investors, according to the "taxation" argument, entrust their money to the managers of corporations in the expectation that it will be put to the most productive use, with the profits returned to the shareholders in the form of dividends. Spending money to pursue social ends is thus a form of taxation without any authority.

Many things are wrong with the "taxation" argument. Even if we accept the main assumption of the argument—that managers have an obligation to operate a corporation in the interests of the legal owners and those of no one else—it does not follow that a corporation has no other obligations that are a part of its social responsibility. A strong case can be made, moreover, for rejecting the underlying assumption of the "taxation" argument. Although shareholders have well-defined legal rights, which are different from those of other members of society, many people have both moral and legal claims that compete with those of investors.

The Question of Means

First, managers of a corporation do not have an obligation to earn the greatest amount of profit for shareholders without regard for the means used. A taxi driver hired to take a passenger to the airport as fast as possible, for example, is not obligated to break traffic laws and endanger everyone else on the road. Similarly, money spent on product safety or pollution control may reduce the potential return to shareholders, but the alternative is to conduct business in a way that threatens the well-being of others in society. Doing business in a country with an oppressive regime might represent the best investment opportunity for a corporation, but would the managers of that corporation be remiss in their duty to the owners if they refused on moral grounds to benefit from violations of human rights? Friedman would insist, of course, that managers carry out their responsibility to shareholders within the "rules of the game," but the moral obligation of managers to be sensitive to the social impact of their actions is more extensive than the minimal restraints listed by Friedman.

Taking a Long-Term View

Second, the obligation of managers is not merely to secure the maximum return but also to preserve the equity invested in a corporation. Securing the maximum return for shareholders consistent with the preservation of invested capital requires managers to take a long-term view that considers the stability and growth of the corporation. For corporations to survive, they must satisfy the legitimate expectations of society and serve the purposes for which they have been created. And among the factors that contribute to the viability of corporations are socially responsible investments in employee and consumer relations and in the local community. Friedman admits the legitimacy of acts of social responsibility as long as they are ultimately in the self-interest of the corporation. The main area of disagreement between proponents and critics of social responsibility is, how much socially responsible behavior is in a corporation's long-term self-interest?

What Are the Interests of Shareholders?

A third objection is that instead of being profligate with the shareholders' money, managers are often more profit-minded than the shareholders themselves. The interests of shareholders are not narrowly economic; corporations are generally expected by their owners to pursue some socially desirable ends. Shareholders are also consumers, environmentalists, and citizens in communities. Consequently, they are affected when corporations fail to act responsibly. In fact, shareholders may be morally opposed to some activities of a corporation and in favor of some changes. One writer contends that "there are conventionally motivated investors who have an interest in the social characteristics of their portfolios *as well as* dividends and capital gains."[34]

If this is so, then managers who exercise social responsibility are not "taxing" shareholders and spending the money contrary to their interests but quite the opposite; managers who do *not* act in a socially responsible manner are using the money of shareholders in ways that are against the interests of their shareholders. A Friedmanite response is, if shareholders want certain social goals, let them use their dividends for that purpose. However, it may be more efficient for corporations to expend funds on environmental protection, for example, than for shareholders to spend the same amount in dividends for the same purpose. Also, corporations do not strive to make the maximum amount of profit. They must make enough profit to attract sufficient capital from investors, of course, but the decision to declare a certain dividend is generally made by balancing several competing goals, of which the interests of shareholders is only one.

Conclusion

For these reasons, then, the "taxation" argument in support of the classical view of corporate social responsibility is not very compelling. Although the property rights of shareholders place some limits on what businesses can justifiably do to address major social concerns, they do not yield the very narrowly circumscribed view of Friedman and others. The taxation argument assumes that the money which corporations spend for socially desirable goals rightly belongs to shareholders as the owners. An alternative view is that this money is spent by corporations in order to realize the purposes for which they have been created by society. And although one end is the making of a profit for shareholders, another is to operate in a socially responsible manner.

THE MANAGERIAL AND STAKEHOLDER VIEWS

The classical view has seldom been adopted in its pure form by the managers of American corporations. In practice, it has been modified by two important concepts, namely, those of *philanthropy* and *trusteeship*. The result is what is sometimes called the *managerial view* of corporate responsibility.[35] In addition to their traditional economic role, corporations have, in this view, the tasks of providing support for worthy causes and of guarding society's resources. This view found increasing favor in the 1920s and the 1930s as a result of a number of historical forces, including the increasing size of corporations, the dispersal of ownership, and the separation between ownership and management.[36]

Philanthropy and Trusteeship

Philanthropy has traditionally been an obligation of individuals and nonprofit organizations such as churches, hospitals, and social welfare agencies. In a famous 1889 article entitled simply "Wealth," Andrew Carnegie popularized the idea that successful business leaders have a responsibility to distribute their riches in ways "best calculated to produce the most beneficial results for the community."[37] Carnegie set an example by contributing generously for libraries, parks, concert halls, and other public facilities. However, the magnitude of social problems in the early decades of the twentieth century exceeded the capacities of even the wealthiest individuals, and organizations turned increasingly to business for contributions. Corporations responded with funds for the Community Chest movement, YMCAs, Red Cross, and a host of other projects.[38]

Although the classical theory permits giving that confers an indirect benefit on a corporation, the concept of corporate philanthropy is based on the recognition of an obligation to serve society without any anticipated return. The argument for holding that corporations have such an obligation is based largely on the idea of corporate citizenship. An illustration is provided by H. Brewster Atwater, Jr., the former chairman and CEO of General Mills, who has written:

> Corporations are classed as citizens under U.S. law, and they enjoy both the privileges and duties of citizenship. This broad concept of corporate citizenship may stem from the view that no citizen can prosper in an unhealthy society. And one of the important duties of each citizen, whether a corporation or an individual, is to work in a multitude of ways for the betterment of society.[39]

The concept of trusteeship—or stewardship, as it is sometimes called—derives from the biblical precept that human beings are not the owners of the earth; rather, it belongs to God, who has entrusted it to people currently living for the benefit of all. Consequently, we have an obligation to use the bounty of creation wisely and to preserve it for future generations. Business leaders, who have command over vast productive and natural resources on which the welfare of workers and the rest of society depends, have a special responsibility to act as trustees or stewards of this accumulated wealth. Unlike the concept of philanthropy, which involves charitable giving out of the earnings of a corporation, trusteeship entails an obligation concerning the total resources of a corporation. In the words of one writer, "It is not the surplus which constitutes the special trust, it is everything the owner owns."[40]

The concept of trusteeship leads corporate managers to be more than profit maximizers for the benefit of shareholders and to take the interests of a diverse constituency into account. According to Robert Hay and Ed Gray:

> The . . . trusteeship manager recognizes that self-interest plays a large role in his actions, but he also recognizes the interest of those people who contribute to his organization—customers, employees, suppliers, owners, creditors, government, and community. He thus operates from self-interest plus the interest of other groups. . . . He is a profit satisficer; that is, he balances the profits of the owners and the organization with the wages for employees, taxes for the government, interest for the creditors, and so forth. Money is important to him, but so are people, because his values tell him that satisfying people's needs is a better goal than just making money.
>
> In balancing the needs of the various contributors to the organization, the trusteeship manager deals with the customers as the chief providers of revenue to the firm. . . . He views employees as having certain rights which must be recognized; they are more than a mere commodity to be traded in the marketplace. His accountability as a manager is to owners as well as customers, employees, suppliers, creditors, government, and the community.[41]

The Managerial View and Social Responsibility

The managerial view, then, with the concepts of philanthropy and trusteeship, is much broader than the classical view, but it is still more limited than the present-day understanding of the social responsibility of corporations to take an active role in addressing major social problems. Trusteeship, for example, is usually interpreted as maintaining a corporation as a going concern, which is compatible with plant closings that devastate communities, strip mining and logging that despoil the environment, and so on.

The concept of philanthropy is similarly inadequate. Although corporations are an important source of support for nonprofit organizations, a very small portion of corporate wealth is actually devoted to charitable giving. The average philanthropic contribution for American corporations has long hovered around 1 percent of pretax profits.[42] Charitable giving, moreover, is concerned with the disposition of the earnings of a corporation and not with the way in which it conducts day-to-day operations. But social responsibility is reflected in all that a corporation does and so cannot be confined to a department of corporate philanthropy.

The Stakeholder Theory

A third concept that goes beyond philanthropy and trusteeship and enlarges the managerial view is that of a *stakeholder*. Instead of serving only the interests of shareholders or stockholders, corporations are *or ought to be* (the distinction is important) operated for the benefit of all those who have a stake in the enterprise, including employees, customers, suppliers, and the local community. A stakeholder is variously defined as "those groups who are vital to the survival and success of the corporation"[43] and as "any group or individual who can affect or is affected by the achievement of the organization's objectives."[44] Although the relation of shareholders, as the owners of a corporation, is different from that of employees, consumers, and so on, all of these constituencies are integral to the operation of a corporation, and their role must be taken into account by managers.

From the fact that there are stakeholders, however, nothing follows about whether corporations have a moral obligation to take their interests into account. Holders of the classical view of social responsibility are perfectly aware that employees, customers, suppliers, and the general public are important to the operation of a corporation. What they deny is the idea that corporations are morally obligated to undertake some actions or refrain from others merely because of the impact on the interests of these groups. Corporations have an obligation to respect the rights of each stakeholder group, but these rights are limited, in the classical view, to the rights of parties in market exchanges, which is to say, the "rules of the game."

To the extent that employees, consumers, and others have a more extensive set of rights that are now recognized in law, corporations have an obligation to act with a regard for the interests of stakeholders in many matters. If employees have a right to a safe and healthy workplace, for example, and consumers have a right to products that are not likely to cause serious injury, then corporations are obligated to take the welfare of these groups into account in making decisions about work routines, product design, and so on. The stakeholder view, then, does not consist merely of the fact that there are many groups besides shareholders who have a stake in a corporation. It has inescapable normative implications about the obligation of corporations to take the interests of other groups into account.

Serious attempts have been made to develop the stakeholder concept into a full-blown view of the corporation that might replace the classical view. In the classical view, as explained earlier in this chapter, business is primarily an economic activity in which economic resources are marshalled for the purpose of making a profit. Employees are critical to this enterprise as a source of labor, but they are merely one *input* that can be "bought" in the market. Customers too are critical, and they receive the *output* of a corporation's activity, namely some good or service. But what customers give and receive is also the result of market exchanges. The resulting view of the corporation is the input-output model displayed in Figure 14.1.

The concept of a stakeholder highlights the fact that corporate activity is not solely a series of market transactions but a cooperative (and competitive) endeavor involving large numbers of people organized in various ways. The corporation or firm is an organizational entity in which and through which many different individuals and groups attempt to achieve their ends. A firm interacts continually with its stakeholder groups, and much of the success of a firm depends on how well all of these stakeholder relations are managed. Managing stakeholder relations, rather than managing inputs and outputs, may provide an adequate model for understanding what people in corporations actually do as well as what they ought to do. Such a stakeholder model of the corporation is displayed in Figure 14.2.

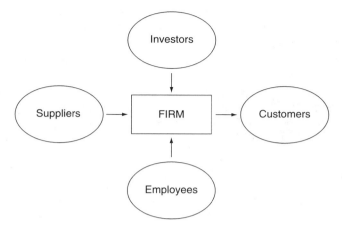

Figure 14.1   The Input-Output Model. *Source:* Thomas Donaldson and Lee E. Preston, "The Stakeholder Theory of the Corporation: Concepts, Evidence, and Implications," *Academy of Management Review,* 20 (1995), 68.

Thomas Donaldson and Lee E. Preston have distinguished three uses of the stakeholder model: descriptive, instrumental, and normative.[45] First, the model can be used as a *description* of the corporation that can enable us to understand the corporation better. That is, a researcher who believes that the stakeholder model accurately describes corporations can use it to answer questions about how corporations are organized and managed or about how people in corporations think about their roles. And the belief that the stakeholder model is an accurate description can be confirmed to the extent that these answers are put to a test and empirically verified. Second, the stakeholder model can be used *instrumentally* as a tool for managers.

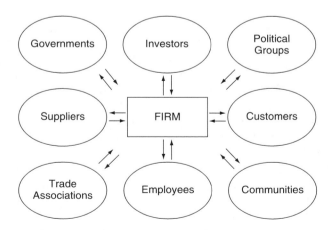

Figure 14.2   The Stakeholder Model. *Source:* Thomas Donaldson and Lee E. Preston, "The Stakeholder Theory of the Corporation: Concepts, Evidence, and Implications," *Academy of Management Review,* 20 (1995), 69.

Even if making a profit is the ultimate goal of corporate activity, this goal does not provide much help in the daily conduct of business. By contrast, telling managers to handle stakeholder relations well is a more practical action guide that may actually lead to greater profit. Certainly, many companies that care deeply about their employees, customers, suppliers, and other affected groups are also highly profitable. Third, the stakeholder model can be used as a *normative* account of how corporations *ought* to treat their various stakeholder groups. The descriptive and instrumental uses of the stakeholder model suggest that corporations must deal with their stakeholders as a matter of practical necessity. Used normatively, the stakeholder model would have managers recognize the interests of employees, customers, and others as worth furthering for their own sakes. As Donaldson and Preston explain, "The interests of all stakeholders are of *"intrinsic value."*[46]

Some writers reject the stakeholder model in its normative use on the ground that the interests of all groups other than shareholders constitute *constraints* on corporate activities in pursuit of the goal of making a profit rather than *goals* themselves. Igor Ansoff, for example, in his classic 1965 book *Corporate Strategy* contends that "responsibilities" and "objectives" are not the same; the former are obligations that limit the achievement of the main objectives of a firm.[47] The stakeholder view, then, confuses the responsibilities of a corporation (which include the obligations to stakeholder groups) with its objectives (one of which is to operate at a profit).

Kenneth E. Goodpaster has criticized the stakeholder model from another direction.[48] Although conceding that corporations have genuine obligations toward various stakeholders that are not merely constraints, Goodpaster insists that the obligations to shareholders are different in kind. The obligation of a manager to the shareholders is that of a *fiduciary*, who is bound to conserve and utilize the assets of the corporation in the interests of these owners. The obligations of managers to employees, customers, and others is morally significant, but they are nonfiduciary obligations. The effect of treating the obligations to shareholders and stakeholders alike is, according to Goodpaster, to obscure an important distinction.

Goodpaster makes an important point, but we also need to keep two other things in mind. First, the stakeholder theory does not deny the obvious fact that the obligations of managers are different for every stakeholder group, but it stresses that they also have a certain commonality. A complete development of a stakeholder theory of the corporation would involve, therefore, a description of the obligations of managers to each stakeholder group—what they have in common as well as how they differ.

Second, although shareholders are legally the owners of a corporation, the corporation itself is a legal entity with interests recognized in law that are not necessarily identical with those of the shareholders. Part of the justification of our system of corporate governance is a version of Adam Smith's "invisible hand" argument, to the effect that stockholders in promoting their own interests will also promote the interests of the corporation, as well as those of society as a whole. For a manager to place special emphasis on serving the interests of shareholders *directly* can be viewed, then, as a way of *indirectly* serving the interests of other stakeholder groups. The creation of a special fiduciary relation between managers and shareholders is designed, in other words, to benefit everyone alike.

A more crucial objection to the stakeholder model is its shortcomings as an action guide for business. Even managers committed to honoring obligations to all stakeholders will find that the stakeholder model leaves many questions unanswered. Many difficult corporate decisions involve trade-offs in which a benefit to one group must be balanced against a loss to another. Thus, increasing the pension benefits of employees might result in higher prices to consumers, or a switch to environmentally safer packaging might lead to the termination of a supplier. A company that protects one community by keeping an unprofitable factory open might become uncompetitive and be forced eventually to close more factories in other communities.

Despite these objections, the stakeholder model remains a very promising version of the managerial view. The concept of a stakeholder is a valuable device for identifying and organizing the multitude of obligations that corporations have to different groups. At the present time, however, the theory is only a framework to help us get started on the very difficult task of deciding exactly what obligations of corporations come under the heading of corporate social responsibility.

Conclusion

The aim of this chapter has been to answer some very practical questions, such as the responsibility of the Campbell Soup Company for the plight of migrant farmworkers in Ohio. In order to do this, however, we are led, of necessity, to consider fundamental issues about the nature and purpose of a corporation. At the center of the debate over corporate social responsibility are two competing positions. One views the modern corporation as a social enterprise sanctioned by society to provide us with goods and services and the means to secure a livelihood. This position measures success by the extent to which corporations contribute to the welfare of the whole of society. The other position holds that corporations are essentially economic institutions for the creation of wealth and that their performance should be judged solely by financial measures. These two positions are not wholly incompatible, and they often lead to similar results in practice because corporations cannot exist without satisfying the legitimate expectations of society. However, companies such as Campbell Soup, which regards itself as being socially responsible, may respond to problems differently from one that takes another view.

CASE 14.2   The Restructuring of Endicott

Bob Endicott, the president and CEO of Endicott Corporation, reviewed the proposal one last time before the start of the board of directors meeting.[49] The main item on the agenda was a plan developed by the newly hired chief financial officer, Mark Bachman, to split Endicott into two separate companies. The restructuring would delight stockholders, but investors in Endicott's bonds could be enraged since most of the gain to stockholders would come at the bondholders' expense. Something needed to be done. Endicott's sales had been growing at a rate of 20 percent each year, and the company earned a consistent 20 percent return on equity. In short, the company was performing very well. The price of Endicott stock was languishing, however, and it currently traded in a range that was one-half of the stock's price only four years ago. Bachman was convinced that the low stock price was due to the inability of investors to evaluate the company because of its diverse holdings. He also believed that investors were unsettled by the large portfolio of hotel properties in a depressed real estate market. The restructuring would enable investors to see more clearly the financial prospects of each company.

Endicott had developed as a traditional hotel chain, owning and managing hotels nationwide. In recent years, the management of hotels had proved to be more profitable than the investment in real estate. Consequently, the company sold many hotel properties to outside investors and retained contracts to manage the hotels under the Endicott name. With the cash from these sales, the company financed the construction of new hotels, which, in turn, were sold to investors with Endicott retaining the management rights. Endicott also expanded aggressively in the highly profitable institutional food service business.

This successful strategy for growth in the 1980s was encountering stiff resistance in the changed environment of the nineties. The hotel industry was entering a period of consolidation because of an oversupply of rooms. At the same time, changes in the tax code made the ownership of hotel properties by private investors less attractive. Endicott currently owned 150 newly built hotels that it could not sell. The new environment also provided possibilities for growth, however. Many fashionable hotels could be bought at rock-bottom prices by anyone with available cash, but Endicott's own portfolio of distressed hotel properties prevented the company from capitalizing on this opportunity.

Mark Bachman's plan—dubbed "Project Camelot"—called for splitting the company in two. Endicott Corporation would be renamed Guest Endicott and would consist primarily of the company's real estate holdings and food concessions at stadiums and toll road plazas. Stockholders would be given, as a special dividend, shares of stock in a new corporation, known as Endicott International, which would be primarily a hotel management and institutional food service company. Endicott International would hold the highly profitable hotel management contracts. The bulk of the company's debt from hotel construction would remain with Guest Endicott. As a result, the renamed Guest Endicott would be responsible for the repayment of $2.5 billion of Endicott Corporation's $3 billion debt but would have only 40 percent of the original company's cash flow along with $300 million in equity. Endicott International would assume the remaining $500 million of debt and have $500 million in equity.

According to projections in the proposal, the combined stock price of the two companies would rise by approximately 30 percent. Guest Endicott bonds would probably be downgraded by the rating services, perhaps to "below investment grade," which is to say, to junk bond status. The loss in value of the investors' $2.5 billion bond holdings could be in the range of 30 percent. Investors who hold their bonds to maturity would be unaffected as long the company remained solvent. Investors in bond mutual funds would suffer losses since the value of bonds in a fund is calculated at market value; and pension funds and insurance companies that are barred from investing in junk bonds would have to sell the downgraded bonds at a loss.

CFO Bachman was confident that Guest Endicott could meet all interest and principal payments, which is all that the company is required to do. Bondholders, unlike shareholders, are guaranteed a fixed return, but a corporation owes bondholders nothing beyond the terms of the bonds' covenants. Bachman noted that nothing in the covenants of Endicott bonds prevented a special dividend—even though no bondholder could have anticipated that the most profitable part of the company would be spun off in this manner!

As Bob Endicott reflected on the proposal, he considered who would be affected. Some jobs would be lost in the restructuring, but maybe more would be created in the long run. Endicott customers would scarcely notice any change. The main victims would be the bondholders. But a bond is like a contract, and he was satisfied that Endicott had upheld their part of the bargain and would continue to do so. Besides, the bondholders could have protected themselves by writing stronger covenants that prohibit this kind of restructuring. "My job," he reminded himself, "is to serve the interests of the stockholders, and that's what I'm doing. The bondholders can look out for themselves."

CASE 14.3   Diller's Dilemma: Street Children and Substance Abuse

---

Walter Diller, chief executive officer of J. G. Diller, Inc., faced a formidable problem.[50] Could the company continue production of its most profitable adhesive product, Endurol, and at the same time manage to maintain its impeccable image for social responsibility?

The executives at J. G. Diller, Inc., first became aware of the substance abuse problem back in 1986 when Honduran newspapers carried articles about police arrests of street children who drugged themselves by sniffing glue. Most of the orphaned or runaway children lived in the poorest slums of the big cities where they scratched out a minimal existence as beggars and illegal squatters. The commonly available adhesive known as Endurol emerged as the substance of choice among these young junkies due to its low price and hallucinogenic qualities. The highly addictive glue induced immediate feelings of elation, grandeur, and power, but it also initiated irreversible liver and brain damage when used over a long period of time. Although the street children abused other substances in addition to Endurol, they soon became tagged as "Enduroleros," a name that eventually became synonymous with all street children, whether they used the drug or not.

Malena Chemical Industries, S.A., one of J. G. Diller's wholly owned subsidiaries, first introduced Endurol to the Central American market in the early 1980s. Malena manufactured and distributed more than a dozen different adhesives under the Endurol brand name in several countries. In Honduras, where Endurol was manufactured, the products had a strong market position. The adhesives were intended primarily for use in shoe manufacturing and repair, leather work, and carpentry. The most common forms of Endurol had properties similar to those of airplane glue or rubber cement and were readily available at household goods stores throughout the country. Malena maintained tight control over the wholesale distribution of Endurol. Nearly all glue products that reached the Enduroleros came from retail outlets, either directly or through street pushers.

In spite of the competitive challenge of operating under unstable political and economic conditions in Central America, Malena managers stressed the objective of going beyond the bottom line in their annual report:

> Malena carries out business with the utmost respect for ethical and legal principles. Its orientation is not solely directed to the customer, who has the highest priority, but also to the shareholders, to employees, and to the communities where it operates.

Diller's founder and Chairman of the Board, J. Grant Diller, had become a legendary figure in the company's home area. He had served several terms in local government and remained active in civic affairs. Diller saw the company through four decades of financial success as president and chief executive officer before handing over the managerial reigns to his son Walter in January 1989.

Three months into Walter's term as president, angry letters began to trickle in from the stockholders. Some of these individuals heard of the Endurol problem through international press releases, while others had witnessed the problem firsthand in Central America. On November 2, 1989, Diller received an irate letter from a shareholder whose daughter worked with an international aid group in Honduras. The man demanded, "How can a company like J. G. Diller claim to have a social conscience and continue to sell Endurol which is practically burning out the brains of children in Latin America?" The letter's timing was uncanny. Walter was about to meet with a national group of socially responsible investors who were considering J. G. Diller's stock for inclusion in their portfolio.

Meanwhile, Walter learned that Malena management had failed to dissuade the Honduran government from regulating Endurol. As a solution to the glue-sniffing problem, the legislature mandated that oil of mustard, allyl isothiocyanate, be added to Endurol to prevent its abuse. They argued that a person attempting to sniff glue with oil of mustard included would find it too powerful to tolerate, like getting an "overdose of horseradish." However, independent toxicology reports revealed that the oil of mustard had some acute side effects. The material could prove fatal if inhaled, swallowed, or absorbed through the skin; it caused severe irritation or burns, and could destroy tissues of the mucous membranes, upper respiratory tract, eyes, and skin. In addition, the Endurol with the oil of mustard included had a shelf life of only six months.

Given J. G. Diller's high visibility as a socially responsible corporation, the glue-sniffing problem had the potential for becoming a public relations nightmare. Diller's staff suggested a number of options, including withdrawal of the product from the market or altering the formula to make Endurol a water-based product. Both would solve the glue-sniffing problem. However, any formula alteration would also affect the strength and durability of the glue, its most valuable properties.

Finally, Diller decided to go to Honduras and see what was going on. Upon his return, he realized that the situation involved more than product misuse and the company's image; it had social and community ramifications as well. The issue was substance abuse by children, regardless of who manufactured the product.

The depth of poverty in Honduras exacerbated the problem. In 1989, 65 percent of all households in Honduras lived in poverty, making it one of the poorest countries in Latin America. The government remained highly unstable with a large turnover rate. Officials usually settled for a quick fix. They seldom stayed in office long enough to manage a long-term policy. By the time of Diller's trip, the oil-of-mustard law had been on the books for several months. However, officials had yet to implement the rule, and the country had scheduled national elections in three months. Diller wondered if his company could do much to solve this complicated social problem.

NOTES

1. Information on this case is taken from "Campbell Soup Company," in JOHN R. BOATRIGHT, ed., *Cases in Ethics and the Conduct of Business* (Englewood Cliffs, NJ: Prentice Hall, 1995), 314–30.

2. *Brandel* v. *United States*, U.S. District Court, Western District of Michigan, Southern Division, 83–1228.

3. For a comprehensive account of the historical development of the concept of corporate social responsibility, see MORRELL HEALD, *The Social Responsibilities of Business: Company and Community, 1900–1960* (Cleveland: Case Western Reserve University Press, 1970). Brief accounts are given in CLARENCE C. WALTON, *Corporate Social Responsibilities* (Belmont, CA: Wadsworth, 1967), 21–53; and JAMES W. McKIE, "Changing Views," in McKIE, ed., *Social Responsibility and the Business Predicament* (Washington, DC: The Brookings Institution, 1974), 17–40.

4. JOSEPH W. McGUIRE, *Business and Society* (New York: McGraw-Hill, 1963), 144. For the point that the assumption of responsibility must be voluntary, see HENRY MANNE and HENRY C. WALLICH, *The Modern Corporation and Social Responsibility* (Washington, DC: American Enterprise Institute for Public Policy Research, 1972), 5.

5. ARCHIE B. CARROLL, "A Three-Dimensional Conceptual Model of Corporate Performance," *Academy of Management Review*, 4 (1979), 497–505.

6. CARROLL, "A Three-Dimensional Conceptual Model of Corporate Performance," 500.

7. *Social Responsibilities of Business Corporations* (New York: Committee for Economic Development, 1971), 15.

8. S. PRAKASH SETHI, "Dimensions of Corporate Social Performance: An Analytical Framework for Measurement and Analysis," *California Management Review*, 17 (Spring 1975), 62. Emphasis in original omitted.

9. For a good survey of socially responsible corporate activities, from which many of the following examples are taken, see TAD TULEJA, *Beyond the Bottom Line: How Business Leaders are Turning Principles into Profits* (New York: Facts on File, 1985).

10. The concept of corporate social responsiveness is developed in ROBERT W. ACKERMAN and RAYMOND A. BAUER, *Corporate Social Responsiveness: The Modern Dilemma* (Reston, VA: Reston, 1976). See also, SETHI, "Dimensions of Corporate Social Performance"; and CARROLL, "A Three-Dimensional Model of Corporate Performance."

11. From an unpublished paper, quoted in CARROLL, "A Three-Dimensional Model of Corporate Performance," 501.

12. For a discussion of the integration of responsiveness into the strategic-planning process, see R. ED-

WARD FREEMAN and DANIEL R. GILBERT, JR., *Corporate Strategy and the Search for Ethics* (Englewood Cliffs, NJ: Prentice Hall, 1988).

13. This point is made by WILLIAM C. FREDERICK, "Toward CSR3: Why Ethical Analysis Is Indispensable and Unavoidable in Corporate Affairs," *California Management Review*, 28 (1986), 131–32.

14. FREDERICK, in "Toward CSR3," proposes as a third concept, beyond corporate social responsibility (CSR1) and corporate social responsiveness (CSR2), CSR3, which is corporate social rectitude. Also see EDWIN M. EPSTEIN, "The Corporate Social Policy Process: Beyond Business Ethics, Corporate Social Responsibility, and Corporate Social Responsiveness," *California Management Review*, 29 (Spring 1987), 99–114, in which corporate social policy is proposed as a fourth concept that unifies and integrates the others in a way that can be implemented in business practice.

15. STEVEN L. WARTICK and PHILIP L. COCHRAN, "The Evolution of the Corporate Social Performance Model," *Academy of Management Review*, 10 (1985), 758–69.

16. DONNA J. WOOD, "Corporate Social Performance Revisited," *Academy of Management Review*, 16 (1991), 693.

17. MILTON FRIEDMAN, *Capitalism and Freedom* (Chicago: University of Chicago Press, 1962), 133.

18. McKIE, "Changing Views," 18–19.

19. FRIEDMAN, *Capitalism and Freedom*, 133. The quotation of Adam Smith is from *The Wealth of Nations*, Book IV, Chapter II. This famous paragraph concludes: "It is an affectation, indeed, not very common among merchants, and very few words need be employed in dissuading them from it."

20. MILTON FRIEDMAN, "The Social Responsibility of Business Is to Increase Its Profits," *New York Times Magazine*, 13 September 1970, 33.

21. FRIEDMAN, "The Social Responsibility of Business Is to Increase Its Profits," 122.

22. See, for example, RICHARD MUSGRAVE, *The Theory of Public Finance* (New York: McGraw-Hill, 1959), in which the three functions of securing efficiency (which includes considerations of externalities), equity, and stability properly belong to government.

23. Holders of the classical view generally favor market solutions over government action in the belief that many externalities result from a lack, rather than an excess, of free market forces and that regulation is often ineffective. Still, they usually admit the principle that government regulation is appropriate in some instances to deal with externalities.

24. For an explanation and discussion of this concept, see ARTHUR M. OKUN, *Equality and Efficiency: The Big Tradeoff* (Washington, DC: The Brookings Institution, 1975).

25. THEODORE LEVITT, "The Dangers of Social Responsibility," *Harvard Business Review*, 36 (September–October 1958), 49.

26. JOHN G. SIMON, CHARLES W. POWERS, and JON P. GUNNEMANN, "The Responsibilities of Corporations and Their Owners," in *The Ethical Investor: Universities and Corporate Responsibility* (New Haven: Yale University Press, 1972), 16–17.

27. KEITH DAVIS, "The Case for and against Business Assumption of Social Responsibilities," *Academy of Management Journal*, 16 (June 1973), 314.

28. KEITH DAVIS, "Five Propositions for Social Responsibility," *Business Horizons*, 18 (June 1975), 20. Italics in the original.

29. KEITH DAVIS and ROBERT L. BLOMSTROM, *Business and Society: Environment and Responsibility*, 3rd ed. (New York: McGraw-Hill, 1975), 50.

30. This objection is formulated in KENNETH E. GOODPASTER and JOHN B. MATTHEWS, JR., "Can a Corporation Have a Conscience?" *Harvard Business Review*, 60 (January–February 1982), 139–40.

31. GOODPASTER and MATTHEWS, "Can a Corporation Have a Conscience?" 140.

32. These points are made in DAVIS, "The Case for and against Assumption of Social Responsibilities," 320. Ironically, another argument is that the assumption of greater social responsibility would weaken the power of corporations by diverting their resources from their most productive use, with the result that they would not be able to fulfill either their economic or social role well. The inconsistency of these arguments has not prevented some critics from using both.

33. SIMON, POWERS, and GUNNEMANN, "The Responsibilities of Corporations and Their Owners."

34. MARVIN A. CHIRELSTEIN, "Corporate Law Reform," in McKIE, *Social Responsibility and the Business Predicament*, 55.

35. The terms "classical view" and "managerial view" are adapted from McKIE, "Changing Views." McKie uses the term "managerial view," however, to denote a view that reached full development in the

present-day conception of corporate social responsibility. The division developed here corresponds more closely to the three phases distinguished in ROBERT HAY and ED GRAY, "Social Responsibilities of Business Managers," *Academy of Management Journal*, 17 (March 1974), 135–43.

36. These developments are described in the classic work by A. A. BERLE, JR., and GARDNER MEANS, *The Modern Corporation and Private Property* (New York: Macmillan, 1932).

37. ANDREW CARNEGIE, "Wealth," *North American Review* (June 1889).

38. For a detailed history of corporate philanthropy, and especially the Community Chest movement, see HEALD, *The Social Responsibilities of Business*. A brief survey is given in BARRY D. KARL, "Corporate Philanthropy: Historical Background," in *Corporate Philanthropy* (Washington, DC: Council on Foundations, 1982), 132–35. A more general history of philanthropy in the United States is provided by ROBERT H. BREMMER, *American Philanthropy* (Chicago: University of Chicago Press, 1960).

39. H. BREWSTER ATWATER, JR., "The Corporation as Good Citizen," in *Corporate Philanthropy*, 17.

40. WILLIAM J. BYRON, "Christianity and Capitalism," *Review of Social Economy*, 40 (1982), 316.

41. HAY and GRAY, "Social Responsibilities of Business Managers," 139.

42. For a compilation of current data, see KATHARINE TROY, "Statistical Analysis of Corporate Philanthropy," in *Corporate Philanthropy*, 136–48. A thorough but dated study is F. EMERSON ANDREWS, *Philanthropic Giving* (New York: Russell Sage Foundation, 1950).

43. WILLIAM M. EVAN and R. EDWARD FREEMAN, "A Stakeholder Theory of the Modern Corporation: Kantian Capitalism," in TOM L. BEAUCHAMP and NORMAN E. BOWIE, eds., *Ethical Theory and Business*, 4th ed. (Englewood Cliffs, NJ: Prentice Hall, 1993), 79. See also R. EDWARD FREEMAN and D. REED, "Stockholders and Stakeholders: A New Perspective on Corporate Governance," in C. HUIZINGA, ed., *Corporate Governance: A Definitive Exploration of the Issues* (Los Angeles: UCLA Extension Press, 1983).

44. R. EDWARD FREEMAN, *Strategic Management: A Stakeholder Approach* (Boston: Pitman, 1984), 46. This book provides a useful discussion of the history of the stakeholder concept and the literature on it.

45. THOMAS DONALDSON and LEE E. PRESTON, "The Stakeholder Theory of the Corporation: Concepts, Evidence, and Implications," *Academy of Management Review*, 20 (1995), 65–91.

46. DONALDSON and PRESTON, "The Stakeholder Theory of the Corporation," 67.

47. IGOR ANSOFF, *Corporate Strategy* (New York: McGraw-Hill, 1965), 38.

48. KENNETH E. GOODPASTER, "Business Ethics and Stakeholder Analysis," *Business Ethics Quarterly*, 1 (1991), 53–73.

49. This case is based on the restructuring of Marriott Corporation. Names have been changed, and some details have been altered. The case was prepared as a basis for class discussion and is not intended to be a description of any actual events.

50. This case was adapted by KAREN MARQUISS and JOANNE B. CIULLA from "H. B. Fuller in Honduras: Street Children and Substance Abuse" prepared by NORMAN E. BOWIE and STEFANIE ANN LENWAY. Copyright 1991 by Columbia Graduate School of Business.

15

Ethics in International Business

The record shows that when U.S. enterprises operate in less developed countries, there is a very high probability that they will be charged from some quarters with various serious failings in terms of social responsibility.[1]

—RAYMOND VERNON

CASE 15.1   The Tragedy at Bhopal

Shortly after midnight on December 3, 1984, Suman Dey, an engineer on duty at the Union Carbide plant in Bhopal, India, noticed that pressure and temperature gauges for tank E610 had suddenly shot up to their maximum readings.[2] Although the instruments in the control room were considered by employees to be unreliable, Dey was concerned this time. Tank E610 contained more than 40 tons of methyl isocyanate (MIC), and workers at that moment were attempting to find the source of a reported leak. The high readings indicated that the normally refrigerated liquid was turning into a hot gas that could rupture the tank. At 12:40 A.M., Dey rushed to the site, where he could hear the rumbling sound of a violent reaction in the tank and feel the intense heat. He ran away in terror just as a six-foot-thick, sixty-foot-long slab of concrete covering three partially submerged MIC tanks began to shake and break apart. Then a safety valve on a vent shaft gave way, allowing the dense gas to escape and form a lethal cloud that silently settled on the surrounding area.

The immediate cause of the accident was the failure of a maintenance worker to block the line leading to tank E610 during a routine washing of the line with water to remove residue. As a result, water was allowed to enter the tank, where it reacted with the highly volatile contents.[3] Three safety systems on the MIC tanks were simultaneously out of order. A refrigeration unit for cooling the tanks in an emergency had been shut down and the coolant used elsewhere in the plant; a scrubber designed to neutralize escaping MIC vapor with a caustic soda solution was switched to a standby position and could not be activated during the crisis; and a flare tower that burned the gas to render it harmless had been turned off so that a piece of corroded pipe could be replaced. A final emergency procedure, spraying the escaping gas with water, proved ineffective when water from fire hoses could not reach the top of the flare tower where the gas was being vented. In any event, none of these systems was designed to contain the amount of MIC that was actually released in the early hours of December 3.

Hundreds of thousands of Indians, most of them desperately poor, lived in makeshift hovels around the plant. Some of these people died in their beds, unable to move, as the gas seared their lungs and caused them to suffocate on the fluid that formed. Others were roused from their sleep by the sounds of a growing panic, and finding themselves nauseous, unable to breathe, and temporarily blinded, they began a stampede to flee the danger. Hospitals were filled to overflowing with desperate people seeking relief from searing chest pains and irritated eyes. Morning found corpses spread across the city, as people lay where they fell. Most were victims of the gas, but some were trampled to death in the stampede. By the end of the week, more than 2,000 were known to have died, and the eventual toll is now estimated to exceed 3,500.[4] At least 200,000 other people were injured in the disaster, many permanently.

Founded as a private company in 1934 for the manufacture of batteries, Union Carbide India Limited (UCIL) became a publicly owned corporation in 1955, with the parent company holding 50.8 percent of the stock. UCIL was a largely autonomous unit staffed by Indian managers, although overall direction was provided by Union Carbide, located in Danbury, Connecticut. At the time of the accident, UCIL was the twenty-first largest corporation in India, with about $170 million in revenues. UCIL entered the pesticide market in the 1960s at the urging of the Indian government, which was conducting a campaign to modernize agricultural production as part of the much touted "Green Revolution." The Indian government also pressed UCIL to build a plant in Bhopal, the capital of Madhya Pradesh, since this populous and impoverished state was in desperate need of modernization. An annual rent of 500 rupees (about $40) per acre was offered to encourage UCIL to locate there. The company accepted the offer, and in 1968, the Agricultural Products Division was transferred to a new facility in Bhopal.

At first the Bhopal plant produced fertilizers and pesticides using chemicals imported from other countries, but the Indian government was anxious to become self-sufficient and prodded UCIL to manufacture finished products from scratch. Also, local production created more jobs and added to the country's output. This policy suited the needs of the American parent company. Increased competition in India from other chemical companies combined with a downturn in farmers' use of fertilizers and pesticides put a squeeze on profits, and Union Carbide Corporation was looking for ways to cut costs. Manufacturing its major pesticide, Sevin, from beginning to end at one plant would be a step in this direction. Because of the toxic nature of the ingredients for Sevin, especially MIC, the expansion of the Bhopal plant was opposed by local officials, but their objections were overruled by the national government. The high expectations of Union Carbide and the Indian government for the new plant at Bhopal were never realized, however. In 1984, the Bhopal plant was losing money for the company and was operating at only 40 percent of capacity. At the time of the accident, in fact, Union Carbide was seeking to sell the facility.

The lack of profitability contributed to the low level of safety at the plant. Although it is possible to manufacture Sevin without producing MIC in an intermediate step, the more hazardous process was adopted for reasons of cost. Storing large quantities of MIC is also not necessary if the chemical is manufactured only as needed, but cost considerations led to the adoption of a system of bulk production. The design of the plant did not incorporate the use of multiple gauges, backup safety devices, and automatic shut-offs that were in common use elsewhere. According to a Union Carbide official, the Bhopal plant was built with a manual rather than an automatic safety system at the insistence of the Indian government, since the former created more jobs.[5] Also, because of cutbacks, the number of employees at the Bhopal plant had been sharply reduced, with a resulting decline in maintenance. Lax safety standards, inadequate training in safety procedures, and a rapid turnover of the work force further contributed to problems at the plant.

INTRODUCTION

Although many firms engage in business abroad, most of the ethical issues in this area arise for the *transnational corporation*, or TNC, which is generally defined as a firm that has a *direct investment* in two or more countries.[6] The forms that foreign direct investment take vary enormously. Usually, though, there is full or partial ownership of affiliates in other countries that are subject to some degree of control from the parent corporation. In some instances, the owners and managers of a TNC are from the home country exclusively; in others, the owners and managers of a firm include people of many different nationalities.

The emergence of TNCs in the second half of the twentieth century has had a profound effect on developed and undeveloped countries alike. Their wealth and power have given rise to concern about the impact on local economies in both home and host countries and about the capacity of governments, even in such countries as the United States, to regulate them effectively.[7] The controversy over transnationals extends beyond their responsibility in less developed countries to include policy prescriptions for national governments in dealing with TNCs and the obligations of the developed countries to share their wealth with the poorer countries of the world. Although important, these are largely political matters that cannot be examined here.

Our concern in this chapter is rather with the moral obligations of managers of transnationals and other firms in dealing with difficult issues, such as those raised by the marketing of pharmaceuticals in the third world. This area, where TNCs have been extensively criticized, is examined first to illustrate the many problems encountered in international business. The main task, though, is to develop an ethical framework for determining the appropriate standards for the different situations in which managers of TNCs find themselves. The framework developed in this chapter is then applied to the problem of risk management in a third world country, looking specifically at the Bhopal tragedy.

MARKETING PHARMACEUTICALS IN THE THIRD WORLD

An ethical framework for international business can be developed by examining the marketing of pharmaceuticals in third world countries. The pharmaceutical industry, more than any other, has been criticized for its activities abroad. Although prescription and over-the-counter drugs have done much to alleviate suffering and increase the well-being of people around the globe, the major drug companies are also faulted for many of their practices. These practices include the following.

1. Different instructions.   One of the most heavily criticized practices is promoting drugs in the third world with more indications for their use and fewer warnings about side effects than in developed countries. A study by the Office of Technology Assessment concluded that 68 percent of a sample of American-made drugs had labels with medically important information missing and unsupported claims added. One example is Lomotil, a treatment for diarrhea marketed by G. D. Searle.

Diarrhea is a life-threatening condition in the third world and the major killer of children under the age of three.[8] This drug does not treat the underlying causes of diarrhea, however, but merely relieves the symptoms by producing constipation. Consequently, the World Health Organization (WHO) has declared Lomotil to be of "no value" in the treatment of diarrhea and a waste of time and money.[9] The drug is also dangerous for young children and should not be prescribed to children under the age of two.[10] But Searle has recommended the drug for diarrhea in children as young as one year in Indonesia and in infants between three and six months in Hong Kong, Thailand, the Philippines, and Central America.[11]

Another example is chloramphenicol. Marketed by Parke-Davis under the brand name of Chloromycetin, this drug is a highly effective treatment for severe life-threatening infections, such a typhoid fever. In a few susceptible people, however, Chloramphenicol can cause a frequently fatal form of aplastic anemia. Accordingly, the *Physicians' Desk Reference* states, "It must not be used in the treatment of trivial infections or where it is not indicated, as in colds, influenza, infections of the throat, or as a prophylactic agent to prevent bacterial infections." WHO has repeatedly issued warnings against indiscriminate use of this drug.[12] Physicians are advised to conduct frequent blood studies, so that treatment can be halted at the first sign of side effects.[13] Parke-Davis claims to have standardized labeling worldwide,[14] but in Mexico and Central America, for example, Chloromycetin has been indicated for tonsillitis, urinary tract infections, bacterial pneumonia, and undulant fever, among other conditions, and it has been sold without the warnings given to doctors in the United States to conduct blood studies every two days.[15]

2. **Drug dumping.**   Another charge against pharmaceutical firms is that they engage in *drug dumping*, the practice of selling abroad drugs that have not been approved or for which approval has been withdrawn in the country where they are manufactured. Combination antibiotics (two or more drugs in a fixed ratio) have been removed from the U.S. market as a result of findings by the FDA that the drugs can interfere with each other and that the fixed ratios prevent doctors from prescribing the proper dose for each patient. Combination antibiotics are still marketed in most developing countries, however, and even command premium prices.[16] A curious case of drug dumping concerns Depo-Provera, an injected contraceptive that protects women against pregnancy for three months or more. In the early 1970s, the FDA refused to approve Depo-Provera because tests conducted since 1965 showed that it can cause extended and even permanent infertility and possible breast tumors and cervical cancer. All the time, Upjohn was promoting this contraceptive outside the United States with no warnings about its side effects.[17] American companies are forbidden by the Food, Drug, and Cosmetic Act of 1938 to export drugs not approved for use in the United States,[18] but many means are available for evading this restriction. Upjohn, for example, was able to manufacture Depo-Provera legally by shifting production to plants in Belgium.[19] In October 1992, the FDA approved Depo-Provera for use in the United States, 35 years after the drug was developed in the Upjohn company laboratories.

3. **Problems with pricing.**   Drug companies are further charged with placing higher prices on some products and lower prices on others in the third world for no apparent reason except what the market will bear.[20] In *Global Reach*, Richard J. Barnet and Ronald E. Muller cite a study showing that the prices for the tranquilizers Valium and Librium in Columbia were, respectively, 82 and 65 times higher than the standard charges elsewhere.[21] *Transfer pricing*, the means by which companies charge their own subsidiaries for goods, makes it possible for transnationals to bypass laws designed to keep profits from being taken out of a country or to limit the taxes paid on profits earned in any given country. This is accomplished by importing raw materials and partially finished products at very low prices into countries with favorable tax and profit repatriation laws and then exporting them to subsidiaries in the third world at artificially high prices so that virtually no profit is recorded there.[22]

Another criticism of the pharmaceutical industry is that the price paid for drugs in third world countries includes the costs of research and development, but priority is commonly given by transnationals to drugs for the treatment of health problems in developed first world countries. Consequently, people suffering from tropical diseases are forced to pay the research and development costs of drugs for cancer therapy, for example, while little or no money goes into the search for drugs to cure sleeping sickness.[23] An apparent exception that only proves the rule is the discovery by Marion Merrell Dow of a new drug, Ornidyl, for the treatment of sleeping sickness. This important discovery was made accidentally, however, by researchers trying to develop a drug for treating cancer.[24]

4. Free samples and bribery. A common practice in the third world is to provide physicians with free samples, which are then sold to patients for extra income. The effect is not only to create a subtle form of bribery (since doctors are encouraged to prescribe a given brand in order to continue the flow of free samples) but also to increase the sale of unneeded drugs by encouraging doctors to unload their stocks on patients. Some doctors are bribed by less subtle means, including free trips, lavish entertainment, and cash payments.[25] In addition, representatives of the major pharmaceutical firms encourage the use of brand-name drugs in the third world rather than cheaper generics, and extensive advertising prompts people to engage in self-medication and to buy all manner of useless pills and tonics.

DEVELOPING AN ETHICAL FRAMEWORK

The crux of the charges against the activities of drug companies abroad is that they adopt a double standard, doing in less developed, third world countries what would be regarded as wrong if done in the developed first world. "The moral failure of the transnationals," according to one critic, "lies in their willingness to settle for much lower standards than at home."[26] However, many of the practices just described are legal in the countries in question and are not considered to be unethical by local standards.

The marketing of pharmaceuticals in the third world illustrates a quandary faced by all transnational corporations; namely, deciding which standards of ethics to follow. Should TNCs be bound by the laws and prevailing morality of the home country and, in the case of American corporations, act everywhere as they do in the United States? Should they follow the practices of the host country and adopt the adage "When in Rome, do as the Romans do"? Or are there special ethical standards that apply when business is conducted across national boundaries? And if so, what are the standards appropriate for international business?

Unfortunately, there are no easy answers to these questions. In some cases, the standards contained in American law and morality ought to be observed beyond our borders; in other cases, there is no moral obligation to do so. Similarly, it is morally permissible for managers of TNCs to follow local practice and "do as the Romans do" in some situations but not others. And even if there are special ethical standards for international business, they cannot be applied without taking into account differences in cultures and value systems, the levels of economic development, and the social and political structures of the foreign countries in which TNCs operate. The existence of special standards, in other words, does not require us to act in the same way in all parts of the world, regardless of the situation. Local circumstances must always be taken into consideration in conducting business abroad.

"No Double Standards!"

Let us consider, first, the position taken by some critics of TNCs: that business ought to be conducted in the same way the world over with no double standards. In particular, U.S. corporations ought to observe domestic law and a single code of conduct in their dealings everywhere. This position might be expressed as, "When in Rome or anywhere else, do as you would at home."[27] A little reflection suffices to show that this high level of conduct is not morally required of TNCs in all instances and that they should not be faulted for every departure from home country standards in doing business abroad. Good reasons can be advanced to show that different practices in different parts of the world are, in some instances, morally justified.

First, the conditions prevailing in other parts of the world are different in some morally relevant respects from those in the United States and other developed countries. If Rome is a significantly different place, then standards that are appropriate at home do not necessarily apply there. Drug laws in the developed world, for example, are very stringent, reflecting greater affluence and better overall health. The standards embodied in these laws are not always appropriate in poorer, less developed countries with fewer medical resources and more severe health problems.

In the United States, the risk of prescribing an antidiarrheal drug such as Lomotil to children is not worth taking. But a physician in Central America, where children frequently die of untreated diarrhea, might evaluate the risk differently. Similarly, the effectiveness of Chloromycetin for massive infections might offset the possibility of aplastic anemia in a country where some people would die without the drug. A missionary in Bolivia who spoke with doctors about the extentive use of chloramphenicol (the generic name for Chloromycetin) reported: "The response was that in the States, because of our better state of general health, we could afford to have the luxury of saving that drug for rare cases. Here, the people's general health is so poor that one must make an all out attack on illness."[28]

Second, some aspects of American law and practice reflect incidental features of our situation, so that not all United States standards express universal moral requirements.[29] The fact that a drug has not been approved in the home country of a transnational or has been withdrawn from the market does not automatically mean that it is unsafe or ineffective. A drug for a tropical disease might never have been submitted for approval, since there is no market for it in the country where it is manufactured. Other drugs might not be approved because of concerns that are unfounded or open to question.

The FDA acted conservatively in initially refusing approval for Depo-Provera, for example; many countries of Western Europe and Canada, with equally strict drug-testing requirements, permitted the use of this drug as a last-resort contraceptive. In borderline cases, there is room for legitimate debate between competent, well-intentioned persons about the correctness of FDA decisions. Also, the approval of drugs in the United States is a lengthy process. Companies convinced of the safety of a drug might be justified in rushing it to market in countries where it is legally permitted, while waiting for approval at home, especially if there is a pressing need abroad. Finally, some critics charge that the long delay in the FDA's approval of Depo-Provera was based on political considerations arising from the opposition of some groups to birth control.

Third, many factors in other countries, especially in the third world, are beyond the control of TNCs, and they often have little choice but to adapt to local conditions—if they are going to do business at all. This position can perhaps be expressed as, "We do not entirely agree with the Romans, but we sometimes find it necessary to do things their way." For example, physicians in the third world often prefer to prescribe multiple drugs for a single ailment. Hence, the demand for combination antibiotics. Although this practice is disapproved by the American medical community, extending the U.S. ban on such drugs to the rest of the world is unlikely to bring about any significant change. If combination antibiotics were not sold, many doctors would continue to issue prescriptions for several different drugs to be taken simultaneously, very possibly in the wrong proportions.

As another example, consider the ethics of marketing prescription drugs directly to consumers. Deep opposition to this practice exists in the United States, and drug companies are severely criticized for ad campaigns that appeal to patients over the heads of physicians. In much of the third world, however, self-medication is a deeply ingrained practice, since many people are too poor to consult a doctor, if, indeed, one is available. And many drugs that are available only by prescription in the United States are freely dispensed by pharmacists in the third world—and even by street corner vendors. Under these conditions, drug companies contend that advertising cannot be effective if it is aimed only at physicians. Drug companies are accused, however, of encouraging self-medication and inducing the population to spend scarce resources on pills, tonics, and other medications when they have so many more pressing needs.

"When in Rome . . ."

The opposite extreme—that the only guide for business conduct abroad is what is legally and morally accepted in any given country where a TNC operates—is equally untenable. "When in Rome do as the Romans do" cannot be followed without exception. In order to see this, however, we need to distinguish at least three different arguments that are used to support this position. These correspond to the objections to the first position just examined and can be sketched briefly as follows:

1. There really are morally relevant differences. The justification for holding a double standard and marketing a drug in a host country that is not approved at home, for example, is that the conditions that prevail in the country are different in morally relevant respects.

2. The people affected have a right to decide. Where different standards exist, the right of a host country to determine which to apply should be respected. The primary responsibility for setting standards properly rests on the government and the people of the country in which business is being conducted.

3. There is no other way of doing business. Where local conditions require that corporations engage in certain practices as a condition of doing business, then those practices are justified. This is a version of the argument "We do not entirely agree with the Romans, but we sometimes find it necessary to do things their way."

The first argument presupposes the existence of general principles of justification, such as the utilitarian principle that justifies practices in terms of their consequences for benefit and harm. As a result, it is possible that no ultimate conflict exists in some cases of apparent double standards; whatever principles are employed simply justify different practices when conditions are different in morally relevant respects. Many of the criticisms directed against TNCs fail to recognize the extent to which the practices in host countries are capable of being justified by the same principles that justify different practices at home. We have already noted some of the relevant differences that might justify different marketing practices for prescription drugs, but there are many other cases that illustrate the point.

Consider whether a double standard is involved, for example, when TNCs pay wages in less developed countries that are a fraction of those in the developed world. One possible position is that although there are vast differences in the actual wages paid by a TNC in the United States and, say, Mexico, the disparity is not unjust *if the same mechanism for setting wages is employed in both cases.* Thus, the wage paid to a worker in the third world must provide a decent standard of living in that country and be arrived at by a process of fair bargaining that fully respects workers as human beings. In order for these conditions to be satisfied, unions might also be necessary to ensure that workers are adequately represented.[30] What is morally objectionable about the wages paid by many TNCs in the third world, then, is not that they are lower than those in the home country but that they are imposed on workers in violation of their rights.

How far this argument is able to justify the use of different standards in host and home countries is a matter for speculation. Although a few of the marketing practices for which the pharmaceutical industry is criticized can perhaps be justified in this manner, it is difficult to believe that the differences between countries are sufficient to justify extensive double standards. A serious effort by TNCs to apply the ethical principles underlying home country standards to the varying conditions they encounter in different parts of the world would be a welcome development—and one that would result, most likely, in many changes in current marketing practices.

Abiding by Local Standards

The argument "The people affected have a right to decide" is not a form of ethical relativism. Just because physicians in some less developed countries routinely sell free samples does not make the practice right. Even when the practice is legal in the country in question and condoned by the local medical community, the indirect payment provided by the sale of free samples that makes it possible for drug companies to bribe physicians can still be branded as morally wrong. The argument is rather an expression of respect for the right of people to govern their own affairs.

Imposing the standards of a developed, first world country in the third world is criticized by some as a form of "ethical imperialism."[31]

Although there is some merit in this argument, it cannot be accepted without considerable qualification. A respect for the right of people to set their own standards does not automatically justify corporations in inflicting grave harm on innocent people, for example, or violating basic human rights. In deciding whether to employ a practice that is regarded as wrong at home but is legal and apparently approved in a host country, a number of factors must be considered.

First, some countries, especially those in the third world, lack the *capacity* to regulate effectively the activities of transnational corporations within their own borders. The governments of these countries are, in many instances, no less committed than those in the United States and Western Europe to protecting their people against harm from prescription and over-the-counter drugs, but they do not always have the resources—the money, skilled personnel, and institutions—to accomplish the task.

The law in Nigeria, for example, prohibits the marketing of any drug in a way that is "false, or misleading, or is likely to create a wrong impression as to its quality, character, value, composition, merit, or safety."[32] Such a law cannot be effective, however, without an agency such as the FDA to acquire information about the vast number of drugs that enter the country and issue detailed guidelines for their use. Such steps can also be thwarted by powerful transnationals. One Nigerian has complained:

> . . . [W]e have a proposed new drug reviewed by a committee of experts—many of them highly competent people trained in England, Canada, and the United States. They review all the evidence, both that submitted by the company and that published in the best scientific journals. They may decide that the proposed drug is not safe or not effective enough, and they reject the application. But then the company goes to court with all its expensive legal talent. It files suit. And sometimes our recommendation is overruled.[33]

Second, some countries with the capacity to regulate transnationals lack the necessary *will.* Often, the local medical community and powerful segments of the population benefit from the unethical marketing practices of the giant drug companies and willingly permit and even encourage their use. TNCs, through the exercise of economic power, including payments to government officials, frequently are able to influence regulatory measures. Third world governments also have to be cautious about offending powerful economic interests in countries of the developed world on which they depend for aid. The absence of laws against unethical marketing practices is sometimes part of a pattern of oppression that exists within the country itself. Drug companies are taking advantage of the immorality of others, therefore, when they use certain practices in third world countries with corrupt governments and elites.

In order for the argument "The people affected have a right to decide" to justify the adoption of different standards, it is necessary to ask whether the standard in a host country, if it is lower than that at home, truly represents the considered judgment of the people in question. Does it reflect the decision that they would make if they had both the capacity to protect their own interests effectively and the means for expressing their collective will? A genuine respect for the right of people to determine which standards to apply in their own country requires a careful and sympathetic consideration of what people would do under certain hypothetical conditions rather than what is actually expressed in the law, conventional morality, and commonly accepted practices.

As in the case of the first argument, it is difficult to speculate on the consequences of applying this one to the broad range of situations faced by TNCs. There is little reason to believe, however, that people in less developed countries, if consulted, would approve the marketing of drugs with more indications and fewer warnings than are provided in the United States, or that they would approve the dumping of drugs that are not permitted to be prescribed in the United States, and so on. The common contention that bribery and other forms of corruption are accepted in the third world often proves to be unfounded. Although common in some countries, these practices are, nevertheless, deeply resented by the bulk of the population and often regretted even by many who stand to benefit. Revelations of official corruption have led to the downfall of more than one government, thus indicating that bribery is not approved in those countries.

The Need to "Go Along"

The final argument, "There is no other way of doing business," like the other two, has some merit. As long as they have a right to operate abroad, corporations ought to be permitted to do what is necessary for the conduct of business—within limits, of course. American firms with contracts for projects in the Middle East, for example, have complied in many instances with requests not to station women and Jewish employees in those countries. Although discrimination of this kind is morally repugnant, it is (arguably) morally permissible when the alternative is to risk losing business in the Arab world. Attempts have been made to justify the practice on the ground that American corporations are forced to go along.

A more complicated case is provided by the Arab boycott of Israel, which was begun by the countries of the Arab League in 1945.[34] In order to avoid blacklisting that would bar them from doing business with participating Arab countries, many prominent American transnationals cooperated by avoiding investment in Israel. Other U.S. corporations, however, refused to cooperate with the boycott for ethical reasons. An executive of RCA, which is now part of General Electric, declared:

> We're a worldwide communications company that has done business with China and Rumania, and we'd like to do business with the Arabs. But we are not going to end relations with Israel to get an Arab contract. This is a moral issue that we feel strongly about.[35]

(The position taken by RCA is now required by law. An amendment to the Export Administration Act, signed into law in June 1977 over vigorous objections by segments of the business community, prohibits American corporations from cooperating with the Arab boycott against Israel.)

As with the other arguments, "There is no other way of doing business" cannot be accepted without some qualifications. First, the alternative is seldom to cease doing business; rather, the claim that a practice is "necessary" often means merely that it is the most profitable way of doing business. Drug companies might lose some business by refusing to market combination antibiotics, for example, but the amount is not likely to be substantial, especially if the changeover is accompanied by a promotional effort to educate doctors about the proper use of drugs. Similarly, direct marketing is less likely to be objectionable if advertising is used to educate consumers about drugs in a way that genuinely contributes to their well-being instead of the profit of the transnationals. The Arab embargo against Israel greatly complicated the problems of doing business in the Middle East, but some companies were able to avoid cooperating with the boycott and still have business relations with Arab countries.

Second, there are some situations in which a company is morally obligated to withdraw if there is no other way to do business. At one time, any company with plants and other production facilities in South Africa was required by law to observe the rigid segregation imposed by apartheid. Some critics held at the time that if the only alternative to participating in racial oppression is to cease all operations there, then the latter is the morally preferable course of action. Subsequently, the South African government allowed U.S. subsidiaries to integrate their work force and abide by the so-called Sullivan Code, which bars discrimination in employment.

However, the Sullivan Code does not address the charge that American firms were still contributing by their presence to the survival of a country that systematically violated the rights of its own people. Also, critics charge that some of the products sold in South Africa contributed to the maintenance of apartheid. Several computer companies in the United States, including IBM, for example, were accused of selling equipment that enabled the South African police to enforce the hated passbook and to keep track of dissidents. American banks have also been criticized for making loans that helped to preserve the economic stability of the white regime. These critics contend that such involvement in an immoral system cannot be justified and that the only moral course was to cease doing business there.

Defenders point out in reply that American companies provided high-paying jobs for blacks in South Africa and that their presence encouraged a gradual process of liberalization. If they had withdrawn, the condition of the oppressed majority would, most likely, not have improved and pressure on the government to make reforms would have been eased. The main consequence would probably have been that other foreign investors and white South Africans would take the place of the departing American firms with worse consequences.

The difficulty with both of the qualifications just discussed lies in finding the appropriate cutoff points. When is conforming to the local way of doing things absolutely necessary and when is it a matter of convenience or mere profitability? When is it morally permissible for a corporation to remain in a country such as South Africa under apartheid and when is a corporation morally obligated to withdraw? Answering these questions requires a careful consideration of the hard realities of the situation and the possibility of justifying each practice. The argument

"There is no other way of doing business," therefore, does not settle the matter in any given case but only serves as a starting point for further ethical inquiry.

Special Standards for International Business

Our results so far have been largely negative. The two extreme positions—"When in Rome, do as the Romans do" and "When in Rome or anywhere else, do as you would at home"—are both inadequate guides in international business. However, the discussion of these positions suggests some principles that can be used to make decisions in difficult cases. These principles recognize that the world of the TNC requires a slightly different approach to issues than the one appropriate to a corporation operating wholly within a single nation-state. This is so for several reasons besides those already mentioned.

First, some of the conditions that create a social responsibility for corporations in a country such as the United States are absent elsewhere. The basis for many of the obligations of American corporations to employees, consumers, and the public at large lies in the extensive powers and privileges that we have conferred upon them. Their responsibility to society rests, in other words, on an implicit "social contract," and that contract does exist to the same degree when corporations operate abroad. The role of TNCs is often limited to marketing goods produced elsewhere, participating in joint ventures with local companies, and so on. Thus, they are not full-fledged "corporate citizens" of a host country, so to speak, but are more like guests. Hence, they have less reason to exhibit the good citizenship that we expect of domestic corporations, although they should still be good "corporate guests."

Second, the lack of effective international law with comprehensive multinational agreements, codes of conduct, and the like creates a less regulated, more competitive environment for international business. One benefit of a legal system is a uniform system of enforceable rules that provides a level playing field for all firms. Business competition within a single country with an extensive set of laws is thus like an athletic competition. International business, by contrast, is more akin to war, which cannot be conducted by the detailed rules of a boxing match, for example. Even war is bound by moral limits, however, such as the concept of a just war and rules such as the Geneva Convention.

Because of these features of international business, it is not appropriate to hold that TNCs have all the same obligations abroad that they have at home and to use the same principles of justification to determine the extent of their obligations in foreign operations. Still, there is a minimal set of obligations that every corporation is morally bound to observe no matter where the activity takes place. An ethical framework for international business consists in part, then, of the moral minimum for corporations operating abroad.

Minimal and Maximal Duties

Thomas Donaldson suggests that we distinguish the minimal and maximal duties of corporations and come to some agreement about the former. A maximal duty or obligation, he says, is one whose fulfillment would be "praiseworthy but not ab-solutely mandatory," whereas a minimal duty is one such that "the persistent failure to observe [it] would deprive the corporation of its moral right to exist."[36] The re-quests of third world countries for help in improving living conditions and devel-oping the local economy, although often expressed as demands for justice, are, in Donaldson's view, pleas for a kind of "corporate philanthropy" that is, at best, a max-imal duty and not a moral minimum.[37] Further impoverishing a people or violating a fundamental human right, such as employing child labor, is, by contrast, a failure to observe minimal obligations that apply to all business enterprises.

What principles might serve to justify the minimal duties or obligations of corporations engaged in international business? Two have been proposed. One is the principle of *negative harm*, which holds that in their dealings abroad, corpora-tions have an obligation not to add substantially to the deprivation and suffering of people.[38] The utilitarian injunction to produce the greatest possible benefit to peo-ple creates a set of maximal obligations of TNCs, but a concern with consequences can take a number of progressively weaker forms that include preventing harm and merely avoiding the infliction of harm. William K. Frankena distinguishes four ver-sions of an obligation of beneficence: (1) One ought not to inflict evil or harm, (2) one ought to prevent evil or harm, (3) one ought to remove evil, and (4) one ought to do or promote good.[39] The negative-harm principle, which is the weakest form, is (arguably) a moral minimum, so that regardless of what other obligations corpora-tions have in foreign operations, they have this one. The only morally justified ex-ceptions to the obligation not to inflict substantial harm on a people are to avoid violating an important right of some kind or to produce a greater benefit in the long run.

A second principle, proposed by Thomas Donaldson, is that corporations have an obligation to respect certain rights; namely, those that ought to be recog-nized as *fundamental international rights*.[40] TNCs are not obligated to extend all the rights of U.S. citizens to people everywhere in the world, but there are certain basic rights that no person or institution, including a corporation, is morally permitted to violate. Fundamental international rights are roughly the same as *natural* or *human* rights, discussed in Chapter 3, and some of these are given explicit recognition in documents ranging from general statements, such as the United Nations Universal Declaration of Human Rights, to the very specific, such as the World Health Orga-nization (WHO) Code of Marketing Breast Milk Substitutes.

Of course, the main problem with a principle to respect fundamental in-ternational rights (or fundamental rights, for short) is specifying the rights in question. Even undeniable human rights that create an obligation for some per-son or institution, such as the government of a country, are not always relevant to a transnational corporation. Everyone has a right to subsistence, for example, but TNCs may be under no obligation to feed the hungry in a country where it operates. It has an obligation, however, not to contribute directly to starvation by, say, converting cultivated land to the production of an export crop. To deal with these complications, Donaldson says that a right must meet the following conditions:

1. The right must protect something of very great importance.
2. The right must be subject to substantial and recurrent threats.
3. The obligations and burdens imposed by the right must be (a) affordable and (b) distributed fairly.[41]

The "fairness-affordability" criterion, expressed in condition 3, serves to relieve corporations of an obligation to do what is beyond its resources and more than its fair share. Although a more extensive list could perhaps be justified by Donaldson's conditions, he suggests the following as a moral minimum:

1. The right to freedom of physical movement.
2. The right to ownership of property.
3. The right to freedom from torture.
4. The right to a fair trial.
5. The right to nondiscriminatory treatment.
6. The right to physical security.
7. The right to freedom of speech and association.
8. The right to minimal education.
9. The right to political participation.
10. The right to subsistence.[42]

Sample applications of these rights, according to Donaldson, include: failing to provide safety equipment, such as goggles, to protect employees from obvious hazards (the right to physical security); using coercive tactics to prevent workers from organizing (the right to freedom of speech and association); employing child labor (the right to minimal education); and bribing government officials to violate their duty or seeking to overthrow democratically elected governments.[43]

APPLYING THE ETHICAL FRAMEWORK

The ethical framework that has been developed in this chapter can now be used to evaluate the conduct of Union Carbide in the Bhopal tragedy. Like most major industrial accidents, the events at Bhopal were caused by a complex interplay of human, organizational, and technological factors.[44] Mistakes by workers on the scene, along with a series of faulty decisions by the management of Union Carbide, defects in the design of the plant, and equipment failures at the time of the accident, all played a part. A heavy responsibility must be borne, though, by Union Carbide, as the parent company, since the safety standards observed at the Bhopal plant were considerably lower than those at facilities in the United States, such as the plant at Institute, West Virginia, where MIC is also produced.[45]

The role of Union Carbide in this immense human tragedy is complicated, however, by differences encountered in international business. Deliberate exposure of any group to death and injury on this scale would certainly be a failure to fulfill the duty not to inflict harm and also a violation of a fundamental human right, the right to physical security. The issue in this case, though, is not the ethics of practices that have known consequences but of operations that pose a certain level of *risk*, and determining what is an acceptable level of risk varies from one setting to another. Thus, a country with a desperate need to raise food for a growing population might accept a trade-off that creates a greater risk of an industrial accident in return for more fertilizers and pesticides. Similarly, a government might accept lower safety standards as the price for gaining local control and creating jobs for its own citizens. Transnational corporations might not find it profitable to invest in less developed countries if they were required to install extensive safety equipment or to employ less hazardous technologies. One reason that companies in developed countries go abroad, in fact, is to take advantage of a looser regulatory environment in order to utilize manufacturing methods that are prohibited at home. Finally, risks are sometimes increased by local conditions beyond the control of TNCs. All of these factors were present in the Bhopal case.

The human toll of the accident was greatly increased by social, political, and economic conditions in the region where the plant was located. As Paul Shrivastava observes, "Bhopal is a textbook example of a rapidly developing city that sought—and obtained—sophisticated Western-style industrialization without making a commensurate investment in industrial infrastructure or rural development."[46] The emphasis on industrial development at the expense of agriculture drove people from the land into Bhopal. As a result, throngs of people occupied hovels right up to the fence of the plant on land that was largely vacant when Union Carbide first arrived. In an effort to improve living conditions, the city passed a law in 1984 granting ownership to the land that squatters already occupied, thus legalizing slums that should never have been allowed in the first place. The plant was also located about a mile from the train station where hundreds of people died on the night of the tragedy.

Ethically Evaluating Union Carbide's Conduct

Under these circumstances, was Union Carbide morally justified in operating the plant at Bhopal and exposing its workers and the local population to the potential harm that became a reality? This question can be repeated for corporations that manufacture asbestos and other hazardous materials abroad, dump toxic wastes in third world countries, pollute the environment, and, in general, create hazards for people around the globe. The negative-harm principle requires us to conduct a risk assessment to ensure that the benefit for the people involved exceeds the harm. Such assessments are routine in evaluating hazards within the United States and other developed countries. Assessing risk in less developed countries is greatly complicated by the difficulty of determining the relative weight that other people place on the various benefits and harms. This is especially true when, as Thomas Donaldson points out, differences in evaluation reflect cultural norms. A Pakistani, for example, might give up some material well-being in order to maintain that country's Moslem heritage[47]

Another impediment to assessing risk in less developed countries is the lack of a market to provide a monetary measure of the relative weight of benefits and harms. The willingness of American workers to accept more dangerous jobs at higher pay offers some indication of the value placed by people in our society on health and safety. Because of massive unemployment in the third world, combined with grinding poverty and a general ignorance of the hazards of many kinds of work, the low wages accepted do not accurately reflect their scale of values. Decisions by the government of a host country are also not always reliable indicators of a people's weighting of benefits and harms. As we have already observed, governments in the third world are often unable or unwilling to protect their own people effectively, and they all too frequently reflect the interests of only a narrow segment of the population.

One means for conducting a risk assessment in less developed countries with very different cultural traditions is to consider as sympathetically as possible how the people affected evaluate the benefits and harms of adopting a certain standard. Thomas Donaldson calls this the test of *rational empathy*, which he describes as putting ourselves in the shoes of a foreigner:

> To be more specific, it makes sense to consider ourselves and our own culture at a level of economic development relevantly similar to that of the other country. And, if, having done this, we find that *under such hypothetically altered social circumstances* we ourselves would accept the lower risk standards, then it is permissible to adopt the standards that appear inferior.[48]

The shortcomings of this method are obvious. Even a limited empathy requires considerable knowledge of other cultures, and truly putting ourselves in the shoes of people of very different cultural traditions is probably a psychological impossibility, even for those who make a sincere effort. Also, the test of rational empathy offers no protection against the coercion that results from dire economic necessity. Desperately poor people might be better off, all things considered, having a hazardous industry in their midst than doing without the jobs and other benefits it provides. Does this fact justify, however, the use of the most profitable technology consistent with ensuring a marginal benefit to the people affected, especially when a slight reduction in profitability could greatly reduce the risk and increase the benefit of an industry to the local population?

Applying the test of rational empathy to the operation of the Union Carbide plant in Bhopal yields inconclusive results. Lower safety standards in the facility are justified to some extent by the desire of the Indian government to boost the industrial output of the country and provide jobs and needed products. UCIL had not been profitable for several years prior to the accident, and the Bhopal plant, in particular, was a liability to the company, even with the use of less costly (and more hazardous) methods of production. Without cutbacks in staffing and maintenance, it is possible that the plant could not have remained open. When the plant closed for good in 1985, 650 people were thrown out of work and an estimated 1,500 other jobs that were related to the presence of Union Carbide were lost.[49] In addition, the city lost an important source of tax revenue.

Certainly, many mistakes by both Union Carbide and the Indian government made a severe accident more likely. The danger that the plant posed to the local population could have been significantly reduced by inexpensive measures, such as a more adequate warning system for the surrounding area. (A manually activated siren was sounded thirty minutes after the release of the gas and was switched off after a few minutes.) If the alternative had been to increase the level of safety to the point that the plant would no longer be profitable to operate, however, it is possible, given India's relative economic underdevelopment, that the benefits of a less safe plant would be sufficient to justify the risk posed by its continued operation.

Objections to the Negative-Harm Principle

Some philosophers contend that the negative-harm principle, as just applied to the Bhopal case, is misconceived. The obligation of a corporation such as Union Carbide is not merely to assess risk in terms of benefit and harm but to avoid inflicting harm (period), or at least to avoid inflicting certain *prohibited harms* except with the consent of the persons involved.[50] The negative-harm principle, in other words, is not a weak version of utilitarianism ("Do more good than evil") but is more akin to Donaldson's right to physical security. Specifically, people have a right not to be harmed in certain prohibited ways without their consent. This interpretation of the negative-harm principle is widely accepted in medical ethics, which holds that a doctor has no right to treat a patient, even for his or her own good, without that person's informed consent.

In this interpretation, Union Carbide would not be justified in operating a hazardous plant merely because the people of Bhopal would accept the risk if they were fully informed (this is what the test of rational empathy seeks to establish), but rather the company has an obligation to inform workers and residents of the dangers they face, so that they can make an informed choice. This interpretation of the negative-harm principle directs our attention not only to the safety standards adopted by Union Carbide at the Bhopal plant but also to the way the company treats the people concerned. Revealing the hazards posed by the plant shows respect for the people of Bhopal and enables them to exercise greater control over their lives.

A major problem of this interpretation of the negative harm principle is specifying the class of prohibited harms. Which harms do people have a right to be informed about? Henry Shue proposes six criteria for distinguishing harms that may not be imposed without the consent of those who will suffer them. According to these criteria, prohibited harms are those that result from a decision that:

> ... (1) may lead to *bodily damage*, (2) that is *serious* and (3) *irreversible*, in circumstances in which the damage is also (4) *unavoidably undetectable* to the person actually suffering it, (5) *unavoidably unpredictable* for the people who may potentially suffer it, and (6) *very likely* to occur.[51]

These criteria reflect the view that people have a right to protect themselves against serious irreversible bodily damage, such as permanently impaired lung capacity and blindness (which afflict the victims of Bhopal today). This is especially true when the source of the hazard is a leak in a tank, for example, that people cannot observe themselves, when they have no way of predicting a leak, and when the probability of a leak is quite high. Although each one of these criteria is subject to some uncertainty (how high must the probability be, for example?), they are all satisfied by the Bhopal case.

Compensating the Victims of the Tragedy

The justification of Union Carbide's operation of the plant in Bhopal is not the only issue raised by the case. The response of the company in the aftermath of the tragedy provides a revealing study of the responsibility of an American corporation to compensate the victims of an accident in a faraway place. Initially, Union Carbide denied that it had any obligation to pay, since it was merely a 51 percent shareholder in Union Carbide India Limited. The company's position was that UCIL bore sole legal liability. Extensive litigation then followed. In April 1985, Union Carbide agreed to pay $5 million for interim relief ordered by a U.S. federal court, but a similar order from a court in the state of Madhya Pradesh in January 1988 to provide $270 million in relief was fought by Union Carbide until the amount was reduced to $190 million.

A $3.3 billion suit by the Indian government, acting on behalf of all the victims of Bhopal, was transferred by a U.S. judge to India, and in February 1989, more than five years after the accident, the Indian Supreme Court ordered Union Carbide to pay $470 million in compensation.[52] In the settlement, blame for the accident was not fixed and all criminal charges against Union Carbide and its executives were dropped. The amount of compensation is about $940 for each of 500,000 claimants. To date, relatively few victims have been compensated, and charges of corruption have been leveled at Indian officials responsible for settling claims.

The American parent company was deeply affected by the whole episode.[53] Coping with the crisis became a full-time job for many top executives, and the barrage of criticism from around the world caused employee morale to suffer. In its weakened state, Union Carbide became the target of a takeover bid by GAF Corporation. To protect itself, Union Carbide adopted a $4.3 billion recapitalization plan that required the company to sell off its consumer products division that marketed such household-name items as Prestone antifreeze, Eveready batteries, and Glad Bags, and to slash its work force by more than half. Union Carbide is now a financially secure but much smaller company. Its reputation has been tarnished, however, and any time the company proposes to build a new plant anywhere in the world, the memory of Bhopal will be rekindled.

Conclusion

The passage from Raymond Vernon that begins this chapter has been amply borne out. Operating abroad, especially in the third world, creates dilemmas that lead to charges of serious ethical failings. Transnational corporations generally recognize a social responsibility and attempt to fulfill their responsibilities everywhere they are located. The major cause of occasional failures to act responsibly is not the lack of effort but the diversity of political and legal systems around the world and differences in economic development. Foreign operations give rise to challenges—and also create opportunities for misconduct—that simply do not exist for purely domestic enterprises.

One quandary facing all TNCs is deciding which standards to follow. We have seen that neither of the two extreme positions is satisfactory. The familiar adage "When in Rome, do as the Romans do" and the opposite, "When in Rome or anywhere else, do as you would at home," are both inadequate guides. The standards of American business practice have been developed for a specific set of conditions and reflect certain choices that we have made as a society. Other, equally justified standards are possible, and some may be more appropriate for the particular circumstances of a third world country. Merely following accepted practices of a country or abiding by the law is no defense, however, when the conduct in question is unethical by any justified standard.

Some guidance is provided by the notion of a moral minimum that specifies a list of minimal obligations or duties for corporations engaged in international business. Two principles, in particular, yield such a list; namely, the principle of negative harm and the principle of respect for fundamental rights. These principles do not escape entirely the difficulties that plague the two positions "When in Rome, do as the Romans do" and "When in Rome or anywhere else, do as you would at home." Still, the two principles under discussion provide a framework for evaluating practices that is capable of yielding reasonably well-supported conclusions in a wide variety of situations. These principles are superceded, of course, by international agreements developed by such bodies as the United Nations, the International Labour Organization, and the Organization for Economic Cooperation and Development. As codes of conduct for transnationals become more detailed and comprehensive, the need for special principles of international business will, it is hoped, diminish.

CASE 15.2   Nike in Indonesia

Nike is a leader in the sports shoe industry with $2 billion in annual sales and a 40 percent share of the American basketball shoe market.[54] With splashy advertising and celebrity endorsements from stars like Michael Jordan, the Oregon-based company has succeeded in making sports shoes a "must have" item for millions of people, most of whom never engage in any kind of athletic activity. Nike has also revolutionized American merchandizing by focusing entirely on design and marketing and leaving the manufacture of their shoes to contractors abroad. Nike employs a mere 8,000 people, mostly in management, distribution, and advertising, and virtually all of the production is in Asia, where local contractors employ about 75,000 workers. By contracting with Asian suppliers, Nike can respond quickly to changes in consumer taste and also pursue the cheapest labor around the globe. Nikes were first produced in South Korea and Taiwan, but these factories have been closed and new ones opened in Indonesia, China, and Thailand, where wages are lower.

A pair of Nike sports shoes manufactured in Indonesia that retails for an average price of $73 costs a mere $5.60 to produce. The secret is young Indonesian women in Korean-owned factories who start at less than 15 cents an hour. With mandatory overtime that usually results in grueling eleven-hour days, some experienced workers receive as much as $2, which is above the $1.22 that the Indonesian government considers necessary to meet "minimum physical needs." The women (many of whom are still girls in their teens) live in fear of their brutal Korean managers, who berate them for failing to meet quotas and withhold pay for any acts of defiance. Indonesian labor laws, lax to begin with, are flouted with impunity by the Koreans, since the government is eager to attract foreign investment. There is little effective union activity in Indonesia, and labor strikes are firmly suppressed by the army.

Such Asian "sweatshop" conditions are not mentioned in the advertising for Nike, and the company denies any responsibility for the people who actually make their shoes. When asked about labor strife in the factories supplying Nike, John Woodman, the company's general manager in Indonesia, responded that he did not know what the causes were and that he had not bothered to find out. "It's not within our scope to investigate," he said. Mr. Woodman defended the company against accusations of exploitation by arguing, "Yes, they are low wages. But we've come in here and given jobs to thousands of people who wouldn't be working otherwise." He could have added that Nike has also given additional employment to Michael Jordan, whose reported $2 million fee in 1992 for promoting Nikes was larger than the payroll that year for all Nike production in Indonesia.

CASE 15.3   Profit before Patriotism?

The National Gallery in London, which houses the royal art collection, is an important symbol for the British people.[55] The director of the museum, Neil McGregor, was delighted, therefore, when a painting in the hands of a London art dealer was tentatively identified as the work of Albrecht Altdorfer, who was a contemporary of Dürer and one of Germany's greatest Renaissance artists. The painting "The Adoration of the Magi," which features richly clad figures against a radiant, mountainous landscape, had been thought to be merely from the workshop of Altdorfer and not by the master himself. An art scholar suspected that the painting was a genuine Altdorfer, and tests using infrared photography supported the suspicion by revealing a kind of underdrawing that was characteristic of his paintings. Colnaghi, a venerable London art firm, bought the painting a year earlier at auction, cleaned and restored it, and was preparing to consign the painting to an auction house with an estimated presale value of £15,000 to £20,000. If genuine, however, the painting could fetch three to four times that price and as much as forty times what Colnaghi paid for it originally.

Mr. McGregor was anxious for the painting to stay in Britain, but he did not have the authority to spend more than £60,000 without the approval of the museum's board of trustees, which could not be obtained quickly. So he asked Stephen Rudge, a codirector of Colnaghi, to bid up to that amount on behalf of the museum, with an understanding that Colnaghi could purchase the painting for themselves if the bidding rose above the museum's limit. In the end, the painting was repurchased by Colnaghi for £68,200. The bidding puzzled some observers, who felt that the price was too high for anyone who believed that the painting was not a genuine Altdorfer and too low if the painting was indeed by the master's hand.

Soon after the sale, the National Gallery informed Colnaghi that they were still interested in acquiring the painting and were willing to pay the dealer "considerably more" than the purchase price. Colnaghi rejected the offer, and the London art world was stunned. The firm was accused of putting profit before patriotism by refusing to make the painting affordable to the nation's preeminent museum. Mr. McGregor said, "The normal convention and the gentlemanly thing would be for a dealer to offer the picture for a very small markup." Another dealer was more blunt: "I haven't heard of this sort of incident in the 40 years I've been in the trade. The question really is which duty comes first—to the nation or to shareholders." Mr. Rudge of Colnaghi denied that there was any conflict of interest since the right of the firm to buy the painting after the bidding exceeded the museum's limit was understood. His primary responsibility, he explained, is to the shareholders of Colnaghi. As for a lack of patriotism, he added, "I'd like to ask any dealer to put their hand on their heart and say how patriotic they are. We're all commercial dealers."

NOTES

1. RAYMOND VERNON, "Foreign Operations," in JAMES W. McKIE, ed., *Social Responsibility and the Business Predicament* (Washington, DC: The Brookings Institution, 1974), 287.

2. Detailed accounts of the accident at Bhopal are provided in DAN KURZMAN, *A Killing Wind: Inside Union Carbide and the Bhopal Catastrophe* (New York: McGraw-Hill, 1987); and PAUL SHRIVASTAVA, *Bhopal: Anatomy of a Crisis* (Cambridge: Ballinger, 1987).

3. Union Carbide has contended that water was pumped into the tank by a disgruntled employee, but this charge has never been substantiated. For details, see KURZMAN, *A Killing Wind*, 185–89.

4. See SANJOY HAZARIKA, "Bhopal Payments Set at $470 Million for Union Carbide," *New York Times*, 15 February 1989, sec. 4, p. 30.

5. KURZMAN, *A Killing Wind*, 25.

6. Some sources, including the United Nations, prefer the term *transnational* instead of the more common *multinational* to emphasize the fact that the corporations in question are usually not owned and operated by people in many nations but are more commonly legally chartered in one country and conduct business across national boundaries. See *Transnational Corporations and Developing Countries: New Policies for a Changing World Economy* (New York: Committee for Economic Development, 1981), 15.

7. A critical view of TNCs is presented in RICHARD J. BARNET and RONALD E. MULLER, *Global Reach: The Power of the Multinational Corporations* (New York: Simon & Schuster, 1974). More approving of transnationals are two books by RAYMOND VERNON, *Sovereignty at Bay* (New York: Basic Books, 1971) and *Storm over the Multinationals* (Cambridge: Harvard University Press, 1977). A study focusing on the United States is C. FRED BERGSTEN, THOMAS HORST, and THEODORE H. MORAN, *American Multinationals and American Interests* (Washington, DC: The Brookings Institution, 1978).

8. CHARLES MEDAWAR and BARBARA FREESE, "Drug Multinationals in the Third World," *Business and Society Review*, 38 (Summer 1981), 23. See also CHARLES MEDAWAR and BARBARA FREESE, *Drug Diplomacy* (London: Social Audit, 1982).

9. MEDAWAR and FREESE, "Drug Multinationals in the Third World," 23.

10. MILTON SILVERMAN, PHILIP R. LEE, and MIA LYDECKER, *Prescriptions for Death: The Drugging of the Third World* (Berkeley and Los Angeles: University of California Press, 1982), 59.

11. MEDAWAR and FREESE, "Drug Multinationals in the Third World," 23; SILVERMAN, LEE, and LYDECKER, *Prescriptions for Death*, 59.

12. MILTON SILVERMAN, *The Drugging of the Americas* (Berkeley and Los Angeles: University of California Press, 1976), 9.

13. SILVERMAN, LEE, and LYDECKER, *Prescriptions for Death*, 21.

14. RALPH J. LEDOGAR, *Hungry for Profits: U.S. and Drug Multinationals in Latin America* (New York: IDOC/North America, 1975), 48–49.

15. SILVERMAN, *The Drugging of the Americas*, 13–15.

16. SILVERMAN, LEE, and LYDECKER, *Prescriptions for Death*, 37–39.

17. LEDOGAR, *Hungry for Profits*, 37–39.

18. This act was amended in 1986 to allow the export of certain nonapproved drugs, such as drugs for the treatment of diseases not found in the United States.

19. SILVERMAN, LEE, and LYDECKER, *Prescriptions for Death*, 136.

20. SILVERMAN, LEE, and LYDECKER, *Prescriptions for Death*, 98. See also MILTON SILVERMAN and PHILIP R. LEE, *Pills, Profits, and Politics* (Berkeley and Los Angeles: University of California Press, 1976), 178–81.

21. BARNET and MULLER, *Global Reach*, 158.

22. BARNET and MULLER, *Global Reach*, 158.

23. SILVERMAN, LEE, and LYDECKER, *Prescriptions for Death*, 98–100.

24. "FDA Clears Drug to Cure African Sleeping Sickness," *Wall Street Journal*, 30 November 1990, B7.

25. See SILVERMAN, LEE, and LYDECKER, *Prescriptions for Death*, chap. 5.

26. JOHN BRAITHWAITE, *Corporate Crime in the Pharmaceutical Industry* (London: Routledge & Kegan Paul, 1984), 246.

27. NORMAN E. BOWIE, "The Moral Obligations of Multinational Corporations," in STEVEN LUPER-FOY, ed., *Problems of International Justice* (Boulder, CO: Westview Press, 1987), 97.

28. Quoted in LEDOGAR, *Hungry for Profits*, 46–47.

29. This point is made by RICHARD T. DEGEORGE, "Ethical Dilemmas for Multinational Enterprise," in W. MICHAEL HOFFMAN, ANN E. LANGE, and DAVID A. FREDO, eds., *Ethics and the Multinational Enterprise* (Lanham, MD: University Press of America, 1986), 40.

30. For an argument of this kind, see HENRY SHUE, "Transnational Transgressions," in TOM REGAN, *Just Business: New Introductory Essays in Business Ethics* (New York: Random House, 1984), 271–91.

31. See, for example, JACK BERMAN, "Should Companies Export Ethics?" *New York Times*, 2 September 1973, sec. 3, p. 12.

32. SILVERMAN, LEE, and LYDECKER, *Prescriptions for Death*, 116.

33. SILVERMAN, LEE, and LYDECKER, *Prescriptions for Death*, 111.

34. For a history of the Arab boycott, see DAN S. CHILL, *The Arab Boycott of Israel* (New York: Praeger, 1976).

35. WALTER GUZZARDI, JR., "That Curious Barrier on the Arab Frontier," *Fortune*, July 1975, 170.

36. THOMAS DONALDSON, *The Ethics of International Business* (New York: Oxford University Press, 1989), 62.

37. DONALDSON, *The Ethics of International Business*, 63.

38. For an application of the negative-harm principle to business in South Africa, see PATRICIA H. WERHANE, "Moral Justifications for Doing Business in South Africa," in HOFFMAN, LANGE, and FREDO, *Ethics and the Multinational Enterprise*, 435–42. The principle is applied to hazardous wastes and technology in HENRY SHUE, "Exporting Hazards," in PETER G. BROWN and HENRY SHUE, eds., *Boundaries: National Autonomy and Its Limits* (Totowa, NJ: Rowman and Littlefield, 1981), 107–45.

39. WILLIAM K. FRANKENA, *Ethics*, 2nd ed. (Englewood Cliffs, NJ: Prentice Hall, 1973), 47.

40. DONALDSON, *The Ethics of International Business*, chap. 5.

41. DONALDSON, *The Ethics of International Business*, 75–76.

42. DONALDSON, *The Ethics of International Business*, 81.

43. DONALDSON, *The Ethics of International Business*, 87–89.

44. For a discussion of this so-called HOT analysis, see SHRIVASTAVA, *Bhopal*, 48–57.

45. This double standard was admitted by Union Carbide CEO Warren Anderson. See STUART DIAMOND, "Warren Anderson: A Public Crisis, A Personal Ordeal," *New York Times*, 19 May 1985, sec. 3, p. 1.

46. SHRIVASTAVA, *Bhopal*, 57.

47. DONALDSON, *The Ethics of International Business*, 113.

48. DONALDSON, *The Ethics of International Business*, 124.

49. SHRIVASTAVA, *Bhopal*, 72.

50. This is the position of Henry Shue, in SHUE "Exporting Hazards," 122.

51. SHUE, "Exporting Hazards," 124.

52. HAZARIKA, "Bhopal Payments Set at $470 Million for Union Carbide."

53. See JONATHAN P. HICKS, "After the Disaster, Carbide is Rebuilt," *New York Times*, 15 February 1989, sec. 4, p. 3.

54. This case is based on information in RICHARD J. BARNET and JOHN CAVANAGH, *Global Dreams: Imperial Corporations and the New World Order* (New York: Simon & Schuster, 1995), 325–328.

55. Material for this case is taken from ANDREW L. YARROW, "London Art Dealer Being Criticized or a Museum Accord Gone Awry," *New York Times*, 14 December 1988, sec. 2, p. 20.

Index